SEARS LIST OF
SUBJECT HEADINGS

Sears List
of
Subject
Headings

13th Edition

Edited by
CARMEN ROVIRA
AND
CAROLINE REYES

New York
The H. W. Wilson Company
1986

Printed in the United States of America

Library of Congress Cataloging in Publication Data

Sears, Minnie Earl, 1873–1933
   Sears list of subject headings

   Bibliography: p.

   1. Subject headings. 1. Rovira, Carmen. II. Reyes, Caroline. III.
Title. IV. Title: List of subject headings.
Z695.S43 1986   025.4′9   86-7734
ISBN 0-8242-0730-0

Table of Contents

Preface

Minnie Earl Sears prepared the first edition of this work in response to demands for a list of subject headings that was more suitable to the needs of the small library than the A.L.A. and the Library of Congress lists. Published in 1923, the *List of Subject Headings for Small Libraries* was based on the headings used by nine small libraries that were known to be well cataloged. However, Minnie Sears early recognized the need for uniformity, and she followed the form of the Library of Congress subject headings with few exceptions. This decision was important and foresighted because it allowed a library to add Library of Congress headings as needed when not provided by the Sears List and to graduate to the full use of Library of Congress headings when collections grew too large for a limited subject heading list.

Minnie Sears used only *See* and "refer from" references in the first edition. In the second (1926) edition she added *See also* references at the request of teachers of cataloging who were using the List as a textbook. To make the List more useful as a textbook she wrote a chapter on "Practical Suggestions for the Beginner in Subject Heading Work" for the third edition (1933).

Isabel Stevenson Monro edited the fourth (1939) and fifth (1944) editions. A new feature of the fourth edition was the inclusion of Dewey Decimal Classification numbers as adapted for the *Standard Catalog for Public Libraries*. The new subjects added to the List were based on those used in the Standard Catalog Series and on the catalog cards issued by The H. W. Wilson Company. Therefore, the original subtitle "Compiled from Lists used in Nine Representative Small Libraries" was dropped. Another new feature was the printing in italics of those subdivisions that had a more general application.

The sixth (1950), seventh (1954), and eighth (1959) editions were prepared by Bertha M. Frick. In recognition of the pioneering and fundamental contributions made by Minnie Sears the title was changed to *Sears List of Subject Headings* with the sixth edition. Since the List was being used by medium-sized libraries as well as small ones, the phrase "for Small Libraries" was deleted from the title. The symbols *x* and *xx* were substituted for the "Refer from (see ref.)" and "Refer from (see also ref.)" phrases to conform to the format adopted by the Library of Congress.

The ninth edition (1965), the first to be prepared by Barbara M. Westby, continued the policies of the earlier editions, with one major exception. The Dewey Decimal Classification numbers were dropped by the publisher. Many users of Sears had called to the attention of the publisher the inconsistency of including classification numbers and at the same time instructing the cataloger to consult the *Dewey Decimal Classification* for numbers. Moreover, it was the expressed opinion of these users that the inclusion of numbers often led to a misuse of the publication due to a misunderstanding of the relationship between subject headings and classification. The publisher decided to omit the Dewey numbers from the ninth and tenth editions, but they were reintroduced in the eleventh edition, largely in response to the needs of librarians in many medium and small-sized libraries who had been left with little or no assistance in the classification of their collections.

The classification numbers with the one exception noted below, are taken from the eleventh edition of the *Abridged Dewey Decimal Classification and Relative Index* (1979), published by Forest Press. In most cases only one number is assigned to a subject heading. There are instances, however, where a given subject is susceptible to more than one point of view, and one number is consequently inadequate for the subject heading. In these cases more than one number may be appropriate, for example: **Food additives 641.4,** and **664.** In the Relative Index these numbers represent the viewpoints of technology and commercial processing, respectively. Occasionally, certain subjects are given the number of an entire class: **Languages, Modern (400's);** and **Literature (800's).** No classification numbers are assigned to some very general

subject headings, e.g. **Charters, Exhibitions, Gifts, Hallmarks, Identification, Indexes,** and **National characteristics.** These headings cannot be classified unless a specific application is identified.

The need for new and expanded classification schedules for computer science and computer engineering, felt by libraries large and small, prompted Forest Press to publish in 1985 a revision of the Dewey Decimal Classification in those fields. The revised schedules use 004 to 006 instead of 001.6 for data processing and computer science, and 621.39 and its subdivisions instead of 621.38195 for computer engineering. Through the courtesy of Forest Press, holders of the copyright of the Dewey Decimal Classification, the editors of Sears have been able to use in this edition the proposed changes for the forthcoming 12th Abridged edition of DDC. The new classification numbers are preceded by an asterisk (*), and appear alongside the old ones under the headings for those subjects.

Few of the numbers selected from the eleventh edition of "Abridged Dewey" are carried out more than four places beyond the decimal point. Except for libraries with large collections, where more detailed numbers may be required, the numbers in this edition of Sears should be adequate. The need for more detailed classification can often be satisfied by the addition of form and geographic subdivisions, as given in the Dewey schedules. Libraries for whom even relatively brief numbers are too long should consult the section entitled "Reduction" (p 31, 32) in the Introduction to the Dewey volume.

The "Practical Suggestions for the Beginner in Subject Heading Work" has been a continuing feature since it was written by Minnie Sears. The chapter as revised by Bertha Frick was reprinted in the ninth edition. Barbara M. Westby revised this chapter for the tenth edition and made further changes in the eleventh. A new section on audiovisual and other materials was also included. The chapter was retitled to emphasize "Principles." The "Principles" appear again in this thirteenth edition, with only slight changes in the examples, reflecting similar modifications in the List.

The headings added to this edition were suggested by librarians representing various sizes and types of libraries and by the catalogers and indexers at The H. W. Wilson Company who are responsible for the headings in the Standard Catalog Series, *Book Review Digest,* and the periodical indexes. In addition, selections were made from *Library of Congress Subject Headings,* 9th edition, and from the *Hennepin County Library Cataloging Bulletin.* No list can hope to keep completely abreast of the information explosion, nor can it provide for every idea, object, process, and relationship. With patterns established and examples provided, the cataloger can add new headings as needed. Guides for the wording of new headings may be found in the works themselves as well as in periodical literature and indexes. Although daily newspaper terminology may be too colloquial for use as headings, it does provide a clue to the way in which a patron may ask for materials, and also suggests terms to be used as cross references.

The selection of new terms for the present edition covers many areas and reflects the continuing interest in health and environment, computer services, space technology, changing family relationships, minorities, consumerism, business and management, among others. At the same time, there is a continuous revision and updating of the existing headings. Some terms have been updated according to usage: **Space shuttles** replaces **Space vehicles, Reusable;** and **Poisonous gases** is used instead of the old-fashioned **Gases, Asphyxiating and poisonous.** A few headings of passing interest have been deleted, such as **Operation Sail 1976,** and others have been changed to more contemporary ones: **Expo '89 (Paris, France)** instead of **Expo '70 (Osaka, Japan).**

The direct form of entry has been preferred to the inverted form, both in new headings and in the revision of those already established, e.g. **Child rearing; Discount stores; Electronic publishing;** etc. **Employment, Part-time** and **Employment, Temporary** are now **Part-time employment** and **Temporary employment;** and the congestion under **Libraries** has been eased by changing the wording of different types of libraries to the direct form: **Children's libraries; Regional libraries; Special libraries,** etc., thus joining the trend previously established by **Business libraries; School libraries;** and others.

The use of scope notes or definitions of the headings used has been increased, sometimes to clarify the meaning of unfamiliar words, or to point out the differences in coverage of related terms.

The successive editors of the Sears List have followed the policy established by Minnie Earl Sears to use the Library of Congress form of subject headings with some modifications for current terminology and spelling. Further modifications, introduced to meet the needs of smaller collections, include the simplification of phrasing and, in some cases, the broadening of a heading. Thus, closely related headings have been combined to create one Sears heading from two Library of Congress headings (e.g. **Bacteriology** for Bacteria and Bacteriology; **Poisons and poisoning** for Poisons and Poisoning). Other compound headings, which the Library of Congress has divided in two separate terms (**Acrobats and acrobatics; Anarchism and anarchists**) have been kept intact in Sears, on the assumption that they were sufficient for the needs of small and medium-sized libraries.

In recent years the Library of Congress has increased the rate of revision and modernization of some of its long-standing subject headings, and this edition of Sears, as the previous ones, has incorporated many of the changes. These range from **Seafood** instead of **Sea food,** to **Decorative arts** instead of **Art industries and trade;** from **Calculators** instead of **Calculating machines,** to **Nuclear energy** instead of **Nuclear power.**

The patent usefulness of the list of "Free-floating subdivisions", which the Library of Congress has established in the last decade, has prompted the editors of the thirteenth edition of Sears to revise and expand the "List of subdivisions" that appeared in the twelfth edition, merging the two existing lists into one and adding other subdivisions which appear under one or two headings, but could obviously be useful under other subjects. Most of these subdivisions also appear in the main list as general *See* references, with instructions and examples of how they can be applied to different subjects. The general references, both to other headings of the same type, and to other headings with a subdivision, increase considerably the coverage of the List and its usefulness.

In accord with a suggestion of the Cataloging of Children's Materials Committee of A.L.A., the headings from *Subject Headings for Children's Literature* (Library of Congress) have been incorporated into the Sears List. Some of the headings were not included specifically because they fell into the category of headings that can be added to Sears as needed; others were omitted because they already existed in Sears in a slightly different form. Since the Sears List is intended for both adult and juvenile collections, two similar headings for the same subject could not be used. Therefore, when Library of Congress has chosen different headings for adult and juvenile use of the same subject, a choice was made for Sears. In cases where the Sears List uses the adult form, the cataloger of children's materials may prefer to use the form found in *Subject Headings for Children's Literature.*

For spelling, hyphenization, and definition the editors consulted *Webster's Third New International Dictionary of the English Language, Unabridged* (1961) and *Webster's Ninth New Collegiate Dictionary* (1985). Capitalization and the forms of corporate entries used as examples are based on the *Anglo-American Cataloging Rules.*

Filing of entries in the present edition of Sears follows the *ALA Filing Rules* (1980) without the exception made in previous editions, that is, all headings are now interfiled disregarding all punctuation. Headings with parenthetical modifiers and phrase headings now appear intermingled with those with dashes and commas (headings with subdivisions and inverted headings). Although this straight alphabetical arrangement may appear to be less logical than the one used before, the increasing use of automation in all types of libraries and the wish to adhere to standard rules have prompted the editors to make this change.

A common criticism of any list concerns the degree of specificity in its headings. The degree or level of specificity depends on the size of a library, its function, the nature of its collection, and its patrons. Practicality rather than theory should determine the degree of specificity, and a balanced blend of theory and practice has been the philosophy of Sears. In a small collection the use of too many specific headings can result in the scattering of like materials. Sears, by example or directive, suggests over 200 classes of headings that may be added by the cata-

loger when more specific subject headings are needed. Combinations of related materials under one heading and the use of subdivisions also affect specificity.

Two "key" headings (**English language** and **United States**) with subdivisions applicable to a similar class of headings were provided in the first edition. Their number has steadily increased. The "key" for individual presidents, provided in the ninth edition, was deleted in the tenth edition in favor of an expansion of the subdivisions applicable to presidents individually and collectively under **Presidents—United States.** Most of the subdivisions under **World War, 1914–1918** have been omitted because they also appear under **World War, 1939–1945.** The latter heading has been made a "key" for all wars. For a list of "key" headings see p xxxvii.

Every heading in the List that may be used as a subject heading is printed in boldface type whether it is in the main file, in a *See also* paragraph, in a "refer from" reference, or an example for an explanation. If a term is not printed in boldface, it is not to be used as a heading.

The list of *See also, x,* and *xx* references follows the format used by the Library of Congress. For a full explanation of cross-referencing see p xxv–xxix.

The editors wish to express their gratitude and heartfelt thanks to the catalogers who responded to our request for suggestions for headings to be added to this edition. Special thanks are due to John P. Comaromi, Editor, Dewey Decimal Classification, for valuable comments on the "Principles," to Eugene T. Frosio, Subject Cataloging Division, Library of Congress, for answering questions on subject headings. Last, but not least, our thanks to The H. W. Wilson Company, to its editors, and to Thomas E. Sullivan, Associate Director of Indexing Services, for specific suggestions, constructive criticism, and editorial assistance.

The publisher, The H. W. Wilson Company, acknowledges its thanks to Forest Press, a division of the Lake Placid Education Foundation, for permission to use the eleventh edition (1979) of the *Abridged Dewey Decimal Classification and Relative Index,* and the *004-006 Data Processing and Computer Science and Changes in Related Disciplines, Revision of Edition 19.*

This Preface incorporates some sections of the text for the Preface of the previous edition, written by Barbara M. Westby, especially when it refers to the history of the earlier editions of the work and the guidelines followed by the earlier editiors beginning with Minnie Earl Sears. The editors hope that this fact emphasizes the continuity, and at the same time the flexibility, of an enterprise which started more than four decades ago, and which has tried to keep up with the changes in library techniques and in the world in which we live. They hope, too, that the users of the List, as in the past, will aid in the improvement of future editions by submitting comments and suggestions and by their constructive criticism. They will all be received with thanks.

Carmen Rovira

Caroline M. Reyes

March 1986

Principles of the Sears List of Subject Headings

This chapter considers some principles and practices of subject cataloging that must be understood before an attempt is made to assign subject headings to library materials. Most of the illustrations refer to the Sears List of Subject Headings but the principles are applicable to other lists of subject headings as well, particularly the one issued by the Library of Congress on which the headings in this List are based.

Purpose of Subject Cataloging. The purpose of subject cataloging is to list under one uniform word or phrase all of the materials on a given subject that a library has in its collection. A subject is the topic treated in a book, videotape, or other work. A subject heading is the word or phrase used in the library catalog to express this topic. A subject entry is placed above the main or author entry as an access point regardless of the format of the catalog records (card, book, microform, or online).

Library materials are given subject entries in the catalog in order to show what information the library has on a given subject, just as author entries are made to show the works that the library has by a given author. Properly made, the subject entry is a very important supplement to the reference tools in the library because it may enable the reader or librarian to find quickly and surely the material needed to answer a question on a subject. Subject entries are sometimes also the fastest way of finding a particular book. Ordinarily one consults the author entry for a specific work, but, if there is uncertainty about the author's name, one may find the individual piece more rapidly under a subject entry. Smith's *Basic Mathematics* would be difficult to find quickly if one did not know the author's first name and had to consult all the cards in the catalog under Smith. What if the author's name were really spelled Smyth? In either case, the book could be found readily under the subject **Mathematics**.

A printed list of subject headings, such as the Sears List, incorporates the thought and experience of many minds in various types of libraries. By using the List as a base, the cataloger has a source on which to rely. Consistency in both the level of specificity and the form of subject headings for the present and for the future is attained by working from an accepted list of subject headings where the choice among possible wordings has been made and recorded. By following the patterns of headings printed in the List, the catalogers will be able to add new headings that will be consistent with the List.

Determining the Subject of the Work. The first step in subject cataloging is to ascertain the real subject of the material and the purpose for which it was produced. Sometimes this is readily determined, e.g. **Butterflies** is obviously the subject of the book titled *Butterfly Book*. In other cases, the subject is not so easy to ascertain because it may be a complex one or the author may not express it in a manner clear to someone unfamiliar with the subject. The subject of a work cannot always be determined from the title alone. The title information is often misleading and undue dependence on it can result in error. A book entitled *Great Masters in*

Art immediately suggests the subject **Artists,** but closer examination reveals the book to be about painters specifically, not artists in general. Therefore, the more exact subject is **Painters,** not **Artists.** Another illustration is "Fundamentals of Instrumentation," part 1 of a *Manual of Instrumentation.* This title may suggest a treatise on musical instruments or music, but actually it is a book on engineering instruments.

   The steps to follow in determining the subject of a work are the same whether one is considering its value for a reader, classifying it, or assigning subject headings to it. After reading the title page of a book to be cataloged, examine the table of contents, and read the preface and introduction. Then, if the subject of the book is still not clear, examine the text carefully and read parts of it, if necessary. For nonbook materials examine the container, the label, any accompanying guides, etc., and view or listen to the contents. The cataloger will be in a position to determine the subject of the item in hand *only* after this preliminary examination has been made. If the meaning of a subject is not clearly understood, one should consult reference sources, not only an unabridged dictionary and general encyclopedias, but also specialized reference books as well. Only when the cataloger has decided on the subject content of the work and *identified it with explicit words,* can the Sears List be used to advantage. The cataloger's own phrasing of the subject must be adapted to the terminology of the List. The library catalog will be more useful if the cataloger considers materials from the reader's point of view. The reader's profile depends on age, background, education, occupation, and geographical location as well as the type of library—school, public, university, or special. When examining a work the cataloger should ask "If I wanted material on this subject, under what words would I look in the catalog?" Then the List is consulted to insure uniformity in choice and form of the words. Local terminology may be used as references to the words in the List. In choosing these words, that is, assigning the proper subject headings, there are certain principles that should be followed. These are considered in the next five sections.

   Specific and Direct Entry. Appreciation of the principle of specific entry is fundamental both in using and in making a modern subject catalog. The rule of specific and direct entry is to enter a work directly under the most specific term, i.e. subject heading, which accurately and precisely represents its content. This word serves as a succinct abstract of the work. If a reader wants information about bridges, the direct approach is to consult the catalog under the heading **Bridges,** not under the large topic **Engineering,** or even the more restricted field, **Civil engineering.** In other words, make direct entry under **Bridges,** not indirectly under **Engineering—Civil Engineering—Bridges.** Or, consider the principle of specific entry from the cataloger's point of view. If one is examining a work about penguins, it is not sufficient to dismiss it as belonging under the subject **Birds,** or even under **Water birds.** It must be entered directly under the most specific heading that expresses the content, that is **Penguins.** If the work is entered under **Birds,** a reader would have to look through may entries in order to find information on penguins. Having found the most specific entry that will fit the item, the cataloger should not then make subject entries under both the specific and the general subject headings. A work with the title *Birds of the Ocean* should not be entered under both **Birds** and **Water birds** but only under **Water birds.** To eliminate this duplication, a network of *See also* references directs the reader from the broader subject headings to the more specific ones, e.g. **Birds.** *See also . . .* **Water birds;** and names of specific birds. . . . In many cases the most specific entry may be a general subject, e.g. *Song Birds of the World* will have the subject heading **Birds.** The specific term, as can be seen, refers to the exact word that summarizes the subject of the book for the user of the catalog. The level of specificity depends on the size of the library, the nature of its collection, its function, and its patrons. The heading should be as specific as possible for the topic it is intended to cover.

   If the name of a specific object is not found in the List, the name of the larger group to which it belongs should be consulted. For example, in assigning subject headings to a work discussing elm and ash trees, the cataloger would find neither **Elm** nor **Ash** listed. However, under the broader subject, **Trees,** the following directions are given: "Names of all trees are not included in this list but are to be added as needed, in the singular form." The cataloger thus

has the authority to use the two headings, **Elm** and **Ash.** (Further directions for adding headings can be found on p xxxvi.)

Materials should be considered in categories. The word or phrase chosen as a subject must fit not only the items being cataloged but also apply to a group of items on the same subject. The cataloger must consider not only the one piece in hand but also the other book and nonbook materials that discuss the same subject, albeit under different titles, in order to select a subject heading that will serve the entire group in the catalog with relation to other groups. In cataloging *Everybody's Cook Book* the inexperienced cataloger might think first of Cookbooks as the term that will give the best description. But there are two other works that belong in the same group: *How's and Why's of Cooking* and *Cooking for Profit.* These contain not only recipes but also other material on cooking. **Cookery** fits the three closely related items better than Cookbooks and it also fits well with the related subject **Cookery for the sick.** Terminology for a subject must be uniform to fit many similar works.

Common Usage. The word or words used to express a subject must represent common usage. In American libraries this means current American spelling and terminology: **Labor** not Labour; **Color** not Colour; **Elevator** not Lift. In British libraries these words would be reversed. Foreign terms are not used unless thay have been incorporated into the English language, e.g. Laissez faire. By the same token contemporary words are to be used: **Home economics** not Domestic economy. Today a more current term might be Homemaking, or Household management, but changing a heading is not always possible or advisable. There may be too many entries to change or, as in the case of **Home economics,** the term is still being used and newer usage may not have stabilized.

A general rule is to use a popular or common, rather than a scientific or technical, name where there is a choice. Subject headings are chosen to fit the needs of the people who are likely to use the catalog. A reader in a small public library will look under **Birds,** not Ornithology, or **Fishes,** not Ichthyology. In a scientific library Ornithology and Ichthyology might be more appropriate. After deciding on the common name as entry word, the cataloger should make a reference from the scientific name to the form used. Such references will be discussed later. A term in common usage and expressed in the language of the user will be understood by that person and will pass the test of comprehensibility.

A decision must be made whether the form of the heading is to be in a singular or plural form. Plural is the most prevalent but in practice both are used. Abstract ideas are usually stated in the singular. A concept or action is singular (**Theater**) whereas objects and things are plural (**Theaters**). The names of fruit trees are stated in the singular so that they can represent either the fruit or the tree. In this case, singular is more inclusive than the plural. In other cases, plural will have the broader coverage (**Art; Arts**).

Some descriptive phrases also carry different connotations, e.g. Arab, Arabian, and Arabic. Their use in headings appears to be inconsistent, but they are used in the following ways: Arab relating to the people; Arabian referring to the geographical area; and Arabic for the language, script, or literature. These subject headings should be consistent, with distinction being made between ethnic, geographical, and linguistic terms.

Uniformity. Another very important factor to be considered is that of uniformity. One uniform term must be selected from several synonyms and this term must be applied consistently to all works on the topic. China, Chinaware, and Porcelain are all entered under **Porcelain.** This example also illustrates the fact that the subject heading must be inclusive and cover the topic. The heading chosen must be unambiguous. If several meanings attach to one word, that word must be qualified: **Masks (Facial); Masks (Plays); Masks (Sculpture).** When variant spellings are in use, one must be selected and uniformly applied: **Color,** not Colour.

Form Headings. In addition to the subject headings that interpret the content of various materials, there are headings of another kind, usually known as form headings, or form subject headings, that have the same appearance as regular subject headings but refer to the literary or artistic form of a work and not to its subject matter, e.g. **Essays, Poetry, Fiction, Hymns,**

Songs, etc. Literary form headings are usually used for collections rather than works of an individual. For example, the form heading **Essays** is used not for works of an individual author but for collections of essays by authors of different nationalities. If the collection includes essays only by American authors, then the more specific heading **American essays** would be used. While the use of form entries for works of individual authors might be helpful, the result in most libraries would not be worth the effort because such entries usually duplicate subject approaches already available in reference sources in the library, e.g. *Short Story Index, Essay and General Literature Index,* etc. The proliferation of entries would be an extra cost and would increase the size of the catalog unnecessarily. Materials of this type are generally classified and arranged on the shelves according to their literary forms, and the reader often has access to the shelves or to the shelf list. Ordinarily individual works of literature are remembered in association with an author, and a reader consults the author or title entry in the catalog for such works.

For a work about the essay as a literary form, e.g. the appreciation of the essay or how to write it, the heading **Essay** represents a true subject and not a form heading. The distinction between form headings and subject headings can sometimes be made by using the singular form for the true subject heading and the plural for the form heading, e.g. **Short story; Short stories.** But the peculiarities of language do not always permit this. For example, the heading **English poetry** is used for a book about English poetry but in order to show that a book is a collection of poetry by several English authors the subdivision *Collected works* must be added, i.e. **English poetry—Collected works.**

In addition to the literary form headings there are some other useful form headings that are determined by the general format of the material and the purpose of the work, e.g. **Almanacs; Encyclopedias and dictionaries; Gazetteers; Yearbooks.**

Classification and Subject Headings. The cataloger should now recognize a fundamental difference between classification and subject headings for the dictionary catalog. In a system of classification, which determines the arrangement of works on the shelves and groups together materials on one subject, a work can obviously stand in only one place. But in a catalog, entries representing the work can appear, if necessary, under more than one subject. The cataloger does not have to decide on one subject to the exclusion of all others, but can make the work useful with entries for as many different points of view as there are distinct subjects in the work (usually, however, not more than three). Classification is used to gather in one numerical place on the shelf works that give similar treatment to a subject. Subject headings gather in one alphabetical place in a catalog all treatments of a subject regardless of shelf location. A piece of material may have more than one subject heading but can have only one class number.

Theoretically, there is no limit to the number of subject entries that could be made for one work, but practically such a policy not only would be expensive but also inefficient for the user of the catalog. For many works, one subject heading will represent the contents accurately. A book such as *Guide to the Trees* is fully and specifically covered by the subject heading **Trees.** Frequently two are necessary as in the title *Field Book of Trees and Shrubs* to which one would assign both **Trees** and **Shrubs.** Occasionally three are required to do justice to the work. More than three should be considered very carefully. The need for more than three may be due to the cataloger's inability to identify precisely the single heading that would cover all the topics in the work. Similarly, a subject heading should not be assigned for a topic that comprises less than one third of a work.

The practice may be stated as follows: As many as three specific subject headings in a given area may be assigned, but if a work treats of more than three, then the next larger inclusive heading is adopted and the specific headings are omitted. A work about lemons and limes would be entered under **Lemon** and **Lime.** If the work also included material on oranges, a third card with the heading **Orange** would be made for the catalog. But if the work discusses grapefruit and citron as well, the only subject heading assigned would be **Citrus fruit.**

Do not assign both a general heading and one of its specific aspects to the same work. In the example cited above, the material may have discussed the orange in a little more detail than the other fruits, but **Citrus fruit** and **Orange** would not be assigned simultaneously.

The following statistics give a practical demonstration of the proportion of books requiring more than one subject entry. Minnie Sears in one of her early editions reported on books cataloged for a high school library, the books having the same characteristics as those in the collections of small public libraries. Of 1241 titles belonging in the first seven classes of the Dewey Decimal Classification, 788, or 63 per cent, required only one subject heading; 358, or 29 per cent, required two subjects; 76, or 6 per cent, received three subjects, and the remaining 2 per cent had received four or five headings. This study showed that the average number of subjects for each title was 1.46.

The cataloger is now aware of another difference between classification and subject cataloging, and one particularly significant for small libraries: classification is by broader subjects and so is not as closely subdivided as the subject entries for the catalog. Material on trees, oak trees, and all of the special kinds of trees are classed together in **582.16.** Another example is found in the treatment of fruit. A book on fruits in general, one on citrus fruits, and one on oranges will all three be classified in one number in a library, while in the catalog each book will have its own specific subject heading: **Fruit; Citrus fruit; Orange.**

It is well to remember this essential difference in the two processes; otherwise, the rule for classifying by broad subject in a small library (large libraries are not considered here) may cause confusion when the librarian assigns subject headings which must be specific in order to achieve maximum usefulness.

The cataloger has learned that subject headings are used for materials that have definite, definable subjects. However, there are a few works in which the subject is so indefinite that it is better not to assign a heading. A work could be a collection of materials produced by several individuals on a variety of subjects or one person's meandering thoughts and ideas. If a cataloger cannot find a definite subject, the reader may not find the item under a makeshift or general heading. Do not use vague terms. They are a disservice to the reader. A book titled *Appreciation* received the heading **Human behavior** from one cataloger while another assigned the word **Happiness.** In reality neither was correct. The book was a personal account of one of the sources of the author's pleasure in life and had no specific subject.

Now that certain principles of subject headings have been considered, the cataloger should understand the structure of subject headings.

Grammar of Subject Headings. (1) *Single Noun.* The simplest form of subject heading consists of a single noun and is the ideal type when the language supplies it. Such terms are not only the simplest in form but often the easiest to comprehend. Most of the large fields of knowledge can be expressed by single words (**Art; Agriculture; Education; Religion;** etc.) as can many specific objects (**Apple; Chairs; Pottery; Trees; Violin;** etc.). But many words have synonyms from which a choice has to be made, and conversely a word may have two or more quite different meanings; for others there is a choice in spelling; another consideration is the use of the singular or plural form. For example, in the case of **Pottery,** other words that might be used are: Crockery; Earthenware; Faience; Fayence; Stoneware. In the Sears List, the term chosen is **Pottery** and references are made from other terms. On the other hand, the word Date may mean a fruit, an historical period, or a social engagement; Files may refer to an arrangement of material or a tool; Forging may mean counterfeiting or metalwork; Bridge may refer among other things to a game or an engineering structure. In the latter case, using the plural removes the possibility of the game but the singular form has to be qualified: **Bridge (Game).** Also the plural **Bridges (Dentistry)** must be distinguished from the engineering structure.

Whenever identical words with different meanings are used in the catalog one of them must be qualified, that is, defined more specifically. In the example of the book on lemons and limes, neither heading is listed in Sears but may be added when needed, as instructed under both **Fruit** or **Citrus fruit.** However, in adding Lime to the List the cataloger finds **Lime** used in relation to **Cement.** The plural Limes should not be used because Sears states that the name of all fruit should be in the singular form. The cataloger would therefore add a qualifier to Lime, i.e. **Lime (Fruit)**. Since **Seals (Animals)** and **Seals (Numismatics)** are already in the List, any subject that must be added to the List but uses the same word must be defined, e.g. **Seals (Christmas, etc.)** or **Seals (Law)**.

Whether to use the singular or the plural or both sometimes depends on the peculiarities of the language since the two forms may express quite different concepts. In many cases, the singular connotes the general, and the plural the specific aspects. Or stated another way, the singular expresses abstract ideas and the plural refers to things. Thus, **Theater** means the art while **Theaters** refers to the buildings. The same parallel exists in the terms, **Essay** and **Essays**, **Short story** and **Short stories**. In all these cases, both forms are necessary, but in general if only one form is required, either the singular or the plural should be adopted. However, the singular form has been chosen for the names of most fruits and nuts so that the more general term (**Apple; Pecan;** etc.) can be used to include works that consider the fruit or the tree or both.

(2) *Compound Headings.* Using two nouns joined by "and" usually groups together under one heading closely related material which cannot be separated easily in concept and which is usually treated together (**Boats and boating; Cities and towns; Publishers and publishing**), or two different subjects that are treated in their relation to each other (**Aeronautics and civilization; Religion and science; Television and children**), or two subjects that are opposites but are usually discussed together (**Belief and doubt; Good and evil; Joy and sorrow**).

The problem in forming such headings is word order. There is no rule to cover all situations although catalogers have been prone to follow the alphabetic when there is no common usage. Whichever order is chosen, reference must be made from the opposite order.

(3) *Adjective with Noun.* Often a specific concept is best expressed by qualifying the noun with an adjective (**American literature; Electric engineering; Tropical fish**). Sometimes the expression is inverted (**Flies, Artificial; Philosophy, Modern**). The reasons for inversion are twofold: 1) an assumption is made that the reader will think first of the noun; or, 2) the noun is placed first in order to keep all aspects of a broad subject together when that result is deemed desirable. Inversion can be made when the first element qualifies the second and the second is an independent unit:

Art, Abstract	**Education, Elementary**	**Insurance, Accident**
Art, American	**Education, Higher**	**Insurance, Fire**
Art, Municipal	**Education, Secondary**	**Insurance, Health**

In formulating this kind of heading it is difficult to decide whether to use the normal word order followed in speaking and writing or the inverted order; some users of the catalog will think of it one way, others in the opposite. There is no precise rule. A reference is usually required from the order not chosen for the subject heading. The best principle is to stress the key word and to avoid scattering material on the same subject throughout the alphabet. It should be noted that some adjective noun phrases could never be inverted because the noun has no significance without the adjective, e.g. **International relations**.

(4) *Phrase Headings.* Some concepts which involve two areas of knowledge can be expressed only by more or less complex phrases. These are the least satisfactory headings as they offer the greatest variation in wording, are often the longest, and may not be thought of readily by either the maker or the user of the catalog—but the English language seems to offer no more compact terminology. Examples are: **Freedom of information; Information storage and retrieval systems**. Sometimes the phrase is inverted to place the important word first, or to facilitate the filing of related subjects together, although this results in an awkward appearance: **Cities and towns, Ruined, extinct, etc.**

Subdivisions. There are other means by which the scope of the List can be enlarged far beyond the actual headings printed. This is through the use of subdivisions of headings. The principle of specific entry can be achieved in some cases only by subdividing a general subject by words or phrases which indicate special aspects:

Birds	**Music**	**Water**
Birds—Eggs and nests	**Music—Acoustics and**	**Water—Analysis**
Birds—Migration	**physics**	**Water—Fluoridation**
Birds—Protection	**Music—Theory**	**Water—Purification**

In each of the special fields above, the subdivisions are appropriate and characteristic of it and those used under one are not applicable to the other two listed here. However, the subdivision *Analysis* would be applicable to a number of other topics besides **Water**; such as **Air; Blood; Food;** etc. Some terms or phrases used as subdivisions are applicable to so many different topics that the subdivisions are not printed under all possible headings. Some are referred to in their alphabetic places with directions for their use. They vary in kind and in value to an individual library.

(1) *Subdivisions by Physical Form.* Some materials present a subject not in expository or narrative form but as lists, outlines, or tables; or, graphically as maps, pictures, or filmstrips. The work may be a directory of chemists, a bibliography of children's literature, a dictionary of psychology, a collection of geological maps, a Bible picture book. In such cases, it is important to show the user of the catalog that they are not works *about* chemists, or children's literature, or psychology, or geology, or the Bible, respectively. If the reader wants a bibliography or dictionary or maps or pictures, etc., it is equally important for him to be able to locate this directly without having to read through all the cards under the main heading. Standard terms known as "form divisions" are the most common subdivisions and may be used whenever appropriate. Since they show what the material *is,* rather than what it is *about,* they are as necessary for a small library as for a large one. Some examples of form divisions are:

Bibliography	*Gazetteers*	*Portraits*
Catalogs	*Indexes*	*Registers*
Dictionaries	*Maps*	*Statistics*
Directories	*Pictorial works*	*Terminology*

Some of these terms are used alone as actual subject headings, but as subdivisions they are usually called form headings. In either case, each of these terms is listed in its alphabetic place in the List with directions for use; for example (entry shortened):

Bibliography
> *See also* **Archives** . . . also names of persons, places, and subjects with the subdivision *Bibliography,* e.g. **Shakespeare, William, 1564–1616—Bibliography; United States—Bibliography; Agriculture—Bibliography;** etc.

Comparable statements are included under each of the other form headings. Applying these directions to the types of materials cited above, the headings would be:

Chemists—Directories	**Geology—Maps**
Children's literature—Bibliography	**Bible—Pictorial works**
Psychology—Dictionaries	

None of these headings appears in this form in the List, unless it has been cited as an example. Therefore, the *See* or *See also* under the name of the form is to be interpreted as directions for use. Only when a heading has been established and added can the words *See* or *See also* be interpreted literally.

(2) *Subdivisions That Show Noncomprehensive Treatment.* Some works though literary in composition and general in subject are not comprehensive in scope. Random essays on a topic, if they do not present a connected and extensive review; yearbooks on a subject; or periodicals in a particular field are representative of this type of treatment. The standard terms for such

noncomprehensive material, which may be used as subdivisions of general subject headings, are:

Addresses and essays	*Societies*
Laboratory manuals	*Yearbooks*
Periodicals	

By following directions under these terms, subject headings such as those listed below could be formulated:

Architecture—Addresses and essays
Chemistry—Laboratory manuals
Engineering—Periodicals
Commerce—Yearbooks

This kind of subdivision is particularly valuable under headings for the large fields of knowledge which are represented by many entries in the catalog. The cataloger must be guided by the character of the content, not by the title. Many works whose titles begin with such expressions as "Outlines of," "Handbook of," "Manual of" are in fact comprehensive works. For example, Wells' *Outline of History,* Locke's *Essay Concerning Human Understanding,* and Rose's *Handbook of Latin Literature* are comprehensive, lengthy treatises and to use the form divisions that the titles suggest would be inaccurate and ridiculous! Other so-titled "Outlines" or "Manuals" or "Handbooks" may prove to be bibliographies, dictionaries, or statistics of the subject.

(3) *Subdivisions That Show Special Aspects.* A general subject may be presented from a particular point of view. The work may be a history of the subject, the most common of the special aspects; or it may deal with the philosophy of the subject, research in the field, the laws about it, or how to study and teach it. These concepts applied to general subjects are expressed by such headings as:

Education—History   **Radio—Law and legislation**
Religion—Philosophy   **Mathematics—Study and teaching**
Aeronautics—Research

(4) *Subdivisions That Show Chronology.* In any catalog, large or small, there will be many works on American history. If they are all entered under the general heading, the library patron must look through many entries to find a specific era. However, with chronological subdivisions corresponding to generally accepted periods of a country's history or to the spans of time most frequently treated in materials, a search can be narrowed to **United States—History—1945–1953,** etc. If a chronological era has been given a specific name, this is included in the heading with dates. The current trend is to use dates in preference to names. This facilitates filing both in the manual and machine modes. In fact, the computer needs very explicit instructions in order to create a chronological file and to ignore a word or phrase preceding a date. Therefore, the Subject Analysis Committee of the ALA Cataloging and Classification Committee recommended that phrases and dates be reversed, e.g. **United States—History—1775–1783, Revolution.** A recommendation was also made that century subdivisions be defined to insure correct numerical filing position, e.g. change 19th century to **1800–1899 (19th century);** and that indefinite subdivisions be written as filed, e.g. To 1500 be changed to **0-1500.** These recommendations were adopted in the twelfth edition of Sears.

The List includes period subdivisions only for those countries for which a library is apt to acquire so many works about their history (United States, Great Britain, France, Germany, Italy and a few others) that it is necessary to separate them into groups according to the period treated, or for contemporary events that have produced a considerable amount of literature, e.g. **Lebanon—History—1982– , Israeli intervention.** Although some countries have a longer history than any of these, period subdivisions of history are not needed because the library acquires so little material about them. Regardless of the period treated all the material would be assigned the general heading, e.g. **India—History.**

Some of the subject and form subdivisions that are applicable to a considerable number of subjects are listed in their alphabetic places in the List and are also gathered together in one list on p XXXVIII–XL. There the cataloger can see readily what possibilities of subdivision are available. History subdivisions, however, are different for each country and so cannot be listed in one place. (The cataloger may wish to consult *LC Period Subdivisions Under Names of Places,* 2nd ed. 1975.)

Geographic Names. Many works limit the discussion of an otherwise general subject to a specific country, state, city, or other region. This is such a common method of treatment that the List has provided directions for many subjects that may be so treated. Other subjects not so identified can be subdivided by the cataloger if this is needed or is desirable. (See the Bibliography on pages XXXI–XXXIII for suggested reference sources to be used in researching and establishing geographic names.)

(1) *Subject Subdivided by Place.* Various subject headings, especially in the fields of science, technology, and economics are followed by a parenthetic statement giving permission to subdivide the heading geographically, such as: **"Agriculture (May subdiv. geog.)."** In application this means that if the work in hand deals with agriculture in general, only the heading **Agriculture** is used; but if it deals with agriculture in Iowa or in France, for example, then the cataloger may assign the heading **Agriculture—Iowa** or **Agriculture—France.**

The unit may be the name of a country, state, city, or other political or geographic area, depending on the nature of the subject and its treatment in the work. There are, however, some topics which would not apply to cities, in which case the note will read: **"(May subdiv. geog. country or state)."**

If the subject is in the field of art or music, then the wording varies slightly since we think of Spanish art, for example (rather than art in Spain), or German music (rather than music in Germany). The List reads **"Art (May subdiv. geog. adjective form, e.g. Art, French)"** and **"Music (May subdiv. geog. adjective form, e.g. Music, American)."** From these directions the work on Spanish art would be assigned the heading **Art, Spanish** and that on German music, **Music, German.**

Observe that the parenthetic note is permissive, not mandatory. If the library has only a few works on a subject for which geographic treatment is suggested, perhaps it would be easier for the user of the catalog to find these under the main heading without geographic subdivision. Some small libraries limit the use of geographic subdivision to countries other than the United States and to nationalities other than American since most of their material, general or special, will be concerned with the United States. The Sears List historically has never distinguished between French art or Art in France (which is not necessarily French). Should a library have sufficient material to warrant such a distinction, **Art—France** could be established in addition to **Art, French** which is suggested. One of the fundamentals of cataloging is to use one's judgment based on the materials on hand and the purpose and needs of the library. Therefore, if a library prefers geographic subdivisions for subjects that are not so indicated in Sears, the library should feel free to add such geographic subdivisions as needed or desired.

Geographic subdivisions can be both direct or indirect. The Sears List prefers the direct place subdivision as the most useful to the reader. In the direct form the name of the place discussed in the work is used directly as the subdivision, e.g. **Theater—Paris** or **Agriculture—Iowa.** The indirect form of place subdivision interposes the name of the country (the larger geographic area) between the subject and the smaller area that may be mentioned in the work, e.g. Theater—France—Paris and Agriculture—United States Iowa.

(2) *Names of Places Subdivided by Subject.* A different procedure is followed for most topics in the fields of history, geography, politics and social sciences, which are treated from a regional point of view. In works discussing the history of California, a census of Peru, the government of Italy, the boundaries of Bolivia, the population of Paris, or the climate of

Alaska, the area treated is the unique factor and its name with the appropriate topical subdivision is the most specific heading for the work. Directions for formulating the headings are given under the general subjects in the same way that subject subdivisions are indicated, for example:

Census
 See also names of countries, cities, etc. with the subdivision *Census,* e.g. **United States—Census;** etc.

The *See also* is to be interpreted as a direction for formulating a heading for the specific area needed and, when placed in the catalog, is a guide to the reader. Similar directions appear under **Boundaries; Climate; Population;** etc., which, applied to the topics cited above, would result in the headings:

California—History	**Bolivia—Boundaries**
Peru—Census	**Paris—Population**
Italy—Politics and government	**Alaska—Climate**

 The name of any country, state, city, or other area could have been used if needed. However, some topics are applicable to countries only (e.g. *Commercial policy; Diplomatic and consular service*); others are used only under names of cities (e.g. *Suburbs and environs*). The subdivision *Description and travel* is used for countries, states, and other large areas but is modified to the single word *Description* when applied to cities; therefore, **New Orleans (La.) —Description,** but **Louisiana—Description and travel.**

 In addition, a list of suggested subject subdivisions which may be used under the name of any city is given in the List under **Chicago (Ill.);** those that may be used under the name of any state are listed under **Ohio;** while under the **United States** are those that may be used under the name of any country or region, except the subdivisions of history. Since each country's history is unique, its periods of history are individual.

 Local materials are an exception to these rules. If the library wishes to keep all of the hometown or area materials together, then (1) and (2) above can be ignored, and all materials listed under the name of the locality with all aspects as subdivisions.

 There are no definite rules on subdividing by place or by subject. In general, subject headings in the field of science, technology, economics, education, and the arts are subdivided by place, while history, geography, politics, and the social sciences are made subdivisions under place. There are, however, exceptions. That aspect of the subject that is most important or has the primary interest is the criterion for decision. When one reads about social life and customs, one asks where the social life exists, e.g. **United States—Social life and customs.** However, one aspect of social life is the **Family.** This is the subject of importance and one asks secondarily where the family is located. (Note that **Family** is not subdivided by place in Sears as it is in the Library of Congress, but if a library has much material on the subject it might be advisable, and is permissible, to do so.)

 In general, the cataloger would enter under place and subdivide by subject those topics whose predominant interest is focused on area or people such as history, geography, or government. One would enter under subject and subdivide by place those topics that are primarily of interest for the subject matter regardless of place. In the field of the social sciences the decision must be made in each instance on the element of predominance because no general rule applies.

 Some headings in the subject areas of biography, language, and literature require subdivisions relevant to their areas, but others do not. Since knowing when not to subdivide is as important as when to use subdivision, the editor has treated these areas in some detail.

 Biography. Works in the field of biography fall into two categories: those in which biography as a form of writing is discussed, a relatively small class covered adequately by the subject heading **Biography (as a literary form);** and lives of persons, a very large class which must be considered in two groups—individual biography and collective biography.

(1) *Individual Biography.* Usually the only subject heading needed for the life of an individual is the name of the person, established in the same way as an author entry. If the work is an autobiography, some catalogers do not make a subject entry for it since the author and the subject are the same. However, since readers have been trained to look under subject entries it seems reasonable to make both an author and a subject heading, especially if there are many other entries as author or if there are subject entries by other authors, or if the library has a divided catalog.

Occasionally a biography will include so much material about the field in which the individual was working that a second subject heading is required in addition to the personal name. A life of Mary Baker Eddy, for example, may include a valuable account of the development of Christian Science that would require the subject heading, **Christian Science—History.** It must be emphasized that such second subject headings should be used *only* when there is a substantial amount of material included and when the book tells more about a person's work than his personal life. It is not used just because the biographee was prominent in the field. Two subject headings should be the exception, not the rule.

There are a few individuals about whom there is a large amount of material that is other than biographical, such as works about their writings or other activities. In such cases, subdivisions are added to the individual's name to separate various aspects treated, among which is *Biography.* Two such outstanding individuals are Jesus Christ and William Shakespeare. The List includes these names with subdivisions appropriate to material written about them. The subdivisions listed under Shakespeare may be used, if needed, under the names of other individuals about whom there is a large amount of varied literature, for example, Dante and Leonardo da Vinci. Subdivisions listed under **Presidents—United States** are to be used where appropriate under the name of any president, or other rulers, if appropriate. It must be noted that this represents the exceptional, not the usual, treatment. For most individual biographies only the name is needed.

(2) *Collective Biography.* This term refers usually to works containing more than three biographies, for if there are no more than three, each subject will be given a heading, consisting of the person's name, as in individual biography. (Some catalogers will treat even larger collections as a group of individual biographies. If they do this, they are analyzing the work, i.e., they are making analytic entries.) There are several varieties of collective biography, each requiring a separate kind of treatment.

> *General.* Collections of biographies not limited to any area or to any class of people are assigned the heading **Biography.** Sometimes the work includes many individuals, such as *International Who's Who;* sometimes a small group, such as *Ten Biographies of Famous Men and Women.*

> *Local Biography.* Very common are the biographies devoted to persons of a particular area, such as *Who's Who in Asia, Who's Who in Latin America, Dictionary of American Biography. Eminent Californians, Leaders in London;* or to ethnic groups, such as *Prominent Jews.* In such works the subject heading is the name of the area or ethnic group with the subdivision *Biography:*

Asia—Biography	**California—Biography**
Latin America—Biography	**London—Biography**
United States—Biography	**Jews—Biography**

If there are many entries under any such heading, the literary works (i.e., those designed for continuous reading) may be separated from the reference works which list a large number of names in alphabetic order, by adding to the heading for the latter, the subdivision *Dictionaries.* The heading for such a work as *Who's Who in America* may be, therefore, **United States—Biography—Dictionaries.**

Classes of Persons. Collective biographies that are devoted to lives of persons of a particular occupation or profession are entered under the term applied to its members, such as **Artists; Authors; Engineers; Librarians; Musicians; Poets; Radiologists, Scientists;** etc., with the subdivision *Biography.*

In a field where there is no adequate term to express its members, or when the name of the class or group refers to the subject in general not to individuals, the heading used for the specific field is subdivided by the term *Biography:*

Catholic Church—Biography	**United States—History—1861–1865, Civil**
Religions—Biography	**War—Biography**
	Women—Biography

N.B. The headings for areas, classes and groups are used for collective biographies only and not for the life of an individual, artist, author, woman, etc. However, reference to names of individuals should be made under the class names, for example: "Artists. See also names of individual artists."

In concluding this discussion on subdivision, another fact should be noted: a subdivided subject can be further subdivided, more than once if necessary. As seen in an example above, **United States—Biography—Dictionaries** was the subject for *Who's Who in America.* For a bibliography of the history of education in the United States the heading would be **Education —United States—History—Bibliography.**

Language and Literature. These fields are closely related, but they differ considerably in the amount of material published and in their treatment in the catalog. Any general library has proportionately a large number of works on literature, often its largest field of interest, and a comparatively small number of works on language. In both areas, but more particularly in language, the major interest is not in the general treatment but in the national aspect, that is, French language or English literature, German grammar or Italian drama, Spanish dictionaries or Hebrew poetry, etc.

Language. The subject heading for a general work about a specific language is the direct phrase: **English language; French language; German language.** If the work deals with a particular aspect or form of that language, terms representing them are used as subdivisions of the name of the language. Examples are:

English language—Etymology	**German language—Grammar**
French language—Dictionaries	**Spanish language—Terms and phrases**

Some of the general form and subject subdivisions will be needed also under names of languages, for example, **Italian language—History.**

Names of some languages are included in this List (and others are to be added as needed) but no subdivisions are listed except under **English language.** This serves as a guide or "key" to the subdivisions that may be used under the name of any language.

Literature. The field of literature includes two classes of material which must be distinguished carefully: (1) works about literature, a relatively small group; (2) examples of literature, that is *belles-lettres,* or the literature itself, a very large group. In the first we are dealing with actual subjects; in the second with literary forms, not subjects.

(1) *Works about Literature.* The subject headings for works about the various literary forms are their specific names, e.g. **Drama; Essay; Fiction; Poetry.** Works about the major literary forms of national literatures are entered also under the direct phrase, not, as in language, as subdivisions; e.g. **Irish drama; Italian poetry; Russian fiction.** Specific aspects are expressed by subdivisions, as for other subjects; e.g. **Drama—Technique; English literature—Dictionaries; Short stories—Indexes; American literature—History and criticism.** It should be noted that the subdivision *History and criticism* is always used in its entirety and corresponds to the subdivision *History* used with other than literature, motion pictures, and music subjects.

Names of some national literatures are included in the List (and others are to be added as needed) but a suggested list of subdivisions which may be used under them is listed only under **English literature** which thus serves as the "key" to subdivisions that may be used under the name of any national literature. The major literary forms may be used for any national literature by substituting its name for the word "English."

(2) *Examples of Literature, i.e. Belles-lettres.* This large class of material must be separated into two categories whose treatment is entirely different.

Individual Authors. In general, the literary works of individual authors receive no subject entry. Literature is known by author and title and readers usually want a specific novel, or a certain play, or poetry by a specific author—material which can be located in the catalog by author and title entries.

Collections of Several Authors. Collections consisting of works of several authors are usually entered in the catalog under the title of the collection. Therefore, as an aid to their location in the catalog, these materials are given a heading that represents the form of literature included in the collection. Since such headings are used also for actual subjects, distinction must be made between the headings for works *describing* a particular literary form and *examples* of it. The singular form is used as an actual subject heading. If it has an acceptable plural, this can be used to represent collections, but if there is no true plural then the subdivision *Collected works* must be added to the name of the literary form:

Subject Heading	Form Heading for Collections
Essay	Essays; American essays; etc.
Parody	Parodies
Short story	Short stories
Drama	Drama—Collected works
French drama	French drama—Collected works
Fiction	Fiction—Collected works
Russian fiction	Russian fiction—Collected works
Literature	Literature—Collected works
German literature	German literature—Collected works
Poetry	Poetry—Collected works
Japanese poetry	Japanese poetry—Collected works

Minor literary forms, such as ballads, fables, fairy tales, parodies, satire, sermons, short stories, and tales, are not listed under the national adjective. If national treatment is needed, the adjective is added after the name of the form, e.g. **Satire, English.** These headings are used not only for collections by several authors but also for works of individual authors and for works about such forms. This departure in treatment from that given to the major literary forms is due to the small number of books involved. If the number of books for any of them is large the heading may be subdivided to separate the works about them from the literature itself, e.g. **Satire, English—History and criticism.**

N.B. Catalogers frequently give novels, poems and plays based on historical events or lives of famous persons a subject entry. Such headings must be distinguished from the headings which are assigned to factual accounts by adding the subdivision *Drama; Fiction;* or *Poetry,* as the case may be:

Slavery—United States—Drama
Lincoln, Abraham, 1809–1865—Fiction
Bunker Hill (Boston, Mass.), Battle of, 1775—Poetry

Nonbook materials. The assignment of subject headings for audiovisual and special instructional materials should follow the same principles that are applied to books. The heading most specifically describing the contents of the material should be used, and the same headings should be applied to book and nonbook materials alike. This is especially important if the catalog integrates all media. One integrated catalog would seem to be preferable because this would bring all materials on one subject together regardless of format. For this edition of the List almost all of the subjects and subdivisions which include the word book have been changed to make them applicable to all materials. Two exceptions are *Handbooks, manuals, etc.* and *Yearbooks.*

Because nonbook materials often concentrate on very small aspects of larger subjects, the cataloger may not find in the List the specific heading that should be used. In such instances the cataloger should be generous in adding new subjects (see p xxx–xxxi). It may also be necesssary to use a form heading for the format of the material, as well as a subject heading for the content. **Biographical films,** for example, could be created as a subject if needed to describe a specific type of film.

Subject headings for nonbook materials should not include form subdivisions to describe physical format, i.e. motion pictures, slides, sound recordings, music, etc. Some libraries may choose to maintain a separate catalog for each format; others may choose to list all materials in an omnimedia catalog. For libraries using omnimedia catalogs, AACR2 provides the option of using general materials designations (GMD), which are placed at the end of the title proper and alert users to the general class to which an item belongs. The appropriate GMD is selected from either the North American list or the British list. Additional information on this aspect of descriptive cataloging can be found in the *Anglo-American Cataloging Rules,* 2nd edition, and in *Commonsense Cataloging.*

Terminology. The subject headings for the general fields of knowledge and for concrete objects are simple to comprehend, but terms for abstract ideas may offer some difficulty. By looking through the *See also* references under a given heading, or noting the *See* references to it, a cataloger may often find how the term is used.

Sometimes two or more terms may seem to cover the same subject, unless the exact meaning and limitations of each is appreciated. Some headings in the List are accompanied by a scope note explaining their limitations as an aid to differentiating between overlapping subjects. For example, the headings **Alcoholism; Drinking of alcoholic beverages; Liquor industry; Prohibition; Temperance** overlap to a certain degree, but because of doubt in their distinctions one should not use all of them for any one book. By means of the scope notes included with these terms, it is understood that **Alcoholism** is used for medical works and works on drunkenness; **Drinking of alcoholic beverages** includes works on drinking in its social aspects and as a social problem; **Liquor industry** is used for works on the liquor industry and trade; **Prohibition** for works dealing with the legal prohibition of liquor traffic and liquor manufacture; and **Temperance** is used for general works on the temperance question and the temperance movement.

A cataloger must consult the library's own catalog in order to see how a subject heading has been used. Printed catalogs such as the *Cumulative Book Index* and the "Standard Catalog Series" are also of value in order to see what kind of works are included under a given subject. Other cataloging aids are the *Weekly Record* and its monthly and annual cumulations, the *American Book Publishing Record, Subject Guide to Books in Print,* and the *Library of Congress Catalogs: Subject Catalog.* The *Readers' Guide to Periodical Literature* and other indexes are also useful. Aid in interpreting the scope and meaning of a subject heading may be found by looking up its classification number or numbers in the *Dewey Decimal Classification.* There the topic can be studied in its relation to other topics, a development usually impossible to see directly in an alphabetic arrangement.

Each cataloger will have individual problems in interpretation of subjects. Whenever a decision has been made on the scope of a term where there has been doubt, a definition or explanation should be recorded for future use. Such notes are a necessity for catalogers and they may be helpful also to users of the catalog. Whenever it is felt that such an explanation would be of general value, it may be entered in the catalog and filed preceding the entries under the subject heading. Of course, the wording may have to be adapted slightly from that in the List which is addressed to catalogers.

References. After an item has been assigned a subject heading, attention must be directed to insuring that the reader who is searching for this material will not fail to find it because of insufficient references to the proper heading. The following is a summary of the types, methods of formulation, and use of references.

(1) *Specific "See" References.* These refer the reader from terms or phrases not used as subject headings to terms or phrases that are used. They are, therefore, absolutely essential to the success of the catalog. The reader must be directed from variant spellings and terminology to the one word or phrase that has been selected to represent the subject. While a subject heading may be used on as many entries as the library has works on the subject, the *See* reference is made only once. For example, the first time the heading **Agriculture** is used, the cataloger (following the suggestion in the *x* paragraph under **Agriculture** in the List) will make an entry for the catalog that reads: "Farming. See Agriculture." This will not be made again, no matter how many times the heading **Agriculture** is used, and no work will ever be assigned the word Farming as a heading.

See references are made:

(1) from synonyms or from terms so neary synonymous that they would cover the same kind of material
(2) from the second part of a compound heading, e.g. **Desertion and nonsupport** requires a reference from Nonsupport
(3) from the second part of an inverted heading, e.g. **Chemistry, Technical** requires a reference from Technical chemistry
(4) sometimes from an inverted heading to normal order, e.g. **Adult education** requires a reference from Education, Adult. (Note the number of used headings that begin with the word Education.)
(5) from variant spellings to the spelling used, e.g. **Color** requires a reference from Colour
(6) from opposites when they are included without being specifically mentioned, e.g. **Temperance** requires a reference from Intemperance
(7) from the singular to the plural when the two forms would not file together in the catalog, e.g. **Mice** requires a reference from Mouse; **Cats** requires a reference from Cat. (Note the long list of headings between the singular and the plural of each of these two words.)

(2) *Specific "See also" References.* The *See* references are concerned mainly with terminology, guiding the reader from words he may think of to those actually used for subject headings. But the *See also* references are concerned entirely with guiding the reader from headings where he has found information to other headings that list materials on related or more specific aspects of the subject. Consequently such references cannot be made without knowing whether the library has material under the other subjects.

In general, *See also* references are made from the general subject to more specific parts of it, and not ordinarily from the specific to the general. For example, "Science. See also Mathematics," but not the other way around. Proceeding one step at a time to the next more specific topic would result in: "Mathematics. See also Arithmetic"; and "Arithmetic. See also Business arithmetic." *See also* references are also made between related subjects of more or less equal specificity, for example, "Drawing. See also Painting."

See also "refer from" references are much more difficult than *See* references both to make and to understand, and their value is not so unquestioned. They have been included freely under headings (in the *xx* paragraph) in the List but only knowledge of the library's collection can determine whether any of these suggestions should be followed. For example, a work that discusses both inventions and patents will be entered in the catalog under **Inventions** and under **Patents.** The List suggests the reference, "Inventions. See also Patents," but it must not be made if the only material that is to be found in the catalog under **Patents** is this work which is already listed under **Inventions.** If there is a choice between two headings, the predominant one should be chosen.

(3) *General References.* In addition to specific references, there are general *See* and *See also* references which, instead of referring to many individual headings, serve as blanket references to all headings of a particular group. Some references are a combination of specific and general. It is the general references which give the cataloger directions for adding specific headings that have been omitted from the List, as explained previously. Their use and value in the public catalog are somewhat different. The most common types of general references are ones to:

(1) Common names of different species of a class, e.g.

> **Flowers**
>> *See also* **Annuals (Plants)** . . . also names of flowers, e.g. **Roses;** etc.

(2) Names of individual persons, e.g.

> **Artists**
>> *See also* **Architects** . . . also names of individual artists

(3) Names of particular institutions, buildings, societies, etc., e.g.

> **Abbeys**
>> *See also* **Cathedrals** . . . also names of individual abbeys, e.g. **Westminster Abbey;** etc.

> **Labor unions**
>> *See also* **Arbitration, Industrial** . . . also names of types of unions and names of individual labor unions, e.g. **Librarians' unions; United Steelworkers of America;** etc.

(4) Names of particular geographic features, e.g.

> **Mountains**
>> *See also* **Mountaineering** . . . also names of mountain ranges, e.g. **Rocky Mountains;** etc.; and names of mountains, e.g. **Elk Mountain (Wyo.);** etc.

(5) Geographic treatment of a general subject, e.g.

> **Population**
>> *See also* **Birth control** . . . also names of countries, cities, etc. with the subdivision *Population,* e.g. **United States—Population; Chicago (Ill.)—Population;** etc.

(6) Form divisions, e.g.

> Glossaries. *See* names of languages or subjects with the subdivision *Dictionaries,* e.g. **English language—Dictionaries; Chemistry—Dictionaries;** etc.

(7) National literatures, e.g.

> **Poetry**
>> *See also* **Ballads** . . . also **American poetry; English poetry;** etc.

It is apparent that the general references in the List save an enormous amount of space both in the List and the library catalog. If all the headings for which directions are given were formulated they would be innumerable. In an individual library relatively few of these headings are used so that it may be preferable to formulate specific references when specific headings are added, particularly if there are only a few in the class. That is, if the cataloger uses the headings **Azaleas; Parakeets; Pineapple** (none of which is in the printed List), these names would be added to the *See also* references under the respective groups represented. For example, assuming that the headings **Fruit; Berries;** and **Citrus fruit** had been used for materials in the library, the reference in the List and in the catalog would now read: "**Fruit.** *See also* **Berries; Citrus fruit; Pineapple.**"

However, when there is a long list of specific headings, catalogers disagree on the policy of adding them to the reference. For example, the heading **Artists** in the List reads: "*See also* . . . names of individual artists." Some catalogers, in preparing this reference for the catalog, would omit the phrase, "names of individual artists," and instead, add the names of all the artists that have been used as subject headings in the library's catalog; other catalogers expect the reader to recall the individual, and the reference is left as printed. Each library must determine this on the basis of the number of specific references that would be needed. But under headings where the individual names may not be numerous or well-known, it is feasible for the cataloger and useful to the reader to list the names rather than to rely on the general reference. However, in the example in the preceding paragraph, the cataloger would be advised to make the reference as follows: "**Fruit.** *See also* **Berries; Citrus fruit;** also names of fruits, e.g., **Pineapple,** etc."

The cataloger should note that under a *See* reference there is never a subject entry for a work, while under *See also* references there are always entries. Reading the reference structure in the List always poses a problem for beginners as does the making of the references for the library catalog. Below is a heading from the List and its reading:

> **Birds** (May subdiv. geog.) **598**
>> Names of all birds are not included in this
>> list but are to be added as needed,
>> in the plural form, e.g. **Canaries;**
>> **Robins;** etc.
>> *See also* classes of birds, e.g. **Birds of prey;**
>> **Cage birds; Game and game birds;**
>> **State birds; Water birds;** etc.; and
>> names of specific birds, e.g.
>> **Canaries; Robins;** etc.
> *x* Bird; Ornithology
> *xx* **Vertebrates; Zoology**

Note that the *See also* references read in direct order from top to bottom: **Birds.** *See also* **Birds of Prey; Cage birds; Game and game birds;** . . . The *See* references read in the reverse order, from bottom to top, that is, from the word opposite the *x* up to the heading: Bird. *See* **Birds.** Ornithology. *See* **Birds.** *See also* "refer from" references also read from the bottom to the top, that is, from the word opposite the *xx* up to the heading: **Vertebrates.** *See also* **Birds. Zoology.** *See also* **Birds.**

To maintain a subject authority file on cards rather than checking in the book as described on p XXXIV-XXXV the cataloger would make cards for those subjects (including the printed instructions and scope notes) used from the List.

The set of cards on the next page illustrates one type of spacing.

Birds

See also

Birds of prey
Cage birds
Game and game birds
State birds
Water birds
    and names of birds, e.g. **Canaries, Robins,** etc.

Bird

See

Birds

Ornithology

See

Birds

Vertebrates

See also

Birds

Zoology

See also

Birds

The directions and scope notes printed in the List for the guidance of the cataloger should be modified for the catalog if the cataloger feels that a note is needed for the patron. Following is an example of a rewording:

As it appears in the List for the cataloger:

> **Space ships   629.45**
>> Use for materials on space vehicles with people on board. Materials on spacecraft both with and without people are entered under **Space vehicles.**
>>
>> *See also* **Orbital rendezvous (Space flight); Rocket planes**
>> *x* Space craft
>> *xx* **Astronautics; Life support systems (Space environment); Rocketry; Space vehicles**

As it appears in the catalog for the reader:

Space ships

Here are listed materials on space vehicles with people on board.

Materials on spacecraft both with and without people are entered under **Space vehicles.**

○

New Terminology for Old Subjects. The English language is changing constantly so that from time to time new terms appear for subjects which are not new. Through the years many changes have had to be made: **Child welfare** was formerly *Children—Charities, protection, etc.;* **Radio advertising** started out as *Radio broadcasting—Business applications; House decoration* was in use before the present **Interior decoration;** and *Profession, Choice of* before **Vocational guidance.**

It is impossible for the subject headings to reflect all the newest language styles, particularly in fields whose terminology fluctuates frequently. A term that is current today may soon be superseded by another, or a term considered passé may return to favor. But at least new terms can be represented in the catalog by *See* references to the heading used.

Of course, if a heading is found to be incorrect or is no longer in common usage, or suddenly assumes a pejorative or biased connotation, changes must be made. The adoption of a new term means changing not only all the old entries to the new form but also the various references to and from it. It is impossible to state at what stage in the development of the language such changes should be made. Each heading must be considered individually. If change is desirable but the number of entries to be changed is prohibitive, one can accomplish the change by *See also* references. Using one of the aforementioned changes as an example, the cataloger would make the following entry substituting for (date) the calendar year in which the change is made:

Space vehicles, Reusable

      For materials issued after (date) consult
the following heading

      Space shuttles

Space shuttles

      For materials issued before (date) consult
the following heading

      Space vehicles, Reusable

These references could also assume the following format for a card catalog. A guide card that protrudes above the other cards in the tray is more readily seen by the user of the catalog.

Space vehicles, Reusable.
      For materials issued after (date) see **Space shuttles**

Space shuttles. For materials issued before (date) see
      Space vehicles, Reusable

New Subjects. No printed list of subject headings can be entirely up to date. There are constantly new ideas, new inventions, or new countries being created. Headings for these new topics of current interest will have to be added by the cataloger as needed. They should be constructed in the same way as headings for related topics and as the cataloger has been shown in this text.

First aid is supplied by the periodical indexes, such as the *Readers' Guide to Periodical Literature, Applied Science & Technology Index,* etc., since their editors must assign subject headings to material as soon as it is published. As the new subject develops, some change in the heading may be made in succeeding issues of the index. By the time a book is written about a new subject, the terminology may have changed and become stabilized since the first periodical index article appeared. Therefore, the catalogs of new works such as *Booklist, Cumulative Book Index,* and *Book Review Digest* are valuable aids. The Library of Congress includes headings for new subjects in the quarterly supplements to its list of Subject Headings. The *Weekly Record* publishes Library of Congress cataloging information which is cumulated in monthly and annual issues of the *American Book Publishing Record.* Through the Cataloging in Publication program the Library of Congress cataloging information will usually appear on the verso of the title page in books of those publishers cooperating in the program.

It is not always possible to decide at once on the permanent form for a new subject heading, but the cataloger cannot always wait for the subject to develop before giving headings to new material. Tentative headings can be assigned and used until the terminology becomes standardized. A list of these tentative headings should be kept (it will never be long) so that they can be reconsidered later and either adopted permanently or changed, as the case may be, and added to the List. One must be sure that the new term is not merely a new name or a colloquialism for a subject already in the catalog.

Recording Headings and References. The cataloger should keep a list of subject headings used and references made for them. This may be kept on cards and filed in the catalog department or a copy of the Sears List may be checked whenever a heading is used for the first time. Additions to the List should be written in and references should be recorded as needed. Detailed directions for checking the List and a Sample Page illustrating them will be found on p XXXIV–XXXV.

Bibliography

Akers, Susan Grey. *Akers' Simple Library Cataloging.* 7th ed. Completely revised and rewritten by Arthur Curley and Jana Varlejs. Metuchen, N.J.: Scarecrow Press, 1984. (Chapter 2)

American Library Association. Filing Committee. *ALA Filing Rules.* Chicago: American Library Association, 1980.

Bakewell, K. G. B. *A Manual on Cataloging Practice.* New York: Pergamon Press, 1972. (Chapter 5)

Bernhardt, Frances S. *Introduction to Library Technical Services.* New York: The H. W. Wilson Co., 1979. (pp. 155–174)

Chan, Lois Mai. *Cataloging and Classification: an introduction.* New York: McGraw-Hill, 1981.

Chan, Lois Mai. *Library of Congress Subject Headings: Principles and Application.* 2nd ed. Littleton, Colo.: Libraries Unlimited, 1986.

Coates, E. J. *Subject Catalogues: Headings and Structure.* London: Library Association, 1960.

The Columbia Lippincott Gazetteer of the World. Edited by Leon E. Seltzer with the geographical research staff of Columbia University Press and with the cooperation of the American Geographical Society; with 1961 supplement. New York: Columbia University Press, 1952.

Dewey, Harry. *An Introduction to Library Cataloging and Classification.* 4th ed. rev. and enl. Madison, Wis.: Capital Press, 1957. (Chapters 10–13 and 15)

Dewey, Melvil. *Abridged Dewey Decimal Classification and Relative Index.* 11th ed. Edited under the direction of Benjamin A. Custer. Albany, N.Y.: Forest Press, 1979.

Dewey, Melvil. *DDC, Dewey Decimal Classification: 004–006 Data Processing and Computer Science and Changes in Related Disciplines.* Revision of edition 19. Prepared by Julianne Beall et. al. Albany, N.Y.: Forest Press, 1985.

Dowell, Arlene T. *Cataloging with Copy: a Decision-Maker's Handbook.* Littleton, Colo.: Libraries Unlimited, 1976. (pp. 111–134)

Dunkin, Paul S. *Cataloging U. S. A.* Chicago: American Library Association, 1969. (Chapter 5)

Eaton, Thelma. *Cataloging and Classification: an Introductory Manual.* 4th ed. Ann Arbor, Mich.: Edwards Brothers, 1967. (Chapters 5–6)

Elrod, J. McRee. *Choice of Subject Headings.* [programmed text] 3rd ed. Metuchen, N.J.: Scarecrow Press, 1980.

Foskett, A. C. *The Subject Approach to Information.* 4th ed. Hamden, Conn.: Linnet Books, 1982.

Frarey, Carlyle James. "Subject Headings." In *The State of the Library Art,* vol. 1, part 2, edited by Ralph R. Shaw. New Brunswick, N.J.: Graduate School of Library Service, Rutgers, The State University, 1960.

Harris, Jessica Lee. *Subject Analysis: Computer Implications of Rigorous Definition.* Metuchen, N.J.: Scarecrow Press, 1970.

Haycock, Ken, and Lynne Isberg Lighthall. *Sears List of Subject Headings: Canadian Companion.* 2nd ed. New York: The H. W. Wilson Co., 1983.

Haykin, David Judson. *Subject Headings: a Practical Guide.* Washington: U.S. Government Printing Office, 1951. Reprint. New York: Gordon Press, 1978.

Hennepin County Library. *HCL Cataloging Bulletin.* Edina, Minn.

Hennepin County Library. *Hennepin County Library Microfiche Authority List.*

Library Literature: an Index to Library and Information Science. New York: The H. W. Wilson Co., 1921-

Library of Congress. Subject Cataloging Division. *Subject Cataloging Manual: Subject Headings.* Rev. ed. Washington: Library of Congress, 1985.

Mann, Margaret. *Introduction to Cataloging and the Classification of Books.* 2nd ed. Chicago: American Library Association, 1943. (Chatpers 9–10)

Miksa, Francis L. *The Subject in the Dictionary Catalog from Cutter to the Present.* Chicago: American Library Association, 1983.

Miller, Rosalind E. and Jane C. Terwillegar. *Commonsense Cataloging: a Cataloger's Manual.* 3rd ed. Revised edition of the 2nd edition of *Commonsense Cataloging* by Esther J. Piercy. New York: The H. W. Wilson Co., 1983. (Chapters 6–8)

National Geographic Society. *National Geographic Atlas of the World.* 5th ed. Washington: National Geographic Society, 1981.

Pettee, Julia. *Subject Headings: the History and Theory of the Alphabetical Subject Approach to Books.* New York: The H. W. Wilson Co., 1946.

Sears, Minnie Earl. *Sears: Lista de encabezamientos de materia.* Traducción y adaptación de la *12a edición en inglés, editada por Barbara M. Westby* por Carmen Rovira. New York: The H. W. Wilson Co., 1984. A Spanish translation by Carmen Rovira of the 12th edition of Sears, including the "Principles" section.

Tauber, Maurice Falcolm. *Technical Services in Libraries; Acquisitions, Cataloging, Classification, Binding, Photographic Reproduction, and Circulation Operations.* New York: Columbia University Press, 1954. (Chapters 10–11)

Theory of Subject Analysis: a sourcebook. Edited by Lois Mai Chan, Phyllis A. Richmond, and Elaine Svenonius. Littleton, Colo.: Libraries Unlimited, 1985.

Times Atlas of the World. 7th comprehensive ed. Times Books in collaboration with John Bartholomew & Son Limited. New York: Times Books, 1985.

Webster's New Geographical Dictionary. Springfield, Mass.: Merriam-Webster, 1984.

Wynar, Bohdan S. *Introduction to Cataloging and Classification.* 7th ed. by Arlene G. Taylor. Littleton, Colo.: Libraries Unlimited, 1985.

CHECKING AND ADDING HEADINGS

See Sample Page opposite

1. *Check the subject heading used.* When the subject heading **Birds** is used for the first time, a check mark is placed in front of it.

2. *Make and check "See" references to the heading.* The *x* terms under **Birds** are considered and the cataloger decides to make a reference from Bird and from Ornithology as suggested. Cards are made for the catalog reading: "Bird. See Birds" and "Ornithology. See Birds." The terms Bird and Ornithology are checked both in their alphabetic places in the List and in the *x* references under **Birds.**

3. *Make and check "See also" and "See also refer from" references to the heading.* The *xx* headings given under **Birds** are examined to see whether they have been used in the catalog. The heading **Vertebrates** has a check mark beside it showing that it has been used. The cataloger decides to place a reference in the catalog reading: "Vertebrates. See also Birds." It is recorded in the List:

    under **Birds,** in the *xx* paragraph, **Vertebrates** is checked
    under **Vertebrates,** in the *See also* paragraph, **Birds** is checked

    For purposes of this explanation, the assumption is made that **Zoology** has not yet been used.

4. *Adding headings to the List.* The library acquires material about ostriches. The term is not in the List but the directions given in the note under **Birds** tell the cataloger that the heading **Ostriches** may be added. It is written in the margin in its alphabetic place and checked. To the public catalog is added the reference: "Birds. See also Ostriches." It is recorded in the List:

    under **Birds,** to the *See also* paragraph is added, **Ostriches,** and checked
    under **Ostriches,** is added, *xx* **Birds,** and checked

    The library acquires material on birds in Maine. Following the permission given with the heading **Birds,** "(May subdiv. geog.)," the cataloger uses the heading, **Birds—Maine,** writing it in the margin in its alphabetic place and checking it. Since the library has very little material about this region, it is decided to make a reference for the catalog reading, "Maine—Birds. See Birds—Maine." This reference is added also to the List and traced under the new heading by adding *x* Maine—Birds.

5. *Canceled subjects.* If all entries for a subject are withdrawn from the catalog, turn to the subject heading in the List, find what references have been made and remove them (if they are individual references) or cancel the heading (if other references are listed). At the same time, erase or cross off the check marks in the List to show that the subject and its references are not now used.

SAMPLE PAGE OF CHECKING

Abbreviated entries taken from various pages of the Sears List. A check (√) indicates that the heading or reference has been used in the library's catalog, marginal notes show how subjects may be added when needed

√ **Birds** (May subdiv. geog.)   **598**

     Names of all birds are not included in this list but are to be added as needed, in the plural form, e.g. **Canaries; Robins;** etc.

     See also classes of birds, e.g. **Birds of prey; Cage birds; Game and game birds; State birds; Water birds;** etc.; and names of specific birds, e.g. **Canaries; Robins;** etc.

     x √ Bird; Ornithology
     xx √ **Vertebrates; Zoology**

√ Ostriches

Birds—Flight   **598**
Birds—Habits and behavior   **598**

√ **Birds – Maine**
    x √ **Maine – Birds**
√ **Maine – Birds.** *See* **Birds – Maine**

Mail service. *See* **Postal service**
Mainstreaming in education   **371.9**

Ornamental plants. *See* **Plants, Ornamental**
√ Ornithology. *See* **Birds**
Orphan drugs   **615**

     Use for materials on drugs which appear to be useful for the treatment of rare disorders but due to their limited commercial value have difficulty in finding funding for research and marketing.

     x Drugs, Orphan
     xx **Drugs**

Osteopathy   **615.5**
     See also **Chiropractic; Massage**
     xx **Massage; Medicine; Medicine—Practice**

√ Ostriches
    xx √ **Birds**

Ostrogoths. *See* **Teutonic peoples**

Versification   **808.1**
     See also **Poetry; Rhyme**
     x English language—Versification; Meter; Prosody
     xx **Authorship; Poetics; Rhythm**
√ **Vertebrates**   **596**
     See also **Amphibians; Birds; Fishes; Mammals; Reptiles**
     xx **Animals; Zoology**

HEADINGS TO BE ADDED BY THE CATALOGER

It is neither possible nor necessary to enter all proper and common nouns including corporate names in a subject heading list such as Sears. If a specific name is not included in the List, the cataloger must establish a heading for it, using available reference sources.

A. PROPER NAMES

       1. Names of persons

       2. Names of families

       3. Names of places

           a. Political units: countries, states, cities, provinces, counties, etc.

           b. Groups of states or countries: e.g. **Atlantic States; Baltic States;** etc.

           c. Geographic features: Mountain ranges and individual mountains; island groups and individual islands; river valleys and individual rivers; regions; oceans; lakes; etc.

       4. Names of nationalities

       5. Names of national languages and literatures

       6. Names of wars and battles

       7. Names of treaties

       8. Names of Indian peoples

       9. Names of corporate bodies

           a. Names of associations, societies, clubs, etc.

           b. Names of institutions: colleges, libraries, hospitals, etc.

           c. Names of church denominations

           d. Names of government bodies

           e. Names of buildings, parks, ships, etc.

B. COMMON NAMES

       1. Names from such categories as:

animals	fruits	sports
birds	games	tools
fishes	musical	trees
flowers	instruments	vegetables
foods	nuts	

       2. Names of diseases

       3. Names of organs and regions of the body

       4. Names of chemicals

       5. Names of minerals

N.B. Wherever the List cites, "*See also* [or *See*] names of . . .," the specific name may be added even though not included in the List

"KEY" HEADINGS

To enable the cataloger to see the full display of possible subdivisions that may be used with some of the more popular categories, the editor has provided certain prominent names in the List to serve as "keys":

Persons:

Presidents—United States (to illustrate subdivisions which may be used under presidents, prime ministers and other rulers)

Shakespeare, William, 1564–1616 (to illustrate subdivisions which may be used under any voluminous author)

Peoples:

Indians of North America (to illustrate subdivisions which may be used under names of peoples and linguistic families)

Places:

United States; Ohio; Chicago (Ill.) (to illustrate subdivisions under geographic names, except for historical periods)

Languages and Literatures:

English language (to illustrate subdivisions which may be used with any language)

English literature (to illustrate subdivisions which may be used with any literature)

N.B. Most of the principal languages and literatures will be found in the List

Wars:

World War, 1939–1945 (to illustrate subdivisions which may be used under any war or battle)

N.B. The subdivisions under the "Keys" are illustrative, not exclusive.

LIST OF COMMONLY USED SUBDIVISIONS

In addition to the subdivisions listed under the "keys" mentioned in the preceding page, a large number of general, form, or topical subdivisions may be used under subjects as needed. These subdivisions are also known as "free-floating subdivisions."

The following list is not all inclusive. The subdivisions which appear under the "key" headings are not repeated here, except when they may also be used under other subjects:

Accidents
Accounting
Addresses and essays
Administration
Air conditioning
Alcohol use
Analysis
Anatomy
Anecdotes, facetiae, satire, etc.
Antiquities
Assassination
Atlases
Attitudes
Audiovisual aids
Automation
Bibliography
Bio-bibliography
Biography
Books and reading
Buildings
Care and hygiene
Cartoons and caricatures
Case studies
Catalogs
Censorship
Chemotherapy
Chronology
Citizen participation
Civil rights
Collected works
Collectibles
Collection and preservation
Collectors and collecting
Colonies
Color
Communication systems
Competitions
Composition
Computer assisted instruction
Computer programs
Concordances
Congresses
Conservation and restoration
Contracts and specifications

Control
Correspondence
Corrupt practices
Costs
Costume
Curricula
Data processing
Desertions
Design
Design and construction
Designs and plans
Dictionaries
Diet therapy
Directories
Directories—Telephone
Discography
Diseases
Diseases and pests
Documentation
Drama
Drug use
Economic aspects
Economic conditions
Education
Employment
Entrance requirements
Environmental aspects
Equipment and supplies
Estimates
Examinations, questions, etc.
Exhibitions
Experiments
Fiction
Filmography
Finance
Fires and fire prevention
Folklore
Food
Fuel consumption
Genetic aspects
Geographical distribution
Government policy
Growth
Guidebooks

Habits and behavior
Handbooks, manuals, etc.
Health and hygiene
Heating and ventilation
Historiography
History (for all works except literature,
   film, and music)
History and criticism (for literature, film,
   and music)
Home care
Housing
Identification
In-service training
Indexes
Industrial applications
Insignia
Inspection
Institutional care
Integration
Intellectual life
International cooperation
Jargon
Kings, queens, rulers, etc.
Labeling
Labor productivity
Laboratory manuals
Language
Law and legislation
Lighting
Maintenance and repair
Malpractice
Management
Maps
Marketing
Materials
Mathematical models
Mathematics
Measurement
Medals, badges, decorations, etc.
Medical care
Methodology
Miscellanea
Models
Moral and religious aspects
Noise
Nursing
Nutrition
Officials and employees
Origin
Outlines, syllabi, etc.
Patterns
Periodicals
Philosophy
Photographs from space

Physiological effect
Pictorial works
Poetry
Political activity
Portraits
Practice
Preservation
Prevention
Prices
Problems, exercises, etc.
Production standards
Professional ethics
Programmed instruction
Prophecies
Protection
Protests, demonstrations, etc.
Psychological aspects
Psychology
Public opinion
Quality
Quality control
Quotations
Rating
Reading materials
Recreation
Recruiting
Recycling
Registers
Rehabilitation
Religion
Religious life
Remodeling
Repairing
Research
Reviews
Safety appliances
Safety measures
Security measures
Segregation
Sexual behavior
Social aspects
Social conditions
Social life and customs
Societies
Songs and music
Sources
Statistics
Stories, plots, etc.
Study and teaching
Suffrage
Surgery
Tables, etc.
Taxation
Technique

Terminology
Testing
Texts
Therapeutic use
Thermodynamics
Tournaments
Toxicology

Training
Transplantation
Transportation
Tropics
Vocational guidance
Voyages and travels
Yearbooks

SEARS LIST OF SUBJECT HEADINGS

3 mile limit. *See* **Territorial waters**
4-H clubs 630.6
>   *x* Boys' agricultural clubs; Four-H clubs; Girls'
>   agricultural clubs
>   *xx* **Agriculture—Societies; Boys' clubs; Girls'
>   clubs**

4th of July. *See* **Fourth of July**
17 year locusts. *See* **Cicadas**
100 years' war. *See* **Hundred Years' War, 1339-
    1453**
200 mile limit. *See* **Territorial waters**
1200-1299 (13th century). *See* **Thirteenth century**
1500-1599 (16th century). *See* **Sixteenth century**
1600-1699 (17th century). *See* **Seventeenth century**
1700-1799 (18th century). *See* **Eighteenth century**
1800-1899 (19th century). *See* **Nineteenth century**
1900-1999 (20th century). *See* **Twentieth century**
2000-2099 (21st century). *See* **Twenty-first century**
A.B.C.'s. *See* **Alphabet**
A.B.M.'s. *See* **Antimissile missiles**
A bomb victims. *See* **Atomic bomb victims**
A.D.C. *See* **Child welfare**
A.I.D.S. (Disease). *See* **AIDS (Disease)**
A.T.V.'s. *See* **All terrain vehicles**
Abacus 513.028
Abandoned children 362.7
>   *See also* **Orphans**
>   *x* Children, Abandoned
>   *xx* **Child welfare; Children; Orphans**

Abandoned towns. *See* **Cities and towns, Ruined,
    extinct, etc.; Ghost towns**
Abandonment of family. *See* **Desertion and non-
    support**
Abbeys 271; 726
>   *See also* **Cathedrals; Convents; Monasteries;** also
>   names of individual abbeys, e.g.
>   **Westminster Abbey;** etc.
>   *xx* **Church architecture; Church history; Con-
>   vents; Monasteries**

Abbreviations 421; 423; etc.
>   *See also* **Acronyms; Ciphers; Code names; Short-
>   hand; Signs and symbols**
>   *x* Contractions; Symbols
>   *xx* **Ciphers; Shorthand; Signs and symbols; Writ-
>   ing**

ABCs. *See* **Alphabet**
Abduction. *See* **Kidnapping**
Ability 153.9
>   *See also* types of ability, e.g. **Creative ability;
>   Executive ability; Leadership; Musical abil-
>   ity;** etc.

1

Ability—*Continued*
    xx **Success**
Ability grouping in education 371.2
    See also **Nongraded schools**
    x Grouping by ability
    xx **Grading and marking (Students)**
Ability—Testing 153.9; 371.2
    x Aptitude testing
    xx **Educational tests and measurements; Mental tests**
ABMs. *See* **Antimissile missiles**
Abnormal children. *See* **Exceptional children; Handicapped children**
Abnormal psychology. *See* **Psychology, Pathological**
Abolition of slavery. *See* **Abolitionists; Slavery**
Abolitionists 326; 920
    x Abolition of slavery
    xx **Slavery—United States**
Aborigines. *See* **Ethnology**
Abortion 179; 363.4; 618.8
    x Fetal death; Pregnancy, Termination of; Termination of pregnancy
    xx **Birth control**
Abortion—Catholic Church 241
    xx **Catholic Church**
Abortion—Moral and religious aspects 179; 241; 291.5
    x Pro-choice movement; Pro-life movement; Right to choose movement; Right to life movement
Abortion, Spontaneous. *See* **Miscarriage**
Abrasives 553.6; 621.9
Absence from school. *See* **School attendance**
Absenteeism (Labor) 331.25; 658.3
    See also **Employee morale**
    x Employee absenteeism; Labor absenteeism
    xx **Labor; Personnel management**
Absenteeism (School). *See* **School attendance**
Abstinence. *See* **Fasting; Temperance**
Abstract art. *See* **Art, Abstract**
Abuse of animals. *See* **Animal abuse**
Abuse of children. *See* **Child abuse**
Abuse of husbands. *See* **Husband abuse**
Abuse of substances. *See* **Substance abuse**
Abuse of the elderly. *See* **Elderly abuse**
Abuse of wives. *See* **Wife abuse**
Abuse, Verbal. *See* **Invective**
Academic advising. *See* **Educational counseling**
Academic degrees. *See* **Degrees, Academic**
Academic dissertations. *See* **Dissertations, Academic**
Academic freedom 371.1; 378
    Use for materials on the freedom of the members of the academic community to carry on their functions, including the right to teach, publish, learn, communicate, conduct research, etc.
    See also **Church and education**
    x Educational freedom; Freedom, Academic;

Academic freedom—*Continued*
        Freedom of teaching; Teaching, Freedom of
  xx **Censorship; Church and education; Civil**
        rights; Freedom; Intellectual freedom; Tol-
        eration
Academic libraries 027.7
  x College and university libraries; Libraries,
        College; Libraries, University; University li-
        braries
  xx **Colleges and universities; Libraries**
Accelerated reading. *See* **Rapid reading**
Accident insurance. *See* **Insurance, Accident**
Accidents 363.3
  See also

Disasters	**Occupations, Dangerous**
Explosions	**Poisons and poisoning**
Fires	**Shipwrecks**
First aid	**Traffic accidents**
Home accidents	**Wounds and injuries**

    also subjects with the subdivision *Accidents,* e.g.
        Aeronautics—Accidents; Railroads—
        Accidents; etc.
  x Emergencies; Injuries
  xx **Disasters; First aid**
Accidents—Prevention 363.3; 658.3; 658.38
  See also **Safety appliances; Safety education;** also
        subjects with the subdivision *Safety appli-*
        ances or *Safety measures,* e.g.
        Aeronautics—Safety measures; Railroads—
        Safety appliances; etc.
  x Prevention of accidents; Safety measures
  xx **Safety appliances; Safety education**
Accidents, Spacecraft. *See* **Astronautics—Accidents**
Acclimatization. *See* **Adaptation (Biology); Man—**
        Influence of environment; Plant introduction
Accompaniment, Musical. *See* **Musical accompani-**
        ment
Accountability. *See* **Liability (Law)**
Accountants 657.092; 920
  x Bookkeepers; Certified public accountants
Accounting 657
  See also **Auditing; Bookkeeping; Cost accounting;**
        also names of industries, professions, etc.
        with the subdivision *Accounting,* e.g.
        Corporations—Accounting; etc.
  x Financial accounting
  xx **Auditing; Bookkeeping; Business; Business**
        arithmetic; Business education
Accounting machines. *See* **Calculators**
Accounts, Collecting of. *See* **Collecting of accounts**
Acculturation 303.4
  See also **East and West; Ethnic relations; Inter-**
        cultural education; Socialization
  x Culture contact
  xx **Anthropology; Civilization; Culture; East and**
        West; Ethnology; Race relations
Acetate silk. *See* **Rayon**
Achievement tests. *See* **Examinations**
Acid precipitation. *See* **Acid rain**

Acid rain 363.7

   x Acid precipitation; Rain, Acid

   xx **Air—Pollution; Rain and rainfall; Water—Pollution**

Acids 546; 547; 661

   Names of all acids are not included in this list but are to be added as needed, e.g. **Carbolic acid;** etc.

   See also names of acids, e.g. **Carbolic acid;** etc.

   xx **Chemicals; Chemistry**

Acne 616.5

   xx **Skin—Diseases**

Acoustics. *See* **Architectural acoustics; Hearing; Music—Acoustics and physics; Sound**

Acquired immune deficiency syndrome. *See* **AIDS (Disease)**

Acquisitions (Libraries). *See* **Libraries—Acquisitions**

Acrobats and acrobatics 791; 791.3; 791.3092

   See also **Gymnastics; Stunt men and women;** also names of acrobatic feats, e.g. **Tumbling;** etc.

   xx **Circus; Gymnastics**

Acronyms 421; 423; etc.

   x English language—Acronyms; Initialisms

   xx **Abbreviations; Code names**

Acting 791.4; 791.43-791.45; 792

   Use for general materials on the art and technique of acting in any medium (stage, television, etc.), on the presentation of plays, and on acting as a profession. Materials limited to the presentation of plays are entered under **Amateur theater** or **Theater—Production and direction.** Materials about members of the profession are entered under **Actors and actresses.**

   See also **Actors and actresses; Drama in education; Mime; Pageants; Pantomimes; Theater**

   x Dramatic art; Histrionics; Stage

   xx **Actors and actresses; Amateur theater; Drama; Drama in education; Public speaking; Theater**

Acting—Costume. *See* **Costume**

Action, Social. *See* **Social action**

Actions and defenses 347

   See also **Arbitration and award**

   x Civil law suits; Defense (Law); Law suits; Litigation; Personal actions (Law); Suing (Law); Suits (Law)

   xx **Law**

Activism, Social. *See* **Social action**

Activities curriculum. *See* **Creative activities**

Activity schools. *See* **Education—Experimental methods**

Actors and actresses (May subdiv. geog. adjective form, e.g. **Actors and actresses, American;** etc.) **791.092; 920**

   See also **Acting; Black actors and actresses; Comedians; Theater;** also names of individual actors and actresses

   x Actresses; Motion picture actors and actresses;

4

Actors and actresses—*Continued*
        Stage; Television actors and actresses
    xx **Acting; Celebrities; Entertainers; Theater**
Actors and actresses, American 791.092; 920
    x American actors and actresses; United
        States—Actors and actresses
Actresses. *See* **Actors and actresses**
Acupressure 615.8
    x Finger pressure therapy; Myotherapy
    xx **Acupuncture; Alternative medicine; Massage**
Acupuncture 615.8
    See also **Acupressure**
    xx **Alternative medicine; Medicine**
Adages. *See* **Proverbs**
Adaptability (Psychology). *See* **Adjustment (Psy-
        chology)**
Adaptation (Biology) 574.5; 581.5; 591.5
    See also **Man—Influence of environment**
    x Acclimatization
    xx **Biology; Ecology; Evolution; Genetics; Varia-
        tion (Biology)**
Adaptation (Psychology). *See* **Adjustment (Psychol-
        ogy)**
Addiction. *See* **Substance abuse**
Addiction to drugs. *See* **Drug abuse; Narcotic habit**
Addictive behavior. *See* **Substance abuse**
Addicts, Drug. *See* **Drug addicts**
Adding machines. *See* **Calculators**
Additives, Food. *See* **Food additives**
Addresses. *See* **Lectures and lecturing; Speeches,
        addresses, etc.;** and general subjects with
        the subdivision *Addresses and essays,* e.g.
        **Agriculture—Addresses and essays; United
        States—History—Addresses and essays;
        World War, 1939-1945—Addresses and es-
        says;** etc.
Adhesives 620.1; 668; 691
    See also names of adhesives, e.g. **Cement; Glue;
        Mortar;** etc.
Adjustment (Psychology) 155.2; 155.4; 155.67
    x Adaptability (Psychology); Adaptation (Psy-
        chology); Coping behavior; Maladjustment
        (Psychology)
    xx **Psychology**
Adjustment, Social. *See* **Social adjustment**
Administration. *See* **Civil service; Management;
        Political science; Public administration;
        State, The;** and types of institutions and
        names of individual institutions with the
        subdivision *Administration,* e.g.
        **Libraries—Administration; Schools—
        Administration;** etc.; and names of coun-
        tries, cities, etc. with the subdivision *Politics
        and government,* e.g. **United States—
        Politics and government;** etc.
Administration of criminal justice. *See* **Criminal
        justice, Administration of**
Administration of justice. *See* **Justice, Administra-
        tion of**
Administrative ability. *See* **Executive ability**

5

Administrative agencies—Reorganization. *See*
     United States—Executive departments—
     Reorganization
Administrative law   342
   See also **Civil service; Constitutional law; Local**
     government; Ombudsman; Public adminis-
     tration
   x Law, Administrative
   xx **Constitutional law; Law; Public administration**
Administrators and executors. *See* **Executors and**
     administrators
Admirals   359.092; 920
Adolescence   155.5; 305.2
   x Age
   xx **Youth**
Adolescent mothers   305.2; 362.7
   See also **Pregnancy, Adolescent**
   x School age mothers; Schoolgirl mothers;
     Teenage mothers
   xx **Mothers; Pregnancy, Adolescent**
Adolescent pregnancy. *See* **Pregnancy, Adolescent**
Adolescent prostitution. *See* **Prostitution, Juvenile**
Adolescent psychiatry   616.89
   x Psychiatry, Adolescent
   xx **Child psychiatry; Psychiatry**
Adolescent psychology   155.5
   See also **Separation anxiety in children**
   x Psychology, Adolescent
   xx **Psychology**
Adolescents. *See* **Youth**
Adopted children. *See* **Children, Adopted**
Adoptees   346.01; 362.7
   Use for materials on anyone formally adopted as
     a dependent.
   See also **Birthparents; Children, Adopted**
   x Adult adoptees
   xx **Adoption; Birthparents; Children, Adopted**
Adoption   346.01; 362.7
   See also **Adoptees; Children, Adopted; Foster**
     home care; Interracial adoption
   x Child placing; Children—Adoption; Chil-
     dren—Placing out
   xx **Foster home care**
Adoption—Corrupt practices   364.1
   x Black market children; Corrupt practices; In-
     fants, Sale of; Sale of infants; Selling of in-
     fants
   xx **Criminal law**
Adoption, Interracial. *See* **Interracial adoption**
Adult adoptees. *See* **Adoptees**
Adult education   374
   See also **Agricultural extension work; Continuing**
     education; Evening and continuation schools;
     Prisoners—Education
   x Education, Adult; Education of adults; Life-
     long education
   xx **Continuing education; Education; Education,**
     Higher; Education, Secondary; Evening and
     continuation schools; University extension
Adulteration of food. *See* **Food adulteration and in-**

Adulteration of food—*Continued*
>> spection

Adultery 306.7; 363.4
>> *x* Extramarital relationships; Infidelity, Marital;
>> Marital infidelity
>> *xx* **Sexual ethics**

Adults and children. *See* **Children and adults**

Adults, Runaway. *See* **Runaway adults**

Adventure and adventurers 904; 904.092; 910.4; 920
>> *See also*

Discoveries (in geography)	**Sea stories**
Escapes	**Seafaring life**
Explorers	**Shipwrecks**
Frontier and pioneer life	**Underwater exploration**
Heroes and heroines	**Voyages and travels**

>> *xx* **Voyages and travels**

Adventure and adventurers—Fiction E; Fic; S C
>> *x* Adventure stories

Adventure stories. *See* **Adventure and adventurers—Fiction**

Advertisement writing. *See* **Advertising copy**

Advertising 659.1
>> May be subdivided by topic, e.g.
>> **Advertising—Libraries;** etc.
>> *See also*

Commercial art	**Public relations**
Coupons (Retail trade)	**Publicity**
Electric signs	**Radio advertising**
Mail-order business	**Selling**
Marketing	**Show windows**
Packaging	**Sign painting**
Posters	**Signs and signboards**
Printing—Specimens	**Television advertising**
Propaganda	

>> *xx* **Business; Propaganda; Public relations; Pub-**
>> **licity; Retail trade; Selling**

Advertising and children 659.1
>> *xx* **Children**

Advertising, Art in. *See* **Commercial art**

Advertising copy 659.13
>> *x* Advertisement writing; Copy writing
>> *xx* **Authorship**

Advertising, Fraudulent 343
>> *x* Deceptive advertising; False advertising;
>> Fraudulent advertising; Misleading adver-
>> tising; Truth in advertising

Advertising layout and typography 659.13
>> *xx* **Printing; Type and type founding**

Advertising—Libraries 021.7
>> *x* Libraries—Advertising; Library advertising

Advertising, Newspaper. *See* **Newspaper advertis-
>> ing**

Advertising—Newspapers 659.1
>> Use for materials discussing advertising of news-
>> papers. Materials discussing advertising in
>> newspapers are entered under **Newspaper**
>> **advertising.**
>> *x* Newspapers—Advertising

Advertising, Pictorial. *See* **Commercial art; Posters**

Advertising, Radio. *See* **Radio advertising**

Advertising, Television. *See* **Television advertising**
Advisors. *See* **Consultants**
Aerial bombs. *See* **Bombs**
Aerial navigation. *See* **Navigation (Aeronautics)**
Aerial photography. *See* **Photography, Aerial**
Aerial reconnaissance 355.4; 358.4
> *x* Reconnaissance, Aerial
> *xx* **Aeronautics, Military; Remote sensing**
Aerial rockets. *See* **Rockets (Aeronautics)**
Aerial spraying and dusting. *See* **Aeronautics in agriculture**
Aerobics 613.7; 796.4
> *x* Dancing, Aerobic; Exercises, Aerobic
> *xx* **Dancing; Exercise; Respiration**
Aerobiology. *See* **Air—Microbiology**
Aerodromes. *See* **Airports**
Aerodynamics 533; 629.132
> *See also* **Aeronautics; Ground cushion phenomena**
> *x* Streamlining
> *xx* **Aeronautics; Air; Dynamics; Pneumatics**
Aerodynamics, Supersonic 629.132
> *See also* **Aerothermodynamics**
> *x* High speed aerodynamics; Speed, Supersonic; Supersonic aerodynamics
> *xx* **High speed aeronautics**
Aeronautical instruments 629.135
> *See also* **Airplanes—Electric equipment; Instrument flying;** also names of specific instruments, e.g. **Gyroscope;** etc.
> *x* Airplanes—Instruments; Instruments, Aeronautical
> *xx* **Scientific apparatus and instruments**
Aeronautical sports 797.5
> *See also* names of specific sports, e.g. **Airplane racing; Skydiving;** etc.
> *xx* **Aeronautics; Sports**
Aeronautics 629.13
> Use for materials on the scientific aspects of aircraft and their construction and operation; or for materials dealing collectively with various types of aircraft.
> *See also*

Aerodynamics	**Kites**
Aeronautical sports	**Lasers in aeronautics**
Airplanes	**Meteorology in aeronautics**
Airships	
Astronautics	**Navigation (Aeronautics)**
Balloons	**Parachutes**
Flight	**Radio in aeronautics**
Gliders (Aeronautics)	**Rocketry**
Helicopters	**Rockets (Aeronautics)**
High speed aeronautics	**Unidentified flying objects**

> *x* Aviation; Locomotion
> *xx* **Aerodynamics; Airships; Balloons; Engineering; Flight**
Aeronautics—Accidents 387.7; 629.13
> *See also* **Survival (after airplane accidents, shipwrecks, etc.)**
> *x* Air crashes; Airplane accidents; Airplane

8

Aeronautics—Accidents—*Continued*
>> collisions; Airplanes—Accidents
>> *xx* **Accidents**

Aeronautics and civilization 306
>> *See also* **Astronautics and civilization**
>> *x* Civilization and aeronautics
>> *xx* **Civilization**

Aeronautics, Commercial 387.7
>> *See also* **Air mail service; Airlines; Airplane industry**
>> *x* Air cargo; Air freight; Air transport; Commercial aeronautics; Commercial aviation
>> *xx* **Freight and freightage; Transportation**

Aeronautics, Commercial—Chartering 387.7
>> *x* Air charters; Airlines—Chartering; Airplanes—Chartering; Charter flights

Aeronautics, Commercial—Hijacking. *See* **Hijacking of airplanes**

Aeronautics—Flights 387.7; 629.13
>> *See also* **Space flight**
>> *x* Aeronautics—Voyages; Flights around the world; Transatlantic flights
>> *xx* **Voyages and travels**

Aeronautics, High speed. *See* **High speed aeronautics**

Aeronautics in agriculture 631
>> Use same pattern for aeronautics in other fields of endeavor.
>> *x* Aerial spraying and dusting; Airplanes in agriculture; Crop dusting, Crop spraying
>> *xx* **Agricultural pests; Agriculture; Insects, Injurious and beneficial; Spraying and dusting**

Aeronautics—Medical aspects. *See* **Aviation medicine**

Aeronautics, Meteorology in. *See* **Meteorology in aeronautics**

Aeronautics, Military 358.4
>> *See also*

Aerial reconnaissance	**Air raid shelters**
Air bases	**Aircraft carriers**
Air defenses	**Airplanes, Military**
Air power	**Parachute troops**

>> also names of wars with the subdivision *Aerial operations,* e.g. **World War, 1939-1945—Aerial operations;** etc.
>> *x* Aeronautics, Naval; Air raids—Protective measures; Air warfare; Military aeronautics; Naval aeronautics
>> *xx* **Armaments; Military art and science; War**

Aeronautics, Naval. *See* **Aeronautics, Military**

Aeronautics—Navigation. *See* **Navigation (Aeronautics)**

Aeronautics—Piloting. *See* **Airplanes—Piloting**

Aeronautics, Radio in. *See* **Radio in aeronautics**

Aeronautics—Safety measures 387.7; 629.134
>> *x* Safety measures
>> *xx* **Accidents—Prevention**

Aeronautics—Songs and music 784.6
>> *xx* **Music; Songs**

Aeronautics—Study and teaching 629.1307
    See also **Airplanes—Piloting**
    x Flight training
Aeronautics—Voyages. *See* **Aeronautics—Flights**
Aeroplanes. *See* **Airplanes**
Aeroponics 631.5
    x Agriculture, Soilless; Gardening in space;
        Plants—Soilless culture; Soilless agriculture;
        Space gardening
    xx **Horticulture**
Aerosols 541.3; 551.5; 660.2
    xx **Air—Pollution**
Aerospace industries 338.4
    See also **Airplane industry**
    x Aircraft production
Aerospace law. *See* **Space law**
Aerospace medicine. *See* **Aviation medicine; Space medicine**
    medicine
Aerothermodynamics 629.4; 629.132
    x Thermoaerodynamics
    xx **Aerodynamics, Supersonic; Astronautics; High**
        speed aeronautics; Thermodynamics
Aesthetics. *See* **Esthetics**
Affection. *See* **Friendship; Love**
Affirmative action programs 331.1; 658.3
    xx **Discrimination in employment; Personnel**
        management
Affliction. *See* **Joy and sorrow**
Africa 916; 960
    See also **Africans; Pan-Africanism**
Africa, Central 967
    x Central Africa
Africa, East 967
    x East Africa
Africa, Eastern 967
Africa, French-speaking Equatorial 967
    x French Equatorial Africa
Africa, French-speaking West 966
    x French West Africa
Africa—History 960
Africa—History—1960- 960
Africa, North 961
    x Barbary States; North Africa
Africa, Northeast 960
Africa, Northwest 964
Africa, South. *See* **South Africa**
Africa, Southern 968
    x Southern Africa
Africa—Study and teaching 960
    x African studies
    xx **Area studies**
Africa, Sub-Saharan 960
    x Sub-Saharan Africa
Africa, West 966
    x West Africa
African-Americans. *See* **Blacks**
African civilization. *See* **Civilization, African**
African literature (English) 820
    x English literature—African authors
African relations. *See* **Pan-Africanism**

African songs. *See* **Songs, African**
African studies. *See* **Africa—Study and teaching**
Africans 572.96
  xx **Africa**
Afro-Americans. *See* **Blacks**
After dinner speeches 808.5; 808.85
  See also **Toasts**
  xx **Speeches, addresses, etc.; Toasts**
After school day care. *See* **After school programs**
After school programs 362.7; 372.12
  x After school day care
  xx **Student activities**
Afterlife. *See* **Future life**
Age. *See* **Adolescence; Middle age; Old age**
Age and employment 331.3
  See also **Career changes; Children—**
      Employment; Youth—Employment
  x Employment and age
  xx **Discrimination in employment; Middle age;**
      Old age
Age discrimination 305.2
  x Discrimination, Age
  xx **Discrimination**
Age, Drinking. *See* **Drinking age**
Age—Physiological effect. *See* **Aging**
Aged. *See* **Elderly**
Ageing. *See* **Aging**
Agent Orange 668
  xx **Herbicides**
Agents, Sales. *See* **Sales personnel**
Aggregates. *See* **Set theory**
Aggressive behavior. *See* **Aggressiveness (Psychology)**
Aggressiveness (Psychology) 152.4; 155.2
  See also **Assertiveness (Psychology); Violence**
  x Aggressive behavior
  xx **Human behavior; Psychology**
Aging 574.3; 612
  x Age—Physiological effect; Ageing; Senescence
  xx **Elderly; Gerontology; Longevity; Middle age;**
      Old age
Agnosticism 149; 211
  See also **Atheism; Belief and doubt; Positivism;**
      Rationalism; Skepticism
  xx **Atheism; Belief and doubt; Faith; Free**
      thought; God; Positivism; Rationalism; Reli-
      gion; Skepticism; Truth
Agrarian question. *See* **Agriculture—Economic as-**
      pects; Agriculture—Government policy;
      Land tenure
Agrarian reform. *See* **Land reform**
Agreements. *See* **Contracts**
Agribusiness 338.1
  x Corporate farming; Corporations—Farming
      operations; Farm corporations; Farming
      corporations
  xx **Agricultural industries; Agriculture—**
      Economic aspects
Agricultural bacteriology. *See* **Bacteriology, Agri-**
      cultural

Agricultural botany. *See* **Botany, Economic**

Agricultural chemicals 631.8; 668

 See also **Fertilizers and manures;** also types of chemicals, e.g. **Herbicides; Insecticides; Pesticides;** etc.; and names of individual chemicals

 xx **Agricultural chemistry; Chemicals**

Agricultural chemistry 630.2

 See also **Agricultural chemicals; Chemurgy; Soils**

 x Chemistry, Agricultural

 xx **Chemistry; Soils**

Agricultural clubs. *See* **Agriculture—Societies**

Agricultural cooperation. *See* **Agriculture, Cooperative**

Agricultural credit 332.7

 x Credit, Agricultural; Farm credit; Rural credit

 xx **Agriculture—Economic aspects; Banks and banking; Credit; Mortgages**

Agricultural economics. *See* **Agriculture— Economic aspects**

Agricultural education. *See* **Agriculture—Study and teaching**

Agricultural engineering 631.3

 See also **Drainage; Electricity in agriculture; Irrigation**

 x Agricultural mechanics; Farm mechanics

 xx **Agricultural machinery; Engineering; Farm engines**

Agricultural experiment stations 630.7

 See also **Agricultural extension work**

 x Experimental farms; Farms, Experimental

 xx **Agriculture—Government policy; Agriculture—Research; Agriculture—Study and teaching**

Agricultural extension work (May subdiv. geog.) **630.7**

 See also **Agriculture—Study and teaching; Community development; County agricultural agents**

 x Extension work, Agricultural

 xx **Adult education; Agricultural experiment stations; Agriculture—Government policy; Agriculture—Study and teaching; Community development**

Agricultural industries 338.1

 See also **Agribusiness**

 xx **Agriculture—Economic aspects**

Agricultural laborers 331.7

 See also **Migrant labor; Peasantry**

 x Farm laborers; Laborers

 xx **Labor; Peasantry**

Agricultural machinery 631.3

 See also **Agricultural engineering; Electricity in agriculture; Farm engines;** also names of farm machinery, e.g. **Harvesting machinery; Plows; Tractors;** etc.

 x Agricultural tools; Farm implements; Farm machinery; Farm mechanics; Implements, utensils, etc.

 xx **Machinery; Tools**

12

Agricultural mechanics. *See* Agricultural engineering
Agricultural pests 632
See also **Aeronautics in agriculture; Fungi; In-
sects, Injurious and beneficial; Pests—
Control; Plants—Diseases; Spraying and
dusting; Weeds;** also names of crops, etc.
with the subdivision *Diseases and pests,* e.g.
Fruit—Diseases and pests; etc.
x Diseases and pests; Garden pests
xx **Insects, Injurious and beneficial; Pests; Zool-
ogy, Economic**
Agricultural pests—Biological control. *See* **Pests—
Biological control**
Agricultural policy. *See* **Agriculture—Government
policy**
Agricultural products. *See* **Farm produce**
Agricultural research. *See* **Agriculture—Research**
Agricultural societies. *See* **Agriculture—Societies**
Agricultural tools. *See* **Agricultural machinery**
Agriculture (May subdiv. geog.) **630**
See also

Aeronautics in agriculture	**Fruit culture**
Aquaculture	**Gardening**
Botany, Economic	**Horticulture**
Crop rotation	**Land tenure**
Dairying	**Land use**
Domestic animals	**Organiculture**
Dry farming	**Pastures**
Farmers	**Plant breeding**
Farms	**Reclamation of land**
Forests and forestry	**Soils**

also names of agricultural products, e.g. **Corn;**
etc.; and headings beginning with the words
Agricultural and **Farm**
x Agronomy; Farming; Planting
xx **Life sciences**
Agriculture—Addresses and essays 630
x Addresses
xx **Essays; Lectures and lecturing; Speeches, addresses, etc.**
Agriculture and state. *See* **Agriculture—
Government policy**
Agriculture—Bibliography 016.63
xx **Bibliography**
Agriculture, Cooperative 334
Use for materials dealing with cooperation in the
production and disposal of agricultural
products.
x Agricultural cooperation; Collective farms;
Cooperative agriculture; Farmers' cooperatives
xx **Cooperation**
Agriculture—Documentation 630.2
xx **Documentation**
Agriculture—Economic aspects 338.1
See also **Agribusiness; Agricultural credit; Agricultural industries; Farm management; Farm
produce—Marketing; Land tenure**
x Agrarian question; Agricultural economics;

13

Agriculture—Economic aspects—*Continued*
> Economic aspects
> *xx* **Economics; Farm management; Farm pro-**
> > **duce—Marketing**

Agriculture—Government policy 338.9
> *See also* **Agricultural experiment stations; Agri-**
> > **cultural extension work; Land reform**
> *x* Agrarian question; Agricultural policy; Agri-
> > culture and state; State and agriculture
> *xx* **Industry—Government policy; Land reform**

Agriculture—Research 630.7
> *See also* **Agricultural experiment stations**
> *x* Agricultural research
> *xx* **Research**

Agriculture—Societies 630.6
> *See also* names of agricultural societies, e.g. **4-H**
> > **clubs; Grange;** etc.
> *x* Agricultural clubs; Agricultural societies;
> > Boys' agricultural clubs; Girls' agricultural
> > clubs
> *xx* **Country life; Societies**

Agriculture, Soilless. *See* **Aeroponics; Hydroponics**

Agriculture—Statistics 338.1; 630.2
> *x* Crop reports
> *xx* **Statistics**

Agriculture—Study and teaching 630.7
> *See also* **Agricultural experiment stations; Agri-**
> > **cultural extension work; County agricultural**
> > **agents**
> *x* Agricultural education
> *xx* **Agricultural extension work; Vocational edu-**
> > **cation**

Agriculture—Tenant farming. *See* **Farm tenancy**

Agriculture—Tropics 630
> *xx* **Tropics**

Agriculture—United States 630.973
> *x* United States—Agriculture

Agronomy. *See* **Agriculture**

Ague. *See* **Malaria**

Aid to dependent children. *See* **Child welfare**

Aid to developing areas. *See* **Economic assistance;**
> **Technical assistance**

AIDS (Disease) 616.9
> *x* A.I.D.S. (Disease); Acquired immune defi-
> > ciency syndrome
> *xx* **Diseases**

Air 533; 546
> Use for materials dealing with air as an element
> > and with its chemical and physical proper-
> > ties. Materials on the body of air surround-
> > ing the earth are entered under **Atmosphere.**
> *See also* **Aerodynamics; Atmosphere; Ventilation**
> *xx* **Atmosphere; Hygiene; Meteorology**

Air bases 358.4
> *x* Air stations, Military; Air stations, Naval;
> > Military air bases; Naval air bases
> *xx* **Aeronautics, Military; Airports**

Air bearing lift. *See* **Ground cushion phenomena**

Air bearing vehicles. *See* **Ground effect machines**

Air cargo. *See* **Aeronautics, Commercial**

Air carriers. *See* **Airlines**

Air charters. *See* **Aeronautics, Commercial—
    Chartering**

Air, Compressed. *See* **Compressed air**

Air conditioning 644; 697.9

> *See also* **Refrigeration and refrigerating ma-
>   chinery; Ventilation;** also subjects with the
>   subdivision *Air conditioning,* e.g.
>   **Automobiles—Air conditioning;** etc.
>
> *xx* **Refrigeration and refrigerating machinery;
>   Ventilation**

Air crashes. *See* **Aeronautics—Accidents**

Air cushion vehicles. *See* **Ground effect machines**

Air defenses 363.3

> Use for materials on civilian defense against air
>   attack. Materials on military defense against
>   air raids are entered under **Aeronautics,
>   Military.** General materials on civilian de-
>   fense are entered under **Civil defense.**
>
> *See also* **Air raid shelters; Ballistic missile early
>   warning system; Poisonous gases—War use;
>   Radar defense networks**
>
> *x* Air raids—Protective measures; Air warfare;
>   Defenses, Air
>
> *xx* **Aeronautics, Military; Civil defense**

Air freight. *See* **Aeronautics, Commercial**

Air hostesses. *See* **Airlines—Flight attendants**

Air lines. *See* **Airlines**

Air mail service 383

> *xx* **Aeronautics, Commercial; Postal service**

Air—Microbiology 576

> *x* Aerobiology
>
> *xx* **Microbiology**

Air, Moisture of. *See* **Humidity**

Air navigation. *See* **Navigation (Aeronautics)**

Air pilots 629.13; 920

> *See also* **Astronauts; Women air pilots**
>
> *x* Airplanes—Pilots; Aviators; Pilots, Airplane;
>   Test pilots

Air piracy. *See* **Hijacking of airplanes**

Air planes. *See* **Airplanes**

Air—Pollution (May subdiv. geog.) **363.7; 628.5**

> *See also* **Acid rain; Aerosols; Air—Quality**
>
> *x* Atmosphere—Pollution; Pollution of air
>
> *xx* **Air—Quality; Environmental health; Pollution**

Air—Pollution—Measurement 363.7; 628.5

> *xx* **Measurement**

Air—Pollution—United States 363.7; 628.50973

> *x* United States—Air—Pollution

Air ports. *See* **Airports**

Air power 358.4

> *xx* **Aeronautics, Military**

Air—Quality 363.7

> *See also* **Air—Pollution**
>
> *x* Quality
>
> *xx* **Air—Pollution; Quality control**

Air raid shelters 363.3

> *x* Bomb shelters; Fallout shelters; Public shel-
>   ters; Shelters, Air raid
>
> *xx* **Aeronautics, Military; Air defenses; Civil**

Air raid shelters—*Continued*
> **defense**

Air raids—Protective measures. *See* **Aeronautics, Military; Air defenses**

Air rights law. *See* **Airspace law**

Air routes. *See* **Airways**

Air-ships. *See* **Airships**

Air space law. *See* **Airspace law**

Air stations, Military. *See* **Air bases**

Air stations, Naval. *See* **Air bases**

Air stewardesses. *See* **Airlines—Flight attendants**

Air stewards. *See* **Airlines—Flight attendants**

Air surfing. *See* **Gliding and soaring**

Air terminals. *See* **Airports**

Air traffic control 387.7
> *x* Airports—Traffic control

Air transport. *See* **Aeronautics, Commercial**

Air warfare. *See* **Aeronautics, Military; Air defenses; Airplanes, Military; Chemical warfare;** and names of wars with the subdivision *Aerial operations,* e.g. **World War, 1939-1945—Aerial operations;** etc.

Aircraft. *See* **Airplanes; Airships; Gliders (Aeronautics); Helicopters**

Aircraft carriers 359.3; 623
> *x* Airplane carriers; Carriers, Aircraft
> *xx* **Aeronautics, Military; Warships**

Aircraft production. *See* **Aerospace industries; Airplane industry**

Airdromes. *See* **Airports**

Airlines 387.7
> Use for materials dealing with systems of aerial transportation and with companies engaged in this business. Materials dealing with the routes along which the planes are flown are entered under **Airways.**
>
> *See also* **Airways**
> *x* Air carriers; Air lines
> *xx* **Aeronautics, Commercial; Airways**

Airlines—Chartering. *See* **Aeronautics, Commercial—Chartering**

Airlines—Flight attendants 387.7
> *x* Air hostesses; Air stewardesses; Air stewards; Airlines—Hostesses; Airplane hostesses; Flight attendants; Hostesses, Airline; Stewardesses, Airline; Stewards, Airline

Airlines—Hijacking. *See* **Hijacking of airplanes**

Airlines—Hostesses. *See* **Airlines—Flight attendants**

Airplane accidents. *See* **Aeronautics—Accidents**

Airplane carriers. *See* **Aircraft carriers**

Airplane collisions. *See* **Aeronautics—Accidents**

Airplane engines. *See* **Airplanes—Engines**

Airplane hijacking. *See* **Hijacking of airplanes**

Airplane hostesses. *See* **Airlines—Flight attendants**

Airplane industry 338.4; 387.7
> *x* Aircraft production
> *xx* **Aeronautics, Commercial; Aerospace industries**

Airplane racing 797.5
> *x* Airplanes—Racing
> *xx* **Aeronautical sports**

Airplane spotting. *See* **Airplanes—Identification**

Airplanes 387.7; 629.133
> *See also* **Gliders (Aeronautics); Propellers, Aerial;** also types of airplanes and special makes of airplanes, e.g. **Bombers; Helicopters; Vertically rising airplanes;** etc.
> *x* Aeroplanes; Air planes; Aircraft; Biplanes; Monoplanes
> *xx* **Aeronautics**

Airplanes—Accidents. *See* **Aeronautics—Accidents**

Airplanes—Chartering. *See* **Aeronautics, Commercial—Chartering**

Airplanes—Design and construction 629.134

Airplanes—Electric equipment 629.135
> *x* Airplanes—Instruments
> *xx* **Aeronautical instruments**

Airplanes—Engines 629.134
> *See also* **Jet propulsion**
> *x* Airplane engines; Airplanes—Motors
> *xx* **Engines; Gas and oil engines**

Airplanes—Flight testing. *See* **Airplanes—Testing**

Airplanes—Hijacking. *See* **Hijacking of airplanes**

Airplanes—Identification 623.74; 629.133
> *x* Airplane spotting; Airplanes—Recognition
> *xx* **Identification**

Airplanes in agriculture. *See* **Aeronautics in agriculture**

Airplanes—Inspection 387.7; 629.134

Airplanes—Instruments. *See* **Aeronautical instruments; Airplanes—Electric equipment**

Airplanes, Jet propelled. *See* **Jet planes**

Airplanes—Maintenance and repair 629.134
> *x* Airplanes—Repair

Airplanes—Materials 629.134

Airplanes, Military 623.74
> *See also* types of military airplanes, e.g. **Bombers;** etc.
> *x* Air warfare; Airplanes, Naval; Military airplanes; Naval airplanes
> *xx* **Aeronautics, Military**

Airplanes—Models 629.133
> *x* Miniature objects; Model airplanes; Models
> *xx* **Machinery—Models; Models and model making**

Airplanes—Motors. *See* **Airplanes—Engines**

Airplanes, Naval. *See* **Airplanes, Military**

Airplanes—Noise 629.132
> *xx* **Noise; Noise pollution**

Airplanes—Operation. *See* **Airplanes—Piloting**

Airplanes—Piloting 629.132
> Use for materials on instruction in the mechanics of flying.
> *See also* **Instrument flying;** also types and names of airplanes with the subdivision *Piloting,* e.g. **Helicopters—Piloting;** etc.
> *x* Aeronautics—Piloting; Airplanes—Operation; Flight training; Piloting (Aeronautics)

17

Airplanes—Piloting—*Continued*
  xx Aeronautics—Study and teaching; Navigation
    (Aeronautics)
Airplanes—Pilots. *See* Air pilots
Airplanes—Propellers. *See* Propellers, Aerial
Airplanes—Racing. *See* Airplane racing
Airplanes—Recognition. *See* Airplanes—
    Identification
Airplanes—Repair. *See* Airplanes—Maintenance
    and repair
Airplanes, Rocket propelled. *See* Rocket planes
Airplanes—Testing 629.134
  x Airplanes—Flight testing; Test pilots
Airplanes, Vertically rising. *See* Vertically rising
    airplanes
Airports (May subdiv. geog.) 629.136
  See also Air bases; Heliports; also names of indi-
    vidual airports
  x Aerodromes; Air ports; Air terminals; Air-
    dromes
Airports—Traffic control. *See* Air traffic control
Airships 629.133
    Use for materials on self-propelled aircraft that
      is lighter than air and that can be steered.
  See also Aeronautics; Balloons
  x Air-ships; Aircraft; Balloons, Dirigible;
    Blimps; Dirigible balloons; Zeppelins
  xx Aeronautics
Airspace law 341.4
  x Air rights law; Air space law
  xx Space law
Airways 387.7
    Use for materials dealing with routes along
      which planes are flown and where aids to
      navigation are maintained such as landing
      fields, beacons, etc. Materials dealing with
      the companies engaged in aerial transporta-
      tion are entered under Airlines.
  See also Airlines
  x Air routes
  xx Airlines
Alaska Highway (Alaska and Canada) 388.1;
    917.98
Alchemy 540.1
    Use for materials on the medieval chemical sci-
      ence which sought to transmute baser met-
      als into gold. Modern materials on the
      transmutation of metals are entered under
      Transmutation (Chemistry).
  See also Transmutation (Chemistry)
  x Hermetic art and philosophy; Metals, Trans-
    mutation of; Philosophers' stone; Transmu-
    tation of metals
  xx Chemistry; Occult sciences; Superstition
Alcohol 547; 661
  See also Alcoholic beverages; Alcoholism; Distil-
    lation; Liquor industry; Liquors and liqueurs
  x Intoxicants
  xx Distillation; Stimulants
Alcohol and teenagers. *See* Youth—Alcohol use

Alcohol and youth. *See* **Youth—Alcohol use**

Alcohol as fuel 662

    See also names of alcohol fuels, e.g. **Gasohol;** etc.

    x Alcohol fuel; Ethanol; Ethyl alcohol fuel

    xx **Biomass energy; Fuel**

Alcohol consumption. *See* **Drinking of alcoholic beverages**

Alcohol, Denatured 661

    x Alcohol, Industrial; Denatured alcohol; Industrial alcohol

Alcohol fuel. *See* **Alcohol as fuel**

Alcohol, Industrial. *See* **Alcohol, Denatured**

Alcohol—Physiological effect 613.8; 616.86

    x Physiological effect

    xx **Alcoholism; Temperance**

Alcohol use. *See* classes of people with the subdivision *Alcohol use,* e.g. **Youth—Alcohol use;** etc.

Alcoholic beverage consumption. *See* **Drinking of alcoholic beverages**

Alcoholic beverages 641.2

    See also **Drinking of alcoholic beverages; Liquors and liqueurs; Wine and wine making**

    x Drinks; Intoxicants

    xx **Alcohol; Beverages**

Alcoholics 616.86

    x Drunkards; Inebriates

    xx **Alcoholism**

Alcoholism 616.86

    Use chiefly for medical materials, including works on drunkenness, dipsomania, etc.

    See also **Alcohol—Physiological effect; Alcoholics; Drinking of alcoholic beverages; Temperance;** also classes of people with the subdivision *Alcohol use,* e.g. **Youth—Alcohol use;** etc.

    x Dipsomania; Drinking problem; Drunkenness; Intemperance; Intoxication; Liquor problem

    xx **Alcohol; Drinking of alcoholic beverages; Drug abuse; Substance abuse; Temperance**

Alfalfa 633.3

    xx **Hay**

Algae 561; 589.3

    x Sea mosses; Seaweeds

    xx **Marine plants**

Algebra 512

    See also **Graph theory; Group theory; Logarithms; Number theory; Probabilities**

    xx **Mathematical analysis; Mathematics**

Algebra, Boolean 511

    x Boolean algebra

    xx **Group theory; Logic, Symbolic and mathematical; Set theory**

Algebras, Linear 512

    See also **Topology**

    x Linear algebras

    xx **Mathematical analysis; Topology**

Alienation (Social psychology) 302.5

    x Estrangement (Social psychology); Rebels (Social psychology); Social alienation

    xx **Social psychology**

Aliens 323.6; 325

    See also **Citizenship; Naturalization; Refugees;** also headings such as **Mexicans—United States;** etc.

    x Foreigners; Noncitizens; Nonnationals

    xx **Citizenship; Immigration and emigration; International law; Naturalization**

Aliens from outer space. *See* **Extraterrestrial beings**

Aliens, Illegal 323.6; 325

    x Illegal aliens; Underground aliens

    xx **Immigration and emigration; Underground economy**

Alkoran. *See* **Koran**

All Fools' Day. *See* **April Fools' Day**

All Hallows' Eve. *See* **Halloween**

All terrain vehicles 629.2

    See also types of vehicles, e.g. **Snowmobiles;** etc.

    x A.T.V.'s; ATVs

    xx **Vehicles**

Allegories 808.88

    Use for collections of allegories.

    See also **Fables; Parables**

    xx **Fiction; Parables; Symbolism in literature**

Allegory 704.9; 808

    Use for materials on allegory as a literary form.

Allergy 616.97

    See also **Hay fever**

    xx **Immunity**

Alleys. *See* **Streets**

Allied health personnel 610.69

    See also types of personnel, e.g. **Medical technologists; Nurse practitioners;** etc.

    x Paramedical personnel

Alligators 597.98

    xx **Crocodiles**

Allocation of time. *See* **Time management**

Alloys 669

    See also **Brass; Metallurgy; Pewter;** also names of alloys, e.g. **Aluminum alloys;** etc.

    xx **Chemistry, Technical; Metallurgy;** Metals; **Solder and soldering**

Allusions 808.88

Almanacs 310

    See also **Calendars; Chronology; Nautical almanacs; Yearbooks**

    x Annuals

    xx **Astronomy; Calendars; Chronology; Yearbooks**

Alphabet 411

    Use for materials dealing with the series of characters which form the elements of a written language and for materials teaching children the ABCs. Materials dealing with the styles of alphabets used by artists, etc., are entered

Alphabet—*Continued*
      under **Alphabets.**
    See also **Alphabets; Writing**
      x A.B.C.'s; ABCs; Alphabet books; Letters of
        the alphabet
    xx **Writing**
Alphabet books. *See* **Alphabet**
Alphabetizing. *See* **Files and filing**
Alphabets 745.6
    See note under **Alphabet.**
    See also **Illumination of books and manuscripts;**
        Initials; Lettering; Monograms
    xx **Alphabet; Decoration and ornament; Initials;**
        Lettering; Sign painting
Alpine animals 591.52
    x Mountain animals
    xx **Animals; Wildlife**
Alpine plants 581; 635.9
    x Mountain plants
    xx **Plants**
Alternate energy resources. *See* **Renewable energy**
      resources
Alternate work site. *See* **Telecommuting**
Alternating current machinery. *See* **Electric ma-**
      chinery—Alternating current
Alternating currents. *See* **Electric currents, Alter-**
      nating
Alternative energy resources. *See* **Renewable en-**
      ergy resources
Alternative lifestyle. *See* **Counter culture; Lifestyles**
Alternative medicine 615.5; 615.8
    See also **Self-care, Health;** also types of alterna-
      tive medicine, e.g. **Acupressure; Acupunc-**
      ture; Chiropractic; Holistic medicine; etc.
    xx **Medicine**
Alternative press. *See* **Underground press**
Alternative schools. *See* **Experimental schools**
Alternative universities. *See* **Free universities**
Alternative work schedules. *See* **Hours of labor;**
      Part-time employment
Altitude, Influence of. *See* **Man—Influence of envi-**
      ronment
Altruists. *See* **Philanthropists**
Aluminum 669; 673
    See also **Aluminum foil**
Aluminum alloys 669; 673
    xx **Alloys**
Aluminum foil 673
    xx **Aluminum; Packaging**
Aluminum—Recycling 604.6; 673
    xx **Recycling (Waste, etc.)**
Alzheimer's disease 616.8
    xx **Brain—Diseases**
Amateur motion pictures 778.5
    x Home movies; Motion pictures, Amateur;
      Personal films
    xx **Motion picture photography**
Amateur radio stations 621.3841
    x Ham radio stations; Radio stations, Amateur
    xx **Radio, Shortwave**
Amateur theater 792
    Use for materials on the production of plays,
      skits, recitations, etc. by nonprofessional
      groups. Collections of plays for such groups
      are entered under **American drama—**
      Collected works; Drama—Collected works;
      and similar subjects.

Amateur theater—*Continued*
   See also
   Acting
   Charades
   Children's plays
   College and school drama
   Drama in education
   Little theater movement
   Makeup, Theatrical
   One act plays
   Pantomimes
   Shadow pantomimes and
      plays
   Theater—Production and
      direction
      x Play production; Private theater; Theater,
         Amateur
      xx **Amusements; Drama in education; Theater**
Ambassadors. *See* **Diplomats**
Amendments, Equal rights. *See* **Equal rights
      amendments**
America 917; 970
      Use for general materials on the Western Hemi-
         sphere.
      See also **Central America; Latin America; North
         America; South America;** also names of sep-
         arate countries of these areas
America—Antiquities 970
America—Exploration 970.01; 973.1
      See also **Explorers; Northwest Passage; United
         States—Exploring expeditions**
      x Canada—Exploration; Conquistadores; Explo-
         rations; North America—Exploration;
         South America—Exploration; United
         States—Exploration
      xx **Discoveries (in geography); Explorers**
America—History 970; 973
      x American history
America—Politics and government 970; 973
      See also **Pan-Americanism**
      xx **Pan-Americanism**
American actors and actresses. *See* **Actors and ac-
      tresses, American**
American architecture. *See* **Architecture, American**
American art. *See* **Art, American**
American artificial satellites. *See* **Artificial satel-
      lites, American**
American artists. *See* **Artists, American**
American arts. *See* **Arts, American**
American authors. *See* **Authors, American**
American ballads. *See* **Ballads, American**
American Bicentennial. *See* **American Revolution
      Bicentennial, 1776-1976**
American bison. *See* **Bison**
American characteristics. *See* **National characteris-
      tics, American**
American Civil War. *See* **United States—
      History—1861-1865, Civil War**
American civilization. *See* **Civilization, American;
      United States—Civilization**
American colleges. *See* **Colleges and universities—
      United States**
American colonies. *See* **United States—History—
      1600-1775, Colonial period**
American color prints. *See* **Color prints, American**
American composers. *See* **Composers, American**

22

American decoration and ornament. *See* **Decoration and ornament, American**

American drama 812
  xx **Drama**

American drama—Collected works 812.08
  xx **Drama—Collected works**

American drama—History and criticism 812.09
  xx **Drama—History and criticism**

American dramatists. *See* **Dramatists, American**

American drawing. *See* **Drawing, American**

American economic assistance. *See* **Economic assistance, American**

American engraving. *See* **Engraving, American**

American environmental policy. *See* **Environment—Government policy—United States**

American espionage. *See* **Espionage, American**

American essays 814.08
  xx **Essays**

American ethics. *See* **Ethics, American**

American fiction 813; Fic
  x Fiction, American
  xx **Fiction**

American flag. *See* **Flags—United States**

American folk art. *See* **Folk art, American**

American folk dancing. *See* **Folk dancing, American**

American folk music. *See* **Folk music—United States**

American folk songs *See* **Folk songs—United States**

American furniture. *See* **Furniture, American**

American government. *See* **United States—Politics and government**

American graphic arts. *See* **Graphic arts, American**

American historians. *See* **Historians, American**

American history. *See* **America—History; United States—History**

American hostages. *See* **Hostages, American**

American illustrators. *See* **Illustrators, American**

American Indians. *See* **Indians; Indians of Central America; Indians of Mexico; Indians of North America; Indians of South America; Indians of the West Indies**

American labor unions. *See* **Labor unions—United States**

American letters 816
  xx **Letters**

American literature 810
  May be subdivided geographically by the names of states or regions, e.g. **American literature—Massachusetts; American literature—Southern States.**
  May also be subdivided by the topical subdivisions and literary forms used under **English literature.**
  See also **Authors, American; Ballads, American; Canadian literature; Latin American literature;** also various forms of American literature, e.g. **American poetry; Satire, American**
  x United States—Literature

American literature—American Indian authors 810
> Use same pattern for materials on literatures and literary forms written by other ethnic groups or classes of authors, such as women authors.
> Use for materials on literature written in the English language by American Indian authors. Literature written in an Indian language is entered under **Indians of North America—Literature.**
> *x* Indian literature (American)

American literature—Black authors 810
> Use same pattern for other literary forms, e.g. **American poetry—Black authors;** etc.
> *x* Black literature (American)

American literature—Collected works 810.8
> Use for collections of both poetry and prose by several American authors. Collections consisting of prose only are entered under **American prose literature;** collections of poetry are entered under **American poetry—Collected works.**

American literature—Women authors 810
> *xx* **Women authors**

American Loyalists 973.3
> *x* Loyalists, American; Tories, American
> *xx* **United States—History—1775-1783, Revolution**

American military assistance. *See* **Military assistance, American**

American music. *See* **Music, American**

American musicians. *See* **Musicians, American**

American national characteristics. *See* **National characteristics, American**

American national songs. *See* **National songs, American**

American newspapers 071
> *xx* **Newspapers**

American novelists. *See* **Novelists, American**

American orations. *See* **Speeches, addresses, etc., American**

American painters. *See* **Painters, American**

American painting. *See* **Painting, American**

American periodicals 051
> *xx* **Periodicals**

American personal names. *See* **Names, Personal—United States**

American philosophers. *See* **Philosophers, American**

American philosophy. *See* **Philosophy, American**

American poetry 811
> *xx* **American literature; Poetry**

American poetry—Black authors 811
> *x* Black poetry (American)

American poetry—Collected works 811.08
> *xx* **Poetry—Collected works**

American poetry—History and criticism 811.09
> *xx* **Poetry—History and criticism**

American poets. *See* **Poets, American**

American politicians. *See* **Politicians—United States**

American politics. *See* **United States—Politics and government**

American pottery. *See* **Pottery, American**

American prints. *See* **Prints, American**

American prisoners of war. *See* **Prisoners of war, American**

American propaganda. *See* **Propaganda, American**

American prose literature 818

Use for collections of prose writings by several American authors which may include a variety of literary forms such as essays, fiction, orations, etc. May also be used for general materials about such prose writings.

x Prose literature, American

American refugees. *See* **Refugees, American**

American Revolution. *See* **United States—History—1775-1783, Revolution**

American Revolution Bicentennial, 1776-1976 973.3

x American Bicentennial; Bicentennial celebrations—United States—1976; United States—Bicentennial celebrations; United States—History—1775-1783, Revolution—Centennial celebrations, etc.

xx **United States—Centennial celebrations, etc.**

American Revolution Bicentennial, 1776-1976—Collectibles 973.3075

x Collectibles; Collections of objects

xx **Collectors and collecting**

American satire. *See* **Satire, American**

American science. *See* **Science—United States**

American sculptors. *See* **Sculptors, American**

American sculpture. *See* **Sculpture, American**

American songs. *See* **Songs, American**

American-Spanish War, 1898. *See* **United States—History—1898, War of 1898**

American speeches. *See* **Speeches, addresses, etc., American**

American technical assistance. *See* **Technical assistance, American**

American travelers. *See* **Travelers, American**

American wit and humor 817.08; 817.09

xx **Wit and humor**

American youth. *See* **Youth—United States**

Americana 069.5; 745.1

xx **Antiques—United States; Collectors and collecting; United States—Civilization; United States—History; United States—Popular culture**

Americanisms 427

Use for materials dealing with the usage of words and expressions peculiar to the United States.

x English language—Americanisms

xx **English language—Dialects**

Americanization 325.73

See also **Naturalization; United States—Foreign population; United States—Immigration and emigration**

25

Americans (May subdiv. geog. except U.S.) **920; 973**
  Use for materials on citizens of the United
    States.
  xx **Ethnology—United States; United States**
Americans—Greece **325.495**
Amerindians. *See* **Indians; Indians of Central**
    America; Indians of Mexico; Indians of
    North America; Indians of South America;
    Indians of the West Indies
Amish **289.7**
  xx **Mennonites**
Ammunition **623.4**
  See also types of ammunition, e.g. **Bombs; Gun-**
    powder; etc.
  xx **Armaments; Explosives; Gunpowder; Projec-**
    tiles
Amnesty **355.1; 364.6**
  See also **Pardon**
  xx **Desertion, Military; Pardon**
Amniocentesis **618.3**
  xx **Prenatal diagnosis**
Amphibians **567; 597**
  See also names of amphibians, e.g. **Frogs; Sala-**
    manders; etc.
  x Batrachia
  xx **Vertebrates**
Amplifiers (Electronics) **621.381**
  See also special types of amplifiers, e.g.
    Amplifiers, Vacuum tube; Masers; etc.
  xx **Electronics**
Amplifiers, Vacuum tube **621.3815**
  xx **Amplifiers (Electronics); Radio—Equipment**
    and supplies; Vacuum tubes
Amusement parks **791.06**
  See also names of specific parks, e.g. **Walt Dis-**
    ney World (Fla.); etc.
  x Carnivals (Circus); Theme parks
  xx **Parks**
Amusements (May subdiv. geog.) **790**
  Use for general materials on various kinds of en-
    tertainment and pastimes. All types of
    amusements are not included in this list but
    are to be added as needed.
  See also

Amateur theater	**Mathematical recreations**
Charades	**Motion pictures**
Church entertainments	**Play**
Circus	**Puzzles**
Concerts	**Recreation**
Creative activities	**Riddles**
Dancing	**Scientific recreations**
Entertaining	**Shadow pictures**
Fortune telling	**Sports**
Games	**Theater**
Hobbies	**Toys**
Indoor games	**Vaudeville**
Literary recreations	**Ventriloquism**
Magic	

  x Entertainments; Pastimes

  xx **Entertaining; Games; Indoor games; Play;**

26

Amusements—*Continued*
        Recreation; Sports
Anaesthetics. *See* **Anesthetics**
Analysis (Chemistry). *See* **Chemistry, Analytic;**
        and names of substances with the subdivi-
        sion *Analysis,* e.g. **Food—Analysis;** etc.
Analysis (Mathematics). *See* **Calculus; Mathemati-**
        cal analysis
Analysis, Microscopic. *See* **Metallography; Micro-**
        scope and microscopy
Analysis of food. *See* **Food adulteration and inspec-**
        tion; Food—Analysis
Analysis situs. *See* **Topology**
Analysis, Spectrum. *See* **Spectrum analysis**
Analytical chemistry. *See* **Chemistry, Analytic**
Analytical geometry. *See* **Geometry, Analytic**
Anarchism and anarchists 320.5; 335
    See also **Terrorism**
    xx **Freedom; Political crimes and offenses; Politi-**
        cal science; Syndicalism
Anatomical gifts. *See* **Donation of organs, tissues,**
        etc.
Anatomy 574.4; 611
    See also **Anatomy, Comparative; Anatomy, Hu-**
        man; Bones; Musculoskeletal system; Ner-
        vous system; Physiology; also subjects with
        the subdivision *Anatomy,* e.g.
        Birds—Anatomy; Botany—Anatomy; etc.
    x Morphology
    xx **Biology; Medicine; Physiology**
Anatomy, Artistic 704.9; 743
    See also **Figure drawing; Figure painting**
    x Artistic anatomy; Human figure in art
    xx **Art; Drawing**
Anatomy, Comparative 574.4; 591.4
    See also **Man—Origin**
    x Comparative anatomy; Morphology
    xx **Anatomy; Evolution; Man—Origin; Zoology**
Anatomy, Dental. *See* **Teeth**
Anatomy, Human 611
    See also names of organs and regions of the
        body, e.g. **Heart;** etc.
    x Body, Human; Human anatomy; Human
        body
    xx **Anatomy**
Anatomy, Human—Atlases 611
    xx **Atlases**
Anatomy of plants. *See* **Botany—Anatomy**
Anatomy, Vegetable. *See* **Botany—Anatomy**
Ancestor worship 291.2; 291.3
    x Dead, Worship of the
    xx **Cults; Religion**
Ancestry. *See* **Genealogy; Heredity**
Ancient architecture. *See* **Architecture, Ancient**
Ancient art. *See* **Art, Ancient**
Ancient civilization. *See* **Civilization, Ancient**
Ancient geography. *See* **Geography, Ancient**
Ancient history. *See* **History, Ancient**
Ancient philosophy. *See* **Philosophy, Ancient**

Androgyny 155.3; 305.3; 305.4

Use for materials on the integration of male and female characteristics, including biological traits, personality traits, behavior, roles, etc.

See also **Sex differences (Psychology); Sex role**

x Unisexuality

xx **Sex (Biology); Sex differences (Psychology); Sex role; Sexual behavior**

Androids. *See* **Robots**

Anecdotes 808.88; 818; etc.

See also subjects with the subdivision *Anecdotes, facetiae, satire, etc.,* e.g. **Music—Anecdotes, facetiae, satire, etc.;** etc.

x Facetiae; Stories

xx **Wit and humor**

Anesthetics 615

x Anaesthetics

xx **Materia medica; Pain; Surgery**

Angels 235

x Spirits

xx **Heaven**

Angina pectoris. *See* **Heart—Diseases**

Anglican Church. *See* **Church of England**

Angling. *See* **Fishing**

Anglo-French intervention in Egypt, 1956. *See* **Sinai Campaign, 1956**

Anglo-Saxon language 429

x English language—0-1100; Old English language

Anglo-Saxon literature 829

x English literature—0-1100; Old English literature

Anglo-Saxons 572.9361; 941.01

x Saxons

xx **Great Britain—History—0-1066; Teutonic peoples**

Animal abuse 179

See also **Animal shelters; Vivisection**

x Abuse of animals; Animal rights; Animals, Cruelty to; Animals—Mistreatment; Animals—Protection; Animals—Treatment; Cruelty to animals; Prevention of cruelty to animals; Protection of animals

xx **Domestic animals; Vivisection**

Animal attacks 591.6

x Attacks by animals

xx **Dangerous animals**

Animal babies. *See* **Animals—Infancy**

Animal behavior. *See* **Animals—Habits and behavior**

Animal camouflage. *See* **Camouflage (Biology)**

Animal chemistry. *See* **Physiological chemistry**

Animal communication 591.59

x Animal language; Animal sounds; Animals—Language; Animals—Sounds; Communication among animals

Animal drawing. *See* **Animal painting and illustration**

Animal-facilitated therapy. *See* **Pet therapy**

Animal food 641.3

Use for materials on human food of animal origin. Materials on the food and food habits of animals are entered under **Animals—Food.**

x Animals as food; Animals, Edible

xx **Food**

Animal homes. *See* **Animals—Habitations**

Animal husbandry. *See* **Livestock**

Animal industry. *See* **Domestic animals; Livestock**

Animal instinct. *See* **Instinct**

Animal intelligence 591.51

See also **Animals—Habits and behavior; Instinct; Learning, Psychology of; Psychology, Comparative;** also names of animals with the subdivision *Psychology,* e.g. **Dogs—Psychology;** etc.

x Animal psychology; Intelligence of animals

xx **Animals—Habits and behavior; Instinct; Psychology, Comparative**

Animal kingdom. *See* **Zoology**

Animal language. *See* **Animal communication**

Animal light. *See* **Bioluminescence**

Animal locomotion 591.1

x Animals—Movements; Locomotion; Movements of animals

Animal lore. *See* **Animals—Folklore; Animals in literature; Animals, Mythical; Natural history**

Animal magnetism. *See* **Hypnotism**

Animal migration. *See* **Animals—Migration**

Animal oils. *See* **Oils and fats**

Animal painting and illustration 704.9; 743; 758

Use for materials on the art and methods of painting and drawing animals. Materials about representations of animals in works of art (painting, sculpture, etc.), or reproductions of them, are entered under **Animals in art.** Materials consisting of photographs or illustrations of animals are entered under **Animals—Pictorial works.**

See also **Animals in art; Animals—Pictorial works; Photography of animals**

x Animal drawing

xx **Animals in art; Animals—Pictorial works; Painting; Photography of animals**

Animal parasites. *See* **Parasites**

Animal photography. *See* **Photography of animals**

Animal physiology. *See* **Zoology**

Animal pictures. *See* **Animals—Pictorial works**

Animal pounds. *See* **Animal shelters**

Animal products. *See* names of special products, e.g. **Hides and skins; Ivory; Wool;** etc.

Animal psychology. *See* **Animal intelligence; Psychology, Comparative**

Animal rights. *See* **Animal abuse**

Animal shelters 179

x Animal pounds; Shelters, Animal

xx **Animal abuse**

Animal signs. *See* **Animal tracks**

Animal sounds. *See* **Animal communication**

Animal stories. *See* **Animals—Fiction**

Animal tracks 591

   x Animal signs; Tracks of animals

   xx **Tracking and trailing**

Animal training. *See* **Animals—Training**

Animals (May subdiv. geog.) **590; 591**

   Use for descriptive and nonsystematic or non-technical material.

   Subdivisions used under this heading may be used under names of orders and classes of the animal kingdom and under names of individual animals.

   See also

Alpine animals	**Pets**
Dangerous animals	**Poisonous animals**
Desert animals	**Prehistoric animals**
Domestic animals	**Rare animals**
Forest animals	**Stream animals**
Freshwater animals	**Swamp animals**
Furbearing animals	**Wildlife**
Game and game birds	**Working animals**
Jungle animals	**Zoology**
Marine animals	**Zoos**
Natural history	

   also names of orders and classes of the animal kingdom, e.g. **Vertebrates; Mammals; Primates;** etc.; and names of individual animals, e.g. **Monkeys;** etc.

   x Beasts; Fauna; Wild animals

   xx **Zoology**

Animals and the handicapped 636.08

   See also **Guide dogs; Hearing ear dogs; Pet therapy**

   x Handi-animals; Handicapped and animals

   xx **Animals—Training**

Animals, Aquatic. *See* **Freshwater animals; Marine animals**

Animals as food. *See* **Animal food**

Animals—Camouflage. *See* **Camouflage (Biology)**

Animals—Color 591.19; 591.57

   xx **Color**

Animals—Courtship 591.56

   x Courtship of animals

   xx **Animals—Habits and behavior**

Animals, Cruelty to. *See* **Animal abuse**

Animals—Diseases 591.2; 636.089

   See also names of animals with the subdivision *Diseases,* e.g. **Cattle—Diseases;** etc.

   x Diseases of animals; Domestic animals—Diseases

   xx **Diseases; Veterinary medicine**

Animals, Domestic. *See* **Domestic animals**

Animals, Edible. *See* **Animal food**

Animals, Extinct. *See* **Extinct animals**

Animals—Fiction Fic

   See note under **Animals in literature.**

   See also **Animals in literature;** also names of animals with the subdivision *Fiction,* e.g. **Dogs—Fiction;** etc.

Animals—Fiction—*Continued*
    x Animal stories; Animals—Stories
    xx **Animals in literature; Fables; Fiction**
Animals, Fictitious. *See* **Animals, Mythical**
Animals—Filmography 016.591
    x Filmography
Animals—Folklore 398; 398.2
    See also **Animals, Mythical; Dragons; Monsters**
    x Animal lore
    xx **Animals, Mythical; Folklore**
Animals—Food 591.51; 591.53
    Use for materials on the food and food habits of
        animals. Materials on human food of ani-
        mal origin are entered under **Animal food.**
    See also **Carnivores; Food chains (Ecology);** also
        names of animals with the subdivision
        Food, e.g. **Fishes—Food;** etc.
    x Feeding behavior in animals
    xx **Animals—Habits and behavior; Food**
Animals, Fossil. *See* **Fossils**
Animals, Freshwater. *See* **Freshwater animals**
Animals—Habitations 591.52
    x Animal homes; Habitations of animals;
        Houses of animals
Animals—Habits and behavior 591.51
    See also **Animal intelligence; Animals—Food;**
        Instinct; Nature study; Tracking and trail-
        ing; also types of specific behavior, e.g.
        Animals—Courtship; Animals—
        Hibernation; Animals—Migration; etc.; and
        names of animals with the subdivision
        Habits and behavior, e.g. **Primates—Habits**
        and behavior; Monkeys—Habits and behav-
        ior; etc.
    x Animal behavior; Behavior; Habits of animals
    xx **Animal intelligence; Nature study**
Animals—Hibernation 591.54
    x Hibernation of animals
    xx **Animals—Habits and behavior**
Animals, Imaginary. *See* **Animals, Mythical**
Animals in art 704.9
    Use for materials about representations of ani-
        mals in works of art (painting, sculpture,
        etc.) or reproductions of them. Materials on
        the art and methods of painting and draw-
        ing animals are entered under **Animal paint-**
        ing and illustration. Materials consisting of
        photographs or illustrations of animals are
        entered under **Animals—Pictorial works.**
    See also **Animal painting and illustration; Ani-**
        mals—Pictorial works
    xx **Animal painting and illustration; Animals—**
        Pictorial works; Art
Animals in literature 808.8; 809
    Use for materials on the theme of animals in lit-
        erature. Poems or stories about animals are
        entered under **Animals—Poetry; Animals—**
        Fiction.
    See also **Animals—Fiction; Animals—Poetry;**
        Bible—Natural history; also phrase

31

Animals in literature—*Continued*
    headings of specific animals in literature, e.g.
    Dogs in literature; etc.
  x Animal lore
  xx **Animals—Fiction; Animals—Poetry; Nature in literature**
Animals in motion pictures 791.43
  xx **Motion pictures**
Animals in police work 363.2; 636.08
  xx **Police; Working animals**
Animals—Infancy 591.3
  x Animal babies; Baby animals
Animals—Language. *See* **Animal communication**
Animals, Marine. *See* **Marine animals**
Animals—Migration 591.52
  See also names of animals with the subdivision
    Migration, e.g. **Birds—Migration;** etc.
  x Animal migration; Migration of animals
  xx **Animals—Habits and behavior**
Animals—Mistreatment. *See* **Animal abuse**
Animals—Movements. *See* **Animal locomotion**
Animals, Mythical 398.2; Fic
  See also **Animals—Folklore;** also names of
    mythical animals, e.g. **Dragons; Giants;
    Mermaids and mermen; Vampires;** etc.
  x Animal lore; Animals, Fictitious; Animals,
    Imaginary; Creatures, Imaginary; Fictitious
    animals; Imaginary animals; Mythical ani-
    mals
  xx **Animals—Folklore; Mythology**
Animals—Photography. *See* **Photography of ani-
    mals**
Animals—Pictorial works 591.022; 743; 778.9
  See note under **Animal painting and illustration.**
  See also **Animal painting and illustration; Ani-
    mals in art; Photography of animals**
  x Animal pictures; Illustrations; Pictorial works
  xx **Animal painting and illustration; Animals in
    art; Photography of animals; Pictures**
Animals—Poetry 808.1; 808.81; 811; 811.08; etc.
  See note under **Animals in literature.**
  See also **Animals in literature**
  xx **Animals in literature; Poetry**
Animals, Prehistoric. *See* **Prehistoric animals**
Animals—Protection. *See* **Animal abuse**
Animals, Rare. *See* **Rare animals**
Animals, Sea. *See* **Marine animals**
Animals—Sounds. *See* **Animal communication**
Animals—Stories. *See* **Animals—Fiction**
Animals—Temperature. *See* **Body temperature**
Animals—Training 636.08
  See also **Animals and the handicapped;** also
    names of animals with the subdivision
    Training, e.g. **Dogs—Training; Horses—
    Training;** etc.
  x Animal training; Training of animals
  xx **Circus**
Animals—Treatment. *See* **Animal abuse**
Animals—United States 591.9
  x United States—Animals

Animals, Useful and harmful. *See* **Zoology, Economic**

Animals, Visiting. *See* **Pet therapy**

Animals—War use 355.4
    See also **Dogs—War use**
    x War use of animals
    xx **Working animals**

Animals, Working. *See* **Working animals**

Animated cartoons. *See* **Motion picture cartoons**

Animation (Cinematography) 741.5; 778.5; 791.43
    See also **Motion picture cartoons**
    xx **Motion picture cartoons**

Anniversaries. *See* **Holidays;** and names of special days, e.g. **Fourth of July;** etc.

Annual income. *See* **Wages—Annual wage**

Annual wage plans. *See* **Wages—Annual wage**

Annuals. *See* **Almanacs; Calendars; Yearbooks;** and general subjects and names of organizations with the subdivision *Yearbooks,* e.g. **Literature—Yearbooks; United Nations—Yearbooks;** etc.

Annuals (Plants) 582; 635.9
    xx **Flower gardening; Flowers; Plants, Cultivated**

Annuities 368.3
    See also **Insurance, Life; Pensions**
    xx **Insurance, Life; Investments; Retirement income**

Annulment of marriage. *See* **Marriage—Annulment**

Anonyms. *See* **Pseudonyms**

Anorexia nervosa 613.2; 616.3
    x Self-starvation; Starvation, Self-imposed
    xx **Eating disorders**

Answers to questions. *See* **Questions and answers**

Ant. *See* **Ants**

Antarctic expeditions. *See* **Antarctic regions;** and names of expeditions, e.g. **Byrd Antarctic Expedition;** etc.

Antarctic regions 919.8; 998
    See also **South Pole**
    x Antarctic expeditions; Expeditions, Antarctic and Arctic; Polar expeditions
    xx **Discoveries (in geography); Earth; Polar regions; Scientific expeditions; South Pole; Voyages and travels**

Antenuptial contracts. *See* **Marriage contracts**

Anthems, National. *See* **National songs**

Anthracite coal. *See* **Coal**

Anthropogeography 572.9
    See also **Geopolitics; Man—Influence of environment**
    x Geographical distribution of people; Geography, Social
    xx **Anthropology; Ethnology; Geography; Geopolitics; History; Human ecology; Immigration and emigration**

Anthropology 301; 573
    See also

Acculturation	**Anthropometry**
Anthropogeography	**Archeology**

Anthropology—*Continued*
    Civilization   **Man**
    Ethnology   **National characteristics**
    Ethnopsychology   **Physical anthropology**
    Eugenics   **Social change**
    Language and languages
        also names of races and peoples, e.g. **Semitic peoples; Navajo Indians;** etc.; and names of countries, cities, etc. with the subdivision *Race relations,* e.g. **United States—Race relations;** etc.
    x Human race
    xx **Civilization; Ethnology; Man**
Anthropology, Physical. *See* **Physical anthropology**
Anthropometry 573
    See also **Fingerprints**
    x Skeletal remains
    xx **Anthropology; Ethnology; Man**
Anti-Americanism. *See* **United States—Foreign opinion**
Anti-apartheid movement (May subdiv. geog.) **172; 320.5; 323.1**
    x Apartheid, Movement against
    xx **Civil rights; Social movements; South Africa—Race relations**
Anti-poverty programs. *See* **Economic assistance, Domestic**
Anti-Reformation. *See* **Reformation**
Antiamericanism. *See* **United States—Foreign opinion**
Antiballistic missiles. *See* **Antimissile missiles**
Antibiotics 615
    See also names of specific antibiotics, e.g. **Penicillin;** etc.
    xx **Chemotherapy**
Antibusing. *See* **Busing (School integration)**
Anticommunist movements 322.4
    x Underground, Anticommunist
    xx **Communism**
Anticorrosive paint. *See* **Corrosion and anticorrosives**
Antimissile missiles 623.4
    x A.B.M.'s; ABMs; Antiballistic missiles
    xx **Guided missiles**
Antinuclear movement (May subdiv. geog.) **172; 333.79; 355**
    See also **Nuclear power plants**
    x Nuclear freeze movement
    xx **Arms control; Nuclear power plants; Nuclear weapons; Social movements**
Antipathies. *See* **Prejudices**
Antipoverty programs. *See* **Economic assistance, Domestic**
Antiques (May subdiv. geog.) **745.1**
    See also **Art objects; Collectors and collecting**
    xx **Antiquities; Decoration and ornament; Decorative arts**
Antiques—United States 745.1
    See also **Americana**
    x United States—Antiques

Antiquities   930.1

    See also **Antiques; Archeology; Bible— Antiquities; Christian antiquities; Classical antiquities; Man, Prehistoric;** also names of groups of people and names of regions, countries, cities, etc. with the subdivision *Antiquities,* e.g. **Indians of North America— Antiquities; United States—Antiquities;** etc.

    x Archeological specimens

    xx **Archeology**

Antiquities, Biblical.   *See* **Bible—Antiquities**

Antiquities, Christian.   *See* **Christian antiquities**

Antiquities, Classical.   *See* **Classical antiquities**

Antiquities—Collection and preservation   069.5

    x Preservation of antiquities

    xx **Collectors and collecting**

Antiquities, Ecclesiastical.   *See* **Christian antiquities**

Antiquity of man.   *See* **Man—Origin**

Antireformation.   *See* **Reformation**

Antisemitism   155.9; 323.1

    See also **Holocaust, Jewish (1933-1945); Jews— Persecutions**

    xx **Jews and Gentiles; Prejudices**

Antiseptics   615

    See also **Disinfection and disinfectants**

    xx **Disinfection and disinfectants; Surgery; Therapeutics**

Antislavery.   *See* **Slavery**

Antitrust law   343

    x Trusts, Industrial—Law and legislation

    xx **Commercial law; Trusts, Industrial**

Antivivisection.   *See* **Vivisection**

Antiwar movements.   *See* names of wars with the subdivision *Protests, demonstrations, etc.,* e.g. **World War, 1939-1945—Protests, demonstrations, etc.;** etc.

Antonyms.   *See* names of languages with the subdivision *Synonyms and antonyms,* e.g. **English language—Synonyms and antonyms;** etc.

Ants   595.7

    x Ant; Hymenoptera

    xx **Insects**

Anxiety.   *See* **Fear; Stress (Psychology); Worry**

Apartheid.   *See* **Segregation; South Africa—Race relations**

Apartheid, Movement against.   *See* **Anti-apartheid movement**

Apartment houses   647; 728.3

    See also **Condominiums**

    x Flats

    xx **Architecture, Domestic; Houses; Housing; Landlord and tenant**

Apiculture.   *See* **Bees**

Apollo project   629.45

    See also headings beginning with **Lunar** and **Moon**

    x Project Apollo

    xx **Life support systems (Space environment); Orbital rendezvous (Space flight); Space flight**

Apollo project—*Continued*
　　　to the moon
Apologetics 239
　　See also **Natural theology; Religion and science**
　　x Christianity—Apologetic works; Christianity—Evidences; Evidences of Christianity; Fundamental theology
Apostles 225; 920
　　x Disciples, Twelve
　　xx **Christian saints; Church history—30(ca.)-600, Early church**
Apostles' Creed 238
　　xx **Creeds**
Apostolic Church. *See* **Church history—30(ca.)-600, Early church**
Apparatus, Chemical. *See* **Chemical apparatus**
Apparatus, Electric. *See* **Electric apparatus and appliances**
Apparatus, Electronic. *See* **Electronic apparatus and appliances**
Apparatus, Scientific. *See* **Scientific apparatus and instruments**
Apparitions 133.1
　　See also **Demonology; Ghosts; Hallucinations and illusions; Miracles; Spiritualism; Visions**
　　x Phantoms; Specters; Spirits
　　xx **Demonology; Ghosts; Hallucinations and illusions; Psychical research; Spiritualism; Superstition; Visions**
Apperception 153.7
　　See also **Attention; Consciousness; Knowledge, Theory of; Number concept; Perception**
　　xx **Educational psychology; Knowledge, Theory of; Perception; Psychology**
Appetite disorders. *See* **Eating disorders**
Apple 582; 634
　　xx **Fruit**
Appliances, Electric. *See* **Electric apparatus and appliances; Household appliances, Electric**
Appliances, Electronic. *See* **Electronic apparatus and appliances**
Applications for positions 331.12
　　See also **Interviewing; Résumés (Employment)**
　　x Employment applications; Employment references; Job applications; Letters of recommendation; Recommendations for positions
　　xx **Job hunting; Personnel management**
Applied arts. *See* **Decorative arts**
Applied mechanics. *See* **Mechanics, Applied**
Applied psychology. *See* **Psychology, Applied**
Applied science. *See* **Technology**
Apportionment (Election law) 324; 328
　　x Legislative reapportionment; Reapportionment (Election law)
　　xx **Representative government and representation**
Appraisal. *See* **Assessment; Valuation**
Appraisal of books. *See* **Books and reading; Books and reading—Best books; Books—Reviews; Criticism; Literature—History and criticism**

Appreciation of art.   *See* **Art appreciation**
Appreciation of music.   *See* **Music—Analysis, ap-
preciation**
Apprentices 331.5
> *See also* **Employees—Training**
> *xx* **Children—Employment; Employees—
> Training; Labor; Technical education**
April Fools' Day 394.2
> *x* All Fools' Day
Aptitude testing.   *See* **Ability—Testing**
Aquaculture 639
> *See also* **Fisheries**
> *x* Aquiculture; Freshwater aquaculture; Maricul-
> ture; Marine aquaculture; Ocean farming;
> Sea farming
> *xx* **Agriculture; Food supply; Marine resources**
Aquanauts 627.092; 920
> *x* Oceanauts
> *xx* **Undersea research stations; Underwater ex-
> ploration**
Aquariums 639
> *See also* **Fish culture; Goldfish; Marine aquari-
> ums;** also names of specific aquariums
> *xx* **Fishes; Freshwater animals; Freshwater biol-
> ogy; Freshwater plants; Indoor gardening;
> Natural history**
Aquariums, Saltwater.   *See* **Marine aquariums**
Aquatic animals.   *See* **Freshwater animals; Marine
animals**
Aquatic birds.   *See* **Water birds**
Aquatic plants.   *See* **Freshwater plants; Marine
plants**
Aquatic sports.   *See* **Water sports**
Aqueducts 628.1
> *x* Conduits; Water conduits
> *xx* **Civil engineering; Hydraulic structures; Water
> supply**
Aquiculture.   *See* **Aquaculture**
Arab civilization.   *See* **Civilization, Arab**
Arab countries 915.6; 956
> *xx* **Islamic countries; Middle East**
Arab countries—Politics and government 956
> *See also* **Panarabism**
Arab-Israel War, 1948-1949.   *See* **Israel-Arab War,
1948-1949**
Arab-Israel War, 1956.   *See* **Sinai Campaign, 1956**
Arab-Israel War, 1967.   *See* **Israel-Arab War, 1967**
Arab-Israel War, 1973.   *See* **Israel-Arab War, 1973**
Arab-Jewish relations.   *See* **Jewish-Arab relations**
Arabia.   *See* **Arabian Peninsula**
Arabian Peninsula 915.3; 953
> *x* Arabia
> *xx* **Peninsulas**
Arabs 572.953; 909
> *See also* names of specific Arab peoples, e.g.
> **Bedouins; Moors;** etc.
Arabs—Palestine.   *See* **Palestinian Arabs**
Arachnida.   *See* **Spiders**
Arbitration and award 347
> Use for materials on the settlement of civil dis-

Arbitration and award—*Continued*
putes by arbitration instead of a court trial.
x Awards (Law); Mediation
xx **Actions and defenses; Commercial law; Courts**
Arbitration, Industrial 331.89
See also **Collective bargaining; Strikes and lockouts**
x Conciliation, Industrial; Industrial arbitration; Industrial conciliation; Labor arbitration; Labor negotiations; Mediation, Industrial; Trade agreements (Labor)
xx **Collective bargaining; Industrial relations; Labor; Labor disputes; Labor unions; Strikes and lockouts**
Arbitration, International 341.5
See also **Arms control; League of Nations; Peace; United Nations**
x International arbitration; International mediation; Mediation, International
xx **Arms control; International cooperation; International law; International relations; Peace; Security, International; Treaties**
Arboriculture. *See* **Forests and forestry; Fruit culture; Trees**
Arc light. *See* **Electric lighting**
Arc welding. *See* **Electric welding**
Archaeology. *See* **Archeology**
Archeological specimens. *See* **Antiquities**
Archeologists 920; 930.1092
xx **Historians**
Archeology (May subdiv. geog.) **930.1**
See also

Antiquities	**Historic sites**
Architecture, Ancient	**Inscriptions**
Arms and armor	**Iron Age**
Bible—Antiquities	**Man, Prehistoric**
Brasses	**Mounds and mound builders**
Bronze Age	
Bronzes	**Mummies**
Christian antiquities	**Numismatics**
Christian art and symbolism	**Obelisks**
	Pottery
Cities and towns, Ruined, extinct, etc.	**Pyramids**
	Radiocarbon dating
Classical antiquities	**Religious art and symbolism**
Cliff dwellers and cliff dwellings	
Ethnology	**Rock drawings, paintings, and engravings**
Excavations (Archeology)	**Stone Age**
Funeral rites and ceremonies	**Stone implements**
	Temples
Gems	**Tombs**
Heraldry	

also names of groups of people and names of regions, countries, cities, etc. with the subdivision *Antiquities,* e.g. **Indians of North America—Antiquities; United States—Antiquities;** etc.
x Archaeology; Prehistory; Ruins
xx **Anthropology; Antiquities; Art; Bronze Age;**

Archeology—*Continued*
> Civilization; Classical antiquities; Ethnology; History; History, Ancient; Iron Age; Stone Age

Archeology, Biblical. *See* **Bible—Antiquities**

Archeology, Christian. *See* **Christian antiquities**

Archeology, Classical. *See* **Classical antiquities**

Archery 799.3
> *See also* **Bow and arrow**
> *xx* **Bow and arrow; Martial arts; Shooting**

Architects 720.92; 920
> *xx* **Artists**

Architectural acoustics 690; 729
> *See also* **Soundproofing**
> *x* Acoustics
> *xx* **Sound**

Architectural decoration and ornament. *See* **Decoration and ornament, Architectural**

Architectural design. *See* **Architecture—Details**

Architectural designs. *See* **Architecture—Designs and plans**

Architectural details. *See* **Architecture—Details**

Architectural drawing 720.28
> *See also* **Architecture—Designs and plans; Architecture—Details**
> *x* Drawing, Architectural; Plans
> *xx* **Drawing; Mechanical drawing**

Architectural engineering. *See* **Building; Building, Iron and steel; Strains and stresses; Strength of materials; Structures, Theory of**

Architectural metalwork 721
> *x* Metalwork, Architectural
> *xx* **Metalwork**

Architectural orders. *See* **Architecture—Orders**

Architectural perspective. *See* **Perspective**

Architecture (May subdiv. geog. adjective form, e.g. **Architecture, Greek;** etc.) **720**
> All types of architecture and buildings are not included in this list but are to be added as needed.
> *See also*

Building	**Obelisks**
Building materials	**Palaces**
Castles	**Public buildings**
Cathedrals	**School buildings**
Church architecture	**Skyscrapers**
Concrete construction	**Spires**
Decoration and ornament, Architectural	**Strains and stresses**
Farm buildings	**Strength of materials**
Historic buildings	**Structural engineering**
Industrial buildings	**Synagogues**
Library architecture	**Temples**
Monuments	**Theaters**
Mosques	**Tombs**
Naval architecture	**Underground architecture**

> also styles of architecture, e.g. **Architecture, Byzantine;** etc.; and types of buildings; and headings beginning with the word **Architectural**

Architecture—*Continued*

    x Construction

    xx **Art; Building**

Architecture, American 720.9; 720.973

    x American architecture; United States—
        Architecture

Architecture, Ancient 722

    See also **Architecture, Greek; Architecture, Roman; Pyramids; Temples**

    x Ancient architecture

    xx **Archeology**

Architecture and the handicapped 720

    x Barrier free design; Handicapped and architecture

Architecture, Asian 722

    See also **Mosques; Temples**

    x Asian architecture; Oriental architecture

Architecture, Baroque 724

    x Baroque architecture

Architecture, Byzantine 723

    x Byzantine architecture

    xx **Architecture**

Architecture, Church. *See* **Church architecture**

Architecture, Colonial 724

    See also **Historic buildings—United States**

    x Colonial architecture

Architecture—Composition, proportion, etc. 729

    x Architecture—Proportion; Proportion (Architecture)

    xx **Composition (Art)**

Architecture—Conservation and restoration 690; 720.28

    See also **Buildings—Maintenance and repair**

    x Architecture—Restoration; Buildings, Restoration of; Conservation of buildings; Preservation of buildings; Restoration of buildings

    xx **Buildings—Maintenance and repair**

Architecture—Decoration and ornament. *See* **Decoration and ornament, Architectural**

Architecture—Designs and plans 729

    See also **Architecture, Domestic—Designs and plans**

    x Architectural designs; Architecture—Plans; Designs, Architectural

    xx **Architectural drawing**

Architecture—Details 729

    See also

Chimneys	**Foundations**
Doors	**Roofs**
Fireplaces	**Windows**
Floors	**Woodwork**

    x Architectural design; Architectural details; Design, Architectural; Details, Architectural

    xx **Architectural drawing**

Architecture, Domestic 728

    See also **Apartment houses; Farm buildings; House construction; Houses; Prefabricated houses; Solar homes**

    x Architecture, Rural; Country houses;

Architecture, Domestic—*Continued*
> Domestic architecture; Dwellings; Habitations, Human; Residences; Rural architecture; Suburban homes; Summer homes; Villas

Architecture, Domestic—Designs and plans 728
> *x* Home designs; House plans
> *xx* **Architecture—Designs and plans**

Architecture, Ecclesiastical. *See* **Church architecture**

Architecture, Gothic 723
> *See also* **Cathedrals; Church architecture**
> *x* Gothic architecture
> *xx* **Cathedrals; Christian antiquities; Church architecture**

Architecture, Greek 722
> *x* Greek architecture
> *xx* **Architecture, Ancient**

Architecture, Medieval 723
> *See also* **Architecture, Romanesque; Castles; Cathedrals**
> *x* Medieval architecture
> *xx* **Middle Ages**

Architecture, Modern 724
> *x* Modern architecture

Architecture, Modern—1600-1799 (17th and 18th centuries) 724

Architecture, Modern—1900-1999 (20th century) 724.9

Architecture, Naval. *See* **Naval architecture; Shipbuilding**

Architecture—Orders 729
> *x* Architectural orders; Orders, Architectural

Architecture—Plans. *See* **Architecture—Designs and plans**

Architecture—Proportion. *See* **Architecture—Composition, proportion, etc.**

Architecture, Renaissance 724
> *xx* **Renaissance**

Architecture—Restoration. *See* **Architecture—Conservation and restoration**

Architecture, Roman 722
> *x* Roman architecture
> *xx* **Architecture, Ancient**

Architecture, Romanesque 723
> *x* Romanesque architecture
> *xx* **Architecture, Medieval**

Architecture, Rural. *See* **Architecture, Domestic; Farm buildings**

Archives (May subdiv. geog.) 025.17
> *See also* **Charters; Libraries; Manuscripts**
> *x* Documents; Government records—Preservation; Historical records—Preservation; Preservation of historical records; Public records—Preservation; Records—Preservation
> *xx* **Bibliography; Charters; Documentation; History—Sources; Information services; Libraries**

Archives—United States 025.17
> *x* United States—Archives

Arctic expeditions. *See* **Arctic regions**
Arctic regions   919.8; 998
See also **North Pole; Northeast Passage; Northwest Passage**
  x Arctic expeditions; Expeditions, Antarctic and Arctic; Polar expeditions
  xx **Discoveries (in geography); Earth; North Pole; Polar regions; Scientific expeditions**
Ardennes, Battle of the, 1944-1945   940.54
  x Bastogne, Battle of; Battle of the Bulge; Bulge, Battle of the
  xx **Battles; World War, 1939-1945; World War, 1939-1945—Campaigns**
Area studies   940-990
See also areas, countries with the subdivision *Study and teaching,* e.g. **Africa—Study and teaching;** etc.
  x Foreign area studies
  xx **Education**
Arena theater   725
  x Round stage; Theater-in-the-round
  xx **Theater**
Argentine rummy. *See* **Canasta (Game)**
Argumentation. *See* **Debates and debating; Logic**
Aristocracy   305.5
See also **Democracy; Nobility; Upper classes**
  xx **Democracy; Equality; Nobility; Political science; Social classes; Sociology**
Arithmetic   513
See also

Average	**Numeration**
Business arithmetic	**Percentage**
Calculators	**Ratio and proportion**
Cube root	**Square root**
Fractions	

  also names of specific arithmetic operations, e.g. **Multiplication; Subtraction;** etc.
  xx **Mathematics; Set theory**
Arithmetic, Commercial. *See* **Business arithmetic**
Arithmetic, Mental   513
  x Mental arithmetic; Oral arithmetic
Arithmetic—Study and teaching   372.7; 513.07
See also **Counting; Number games**
Armada, 1588   942.05
  x Spanish Armada
  xx **Great Britain—History—1485-1603, Tudors**
Armaments   355.8
  Use for materials on military strength, including military personnel, munitions, natural resources and industrial war potential. Materials on the implements of war and the industries producing them are entered under the heading **Munitions.** Materials on the armament of a particular country are entered under the name of the country with the subdivision *Defenses,* e.g. **United States—Defenses;** etc.
See also

Aeronautics, Military	**Armed forces**
Ammunition	**Armies**

Armaments—*Continued*
    Arms control   **Munitions**
    Arms race   **Navies**
    Industrial mobilization   **Ordnance**
   xx **Military art and science**

Armaments race. *See* **Arms race**

Armed forces 343; 355
   See also **Armies; Military personnel; Military
      service, Voluntary; Navies;** also specific
      branches of the armed forces under names
      of countries, e.g. **United States. Army;** and
      names of countries and international organi-
      zations with the subdivision *Armed forces,*
      e.g. **United States—Armed forces; United
      Nations—Armed forces;** etc.
   x Armed services
   xx **Armaments; Military art and science**

Armed services. *See* **Armed forces**

Armies 355.3
   See also **Arms control; Military art and science;
      Military service, Compulsory; Navies; Sol-
      diers; War; World War, 1939-1945—
      Human resources;** also names of countries
      with the subhead *Army,* e.g. **United States.
      Army;** etc.; and headings beginning with the
      word **Military**
   x Army; Military forces; Military power
   xx **Armaments; Armed forces; Military art and
      science; Military personnel; Navies; Strat-
      egy; War**

Armies—Medical care 355.3
   See also **Medicine, Military; Military health;**
      also names of wars with the subdivision
      Health aspects or *Medical care,* e.g. **World
      War, 1939-1945—Health aspects; World
      War, 1939-1945—Medical care;** etc.
   xx **Medicine, Military; Military health**

Armistice Day. *See* **Veterans Day**

Armistices. *See* names of wars with the subdivi-
      sion *Armistices,* e.g. **World War, 1939-
      1945—Armistices;** etc.

Armor. *See* **Arms and armor**

Armored cars (Tanks). *See* **Tanks (Military sci-
      ence)**

Arms aid. *See* **Military assistance**

Arms and armor 355.8; 623.4; 739.7
   See also **Firearms; Ordnance; Rifles**
   x Armor; Weapons and weaponry
   xx **Archeology; Costume; Military art and science**

Arms, Coats of. *See* **Heraldry**

Arms control 327.1; 341.7
   See also **Antinuclear movement; Arbitration, In-
      ternational; Arms race; Peace; Sea power;
      Security, International**
   x Disarmament; Limitation of armament; Mili-
      tary power; Non-proliferation of nuclear
      weapons; Nuclear test ban; Nuclear weap-
      ons and disarmament
   xx **Arbitration, International; Armaments; Ar-
      mies; International relations; Military art**

Arms control—*Continued*
　　　　and science; **Navies; Peace; Sea power; Security, International; War**
Arms proliferation. *See* **Arms race**
Arms race 355
　　　Use for materials on the competitive buildup
　　　　and improvement of the military power of
　　　　two or more nations or blocs.
　　　x Armaments race; Arms proliferation; Proliferation of arms
　　　xx **Armaments; Arms control; Munitions**
Arms sales. *See* **Military assistance; Munitions**
Army. *See* **Armies; Military art and science;** and
　　　　names of countries with the subhead *Army,*
　　　　e.g. **United States. Army;** etc.
Army desertion. *See* **Desertion, Military**
Army life. *See* **Soldiers;** and names of armies with
　　　　the subdivision *Military life,* e.g. **United
　　　　States. Army—Military life;** etc.
Army posts. *See* **Military posts**
Army schools. *See* **Military education**
Army tests. *See* **United States. Army—
　　　　Examinations**
Army vehicles. *See* **Vehicles, Military**
Aromatic plant products. *See* **Essences and essential oils**
Arrow. *See* **Bow and arrow**
Art (May subdiv. geog. adjective form, e.g. **Art,
　　　　French;** etc.) **700**
　　　Subdivisions listed under this heading may be
　　　　used under other art media where applicable.
　　　Names of all types of art are not included in this
　　　　list but are to be added as needed.
　　　Materials on special themes in art are entered
　　　　under phrase headings of the type [subject]
　　　　in art, e.g. **Animals in art.**
　　　See also

Anatomy, Artistic	**Futurism (Art)**
Archeology	**Gems**
Architecture	**Graphic arts**
Art objects	**Illumination of books and**
Arts and crafts movement	**manuscripts**
Brasses	**Illustration of books**
Bronzes	**Interior design**
Christian art and symbolism	**Painting**
ism	**Photography, Artistic**
Collage	**Pictures**
Collectors and collecting	**Portraits**
Commercial art	**Religious art and symbolism**
Composition (Art)	**ism**
Decoration and ornament	**Rock drawings, paintings,**
Decorative arts	**and engravings**
Drawing	**Sculpture**
Engraving	**Surrealism**
Esthetics	**Symbolism**
Etching	**Video art**
Folk art	**World War, 1939-1945—**
Forgery of works of art	**Art and the war**

　　　also subjects and themes in art, e.g. **Animals in**

Art—*Continued*
>> **art; Blacks in art; Children in art; Plants in art; Women in art;** etc.
>
> *x* Iconography
> *xx* **Civilization; Humanities**

Art, Abstract 709.04
> *See also* types of abstract art, e.g. **Kinetic art;** etc.
>
> *x* Abstract art; **Art, Nonobjective; Nonobjective art; Painting, Abstract**
> *xx* **Art, Modern—1900-1999 (20th century)**

Art, American 709.73
> *See also* **Folk art, American**
>
> *x* American art; United States—Art

Art—Analysis, interpretation, appreciation. *See* **Art appreciation; Art criticism; Art—Study and teaching**

Art, Ancient 709.01
> *See also* **Classical antiquities**
>
> *x* Ancient art

Art and mythology 704.9
> Use same pattern for art and other subjects.
>
> *x* Mythology in art
> *xx* **Art and religion; Mythology**

Art and religion 704.9
> *See also* **Art and mythology; Religious art and symbolism**
>
> *x* Religion and art
> *xx* **Art and society; Religious art and symbolism**

Art and society 701
> *See also* **Art and religion; Art patronage; Folk art**
>
> *x* Society and art

Art, Applied. *See* **Design, Industrial**

Art appreciation 701
> *x* Appreciation of art; Art—Analysis, interpretation, appreciation
> *xx* **Art criticism; Esthetics**

Art, Asian 709.5
> *x* **Art, Oriental;** Asian art; Oriental art

Art, Baroque 709.03
> *x* Baroque art

Art, Black. *See* **Black art**

Art, Buddhist 709.17
> *x* Buddhist art

Art, Byzantine 709.02
> *x* Byzantine art
> *xx* **Art, Medieval**

Art, Christian. *See* **Christian art and symbolism**

Art, Classical. *See* **Art, Greek; Art, Roman**

Art, Commercial. *See* **Commercial art**

Art—Composition. *See* **Composition (Art)**

Art, Computer. *See* **Computer art**

Art criticism 701
> *See also* **Art appreciation**
>
> *x* Art—Analysis, interpretation, appreciation
> *xx* **Criticism**

Art, Decorative. *See* **Decoration and ornament**

Art, Ecclesiastical. *See* **Christian art and symbolism**

Art education. *See* **Art—Study and teaching**

Art, Electronic. *See* **Computer art; Video art**

Art, Erotic. *See* **Erotic art**
Art—Exhibitions 707.4
> *xx* **Exhibitions**

Art forgeries. *See* **Forgery of works of art**
Art galleries. *See* **Art—Museums**
Art, Graphic. *See* **Graphic arts**
Art, Greek 709.38; 709.495
> *x* Art, Classical; Classical art; Greek art
> *xx* **Classical antiquities**

Art—History 709
> *xx* **History**

Art, Immoral. *See* **Erotic art**
Art in advertising. *See* **Commercial art**
Art in motion. *See* **Kinetic art**
Art, Indian. *See* **Indians of North America—Art**
Art industries and trade. *See* **Decorative arts**
Art, Islamic 709.1
> *x* Art, Mohammedan; Islamic art; Moham-
> medan art; Moslem art

Art, Kinetic. *See* **Kinetic art**
Art, Medieval 709.02
> *See also* **Art, Byzantine; Art, Romanesque; Illu-
> mination of books and manuscripts**
> *x* Medieval art; Religious art
> *xx* **Civilization, Medieval; Middle Ages**

Art metalwork 739; 745.56
> *See also* kinds of art metalwork, e.g. **Bronzes;
> Goldwork; Jewelry; Silverwork;** etc.
> *x* Decorative metalwork; Metalwork, Art
> *xx* **Decorative arts; Metalwork**

Art, Modern 709.03
> *x* Modern art

Art, Modern—1800-1899 (19th century) 709.03
> *See also* **Postimpressionism (Art)**

Art, Modern—1900-1999 (20th century) 709.04
> *See also* names of modern art, e.g. **Art, Ab-
> stract; Computer art; Earthworks (Art); Ki-
> netic art; Video art;** etc.
> *x* Contemporary art

Art, Mohammedan. *See* **Art, Islamic**
Art, Municipal 711
> *See also* **City planning; Public buildings**
> *x* Civic art; Municipal art; Municipal improve-
> ments
> *xx* **Cities and towns; City planning**

Art—Museums 708; 727
> *x* Art galleries; Galleries, Art; Picture galleries
> *xx* **Museums**

Art, Nonobjective. *See* **Art, Abstract**
Art objects 745.1
> Use for general materials about decorative arti-
> cles of artistic merit such as snuff boxes,
> brasses, pottery, needlework, glassware, etc.
> Materials on old decorative objects having
> historical or financial value are entered un-
> der **Antiques.**
> *See also* classes of art objects, e.g. **Furniture;
> Pottery;** etc.
> *xx* **Antiques; Art; Decoration and ornament; Dec-
> orative arts**

Art objects, Forgery of. *See* **Forgery of works of art**

Art, Oriental. *See* **Art, Asian**

Art patronage 700
> Use for materials dealing with patronage of the arts by individuals or corporations. Materials on government support of the arts are entered under **Arts—Government policy.**
>
> *See also* **Arts—Government policy**
>
> *x* Art patrons; Business patronage of the arts; Corporate patronage of the arts; Corporations—Art patronage; Funding for the arts; Patronage of the arts; Private funding of the arts
>
> *xx* **Art and society; Arts—Government policy**

Art patrons. *See* **Art patronage**

Art, Prehistoric 709.01
> *See also* **Rock drawings, paintings, and engravings**
>
> *x* Prehistoric art

Art—Prices 707.5
> *xx* **Prices**

Art, Renaissance 709.02
> *xx* **Renaissance**

Art robberies. *See* **Art thefts**

Art, Roman 709.37
> *x* Art, Classical; Classical art; Roman art
>
> *xx* **Classical antiquities**

Art, Romanesque 709.02
> *See also* **Painting, Romanesque**
>
> *x* Romanesque art
>
> *xx* **Art, Medieval**

Art schools. *See* **Art—Study and teaching**

Art—Study and teaching 707
> *x* Art—Analysis, interpretation, appreciation; Art education; Art schools
>
> *xx* **Study, Method of**

Art—Technique 702.8

Art thefts 704
> *x* Art robberies; Thefts, Art

Art, Video. *See* **Video art**

Artesian wells. *See* **Wells**

Arthritis 616.7; 618.97
> *xx* **Gout; Rheumatism**

Arthur, King—Romances. *See* **Arthurian romances**

Arthurian romances 398.2; 800's
> *See also* **Grail**
>
> *x* Arthur, King—Romances; Knights of the Round Table
>
> *xx* **Grail; Romances**

Articles of war. *See* **Military law**

Articulation (Education) 371.2
> Use for materials that discuss the integration of various elements of the school system so as to provide for continuous progress by the student. This may be the adjustments and relationships between different levels (e.g. elementary and secondary schools, high school and college); the integration between subjects (e.g. humanities and social studies); or the relationship between the school's pro-

Articulation—*Continued*

gram and outside factors (e.g. church, scouts, welfare agencies).

x Integration in education

xx **Education—Curricula; Schools— Administration**

Artificial flies.   *See* **Flies, Artificial**

Artificial flowers   745.59

x Flowers, Artificial

Artificial food.   *See* **Food, Artificial**

Artificial fuels.   *See* **Synthetic fuels**

Artificial heart   617

xx **Artificial organs; Heart**

Artificial insemination   636.08

Use for general materials and materials on artificial insemination of livestock, etc. Materials limited to artificial insemination in humans are entered under **Artificial insemination, Human.**

x Impregnation, Artificial; Insemination, Artificial

xx **Reproduction**

Artificial insemination, Human   176; 618.1

xx **Sexual ethics**

Artificial intelligence   001.53; *006.3

x Brain, Electronic; Electronic brains; Intelligence, Artificial; Machine intelligence

xx **Bionics**

Artificial islands.   *See* **Drilling platforms**

Artificial limbs   617

x Extremities, Artificial; Limbs, Artificial; Prosthesis

Artificial organs   617

See also names of artificial organs, e.g. **Artificial heart;** etc.

x Organs, Artificial; Prosthesis

Artificial respiration   616.02

x Pulmonary resuscitation; Respiration, Artificial; Resuscitation, Pulmonary

xx **First aid**

Artificial rubber.   *See* **Rubber, Artificial**

Artificial satellites (May subdiv. geog. adjective form)   **629.43; 629.46**

See also types of satellites, e.g. **Meteorological satellites; Space stations; Space vehicles;** etc.; also names of specific satellites, e.g. **Explorer (Artificial satellite);** etc.

x Orbiting vehicles; Satellites, Artificial

xx **Astronautics; Space vehicles**

Artificial satellites, American   629.43; 629.46

x American artificial satellites; United States— Artificial satellites

Artificial satellites—Control systems   629.8

Artificial satellites in telecommunication   621.38

See also names of specific satellites or projects, e.g. **Telstar project;** etc.

x Communication satellites; Communications relay satellites; Global satellite communications systems; Satellite communication systems

Artificial satellites in telecommunication—*Continued*
   xx **Telecommunication**
Artificial satellites—Launching 629.47
   x Launching of satellites
   xx **Rockets (Aeronautics)**
Artificial satellites—Law and legislation. *See* **Space law**
Artificial satellites—Orbits 629.43
   xx **Astrodynamics**
Artificial satellites, Russian 629.43; 629.46
   x Russian artificial satellites; Sputniks
Artificial satellites—Tracking 629.43
   x Tracking of satellites
Artificial silk. *See* **Rayon**
Artificial sweeteners. *See* **Sugar substitutes**
Artificial weather control. *See* **Weather—Control**
Artillery 355.7
   See also **Ordnance**
Artistic anatomy. *See* **Anatomy, Artistic**
Artistic photography. *See* **Photography, Artistic**
Artists (May subdiv. geog. adjective form) **709.2; 920**
   See also

Architects	**Illustrators**
Black artists	**Painters**
Child artists	**Potters**
Engravers	**Sculptors**
Etchers	**Women artists**

   also names of individual artists
   xx **Painters**
Artists, American 709.2; 920
   x American artists; United States—Artists
Artists, Black. *See* **Black artists**
Artists' materials 741.2; 751.2
   x Drawing materials; Painters' materials
Arts (May subdiv. geog. adjective form) **700**
   Use for materials on the arts in general, including the visual arts, literature, and the performing arts. Materials on the visual arts only (architecture, painting, etc.) are entered under **Art.**
   See also **Visual literacy**
   x Arts, Fine; Fine arts
Arts, American 709.73
   x American arts
Arts and crafts movement 745
   Use for materials on the movement that promoted craftsmanship and a reform of applied design or decorative arts. Originating in England in the second half of the 19th century under the influence of William Morris and spreading to the United States, Germany, and Austria, the movement grew as a response to the Industrial Revolution and incorporated ideas of socialism and the moral need for integrating beauty with the accessories of daily life.
   See also **Handicraft**
   x Crafts (Arts)
   xx **Art; Decoration and ornament; Decorative**

Arts and crafts movement—*Continued*
   arts; Folk art; Handicraft
Arts and state. *See* Arts—Government policy
Arts, Applied. *See* Decorative arts
Arts, Decorative. *See* Decoration and ornament;
   Decorative arts; Interior design
Arts, Fine. *See* Arts
Arts—Government policy 351.85; 700
  See also Art patronage
  x Arts and state; Funding for the arts; State and
    the arts; State encouragement of the arts
  xx Art patronage
Arts, Graphic. *See* Graphic arts
Arts, Minor. *See* Decorative arts
Arts, Useful. *See* Industrial arts; Technology
Asbestos 620.1; 666; 691
  xx Geology, Economic
Asceticism 248; 291.4
  xx Fanaticism; Fasting; Religious orders
Asia 915; 950
  See also areas of Asia, e.g. East Asia; Middle
    East; Southeast Asia; etc.
  x East; Orient
Asia, East. *See* East Asia
Asia—Politics and government 950
  x Politics
Asia, Southeast. *See* Southeast Asia
Asian architecture. *See* Architecture, Asian
Asian art. *See* Art, Asian
Asian civilization. *See* Civilization, Asian
Asphalt 625.8028; 665.5
  xx Concrete; Pavements
Asphyxiating gases. *See* Poisonous gases
Assassination 364.1
  See also Murder; Terrorism; also names of per-
    sons and groups with the subdivision
    Assassination, e.g. Presidents—United
    States—Assassination; etc.
  xx Crime; Murder; Offenses against the person;
    Political crimes and offenses
Assault, Criminal. *See* Rape
Assembly programs, School. *See* School assembly
   programs
Assembly, Right of. *See* Freedom of assembly
Assertive behavior. *See* Assertiveness (Psychology)
Assertiveness (Psychology) 152.4; 155.2
  x Assertive behavior
  xx Aggressiveness (Psychology); Psychology
Assessment 336.2
  Use for general materials only. Materials on the
    assessment of a given locality are entered
    under Taxation followed by the appropriate
    geographical division.
  See also Taxation; Valuation
  x Appraisal
  xx Taxation
Assessments, Political. *See* Campaign funds
Assistance in emergencies. *See* Helping behavior
Assistance to developing areas. *See* Economic as-
   sistance; Technical assistance

Association, Freedom of.   *See* **Freedom of association**
Associations   060; 302.3; 366
   See also **Clubs; Community life; Cooperation; Social group work; Societies; Voluntarism;** also
names of types of associations, e.g. **Trade
and professional associations;** etc.; and subjects with the subdivision *Societies,* e.g.
Agriculture—Societies; etc.; and names of
specific associations
   x Organizations; Voluntary associations
   xx **Societies; Voluntarism**
Associations, International.   *See* **International agencies**
Astrobiology.   *See* **Life on other planets; Space biology**
Astrodynamics   521; 629.4
   See also **Artificial satellites—Orbits; Astronautics; Navigation (Astronautics); Space flight**
   xx **Astronautics; Dynamics; Space flight**
Astrogeology   523.9
   See also **Lunar geology;** also names of planets
with the subdivision *Geology,* e.g. **Mars
(Planet)—Geology;** etc.
   xx **Geology**
Astrology   133.5
   See also **Horoscopes; Occult sciences**
   x Hermetic art and philosophy
   xx **Astronomy; Divination; Fortune telling; Occult
sciences; Prophecies (Occult sciences);
Stars; Superstition**
Astronautical accidents.   *See* **Astronautics—
Accidents**
Astronautical communication systems.   *See* **As-
tronautics—Communication systems**
Astronautical instruments   629.4
   See also **Astronautics—Communication systems**
   x Instruments, Astronautical; Space vehicles—
Instruments
   xx **Astronautics—Communication systems; Navi-
gation (Astronautics); Space optics**
Astronautics (May subdiv. geog.) **629.4**
   See also

Aerothermodynamics	**Space flight**
Artificial satellites	**Space flight to the moon**
Astrodynamics	**Space sciences**
Interplanetary voyages	**Space ships**
Navigation (Astronautics)	**Space stations**
Outer space	**Space vehicles**
Rocketry	**Unidentified flying objects**

   xx **Aeronautics; Astrodynamics; Space sciences;
Space vehicles**
Astronautics—Accidents   629.4
   x Accidents, Spacecraft; Astronautical accidents;
Space ships—Accidents; Space vehicles—
Accidents
Astronautics and civilization   306
   See also **Religion and astronautics; Space colo-
nies; Space law**
   x Civilization and astronautics; Outer space and

Astronautics and civilization—*Continued*
  civilization; Space age; Space power
  xx **Aeronautics and civilization; Civilization**
Astronautics and religion. *See* **Religion and as-**
    tronautics
Astronautics—Communication systems 629.47
  See also **Astronautical instruments; Radio in as-**
    tronautics; Television in astronautics
  x Astronautical communication systems; Space
    communication
  xx **Astronautical instruments; Interstellar commu-**
    nication; Telecommunication
Astronautics—International cooperation 629.4
  x International space cooperation
  xx **International cooperation**
Astronautics—Law and legislation. *See* **Space law**
Astronautics, Photography in. *See* **Space photogra-**
    phy
Astronautics—United States 629.4
  x United States—Astronautics
Astronauts 629.45; 920
  See also **Space vehicles—Piloting**
  x Cosmonauts; Space ships—Pilots
  xx **Air pilots; Space flight**
Astronauts—Clothing 629.47
  x Pressure suits; Space suits
  xx **Life support systems (Space environment)**
Astronauts—Food 629.47
  x Meals for astronauts; Menus for space flight
  xx **Astronauts—Nutrition**
Astronauts—Nutrition 629.47
  See also **Astronauts—Food**
  x Space nutrition
  xx **Nutrition**
Astronavigation. *See* **Navigation (Astronautics)**
Astronomers 520.92; 920
  xx **Scientists**
Astronomical instruments 522
  See also **Astronomical photography;** also names
    of instruments, e.g. **Telescope;** etc.
  x Instruments, Astronomical
  xx **Scientific apparatus and instruments; Space**
    optics
Astronomical observatories 522
  x Observatories, Astronomical
Astronomical photography 522
  x Astrophotography; Photography, Astronomi-
    cal
  xx **Astronomical instruments; Photography**
Astronomical physics. *See* **Astrophysics**
Astronomy 520-523
  See also

Almanacs	**Eclipses, Solar**
Astrology	**Galaxies**
Astrophysics	**Life on other planets**
Bible—Astronomy	**Meteorites**
Black holes (Astronomy)	**Meteors**
Chronology	**Moon**
Comets	**Nautical astronomy**
Eclipses, Lunar	**Outer space**

Astronomy—*Continued*
> **Planetariums**
> **Planets**
> **Quasars**
> **Radio astronomy**
> **Seasons**
> **Solar system**
> **Space environment**
> **Space sciences**
> **Spectrum analysis**
> **Stars**
> **Sun**
> **Tides**
> **Zodiac**
>> *x* Constellations
>> *xx* **Science; Space sciences; Stars; Universe**

Astronomy—Atlases. *See* **Stars—Atlases**

Astronomy—Collected works 500
> *x* Collections of literature

Astronomy—Mathematics 521
> *xx* **Mathematics**

Astronomy, Nautical. *See* **Nautical astronomy**

Astrophotography. *See* **Astronomical photography**

Astrophysics 523.01
> *See also* **Black holes (Astronomy); Spectrum analysis**
>> *x* Astronomical physics; Physics, Astronomical
>> *xx* **Astronomy; Physics; Stars**

Astros (Baseball team). *See* **Houston Astros (Baseball team)**

Asylum, Right of 341.4
> *See also* **Refugees, Political**
>> *x* Political asylum; Right of asylum; Sanctuary (Law)
>> *xx* **International law**

Asylums. *See* **Institutional care;** and classes of people with the subdivision *Institutional care,* e.g. **Blind—Institutional care; Deaf—Institutional care; Mentally ill—Institutional care;** etc.

At-home employment. *See* **Home business; Telecommuting**

Atheism 211
> *See also* **Agnosticism; Deism; Rationalism; Skepticism; Theism**
>> *xx* **Agnosticism; Deism; Faith; God; Rationalism; Religion; Secularism; Theism; Theology**

Athletes 796.092; 920
> *See also* **Black athletes**

Athletes, Black. *See* **Black athletes**

Athletic coaching. *See* **Coaching (Athletics)**

Athletic medicine. *See* **Sports medicine**

Athletics 796
> *See also* **Coaching (Athletics); Martial arts; Olympic games; Physical education; Sports;** also names of specific athletic activities, e.g. **Boxing; Gymnastics; Rowing; Track athletics; Weight lifting;** etc.
>> *x* College athletics; Intercollegiate athletics
>> *xx* **Physical education; Sports**

Atlantic cable. *See* **Cables, Submarine**

Atlantic Ocean
> *xx* **Ocean**

Atlantic States 917.4; 917.5; 974; 975
> *x* Eastern Seaboard; Middle Atlantic States; South Atlantic States

Atlantic States—*Continued*
   xx **United States**
Atlas (Missile) 623.4; 629.47
   xx **Ballistic missiles; Intercontinental ballistic missiles**
Atlases 912
   Use as a form heading for geographical atlases of world coverage. General materials about maps and their history are entered under **Maps.**
   See also **Bible—Geography;** also names of scientific and technical subjects with the form subdivision *Atlases,* e.g. **Anatomy, Human—Atlases; Stars—Atlases;** etc.; and countries, cities, etc. with the subdivision *Maps,* e.g. **United States—Maps; Chicago (Ill.)—Maps;** etc.
   x Geographical atlases
   xx **Geography; Maps**
Atlases, Astronomical. *See* **Stars—Atlases**
Atlases, Historical 911
   x Geography, Historical—Maps; Historical atlases; Historical geography; History—Atlases; Maps, Historical
Atmosphere 551.5
   Use for materials on the body of air surrounding the earth as distinguished from the upper rarefied air. Materials dealing with air as an element and with its chemical and physical properties are entered under **Air.**
   See also **Air; Meteorology**
   xx **Air; Earth; Meteorology**
Atmosphere—Pollution. *See* **Air—Pollution**
Atmosphere, Upper 551.5
   See also **Stratosphere**
   x Upper atmosphere
Atmospheric humidity. *See* **Humidity**
Atolls. *See* **Coral reefs and islands**
Atom smashing. *See* **Cyclotron**
Atomic bomb 623.4
   See also **Hydrogen bomb; Radioactive fallout**
   xx **Bombs; Hydrogen bomb; Nuclear energy; Nuclear warfare; Nuclear weapons**
Atomic bomb—Physiological effect 616.9
   See also **Radiation—Physiological effect**
   xx **Radiation—Physiological effect**
Atomic bomb—Testing 623.4
Atomic bomb victims 940.54
   Use for materials on the victims of atomic bomb warfare.
   x A-bomb victims; Victims of atomic bombings
Atomic energy. *See* **Nuclear energy**
Atomic industry. *See* **Nuclear industry**
Atomic medicine. *See* **Nuclear medicine**
Atomic nuclei. *See* **Nuclear physics**
Atomic piles. *See* **Nuclear reactors**
Atomic power. *See* **Nuclear energy**
Atomic power plants. *See* **Nuclear power plants**
Atomic powered vehicles. *See* **Nuclear propulsion**
Atomic submarines. *See* **Nuclear submarines**

Atomic theory 539.7; 541.2

> *See also* **Nuclear energy; Quantum theory**
>
> *xx* **Chemistry, Physical and theoretical; Quantum theory**

Atomic warfare. *See* **Nuclear warfare**

Atomic weapons. *See* **Nuclear weapons**

Atoms 539; 541

> *See also* **Cyclotron; Electrons; Nuclear physics; Transmutation (Chemistry)**
>
> *xx* **Chemistry, Physical and theoretical; Neutrons; Protons**

Atonement—Christianity 232; 234

> *x* Jesus Christ—Atonement; Vicarious atonement
>
> *xx* **Christianity; Jesus Christ; Sacrifice; Salvation**

Atonement, Day of. *See* **Yom Kippur**

Atonement—Judaism 296.3

> *xx* **Judaism**

Atrocities 179

> *See also* **Massacres; Persecution**
>
> *xx* **Crime; Cruelty**

Atrocities, Military. *See* names of wars with the subdivision *Atrocities,* e.g. **World War, 1939-1945—Atrocities;** etc.; and names of specific atrocities

Attacks by animals. *See* **Animal attacks**

Attendance, School. *See* **School attendance**

Attention 153.7

> *See also* **Listening**
>
> *x* Concentration
>
> *xx* **Apperception; Educational psychology; Listening; Memory; Psychology; Thought and thinking**

Attitude (Psychology) 152.4

> *See also* **Conformity; Job satisfaction; Prejudices; Public opinion; Racism; Sexism;** also names of groups of people with the subdivision *Attitudes,* e.g. **Youth—Attitudes;** etc.
>
> *x* Frustration
>
> *xx* **Emotions; Psychology; Public opinion; Social psychology**

Attorneys. *See* **Lawyers**

ATVs. *See* **All terrain vehicles**

Auction bridge. *See* **Bridge (Game)**

Auctions 658.8

> *x* Sales, Auction

Audiodisc players. *See* **Compact disc players**

Audiodiscs. *See* **Sound recordings**

Audiorecords. *See* **Sound recordings**

Audiovisual education 371.3

> *See also* **Audiovisual materials; Motion pictures in education; Radio in education; Sound recordings; Television in education;** also subjects with the subdivision *Audiovisual aids,* e.g. **Library education—Audiovisual aids;** etc.
>
> *x* Visual instruction
>
> *xx* **Education**

Audiovisual materials 025.17; 371.3

> *See also* names of specific materials, e.g.

Audiovisual materials—*Continued*
        **Filmstrips; Motion pictures; Sound record-
        ings; Videodiscs; Videotapes;** etc.; and sub-
        jects with the subdivision *Audiovisual aids,*
        e.g. **Library education—Audiovisual aids;**
        etc.
   x Multimedia materials; Nonbook materials;
      Nonprint materials
   xx **Audiovisual education; Teaching—Aids and
      devices**
Audiovisual materials centers. *See* **Instructional
       materials centers**
Auditing 657
   See also **Accounting**
   xx **Accounting; Bookkeeping**
Aurora borealis. *See* **Auroras**
Auroras 523.01; 538
   x Aurora borealis; Northern lights; Polar lights
   xx **Geophysics; Meteorology**
Author and publisher. *See* **Authors and publishers**
Authoritarianism. *See* **Fascism; Totalitarianism**
Authors (May subdiv. geog. adjective form, e.g.
        Authors, English; etc.) **808.092; 920**
   See also **Black authors; Child authors; Litera-
      ture—Bio-bibliography; Literature—History
      and criticism; Pseudonyms; Women authors;**
      also classes of writers, e.g. **Dramatists; Nov-
      elists; Poets;** etc.; and names of individual
      authors
   x Writers
   xx **Books; Literature—Bio-bibliography; Litera-
      ture—History and criticism**
Authors, American 808.092; 920
   x American authors; United States—Authors
   xx **American literature**
Authors and publishers 070.5
   Use for materials on the relations between au-
      thor and publisher.
   See also **Copyright**
   x Author and publisher; Publishers and authors
   xx **Authorship; Contracts; Copyright; Publishers
      and publishing**
Authors, Black. *See* **Black authors**
Authors—Correspondence 92
   x Correspondence
Authors, English 808.092; 920
   See also **English literature—Bio-bibliography**
   x English authors
   xx **English literature**
Authors—Homes and haunts. *See* **Literary land-
      marks**
Authorship 808
   Use for general materials dealing with the means
      of becoming an author. Materials concern-
      ing the composition of special types of liter-
      ature are entered under more specific head-
      ings such as **Fiction—Technique; Love
      stories—Technique; Short story;** etc.

Authorship—*Continued*

   See also

Advertising copy	**Love stories—Technique**
Authors and publishers	**Plots (Drama, fiction, etc.)**
Biography (as a literary	**Radio authorship**
form)	**Report writing**
Copyright	**Short story**
Creative writing	**Technical writing**
Drama—Technique	**Television authorship**
Fiction—Technique	**Versification**
Journalism	

   x Writing (Authorship)

   xx **Literature**

Authorship—Handbooks, manuals, etc. 808

   See also **Printing—Style manuals**

   xx **Printing—Style manuals**

Autism 616.89; 618.92

   xx **Child psychiatry**

Auto courts. *See* **Hotels, motels, etc.**

Autobiographies 920

   Use for collections of autobiographies.

   See also subjects with the subdivision
      Biography or *Correspondence,* e.g.
      Women—Biography; Authors—
      Correspondence; etc.; and names of wars
      with the subdivision *Personal narratives,*
      e.g. **World War, 1939-1945—Personal nar-**
      ratives; etc.

   x Diaries; Memoirs; Personal narratives

   xx **Biography**

Autobiography (as a literary form). *See* **Biography**
      (as a literary form)

Autobiography—Technique. *See* **Biography (as a**
      literary form)

Autocodes. *See* **Programming languages (Comput-**
      ers)

Autographs 929.8

   See also **Manuscripts**

   xx **Biography; Manuscripts; Writing**

Automata. *See* **Robots**

Automated genetic engineering. *See* **Genetic engi-**
      neering, Automated

Automated information networks. *See* **Information**
      networks

Automatic computers. *See* **Computers**

Automatic control. *See* **Automation; Cybernetics;**
      Electric controllers; Servomechanisms

Automatic data processing. *See* **Electronic data**
      processing

Automatic drafting. *See* **Computer graphics**

Automatic drawing. *See* **Computer graphics**

Automatic information retrieval. *See* **Information**
      storage and retrieval systems

Automatic programming languages. *See* **Program-**
      ming languages (Computers)

Automatic speech recognition 001.53; 001.54; 621.
      389; *006.4; *621.39

   x Mechanical speech recognition; Speech recog-
      nition, Automatic

   xx **Voice**

Automatic teaching. *See* **Teaching machines**

Automation 629.8

> *See also* **Feedback control systems; Servomechanisms; Systems engineering; Telecommuting;** also subjects with the subdivision *Automation,* e.g. **Libraries—Automation;** etc.
>
> *x* Automatic control; Computer control; Machinery, Automatic
>
> *xx* **Machinery in industry**

Automobile accidents. *See* **Traffic accidents**

Automobile driver education. *See* **Automobile drivers—Education**

Automobile drivers 629.28

> *x* Automobile driving; Automobiles—Driving; Drivers, Automobile

Automobile drivers—Education 629.28

> *x* Automobile driver education; Driver education
>
> *xx* **Education**

Automobile driving. *See* **Automobile drivers**

Automobile engines. *See* **Automobiles—Engines**

Automobile guides. *See* **Automobiles—Road guides**

Automobile industry 338.4; 388.3

Automobile insurance. *See* **Insurance, Automobile**

Automobile parts. *See* **Automobiles—Parts**

Automobile pools. *See* **Car pools**

Automobile racing 796.7

> *See also* **Karts and karting;** also names of types of automobile races and names of specific races
>
> *x* Automobiles—Racing; Racing

Automobile repairs. *See* **Automobiles—Maintenance and repair**

Automobile touring. *See* **Automobiles—Touring**

Automobile trailers. *See* **Automobiles—Trailers**

Automobile transmission. *See* **Automobiles—Transmission devices**

Automobile trucks. *See* **Trucks**

Automobiles 629.2

> *See also* **Buses; Sports cars; Trucks;** also names of specific makes and models of automobiles, e.g. **Ford automobile;** etc.
>
> *x* Cars (Automobiles); Locomotion; Motor cars
>
> *xx* **Transportation, Highway; Vehicles**

Automobiles—Accidents. *See* **Traffic accidents**

Automobiles—Air conditioning 629.2

> *xx* **Air conditioning**

Automobiles—Brakes 629.2

> *xx* **Brakes**

Automobiles, Compact 629.2

> *See also* names of specific makes and models
>
> *x* Compact automobiles; Compact cars

Automobiles—Design and construction 629.2

Automobiles, Diesel 629.2

> *x* Diesel automobiles

Automobiles—Driving. *See* **Automobile drivers**

Automobiles, Electric 629.2

> *x* Electric automobiles

Automobiles—Electric equipment 629.2
   x Electric equipment of automobiles
Automobiles—Engines 629.2
   x Automobile engines; Automobiles—Motors
   xx **Engines; Gas and oil engines**
Automobiles, Foreign 629.2
   See also names of specific makes and models
   x Foreign automobiles
Automobiles—Fuel consumption 629.28
   x Fuel consumption
   xx **Energy consumption; Fuel**
Automobiles—Gearing. *See* **Automobiles—**
      Transmission devices
Automobiles—Law and legislation 343; 629.2026
   See also **Traffic regulations**
   x Laws
   xx **Law; Legislation; Traffic regulations**
Automobiles—Maintenance and repair 629.28
   See also **Automobiles—Restoration**
   x Automobile repairs; Automobiles—Repairing;
      Maintenance and repair
   xx **Repairing**
Automobiles—Models 629.2
   x Model cars
   xx **Machinery—Models**
Automobiles—Motors. *See* **Automobiles—Engines**
Automobiles—Parts 629.28
   x Automobile parts
Automobiles—Pollution control devices 629.2
   x Pollution control devices (Motor vehicles)
Automobiles—Pools. *See* **Car pools**
Automobiles—Racing. *See* **Automobile racing**
Automobiles—Repairing. *See* **Automobiles—**
      Maintenance and repair
Automobiles—Restoration 629.28
   x Restoration of automobiles
   xx **Automobiles—Maintenance and repair**
Automobiles—Road guides 910.22
   See also **Road maps**
   x Automobile guides
   xx **Maps; Road maps**
Automobiles—Service stations 629.28
   x Filling stations; Gas stations; Service stations,
      Automobile
Automobiles—Touring 796.7
   x Automobile touring; Motoring
   xx **Travel**
Automobiles—Trailers 629.2
   See also **Travel trailers and campers**
   x Automobile trailers; Trailers
Automobiles—Transmission devices 629.2
   x Automobile transmission; Automobiles—
      Gearing; Transmissions, Automobile
   xx **Gearing**
Autosuggestion. *See* **Hypnotism; Mental suggestion**
Autumn 525
   x Fall
   xx **Seasons**
Avant-garde churches. *See* **Noninstitutional**
      churches

Avant-garde films. *See* **Experimental films**
Avant-garde theater. *See* **Experimental theater**
Avenues. *See* **Streets**
Average 519.5
> *xx* **Arithmetic; Probabilities; Statistics**
Aviation. *See* **Aeronautics**
Aviation medicine 616.9
> *See also* **Jet lag; Space medicine**
> *x* Aeronautics—Medical aspects; Aerospace
> medicine; Medicine, Aviation
> *xx* **Medicine; Space medicine**
Aviators. *See* **Air pilots**
Avocations. *See* **Hobbies**
Awakening, Religious. *See* **Religious awakening**
Awards. *See* **Rewards (Prizes, etc.);** and names of
> awards
Awards (Law). *See* **Arbitration and award**
Awards, Literary. *See* **Literary prizes**
Axiology. *See* **Values**
Aztecs 970.004; 972
> *xx* **Indians of Mexico**
B-52 bomber 623.74
> *xx* **Bombers**
Babies. *See* **Infants**
Babies, Test tube. *See* **Fertilization in vitro, Human**
Baby animals. *See* **Animals—Infancy**
Baby sitters 649
> *xx* **Children—Care and hygiene; Infants—Care
> and hygiene**
Bacilli. *See* **Bacteriology; Germ theory of disease**
Back packing. *See* **Backpacking**
Backpacking 796.5
> *x* Back packing; Pack transportation
> *xx* **Camping; Hiking**
Bacon-Shakespeare controversy. *See* **Shakespeare,
> William, 1564-1616—Authorship**
Bacon's Rebellion, 1676 973.2
> *xx* **United States—History—1600-1775, Colonial
> period**
Bacteria. *See* **Bacteriology**
Bacterial warfare. *See* **Biological warfare**
Bacteriology 589.9
> *See also* **Disinfection and disinfectants; Fermen-
> tation; Germ theory of disease; Immunity;
> Microorganisms;** also subjects with the sub-
> division *Bacteriology,* e.g.
> **Cheese—Bacteriology;** etc.
> *x* Bacilli; Bacteria; Disease germs; Germs; Mi-
> crobes
> *xx* **Communicable diseases; Fermentation; Fungi;
> Germ theory of disease; Medicine; Microbi-
> ology; Microorganisms; Parasites; Pathol-
> ogy; Science**
Bacteriology, Agricultural 630.2
> *See also* **Soils—Bacteriology;** also names of
> crops, etc. with the subdivision *Diseases and
> pests,* e.g. **Fruit—Diseases and pests;** etc.
> *x* Agricultural bacteriology; Diseases and pests
> *xx* **Soils—Bacteriology**

60

Badges of honor. *See* **Decorations of honor; Insignia; Medals**

Baha'i Faith. *See* **Bahaism**

Bahaism 297
> *x* Baha'i Faith
> *xx* **Islam; Religions**

Baking 641.7
> *See also* **Pastry**; also names of baked products, e.g. **Bread; Cake; Pastry,** etc.
> *xx* **Cookery**

Balance of nature. *See* **Ecology**

Balance of payments 382.1
> *See also* **Balance of trade**
> *xx* **Balance of trade; International economic relations**

Balance of power 327.1
> *x* Power politics

Balance of trade 382.1
> *See also* **Balance of payments**
> *x* Trade, Balance of
> *xx* **Balance of payments; Commerce; Economics; Free trade and protection; Tariff**

Ball bearings. *See* **Bearings (Machinery)**

Ball games 796.3
> *See also* names of games, e.g. **Baseball; Basketball; Soccer;** etc.; and names of competitions
> *xx* **Games**

Ballads 808.81; 811.08; etc.
> Use for collections of ballads and for materials about ballads. Materials dealing with the folk tunes associated with these ballads, and collections that include both words and music are entered under **Folk songs.**
> *See also* **Folk songs**
> *xx* **Folk songs; Literature; Poetry; Songs**

Ballads, American 811.08
> *x* American ballads; United States—Ballads
> *xx* **American literature**

Ballet 792.8
> *See also* **Pantomimes**
> *xx* **Dancing; Drama; Opera; Performing arts; Theater**

Ballet dancers 792.8
> *xx* **Dancers**

Ballet, Water. *See* **Synchronized swimming**

Ballets 792.8

Ballets—Stories, plots, etc. 792.8
> *x* Stories
> *xx* **Plots (Drama, fiction, etc.)**

Ballistic missile early warning system 621.3848
> *x* BMEWS; Early warning system, Ballistic missile
> *xx* **Air defenses; Radar defense networks**

Ballistic missiles 623.4
> *See also* types of ballistic missiles, e.g. **Intercontinental ballistic missiles;** etc.; also names of specific missiles, e.g. **Atlas (Missile);** etc.
> *x* Missiles, Ballistic

Ballistic missiles—*Continued*
    xx **Guided missiles; Nuclear weapons; Rocketry;**
        Rockets (Aeronautics)
Balloons 623.74; 629.133
    See also **Aeronautics**
    xx **Aeronautics; Airships**
Balloons, Dirigible. *See* **Airships**
Ballot. *See* **Elections**
Band music 785.1
    xx **Instrumental music; Military music**
Bandages and bandaging 616.02
    xx **First aid**
Bandits. *See* **Robbers and outlaws**
Bandmasters. *See* **Conductors (Music)**
Bands (Music) 785.06
    See also **Conducting; Drum majoring; Instrumen-**
        tation and orchestration; Orchestra; Wind
        instruments; also names of types of bands
        and specific bands
    xx **Conducting; Orchestra; Wind instruments**
Bank failures 332.1
    x Failure of banks
    xx **Bankruptcy; Banks and banking; Business**
        failures
Banking. *See* **Banks and banking**
Bankruptcy 332.7; 336.3; 346
    See also **Bank failures**
    x Business mortality; Failure in business; Insol-
        vency
    xx **Business failures; Commercial law; Debtor**
        and creditor; Finance
Banks and banking (May subdiv. geog.) **332.1**
    See also

Agricultural credit	**Investment trusts**
Bank failures	**Investments**
Consumer credit	**Money**
Credit	**Negotiable instruments**
Federal Reserve banks	**Savings and loan associa-**
Foreign exchange	**tions**
Interest (Economics)	**Trust companies**

    also names of individual banks
    x Banking; Savings banks
    xx **Business; Capital; Commerce; Credit; Finance;**
        Money; Trust companies
Banks and banking, Cooperative 334
    See also **Credit unions**
    x Cooperative banks; People's banks
    xx **Cooperation; Cooperative societies; Personal**
        loans
Banks and banking—Data processing 332.1028
    x Data processing
    xx **Electronic data processing**
Banks and banking—United States 332.1
    x United States—Banks and banking
Banned books. *See* **Books—Censorship**
Banners. *See* **Flags**
Banquets. *See* **Dinners and dining**
Baptism 234; 265
    See also **Regeneration (Theology)**
    x Christening; Immersion, Baptismal

Baptism—*Continued*
>> *xx* **Rites and ceremonies; Sacraments; Theology**

Baptists 286; 920
>> *See also* **Mennonites**

Bar. *See* **Lawyers**

Barbary corsairs. *See* **Pirates**

Barbary States. *See* **Africa, North**

Barbecue cookery 641.7
>> *x* Cookery, Barbecue; Grill cookery
>> *xx* **Outdoor cookery**

Barns 631.2
>> *xx* **Farm buildings**

Barometer 551.5028
>> *xx* **Meteorological instruments**

Baronage. *See* **Nobility**

Baroque architecture. *See* **Architecture, Baroque**

Baroque art. *See* **Art, Baroque**

Barrier free design. *See* **Architecture and the handicapped**

Barristers. *See* **Lawyers**

Barrows. *See* **Mounds and mound builders**

Bars and restaurants. *See* **Restaurants, bars, etc.**

Barter 332.5
>> *x* Exchange, Barter
>> *xx* **Commerce; Economics; Money; Subsistence economy; Underground economy**

Baseball 796.357
>> *See also* **Little league baseball; Softball**
>> *xx* **Ball games; College sports; Sports**

Baseball clubs 796.357
>> *See also* names of individual baseball clubs, e.g. **Houston Astros (Baseball team)**; etc.

Basements 721
>> *x* Cellars
>> *xx* **Foundations; Underground architecture**

Bases (Chemistry) 661
>> *xx* **Chemistry**

Bashfulness 152.4
>> *x* Shyness
>> *xx* **Emotions**

Basic education 375
>> *x* Basic skills education; Fundamental education
>> *xx* **Education**

Basic life skills. *See* **Life skills**

Basic skills education. *See* **Basic education**

Basket making 746.41
>> *xx* **Weaving**

Basketball 796.32
>> *xx* **Ball games; College sports; Sports**

Bastardy. *See* **Illegitimacy**

Bastogne, Battle of. *See* **Ardennes, Battle of the, 1944-1945**

Bat. *See* **Bats**

Baths 613; 615.8
>> *See also* **Hydrotherapy**
>> *xx* **Cleanliness; Hydrotherapy; Hygiene; Physical therapy**

Bathyscaphe 623.8
>> *xx* **Oceanography—Research; Submersibles**

Batik 746.6
> *xx* **Dyes and dyeing**

Baton twirling 785.06
> *See also* **Drum majoring**
> *xx* **Drum majoring**

Batrachia. *See* **Amphibians**

Bats 599.4
> *x* Bat
> *xx* **Mammals**

Battered children. *See* **Child abuse**

Battered elderly. *See* **Elderly abuse**

Battered husbands. *See* **Husband abuse**

Battered men. *See* **Husband abuse**

Battered wives. *See* **Wife abuse**

Battered women. *See* **Wife abuse**

Batteries, Electric. *See* **Electric batteries; Storage batteries**

Batteries, Solar. *See* **Solar batteries**

Battle of the Bulge. *See* **Ardennes, Battle of the, 1944-1945**

Battle ships. *See* **Warships**

Battle songs. *See* **War songs**

Battles 355.4; 904
> Names of all battles are not included in this list but are to be added as needed, e.g. **Ardennes, Battle of the, 1944-1945;** etc.
> *See also* **Naval battles;** also names of wars with the subdivision *Campaigns,* e.g. **United States—History—1861-1865, Civil War—Campaigns; World War, 1939-1945—Campaigns;** etc.; and names of individual battles, e.g. **Ardennes, Battle of the, 1944-1945;** etc.
> *x* Fighting; Sieges
> *xx* **Military art and science; Military history; Naval battles; War**

Battleships. *See* **Warships**

Bay of Pigs invasion. *See* **Cuba—History—1961, Invasion**

Bazaars. *See* **Fairs**

Beaches 551.4
> *xx* **Seashore**

Beadwork 746.5
> *xx* **Crocheting; Embroidery; Weaving**

Bearings (Machinery) 621.8
> *See also* **Lubrication and lubricants**
> *x* Ball bearings; Journals (Machinery)
> *xx* **Lubrication and lubricants; Machinery**

Beasts. *See* **Animals; Domestic animals**

Beat generation. *See* **Bohemianism**

Beatniks. *See* **Bohemianism**

Beautification of landscape. *See* **Landscape protection**

Beauty. *See* **Esthetics**

Beauty, Personal. *See* **Grooming, Personal**

Beauty shops 646.7
> *See also* **Cosmetics**

Beavers 599.3
> *xx* **Freshwater animals; Furbearing animals**

Bed and breakfast accommodations. *See* **Hotels,**

Bed and breakfast accommodations—*Continued*
          motels, etc.
Bedouins   572.953; 909
  xx **Arabs**
Bedspreads   746.9
  x Coverlets
  xx **Interior design**
Bedtime   E
  See also **Lullabies**
  x Getting ready for bed
  xx **Night; Sleep**
Bee. *See* **Bees**
Beef   641.3; 664
  xx Meat
Beef cattle   636.2
  See also names of breeds of beef cattle, e.g.
          Hereford cattle; etc.
  x Steers
  xx **Cattle**
Bees   595.79; 638
  See also **Honey**
  x Apiculture; Bee; Hymenoptera
  xx **Honey; Insects**
Begging   362.5
  See also **Tramps**
  x Mendicancy
  xx **Tramps**
Beginning reading materials. *See* **Easy reading ma-
          terials**
Behavior. *See* **Animals—Habits and behavior; Hu-
          man behavior**
Behavior genetics   155.7
  x Psychogenetics
  xx **Genetics; Psychology**
Behavior modification   152
  See also **Brainwashing**
  xx **Human behavior; Learning, Psychology of;
          Psychology, Applied**
Behavior problems (Children). *See* **Emotionally
          disturbed children**
Behaviorism   150.19
      Use for materials on the conception of psychol-
          ogy which claims that its subject matter is
          the objectively observable actions of organ-
          isms and not the study of mental phenom-
          ena.
  xx **Human behavior; Psychology; Psychology,
          Physiological**
Belief and doubt   121
      Use for materials on belief and doubt from the
          philosophical standpoint. Materials on reli-
          gious belief and doubt are entered under
          Faith.
  See also **Agnosticism; Rationalism; Skepticism;
          Truth**
  x Certainty; Doubt
  xx **Agnosticism; Emotions; Knowledge, Theory of;
          Philosophy; Rationalism; Religion; Skepti-
          cism**
Bell System Telstar satellite. *See* **Telstar project**

65

Belles-lettres. *See* **Literature**
Bells 621.389; 789
    x Carillons; Chimes; Church bells
Belts and belting 621.8
    See also **Power transmission**
    x Chain belting
    xx **Machinery; Power transmission**
Benevolent institutions. *See* **Institutional care**
Bequests. *See* **Gifts; Inheritance and succession;**
    Wills
Bereavement 152.4
    See also **Sympathy**
    xx **Death; Sympathy**
Bermuda Triangle 001.9
    x Devil's Triangle; Graveyard of the Atlantic
Berries 634
    Names of all berries are not included in this list
        but are to be added as needed in the plural
        form, e.g. **Strawberries;** etc.
    See also names of berries, e.g. **Strawberries;** etc.
    xx **Fruit; Fruit culture**
Best books. *See* **Books and reading—Best books**
Best sellers (Books) 028; 070.5
    x Books—Best sellers
    xx **Book industries and trade; Books and reading**
Betting. *See* **Gambling**
Bevel gearing. *See* **Gearing**
Beverages 613; 641.2; 641.8; 663
    See also names of types of beverages, e.g.
        Alcoholic beverages; Liquors and liqueurs;
        etc.; also names of specific beverages, e.g.
        Cocoa; Coffee; etc.
    x Drinks
    xx **Diet; Food**
Bias (Psychology). *See* **Prejudices**
Bible 220
    The subject subdivisions under **Bible** may be
        used also for any part of the Bible, under
        the same form of entry as for the texts of
        such parts, e.g. **Bible. O.T.—Biography; Bi-**
        ble. O.T. Pentateuch—Commentaries; Bible.
        O.T. Psalms—History; Bible. N.T. Gos-
        pels—Inspiration; etc.
    x Holy Scriptures; Scriptures, Holy
    xx **Hebrew literature; History, Ancient; Jewish**
        literature; Sacred books
Bible and science 220.8
    x Bible—Science; Science and the Bible
    xx **Religion and science**
Bible—Animals. *See* **Bible—Natural history**
Bible—Antiquities 220.9
    See also **Christian antiquities**
    x Antiquities, Biblical; Archeology, Biblical;
        Biblical archeology
    xx **Antiquities; Archeology**
Bible as literature 220.6
    See also **Bible—Criticism, interpretation, etc.;**
        Bible—Parables; Religious literature
    x Bible—Language, style, etc.; Bible—Literary
        character

Bible as literature—*Continued*
   xx **Religious literature**
Bible—Astronomy 220.8
   xx **Astronomy**
Bible—Biography 220.9
   See also **Women in the Bible**
   x Biblical characters
Bible—Birds. *See* **Bible—Natural history**
Bible—Botany. *See* **Bible—Natural history**
Bible—Catechisms, question books 238
   x Bible—Question books
   xx **Bible—Study; Catechisms**
Bible—Chronology 220.9
   Use for materials on the dates of events related
        in the Bible and their correlation with the
        dates of general history.
   x Bible—History of biblical events—
        Chronology; Chronology, Biblical
Bible classes. *See* **Bible—Study; Summer schools,**
        Religious; Sunday schools
Bible—Commentaries 220.7
   x Bible—Interpretation; Commentaries, Biblical
Bible—Concordances 220.4-220.5
   x Bible—Indexes; Concordances
   xx **Bible—Dictionaries**
Bible—Criticism, interpretation, etc. 220.6
   x Bible—Exegesis; Bible—Hermeneutics; Bi-
        ble—Interpretation; Exegesis, Biblical; Her-
        meneutics, Biblical; Higher criticism
   xx **Bible as literature; Criticism**
Bible—Dictionaries 220.3
   See also **Bible—Concordances**
   x Bible—Indexes
Bible—Drama 808.2; 808.82, 812; etc.
   See also **Mysteries and miracle plays**
   x Bible plays; Plays, Bible
   xx **Religious drama**
Bible—Evidences, authority, etc. 220.1
   See also **Miracles—Christianity**
   x Evidences of the Bible
   xx **Free thought**
Bible—Exegesis. *See* **Bible—Criticism, interpreta-**
        tion, etc.
Bible—Fiction. *See* **Bible—History of biblical**
        events—Fiction
Bible—Flowers. *See* **Bible—Natural history**
Bible—Gardens. *See* **Bible—Natural history**
Bible—Geography 220.9
   x Bible—Maps; Geography, Biblical
   xx **Atlases**
Bible—Hermeneutics. *See* **Bible—Criticism, inter-**
        pretation, etc.
Bible—History 220.9
   Use for materials on the origin, authorship and
        composition of the Bible as a book. Materi-
        als dealing with historical events as de-
        scribed in the Bible are entered under
        Bible—History of biblical events.
Bible—History of biblical events 220.9
   See note under **Bible—History.**

Bible—History of biblical events—*Continued*
 x History, Biblical
Bible—History of biblical events—Chronology. *See*
  Bible—Chronology
Bible—History of biblical events—Fiction Fic
 See note under **Bible stories.**
 x Bible—Fiction
Bible—Illustrations. *See* **Bible—Pictorial works**
Bible in literature 809
 Use for materials that discuss the Bible as a
  theme in literature. An additional subject
  heading may be necessary for the name of
  the literature or the name of the author dis-
  cussed.
 See also **Religion in literature**
 xx **Literature; Religion in literature**
Bible in the schools. *See* **Religion in the public
  schools**
Bible—Indexes. *See* **Bible—Concordances; Bible—
  Dictionaries**
Bible—Inspiration 220.1
 x Inspiration, Biblical
Bible—Interpretation. *See* **Bible—Commentaries;
  Bible—Criticism, interpretation, etc.**
Bible—Introductions. *See* **Bible—Study**
Bible—Language, style, etc. *See* **Bible as literature**
Bible—Literary character. *See* **Bible as literature**
Bible—Maps. *See* **Bible—Geography**
Bible—Miracles. *See* **Miracles—Christianity**
Bible. N.T. 225
 Use same subject subdivisions as those given
  under **Bible.** They may be used also for
  groups of books (e.g. **Bible. N.T. Gospels;**
  etc.) and for single books (e.g. **Bible. N.T.
  Matthew;** etc.)
 x New Testament
Bible—Natural history 220.8
 x Bible—Animals; Bible—Birds; Bible—
  Botany; Bible—Flowers; Bible—Gardens;
  Bible—Plants; Bible—Zoology; Botany of
  the Bible; Natural history, Biblical; Zoology
  of the Bible
 xx **Animals in literature; Birds in literature**
Bible. O.T. 221
 Use same subject subdivisions as those given
  under **Bible.** They may be used also for
  groups of books (e.g. **Bible. O.T. Penta-
  teuch;** etc.) and for single books (e.g. **Bible.
  N.T. Psalms;** etc.)
 x Old Testament
Bible—Parables 220; 226
 See also **Jesus Christ—Parables**
 xx **Bible as literature; Parables**
Bible—Pictorial works 220.22
 x Bible—Illustrations
 xx **Christian art and symbolism; Jesus Christ—
  Art**
Bible—Plants. *See* **Bible—Natural history**
Bible plays. *See* **Bible—Drama; Mysteries and miracle plays**

Bible—Prophecies 220.1
>   *See also* **Jesus Christ—Prophecies**
>   *x* Prophecies (Bible)

Bible—Psychology 220.8
>   *x* Psychology, Biblical

Bible—Question books. *See* **Bible—Catechisms,
    question books**

Bible—Reading 220.5

Bible—Science. *See* **Bible and science**

Bible stories 220.9
>   Use for materials that retell or adapt stories
>   from the Bible. May also be used for materi-
>   als about Bible stories. Fiction in which
>   characters and settings are taken from the
>   Bible is entered under **Bible—History of
>   biblical events—Fiction.**
>   *x* Stories

Bible—Study 220.6; 230
>   *See also* **Bible—Catechisms, question books**
>   *x* Bible classes; Bible—Introductions
>   *xx* **Christian education; Sunday schools**

Bible—Use 220.6
>   Use for materials that show how the Bible is
>   used as a guide to living, to cultivation of a
>   spiritual life, and to problems of doctrine.

Bible—Versions 220; 220.5
>   Use for history of versions, including materials
>   on both the Old Testament and the New
>   Testament.

Bible—Women. *See* **Women in the Bible**

Bible—Zoology. *See* **Bible—Natural history**

Biblical archeology. *See* **Bible—Antiquities**

Biblical characters. *See* **Bible—Biography**

Bibliographic control 025.3
>   *See also* **Cataloging; Indexing; Information stor-
>   age and retrieval systems; MARC system**
>   *x* Universal bibliographic control
>   *xx* **Documentation**

Bibliographic data in machine readable form. *See*
        Machine readable bibliographic data

Bibliography 010-016
>   *See also*

Archives	**Information storage and**
Bookbinding	**retrieval systems**
Books	**Library science**
Cataloging	**Manuscripts**
Classification—Books	**Printing**
Indexes	**Serial publications**
Indexing	

>   also names of persons, places, and subjects with
>   the subdivision *Bibliography,* e.g.
>   **Shakespeare, William, 1564-1616—
>   Bibliography; United States—Bibliography;
>   Agriculture—Bibliography;** etc.
>   *xx* **Books; Cataloging; Documentation; Library
>   science**

Bibliography—Best books. *See* **Books and read-
        ing—Best books**

Bibliography—Bilingual books. *See* **Bilingual
        books**

Bibliography—Editions 016
   See also **Paperback books; Rare books**
   x Bibliography—Reprints; Editions; Reprints
Bibliography—First editions 016
   x Books—First editions; First editions
Bibliography—Reprints. *See* **Bibliography—Editions**
Bibliomania. *See* **Book collecting**
Bibliophily. *See* **Book collecting**
Bicentennial celebrations—United States—1976. *See* **American Revolution Bicentennial, 1776-1976**
Biculturalism (May subdiv. geog.) **306**
   xx **Civilization; Culture**
Biculturalism—United States 306
   x United States—Biculturalism
Bicycle racing 796.6
   x Racing
   xx **Bicycles and bicycling**
Bicycles and bicycling 629.2; 796.6
   See also **Bicycle racing; Minibikes; Motorcycles; Tricycles**
   x Biking; Cycling
Big band music. *See* **Dance music**
Big bang theory. *See* **Universe**
Bigotry. *See* **Prejudices; Toleration**
Biking. *See* **Bicycles and bicycling**
Bilingual books (May subdiv. by languages)
   x Bibliography—Bilingual books
   xx **Books**
Bilingual books—English-Spanish
Bilingual education. *See* **Education, Bilingual**
Bilingualism (May subdiv. geog.) **400**
   See also **Education, Bilingual**
   xx **Language and languages**
Bilingualism—United States 400
   x United States—Bilingualism
Billboards. *See* **Signs and signboards**
Bills and notes. *See* **Negotiable instruments**
Bills of credit. *See* **Credit; Negotiable instruments; Paper money**
Bills of fare. *See* **Menus**
Bimetallism. *See* **Gold; Monetary policy; Silver**
Binary system (Mathematics) 513
   x Pair system
   xx **Mathematics; Numeration**
Binding of books. *See* **Bookbinding**
Bio-bibliography. *See* names of persons, subjects and names of countries, cities, etc. with the subdivision *Bio-bibliography,* e.g. **English literature—Bio-bibliography; United States—Bio-bibliography;** etc.
Bioastronautics. *See* **Space biology; Space medicine**
Biochemistry 574.19
   See also **Metabolism; Molecular biology; Physiological chemistry**
   x Biological chemistry; Chemistry, Biological
   xx **Chemistry; Physiological chemistry**
Bioconversion. *See* **Biomass energy**

Bioethics 174

> *See also* **Medical ethics; Transplantation of organs, tissues, etc.—Moral and religious aspects**
>
> *x* Biological ethics; Biology—Ethics; Biomedical ethics; Ethics, Biological; Life sciences ethics
>
> *xx* **Social ethics**

Biofeedback training 152.1

> *x* Visceral learning
>
> *xx* **Feedback (Psychology); Learning, Psychology of; Mind and body; Psychotherapy**

Biogeography 574.9

> *See also* names of plants and animals with the subdivision *Geographical distribution,* e.g. **Fishes—Geographical distribution; Plants—Geographical distribution;** etc.
>
> *x* Distribution of animals and plants; Geographical distribution of animals and plants; Paleobiogeography; Zoogeography
>
> *xx* **Ecology; Geography; Natural history**

Biographical dictionaries. *See* **Biography—Dictionaries**

Biography 920

> Use for collections of biographies which are not limited to one country or to one class of people. Materials that deal with the writing of biography are entered under **Biography (as a literary form).**
>
> *See also*

Autobiographies	**Men—Biography**
Autographs	**Musicians—Biography**
Celebrities	**Obituaries**
Chicago (Ill.)—Biography	**Portraits**
Epitaphs	**Religions—Biography**
Genealogy	**United States—Biography**
Heraldry	**Women—Biography**

> also subjects with the subdivision *Biography* or *Correspondence;* and names of wars with the subdivision *Personal narratives,* e.g. **World War, 1939-1945—Personal narratives;** etc.
>
> *x* Life histories; Memoirs; Personal narratives
>
> *xx* **Genealogy; History**

Biography (as a literary form) 808

> Use for materials dealing with the writing of biography.
>
> *x* Autobiography (as a literary form); Autobiography—Technique; Biography—Technique
>
> *xx* **Authorship; Literature**

Biography—Dictionaries 920.03

> Use for collections of biographies that are not limited to one class of people and that are arranged in dictionary form.
>
> *See also* names of countries with the subdivision *Biography—Dictionaries,* e.g. **United States—Biography—Dictionaries;** etc.
>
> *x* Biographical dictionaries; Dictionaries, Biographical
>
> *xx* **Encyclopedias and dictionaries**

Biography—Technique. *See* **Biography (as a literary form)**

Biological anthropology. *See* **Physical anthropology**

Biological chemistry. *See* **Biochemistry**

Biological clocks. *See* **Biological rhythms**

Biological control of pests. *See* **Pests—Biological control**

Biological ethics. *See* **Bioethics**

Biological oceanography. *See* **Marine biology; Marine ecology**

Biological parents. *See* **Birthparents**

Biological physics. *See* **Biophysics**

Biological rhythms 574.1

> *See also* **Jet lag**
> *x* Biological clocks; Biology—Periodicity; Biorhythms
> *xx* **Periodicity**

Biological warfare 358; 623.4

> *x* Bacterial warfare; Germ warfare
> *xx* **Communicable diseases; Military art and science; Tactics**

Biologists 574.092; 920

> *xx* **Naturalists**

Biology 574

> *See also*

Adaptation (Biology)	**Life (Biology)**
Anatomy	**Marine biology**
Biomathematics	**Microbiology**
Biophysics	**Natural history**
Botany	**Physiology**
Cells	**Protoplasm**
Cryobiology	**Radiobiology**
Death	**Reproduction**
Embryology	**Sex (Biology)**
Evolution	**Space biology**
Freshwater biology	**Variation (Biology)**
Genetics	**Zoology**
Heredity	

> *x* Morphology
> *xx* **Evolution; Life (Biology); Life sciences; Natural history; Science**

Biology—Ecology. *See* **Ecology**

Biology, Economic. *See* **Botany, Economic; Zoology, Economic**

Biology—Ethics. *See* **Bioethics**

Biology, Marine. *See* **Marine biology**

Biology, Molecular. *See* **Molecular biology**

Biology—Periodicity. *See* **Biological rhythms**

Biology—Social aspects. *See* **Sociobiology**

Bioluminescence 574.19

> *x* Animal light; Light production in animals; Luminescence, Animal
> *xx* **Phosphorescence**

Biomass energy 333.79

> Use for materials on the production of energy from a composition of living matter and organic waste.
> *See also* names of matter as fuels, e.g. **Alcohol as fuel; Waste products as fuel;** etc.
> *x* Bioconversion; Energy, Biomass; Energy con-

Biomass energy—*Continued*
    version, Microbial; Microbial energy conversion
  xx **Energy resources; Fuel; Waste products as fuel**
Biomass energy industries 338.2; 338.4
Biomathematics 510
  xx **Biology; Mathematics**
Biomechanics. *See* **Human engineering**
Biomedical ethics. *See* **Bioethics**
Bionics 001.53
  Use for materials on the science of technological systems that function in the manner of living systems.
  See also **Artificial intelligence; Optical data processing**
  xx **Biophysics; Cybernetics; Systems engineering**
Biophysics 574.19
  See also **Bionics; Molecular biology; Radiobiology**
  x Biological physics; Molecular physiology; Physics, Biological; Physiology, Molecular
  xx **Biology; Physics**
Biorhythms. *See* **Biological rhythms**
Biosciences. *See* **Life sciences**
Biosociology. *See* **Sociobiology**
Biotechnology 574.6
  Use for materials on the application of living organisms or their biological systems or processes to the manufacture of products.
  See also **Genetic engineering**
  xx **Chemical engineering; Genetic engineering; Microbiology**
Biplanes. *See* **Airplanes**
Bird. *See* **Birds**
Bird decoys (Hunting). *See* **Decoys (Hunting)**
Bird houses 598
Bird photography. *See* **Photography of birds**
Bird song 598
  x Birds—Song
Bird watching 598.07
Birdbanding 598.07
  x Birds—Banding; Birds—Marking
Birds (May subdiv. geog.) **598**
  Names of all birds are not included in this list but are to be added as needed, in the plural form, e.g. **Canaries; Robins;** etc.
  See also classes of birds, e.g. **Birds of prey; Cage birds; Game and game birds; State birds; Water birds;** etc.; and names of specific birds, e.g. **Canaries; Robins;** etc.
  x Bird; Ornithology
  xx **Vertebrates; Zoology**
Birds—Anatomy 598
  xx **Anatomy**
Birds, Aquatic. *See* **Water birds**
Birds—Banding. *See* **Birdbanding**
Birds—Collection and preservation 579
  x Collections of natural specimens; Specimens, Preservation of
  xx **Collectors and collecting; Taxidermy; Zoologi-**

Birds—Collection and preservation—*Continued*
      cal specimens—Collection and preservation
Birds—Color 598
  xx Color
Birds' eggs. *See* Birds—Eggs and nests
Birds—Eggs and nests 598
  x Birds' eggs; Birds' nests; Nests
  xx Eggs
Birds—Flight 598
Birds—Habits and behavior 598
Birds in literature 809
  See also Bible—Natural history
  xx Nature in literature
Birds—Marking. *See* Birdbanding
Birds—Migration 598
  x Migration of birds
  xx Animals—Migration
Birds' nests. *See* Birds—Eggs and nests
Birds of prey 598
  See also names of birds of prey, e.g. Eagles; etc.
  xx Birds
Birds—Photography. *See* Photography of birds
Birds—Protection 333.95
  See also Game protection
  x Protection of birds
  xx Game protection; Wildlife conservation
Birds—Song. *See* Bird song
Birds—United States 598
  x United States—Birds
Birth. *See* Childbirth
Birth control 344; 613.9
  See also Abortion; Birthrate; Childlessness; Fertility, Human; Sterilization (Birth control)
  x Conception—Prevention; Contraception; Family planning; Fertility control; Planned parenthood
  xx Birth rate; Eugenics; Fertility, Human; Population; Sexual ethics; Sexual hygiene
Birth control—Moral and religious aspects 176; 241; 261.8
  x Moral and religious aspects
  xx Ethics
Birth, Multiple 618.2
  See also names of multiple births, e.g. Twins; etc.
  x Multiple birth
  xx Childbirth
Birth rate. *See* Birthrate
Birth records. *See* Registers of births, etc.
Birthdays 392
  x Days
Birthparents 306.8
  Use for materials on natural, i.e. biological, parents who relinquished their children for adoption.
  See also Adoptees
  x Biological parents; Natural parents; Parents, Biological
  xx Adoptees

Birthrate 304.6
> *See also* **Birth control; Fertility, Human; Population**
> *x* Birth rate
> *xx* **Birth control; Population**

Births, Registers of. *See* **Registers of births, etc.**

Bison 599.73; 636.2
> *x* American bison; Buffalo, American
> *xx* **Endangered species**

Bituminous coal. *See* **Coal**

Black actors and actresses 791.092; 920
> *xx* **Actors and actresses**

Black Americans. *See* **Blacks**

Black art 704
> See note under **Blacks in art.**
> *See also* **Black artists**
> *x* Art, Black; Blacks—Art
> *xx* **Black artists**

Black art (Magic). *See* **Witchcraft**

Black artists 709.2; 920
> Use same pattern for Blacks in other occupa-
> tions and professions, e.g. **Black librarians;**
> etc.
> *See also* **Black art**
> *x* Artists, Black
> *xx* **Artists; Black art**

Black athletes 796.092; 920
> *x* Athletes, Black
> *xx* **Athletes**

Black authors 808.092; 920
> *x* Authors, Black
> *xx* **Authors**

Black business people 920
> *x* Business people, Black
> *xx* **Blacks—Employment; Business people**

Black death. *See* **Plague**

Black folk songs. *See* **Black songs**

Black folklore. *See* **Blacks—Folklore**

Black Friars. *See* **Dominicans**

Black Hawk War, 1832 973.5
> *xx* **Indians of North America—Wars; United
> States—History—1815-1861**

Black holes (Astronomy) 523.1; 523.8
> *x* Frozen stars
> *xx* **Astronomy; Astrophysics; Stars**

Black lead. *See* **Graphite**

Black librarians 020.92; 920
> *x* Librarians, Black
> *xx* **Librarians**

Black literature (American). *See* **American literature—Black authors**

Black magic (Witchcraft). *See* **Witchcraft**

Black market children. *See* **Adoption—Corrupt
practices**

Black minstrels 791
> *x* Minstrels, Black
> *xx* **Minstrels**

Black music 781.7
> *See also* **Black songs; Blacks—Songs and music;
> Spirituals (Songs)**

Black music—*Continued*
> *x* Music, Black
> *xx* **Blacks—Songs and music**

Black musicians 780.92; 920
> *x* Musicians, Black

Black Muslims 297
> *x* Muslims, Black; Nation of Islam
> *xx* **Black nationalism; Blacks—Religion; Muslims—United States; United States—Race relations**

Black nationalism 320.5
> *See also* **Black Muslims**
> *x* Black separatism; Nationalism, Black; Separatism, Black
> *xx* **Blacks—Political activity; Blacks—Race identity**

Black poetry (American). *See* **American poetry—Black authors**

Black power 322.4
> *xx* **Blacks—Civil rights; Blacks—Economic conditions; Blacks—Political activity**

Black separatism. *See* **Black nationalism**

Black songs 784.7
> *See also* **Blacks—Songs and music; Blues (Songs, etc.); Spirituals (Songs)**
> *x* Black folk songs; Folk songs, Black (American)
> *xx* **Black music; Blacks—Songs and music; Music, American; Songs; Songs, American; Spirituals (Songs)**

Black spirituals. *See* **Spirituals (Songs)**

Black suffrage. *See* **Blacks—Suffrage**

Black women 305.4
> *x* Women, Black
> *xx* **Women**

Blackboard drawing. *See* **Chalk talks; Crayon drawing**

Blackouts, Electric power. *See* **Electric power failures**

Blackouts in war. *See* **Civil defense**

Blacks (May be subdiv. geog.) **305.8**
> Use for materials dealing collectively with Blacks in the United States or with Blacks in geographic areas outside the United States.
> Geographic subdivisions may be used for materials limited in scope to a particular area of the United States, e.g. **Blacks—Arkansas; Blacks—Chicago (Ill.); Blacks—Southern States.** Geographic subdivisions may also be used for materials dealing with Blacks in other regions, countries, etc., e.g. **Blacks—Africa; Blacks—France;** etc.
> *See also* **Libraries and Blacks; Slavery—United States**
> *x* African-Americans; Afro-Americans; Black Americans; Blacks—United States; Negroes
> *xx* **Ethnology; Slavery—United States**

Blacks—Africa 572.96

Blacks and libraries. *See* **Libraries and Blacks**

Blacks—Arkansas 572.9767
Blacks—Art. *See* Black art
Blacks—Biography 920
Blacks—Chicago (Ill.) 572.9773
Blacks—Civil rights 323.4
>   *See also* Black power
>   *x* Demonstrations for Black civil rights—
>   United States; Freedom marches—United
>   States; Marches for Black civil rights—
>   United States
>   *xx* Blacks—Political activity; Civil rights

Blacks—Economic conditions 330.973
>   *See also* Black power
>   *xx* Economic conditions

Blacks—Education 370.19
>   *See also* School integration; Segregation in edu-
>   cation
>   *xx* Education

Blacks—Employment 331.6
>   *See also* Black business people
>   *x* Blacks—Occupations
>   *xx* Discrimination in employment; Employment

Blacks—Folklore 398.2
>   *x* Black folklore; Folklore, Black
>   *xx* Folklore

Blacks—France 572.944

Blacks—Housing 307
>   *x* Housing, Black
>   *xx* Housing

Blacks in art 704.9
>   Use for materials on Blacks depicted in works of
>   art. Materials on the attainments of Blacks
>   in the area of art are entered under **Black
>   artists.** Materials on works of art by Black
>   artists are entered under **Black art.**
>   *xx* Art

Blacks in literature 809
>   Use for materials on the theme of Blacks in
>   works of literature. Materials on the attain-
>   ments of Blacks in the area of literature are
>   entered under **Black authors.** Materials on
>   works of literature by Black authors are en-
>   tered under individual literatures and forms
>   of literature with the subdivision *Black au-
>   thors,* e.g. **American literature—Black au-
>   thors; American poetry—Black authors;** etc.
>   *xx* Characters and characteristics in literature;
>   Literature

Blacks in motion pictures 791.43
>   Use for materials on Blacks depicted in motion
>   pictures. Materials on Black actors and ac-
>   tresses are entered under **Black actors and
>   actresses.**
>   *xx* Motion pictures

Blacks—Integration 302
>   *See also* School integration
>   *x* Integration, Racial

Blacks—Intellectual life 305.8
>   *x* Intellectual life

Blacks—Occupations. *See* Blacks—Employment

Blacks—Political activity 322.4; 324
    See also **Black nationalism; Black power;**
        Blacks—Civil rights
Blacks—Race identity 305.8
    See also **Black nationalism**
    x Negritude; Race identity; Racial identity
    xx **Race awareness**
Blacks—Religion 277.3; 299
    See also **Black Muslims**
    xx **Religion**
Blacks—Segregation 305.8
    See also **Segregation in education**
    xx **Segregation**
Blacks—Social conditions 305.8
    xx **Social conditions**
Blacks—Social life and customs 305.8
Blacks—Songs and music 784.7
    See also **Black music; Black songs**
    xx **Black music; Black songs**
Blacks—Southern States 572.975
Blacks—Suffrage 324.6
    x Black suffrage
    xx **Suffrage**
Blacks—United States. *See* **Blacks**
Blacksmithing 682
    See also **Forging; Welding**
    x Farriering; Horseshoeing
    xx **Forging; Ironwork**
Blast furnaces 669
    xx **Furnaces; Smelting**
Bleaching 667
    See also **Dyes and dyeing**
    xx **Chemistry, Technical; Cleaning; Dyes and**
        dyeing; Textile industry
Blimps. *See* **Airships**
Blind 362.4
    xx **Physically handicapped; Vision disorders**
Blind—Books and reading 027.6
    See also **Large print books; Talking books**
    x Books for the blind; Braille books
Blind, Dogs for the. *See* **Guide dogs**
Blind—Education 371.91
    x Blind—Rehabilitation; Education of the blind
    xx **Vocational education; Vocational guidance**
Blind—Institutional care 362.4
    x Asylums; Charitable institutions; Homes (In-
        stitutions)
    xx **Institutional care**
Blind—Rehabilitation. *See* **Blind—Education**
Blizzards 551.5
    xx **Storms**
Block grants. *See* **Grants-in-aid**
Block printing. *See* **Color prints; Linoleum block**
        printing; Textile printing; Wood engraving;
        Woodcuts
Block signal systems. *See* **Railroads—Signaling**
Blood 612
    xx **Physiology**
Blood—Circulation 574.1; 612
    See also **Blood pressure; Cardiovascular system**

78

Blood—Circulation—*Continued*
    x Circulation of the blood
    xx **Blood pressure; Cardiovascular system; Heart**
Blood—Diseases 616.1
    See also names of blood diseases, e.g. **Leukemia;**
        etc.
    x Diseases of the blood
Blood groups 612
    See also **Blood—Transfusion**
    x Rh factor
    xx **Heredity**
Blood pressure 574.1; 612
    See also **Blood—Circulation; Hypertension**
    xx **Blood—Circulation**
Blood—Transfusion 615
    xx **Blood groups**
Blowing the whistle. *See* **Whistle blowing**
Blowouts, Oil well. *See* **Oil wells—Blowouts**
Blue collar workers. *See* **Labor**
Blue prints. *See* **Blueprints**
Blueprints 604.2; 692
    x Blue prints
Blues (Songs, etc.) 784.5
    xx **Black songs; Jazz music; Music, Popular**
        (Songs, etc.); Spirituals (Songs)
BMEWS. *See* **Ballistic missile early warning system**
Board sailing. *See* **Windsurfing**
Boarding houses. *See* **Hotels, motels, etc.**
Boarding schools. *See* **Private schools**
Boards of education. *See* **School boards**
Boards of health. *See* **Health boards**
Boards of trade. *See* **Chambers of commerce**
Boat building. *See* **Boatbuilding**
Boat racing 797.1
    See also names of races
    x Motorboat racing; Racing; Yacht racing
    xx **Boats and boating**
Boatbuilding 623.8
    See also **Shipbuilding; Yachts and yachting**
    x Boat building
    xx **Boats and boating; Naval architecture; Ship-**
        building
Boating. *See* **Boats and boating**
Boats and boating 797.1
    See also

Boat racing	**Motorboats**
Boatbuilding	**Rowing**
Canoes and canoeing	**Sailing**
Catamarans	**Ships**
Houseboats	**Steamboats**
Iceboats	**Submarines**
Marinas	**Yachts and yachting**

    x Boating; Locomotion
    xx **Sailing; Ships; Water sports**
Boats, Submarine. *See* **Submarines; Submersibles**
Body and mind. *See* **Mind and body**
Body building. *See* **Bodybuilding**
Body care. *See* **Hygiene**
Body heat. *See* **Body temperature**

Body, Human. *See* **Anatomy, Human; Physiology**
Body language 153.6
  xx **Nonverbal communication**
Body temperature 591.1; 612
  See also **Fever**
  x Animals—Temperature; Body heat; Temperature, Animal and human; Temperature, Body
  xx **Diagnosis; Fever; Physiology**
Body weight control. *See* **Reducing**
Bodybuilding 646.7
  See also **Weight lifting**
  x Body building; Physique
  xx **Exercise; Physical fitness; Weight lifting**
Bodybuilding (Weight lifting). *See* **Weight lifting**
Bogs. *See* **Marshes**
Bohemianism 305.5
  See also **Hippies**
  x Beat generation; Beatniks
  xx **Collective settlements; Counter culture; Manners and customs**
Bolshevism. *See* **Communism**
Bomb shelters. *See* **Air raid shelters**
Bombers 358.4; 623.74
  See also names of bombers, e.g. **B-52 bomber;** etc.
  xx **Airplanes; Airplanes, Military**
Bombs 623.4
  Use for materials on bombs in general and those to be launched from aircraft.
  See also names of types of bombs, e.g. **Atomic bomb; Guided missiles; Hydrogen bomb; Incendiary bombs; Neutron bombs;** etc.
  x Aerial bombs
  xx **Ammunition; Ordnance; Projectiles**
Bombs, Flying. *See* **Guided missiles**
Bombs, Incendiary. *See* **Incendiary bombs**
Bonds 332.63
  See also **Debts, Public; Stocks**
  xx **Debts, Public; Finance; Investments; Negotiable instruments; Securities; Stock exchange; Stocks**
Bonds—Rating 332.63
  x Rating
  xx **Performance standards**
Bones 611; 612
  See also **Fractures; Skeleton**
  x Osteology
  xx **Anatomy; Musculoskeletal system; Physiology; Skeleton**
Bonsai 635.9
  x Kamuti
  xx **Dwarf trees**
Bonus, Soldiers'. *See* **Pensions, Military**
Book awards. *See* **Literary prizes;** and names of awards, e.g. **Caldecott Medal books; Newbery Medal books;** etc.
Book buying (Libraries). *See* **Libraries—Acquisitions**
Book catalogs. *See* **Catalogs, Book**

Book collecting 002.075
    x Bibliomania; Bibliophily
    xx **Book selection; Collectors and collecting**
Book fairs. *See* **Book industries and trade—**
        Exhibitions
Book illustration. *See* **Illustration of books**
Book industries and trade 686
    See also **Best sellers (Books); Bookbinding;**
        Booksellers and bookselling; Paper making
        and trade; Printing; Publishers and publish-
        ing
    x Book trade
    xx **Booksellers and bookselling; Paper making**
        and trade; Publishers and publishing
Book industries and trade—Exhibitions 686.074
    See also **Printing—Exhibitions**
    x Book fairs; Books—Exhibitions
    xx **Printing—Exhibitions**
Book lending. *See* **Library circulation**
Book numbers, Publishers' standard. *See* **Publish-**
        ers' standard book numbers
Book plates. *See* **Bookplates**
Book prices. *See* **Books—Prices**
Book prizes. *See* **Literary prizes;** and names of
        prizes, e.g. **Caldecott Medal books; Newbery**
        Medal books; etc.
Book rarities. *See* **Rare books**
Book reviews. *See* **Books—Reviews**
Book sales. *See* **Books—Prices**
Book selection 025.2
    Use for materials that discuss the principles of
        book appraisal and how to select books for
        libraries. Lists of recommended books are
        entered under **Books and reading—Best**
        books.
    See also **Book collecting; Books and reading—**
        Best books
    x Books—Appraisal; Books—Selection; Choice
        of books
    xx **Books and reading—Best books, Libraries—**
        Acquisitions; Libraries—Collection develop-
        ment
Book trade. *See* **Book industries and trade; Book-**
        sellers and bookselling; Publishers and pub-
        lishing
Book week, National. *See* **National book week**
Bookbinding 025.7; 686.3
    x Binding of books
    xx **Bibliography; Book industries and trade; In-**
        dustrial arts; Leather industry and trade
Bookkeepers. *See* **Accountants**
Bookkeeping 657
    See also **Accounting; Auditing; Cost accounting;**
        Office equipment and supplies; also names
        of industries, professions, etc. with the sub-
        division *Accounting,* e.g.
        Corporations—Accounting; etc.
    xx **Accounting; Business; Business arithmetic;**
        Business education

Bookmobiles 027.4
> *xx* **Library extension**

Bookplates 025.7
> *x* Book plates; Ex libris

Books 002
> *See also*

Authors	**Libraries**
Bibliography	**Literature**
Bilingual books	**Manuscripts**
Cataloging	**Paperback books**
Chapbooks	**Printing**
Illumination of books and	**Publishers and publishing**
manuscripts	**Serial publications**
Illustration of books	

> also headings beginning with the word **Book**
>
> *xx* **Bibliography; Literature; Printing; Publishers
> and publishing; Serial publications**

Books and reading 028
> Use for general materials on reading for infor-
> mation and culture, advice to readers, and
> surveys of reading habits.
>
> *See also* **Best sellers (Books); Books—Reviews;
> Children's literature; Libraries; Literature;
> National book week; Reference books;** also
> names of individuals and classes of people
> with the subdivision *Books and reading,*
> e.g. **Blind—Books and reading;** etc.
>
> *x* Appraisal of books; Books—Appraisal; Choice
> of books; Evaluation of literature; Litera-
> ture—Evaluation; Reading interests
>
> *xx* **Communication; Education; Reading**

Books and reading—Best books 010
> Use for lists of recommended books.
>
> *See also* **Book selection**
>
> *x* Appraisal of books; Best books; Bibliogra-
> phy—Best books; Books—Appraisal;
> Choice of books; Evaluation of literature;
> Literature—Evaluation
>
> *xx* **Book selection; Reference books**

Books—Appraisal. *See* **Book selection; Books and
reading; Books and reading—Best books;
Books—Reviews; Criticism; Literature—
History and criticism**

Books—Best sellers. *See* **Best sellers (Books)**

Books—Catalogs. *See* **Catalogs, Book; Catalogs,
Booksellers'; Catalogs, Publishers'**

Books—Censorship 025.2; 323.44
> *x* Banned books; Index librorum prohibitorum;
> Prohibited books
>
> *xx* **Censorship; Freedom of the press**

Books—Copyright. *See* **Copyright—Books**

Books—Exhibitions. *See* **Book industries and
trade—Exhibitions; Printing—Exhibitions**

Books—First editions. *See* **Bibliography—First
editions**

Books for children. *See* **Children's literature**

Books for sight saving. *See* **Large print books**

Books for the blind. *See* **Blind—Books and reading**

Books—Large print. *See* **Large print books**

Books, Paperback. *See* **Paperback books**

Books—Preservation. *See* **Library resources—Conservation and restoration**

Books—Prices 002.075; 338.402
>   *x* Book prices; Book sales; Manuscripts—Prices
>   *xx* **Booksellers and bookselling; Prices**

Books, Rare. *See* **Rare books**

Books—Reviews 028.1; 808
>   *x* Appraisal of books; Book reviews; Books—Appraisal; Evaluation of literature; Literature—Evaluation; Reviews
>   *xx* **Books and reading; Criticism**

Books, Sacred. *See* **Sacred books**

Books—Selection. *See* **Book selection**

Books, Talking. *See* **Talking books**

Booksellers and bookselling 658.8
>   *See also* **Book industries and trade; Books—Prices; Catalogs, Booksellers'; Publishers and publishing**
>   *x* Book trade
>   *xx* **Book industries and trade; Publishers and publishing; Sales personnel; Selling**

Booksellers' catalogs. *See* **Catalogs, Booksellers'**

Boolean algebra. *See* **Algebra, Boolean**

Boots. *See* **Shoes**

Border life. *See* **Frontier and pioneer life**

Borders (Geography). *See* **Boundaries**

Boring 622.028
>   Use for materials on the operation of cutting holes in earth or rock. Materials dealing with workshop operations in metal, wood, etc. are entered under **Drilling and boring.**
>   *See also* **Wells**
>   *x* Drilling and boring (Earth and rocks); Shaft sinking; Well boring
>   *xx* **Hydraulic engineering; Mining engineering; Natural gas; Petroleum; Tunnels; Water supply engineering; Wells**

Boring (Metal, wood, etc.). *See* **Drilling and boring**

Born again Christians. *See* **Regeneration (Christianity)**

Borrowing money. *See* **Loans**

Boss rule. *See* **Corruption in politics**

Botanical chemistry 581.1
>   *See also* **Plants—Analysis**
>   *x* Chemistry, Botanical; Plant chemistry
>   *xx* **Chemistry**

Botanical gardens 580.74
>   *See also* names of botanical gardens
>   *xx* **Gardens; Parks**

Botanical specimens—Collection and preservation. *See* **Plants—Collection and preservation**

Botanists 581.092; 920
>   *xx* **Naturalists**

Botany (May subdiv. geog.) **580**
>   *See also*

Bulbs	**Grafting**
Flower gardening	**Leaves**
Flowers	**Plant physiology**
Fruit	**Plants**

Botany—*Continued*

Plants, Fossil	**Variation (Biology)**
Seeds	**Vegetables**
Shrubs	**Weeds**
Trees	

 x Flora; Vegetable kingdom

 xx **Biology; Natural history; Nature study; Science**

Botany, Agricultural. *See* **Botany, Economic**

Botany—Anatomy 581.4

 x Anatomy of plants; Anatomy, Vegetable; Botany—Structure; Morphology; Plant anatomy; Plants—Anatomy; Structural botany; Vegetable anatomy

 xx **Anatomy**

Botany—Ecology 581.5

 See also **Desert plants**

 x Plants—Ecology; Symbiosis

 xx **Ecology; Forest influences**

Botany, Economic 581.6

 See also

Cotton	**Plant introduction**
Forest products	**Plants, Edible**
Grain	**Poisonous plants**
Grasses	**Weeds**
Plant conservation	

 x Agricultural botany; Biology, Economic; Botany, Agricultural; Economic botany; Plants, Useful

 xx **Agriculture**

Botany, Fossil. *See* **Plants, Fossil**

Botany, Medical 581.6

 x Drug plants; Herbal medicine; Herbals; Herbs, Medical; Medical botany; Medicinal plants; Plants, Medicinal

 xx **Medicine; Pharmacy**

Botany—Nomenclature. *See* **Botany—Terminology; Plant names, Popular**

Botany of the Bible. *See* **Bible—Natural history**

Botany—Pathology. *See* **Plants—Diseases**

Botany—Physiology. *See* **Plant physiology**

Botany—Structure. *See* **Botany—Anatomy**

Botany—Terminology 580.3

 Use for materials on the scientific names of plants, etc. Materials on popular names are entered under **Plant names, Popular.**

 See also **Plant names, Popular**

 x Botany—Nomenclature; Nomenclature; Plant names, Scientific; Terminology

 xx **Plant names, Popular**

Botany—United States 581.973

 x United States—Botany

Boulder Dam (Ariz. and Nev.). *See* **Hoover Dam (Ariz. and Nev.)**

Boulevards. *See* **Streets**

Boundaries 320.1; 341.4

 See also **Geopolitics;** also names of wars with the subdivision *Territorial questions,* e.g. **World War, 1939-1945—Territorial questions;** etc.; and names of countries, cities, etc. with

Boundaries—*Continued*

    the subdivision *Boundaries,* e.g. **United States—Boundaries;** etc.

  x Borders (Geography); Frontiers; Geography, Political; Political boundaries; Political geography

  xx **Geography; Geopolitics; International law; International relations**

Bounties. *See* **Subsidies**

Bourgeoisie. *See* **Middle classes**

Bow and arrow 799.3

  See also **Archery**

  x Arrow

  xx **Archery**

Bowed instruments. *See* **Stringed instruments**

Bowling 794.6; 796.31

  x Tenpins

Boxing 796.8

  x Fighting; Prize fighting; Pugilism; Sparring

  xx **Athletics; Self-defense**

Boy Scouts (May subdiv. geog.) **369.43**

  x Cub Scouts

  xx **Boys' clubs; Scouts and scouting**

Boycott 322.4; 331.89

  xx **Passive resistance**

Boys 155.4; 305.2

  See also **Children; Fathers and sons; Mothers and sons; Young men; Youth**

  xx **Children; Men; Young men; Youth**

Boys' agricultural clubs. *See* **4-H clubs; Agriculture—Societies; Boys' clubs**

Boys' clubs 369.42

  See also **4-H clubs; Boy Scouts**

  x Boys' agricultural clubs; Boys—Societies

  xx **Clubs; Men—Societies; Social settlements; Societies**

Boys—Employment. *See* **Children—Employment**

Boys—Societies. *See* **Boys' clubs**

Boys' towns. *See* **Children—Institutional care**

Brahmanism 294.5

  See also **Caste; Hinduism**

  xx **Buddhism; Hinduism; Religions**

Braille books. *See* **Blind—Books and reading**

Brain 611; 612

  See also

Dreams	**Nervous system**
Head	**Phrenology**
Memory	**Psychology**
Mind and body	**Sleep**

  xx **Head; Nervous system**

Brain damaged children 618.92

  xx **Exceptional children; Handicapped children**

Brain death 616.07

  x Irreversible coma

  xx **Death**

Brain—Diseases 616.8

  See also **Alzheimer's disease; Cerebral palsy**

Brain, Electronic. *See* **Artificial intelligence; Computers**

Brain storming. *See* **Problem solving, Group**

Brainwashing 153.8

Use for materials on the forcible indoctrination of an individual or group in order to alter basic political, social, religious, or moral beliefs.

x Deprogramming; Forced indoctrination; Indoctrination, Forced; Mind control; Thought control; Will

xx **Behavior modification; Learning, Psychology of; Mental suggestion; Psychological warfare**

Brakes 625.2; 629.2

See also subjects with the subdivision *Brakes,* e.g. **Automobiles—Brakes;** etc.

xx **Railroads—Safety appliances**

Branch stores. *See* **Chain stores**

Brand name products 380.1; 658.8

See also **Trademarks**

x Products, Brand name

xx **Commercial products; Manufactures; Trademarks**

Brass 669; 673

See also **Brasses**

xx **Alloys; Founding; Zinc**

Brass instruments. *See* **Wind instruments**

Brasses 739

x Monumental brasses; Sepulchral brasses

xx **Archeology; Art; Brass; Inscriptions; Sculpture; Tombs**

Bravery. *See* **Courage**

Brazilian literature 869

May use same subdivisions and names of literary forms as for **English literature.**

See also **Portuguese literature**

xx **Latin American literature; Portuguese literature**

Brazing. *See* **Solder and soldering**

Bread 641.8; 664

xx **Baking; Cookery; Food**

Breadstuffs. *See* **Flour; Grain; Wheat**

Break dancing 793.3

xx **Dancing**

Breakfast cereals. *See* **Cereals, Prepared**

Breast feeding 649

x Nursing (Infant feeding)

xx **Infants—Nutrition**

Breathing. *See* **Respiration**

Breeder reactors. *See* **Nuclear reactors**

Breeding 581.1; 631.5; 636.08

See also **Domestic animals; Genetics; Heredity; Mendel's law; Plant breeding;** also subdivision *Breeding* under particular animals, e.g. **Dogs—Breeding; Horses—Breeding; Livestock—Breeding;** etc.

x Selection, Artificial

xx **Genetics**

Bricklaying 693

See also **Masonry**

xx **Bricks; Building; Masonry**

Bricks 666; 691
>*See also* **Bricklaying; Tiles**
>*xx* **Building materials; Clay; Clay industries**

Bridal customs. *See* **Marriage customs and rites**

Bridge (Game) 795.4
>*x* Auction bridge; Contract bridge; Duplicate
>bridge
>*xx* **Card games**

Bridges (May subdiv. geog. by countries, states, cities, etc. and by rivers) **624**
>*See also* names of bridges, e.g. **Golden Gate
>Bridge (San Francisco, Calif.);** etc.
>*x* Suspension bridges; Viaducts
>*xx* **Building, Iron and steel; Civil engineering;
>Masonry; Transportation**

Bridges—Chicago (Ill.) 624
>*x* Chicago (Ill.)—Bridges

Bridges—Hudson River (N.Y.) 624
>*x* Hudson River (N.Y.)—Bridges

Brigands. *See* **Robbers and outlaws**

Bright children. *See* **Gifted children**

British Commonwealth of Nations. *See* **Commonwealth of Nations**

British Dominions. *See* **Commonwealth of Nations**

Broadcast journalism 070
>*See also* **Journalism**
>*x* News broadcasting; Radio journalism; Radio
>news; Television journalism; Television
>news
>*xx* **Broadcasting; Journalism; Press**

Broadcast videotex systems. *See* **Teletext systems**

Broadcasting 384.5
>*See also* **Broadcast journalism; Minorities in
>broadcasting; Radio broadcasting; Television
>broadcasting**
>*xx* **Telecommunication**

Bronze Age 930
>*See also* **Archeology; Iron Age**
>*x* Prehistory
>*xx* **Archeology; Iron Age; Man, Prehistoric**

Bronzes 739
>*xx* **Archeology; Art; Art metalwork; Decoration
>and ornament; Metalwork; Sculpture**

Brothers and sisters 155.4; 306.8
>*See also* **Twins**
>*x* Siblings; Sisters and brothers
>*xx* **Family; Twins**

Brownouts. *See* **Electric power failures**

Brutality. *See* **Cruelty**

Bubonic plague. *See* **Plague**

Buccaneers. *See* **Pirates**

Buddhism 294.3
>*See also* **Brahmanism; Zen Buddhism**
>*xx* **Religions**

Buddhist art. *See* **Art, Buddhist**

Budget (May subdiv. geog.) **351.72**
>Use for materials on the budget or reports on the
>appropriations and expenditures of a gov-
>ernment.
>*See also* **Finance**

Budget—*Continued*

   xx **Finance**

Budget—United States 353.007

   See also **United States—Appropriations and ex-**
       penditures

   x Federal budget; United States—Budget

Budgets, Business 658.1

   x Business—Budget

   xx **Business**

Budgets, Household 640

   x Domestic finance; Family budget; Finance,
       Household; Home economics—Accounting;
       Household budget; Household finances

   xx **Cost of living; Finance, Personal**

Budgets, Personal. *See* **Finance, Personal**

Buffalo, American. *See* **Bison**

Buffing. *See* **Grinding and polishing**

Bugging, Electronic. *See* **Eavesdropping**

Building 690

   See also

Architecture	**Foundations**
Bricklaying	**House construction**
Carpentry	**Masonry**
Chimneys	**Roofs**
Concrete construction	**Sanitary engineering**
Doors	**Strength of materials**
Engineering	**Walls**
Floors	**Windows**

   x Architectural engineering; Construction

   xx **Architecture; Carpentry; Houses; Structural**
       engineering; Structures, Theory of; Technol-
       ogy

Building and earthquakes. *See* **Buildings—**
      Earthquake effects

Building and loan associations. *See* **Savings and**
      loan associations

Building, Concrete. *See* **Concrete construction**

Building contracts. *See* **Building—Contracts and**
      specifications

Building—Contracts and specifications 692

   x Building contracts; Building—Specifications

   xx **Contracts**

Building—Estimates 692

   x Estimates

Building failures 690; 721

   xx **Structural failures**

Building, House. *See* **House construction**

Building, Iron and steel 693

   See also **Bridges; Roofs; Skyscrapers; Steel,**
       Structural; Strength of materials; Structures,
       Theory of

   x Architectural engineering; Iron and steel
      building; Steel construction

   xx **Iron; Steel; Steel, Structural**

Building materials 691

   All types of building materials are not included
      in this list but are to be added as needed.

   See also

Bricks	**Concrete**
Cement	**Concrete, Reinforced**

Building materials—*Continued*

Glass construction	Stucco
Steel, Structural	Terra cotta
Stone	Tiles
Strength of materials	Wood
Structural engineering	

    x Structural materials

    xx **Architecture; Engineering; Materials; Strength of materials**

Building repair. *See* **Buildings—Maintenance and repair**

Building—Repair and reconstruction. *See* **Buildings—Maintenance and repair**

Building security. *See* **Burglary protection**

Building—Specifications. *See* **Building—Contracts and specifications**

Buildings (May subdiv. geog.) **690; 720**

    See also **Historic buildings;** also names of types of buildings and construction, e.g. **Buildings, Prefabricated; Farm buildings; Industrial buildings; School buildings;** etc.; also names of institutions with the subdivision *Buildings,* e.g. **Colleges and universities—Buildings;** etc.; and names of specific buildings

Buildings, College. *See* **Colleges and universities—Buildings**

Buildings—Earthquake effects 693.8

    Use for materials on the design and construction of buildings to withstand earthquakes.

    x Building and earthquakes; Earthquakes and building

    xx **Earthquakes**

Buildings, Farm. *See* **Farm buildings**

Buildings, Historic. *See* **Historic buildings**

Buildings, Industrial. *See* **Industrial buildings**

Buildings, Library. *See* **Library architecture**

Buildings—Maintenance and repair 690

    See also **Architecture—Conservation and restoration; Houses—Maintenance and repair**

    x Building repair; Building—Repair and reconstruction; Maintenance and repair

    xx **Architecture—Conservation and restoration; Repairing**

Buildings, Office. *See* **Office buildings**

Buildings, Prefabricated 693

    See also **Prefabricated houses**

    xx **Buildings**

Buildings, Public. *See* **Public buildings;** and names of countries, cities, etc. with the subdivision *Public buildings,* e.g. **Chicago (Ill.)—Public buildings;** etc.

Buildings—Remodeling 643; 690

    x Remodeling of buildings

Buildings, Restoration of. *See* **Architecture—Conservation and restoration**

Buildings, School. *See* **School buildings**

Buildings—Security. *See* **Burglary protection**

Built-in furniture 684.1; 749

    x Furniture, Built in

Built-in furniture—*Continued*
   xx **Furniture**
Bulbs 581.3; 635.9
   xx **Botany; Flower gardening; Gardening**
Bulge, Battle of the. *See* **Ardennes, Battle of the, 1944-1945**
Bulletin boards 021.7; 371.3
   See also **Computer bulletin boards**
   xx **Teaching—Aids and devices**
Bullets. *See* **Projectiles**
Bullfights 791
   x Fighting
Bullion. *See* **Gold; Money; Silver**
Bunker Hill (Boston, Mass.), Battle of, 1775—Poetry 811
   xx **Poetry**
Bureaucracy 350-354
   See also **Civil service**
   xx **Civil service; Political science; Public administration**
Burglar alarms 621.389
   xx **Burglary protection; Electric apparatus and appliances**
Burglars. *See* **Robbers and outlaws**
Burglary protection 621.389
   See also types of protective devices, e.g. **Burglar alarms; Locks and keys;** etc.; also types of buildings with the subdivision *Security measures,* e.g. **Nuclear power plants—Security measures;** etc.
   x Building security; Buildings—Security; Protection against burglary; Residential security
Burial. *See* **Catacombs; Cemeteries; Cremation; Cryonics; Epitaphs; Funeral rites and ceremonies; Mounds and mound builders; Mummies; Tombs**
Burial statistics. *See* **Mortality; Registers of births, etc.; Vital statistics;** and names of countries, cities, etc. with the subdivision *Statistics,* e.g. **United States—Statistics;** etc.
Buried cities. *See* **Cities and towns, Ruined, extinct, etc.**
Buried treasure 910.4
   x Hidden treasure; Sunken treasure; Treasure trove
Burn out (Psychology) 158.7
   x Burnout syndrome
   xx **Job satisfaction; Job stress; Mental health; Motivation (Psychology); Occupational health and safety; Stress (Psychology)**
Burnout syndrome. *See* **Burn out (Psychology)**
Burying grounds. *See* **Cemeteries**
Buses 388.4; 629.2
   x Motor buses
   xx **Automobiles; Local transit; Transportation, Highway**
Bush survival. *See* **Wilderness survival**

X **Business 650**

See also

Accounting	**Home business**
Advertising	**Industrial management**
Banks and banking	**Instalment plan**
Bookkeeping	**Mail-order business**
Budgets, Business	**Manufactures**
Business failures	**Marketing**
Business people	**Markets**
Commercial law	**Merchants**
Competition	**Occupations**
Corporations	**Office management**
Credit	**Profit**
Department stores	**Real estate business**
Economic conditions	**Selling**
Efficiency, Industrial	**Small business**
Entrepreneurs	**Trust companies**

   x Trade

  xx **Commerce; Economics; Industrial manage-**
     ment

Business administration. *See* **Industrial manage-**
    ment

Business and government. *See* **Industry—**
    Government policy

Business and politics 658

   x Business—Political activity; Politics and busi-
    ness

  xx **Politics, Practical**

Business arithmetic 513

   See also **Accounting; Bookkeeping; Interest (Eco-**
    nomics)

   x Arithmetic, Commercial; Commercial arith-
    metic

  xx **Arithmetic**

Business—Budget. *See* **Budgets, Business**

Business colleges. *See* **Business education**

Business combinations. *See* **Conglomerate corpora-**
    tions; Trusts, Industrial

Business correspondence. *See* **Business letters**

Business cycles 338.5

   See also **Economic forecasting;** also names of
    types of business cycles, e.g. **Depressions,**
    Economic; etc.

   x Business depressions; Cycles, Business; Eco-
    nomic cycles; Stabilization in industry

  xx **Economic conditions**

Business depressions. *See* **Business cycles; Depres-**
    sions, Economic; Economic conditions

Business education 650

   Use for materials on how to teach business and
    for descriptions of business operations.

   See also **Accounting; Bookkeeping; Commercial**
    law; Handwriting; Secretaries; Shorthand;
    Typewriting

   x Business colleges; Business schools; Clerical
    work—Training; Commercial education;
    Commercial schools; Education, Business;
    Office work—Training; Schools, Commer-
    cial

  xx **Education**

Business English. *See* **English language—Business English**

Business enterprises, International. *See* **International business enterprises**

Business enterprises—Management. *See* **Industrial management**

Business entertaining 395; 658

    xx **Entertaining; Public relations**

Business ethics 174

    See also **Competition; Success**

    x Ethics, Business

    xx **Ethics; Professional ethics**

Business failures 338; 658

    See also **Bank failures; Bankruptcy**

    x Business mortality; Failure in business

    xx **Business; Industry**

Business forecasting 338.5

    xx **Economic forecasting; Forecasting**

Business—Information services 658.4

    xx **Information services**

Business—International aspects. *See* **International business enterprises**

Business law. *See* **Commercial law**

Business letters 651.7

    See also **English language—Business English**

    x Business correspondence; Commercial correspondence; Correspondence

    xx **English language—Business English; Letter writing**

Business libraries 026

    Use for materials on libraries with a subject focus in business. Materials on libraries located within companies, firms, or private businesses, and covering any subject area, are entered under **Corporate libraries.**

    x Libraries, Business

    xx **Special libraries**

Business machines. *See* **Office equipment and supplies**

Business mortality. *See* **Bankruptcy; Business failures**

Business patronage of the arts. *See* **Art patronage**

Business people 650.1; 920

    See also **Black business people; Businessmen; Businesswomen; Capitalists and financiers; Entrepreneurs**

    x Businesspeople

    xx **Business; Commerce; Industry**

Business people, Black. *See* **Black business people**

Business—Political activity. *See* **Business and politics**

Business schools. *See* **Business education**

Business, Small. *See* **Small business**

Businessmen 650.1; 920

    x Men in business

    xx **Business people**

Businesspeople. *See* **Business people**

Businesswomen 331.4; 650.1; 920

    x Women in business

    xx **Business people**

Busing (School integration) 344; 370.19
    x Antibusing; Racial balance in schools; School
        busing; Student busing
    xx **School children—Transportation; School inte-**
        gration; Segregation in education
Butter 637; 641.3
    See also **Margarine**
    xx **Dairy products; Milk**
Butter, Artificial. *See* **Margarine**
Butterflies 595.7
    See also **Caterpillars; Moths**
    x Cocoons; Lepidoptera
    xx **Insects; Moths**
Buttons 687
    xx **Clothing and dress**
Buy American policy. *See* **Buy national policy—**
    United States
Buy national policy (May subdiv. geog.) **351.71;**
    352.1
    Use for materials on the requirement that the
    government procure goods produced within
    the nation.
    xx **Commercial policy; Government purchasing**
Buy national policy—United States 353.0071
    x Buy American policy
Buyers' guides. *See* **Consumer education; Shopping**
Buying 351.71; 352.1; 658.7
    Use for materials on buying by government
    agencies and by commercial and industrial
    enterprises. Materials on buying by the con-
    sumer are entered under **Consumer educa-**
    tion; Shopping. See notes under these head-
    ings.
    See also **Consumer education; Government pur-**
    chasing; Instalment plan; Shopping
    x Purchasing
    xx **Consumer education; Industrial management;**
    Shopping
By-products. *See* **Waste products**
Byrd Antarctic Expedition 919.8
    x Antarctic expeditions; Expeditions, Antarctic
    and Arctic
Byzantine architecture. *See* **Architecture, Byzantine**
Byzantine art. *See* **Art, Byzantine**
Byzantine Empire 949.5
    x Eastern Empire
C.A.T.V. *See* **Cable television**
C.B. radio. *See* **Citizens band radio**
C.R.T.'s. *See* **Cathode ray tubes**
Cabala 296.1
    See also **Symbolism of numbers**
    x Cabbala; Kabbala
    xx **Hebrew literature; Jewish literature; Judaism;**
        Mysticism; Occult sciences; Symbolism of
        numbers
Cabbala. *See* **Cabala**
Cabinet officers 351.004092; 353.04092; 920
    See also **Prime ministers**
    x Ministers of state

Cabinet work 684.1
>   See note under **Carpentry.**
>   *See also* **Veneers and veneering; Woodwork**
>   *xx* **Carpentry; Furniture; Woodwork**

Cabins. *See* **Log cabins and houses**

Cable codes. *See* **Cipher and telegraph codes**

Cable railroads 385; 625.1
>   *See also* **Street railroads**
>   *x* Funicular railroads; Railroads, Cable
>   *xx* **Street railroads**

Cable television 384.55
>   *See also* **Home Box Office; Telemarketing**
>   *x* C.A.T.V.; CATV; Community antenna television; Pay television, Cable; Television, Cable
>   *xx* **Television broadcasting**

Cables 384.6; 624.1
>   *xx* **Power transmission; Rope**

Cables, Submarine 384.6; 621.382; 624.1
>   *x* Atlantic cable; Ocean cables; Pacific cable; Submarine cables; Submarine telegraph; Telegraph, Submarine
>   *xx* **Telecommunication; Telegraph**

Cactus 635.9
>   *xx* **Desert plants**

Cafeterias. *See* **Restaurants, bars, etc.**

Cage birds 636.6
>   *See also* names of cage birds, e.g. **Canaries;** etc.
>   *xx* **Birds**

Cake 641.8; 664
>   *xx* **Baking; Cookery**

Cake decorating 641.8
>   *xx* **Confectionery**

Calculating machines. *See* **Calculators**

Calculators 513.028; 651.8; 681
>   Use for materials on present-day calculators and on calculating machines and mechanical computers made before 1945. Materials on modern electronic computers developed after 1945 are entered under **Computers.**
>   *See also* **Computers; Cybernetics; Slide rule**
>   *x* Accounting machines; Adding machines; Calculating machines; Pocket calculators
>   *xx* **Arithmetic; Computers; Office equipment and supplies**

Calculus 515
>   *x* Analysis (Mathematics)
>   *xx* **Mathematical analysis; Mathematics**

Caldecott Medal books 028.5
>   *x* Book awards; Book prizes
>   *xx* **Children's literature; Illustration of books; Literary prizes**

Calendars 529
>   *See also* **Almanacs; Devotional calendars; Months; Week**
>   *x* Annuals
>   *xx* **Almanacs; Time; Yearbooks**

California—Gold discoveries 979.4
>   *x* Gold rush

Calisthenics. *See* **Gymnastics; Physical education**

Calligraphy 745.6

   xx **Decorative arts; Handwriting; Writing**

Calvinism 284

   See also **Congregationalism; Predestination; Puritans**

   xx **Congregationalism; Puritans; Reformation**

Cambistry. *See* **Foreign exchange; Weights and measures**

Camels 599.73; 636.2

   x Dromedaries

   xx **Desert animals**

Cameras 771.3

   See also names of types of cameras and of individual makes of cameras, e.g. **Motion picture cameras; Kodak camera;** etc.

   xx **Photography; Photography—Equipment and supplies**

Camouflage (Biology) 591.57

   x Animal camouflage; Animals—Camouflage

Camouflage (Military science) 355.4; 359.4; 623.7

   xx **Military art and science; Naval art and science**

Camp cooking. *See* **Outdoor cookery**

Camp Fire Girls 369.47

   xx **Girls' clubs**

Camp sites. *See* **Campgrounds**

Campaign funds (May subdiv. geog.) 324.7

   x Assessments, Political, Elections—Finance; Political assessments; Political parties—Finance

   xx **Corruption in politics; Elections; Politics, Practical**

Campaign funds—United States 324.7

   x Elections—United States—Finance; United States—Campaign funds

Campaign literature (May subdiv. by date and party) 324.2

   xx **Politics, Practical**

Campaigns, Political. *See* **Politics, Practical**

Campaigns, Presidential—United States. *See* **Presidents—United States—Election**

Campers and trailers. *See* **Travel trailers and campers**

Campgrounds 796.54

   See also **Trailer parks**

   x Camp sites

Camping 796.54

   See note under **Camps.**

   See also **Backpacking; Outdoor cookery; Outdoor life; Tents; Travel trailers and campers; Wilderness survival**

   xx **Outdoor life; Outdoor recreation**

Camps 796.54

   Use for materials on camps with a definite program of activities. Materials on the technique of camping are entered under **Camping.**

   x Summer camps

Camps (Military) 355.7

   See also **Concentration camps**

Camps (Military)—*Continued*
   x Military camps
   xx **Military art and science**
Campus disorders.   *See* **College students—Political activity**
Canada   917.1; 971
   See also **Northwest, Canadian;** also names of individual provinces and territories
Canada—English-French relations   305.8
   See also **Québec (Province)—History— Autonomy and independence movements**
   x Canada—French-English relations
Canada—Exploration.   *See* **America—Exploration**
Canada—French-English relations.   *See* **Canada— English-French relations**
Canada—History—0-1763 (New France)   971.01
   x New France—History
Canada—History—1763-1791   971.02
Canada—History—1800-1899 (19th century) 971.03-971.05
Canada—History—1914-1945   971.06
Canada—History—1945-   971.06
Canada, Northwest.   *See* **Northwest, Canadian**
Canadian Indians.   *See* **Indians of North America— Canada**
Canadian Invasion, 1775-1776   973.3
   xx **United States—History—1775-1783, Revolution**
Canadian literature   810; 820; 840
   May use same subdivision and names of literary forms as for **English literature.**
   See also **French Canadian literature**
   xx **American literature**
Canadian literature, French.   *See* **French Canadian literature**
Canadian Northwest.   *See* **Northwest, Canadian**
Canadians   971
   See also **French Canadians**
Canals (May subdiv. geog.)   **386; 627**
   See also **Inland navigation;** also names of canals, e.g. **Panama Canal;** etc.
   xx **Civil engineering; Hydraulic structures; Inland navigation; Transportation; Waterways**
Canaries   598.8; 636.6
   xx **Birds; Cage birds**
Canasta (Game)   795.4
   x Argentine rummy
   xx **Card games**
Cancer   616.99
   See also **Leukemia**
   x Carcinoma; Malignant tumors
   xx **Tumors**
Cancer—Chemotherapy   616.99
   xx **Chemotherapy**
Cancer—Diet therapy   616.99
   xx **Diet therapy**
Cancer—Genetic aspects   616.99
   x Genetic aspects
   xx **Medical genetics**

Cancer—Nursing 616.99
    xx **Nursing**
Cancer—Surgery 616.99
    xx **Surgery**
Candles 665
    xx **Lighting**
Candy. *See* **Confectionery**
Caning of chairs. *See* **Chair caning**
Canned goods. *See* **Canning and preserving**
Cannibalism 291.3; 394
    xx **Ethnology; Human behavior**
Canning and preserving 641.4; 664
    See also names of foods with the subdivision
        Preservation, e.g. **Fruit—Preservation; Veg-**
        etables—Preservation; etc.
    x Canned goods; Food, Canned; Pickling; Pre-
        serving
    xx **Chemistry, Technical; Cookery; Food—**
        Preservation
Cannon. *See* **Ordnance**
Canoes and canoeing 797.1
    xx **Boats and boating; Water sports**
Canon law. *See* **Ecclesiastical law**
Cantatas 783.4
    See also **Choral music**
    xx **Vocal music**
Canvas embroidery. *See* **Needlepoint**
Capital 332
    See also

Banks and banking	**Monopolies**
Capitalism	**Profit**
Interest (Economics)	**Trusts, Industrial**
Investments	**Wealth**

    xx **Capitalism; Economics; Finance; Income;**
        Money; Wealth
Capital and labor. *See* **Industrial relations**
Capital punishment (May subdiv. geog.) 179; 364.6
    x Death penalty; Executions; Hanging
    xx **Crime; Criminal law; Murder; Punishment**
Capital punishment—United States 179; 364.6
    x United States—Capital punishment
Capitalism 330.12
    See also **Capital; Socialism**
    xx **Capital; Economics; Labor; Monopolies;**
        Profit; Socialism; Trusts, Industrial
Capitalists and financiers 332.092; 920
    See also **Millionaires**
    x Financiers
    xx **Business people; Wealth**
Capitalization (Finance). *See* **Corporations—**
        Finance; Railroads—Finance; Securities;
        Valuation
Capitals (Cities)
    Use for materials on the capital cities of several
        countries or states.
Capitols 725
Car pools 388.3
    x Automobile pools; Automobiles—Pools; Car-
        pools; Ride sharing; Van pools
    xx **Traffic engineering; Transportation**

Car wheels. *See* **Wheels**

Carbines. *See* **Rifles**

Carbolic acid   546; 547; 661

  xx **Acids; Chemicals**

Carbon   546; 547; 661; 662

  See also **Charcoal; Coal; Diamonds; Graphite**

Carbon 14 dating. *See* **Radiocarbon dating**

Carburetors   621.43

  xx **Gas and oil engines**

Carcinoma. *See* **Cancer**

Card catalogs. *See* **Catalogs, Card**

Card games   795.4

  See also **Card tricks; Tarot;** also names of card
      games, e.g. **Bridge (Game); Canasta (Game);**
      etc.

  x Cards, Playing; Playing cards

  xx **Gambling; Games**

Card tricks   795.4

  xx **Card games; Magic; Tricks**

Cardiac diseases. *See* **Heart—Diseases**

Cardiac resuscitation   615.8; 616.02

  x Heart resuscitation; Resuscitation, Heart

  xx **First aid**

Cardinals   262; 920

  xx **Catholic Church—Clergy**

Cardiovascular system   612

  See also **Blood—Circulation; Heart**

  x Circulatory system; Vascular system

  xx **Blood—Circulation**

Cards, Greeting. *See* **Greeting cards**

Cards, Playing. *See* **Card games**

Career changes   331.7; 371.4

  x Changing careers; Mid-career changes

  xx **Age and employment; Vocational guidance**

Career education. *See* **Vocational education**

Career guidance. *See* **Vocational guidance**

Careers. *See* **Occupations; Professions**

Caricatures. *See* **Cartoons and caricatures**

Carillons. *See* **Bells**

Carnivals. *See* **Festivals**

Carnivals (Circus). *See* **Amusement parks**

Carnivores   599.74

  See also names of carnivorous animals

  x Meat-eating animals

  xx **Animals—Food; Mammals**

Carols   783.6

  x Christmas carols; Easter carols

  xx **Christmas—Poetry; Church music; Folk
    songs; Hymns; Religious poetry; Songs; Vo-
    cal music**

Carpentry   694

  Use for materials dealing with the construction
    of a wooden building or the wooden portion
    of any building. Materials dealing with the
    making and finishing of fine woodwork,
    such as furniture or interior details, are en-
    tered under **Cabinet work.**

  See also

Building	**Doors**
Cabinet work	**Floors**

Carpentry—*Continued*
    Roofs   **Walls**
    Turning   **Woodwork**
    xx **Building; Woodwork**
Carpentry—Tools 694
    See also names of tools, e.g. **Saws;** etc.
    xx **Tools**
Carpetbag rule. *See* **Reconstruction (1865-1876)**
Carpets 645; 677; 746.7
    Use for materials on heavy woven or felted fab-
        rics used as floor coverings, usually covering
        large areas. Consider also **Rugs.**
    See also **Rugs; Weaving**
    xx **Decoration and ornament; Interior design;**
        Rugs; Textile industry; Weaving
Carpools. *See* **Car pools**
Carriages and carts 688.6
    x Carts; Coaches, Stage; Stagecoaches; Wagons
Carriers, Aircraft. *See* **Aircraft carriers**
Cars, Armored (Tanks). *See* **Tanks (Military sci-
    ence)**
Cars (Automobiles). *See* **Automobiles**
Cartels. *See* **Trusts, Industrial**
Cartography. *See* **Charts; Map drawing; Maps**
Cartoons and caricatures 741.5
    Use for general collections of pictorial humor
        and for materials about caricatures and car-
        toons.
    See also **Comic books, strips, etc.; Motion picture**
        cartoons; also subjects with the subdivision
        Cartoons and caricatures, e.g.
        Computers—Cartoons and caricatures; and
        names of wars with the subdivision *Humor,*
        caricatures, etc., e.g. **World War, 1939-**
        1945—Humor, caricatures, etc.; etc.
    x Caricatures; Humorous pictures; Illustrations,
        Humorous; Pictures, Humorous
    xx **Comic books, strips, etc.; Pictures; Portraits**
Carts. *See* **Carriages and carts**
Carving (Arts). *See* kinds of carving, e.g. **Wood
    carving;** etc.
Carving (Meat, etc.) 642
    xx **Dinners and dining**
Carving, Wood. *See* **Wood carving**
Case studies. *See* subjects with the subdivision
    Case studies, e.g. **Juvenile deliquency—
    Case studies;** etc.
Case work, Social. *See* **Social case work**
Cassette books. *See* **Talking books**
Cassette recorders and recording. *See* **Magnetic re-
    corders and recording**
Cassette tape recordings, Video. *See* **Videotapes**
Castaways. *See* **Survival (after airplane accidents,
    shipwrecks, etc.)**
Caste 294.5; 305.5; 323.3
    See also **Social classes**
    xx **Brahmanism; Hinduism; Manners and cus-
    toms**
Casting. *See* **Founding; Plaster casts**

Castles (May subdiv. geog.) **728.8**
    x Chateaux
    xx **Architecture; Architecture, Medieval**
Casts, Plaster. *See* **Plaster casts**
Casualty insurance. *See* **Insurance, Casualty**
Cat. *See* **Cats**
Catacombs 393; 726
    See also **Church history—30(ca.)-600, Early**
        church
    x Burial
    xx **Cemeteries; Christian antiquities; Christian**
        art and symbolism; Church history—30(ca.)
        -600, Early church; Tombs
Cataloging 025.3
    May be subdivided by topic, e.g.
        Cataloging—Music; etc.
    See also **Bibliography; Classification—Books;**
        Indexing; Machine readable bibliographic
        data; Subject headings
    x Cataloguing
    xx **Bibliographic control; Bibliography; Books;**
        Documentation; Indexing; Library science;
        Library technical processes
Cataloging data in machine readable form. *See*
    Machine readable bibliographic data
Cataloging—Data processing 025.3
Cataloging—Music 025.3
    Use same form for the cataloging of other types
        of materials.
    x Music—Cataloging
Catalogs. *See* **Catalogs, Booksellers'; Catalogs,**
    Publishers'; Library catalogs; and subjects
    with the subdivision *Catalogs,* e.g. **Motion**
    pictures—Catalogs; etc.
Catalogs, Book 010
    x Book catalogs; Books—Catalogs; Catalogs in
        book form
    xx **Library catalogs**
Catalogs, Booksellers' 017; 018; 019
    x Books—Catalogs; Booksellers' catalogs; Cata-
        logs
    xx **Booksellers and bookselling**
Catalogs, Card 017; 018; 019
    x Card catalogs
    xx **Library catalogs**
Catalogs, Classified 017
    See also **Classification—Books**
    x Catalogs, Systematic; Classed catalogs; Classi-
        fied catalogs
    xx **Classification—Books; Library catalogs**
Catalogs, COM. *See* **Library catalogs on microfilm**
Catalogs in book form. *See* **Catalogs, Book**
Catalogs, Library. *See* **Library catalogs**
Catalogs on microfilm. *See* **Library catalogs on mi-**
    crofilm
Catalogs, Online 025.3
    x Online catalogs
    xx **Library catalogs**
Catalogs, Publishers' 015
    x Books—Catalogs; Catalogs; Publishers'

Catalogs, Publishers'—*Continued*
    catalogs
  xx **Publishers and publishing**
Catalogs, Subject 017
  See also **Subject headings**
  xx **Library catalogs**
Catalogs, Systematic. *See* **Catalogs, Classified**
Cataloguing. *See* **Cataloging**
Catalysis 541.3
  xx **Chemistry, Physical and theoretical**
Catamarans 797.1
  xx **Boats and boating**
Catastrophes. *See* **Disasters**
Catechisms 238; 268
  See also **Bible—Catechisms, question books;**
    Creeds
  xx **Christian education; Creeds; Theology—Study**
    and teaching
Caterers and catering 642
  See also **Desserts; Dinners and dining; Lunch-**
    eons; Menus
  xx **Cookery; Food service; Menus**
Caterpillars 595.78
  x Cocoons
  xx **Butterflies; Moths**
Cathedrals (May subdiv. geog.) **726**
  See also **Architecture, Gothic;** also names of in-
    dividual cathedrals
  xx **Abbeys; Architecture; Architecture, Gothic;**
    Architecture, Medieval; Christian art and
    symbolism; Church architecture; Churches
Cathedrals—United States 726
  x United States—Cathedrals
Cathode ray tubes 537.5; 621.3815
  x C.R.T.'s; CRTs
  xx **Vacuum tubes**
Catholic Church (May subdiv. geog.) **282**
  See also **Inquisition; Papacy;** also subjects with
    the subdivision *Catholic Church,* e.g.
    Abortion—Catholic Church; etc.
  x Roman Catholic Church
  xx **Christianity**
Catholic Church—Charities 361.7
  xx **Charities**
Catholic Church—Clergy 253
  See also **Cardinals; Ex-priests**
  xx **Clergy; Priests**
Catholic Church—Converts. *See* **Converts, Catho-**
  lic
Catholic Church—Foreign relations. *See* **Catholic**
  Church—Relations (Diplomatic)
Catholic Church—Liturgy 264
  Use for materials on the forms of prayers, ritu-
    als, and ceremonies used in the official pub-
    lic worship of the Catholic Church.
  xx **Liturgies; Rites and ceremonies**
Catholic Church—Missions 266
  xx **Missions, Christian**

Catholic Church—Relations (May subdiv. by church or religion) **282**
> Use for materials on relations between the Catholic Church and other churches and religions.

Catholic Church—Relations (Diplomatic) (May subdiv. geog. by appropriate political jurisdiction) **282; 914.5**
> Use for materials on the dealings and relations between the Catholic Church and political jurisdictions.
>
> *x* Catholic Church—Foreign relations; Vatican City—Foreign relations
>
> *xx* **International relations**

Catholic Church—United States 282
> *x* United States—Catholic Church

Catholic converts. *See* **Converts, Catholic**

Catholic ex-priests. *See* **Ex-priests**

Catholic laity. *See* **Laity—Catholic Church**

Catholic literature 282; 808
> *x* Index librorum prohibitorum
>
> *xx* **Christian literature; Literature; Religious literature**

Catholics (May subdiv. geog.) **305.6**

Catholics—United States 305.6
> *x* United States—Catholics

Cats 599.74; 636.8
> *See also* names of specific breeds
>
> *x* Cat
>
> *xx* **Domestic animals; Pets**

Cattle 636.2
> Use for materials on domesticated bovine animals, usually kept on a farm or a ranch.
>
> *See also* **Beef cattle; Dairy cattle; Dairying; Pastures**
>
> *x* Cows
>
> *xx* **Dairying; Domestic animals; Livestock**

Cattle brands 636.2

Cattle—Diseases 636.2
> *x* Cows—Diseases
>
> *xx* **Animals—Diseases; Veterinary medicine**

CATV. *See* **Cable television**

Cave drawings 743; 759.01
> *See also* **Rock drawings, paintings, and engravings**
>
> *xx* **Mural painting and decoration; Picture writing; Rock drawings, paintings, and engravings**

Cave dwellers 572
> *xx* **Man, Prehistoric**

Caves 551.4; 796.5
> *x* Grottoes; Speleology

CB radio. *See* **Citizens band radio**

CD players. *See* **Compact disc players**

Celebrities 920
> *See also* types of celebrities, e.g. **Actors and actresses;** etc.
>
> *x* Famous people; Public figures
>
> *xx* **Biography**

Celery 633; 635

xx **Vegetables**

Celibacy 176; 253

xx **Marriage; Religious orders**

Cellars. *See* **Basements**

Cello. *See* **Violoncello**

Cells 574.87; 581.87; 591.87

See also **DNA; Embryology; Protoplasm; Proto-zoa**

x Cytology

xx **Biology; Embryology; Physiology; Protoplasm; Reproduction**

Cells, Electric. *See* **Electric batteries**

Celtic legends. *See* **Legends, Celtic**

Celts 572.9364; 936.4

See also **Druids and Druidism**

x Gaels

xx **France—History—0-1328; Great Britain—History—0-1066**

Cement 620.1; 666; 691

See also **Concrete; Pavements**

x Hydraulic cement

xx **Adhesives; Building materials; Ceramics; Concrete; Lime; Masonry; Plaster and plastering**

Cemeteries (May subdiv. geog.) 393; 718

See also **Catacombs; Epitaphs; Tombs;** also names of cemeteries

x Burial; Burying grounds; Churchyards; Graves; Graveyards

xx **Public health; Sanitation; Tombs**

Censorship 303.3

Use for general materials on the limitation of freedom of expression in various fields.

See also **Academic freedom; Free speech; Freedom of information; Freedom of the press;** also subjects with the subdivision *Censorship,* e.g. **Books—Censorship; Motion pictures—Censorship; Television—Censorship;** etc.

xx **Freedom of information; Intellectual freedom**

Census 312

See also names of countries, cities, etc. with the subdivision *Census,* e.g. **United States—Census;** etc.

xx **Population; Statistics; Vital statistics**

Centers for the performing arts 725

See also **Theaters;** also names of individual centers

xx **Performing arts**

Central Africa. *See* **Africa, Central**

Central America 972.8

xx **America**

Central Europe 943

Use for materials on the area included in the basins of the Danube, Elbe and Rhine rivers.

x Europe, Central

Central States. *See* **Middle West**

Centralization of schools. *See* **Schools—Centralization**

Centralized processing (Libraries). *See* **Library technical processes**

Ceramic industries 338.4
See also types of ceramic industries, e.g. **Glass manufacture;** etc.

Ceramic materials 666; 738.1
See also names of individual materials, e.g. **Clay;** etc.

Ceramics 666
Use for materials on the technology of fired earth products or clay products intended for industrial use. Earthenware, chinaware, and porcelain are entered under **Pottery** and **Porcelain.**

See also **Cement; Glass; Glazes; Pottery; Tiles**
x Keramics
xx **Decorative arts**

Cereals. *See* **Cereals, Prepared; Grain**

Cereals, Prepared 641.3; 664
x Breakfast cereals; Cereals

Cerebral palsy 616.8
x Palsy, Cerebral; Paralysis, Cerebral; Paralysis, Spastic; Spastic paralysis
xx **Brain—Diseases**

Ceremonies. *See* **Etiquette; Manners and customs; Rites and ceremonies**

Certainty. *See* **Belief and doubt; Probabilities; Truth**

Certified public accountants. *See* **Accountants**

Chain belting. *See* **Belts and belting**

Chain stores 658.8
x Branch stores; Stores
xx **Retail trade**

Chair caning 684.1
x Caning of chairs

Chairs 684.1; 749
xx **Furniture**

Chalk talks 741.2
x Blackboard drawing

Challenger (Space shuttle) 629.44
xx **Space shuttles**

Chamber music 785.7
xx **Instrumental music; Music; Orchestral music**

Chambers of commerce 381
x Boards of trade; Trade, Boards of
xx **Commerce**

Change of life in men. *See* **Climacteric, Male**

Change of life in women. *See* **Menopause**

Change of sex. *See* **Transsexuality**

Change, Social. *See* **Social change**

Changing careers. *See* **Career changes**

Chanties. *See* **Sea songs**

Chants (Plain, Gregorian, etc.) 783.5
x Gregorian chant; Plain chant; Plainsong
xx **Church music**

Chanukah. *See* **Hanukkah**

Chapbooks 398
See also **Comic books, strips, etc.**
x Jestbooks
xx **Books; Comic books, strips, etc.; Folklore;**

Chapbooks—*Continued*
>> **Literature; Pamphlets; Periodicals; Wit and humor**

Chaplains 253
> *See also* names of bodies or institutions having chaplains, with the subdivision *Chaplains,* e.g. **United States. Army—Chaplains;** etc.
> *xx* **Clergy**

Character 155.2
> *See also* **Human behavior; Temperament**
> *xx* **Personality; Temperament**

Character assassination. *See* **Libel and slander**

Character education. *See* **Moral education**

Characteristics, National. *See* **National characteristics**

Characters and characteristics in literature 809; 810.9; 820.9; etc.
> *See also* **Blacks in literature; Children in literature; Drama—Technique; Plots (Drama, fiction, etc.); Women in literature;** also names of prominent authors with the subdivision *Characters,* e.g. **Shakespeare, William, 1564-1616—Characters;** etc.; and names of individual characters in literature
> *x* Literary characters
> *xx* **Literature**

Charades 793.2
> *xx* **Amateur theater; Amusements; Literary recreations; Riddles**

Charcoal 662
> *xx* **Carbon; Fuel**

Charitable institutions. *See* **Charities; Institutional care; Orphanages;** and classes of people with the subdivision *Institutional care,* e.g. **Blind—Institutional care; Deaf—Institutional care; Mentally ill—Institutional care;** etc.

Charities (May subdiv. geog.) 361.7-361.8
> Use for materials on privately supported welfare activities. Materials on tax supported welfare activities are entered under **Public welfare.** Materials on the methods employed in welfare work, public or private, are entered under **Social work.**
>
> *See also*

Charities, Medical	**Institutional care**
Charity organization	**Orphanages**
Child care centers	**Public welfare**
Child welfare	**Social settlements**
Disaster relief	**Unemployed**
Endowments	**Voluntarism**
Food relief	

> also names of appropriate corporate bodies with the subdivision *Charities,* e.g. **Catholic Church—Charities;** etc.; and names of wars with the subdivision *Civilian relief,* e.g. **World War, 1939-1945—Civilian relief;** etc.
> *x* Charitable institutions; Endowed charities; Homes (Institutions); Institutions, Charitable and philanthropic; Philanthropy; Poor

Charities—*Continued*
     relief; Social welfare; Welfare agencies; Welfare work
  xx **Charity organization; Endowments; Poverty; Public welfare; Social problems; Social work; Voluntarism**
Charities, Legal. *See* **Legal aid**
Charities, Medical 362
     See also **Hospitals; Institutional care**
     x Medical charities; Socialized medicine
     xx **Charities; Medical care; Medicine, State; Public health**
Charities, Public. *See* **Public welfare**
Charity 177
     See also **Love (Theology)**
     xx **Ethics; Human behavior**
Charity organization 361
     See also **Charities**
     x Philanthropy
     xx **Charities**
Charlatans. *See* **Impostors and imposture**
Charms 133.4
     x Spells; Talismans
     xx **Demonology; Folklore; Superstition; Witchcraft**
Charter flights. *See* **Aeronautics, Commercial—Chartering**
Charters
     See also **Archives; Manuscripts**
     x Documents
     xx **Archives; History—Sources; Manuscripts**
Chartography. *See* **Charts; Map drawing; Maps**
Charts 912
     See also **Maps**
     x Cartography; Chartography
     xx **Maps**
Chateaux. *See* **Castles**
Chattel mortgages. *See* **Mortgages**
Cheating in sports. *See* **Sports—Corrupt practices**
Checkers 794.2
     x Draughts
Cheers and cheerleading 371.8
Cheese 637; 641.3
     xx **Dairy products; Milk**
Cheese—Bacteriology 637
     xx **Bacteriology**
Chemical analysis. *See* **Chemistry, Analytic;** and names of substances with the subdivision *Analysis,* e.g. **Water—Analysis;** etc.
Chemical apparatus 542
     x Apparatus, Chemical; Chemistry—Apparatus
     xx **Scientific apparatus and instruments**
Chemical elements 546
     See also **Periodic law;** also names of elements, e.g. **Hydrogen;** etc.
     x Elements, Chemical
Chemical engineering 660.2
     See also **Biotechnology; Chemistry, Technical; Metallurgy**
     x Chemistry, Industrial; Industrial chemistry

Chemical engineering—*Continued*
    xx **Chemistry, Technical; Engineering; Metal-**
        lurgy
Chemical equations 540
    x Equations, Chemical
    xx **Chemical reactions**
Chemical geology. *See* **Geochemistry**
Chemical industries 338.4; 660
    Use for materials about industries based mainly
        on chemical processes. Materials on the
        manufacture of chemicals as such are en-
        tered under **Chemicals.**
    See also names of industries, e.g. **Paper making**
        and trade; etc.
    x Chemistry, Industrial; Industrial chemistry;
        Industries, Chemical
    xx **Chemicals; Chemistry, Technical**
Chemical landfills. *See* **Hazardous waste sites**
Chemical reactions 540-547
    See also **Chemical equations**
    x Reactions, Chemical
Chemical societies. *See* **Chemistry—Societies**
Chemical technology. *See* **Chemistry, Technical**
Chemical warfare 358
    See also **Incendiary weapons; Poisonous gases—**
        War use; also names of wars with the subdi-
        vision *Chemical warfare,* e.g. **World War,**
        1939-1945—Chemical warfare; etc.
    x Air warfare
    xx **Military art and science; War**
Chemicals 661
    Use for general materials on chemicals, includ-
        ing their manufacture. See note under
        Chemical industries.
    See also **Chemical industries; Chemistry, Techni-**
        cal; also groups of chemicals, e.g. **Acids; Ag-**
        ricultural chemicals; Petrochemicals; etc.;
        and names of individual chemicals, e.g.
        Carbolic acid; etc.
    xx **Chemistry, Technical**
Chemiculture. *See* **Hydroponics**
Chemistry 540
    See also

Acids	**Fire**
Agricultural chemistry	**Geochemistry**
Alchemy	**Microchemistry**
Bases (Chemistry)	**Pharmacy**
Biochemistry	**Photographic chemistry**
Botanical chemistry	**Physiological chemistry**
Color	**Poisons and poisoning**
Combustion	**Space chemistry**
Explosives	**Spectrum analysis**
Fermentation	

    also headings beginning with the word **Chemical**
    xx **Science**
Chemistry, Agricultural. *See* **Agricultural chemistry**
Chemistry, Analytic 543-545
    See also names of substances with the subdivi-
        sion *Analysis,* e.g. **Water—Analysis;** etc.
    x Analysis (Chemistry); Analytical chemistry;

Chemistry, Analytic—*Continued*
      Chemical analysis; Qualitative analysis;
      Quantitative analysis
Chemistry, Animal. *See* **Physiological chemistry**
Chemistry—Apparatus. *See* **Chemical apparatus**
Chemistry, Biological. *See* **Biochemistry**
Chemistry, Botanical. *See* **Botanical chemistry**
Chemistry, Clinical. *See* **Chemistry, Medical and
    pharmaceutical**
Chemistry—Dictionaries 540.3
  xx **Encyclopedias and dictionaries**
Chemistry—Experiments 540; 542
  x Experiments, Scientific; Scientific experiments
  xx **Science—Experiments**
Chemistry, Industrial. *See* **Chemical engineering;
    Chemical industries; Chemistry, Technical**
Chemistry, Inorganic 546
  See also **Metals**
  x Inorganic chemistry
Chemistry—Laboratory manuals 540
  x Laboratory manuals
Chemistry, Medical and pharmaceutical 615
  See also **Disinfection and disinfectants; Drugs;
    Materia medica; Pharmacy; Poisonous
    plants; Poisons and poisoning**
  x Chemistry, Clinical; Chemistry, Pathological;
    Chemistry, Pharmaceutical; Medical chem-
    istry; Pathological chemistry; Pharmaceuti-
    cal chemistry
  xx **Medicine; Pharmacy; Physiological chemistry;
    Therapeutics**
Chemistry of food. *See* **Food—Analysis; Food—
    Composition**
Chemistry, Organic 547
  x Organic chemistry
  xx **Physiological chemistry**
Chemistry, Organic—Synthesis 547
  See also **Plastics; Polymers and polymerization;
    Synthetic products**
  x Chemistry, Synthetic; Synthetic chemistry
  xx **Plastics**
Chemistry, Pathological. *See* **Chemistry, Medical
    and pharmaceutical; Physiological chemistry**
Chemistry, Pharmaceutical. *See* **Chemistry, Medi-
    cal and pharmaceutical**
Chemistry, Photographic. *See* **Photographic chem-
    istry**
Chemistry, Physical and theoretical 541
  See also

Atomic theory	**Periodic law**
Atoms	**Polymers and polymeriza-**
Catalysis	**tion**
Colloids	**Quantum theory**
Crystallography	**Radiochemistry**
Electrochemistry	**Solids**
Molecules	**Thermodynamics**
Nuclear physics	

  x Physical chemistry; Theoretical chemistry
  xx **Nuclear physics; Physics; Quantum theory**
Chemistry, Physiological. *See* **Physiological**

Chemistry, Physiological—*Continued*
> **chemistry**

Chemistry—Problems, exercises, etc. 540.76
> *x* Problems, exercises, etc.

Chemistry—Societies 540.6
> *x* Chemical societies

Chemistry, Synthetic. *See* **Chemistry, Organic—**
> **Synthesis**

Chemistry, Technical 660
> *See also*

Alloys	**sives**
Bleaching	**Electrochemistry**
Canning and preserving	**Food—Analysis**
Chemical engineering	**Gums and resins**
Chemical industries	**Synthetic products**
Chemicals	**Tanning**
Chemurgy	**Textile chemistry**
Corrosion and anticorro-	**Waste products**

> also names of specific industries and products,
> e.g. **Clay industries; Dyes and dyeing;** etc.
> *x* Chemical technology; Chemistry, Industrial;
> Industrial chemistry; Technical chemistry
> *xx* **Chemical engineering; Chemicals; Metallurgy;**
> **Technology**

Chemistry, Textile. *See* **Textile chemistry**

Chemists 540.92; 920
> *xx* **Scientists**

Chemotherapy 615
> *See also* **Antibiotics;** also names of diseases with
> the subdivision *Chemotherapy,* e.g.
> **Cancer—Chemotherapy;** etc.
> *x* Drug therapy; Pharmacotherapy
> *xx* **Pharmacology**

Chemurgy 660.2
> Use for materials that deal with the advance-
> ment of the industrial use of farm products
> by means of applied science.
> *See also* **Synthetic products**
> *xx* **Agricultural chemistry; Chemistry, Technical;**
> **Synthetic products**

Chess 794.1
> *xx* **Games**

Chicago (Ill.) 917.73; 977.3
> Subdivisions have been given under this subject
> to serve as a guide to the subdivisions that
> may be used under the name of any city.
> They are examples of the application of di-
> rections given in the general references un-
> der various headings throughout the list.
> References are given only for those headings
> that are cited specifically under the general
> references. The subdivisions under **United**
> **States** may be consulted as a guide for for-
> mulating other references that may be
> needed.
> Until early 1985, certain topical headings in
> *Library of Congress Subject Headings* had
> provision for indirect local subdivision, but
> were not divided indirectly to the city level.
> Instead, the topic was used as a subdivision

Chicago (Ill.)—*Continued*

under the heading for the city. The term "city flip" was used informally to refer to this practice, which has been discontinued by the Library of Congress. In the interest of standardization, the "city flip" has been discontinued in this edition of the Sears List. Therefore, the topical headings formerly used as subdivisions under cities only have been removed from under **Chicago (Ill.),** and the appropriate headings have received subdivision notes, e.g. **Bridges.**

Chicago (Ill.)—Antiquities 977.3

Chicago (Ill.)—Bibliography 015.9773

Chicago (Ill.)—Bio-bibliography 016.92

Chicago (Ill.)—Biography 920

xx **Biography**

Chicago (Ill.)—Biography—Portraits 920

Chicago (Ill.)—Boundaries 352.0773; 977.3

Chicago (Ill.)—Bridges. *See* **Bridges—Chicago (Ill.)**

Chicago (Ill.)—Census 317.73

Chicago (Ill.)—Civil defense 363.3

xx **Civil defense**

Chicago (Ill.)—Climate 551.69773

Chicago (Ill.)—Commerce 381

Chicago (Ill.)—Description 917.73

x Description

Chicago (Ill.)—Description—Guidebooks 917.73

x Chicago (Ill.)—Guidebooks; Guidebooks

Chicago (Ill.)—Description—Maps. *See* **Chicago (Ill.)—Maps**

Chicago (Ill.)—Description—Views 917.73

x Chicago (Ill.)—Pictures; Chicago (Ill.)—Views; Scenery

xx **Pictures; Views**

Chicago (Ill.)—Directories 977.3025

Use for lists of names and addresses. Lists of names without addresses are entered under **Chicago (Ill.)—Registers.**

See also **Chicago (Ill.)—Registers**

xx **Chicago (Ill.)—Registers**

Chicago (Ill.)—Directories—Telephone 384.6025

x Directories—Telephone; Telephone directories

Chicago (Ill.)—Economic conditions 330.9773

Chicago (Ill.)—Foreign population 305.8; 325.773

x Foreign population; Population, Foreign

Chicago (Ill.)—Government. *See* **Chicago (Ill.)—Politics and government**

Chicago (Ill.)—Government publications 015.773

Chicago (Ill.)—Guidebooks. *See* **Chicago (Ill.)—Description—Guidebooks**

Chicago (Ill.)—Historic buildings. *See* **Historic buildings—Chicago (Ill.)**

Chicago (Ill.)—History 977.3

Chicago (Ill.)—History—Societies 977.306

Chicago (Ill.)—Industries 338.09

x Chicago (Ill.)—Manufactures

xx **Manufactures**

Chicago (Ill.)—Intellectual life 001.2; 977.3

Chicago (Ill.)—Manufactures. *See* **Chicago (Ill.)—
Industries**
Chicago (Ill.)—Maps 912
x Chicago (Ill.)—Description—Maps
xx **Maps; Road maps**
Chicago (Ill.)—Moral conditions 977.3
Chicago (Ill.)—Occupations 331.7
xx **Occupations**
Chicago (Ill.)—Officials and employees 352.09773
x Employees and officials; Municipal employ-
ees; Officials
xx **Civil service**
Chicago (Ill.)—Pictures. *See* **Chicago (Ill.)—
Description—Views**
Chicago (Ill.)—Poetry 808.81; 811; 811.08; etc.
xx **Poetry**
Chicago (Ill.)—Politics and government 977.3
x Chicago (Ill.)—Government; Politics
xx **Municipal government**
Chicago (Ill.)—Popular culture 977.3
Chicago (Ill.)—Population 304.6; 312
xx **Population**
Chicago (Ill.)—Protests, demonstrations, etc. *See*
Protests, demonstrations, etc.—Chicago (Ill.)
Chicago (Ill.)—Public buildings 720.9773; 725
x Buildings, Public
xx **City planning; Public buildings**
Chicago (Ill.)—Public works 352.7
x Municipal improvements
xx **City planning; Public works**
Chicago (Ill.)—Race relations 305.8
xx **Race relations**
Chicago (Ill.)—Registers 977.3025
Use for lists of names without addresses. Lists of
names that include addresses are entered
under **Chicago (Ill.)—Directories.**
See also **Chicago (Ill.)—Directories**
xx **Chicago (Ill.)—Directories**
Chicago (Ill.)—Social conditions 977.3
xx **Social conditions**
Chicago (Ill.)—Social life and customs 977.3
Chicago (Ill.)—Social policy 977.3
Chicago (Ill.)—Statistics 317.73
xx **Statistics**
Chicago (Ill.)—Streets. *See* **Streets—Chicago (Ill.)**
Chicago (Ill.)—Suburbs and environs 307.7; 977.3
See also **Chicago metropolitan area (Ill.)**
xx **Suburban life**
Chicago (Ill.)—Urban renewal. *See* **Urban renew-
al—Chicago (Ill.)**
Chicago (Ill.)—Views. *See* **Chicago (Ill.)—
Description—Views**
Chicago metropolitan area (Ill.) 307.7; 977.3
xx **Chicago (Ill.)—Suburbs and environs; Metro-
politan areas**
**Chicago metropolitan area (Ill.)—Politics and govern-
ment 977.3**
xx **Metropolitan government**
Chicanos. *See* **Mexican Americans**
Chief justices. *See* **Judges**

Child abuse 362.7

> *See also* **Child molesting; Prostitution, Juvenile**
> *x* Abuse of children; Battered children; Child
>   battering; Child neglect; Children—Abuse;
>   Children, Cruelty to; Cruelty to children
> *xx* **Child rearing; Child welfare; Family violence;**
>   **Parent and child**

Child abuse, Sex. *See* **Child molesting**

Child and parent. *See* **Parent and child**

Child artists 704; 709.2; 920

> Use for materials on children as artists and on
>   works of art by children.
> *See also* **Finger painting**
> *x* Children as artists
> *xx* **Artists; Gifted children**

Child authors 028.5; 920

> Use for materials on children as authors and on
>   works written by children.
> *x* Children as authors
> *xx* **Authors; Gifted children**

Child battering. *See* **Child abuse**

Child birth. *See* **Childbirth**

Child care centers 362.7

> *See also* **Nursery schools**
> *x* Children—Day care; Children's day care cen-
>   ters; Day care centers; Day nurseries; Nur-
>   series, Day
> *xx* **Charities; Child welfare; Children—**
>   **Institutional care; Nursery schools**

Child custody 306.8; 346.01; 362.7

> *See also* **Kidnapping, Parental**
> *x* Children—Custody; Custody of children;
>   Joint custody of children; Parental custody;
>   Shared custody
> *xx* **Divorce mediation; Parent and child**

Child development 155.4; 362.7

> *See also* **Child psychology; Child rearing; Chil-**
>   **dren—Growth; Home instruction**
> *x* Child study; Children—Development
> *xx* **Child rearing; Children; Home instruction**

Child labor. *See* **Children—Employment; Youth—**
>   **Employment**

Child molesting 362.7; 364.1

> *x* Child abuse, Sex; Child sex abuse; Children—
>   Molesting; Molesting of children
> *xx* **Child abuse; Incest; Sex crimes; Sexual ha-**
>   **rassment**

Child neglect. *See* **Child abuse**

Child placing. *See* **Adoption; Foster home care**

Child prostitution. *See* **Prostitution, Juvenile**

Child psychiatry 616.89; 618.92

> *See also* **Adolescent psychiatry; Autism; Child**
>   **psychology; Mentally handicapped children;**
>   **Mentally ill children**
> *x* Children—Mental health; Pediatric psychia-
>   try; Psychiatry, Child
> *xx* **Psychiatry**

Child psychology 155.4

> *See also* **Child rearing; Children and adults; Edu-**
>   **cational psychology; Learning, Psychology**

Child psychology—*Continued*
    of; Mental tests; Separation anxiety in chil-
        dren
    x Child study; Children—Psychology; Psychol-
        ogy, Child
    xx **Child development; Child psychiatry; Child
        rearing; Educational psychology; Psychol-
        ogy**
Child rearing 392; 649
    Use for materials on the principles and tech-
        niques of raising children. Materials on the
        psychological and social interaction between
        parents and their minor children are entered
        under **Parent and child.** Materials on the
        skills, attributes, and attitudes needed for
        parenthood are entered under **Parenting.**
    See also **Child abuse; Child development; Child
        psychology; Children—Care and hygiene;
        Home instruction; Parenting; Socialization**
    x Children—Management; Children—Training;
        Training of children
    xx **Child development; Child psychology; Chil-
        dren and adults; Home instruction; Parent
        and child; Parenting**
Child sex abuse. *See* **Child molesting**
Child snatching by parents. *See* **Kidnapping, Pa-
    rental**
Child study. *See* **Child development; Child psychol-
    ogy**
Child support 306.8; 346.01; 362.7
    x Support of children
    xx **Child welfare; Desertion and nonsupport; Di-
        vorce mediation**
Child welfare 362.7
    Use for materials on the aid, support, and pro-
        tection of children, by the state or by pri-
        vate welfare organizations.
    See also

Abandoned children	care
Child abuse	**Children's hospitals**
Child care centers	**Foster home care**
Child support	**Juvenile delinquency**
Children—Care and hy-	**Mothers' pensions**
giene	**Orphanages**
Children—Employment	**Playgrounds**
Children—Institutional	

    x A.D.C.; Aid to dependent children; Chil-
        dren—Charities, protection, etc.; Depen-
        dent children; Protection of children
    xx **Charities; Children's hospitals; Juvenile delin-
        quency; Mothers' pensions; Orphanages;
        Public welfare**
Childbirth 618.2
    See also **Birth, Multiple; Natural childbirth;
        Pregnancy**
    x Birth; Child birth; Labor (Childbirth); Mid-
        wifery; Obstetrics
    xx **Medicine—Practice; Pregnancy**
Childbirth, Natural. *See* **Natural childbirth**

Childlessness 304.6; 306.8

    See also **Infertility**

    xx **Birth control; Children; Family; Fertility, Human; Marriage**

Childnapping. *See* **Kidnapping, Parental**

Children (May subdiv. geog.) **305.2**

    The term is popularly applied to any age up to fifteen or even later. Materials limited to the first two years of a child's life are entered under **Infants.**

    See also

Abandoned children	**Kindergarten**
Advertising and children	**Missing children**
Boys	**Motion pictures and children**
Child development	
Childlessness	**Orphans**
Computers and children	**Play**
Education, Elementary	**Playgrounds**
Exceptional children	**Runaway children**
Girls	**School children**
Handicapped children	**Television and children**
Heredity	**World War, 1939-1945—**
Indians of North America—Children	**Children**
	Youth
Infants	

    x Preschool children

    xx **Boys; Family; Girls; Infants; Youth**

Children, Abandoned. *See* **Abandoned children**

Children, Abnormal. *See* **Exceptional children; Handicapped children**

Children—Abuse. *See* **Child abuse**

Children, Adopted 362.7

    See also **Adoptees; Orphans**

    x Adopted children

    xx **Adoptees; Adoption; Orphans**

Children—Adoption. *See* **Adoption**

Children and adults 305.2; 362.7; 649

    See also **Child rearing; Children and strangers; Conflict of generations; Parent and child; Teacher-student relationships**

    x Adults and children

    xx **Child psychology**

Children and motion pictures. *See* **Motion pictures and children**

Children and prostitution. *See* **Prostitution, Juvenile**

Children and strangers 362.7

    x Infants and strangers; Strangers and children

    xx **Children and adults**

Children and television. *See* **Television and children**

Children as artists. *See* **Child artists**

Children as authors. *See* **Child authors**

Children as consumers. *See* **Young consumers**

Children—Care and hygiene 618.92; 649

    Use for general materials on the physical care of children. Materials limited to their physical care in school are entered under **School hygiene.**

Children—Care and hygiene—*Continued*
   See also

Baby sitters	**Infants—Care and hygiene**
Children—Diseases	**Nursing**
Children—Nutrition	**School children—Food**
Children's hospitals	**School hygiene**
Health education	**School nurses**

   x Children—Health; Health of children; Pediatrics
   xx **Child rearing; Child welfare; Health; Hygiene; Nursing**
Children—Charities, protection, etc. *See* **Child welfare**
Children—Civil rights 323.4; 342
Children—Clothing. *See* **Children's clothing**
Children—Costume 391
   Use for descriptive and historical materials on children's costume among various nations and at different periods. Materials dealing with children's clothing from a practical standpoint are entered under **Children's clothing.**
   xx **Costume**
Children, Crippled. *See* **Physically handicapped children**
Children, Cruelty to. *See* **Child abuse**
Children—Custody. *See* **Child custody**
Children—Day care. *See* **Child care centers**
Children, Delinquent. *See* **Juvenile delinquency**
Children—Development. *See* **Child development**
Children—Diseases 618.92
   See also **Children's hospitals;** also names of diseases, e.g. **Diphtheria;** etc.
   x Children's diseases; Diseases of children; Medicine, Pediatric; Pediatrics
   xx **Children—Care and hygiene; Children's hospitals; Diseases; Medicine—Practice**
Children—Education. *See* **Education, Elementary; Education, Preschool**
Children, Emotionally disturbed. *See* **Emotionally disturbed children**
Children—Employment (May subdiv. geog.) **331.3**
   See also **Apprentices; Hours of labor; Money-making projects for children**
   x Boys—Employment; Child labor; Employment of children; Girls—Employment; Working boys; Working girls
   xx **Age and employment; Child welfare; Education, Compulsory; Hours of labor; Labor; Labor supply; School attendance; Social problems**
Children—Employment—United States 331.3
   x United States—Children—Employment
Children, Exceptional. *See* **Exceptional children**
Children—Food 641.5
   x Children's food
   xx **Children—Nutrition**
Children, Gifted. *See* **Gifted children**
Children—Growth 612
   xx **Child development; Growth**

Children—Health. *See* **Children—Care and hygiene; School hygiene**
Children—Hospitals. *See* **Children's hospitals**
Children, Hyperactive. *See* **Hyperactive children**
Children, Illegitimate. *See* **Illegitimacy**
Children in art 704.9
    Use for materials on children depicted in works of art. Materials on children as artists are entered under **Child artists.**
  xx **Art**
Children in literature 809
    Use for materials on the theme of children in works of literature. Materials about children as authors and works written by children are entered under **Child authors.**
  xx **Characters and characteristics in literature; Literature**
Children—Institutional care 362.7
  See also **Child care centers; Foster home care; Orphanages; Reformatories**
  x Boys' towns; Children's homes; Homes (Institutions)
  xx **Child welfare; Foster home care; Institutional care**
Children—Language 155.4
  xx **Language and languages**
Children—Management. *See* **Child rearing**
Children—Mental health. *See* **Child psychiatry**
Children—Molesting. *See* **Child molesting**
Children—Nutrition 641.1; 649
  See also **Children—Food**
  xx **Children—Care and hygiene; Nutrition**
Children of divorced parents 306.8; 646.7
  See also **Parenting, Part-time**
  xx **Divorce; Parent and child; Parenting, Part-time; Single parent family**
Children of immigrants 305.2
  x First generation children
  xx **Immigration and emigration**
Children of working parents 306.8; 640
  See also **Latchkey children**
  x Working parents, Children of
  xx **Parent and child**
Children—Placing out. *See* **Adoption; Foster home care**
Children—Psychology. *See* **Child psychology**
Children, Retarded. *See* **Mentally handicapped children; Slow learning children**
Children, Runaway. *See* **Runaway children**
Children—Socialization. *See* **Socialization**
Children—Training. *See* **Child rearing**
Children—United States 305.2
  x United States—Children
Children's books. *See* **Children's literature**
Children's clothing 646; 649
  See note under **Children—Costume.**
  x Children—Clothing
  xx **Clothing and dress**
Children's courts. *See* **Juvenile courts**
Children's day care centers. *See* **Child care centers**

Children's diseases. *See* **Children—Diseases**
Children's food. *See* **Children—Food**
Children's homes. *See* **Children—Institutional care**
Children's hospitals 362.7
> *See also* **Child welfare; Children—Diseases**
> *x* Children—Hospitals
> *xx* **Child welfare; Children—Care and hygiene;**
> **Children—Diseases; Hospitals; Public wel-**
> **fare**
Children's libraries 027.62
> *See also* **Children's literature; Libraries and**
> **schools; School libraries (Elementary**
> **school); Young adults' library services**
> *x* Libraries and children; Libraries, Children's;
> Library services to children
> *xx* **Children's literature; Libraries and schools;**
> **School libraries; School libraries (Elemen-**
> **tary school); Young adults' library services**
Children's literature 028.5
> Use for materials on the development of juve-
> nile literature, discussions of good books for
> children, etc. Materials written by children
> and books about children as authors are en-
> tered under **Child authors.**
>
> *See also*

Caldecott Medal books	**Libraries and schools**
Children's libraries	**Newbery Medal books**
Children's plays	**Picture books for children**
Children's poetry	**Plot-your-own stories**
Easy reading materials	**Reading materials**
Fairy tales	**Storytelling**

> *x* Books for children; Children's books; Chil-
> dren's stories; Juvenile literature
> *xx* **Books and reading; Children's libraries; Li-**
> **braries and schools; Literature; School li-**
> **braries**
Children's moneymaking projects. *See* **Moneymak-**
> **ing projects for children**
Children's parties 395; 793.2
> *xx* **Games; Parties**
Children's plays 808.82; 812; 812.08; etc.
> Use for collections of plays for children by one
> or more authors and for materials about
> children's plays.
> *x* Plays for children; School plays
> *xx* **Amateur theater; Children's literature; Drama;**
> **Drama—Collected works; Theater**
Children's poetry 808.81; 811; 811.08; etc.
> Use for collections of poetry for children by one
> or more authors and for materials about
> children's poetry. Materials on poetry writ-
> ten by children are entered under **Child au-**
> **thors.**
> *See also* **Children's songs; Lullabies; Nonsense**
> **verses; Nursery rhymes; Tongue twisters**
> *x* Poetry for children
> *xx* **Children's literature; Poetry; Poetry—**
> **Collected works**
Children's reading. *See* **Reading**

Children's songs 784.6
>   *See also* **Lullabies; Nursery rhymes**
>   *xx* **Children's poetry; School songbooks; Songs**

Children's stories.   *See* **Children's literature; Fairy tales**

Chimes.   *See* **Bells**

Chimneys 697; 729
>   *x* Smoke stacks
>   *xx* **Architecture—Details; Building; Fireplaces; Heating; Ventilation**

China 951
>   Use as a heading or as a geographic subdivision for works discussing mainland China or the People's Republic of China, regardless of time period. Materials discussing the post-1948 Republic of China or the island of Taiwan are entered under **Taiwan,** regardless of time period.
>   Appropriate period subdivisions may be added as needed.
>   *x* China (People's Republic of China: 1949-   ); People's Republic of China

China—History 951

China—History—1912-1949 951.04

China—History—1949-1976 951.05

China—History—1976- 951.05

China painting 738.2
>   *x* Porcelain painting
>   *xx* **Decoration and ornament; Painting; Porcelain**

China (People's Republic of China, 1949-   ). *See* **China**

China (Porcelain).   *See* **Porcelain**

China (Republic of China, 1949-   ). *See* **Taiwan**

Chinaware. *See* **Porcelain**

Chinese Americans 305.8

Chinese satellite countries. *See* **Communist countries**

Chipmunks 599.32
>   *xx* **Squirrels**

Chiropody. *See* **Podiatry**

Chiropractic 615.5
>   *See also* **Naturopathy**
>   *xx* **Alternative medicine; Massage; Medicine; Osteopathy**

Chivalry 394
>   *See also* **Civilization, Medieval; Crusades; Feudalism; Heraldry; Knights and knighthood; Romances**
>   *xx* **Civilization, Medieval; Crusades; Feudalism; Heraldry; Knights and knighthood; Manners and customs; Middle Ages**

Chivalry—Romances. *See* **Romances**

Chocolate 633.7; 641.3
>   *See also* **Cocoa**
>   *xx* **Cocoa**

Choice, Freedom of. *See* **Free will and determinism**

Choice of books. *See* **Book selection; Books and reading; Books and reading—Best books**

Choice of college. *See* **College choice**

Choice of profession, occupation, vocation, etc. *See*
　　Vocational guidance
Choice (Psychology) 153.8
　　See also **Decision making**
　　xx **Decision making; Psychology**
Choirs (Music) 783.8
　　See also **Choral music; Choral societies; Con-**
　　　ducting, Choral; Singing
　　xx **Choral music; Choral societies; Church music;**
　　　Conducting, Choral; Singing
Cholesterol content of food. *See* **Food—Cholesterol**
　　content
Choose-your-own story plots. *See* **Plot-your-own**
　　stories
Choral conducting. *See* **Conducting, Choral**
Choral music 783.8
　　See also **Choirs (Music); Choral societies; Con-**
　　　ducting, Choral
　　x Music, Choral
　　xx **Cantatas; Choirs (Music); Choral societies;**
　　　Church music; Conducting, Choral; Vocal
　　　music
Choral societies 783.806
　　See also **Choirs (Music); Choral music**
　　x Singing societies
　　xx **Choirs (Music); Choral music; Societies**
Choral speaking 808.5
　　x Speaking choirs; Unison speaking
Christ. *See* **Jesus Christ**
Christening. *See* **Baptism**
Christian antiquities 225.9; 270
　　See also **Architecture, Gothic; Catacombs; Chris-**
　　　tian art and symbolism; Church architecture;
　　　Church furniture
　　x Antiquities, Christian; Antiquities, Ecclesiasti-
　　　cal; Archeology, Christian; Church antiqui-
　　　ties; Ecclesiastical antiquities
　　xx **Antiquities; Archeology; Bible—Antiquities;**
　　　Christian art and symbolism
Christian art and symbolism 246
　　See also

Bible—Pictorial works	**Illumination of books and**
Catacombs	**manuscripts**
Cathedrals	**Jesus Christ—Art**
Christian antiquities	**Mary, Blessed Virgin,**
Church architecture	**Saint—Art**
Church furniture	**Symbolism of numbers**

　　x Art, Christian; Art, Ecclesiastical; Christian
　　　symbolism; Ecclesiastical art; Iconography;
　　　Sacred art
　　xx **Archeology; Art; Christian antiquities; Jesus**
　　　Christ—Art; Religious art and symbolism;
　　　Symbolism
Christian biography. *See* **Christianity—Biography**
Christian civilization. *See* **Civilization, Christian**
Christian devotional calendars. *See* **Devotional cal-**
　　endars
Christian doctrine. *See* **Theology, Doctrinal**

Christian education 268
>See note under **Church and education.**
>*See also* **Bible—Study; Catechisms; Church and education; Fundamentalism and education; Theology—Study and teaching**
>*x* Education, Christian
>*xx* **Christian life; Fundamentalism and education; Religious education; Theology—Study and teaching**

Christian ethics 241; 248.4
>*See also* **Christian life; Christianity and economics; Conscience; Psychology, Pastoral; Sin**
>*x* Christian moral theology; Ethics, Christian; Moral theology, Christian
>*xx* **Christian life; Ethics**

Christian life 248.4
>*See also* **Christian education; Christian ethics; Conversion; Revivals**
>*x* Life, Christian; Religious life (Christian)
>*xx* **Christian ethics**

Christian literature 280
>*See also* **Catholic literature; Devotional literature**
>*xx* **Religious literature**

Christian literature—30(ca.)-600, Early 281
>Use for materials about writings of Christian authors to the time of Gregory the Great in the West and John of Damascus in the East. Collections of such writings are entered under this heading with subdivision *Collected works.*
>*See also* **Church history—30(ca.)-600, Early church**
>*x* Early Christian literature
>*xx* **Latin literature; Literature; Literature, Medieval; Religious literature**

Christian ministry. *See* **Ministry, Christian**
Christian missions. *See* **Missions, Christian**
Christian moral theology. *See* **Christian ethics**
Christian names. *See* **Names, Personal**
Christian new birth. *See* **Regeneration (Christianity)**
Christian regeneration. *See* **Regeneration (Christianity)**
Christian saints 920
>*See also* **Apostles**
>*xx* **Saints**

Christian Science 289.5
>*See also* **Mental healing; Spiritual healing**
>*x* Church of Christ, Scientist; Divine healing; Mind cure
>*xx* **Medicine and religion; Mental healing; Spiritual healing**

Christian sociology. *See* **Sociology, Christian**
Christian symbolism. *See* **Christian art and symbolism**
Christian unity 262; 270.8
>Use for materials on the worldwide movement towards bringing all Christian faiths into cooperation, fellowship and eventually one organization.

Christian unity—*Continued*
    See also **Community churches; Interfaith relations**
    x Church unity; Ecumenical movement
    xx **Church**
Christianity 200
    See also

Atonement—Christianity	**Miracles—Christianity**
Civilization, Christian	**Missions, Christian**
Councils and synods	**Protestantism**
Deism	**Reformation**
God—Christianity	**Theology**
Jesus Christ	

    also names of Christian churches and sects, e.g. **Catholic Church; Huguenots;** etc. and headings beginning with the words **Christian** and **Church**
    xx **Church; Deism; God—Christianity; Jesus Christ; Religions; Theism; Theology**
Christianity and economics 261.8
    Use same form for Christianity and other subjects.
    See also **Church and labor**
    x Economics and Christianity
    xx **Christian ethics; Church and labor; Communism and religion; Economics; Sociology, Christian**
Christianity and other religions 261.2
    See also **Paganism**
    x Christianity—Relations; Comparative religion
Christianity and politics 261.7
    x Politics and Christianity
    xx **Church—Government policy; Religion and politics**
Christianity and war. *See* **War and religion**
Christianity—Apologetic works. *See* **Apologetics**
Christianity—Biography 920
    x Christian biography; Ecclesiastical biography; Religious biography
    xx **Religions—Biography**
Christianity—Evidences. *See* **Apologetics**
Christianity—History. *See* **Church history**
Christianity—Origin. *See* **Church history—30(ca.)-600, Early church**
Christianity—Philosophy 201
    x Theology—Philosophy
Christianity—Psychology 201; 253.5; 261.5
    xx **Psychology, Religious**
Christianity—Relations. *See* **Christianity and other religions**
Christians—Persecutions. *See* **Persecution**
Christmas (May subdiv. geog.) **263; 394.2**
    See also **Christmas entertainments; Jesus Christ—Nativity; Santa Claus**
    x Days; Religious festivals
    xx **Jesus Christ—Nativity**
Christmas cards. *See* **Greeting cards**
Christmas carols. *See* **Carols**
Christmas decorations 745.59
    x Christmas ornaments

Christmas—Drama 394.2; 791; 808.82; 812.08; etc.
    x Christmas plays; Plays, Christmas
    xx **Christmas entertainments; Religious drama**
Christmas entertainments 394.2; 791
    See also **Christmas—Drama**
    x Entertainments
    xx **Christmas**
Christmas ornaments. *See* **Christmas decorations**
Christmas plays. *See* **Christmas—Drama**
Christmas—Poetry 808.81; 811; etc.
    See also **Carols**
    xx **Poetry—Collected works**
Christmas—United States 394.2
    x United States—Christmas
Christology. *See* **Jesus Christ**
Chromosomes 574.8
    See also **Genetic recombination**
    xx **Genetics; Heredity**
Chronology 529
    Use for materials on the science that deals with measuring time by regular divisions and that assigns proper dates to events.
    See also **Almanacs; Day; Months; Night; Week;** also subjects with the subdivision *Chronology,* e.g. **Bible—Chronology; Indians of North America—Chronology;** etc.
    x Hours (Time)
    xx **Almanacs; Astronomy; History; Time**
Chronology, Biblical. *See* **Bible—Chronology**
Chronology, Historical 902
    Use for materials in which events are arranged by date.
    See also names of countries, cities, etc. with the subdivision *History—Chronology,* e.g. **United States—History—Chronology;** etc.
    x Dates, Historical; Historical chronology; History—Chronology
Church 260
    See also **Christian unity; Christianity**
    xx **Christianity; Theology**
Church and education 261.1
    Use same form for the church and other subjects.
    Use for materials on the relation of the church to education in general, and for materials on the history of the part that the church has taken in secular education. Materials on church supported and controlled elementary and secondary schools are entered under **Church schools.** Materials on the instruction of religion in schools and private life are entered under **Religious education,** and on Christian religion under **Christian education.**
    See also **Academic freedom; Fundamentalism and education; Religion in the public schools; Theology—Study and teaching**
    x Education and church; Education and religion; Religion and education
    xx **Academic freedom; Christian education;**

Church and education—*Continued*
> Church—Government policy; Education;
> Theology—Study and teaching

Church and labor 261.8
> *See also* **Christianity and economics**
> *x* Labor and the church
> *xx* **Christianity and economics; Labor**

Church and race relations 261.8
> *x* Integrated churches; Race relations and the
> church

Church and social problems 261.1; 261.8
> Use for materials dealing with the practical treat-
> ment of social problems from the point of
> view of the church. For materials on social
> theory from a Christian point of view use
> **Sociology, Christian.**
> *See also* **Church work; Liberation theology;**
> **Sanctuary movement (Refugee aid); Sociol-**
> **ogy, Christian**
> *x* Religion and social problems; Social problems
> and the church
> *xx* **Church work**

Church and state. *See* **Church—Government policy**
Church and war. *See* **War and religion**
Church antiquities. *See* **Christian antiquities**
Church, Apostolic. *See* **Church history—30(ca.)-**
> **600, Early church**

Church architecture 726
> *See also* **Abbeys; Architecture, Gothic; Cathe-**
> **drals; Churches; Mosques; Spires; Temples**
> *x* Architecture, Church; Architecture, Ecclesias-
> tical; Ecclesiastical architecture; Religious
> art
> *xx* **Architecture; Architecture, Gothic; Christian**
> **antiquities; Christian art and symbolism;**
> **Churches**

Church attendance. *See* **Public worship**
Church bells. *See* **Bells**
Church councils. *See* **Councils and synods**
Church denominations. *See* **Sects;** and names of
> particular denominations and sects, e.g.
> **Presbyterian Church;** etc.

Church entertainments 259
> *x* Church sociables; Entertainments; Socials
> *xx* **Amusements; Church work**

Church festivals. *See* **Fasts and feasts**
Church finance 254.8
> *See also* **Tithes**
> *x* Finance, Church
> *xx* **Finance**

Church furniture 247; 729
> *x* Ecclesiastical furniture
> *xx* **Christian antiquities; Christian art and sym-**
> **bolism; Furniture**

Church—Government policy (May subdiv. geog.)
> **261.7; 322**
> *See also* **Christianity and politics; Church and**
> **education; Ecclesiastical law; Freedom of**
> **conscience; Popes—Temporal power; Reli-**
> **gion in the public schools; Religious freedom**

Church—Government policy—*Continued*
    x Church and state; Religion and state; State
       and church; State church
  xx **Popes—Temporal power; Religious freedom**
Church—Government policy—United States 261.7;
    322
    x United States—Church—Government policy
Church history 209; 270
    Use for materials dealing with the development
       of Christianity and church organization.
    See also

Abbeys	Persecution
Councils and synods	Popes
Creeds	Protestant churches
Jews	Protestantism
Martyrs	Reformation
Miracles—Christianity	Revivals
Missions, Christian	Sects
Papacy	

    also names of countries, states, etc. with the sub-
       division *Church history,* e.g. **United
       States—Church history;** etc.; names of de-
       nominations, sects, churches, etc.; and head-
       ings beginning with the word **Christian**
    x Christianity—History; Ecclesiastical history;
       History, Church; Religious history
  xx **History**
Church history—30(ca.)-600, Early church 209;
    270.1; 270.2
    See also **Apostles; Catacombs; Gnosticism**
    x Apostolic Church; Christianity—Origin;
       Church, Apostolic; Primitive Christianity
  xx **Catacombs; Christian literature—30(ca.)-600,
    Early**
Church history—600-1500, Middle Ages
    270.2-270.5
    See also **Crusades; Inquisition; Popes—Temporal
    power**
  xx **Middle Ages**
Church history—1500- , Modern period
    270.5-270.8
Church history—1517-1648, Reformation. *See*
    Reformation
Church law. *See* **Ecclesiastical law**
Church libraries 027.6
    x Libraries, Church; Parish libraries
  xx **Libraries**
Church music 783
    See also

Carols	Hymns
Chants (Plain, Gregorian,	Liturgies
etc.)	Oratorios
Choirs (Music)	Organ music
Choral music	

    x Music, Sacred; Psalmody; Religious music;
      Sacred music
  xx **Hymns; Music**
Church of Christ, Scientist. *See* **Christian Science**
Church of England (May subdiv. geog.) **283**
    x Anglican Church; England, Church of

Church of England—United States 283
>Use for materials on the Episcopal Church in the United States prior to 1789. Materials on the Episcopal Church in the United States after 1789 are entered under **Episcopal Church.**
>*See also* **Episcopal Church; Puritans**
>*x* United States—Church of England
>*xx* **Episcopal Church; Puritans**

Church of Jesus Christ of Latter-day Saints 289.3
>*x* Latter-day Saints; Mormon Church
>*xx* **Mormons**

Church schools 377
>See note under **Church and education.**
>*See also* **Fundamentalism and education**
>*x* Denominational schools; Nonpublic schools; Parochial schools; Schools, Parochial
>*xx* **Fundamentalism and education; Private schools; Schools**

Church service books. *See* **Liturgies**

Church settlements. *See* **Social settlements**

Church sociables. *See* **Church entertainments**

Church unity. *See* **Christian unity**

Church work 250
>*See also*

Church and social problems	**Missions, Christian**
	Psychology, Pastoral
Church entertainments	**Revivals**
Evangelistic work	**Rural churches**
Lay ministry	**Sunday schools**

>*xx* **Church and social problems; Pastoral work**

Church work, Rural. *See* **Rural churches**

Church work with children. *See* **Church work with youth**

Church work with the sick 361.7
>Use same form for church work with other groups of people.

Church work with youth 259
>*x* Church work with children
>*xx* **Youth**

Churches (May subdiv. geog.) **270; 280**
>Use for general descriptive and historical materials on churches which cannot be entered under **Church architecture.**
>*See also* **Cathedrals; Church architecture;** also names of individual churches
>*xx* **Church architecture**

Churches, Avant-garde. *See* **Noninstitutional churches**

Churches, Community. *See* **Community churches**

Churches, Country. *See* **Rural churches**

Churches, Noninstitutional. *See* **Noninstitutional churches**

Churches, Rural. *See* **Rural churches**

Churches, Undenominational. *See* **Community churches**

Churches—United States 277.3; 280; 726
>*x* United States—Churches

Churchyards. *See* **Cemeteries**

Cicadas 595.7; 632

   x 17 year locusts; Locusts, Seventeen-year; Seventeen-year locusts

Cigarettes 679

   xx **Smoking**

Cigars 679

   xx **Smoking**

Cinema. *See* **Motion pictures**

Cinematography. *See* **Motion picture photography**

Cipher and telegraph codes 621.382

   x Cable codes; Codes, Telegraph; Morse code; Telegraph codes

   xx **Telegraph**

Ciphers 652

   See also **Abbreviations; Cryptography; Writing**

   x Contractions

   xx **Abbreviations; Cryptography; Signs and symbols; Writing**

Ciphers (Lettering). *See* **Monograms**

Circuits, Electric. *See* **Electric circuits**

Circulation of library materials. *See* **Library circulation**

Circulation of the blood. *See* **Blood—Circulation**

Circulatory system. *See* **Cardiovascular system**

Circumnavigation. *See* **Voyages around the world**

Circus 791.3

   See also **Acrobats and acrobatics; Animals—Training; Clowns**

   xx **Amusements**

Cities and towns (May subdiv. geog.) 307.7

   Use for general materials on cities and towns. For materials on large cities and their surrounding areas use **Metropolitan areas**. General materials on the government of cities are entered under **Municipal government**; general materials on local government other than that of cities are entered under **Local government**.

   See also

Art, Municipal	**Streets**
City life	**Tenement houses**
Markets	**Urbanization**
Parks	**Villages**
Sociology, Urban	

   also headings beginning with the word **Municipal;** and names of individual cities and towns

   x Municipalities; Towns; Urban areas

   xx **Local government; Metropolitan areas; Municipal government; Sociology; Sociology, Urban**

Cities and towns—Civic improvement 352.9

   See also **City planning; Community centers**

   x Civic improvement; Municipal improvements

Cities and towns—Lighting. *See* **Streets—Lighting**

Cities and towns—Planning. *See* **City planning**

Cities and towns, Ruined, extinct, etc. 930

   See also **Excavations (Archeology); Ghost towns**

   x Abandoned towns; Buried cities; Extinct cities; Ruins; Sunken cities

Cities and towns, Ruined, extinct, etc.—*Continued*
   xx **Archeology; Ghost towns**
Cities and towns—United States 307.7; 973
   x United States—Cities and towns
Cities, Imaginary. *See* **Geographical myths**
Citizen participation. *See* appropriate subjects with
         the subdivision *Citizen participation,* e.g.
         **City planning—United States—Citizen par-
         ticipation;** etc.
Citizens band radio 621.3845
   x C.B. radio; CB radio; Citizens radio service
   xx **Radio, Shortwave**
Citizen's defender. *See* **Ombudsman**
Citizens radio service. *See* **Citizens band radio**
Citizenship 172; 323.6
   See also **Aliens; Naturalization; Patriotism; Suf-
         frage**
   x Civics; Foreigners; Franchise; Nationality
         (Citizenship)
   xx **Aliens; Constitutional law; Naturalization; Po-
         litical ethics; Political science; Social ethics**
Citrus fruit 634
      Names of fruits are not included in this list but
         are to be added as needed, in the singular
         form, e.g. **Orange;** etc.
      See also names of citrus fruits, e.g. **Orange;** etc.
   xx **Fruit**
City and town life. *See* **City life**
City-federal relations. *See* **Federal-city relations**
City government *See* **Municipal government**
City life 307.7
      See also **Community life**
   x City and town life; Town life; Urban life
   xx **Cities and towns; Community life; Sociology,
         Urban**
City manager. *See* **Municipal government by city
         manager**
City planning (May subdiv. geog.) **307; 352.9; 711**
      See also

Art, Municipal	**Social surveys**
Community development	**Urban renewal**
Housing	**Zoning**

      also names of cities with the subdivisions *Public
         buildings* and *Public works,* e.g. **Chicago
         (Ill.)—Public buildings; Chicago (Ill.)—
         Public works;** etc.
   x Cities and towns—Planning; Municipal plan-
         ning; Planning, City; Town planning; Urban
         planning
   xx **Art, Municipal; Cities and towns—Civic im-
         provement; Community development; Hous-
         ing; Regional planning; Tenement houses;
         Urban renewal**
City planning—United States 307; 352.9; 711
   x United States—City planning
**City planning—United States—Citizen participation
         307; 323.6**
   x Citizen participation; Civic involvement
   xx **Social action**
City planning—Zone system. *See* **Zoning**

City-state relations. *See* **State-local relations**

City traffic   388.3

    x Local traffic; Street traffic; Traffic, City; Urban traffic

    xx **Streets; Traffic engineering**

City transit. *See* **Local transit**

Civic art. *See* **Art, Municipal**

Civic improvement. *See* **Cities and towns—Civic improvement**

Civic involvement. *See* appropriate subjects with the subdivision *Citizen participation,* e.g. **City planning—United States—Citizen participation;** etc.

Civics. *See* **Citizenship; Political science; United States—Politics and government**

Civil defense   363.3

    See note under **Air defenses.**

    See also **Air defenses; Air raid shelters; Disaster relief; Rescue work; Survival skills; World War, 1939-1945—Evacuation of civilians;** also names of countries, cities, etc. with the subdivision *Civil defense,* e.g. **Chicago (Ill.) —Civil defense; United States—Civil defense;** etc.

    x Blackouts in war; Civilian defense; Defense, Civil; World War, 1939-1945—Civilian defense

    xx **Disaster relief; Military art and science**

Civil disobedience. *See* **Government, Resistance to; Passive resistance**

Civil disorders. *See* **Riots**

Civil engineering   624

    See also

Aqueducts	**Public works**
Bridges	**Railroad engineering**
Canals	**Reclamation of land**
Dams	**Rivers**
Drainage	**Roads**
Dredging	**Sanitary engineering**
Excavation	**Steel, Structural**
Foundations	**Streets**
Harbors	**Strength of materials**
Highway engineering	**Structural engineering**
Hydraulic engineering	**Subways**
Irrigation	**Surveying**
Marine engineering	**Tunnels**
Masonry	**Walls**
Mechanical engineering	**Water supply**
Military engineering	**Water supply engineering**
Mining engineering	

    xx **Engineering**

Civil government. *See* **Political science; United States—Politics and government**

Civil law suits. *See* **Actions and defenses**

Civil liberty. *See* **Freedom**

Civil rights   323.4

    See also

Academic freedom	**Freedom**
Anti-apartheid movement	**Freedom of assembly**
Free speech	**Freedom of association**

Civil rights—*Continued*
> **Freedom of information**   **Freedom of the press**
> **Freedom of movement**   **Religious freedom**
>> also names of groups of people with the subdivision *Civil rights,* e.g. **Blacks—Civil rights; Men—Civil rights; Women—Civil rights;** etc.
>
> *x* Human rights; Natural law; Rights, Civil
> *xx* **Constitutional law; Discrimination; Freedom; Political science**

Civil service (May subdiv. geog.) **350-352**
> Use for general materials on the history and development of public service. Materials on public personnel administration, including the duties of civil service employees, their salaries, pensions, etc., are entered under the name of the country, state or city with the subdivision *Officials and employees.*
>
> *See also* **Bureaucracy;** also names of countries, cities, etc. with the subdivision *Officials and employees,* e.g. **Chicago (Ill.)—Officials and employees;** etc.
>
> *x* Administration; Employees and officials; Government employees; Government service; Municipal employees; Office, Tenure of; Officials; Tenure of office
> *xx* **Administrative law; Bureaucracy; Political science; Public administration**

Civil service—Examinations **351.3**
> *xx* **Examinations**

Civil service—United States **353**
> *See also* **United States—Officials and employees**
> *x* United States—Civil service
> *xx* **United States—Officials and employees**

Civil War—England. *See* **Great Britain—History—1642-1660, Civil War and Commonwealth**

Civil War—United States. *See* **United States—History—1861-1865, Civil War**

Civilian defense. *See* **Civil defense**

Civilian evacuation. *See* **World War, 1939-1945—Evacuation of civilians**

Civilization **909**
> Use for materials dealing with civilization in general and with the development of social customs, art, industry, religion, etc. of several countries or peoples. Materials confined to the civilization of one country are entered under the name of the country with the subdivision *Civilization.* Materials on peoples whose culture spread beyond their own boundaries are entered under such headings as **Civilization, Asian; Civilization, Greek; Civilization, Occidental; Civilization, Scandinavian;** etc. Add as needed.
>
> *See also*
>> **Acculturation**   **Archeology**
>> **Aeronautics and civilization**   **Art**
>> **Anthropology**   **Astronautics and civilization**

129

Civilization—*Continued*

    Biculturalism

    Culture

    Education

    Ethnology

    Industry

    Inventions

    Learning and scholarship

    Manners and customs

    Popular culture

    Progress

    Religions

    Science and civilization

    Society, Nonliterate folk

    Technology and civilization

    War and civilization

    also names of countries, states, etc. with the subdivision *Civilization,* e.g. **United States—Civilization;** etc.

  xx **Anthropology; Culture; Ethnology; History; History—Philosophy; Progress; Sociology**

Civilization, African 909

  x African civilization

Civilization, American 970; 980

    Use for general materials on the civilization of the Western Hemisphere or of Latin America, and for materials on ancient American civilization, including that of the Mayas, Aztecs, etc. Materials limited to the civilization of the United States are entered under **United States—Civilization.**

  x American civilization

Civilization, Ancient 913; 930

  See also **Man, Prehistoric**

  x Ancient civilization

  xx **History, Ancient**

Civilization and aeronautics. *See* **Aeronautics and civilization**

Civilization and astronautics. *See* **Astronautics and civilization**

Civilization and computers. *See* **Computers and civilization**

Civilization and science. *See* **Science and civilization**

Civilization and technology. *See* **Technology and civilization**

Civilization and war. *See* **War and civilization**

Civilization, Arab 909

  x Arab civilization

Civilization, Asian 909; 950

  x Asian civilization; Civilization, Oriental; Oriental civilization

  xx **East and West**

Civilization, Christian 200.9

  x Christian civilization

  xx **Christianity**

Civilization, Greek 909; 938

    Use same form for materials dealing with the culture of people not confined to one country, e.g. **Civilization, Arab; Civilization, Occidental;** etc.

  See also **Hellenism**

  x Greece—Civilization; Greek civilization

Civilization, Jewish. *See* **Jews—Civilization**

Civilization, Medieval 909.07

  See also **Art, Medieval; Chivalry; Feudalism; Middle Ages; Monasticism**

Civilization, Medieval—*Continued*
    x Medieval civilization
    xx **Chivalry; Middle Ages; Middle Ages—**
        History; Renaissance
Civilization, Modern 909.7; 909.08; 909.82
    Use for materials covering the period after 1453.
    See also **History, Modern; Renaissance**
    x Modern civilization
    xx **History, Modern**
Civilization, Modern, 1950- 909.82-909.83
Civilization, Occidental 909
    x Occidental civilization; Western civilization
    xx **East and West**
Civilization, Oriental. *See* **Civilization, Asian**
Civilization, Scandinavian 948
    x Scandinavian civilization
Clairvoyance
    See also **Divination; Extrasensory perception;**
        Fortune telling; Hypnotism; Mind reading;
        Telepathy
    xx **Divination; Fortune telling; Mind reading; Oc-**
        cult sciences; Psychical research; Spiritual-
        ism; Telepathy
Clans 305.8; 307.7; 390; 941
    See also **Tartans;** also names of families
    x Highland clans; Scottish clans
    xx **Family; Feudalism**
Class conflict. *See* **Social conflict**
Class consciousness 305.5
    xx **Social classes; Social psychology**
Class distinction. *See* **Social classes**
Class struggle. *See* **Social conflict**
Classed catalogs. *See* **Catalogs, Classified**
Classes (Mathematics). *See* **Set theory**
Classical antiquities 937-938
    See also **Archeology; Art, Greek; Art, Roman;**
        Mythology, Classical; also names of coun-
        tries, cities, etc. with the subdivision
        Antiquities, e.g. **Greece—Antiquities;** etc.
    x Antiquities, Classical; Archeology, Classical;
        Classical archeology; Greek antiquities; Ro-
        man antiquities
    xx **Antiquities; Archeology; Art, Ancient**
Classical antiquities—Dictionaries. *See* **Classical**
    dictionaries
Classical archeology. *See* **Classical antiquities**
Classical art. *See* **Art, Greek; Art, Roman**
Classical biography. *See* **Greece—Biography;**
    Rome—Biography
Classical dictionaries 938.03
    x Classical antiquities—Dictionaries; Dictionar-
        ies, Classical
    xx **Encyclopedias and dictionaries; History, An-**
        cient
Classical education 370.11
    See also **Colleges and universities; Humanism;**
        Humanities
    x Education, Classical
    xx **Colleges and universities; Education; Educa-**
        tion, Higher; Humanism; Humanities

Classical geography. *See* **Geography, Ancient**

Classical languages. *See* **Greek language; Latin language**

Classical literature 880
    See also **Greek literature; Latin literature**
    x Literature, Classical
    xx **Greek literature; Latin literature; Literature**

Classical mythology. *See* **Mythology, Classical**

Classification—Books 025.4
    Use same form for classification of other library materials.
    See also **Catalogs, Classified; Classification, Dewey Decimal**
    x Libraries—Classification; Library classification
    xx **Bibliography; Cataloging; Catalogs, Classified; Documentation; Library science; Library technical processes; Subject headings**

Classification, Dewey Decimal 025.4
    x Dewey Decimal Classification
    xx **Classification—Books**

Classified catalogs. *See* **Catalogs, Classified**

Classroom management 371.1
    xx **School discipline; Teaching**

Clay 553.6; 666; 738.1
    See also **Bricks; Modeling**
    xx **Ceramic materials; Soils**

Clay industries 338.4; 666
    See also **Bricks; Pottery; Tiles**
    xx **Chemistry, Technical**

Clay modeling. *See* **Modeling**

Cleaning 648; 667
    See also

Bleaching	**House cleaning**
Cleaning compounds	**Laundry**
Dry cleaning	**Soap**
Dyes and dyeing	**Street cleaning**

Cleaning compounds 648; 667
    See also **Detergents, Synthetic; Soap**
    xx **Cleaning**

Cleanliness 391; 613; 646.7
    See also **Baths; Hygiene; Sanitation**
    x Messiness; Neatness

Clearing of land. *See* **Reclamation of land**

Clergy 253
    See also **Chaplains; Priests; Rabbis;** also church denominations with the subdivision *Clergy,* e.g. **Catholic Church—Clergy;** etc.
    x Curates; Ministers of the gospel; Pastors; Preachers; Rectors
    xx **Pastoral work**

Clergy—Office. *See* **Ministry**

Clergy—Political activity 253

Clerical employees. *See* **Office employees**

Clerical work—Training. *See* **Business education**

Clerks. *See* **Office employees**

Clerks (Retail trade). *See* **Sales personnel**

Cliff dwellers and cliff dwellings 979.004
    See also **Mounds and mound builders**
    xx **Archeology; Indians of North America**

Climacteric, Female. *See* **Menopause**
Climacteric, Male 612
> *x* Change of life in men; Male climacteric
Climate 551.6
> Use for materials on climate as it relates to man
> and to plant and animal life, including the
> effects of changes of climate. Materials lim-
> ited to the climate of a particular region are
> entered under the name of the place with
> the subdivision *Climate.* Materials on the
> state of the atmosphere at a given time and
> place with respect to heat or cold, wetness
> or dryness, calm or storm, are entered under
> **Weather.** Scientific materials on the atmo-
> sphere, especially weather factors, are en-
> tered under **Meteorology.**
>
> *See also* **Forest influences; Meteorology; Rain
> and rainfall; Seasons; Weather;** also names
> of countries, cities, etc. with the subdivision
> *Climate,* e.g. **United States—Climate;** etc.
> *x* Climatology
> *xx* **Earth sciences; Meteorology; Physical geogra-
> phy; Weather**
Climate and forests. *See* **Forest influences**
Climatology. *See* **Climate**
Climbing plants 582.1; 635.9
> *x* Vines
> *xx* **Gardening; Plants**
Clinical genetics. *See* **Medical genetics**
Clipper ships 387.2; 623.8
> *xx* **Ships**
Clippings (Books, newspapers, etc.) 025.17
> *x* Newspaper clippings; Press clippings
> *xx* **Newspapers**
Clocks and watches 681.1
> *See also* **Sundials**
> *x* Horology; Watches
> *xx* **Time**
Clog dancing 793.3
> *xx* **Tap dancing**
Cloisters. *See* **Convents; Monasteries**
Clones and cloning 174; 574.87
> *See also* **Molecular cloning**
> *x* DNA cloning
> *xx* **Genetic engineering**
Cloning, Molecular. *See* **Molecular cloning**
Closed-circuit television 384.55
> *See also* **Television in education**
> *x* Television, Closed-circuit
> *xx* **Intercommunication systems; Microwave com-
> munication systems; Television; Television
> in education**
Closed shop. *See* **Open and closed shop**
Cloth. *See* **Fabrics**
Clothes. *See* **Clothing and dress**
Clothiers. *See* **Clothing trade**
Clothing and dress 646
> Use for materials dealing with clothing from a
> practical standpoint including the art of
> dress. Descriptive and historical materials
> on the costume of particular countries, or
> periods, or peoples, and materials on fancy
> dress and theatrical costumes are entered
> under **Costume.** Materials describing the
> prevailing mode or style of dress are entered
> under **Fashion.**

Clothing and dress—*Continued*
　　See also
　　Children's clothing　　**Fashion**
　　Costume　　　　　　　**Men's clothing**
　　Dress accessories　　**Tailoring**
　　Dressmaking　　　　　**Women's clothing**
　　　also names of articles of clothing and accesso-
　　　　　ries, e.g. **Buttons; Hats; Hosiery; Leather**
　　　　　garments; Shoes; etc.
　　x Clothes; Dress; Garments
　　xx **Costume; Fashion; Manners and customs**
Clothing and dress—Dry cleaning.　*See* **Dry clean-**
　　　ing
Clothing and dress—Repairing 646.2; 646.4
Clothing, Leather.　*See* **Leather garments**
Clothing, Men's.　*See* **Men's clothing**
Clothing trade 338.4; 687
　　See also **Tailoring**
　　x Clothiers
Cloud seeding.　*See* **Weather—Control**
Clouds 551.5
　　xx **Meteorology**
Clowns 791.3; 791.3092; 920
　　xx **Circus; Entertainers**
Clubs 367
　　See also **Boys' clubs; Girls' clubs; Men—**
　　　　Societies; Social group work; Societies;
　　　　Women—Societies
　　xx **Associations; Societies**
Coaches, Stage.　*See* **Carriages and carts**
Coaching (Athletics) 796.07
　　See also names of sports with the subdivision
　　　　Coaching, e.g. **Football—Coaching;** etc.
　　x Athletic coaching; Sports coaching
　　xx **Athletics; College sports; Physical education;**
　　　　School sports; Sports
Coal 553.2
　　See also **Coal mines and mining**
　　x Anthracite coal; Bituminous coal
　　xx **Carbon; Fuel; Geology, Economic**
Coal gas.　*See* **Gas**
Coal gasification 622.028
　　x Gasification of coal
Coal liquefaction 622.028
　　x Liquefaction of coal
Coal miners 622.092; 920
　　xx **Miners**
Coal mines and mining 622
　　See also **Mining engineering**
　　xx **Coal; Mines and mineral resources**
Coal oil.　*See* **Petroleum**
Coal tar products 547.8; 661
　　See also **Gas; Oils and fats**
　　xx **Gas; Petroleum**
Coast pilot guides.　*See* **Pilot guides**
Coastal signals.　*See* **Signals and signaling**
Coats of arms.　*See* **Heraldry**
Cocoa 633.7; 641.3
　　See also **Chocolate**
　　xx **Beverages; Chocolate**

Cocoons. *See* **Butterflies; Caterpillars; Moths; Silk-worms**

Code names 423
    See also **Acronyms**
    xx **Abbreviations; Names**
Codes, Telegraph. *See* **Cipher and telegraph codes**
Coeducation 376
    See also **Education; Men—Education; Women—Education**
    xx **Colleges and universities; Education; Men—Education; Women—Education**
Coffee 633.7; 641.8
    xx **Beverages**
Coffee houses 647
    xx **Restaurants, bars, etc.**
Cog wheels. *See* **Gearing**
Cognition. *See* **Knowledge, Theory of**
Cohabitation. *See* **Unmarried couples**
Coiffure. *See* **Hair and hairdressing**
Coin collecting. *See* **Coins**
Coinage 332.4
    Use for materials on the processing and history of metal money. Lists of coins and materials about coins and coin collecting are entered under **Coins.**
    See also **Counterfeits and counterfeiting; Gold; Mints; Monetary policy; Money; Silver**
    xx **Gold; Mints; Money; Silver**
Coinage of words. *See* **Words, New**
Coins 737.4
    Use for lists of coins, materials about coins and coin collecting. Materials on coins from the point of view of art and archeology are entered under **Numismatics;** materials on the processing of metal money are entered under **Coinage.**
    See also **Numismatics**
    x Coin collecting
    xx **Money; Numismatics**
Cold 551.5
    See also **Cryobiology; Ice; Low temperatures**
    xx **Low temperatures**
Cold (Disease) 616.2
    See also **Influenza**
    x Common cold
Cold—Physiological effect 613
    xx **Cryobiology**
Cold storage 641.4; 664
    See also **Compressed air; Refrigeration and refrigerating machinery**
    xx **Food—Preservation; Meat industry and trade; Refrigeration and refrigerating machinery**
Cold—Therapeutic use 615
    See also **Cryosurgery**
    x Cryotherapy
Cold war. *See* **Psychological warfare; World politics—1945-1965**
Collaborationists. *See* **Treason**
Collage 702.8; 751.4
    xx **Art**

Collapse of structures. *See* **Structural failures**

Collected works. *See* types of art and literature and collections of writings with the subdivision *Collected works,* e.g. **English literature—Collected works;** etc.

Collectibles. *See* names of events with the subdivision *Collectibles,* e.g. **American Revolution Bicentennial, 1776-1976—Collectibles;** etc.; and names of objects collected with the subdivision *Collectors and collecting,* e.g. **Postage stamps—Collectors and collecting;** etc.

Collecting. *See* **Collectors and collecting**

Collecting of accounts 658.8
   x Accounts, Collecting of
   xx **Commercial law; Credit; Debtor and creditor**

Collection development (Libraries). *See* **Libraries—Collection development**

Collections of art, painting, etc. *See* types of art with the subdivision *Collected works,* e.g. **Painting—Collected works;** etc.

Collections of literature. *See* form headings that represent collections of works of several authors, e.g. **American essays; Essays; Parodies; Short stories;** etc.; and names of literatures and literary forms with the subdivision *Collected works,* e.g. **English literature—Collected works; Poetry—Collected works;** etc. For other collections of writings see names of authors, literary or otherwise, or subjects with the subdivision *Collected works,* e.g. **Shakespeare, William, 1564-1616—Collected works; Astronomy—Collected works;** etc.

Collections of natural specimens. *See* **Zoological specimens—Collection and preservation;** and names of specimens with the subdivision *Collection and preservation,* e.g. **Birds—Collection and preservation;** etc.

Collections of objects. *See* **Collectors and collecting;** and names of events with the subdivision *Collectibles,* e.g. **American Revolution Bicentennial, 1776-1976—Collectibles;** etc.; and names of objects collected with the subdivision *Collectors and collecting,* e.g. **Postage stamps—Collectors and collecting;** etc.

Collective bargaining 331.8; 331.89; 658.3
   May be subdivided by topic, e.g. **Collective bargaining—Librarians;** etc.
   See also **Arbitration, Industrial; Labor contract; Labor unions; Management—Employee participation; Strikes and lockouts**
   x Labor negotiations
   xx **Arbitration, Industrial; Industrial relations; Labor; Labor contract; Labor disputes; Labor unions; Management—Employee participation; Strikes and lockouts**

Collective bargaining—Librarians 331.89
 x Librarians—Collective bargaining; Libraries—Collective bargaining
Collective farms. *See* **Agriculture, Cooperative**
Collective labor agreements. *See* **Labor contract**
Collective security. *See* **Security, International**
Collective settlements (May subdiv. geog.) **307.7;
  335**
 See also **Bohemianism; Counter culture;** also
  names of individual communes
 x Communal living; Communes; Cooperative
  living; Group living
 xx **Counter culture**
Collective settlements—Israel 307.7; 335
 x Israel—Collective settlements; Kibbutz
Collective settlements—United States 307.7; 335
 x United States—Collective settlements
Collectivism. *See* **Communism; Socialism**
Collectors and collecting 790.1
 See also **Americana; Book collecting;** also names
  of objects collected with the subdivision
  Collectors and collecting, e.g. **Postage
  stamps—Collectors and collecting;** etc.;
  names of events with the subdivision
  Collectibles, e.g. **American Revolution Bicentennial, 1776-1976—Collectibles;** etc.;
  and names of natural specimens, etc. with
  the subdivsion *Collection and preservation,*
  e.g. **Antiquities—Collection and preservation; Birds—Collection and preservation;
  Plants—Collection and preservation; Zoological specimens—Collection and preservation;** etc.
 x Collecting; Collections of objects
 xx **Antiques; Art; Hobbies**
Collects. *See* **Prayers**
College and school drama 371.8
 Use for materials about college and school
  drama. Collections of plays for production
  in colleges and schools are entered under
  College and school drama—Collected works.
 See also **Drama in education**
 x College drama; School drama; Theatricals,
  College
 xx **Amateur theater; Drama; Drama in education;
  Student activities**
**College and school drama—Collected works 808.82;
  812.08; etc.**
 x College plays; Plays, College; School plays
 xx **Drama—Collected works**
College and school journalism 371.8
 x College journalism; College periodicals;
  School journalism; School newspapers
 xx **Journalism; Student activities**
College and university libraries. *See* **Academic li-
  braries**
College athletics. *See* **Athletics; College sports**
College choice 378
 x Choice of college; Colleges and universities—
  Selection

College choice—*Continued*
    xx **Colleges and universities**
College costs 378.3
    x Tuition
    xx **Colleges and universities—Finance**
College degrees. *See* **Degrees, Academic**
College drama. *See* **College and school drama**
College entrance examinations. *See* **Colleges and universities—Entrance examinations**
College entrance requirements. *See* **Colleges and universities—Entrance requirements;** and names of individual colleges and universities with the subdivision *Entrance requirements*
College fraternities. *See* **Fraternities and sororities**
College graduates 331.11; 338.4; 650.1
    See also **College students**
    x Graduates, College; University graduates
    xx **College students; Professions**
College journalism. *See* **College and school journalism**
College life. *See* **College students**
College periodicals. *See* **College and school journalism**
College plays. *See* **College and school drama—Collected works**
College songs. *See* **Students' songs**
College sororities. *See* **Fraternities and sororities**
College sports 371.8
    See also **Coaching (Athletics);** also names of individual sports, e.g. **Baseball; Basketball; Football; Rowing; Soccer; Track athletics;** etc.
    x College athletics; Intercollegiate athletics; Varsity sports
    xx **School sports; Sports**
College students 378
    See also **College graduates**
    x College life; Colleges and universities—Students; Undergraduates; University students
    xx **College graduates; Students**
College students, Foreign. *See* **Students, Foreign**
College students—Political activity 378
    x Campus disorders; Political participation
    xx **Politics, Practical**
College students—Sexual behavior 371.8; 378
    xx **Sexual behavior**
College teachers. *See* **Colleges and universities—Faculty; Educators; Teachers**
Colleges and universities (May subdiv. geog.) **378**
    See also

Academic libraries	**Fraternities and sororities**
Classical education	**Free universities**
Coeducation	**Junior colleges**
College choice	**Scholarships, fellowships, etc.**
Commencements	
Degrees, Academic	**Teachers colleges**
Dissertations, Academic	**University extension**
Education, Higher	

Colleges and universities—*Continued*

 also headings beginning with the word **College** and names of individual institutions

 x Universities

 xx **Classical education; Education; Education, Higher; Professional education; Schools**

Colleges and universities—Buildings 727

 x Buildings, College

 xx **Buildings**

Colleges and universities—Curricula 378

 x Core curriculum; Courses of study; Curricula (Courses of study); Schools—Curricula; Study, Courses of

 xx **Education—Curricula**

Colleges and universities—Entrance examinations 378

 See also **Graduate record examination; Scholastic aptitude test**

 x College entrance examinations; Entrance examinations for colleges

 xx **Educational tests and measurements; Examinations**

Colleges and universities—Entrance requirements 378

 See also names of individual colleges and universities with the subdivision *Entrance requirements*

 x College entrance requirements; Entrance requirements for colleges and universities

 xx **Examinations; Free universities**

Colleges and universities—Faculty 378

 x College teachers; Faculty (Education)

Colleges and universities—Finance 378

 See also **College costs; Federal aid to education**

 x Tuition

Colleges and universities—Insignia 378

 xx **Insignia**

Colleges and universities, Nonformal. *See* **Free universities**

Colleges and universities—Selection. *See* **College choice**

Colleges and universities—Students. *See* **College students**

Colleges and universities—United States 378.73

 x American colleges; United States—Colleges and universities; United States—Universities

Collies 636.7

 xx **Dogs**

Collisions, Railroad. *See* **Railroads—Accidents**

Colloids 541.3; 547.1

 xx **Chemistry, Physical and theoretical**

Colonial architecture. *See* **Architecture, Colonial**

Colonial furniture (U.S.). *See* **Furniture, American**

Colonial history (U.S.). *See* **United States—History—1600-1775, Colonial period**

Colonialism. *See* **Colonies; Imperialism**

Colonies 325

 Use for materials on general colonial policy. Materials on the policy of settling immigrants

Colonies—*Continued*

or nationals in unoccupied areas are entered under **Colonization.** Materials on migration from one country to another are entered under **Immigration and emigration.** Materials on the movement of population within a country for permanent settlement are entered under **Migration, Internal.** Materials discussing collectively the colonies ruled by a country are entered under the name of the country with the subdivision *Colonies,* e.g. **Great Britain—Colonies;** etc.

See also **Colonization; Immigration and emigration; Land settlement; National liberation movements; Penal colonies;** also names of countries with the subdivision *Colonies,* e.g. **Great Britain—Colonies; United States—Colonies;** etc.

x Colonialism; Dependencies

xx **Colonization; Imperialism**

Colonies, Space. *See* **Space colonies**

Colonization 325

See note under **Colonies.**

See also **Colonies; Immigration and emigration; Jews—Colonization; Migration, Internal; Penal colonies;** also names of countries with the subdivision *Immigration and emigration,* e.g. **United States—Immigration and emigration;** etc.

x Dependencies

xx **Colonies; History; Immigration and emigration; Imperialism; Land settlement**.

Color 535.6; 752

See also **Dyes and dyeing;** also subjects with the subdivision *Color,* e.g. **Animals—Color; Birds—Color; Man—Color;** etc.; and names of individual colors, e.g. **Red;** etc.

x Colour

xx **Chemistry; Esthetics; Light; Optics; Painting; Photometry**

Color blindness 617.7

xx **Color sense; Vision disorders**

Color etchings. *See* **Color prints**

Color photography 778.6

x Color slides; Photography, Color

xx **Photography**

Color printing 686.2

Use for materials on typographic printing in color. Materials on pictures printed in color from engraved metal, wood or stone are entered under **Color prints.**

See also **Illustration of books; Lithography; Silk screen printing**

xx **Printing**

Color prints (May subdiv. geog. adjective form) **769**

See note under **Color printing.**

See also **Linoleum block printing**

x Block printing; Color etchings; Painting—Color reproductions

140

Color prints, American 769
   x American color prints
Color prints, Japanese 769
   x Japanese color prints; Japanese prints
Color—Psychological aspects 152.1
   x Psychology of color
   xx **Color sense; Psychology**
Color sense 152.1
   See also **Color blindness; Color—Psychological
      aspects**
   xx **Psychology, Physiological; Senses and sensa-
      tion; Vision**
Color slides. *See* **Color photography; Slides (Pho-
      tography)**
Color television 621.388
   x Television, Color
   xx **Television**
Colorado River—Hoover Dam. *See* **Hoover Dam
      (Ariz. and Nev.)**
Coloring books 372.5; E
   x Painting books
   xx **Picture books for children**
Colour. *See* **Color**
Columnists. *See* **Journalists**
COM catalogs. *See* **Library catalogs on microfilm**
Combinations in restraint of trade. *See* **Restraint of
      trade**
Combinations, Industrial. *See* **Trusts, Industrial**
Combustion 541.3; 544; 545; 547.1
   See also **Fire; Fuel; Heat**
   x Spontaneous combustion
   xx **Chemistry; Fire; Heat**
Comedians 791.092; 920
   xx **Actors and actresses; Entertainers**
Comedy 792.2
   x Comic literature
   xx **Drama; Wit and humor**
Comets 523.6
   See also **Halley's comet**
   xx **Astronomy; Solar system**
Comic books, strips, etc. 741.5
   Use for materials on printed comic strips, i.e.
      groups of cartoons in narrative sequence,
      and magazines consisting of comic strips,
      etc.
   See also **Cartoons and caricatures; Chapbooks;**
      also names of comic books, comic strips,
      and comic strip characters
   x Comic strips; Funnies; Humorous pictures
   xx **Cartoons and caricatures; Chapbooks**
Comic literature. *See* **Comedy; Parody; Satire**
Comic opera. *See* **Opera; Operetta**
Comic strips. *See* **Comic books, strips, etc.**
Commandments, Ten. *See* **Ten commandments**
Commencements 371.2
   x Graduation
   xx **Colleges and universities; High schools;
      School assembly programs**
Commentaries, Biblical. *See* **Bible—Commentaries**
Commerce 380-382
   Use for general materials on foreign and domes-
      tic commerce. Materials limited to com-
      merce between states are entered under
      Interstate commerce.

Commerce—*Continued*

See also

Balance of trade	Interstate commerce
Banks and banking	Markets
Barter	Merchants
Business	Monopolies
Business people	Prices
Chambers of commerce	Profit sharing
Competition	Restraint of trade
Contracts	Retail trade
Cooperation	Stock exchange
Exchange	Stocks
Free trade and protection	Tariff
Geography, Commercial	Trade routes
Insurance, Marine	Trademarks
International business en- terprises	Transportation Trusts, Industrial

also names of countries, cities, etc. with the subdivision *Commerce,* e.g. **United States—
Commerce;** etc.; names of articles of commerce, e.g. **Cotton;** etc.; and headings beginning with the word **Commercial**

x Distribution (Economics); Exports; Foreign
trade; Imports; International trade; Trade

xx **Economics; Exchange; Finance; Transportation**

Commerce, Interstate. *See* **Interstate commerce**

Commercial aeronautics. *See* **Aeronautics, Commercial**

Commercial arithmetic. *See* **Business arithmetic**

Commercial art 741.6

Use for general materials on the application of
art to business, i.e. in advertising layout,
fashion design, lettering, etc.

See also **Fashion design; Posters; Textile design**

x Advertising, Art in; Advertising, Pictorial;
Art, Commercial; Art in advertising

xx **Advertising; Art; Drawing**

Commercial aviation. *See* **Aeronautics, Commercial**

Commercial correspondence. *See* **Business letters**

Commercial education. *See* **Business education**

Commercial employees. *See* **Office employees**

Commercial endeavors in space. *See* **Space industrialization**

Commercial geography. *See* **Geography, Commercial**

Commercial law 346

See also

Antitrust law	Debtor and creditor
Arbitration and award	Landlord and tenant
Bankruptcy	Maritime law
Collecting of accounts	Mortgages
Contracts	Negotiable instruments
Corporation law	Restraint of trade

x Business law; Law, Business; Law, Commercial; Mercantile law

xx **Business; Business education; Law; Maritime
law**

Commercial paper. *See* **Negotiable instruments**

Commercial photography. *See* **Photography, Commercial**

Commercial policy 380.1; 381-382
> Use for general materials on the various regulations by which governments seek to protect and increase the commerce of a country such as subsidies, tariffs, free ports, etc.
>
> *See also* **Buy national policy; Commercial products; Free trade and protection; Tariff;** also names of countries with the subdivision *Commercial policy,* e.g. **United States—Commercial policy;** etc.
>
> *x* Government regulation of commerce; Reciprocity; Trade barriers; World economics
>
> *xx* **Economic policy; International economic relations**

Commercial products 380.1
> *See also*

Brand name products	**Manufactures**
Forest products	**Marine resources**
Generic products	**Raw materials**
Geography, Commercial	**Substitute products**

> also names of individual products
>
> *x* Consumer goods; Consumer products; Merchandise; Products, Commercial
>
> *xx* **Commercial policy**

Commercial products recall. *See* **Product recall**

Commercial schools. *See* **Business education**

Commercials, Radio. *See* **Radio advertising**

Commercials, Television. *See* **Television advertising**

Commission government. *See* **Municipal government by commission**

Commission government with city manager. *See* **Municipal government by city manager**

Common cold. *See* **Cold (Disease)**

Common law marriage. *See* **Unmarried couples**

Common market. *See* **European Economic Community**

Common schools. *See* **Public schools**

Commonwealth of England. *See* **Great Britain—History—1642-1660, Civil War and Commonwealth**

Commonwealth of Nations 909; 910
> Use for materials dealing collectively with Great Britain and the self-governing dominions.
>
> *See also* **Great Britain—Colonies**
>
> *x* British Commonwealth of Nations; British Dominions; Dominions, British
>
> *xx* **Great Britain**

Commonwealth, The. *See* **Political science; Republics; State, The**

Communal living. *See* **Collective settlements**

Communes. *See* **Collective settlements**

Communicable diseases 616.9
> *See also*

Bacteriology	**Epidemics**
Biological warfare	**Fumigation**
Disinfection and disinfectants	**Germ theory of disease**
	Immunity

Communicable diseases—*Continued*

  Insects as carriers of dis-   Vaccination
    ease

  also names of communicable diseases, e.g.
    Smallpox; etc.

  x Contagion and contagious diseases; Conta-
    gious diseases; Diseases, Communicable;
    Diseases, Contagious; Diseases, Infectious;
    Infection and infectious diseases; Quaran-
    tine

  xx **Diseases; Epidemics; Immunity; Medicine—**
    Practice; Public health

Communicable diseases—Prevention 614.4

Communication 001.54; 302.2

  Use for general materials on communication in
    its broadest sense, including the spoken and
    written word.

  See also

Books and reading	**Nonverbal communication**
Cybernetics	**Popular culture**
Information science	**Postal service**
Language and languages	**Signals and signaling**
Language arts	**Telecommunication**
Mass media	**Writing**

  x Mass communication

Communication among animals. *See* **Animal com-**
    munication

Communication arts. *See* **Language arts**

Communication satellites. *See* **Artificial satellites**
    in telecommunication

Communication systems, Computer. *See* **Computer**
    networks

Communications relay satellites. *See* **Artificial sat-**
    ellites in telecommunication

Communion. *See* **Lord's Supper**

Communism (May subdiv. geog.) **320.5; 321.9;**
    335.43

  See also **Anticommunist movements; Dialectical**
    materialism; Socialism

  x Bolshevism; Collectivism; Marxism

  xx **Cooperation; Individualism; Labor; Political**
    science; Socialism; Sociology; Syndicalism;
    Totalitarianism

Communism and literature 335.4; 809; 810.9; etc.

  Use same pattern for communism and other
    subjects, e.g. **Communism and religion;** etc.

  x Literature and communism

Communism and religion 261.7; 335.4

  See also **Christianity and economics**

  x Religion and communism

Communism—Soviet Union 335.43;
    947.084-947. 085

  x Russian communism; Soviet Union—
    Communism

Communism—United States 335.43; 973.91-973.92

  x United States—Communism

Communist countries 947

  x Chinese satellite countries; Iron curtain coun-
    tries; People's democracies; Russian satel-
    lite countries; Soviet bloc

Communities, Space. *See* **Space colonies**

Community and libraries. *See* **Libraries and community**

Community and school 370.19

> Use for materials on ways in which the community at large, as distinct from government, may aid the school program.
>
> *See also* **Parents' and teachers' associations**
>
> *x* School and community
>
> *xx* **Community life**

Community antenna television. *See* **Cable television**

Community based residences. *See* **Group homes**

Community centers 374

> *See also* **Playgrounds**
>
> *x* Play centers; Recreation centers; School buildings as recreation centers; Schools as social centers
>
> *xx* **Cities and towns—Civic improvement; Community life; Community organization; Playgrounds; Recreation; Social problems; Social settlements**

Community chests. *See* **Fund raising**

Community churches 254

> Use for materials on local churches that have no denominational affiliations.
>
> *x* Churches, Community; Churches, Undenominational; Nondenominational churches; Undenominational churches; Union churches
>
> *xx* **Christian unity**

Community colleges. *See* **Junior colleges**

Community councils. *See* **Community organization**

Community development (May subdiv. geog.) **307; 361.6**

> *See also* **Agricultural extension work; City planning; Technical assistance**
>
> *x* Neighborhood development
>
> *xx* **Agricultural extension work; City planning; Economic assistance, Domestic; Social change; Technical assistance; Urban renewal; Villages**

Community health services 362

> *xx* **Community services; Public health**

Community life 307

> *See also* **City life; Community and school; Community centers; Community organization**
>
> *x* Neighborhood
>
> *xx* **Associations; City life**

Community organization 307

> *See also* **Community centers; Local government; Urban renewal**
>
> *x* Community councils
>
> *xx* **Community life; Social work; Urban renewal**

Community schools. *See* **Schools**

Community services 361.7; 361.8

> *See also* types of services, e.g. **Community health services;** etc.

Community songbooks. *See* **Songbooks**

Community surveys. *See* **Social surveys**

Community theater.   *See* **Little theater movement**
Compact automobiles.   *See* **Automobiles, Compact**
Compact cars.   *See* **Automobiles, Compact**
Compact disc players   621.389; 789.9
> *x* Audiodisc players; CD players; Digital audio
> disc players; Disc players, Compact; Laser
> disc players; Players, Compact disc
>
> *xx* **Phonograph; Sound—Recording and repro-**
> **ducing**

Companies.   *See* **Corporations**
Companies, Trust.   *See* **Trust companies**
Companion-animal partnership.   *See* **Pet therapy**
Company libraries.   *See* **Corporate libraries**
Company symbols.   *See* **Trademarks**
Comparative anatomy.   *See* **Anatomy, Comparative**
Comparative government   320.3
> *See also* names of countries, cities, etc. with the
> subdivision *Politics and government,* e.g.
> **United States—Politics and government;**
> etc.
>
> *x* Government, Comparative
> *xx* **Political science**

Comparative librarianship   020
> *x* Librarianship, Comparative
> *xx* **International education; Library science**

Comparative linguistics.   *See* **Language and lan-**
guages; Philology, Comparative
Comparative literature.   *See* **Literature, Compara-**
tive
Comparative philology.   *See* **Philology, Compara-**
tive
Comparative physiology.   *See* **Physiology, Compar-**
ative
Comparative psychology.   *See* **Psychology, Compar-**
ative
Comparative religion.   *See* **Christianity and other**
religions; Religions
Comparison of cultures.   *See* **Cross cultural studies**
Compass   538.028; 623.89
> *x* Magnetic needle; Mariner's compass
> *xx* **Magnetism; Navigation**

Compassion.   *See* **Sympathy**
Compensation.   *See* **Pensions; Wages; Workers'**
compensation
Compensatory spending.   *See* **Deficit financing**
Competencies, Functional.   *See* **Life skills**
Competition   338.6
> *See also* **Monopolies; Trusts, Industrial**
> *xx* **Business; Business ethics; Commerce; Monop-**
> **olies; Trusts, Industrial**

Competition, Unfair   338.6
> *See also* **Restraint of trade**
> *x* Fair trade; Unfair competition; Unfair trade
> practices
>
> *xx* **Restraint of trade**

Competitions.   *See* **Contests; Rewards (Prizes, etc.);**
and subjects with the subdivision
Competitions, e.g.
Literature—Competitions; etc.

Complaints against police. *See* **Police—Complaints
     against**
Composers (May subdiv. geog. adjective form)
     780.92; 784.092; 920
   x Songwriters
   xx **Musicians**
Composers, American   780.92; 784.092; 920
   x American composers; United States—
       Composers
Composition (Art)   701
   See also **Architecture—Composition, proportion,
       etc.; Painting**
   x Art—Composition
   xx **Art; Painting**
Composition (Music)   781.6
   See also **Counterpoint; Fugue; Harmony; Instru-
       mentation and orchestration; Music, Popular
       (Songs, etc.)—Writing and publishing; Mu-
       sical accompaniment**
   x Music—Composition; Musical composition;
       Song writing
   xx **Music; Music—Study and teaching; Music—
       Theory**
Composition (Printing). *See* **Typesetting**
Composition (Rhetoric). *See* **Rhetoric;** and names
       of languages with the subdivision
       Composition and exercises, e.g. **English lan-
       guage—Composition and exercises;** etc.
Compost   631.8
   xx **Fertilizers and manures; Soils**
Comprehensive health care organizations. *See*
       Health maintenance organizations
Compressed air   621.5
   x Air, Compressed; Pneumatic transmission
   xx **Cold storage; Foundations; Pneumatics; Power
       (Mechanics)**
Compressed work week. *See* **Hours of labor**
Compulsory education. *See* **Education, Compulsory**
Compulsory labor. *See* **Convict labor; Peonage;
       Slavery**
Compulsory military service. *See* **Military service,
       Compulsory**
Compulsory school attendance. *See* **Education,
       Compulsory; School attendance**
Computer art   709.04; 760
     Use for materials on works of art, mostly draw-
       ings and graphics, created or produced with
       the aid of digital computing or plotting de-
       vices.
   x Art, Computer; Art, Electronic; Computer
       drawing; Drawing, Computer; Drawing,
       Electronic; Electronic art; Electronic draw-
       ing
   xx **Art, Modern—1900-1999 (20th century);
       Computer graphics; Computers**
Computer assisted instruction   371.3
     Use for materials on automated instruction in
       which a student interacts directly with a
       computer.
     See also subjects with the subdivision *Computer*

Computer assisted instruction—*Continued*
> *assisted instruction,* e.g.
>> **Mathematics—Computer assisted instruction;** etc.
> *x* Computer teaching; Computers—Educational use; Education—Automation; Education—Data processing; Teaching, Computer; Teaching—Data processing
> *xx* **Electronic data processing; Programmed instruction**

Computer-based information systems. *See* **Information storage and retrieval systems**

Computer bulletin boards   001.64; 384; *004.6; *384.3
> Use for works on computer services which function like a community bulletin board and allow a remote caller to dial a central calling place to enter and receive messages, access bulletins or notices, etc.
> *x* Electronic bulletin boards
> *xx* **Bulletin boards; Computer networks; Electronic data processing; Electronic mail systems; Online data processing**

Computer communication systems. *See* **Computer networks**

Computer control. *See* **Automation**

Computer crimes   364.1
> *See also* **Privacy, Right of**
> *x* Computer fraud; Fraud, Computer
> *xx* **Crime; Privacy, Right of**

Computer drawing. *See* **Computer art**

Computer fraud. *See* **Computer crimes**

Computer graphics   001.64; *006.6
> Use for materials on the technique for producing line drawings, particularly engineering drawings, by the use of digital computing and plotting devices. Representations may be online or hardcopy. Materials on the use of computer graphics to create artistic designs, drawings, or other works of art are entered under **Computer art.**
> *See also* **Computer art**
> *x* Automatic drafting; Automatic drawing; Drafting, Automatic; Drawing, Automatic; Drawing, Electronic; Electronic drawing; Graphics, Computer
> *xx* **Electronic data processing**

Computer hardware. *See* **Computer peripherals**

Computer input-output equipment. *See* **Computer peripherals**

Computer interfaces   001.64; 621.3819; *004.6; *621.398
> Use for materials on equipment and techniques linking computers to peripheral devices or to other computers.
> *x* Interfaces, Computer
> *xx* **Computer peripherals**

Computer keyboards. *See* **Keyboards (Electronics)**

Computer literacy   001.64; *004
> Use for materials on the ability to use and un-

Computer literacy—*Continued*
derstand computers, including their applications and social implications.
x Literacy, Computer
xx **Computers; Computers and civilization; Literacy**

Computer memory systems. *See* **Computer storage devices**

Computer networks **001.64; 384; *004.6; *384.3**
Use for materials on computer systems consisting of two or more interconnected computing units.
See also **Computer bulletin boards**
x Communication systems, Computer; Computer communication systems; Data networks, Computer; Networks, Computer; Teleprocessing networks
xx **Data transmission systems; Electronic data processing; Information networks; Telecommunication**

Computer peripherals **001.64; 621.3819; *004.7; *621.398**
See also **Computer interfaces; Computer storage devices;** also names of types of computer peripherals, e.g. **Computer terminals; Keyboards (Electronics);** etc.
x Computer hardware; Computer input-output equipment; Input equipment (Computers); Output equipment (Computers)
xx **Computer systems**

Computer program languages. *See* **Programming languages (Computers)**

Computer programming. *See* **Programming (Computers)**

Computer programs **001.64; 651.8; *005.3**
See note under **Computer software.**
See also subjects with the subdivision *Computer programs,* e.g. **Oceanography—Computer programs;** etc.; also names of computer programs
x Programs, Computer
xx **Computer software; Programming (Computers)**

Computer software **001.64; 651.8; *005.1; *005.3**
Use for general materials on computer programs along with documentation such as manuals, diagrams and operating instructions, etc. Materials limited to computer programs are entered under **Computer programs.**
See also **Computer programs; Computer software industry; Computers; Programming (Computers); Programming languages (Computers)**
x Software, Computer
xx **Computer systems; Computers; Programming (Computers)**

Computer software industry **338.4; 381**
xx **Computer software**

Computer storage devices **001.64; 621.38; *004.5; *621.397**

Computer storage devices—*Continued*
> *See also* **Optical storage devices**
>> *x* Computer memory systems; Computers—Memory systems; Computers—Storage devices; Direct access storage devices (Data processing); Random access memories (Data processing); Random access storage devices (Data processing); Rotating memory devices (Data processing); Storage devices, Computer
> *xx* **Computer peripherals**

Computer stored cataloging data. *See* **Machine readable bibliographic data**

Computer systems   001.6; *004
> Use for materials on computers, their peripheral devices, and their operating systems.
> *See also* **Computer peripherals; Computer software; Computers**
> *xx* **Electronic data processing**

Computer teaching. *See* **Computer assisted instruction**

Computer terminals   001.64; 621.3819; *004.7; *621.398
> *x* Terminals, Computer
> *xx* **Computer peripherals**

Computers   001.64; 338.4; 621.3819; *004; *621.39
> Use for materials on modern electronic computers developed after 1945. Materials on present-day calculators and on calculating machines and mechanical computers made before 1945 are entered under **Calculators.**
> *See also* **Calculators; Computer art; Computer literacy; Computer software; Electronic data processing; Home computers; Information storage and retrieval systems;** also names of types and of specific computers, e.g. **Microcomputers; Minicomputers; IBM 7090 (Computer);** etc.
> *x* Automatic computers; Brain, Electronic; Computers, Electronic; Computing machines (Electronic); Electronic brains; Electronic calculating machines; Electronic computers; Mechanical brains
> *xx* **Calculators; Computer software; Computer systems; Cybernetics; Electronic apparatus and appliances**

Computers and children   001.64; *004.01
> *xx* **Children**

Computers and civilization   001.64; 303.4; *004.01
> *See also* **Computer literacy**
> *x* Civilization and computers
> *xx* **Technology and civilization**

Computers—Cartoons and caricatures   338.4; 621.3819; 741.5
> *xx* **Cartoons and caricatures**

Computers—Educational use. *See* **Computer assisted instruction**

Computers, Electronic. *See* **Computers**

Computers—Memory systems. *See* **Computer storage devices**

Computers—Programming. *See* **Programming (Computers)**

Computers—Storage devices. *See* **Computer storage devices**

Computing machines (Electronic). *See* **Computers**

Con artists. *See* **Swindlers and swindling**

Con game. *See* **Swindlers and swindling**

Concentration. *See* **Attention**

Concentration camps 365

> *See also* **Prisoners of war;** also names of individual camps; and names of wars with the subdivision *Prisoners and prisons,* e.g. **World War, 1939-1945—Prisoners and prisons;** etc.
>
> *x* Internment camps
>
> *xx* **Camps (Military); Political crimes and offenses; Prisoners of war**

Concept formation. *See* **Concept learning**

Concept learning 153.1; 370.15

> Use for materials on the process of discovering the distinguishing features of particular concepts and the ensuing ability to use the concepts appropriately.
>
> *x* Concept formation; Learning, Concept
>
> *xx* **Concepts; Learning, Psychology of**

Conception—Prevention. *See* **Birth control**

Concepts 153.2

> *See also* **Concept learning;** also types of concepts and images, e.g. **Size and shape;** etc.
>
> *xx* **Perception**

Concerto 785.6

> *xx* **Musical form**

Concertos 785.6

> *xx* **Musical form; Orchestral music**

Concerts 780.73

> *See also* **Music festivals**
>
> *xx* **Amusements; Music**

Conchology. *See* **Shells**

Conciliation, Industrial. *See* **Arbitration, Industrial**

Concordances. *See* **Bible—Concordances;** and names of authors with the subdivision *Concordances,* e.g. **Shakespeare, William, 1564-1616—Concordances;** etc.

Concrete 691; 693.5

> *See also* **Asphalt; Cement; Pavements**
>
> *xx* **Building materials; Cement; Foundations; Masonry; Plaster and plastering**

Concrete construction 693

> *x* Building, Concrete; Construction, Concrete
>
> *xx* **Architecture; Building**

Concrete, Reinforced 693.5

> *x* Reinforced concrete
>
> *xx* **Building materials**

Concrete—Testing 691

> *xx* **Strength of materials**

Condemnation of land. *See* **Eminent domain**

Condensers (Electricity) 621.31

> *x* Electric condensers
>
> *xx* **Induction coils**

Condensers (Steam) 621.1
    xx **Steam engines**
Condominium timesharing. *See* **Timesharing (Real estate)**
Condominiums 643; 647
    See also **Timesharing (Real estate)**
    xx **Apartment houses**
Conduct of life. *See* **Human behavior**
Conducting 781.6
    Use for materials on orchestral conducting or a combination of orchestral and choral conducting. Materials limited to choral conducting are entered under **Conducting, Choral.**
    See also **Bands (Music); Conducting, Choral; Conductors (Music); Orchestra**
    xx **Bands (Music); Conductors (Music); Music—Study and teaching; Orchestra**
Conducting, Choral 784.9
    See note under **Conducting.**
    See also **Choirs (Music); Choral music; Conductors (Music)**
    x Choral conducting
    xx **Choirs (Music); Choral music; Conducting; Conductors (Music)**
Conductors, Electric. *See* **Electric conductors**
Conductors (Music) 780.92; 920
    See also **Conducting; Conducting, Choral**
    x Bandmasters; Music conductors
    xx **Conducting; Conducting, Choral; Musicians; Orchestra**
Conduits. *See* **Aqueducts**
Confectionery 641.8; 664
    See also **Cake decorating**
    x Candy
    xx **Cookery; Ice cream, ices, etc.**
Confederacies. *See* **Federal government**
Confederate States of America 973.7
    xx **United States—History—1861-1865, Civil War**
Confederation of American colonies. *See* **United States—History—1783-1809**
Conference calls (Teleconferencing). *See* **Teleconferencing**
Conferences. *See* **Congresses and conventions**
Conferences, Parent-teacher. *See* **Parent-teacher conferences**
Confessions of faith. *See* **Creeds**
Confidence game. *See* **Swindlers and swindling**
Configuration (Psychology). *See* **Gestalt psychology**
Conflict, Ethnic. *See* **Ethnic relations**
Conflict of cultures. *See* **Culture conflict**
Conflict of generations 306.8
    See also **Parent and child**
    x Generation gap
    xx **Children and adults; Human relations; Parent and child; Social conflict**
Conflict of interests 351.9
    See also **Corruption in politics; Misconduct in office**

152

Conflict of interests—*Continued*
    xx **Political ethics**
Conflict, Social. *See* **Social conflict**
Conformity 153.8; 302.5
    See also **Dissent; Individuality; Social values**
    x Nonconformity; Social conformity
    xx **Attitude (Psychology); Freedom; Individuality**
Confucianism 299
    xx **Religions**
Congenital diseases. *See* **Medical genetics**
Conglomerate corporations 338.8
    x Business combinations; Consolidation and
        merger of corporations; Corporations, Con-
        glomerate; Industrial mergers; Mergers,
        Conglomerate; Mergers, Corporate
    xx **Corporations**
Congregationalism 285.8
    See also **Calvinism; Puritans; Society of Friends;**
        Unitarianism
    xx **Calvinism; Puritans**
Congress—United States. *See* **United States. Con-**
        gress
Congresses and conventions 060
    See also **International organization; Treaties;**
        also names of specific congresses; and sub-
        jects with the subdivision *Congresses,* e.g.
        World War, 1939-1945—Congresses; etc.
    x Conferences; Conventions (Congresses); Inter-
        national conferences
    xx **Intellectual cooperation; International cooper-**
        ation
Congressional investigations. *See* **Governmental in-**
        vestigations
Conjuring. *See* **Magic**
Conquistadores. *See* **America—Exploration**
Conscience 171; 241
    See also **Freedom of conscience**
    xx **Christian ethics; Duty; Ethics**
Conscientious objectors 343; 355.2
    See also **Military service, Compulsory—Draft re-**
        sisters; Pacifism; also names of wars with
        the subdivision *Conscientious objectors,* e.g.
        World War, 1939-1945—Conscientious ob-
        jectors; etc.
    xx **Freedom of conscience; Military service, Com-**
        pulsory—Draft resisters; Pacifism; War and
        religion
Consciousness 126; 153
    See also **Gestalt psychology; Individuality;**
        Knowledge, Theory of; Personality; Self;
        Subconsciousness
    xx **Apperception; Mind and body; Perception;**
        Psychology; Subconsciousness
Conscription, Military. *See* **Military service, Com-**
        pulsory
Conservation of buildings. *See* **Architecture—**
        Conservation and restoration
Conservation of energy. *See* **Energy conservation;**
        Force and energy
Conservation of forests. *See* **Forests and forestry**

Conservation of natural resources 333.7-333.9; 639.9
    See also **Energy conservation; National parks
        and reserves; Nature conservation; Plant
        conservation; Wildlife conservation**
    x Preservation of natural resources; Resource
        management
    xx **Environment—Government policy; Natural re-
        sources**
Conservation of nature. *See* **Nature conservation**
Conservation of plants. *See* **Plant conservation**
Conservation of power resources. *See* **Energy con-
        servation**
Conservation of the soil. *See* **Soil conservation**
Conservation of water. *See* **Water conservation**
Conservation of wildlife. *See* **Wildlife conservation**
Conservation of works of art, books, etc. *See* sub-
        jects with the subdivision *Conservation and
        restoration,* e.g. **Library resources—
        Conservation and restoration; Painting—
        Conservation and restoration;** etc.
Conservatism 320.5
    See also **Right and left (Political science)**
    xx **Right and left (Political science)**
Consolation. *See* **Sympathy**
Consolidation and merger of corporations. *See*
        Conglomerate corporations
Consolidation of schools. *See* **Schools—
        Centralization**
Consortia, Library. *See* **Library cooperation; Li-
        brary information networks**
Constellations. *See* **Astronomy; Stars**
Constitutional history 342
    See also **Democracy; Monarchy; Political sci-
        ence; Representative government and repre-
        sentation; Republics;** also names of coun-
        tries, states, etc. with the subdivision
        Constitutional history, e.g. **United States—
        Constitutional history;** etc.
    x Constitutional law—History; History, Consti-
        tutional
    xx **Constitutions; History; Political science**
Constitutional law 342
    See also

Administrative law	**Monarchy**
Citizenship	**Political science**
Civil rights	**Proportional representa-**
Constitutions	**tion**
Democracy	**Referendum**
Eminent domain	**Representative government**
Executive power	**and representation**
Federal government	**Republics**
Injunctions	**Separation of powers**
Legislation	**Suffrage**
Legislative bodies	

    also names of countries with the subdivision
        Constitutional law, e.g. **United States—
        Constitutional law;** etc.
    x Law, Constitutional
    xx **Administrative law; Constitutions; Law; Politi-
        cal science**

154

Constitutional law—History. *See* **Constitutional history**

Constitutions 342

    See also **Constitutional history; Constitutional law; Equal rights amendments; United States—Constitution**

    xx **Constitutional law; Political science; Representative government and representation**

Constitutions, State 342

    See also **State governments**

    x State constitutions

    xx **Political science; State governments**

Construction. *See* **Architecture; Building; Engineering**

Construction, Concrete. *See* **Concrete construction**

Construction, House. *See* **House construction**

Construction of roads. *See* **Roads**

Consulates. *See* **Diplomatic and consular service**

Consuls. *See* **Diplomats**

Consultants

    See also types of consultants, e.g. **Educational consultants;** etc.

    x Advisors

    xx **Counseling**

Consultative management. *See* **Management—Employee participation**

Consumer behavior. *See* **Consumers**

Consumer credit 332.7

    See also **Credit unions; Instalment plan; Personal loans**

    x Credit, Consumer

    xx **Banks and banking; Credit; Credit unions; Finance, Personal**

Consumer education 640.73

    Use for materials on the selection and most efficient use of consumer goods and services, including methods of educating the consumer. Materials on the economic theory of consumption are entered under **Consumption (Economics).**

    See also **Buying; Shopping**

    x Buyers' guides, Consumers' guides; Shoppers' guides

    xx **Buying; Home economics; Shopping**

Consumer goods. *See* **Commercial products; Manufactures**

Consumer loans. *See* **Personal loans**

Consumer organizations. *See* **Cooperative societies**

Consumer price indexes 338.5

    x Cost of living indexes; Price indexes, Consumer

    xx **Cost of living; Prices**

Consumer products. *See* **Commercial products; Manufactures**

Consumer protection 343

    Use for materials on governmental and private activities which guard the consumer against dangers to his health, safety, or economic well-being.

    See also **Drugs—Adulteration and analysis; Food**

Consumer protection—*Continued*
      adulteration and inspection; Product recall
    x Consumerism
Consumerism. *See* **Consumer protection**
Consumers 640.73; 658.8
    Use for materials on consumer behavior.
    See also **Young consumers**
    x Consumer behavior
    xx **Shopping**
Consumers' cooperative societies. *See* **Cooperative**
    societies
Consumers' guides. *See* **Consumer education**
Consumption (Economics) 339.4
    See note under **Consumer education.**
    See also **Prices**
    xx **Economics**
Consumption of alcoholic beverages. *See* **Drinking**
    of alcoholic beverages
Consumption of energy. *See* **Energy consumption**
Contact lenses 617.7
    xx **Eyeglasses; Lenses**
Contagion and contagious diseases. *See* **Communi-**
    cable diseases
Contagious diseases. *See* **Communicable diseases**
Contaminated food. *See* **Food contamination**
Contamination of environment. *See* **Pollution**
Contemporary art. *See* **Art, Modern—1900-1999**
    (20th century)
Contests 001.4; 790.1
    See also **Rewards (Prizes, etc.);** also types of con-
        tests and names of specific contests, e.g.
        Olympic games; and subjects with the sub-
        division *Competitions* or *Tournaments,*
        e.g. **Literature—Competitions; Tennis—**
        Tournaments; etc.
    x Competitions
    xx **Rewards (Prizes, etc.)**
Continental drift 551.1
    See also **Plate tectonics**
    x Drifting of continents
    xx **Continents; Geology; Plate tectonics**
Continental shelf 551.4
    See also **Territorial waters**
    xx **Geology; Territorial waters**
Continents 551.4
    See also **Continental drift**
Continuation schools. *See* **Evening and continua-**
    tion schools
Continuing education 374
    See also **Adult education; Evening and continua-**
    tion schools
    x Education, Continuing; Lifelong education;
        Permanent education; Recurrent education
    xx **Adult education; Education**
Contraband trade. *See* **Smuggling**
Contraception. *See* **Birth control**
Contract bridge. *See* **Bridge (Game)**
Contract labor 331.5
    See also **Convict labor; Peonage; Slavery**
    x Indentured servants

Contract labor—*Continued*
   xx **Labor; Peonage**
Contractions. *See* **Abbreviations; Ciphers**
Contracts 346
   See also **Authors and publishers; Liability (Law);**
      also types of contracts, e.g. **Labor contract;**
      Mortgages; Negotiable instruments; etc.;
      and subjects with the subdivision *Contracts*
      and specifications, e.g. **Building—Contracts**
      and specifications; etc.
   x Agreements
   xx **Commerce; Commercial law**
Control. *See* subjects with the subdivision *Control,*
      e.g. **Pests—Control; Weather—Control;** etc.
Conundrums. *See* **Riddles**
Convenience foods 641.3; 664
   Use for materials on prepackaged foods that are
      easy to prepare for eating.
   x Fast foods
   xx **Food**
Conventions (Congresses). *See* **Congresses and con-**
      ventions
Conventions, Political. *See* **Political conventions**
Convents 271; 726
   See also **Abbeys; Monasteries; Religious orders**
      for women
   x Cloisters; Nunneries
   xx **Abbeys; Monasteries**
Conversation 808.56
   x Discussion; Table talk; Talking
   xx **Language and languages**
Conversation in foreign languages. *See* **Languages,**
      Modern—Conversations and phrases; and
      names of foreign languages with the subdivi-
      sion *Conversations and phrases,* e.g. **French**
      language—Conversations and phrases; etc.
Conversion 248.2
   See also **Converts; Grace (Theology); Regenera-**
      tion (Theology)
   xx **Christian life; Evangelistic work; Regeneration**
      (Theology); Theology
Conversion of saline water. *See* **Sea water conver-**
      sion
Conversion of waste products. *See* **Recycling**
      (Waste, etc.); Salvage (Waste, etc.)
Converts 248.2
   Use for materials on converts from one religion
      or denomination to another. For persons af-
      filiating with a particular denomination or
      religion use adjective form, e.g. **Converts,**
      Catholic; etc.
   See also **Converts, Catholic**
   xx **Conversion**
Converts, Catholic 282
   x Catholic Church—Converts; Catholic con-
      verts
   xx **Converts**
Conveying machinery 621.8
   See also **Hoisting machinery**
   x Conveyors

Conveying machinery—*Continued*
>   *xx* **Hoisting machinery; Machinery; Materials handling**
Conveyors. *See* **Conveying machinery**
Convict labor   331.5; 365
>   *See also* **Peonage; Prisons**
>   *x* Compulsory labor; Convicts; Forced labor; Prison labor
>   *xx* **Contract labor; Criminals; Labor; Peonage; Prisons**
Convicts. *See* **Convict labor; Criminals; Penal colonies; Prisoners**
Cook books. *See* **Cookery**
Cookery   641.5
>   Use for general materials on cookery, including American cookery. If limited to a particular area in the U.S. may use geog. subdiv., e.g. **Cookery—Maine; Cookery—Southern States;** etc. For materials on foreign cookery, use geog. subdiv. adjective form, e.g. **Cookery, French;** etc. For types of cookery, use direct form, e.g. **Microwave cookery; Outdoor cookery;** etc.
>   *See also*

Baking	**Food**
Bread	**Luncheons**
Cake	**Menus**
Canning and preserving	**Microwave cookery**
Caterers and catering	**Outdoor cookery**
Confectionery	**Pastry**
Cookery for the sick	**Salads**
Desserts	**Sandwiches**
Diet	**Soups**
Dinners and dining	**Vegetarian cookery**
Flavoring essences	

>   *x* Cook books; Cooking; Gastronomy; Recipes
>   *xx* **Diet; Dinners and dining; Food; Home economics**
Cookery, Barbecue. *See* **Barbecue cookery**
Cookery for institutions, etc. *See* **Cookery, Quantity**
Cookery for large numbers. *See* **Cookery, Quantity**
Cookery for the sick   641.5
>   *See also* **Diet therapy;** also names of diets, e.g. **Salt free diet;** etc.
>   *x* Food for invalids; Invalid cookery
>   *xx* **Cookery; Diet in disease; Nursing; Sick**
Cookery, Microwave. *See* **Microwave cookery**
Cookery—Natural foods   641.5
>   Use same form for materials on the cookery of other foods or types of food.
>   *x* Natural food cookery
>   *xx* **Food, Natural**
Cookery, Outdoor. *See* **Outdoor cookery**
Cookery, Quantity   641.5
>   *x* Cookery for institutions, etc.; Cookery for large numbers; Quantity cookery
Cookery—Vegetables   641.6
>   *xx* **Vegetables; Vegetarian cookery**
Cookery, Vegetarian. *See* **Vegetarian cookery**

Cooking. *See* **Cookery**
Cooking utensils. *See* **Household equipment and supplies**
Cooling appliances. *See* **Refrigeration and refrigerating machinery**
Cooperation 334
> Use for general materials on the theory and history of cooperation and the cooperative movement. Materials dealing specifically with cooperative enterprises are entered under **Cooperative societies.**
>
> *See also*

Agriculture, Cooperative	**Labor unions**
Banks and banking, Cooperative	**Profit sharing**
Communism	**Savings and loan associations**
Cooperative societies	**Socialism**
International cooperation	

> *x* Cooperative distribution; Distribution, Cooperative; Rochdale system
>
> *xx* **Associations; Commerce; Economics; Profit sharing**

Cooperation, Intellectual. *See* **Intellectual cooperation**
Cooperation, International. *See* **International cooperation**
Cooperation, Library. *See* **Library cooperation**
Cooperative agriculture. *See* **Agriculture, Cooperative**
Cooperative banks. *See* **Banks and banking, Cooperative**
Cooperative building associations. *See* **Savings and loan associations**
Cooperative distribution. *See* **Cooperation; Cooperative societies**
Cooperative living. *See* **Collective settlements**
Cooperative societies 334; 658.8
> See note under **Cooperation.**
> *See also* types of cooperative societies, e.g. **Banks and banking, Cooperative; Credit unions; Savings and loan associations;** etc.
>
> *x* Consumer organizations; Consumers' cooperative societies; Cooperative distribution; Cooperative stores; Distribution, Cooperative; Societies, Cooperative; Stores
>
> *xx* **Cooperation; Corporations; Societies**

Cooperative stores. *See* **Cooperative societies**
Coping behavior. *See* **Adjustment (Psychology); Life skills**
Copper engraving. *See* **Engraving**
Copperwork 673; 739
> *xx* **Metalwork**

Copy writing. *See* **Advertising copy**
Copybooks. *See* **Handwriting**
Copying processes and machines 686.4
> *See also* names of specific processes, e.g. **Xerography;** etc.
>
> *x* Duplicating processes; Photocopying machines; Reproduction processes; Reprography

Copyright 341.7; 346.04
> May be subdivided by topic, e.g.
>> Copyright—Books; etc.
> *See also* **Authors and publishers; Fair use (Copyright); Publishers and publishing**
> *x* Intellectual property; International copyright; Literary property; Property, Literary
> *xx* **Authors and publishers; Authorship; Publishers and publishing**

Copyright—Books 341.7; 346.04
> *x* Books—Copyright

Coral reefs and islands 551.4
> *x* Atolls
> *xx* **Geology; Islands**

Corals 563; 593.6
> *xx* **Invertebrates; Marine animals**

Core curriculum. *See* **Education—Curricula;** and types of education and schools with the subdivision *Curricula,* e.g. **Library education—Curricula;** etc.

Corn 633.1
> *x* Maize
> *xx* **Agriculture; Forage plants; Grain**

Corn—Therapeutic use 615.5; 633.1
> *xx* **Diet therapy; Therapeutics**

Coronary heart diseases. *See* **Heart—Diseases**

Corporate farming. *See* **Agribusiness**

Corporate libraries 027.6
> See note under **Business libraries.**
> *x* Company libraries; Industrial libraries; Libraries, Company; Libraries, Corporate; Libraries, Industrial
> *xx* **Special libraries**

Corporate patronage of the arts. *See* **Art patronage**

Corporate symbols. *See* **Trademarks**

Corporation law 346
> *See also* **Public service commissions; Public utilities; Trusts, Industrial**
> *x* Law, Corporation
> *xx* **Commercial law; Corporations; Law; Monopolies; Public utilities**

Corporations 338.7; 658.1
> *See also*

Conglomerate corporations	**Municipal ownership**
Cooperative societies	**Public service commissions**
Corporation law	**Public utilities**
Government ownership	**Trust companies**
International business enterprises	**Trusts, Industrial**

> *x* Companies
> *xx* **Business; Public utilities; Stocks; Trusts, Industrial**

Corporations—Accounting 657; 658.1
> *xx* **Accounting; Bookkeeping**

Corporations—Art patronage. *See* **Art patronage**

Corporations, Conglomerate. *See* **Conglomerate corporations**

Corporations—Farming operations. *See* **Agribusiness**

Corporations—Finance 658.1
    x Capitalization (Finance)
Corporations, International. *See* **International business enterprises**
Corporations—Management. *See* **Industrial management**
Corporations, Multinational. *See* **International business enterprises**
Corpulence. *See* **Obesity**
Correctional institutions (May subdiv. geog.) **365**
    See also **Halfway houses;** also types of correctional institutions, e.g. **Prisons; Reformatories;** etc.
    x Penal institutions
Correspondence. *See* **Business letters; Letter writing; Letters;** and subjects with the subdivision *Correspondence,* e.g.
      Authors—Correspondence; etc.
Correspondence schools and courses 374
    x Home education; Home study courses; Self-instruction
    xx **Education; Technical education; University extension**
Corrosion and anticorrosives 620.1
    See also **Paint**
    x Anticorrosive paint; Rust; Rustless coatings
    xx **Chemistry, Technical; Paint**
Corrupt practices. *See* subjects with the subdivision *Corrupt practices,* e.g.
      Adoption—Corrupt practices; Sports—Corrupt practices; etc.
Corruption in politics 324; 351.9; 352
    See also **Campaign funds; Lobbying and lobbyists; Misconduct in office; Whistle blowing;** also names of specific incidents, e.g. **Watergate Affair, 1972-1974;** etc.
    x Boss rule; Graft in politics; Political corruption; Political scandals; Politics—Corrupt practices; Spoils system
    xx **Conflict of interests; Lobbying and lobbyists; Misconduct in office; Political crimes and offenses; Political ethics; Politics, Practical**
Corruption in sports. *See* **Sports—Corrupt practices**
Corruption, Police. *See* **Police—Corrupt practices**
Corsairs. *See* **Pirates**
Cosmetic surgery. *See* **Surgery, Plastic**
Cosmetics 646.7; 668
    See also **Perfumes**
    x Makeup (Cosmetics); Toilet preparations
    xx **Beauty shops; Costume**
Cosmic biology. *See* **Space biology**
Cosmic chemistry. *See* **Space chemistry**
Cosmic rays 539.7
    x Millikan rays
    xx **Nuclear physics; Radiation; Radioactivity; Space environment**
Cosmobiology. *See* **Space biology**
Cosmochemistry. *See* **Space chemistry**
Cosmogony. *See* **Universe**

Cosmogony, Biblical.   *See* **Creation**
Cosmography.   *See* **Universe**
Cosmology.   *See* **Universe**
Cosmology, Biblical.   *See* **Creation**
Cosmonauts.   *See* **Astronauts**
Cost accounting   657
    See also **Efficiency, Industrial**
    xx **Accounting; Bookkeeping**
Cost of living   339.4
    See also **Budgets, Household; Consumer price in-**
        dexes; Prices; Saving and thrift; Subsistence
        economy; Wages
    x Food, Cost of; Household finances; Living,
        Cost of
    xx **Economics; Home economics; Labor; Prices;**
        Saving and thrift; Social conditions; Stan-
        dard of living; Wages
Cost of living indexes.   *See* **Consumer price indexes**
Cost of medical care.   *See* **Medical care—Costs**
Costs.   *See* subjects with the subdivision *Costs,* e.g.
    Medical care—Costs; etc.
Costume (May subdiv. geog.)   **391**
    Use for descriptive and historical materials on
        the costume of particular countries, or peri-
        ods, or peoples, and for materials on fancy
        dress and theatrical costumes. Materials
        dealing with clothing from a practical stand-
        point, including the art of dress, are entered
        under **Clothing and dress.** Materials de-
        scribing the prevailing mode or style of
        dress are entered under **Fashion.**
    See also

Arms and armor	**Hats**
Clothing and dress	**Makeup, Theatrical**
Cosmetics	**Millinery**
Fans	**Uniforms, Military**
Fashion	**Wigs**

    also classes of people with the subdivision
        Costume, e.g. **Children—Costume;** etc.
    x Acting—Costume; Fancy dress; Style in dress;
        Theatrical costume
    xx **Clothing and dress; Decorative arts; Ethnol-**
        ogy; Fashion; Manners and customs
Costume design.   *See* **Fashion design**
Costume jewelry.   *See* **Jewelry**
Costume, Military.   *See* **Uniforms, Military**
Cottage industry.   *See* **Home business**
Cottage industry, Electronic.   *See* **Telecommuting**
Cottages.   *See* **Houses**
Cotton   633.5
    See also **Fibers**
    xx **Botany, Economic; Commerce; Fibers; Yarn**
Cotton manufacture   677
    xx **Textile industry**
Councils and synods   262
    See also names of special councils and synods,
        e.g. **Vatican Council (2nd : 1962-1965);** etc.
    x Church councils; Ecumenical councils; Synods
    xx **Christianity; Church history**

Counseling 361.3; 371.4

  Use for materials dealing with the principles or practices used in various types of guidance work—student, employment, veterans, personnel.

  See also **Consultants; Crisis centers; Interviewing; School counseling; Social case work; Vocational guidance;** also types of counseling, e.g. **Educational counseling; Health counseling; Hotlines (Telephone counseling); Marriage counseling;** etc.; and classes of persons with the subdivision *Counseling of,* e.g. **Elderly—Counseling of;** etc.

  x Guidance; Peer counseling

  xx **Helping behavior; Interviewing; Personnel management; Psychology, Applied; Social case work; Welfare work in industry**

Counter culture 306

  See also **Bohemianism; Collective settlements**

  x Alternative lifestyle; Counterculture; Escape lifestyle; Nonconformity; Subculture

  xx **Collective settlements; Lifestyles; Social conditions**

Counter-Reformation. *See* **Reformation**

Counterculture. *See* **Counter culture**

Counterespionage. *See* **Intelligence service**

Counterfeits and counterfeiting 332.9; 364.1

  See also **Credit card crimes**

  xx **Coinage; Crime; Forgery; Impostors and imposture; Money; Swindlers and swindling**

Counterintelligence. *See* **Intelligence service**

Counterpoint 781.4

  See also **Fugue**

  xx **Composition (Music); Music—Theory**

Counterreformation. *See* **Reformation**

Counting 513; E

  Use for materials on counting, including counting books, etc. Materials on the systems of numeration and the theory of numeration are entered under **Numeration.** Materials on the psychology of numeration are entered under **Number concept.**

  See also **Number games; Numeration**

  x Counting books

  xx **Arithmetic—Study and teaching; Numeration**

Counting books. *See* **Counting**

Country and western music. *See* **Country music**

Country churches. *See* **Rural churches**

Country houses. *See* **Architecture, Domestic**

Country life (May subdiv. geog.) **307.7; 630.1**

  Use for descriptive, popular and literary materials on living in the country. Materials dealing with social organization and conditions in rural communities are entered under **Sociology, Rural.**

  See also **Agriculture—Societies; Farm life; Farmers; Outdoor life; Sociology, Rural**

  x Rural life

  xx **Farm life; Outdoor life; Sociology, Rural**

Country life—United States 630.1
  x United States—Country life
Country music 784.5
  x Country and western music; Hillbilly music;
      Western and country music
  xx Folk music—United States; Music, Popular
      (Songs, etc.)
Country schools. *See* Rural schools
County agricultural agents 630.7
  xx Agricultural extension work; Agriculture—
      Study and teaching
County government 352
  x County officers
  xx Local government
County libraries 027.4
  x Libraries, County
  xx Library extension; Public libraries; Regional
      libraries
County officers. *See* County government
County planning. *See* Regional planning
Coupons (Retail trade) 659
  xx Advertising
Coups d'état. *See* Revolutions
Courage 179
  See also Fear; Heroes and heroines; Morale
  x Bravery; Heroism
  xx Heroes and heroines; Human behavior
Courses of study. *See* Education—
      Curricula; and types of education and
      schools with the subdivision *Curricula,* e.g.
      Library education—Curricula; etc.
Court life. *See* Courts and courtiers
Court martial. *See* Courts martial and courts of in-
      quiry
Courtesy 177; 395
  See also Human behavior
  x Manners; Politeness
  xx Etiquette; Human behavior
Courtiers. *See* Courts and courtiers
Courting. *See* Dating (Social customs)
Courts (May subdiv. geog.) 347
  See also Arbitration and award; Courts martial
      and courts of inquiry; Criminal procedure;
      Judges; Jury; Justice, Administration of; Ju-
      venile courts
  x Judiciary
  xx Judges; Justice, Administration of; Law
Courts and courtiers 390; 929.7
  See also Kings, queens, rulers, etc.
  x Court life; Courtiers
  xx Kings, queens, rulers, etc.; Manners and cus-
      toms
Courts martial and courts of inquiry 343
  See also Military law
  x Court martial; Military courts
  xx Courts; Military law; Trials
Courts—United States 347.73
  x Federal courts; United States—Courts
Courtship. *See* Dating (Social customs)
Courtship of animals. *See* Animals—Courtship

Covens. *See* **Witches**

Coverlets. *See* **Bedspreads; Quilts**

Cowboys. *See* **Cowhands**

Cowgirls. *See* **Cowhands**

Cowhands 390; 978
 See also **Rodeos**
  x Cowboys; Cowgirls; Gauchos
  xx **Frontier and pioneer life; Ranch life**

Cowhands—Songs and music 784.7
  xx **Music; Songs**

Cows. *See* **Cattle**

Cows—Diseases. *See* **Cattle—Diseases**

Crabs 565; 595.3
  xx **Crustacea; Shellfish**

Cradle songs. *See* **Lullabies**

Craft festivals. *See* **Craft shows**

Craft shows 745
  x Craft festivals; Shows, Craft
  xx **Exhibitions; Festivals; Handicraft**

Crafts (Arts). *See* **Arts and crafts movement; Hand-icraft**

Cranes, derricks, etc. 621.8
  x Derricks
  xx **Hoisting machinery**

Cranks. *See* **Eccentrics and eccentricities**

Crayon drawing 741.2
 See also **Pastel drawing**
  x Blackboard drawing
  xx **Drawing; Pastel drawing; Portrait painting**

Creation 213; 233
 See also

Earth	**Man**
Evolution	**Mythology**
Geology	**Theology**
God	**Universe**

  x Cosmogony, Biblical; Cosmology, Biblical
  xx **Earth; Evolution; Geology; God; Man; Natural theology; Religion and science; Universe**

Creation (Literary, artistic, etc.) 153.3
 See also **Creative ability; Creative writing**
  x Inspiration
  xx **Creative ability; Genius; Imagination; Intellect; Inventions**

Creation—Study and teaching 213; 233
 See also Evolution—Study and teaching; Fundamentalism and education
  x Creationism
  xx **Evolution—Study and teaching; Fundamentalism and education**

Creationism. *See* **Creation—Study and teaching**

Creative ability 153.3; 701; 801
 See also **Creation (Literary, artistic, etc.); Creative thinking**
  x Creativity
  xx **Ability; Creation (Literary, artistic, etc.); Creative thinking**

Creative activities 372.5; 372.8
  Use for materials on play or work activities for children that initiate new interests, facilitate the seeing of new relationships in thinking

Creative activities—*Continued*
and learning, and result in some form of expressional art, i.e. painting, cooking, drama, etc.

x Activities curriculum

xx **Amusements; Education, Elementary; Handicraft; Kindergarten**

Creative movement. *See* **Movement education**

Creative thinking 153.4

See also **Creative ability**

xx **Creative ability**

Creative writing 808

x Writing (Authorship)

xx **Authorship; Creation (Literary, artistic, etc.); Language arts**

Creativity. *See* **Creative ability**

Creatures, Imaginary. *See* **Animals, Mythical**

Credibility. *See* **Truthfulness and falsehood**

Credit 332.7

See also

Agricultural credit	**Debts, Public**
Banks and banking	**Instalment plan**
Collecting of accounts	**Loans**
Consumer credit	**Mortgages**
Credit cards	**Negotiable instruments**
Debtor and creditor	

x Bills of credit; Letters of credit

xx **Banks and banking; Business; Debtor and creditor; Economics; Finance; Money**

Credit, Agricultural. *See* **Agricultural credit**

Credit card crimes 364.1

x Fraud, Credit card

xx **Counterfeits and counterfeiting; Swindlers and swindling**

Credit cards 332.7

xx **Credit**

Credit, Consumer. *See* **Consumer credit**

Credit unions 334

Use for materials on cooperative associations that make small loans to its members at low interest rates.

See also **Consumer credit**

xx **Banks and banking, Cooperative; Consumer credit; Cooperative societies; Loans; Personal loans**

Creeds 238

See also **Apostles' Creed; Catechisms; Nicene Creed**

x Confessions of faith; Faith, Confessions of

xx **Catechisms; Church history; Theology**

Cremation 393; 614

See also **Funeral rites and ceremonies**

x Burial; Incineration; Mortuary customs

xx **Funeral rites and ceremonies; Public health; Sanitation**

Creoles 305.8; 976

Crests. *See* **Heraldry**

Crewelwork 746.44

xx **Embroidery**

Crime (May subdiv. geog.) **364**

All types of crime are not included in this list but are to be added as needed.

Crime—*Continued*

    See also

Assassination	**Parole**
Atrocities	**Police**
Capital punishment	**Prisons**
Computer crimes	**Prostitution**
Counterfeits and counter-	**Punishment**
feiting	**Racketeering**
Crime prevention	**Reformatories**
Crimes without victims	**Riots**
Criminal law	**Sex crimes**
Criminals	**Smuggling**
Forgery	**Swindlers and swindling**
Justice, Administration of	**Treason**
Juvenile delinquency	**Trials**
Lynching	**Victims of crime**
Murder	**Vigilance committees**
Organized crime	

    x Crimes; Criminology; Felony; Vice

    xx **Criminal justice, Administration of; Justice, Administration of; Police; Prisons; Punishment; Social ethics; Social problems; Trials**

Crime and narcotics. *See* **Narcotics and crime**

Crime prevention 364.4

    See also **Criminal psychology**

    x Prevention of crime

    xx **Crime**

Crime syndicates. *See* **Organized crime; Racketeering**

Crime—United States 364

    x United States—Crime

Crime victims. *See* **Victims of crime**

Crimean War, 1853-1856 947

    x Great Britain—History—1853-1856, Crimean War; Russo-Turkish War, 1853-1856

Crimes. *See* **Crime**

Crimes against public safety. *See* **Offenses against public safety**

Crimes against the person. *See* **Offenses against the person**

Crimes, Military. *See* **Military offenses**

Crimes, Political. *See* **Political crimes and offenses**

Crimes, Sex. *See* **Sex crimes**

Crimes without victims 364.1

    See also names of crimes, e.g. **Drug abuse; Gambling;** etc.

    x Non-victim crimes; Nonvictim crimes; Victimless crimes

    xx **Crime; Criminal law**

Criminal assault. *See* **Rape**

Criminal investigation 363.2

    See also

Criminals—Identification	**Missing children**
Detectives	**Missing persons**
Eavesdropping	**Police**
Fingerprints	**Wiretapping**
Medical jurisprudence	

    xx **Detectives; Police**

Criminal justice, Administration of 345

    See also **Crime; Pardon; Parole; Prisons;**

Criminal justice, Administration of—*Continued*
      Punishment
    x Administration of criminal justice
    xx **Criminal law**
Criminal law 345
    See also

Adoption—Corrupt practices
Capital punishment
Crimes without victims
Criminal justice, Administration of
Criminal procedure
Jury
Kidnapping
Medical jurisprudence
Military offenses

Misconduct in office
Offenses against public safety
Offenses against the person
Poisons and poisoning
Probation
Punishment
Trials
Vigilance committees

    also names of crimes, e.g. **Murder;** etc.
    x Law, Criminal; Misdemeanors (Law); Penal codes; Penal law
    xx **Crime; Criminal procedure; Law; Prisons; Punishment**
Criminal procedure 345
    See also **Criminal law**
    xx **Courts; Criminal law**
Criminal psychology 364.3
    See also **Psychology, Pathological**
    x Psychology, Criminal
    xx **Crime prevention; Psychology, Pathological**
Criminals 364.1
    See also **Convict labor; Penal colonies; Pirates; Prisoners; Robbers and outlaws; Swindlers and swindling**
    x Convicts; Delinquents; Gangs; Reform of criminals
    xx **Crime**
Criminals—Drug use 362.2; 364.3
    x Drug use; Drugs and criminals
    xx **Drug abuse; Drug addicts; Drugs; Narcotic habit**
Criminals—Identification 363.2
    See also **Fingerprints**
    xx **Criminal investigation; Identification**
Criminology. *See* **Crime**
Crippled children. *See* **Physically handicapped children**
Crippled people. *See* **Physically handicapped**
Crisis centers 361.3; 362
    See also types of crisis centers, e.g. **Hotlines (Telephone counseling;** etc.
    x Crisis intervention centers
    xx **Counseling; Hotlines (Telephone counseling); Social work**
Crisis counseling. *See* **Hotlines (Telephone counseling)**
Crisis intervention centers. *See* **Crisis centers**
Crisis intervention telephone service. *See* **Hotlines (Telephone counseling)**

Crisis management 658.4
    xx **Management; Problem solving**
Critical thinking 153.4; 160
    Use for materials on thinking that is based on
        the careful evaluation of premises and evi-
        dence and that comes to conclusions as ob-
        jectively as possible through the consider-
        ation of all pertinent factors and the use of
        logical procedures.
    xx **Decision making; Logic; Problem solving;**
        Reasoning; Thought and thinking
Criticism 801
    Use for materials on the history, principles,
        methods, etc. of criticism in general and of
        literary criticism in particular. Criticism in a
        specific field is entered under the subject in
        variant forms as listed below. Criticism of
        the work of an individual author, artist,
        composer, etc. is entered under his/her
        name as subject; only in the case of volumi-
        nous authors is it necessary to add the sub-
        division *Criticism, interpretation, etc.* Criti-
        cism of a single work is entered under the
        person's name followed by the title of the
        work.
    See also **Art criticism; Bible—Criticism, interpre-**
        tation, etc.; Books—Reviews; Dramatic criti-
        cism; Shakespeare, William, 1564-1616—
        Criticism, interpretation, etc.; Style, Liter-
        ary; also literature, film, and music subjects
        with the subdivision *History and criticism,*
        e.g. **English literature—History and criti-**
        cism; English poetry—History and criticism;
        Music—History and criticism; etc.
    x Appraisal of books; Books—Appraisal; Evalu-
        ation of literature; Literary criticism; Liter-
        ature—Evaluation
    xx **Esthetics; Literature; Literature—History and**
        criticism; Rhetoric; Style, Literary
Cro-Magnons 573.3
    x Cromagnons
    xx **Man, Prehistoric**
Crocheting 746.43
    See also **Beadwork; Lace and lace making**
Crockery. *See* **Pottery**
Crocodiles 597.98
    See also **Alligators**
    xx **Reptiles**
Cromagnons. *See* **Cro-Magnons**
Crop dusting. *See* **Aeronautics in agriculture**
Crop reports. *See* **Agriculture—Statistics**
Crop rotation 631.4
    x Crops, Rotation of; Rotation of crops
    xx **Agriculture**
Crop spraying. *See* **Aeronautics in agriculture**
Crops. *See* **Farm produce**
Crops, Rotation of. *See* **Crop rotation**
Cross cultural conflict. *See* **Culture conflict**
Cross cultural psychology. *See* **Ethnopsychology**

Cross cultural studies 155.8; 306
>   Use for materials on the systematic comparison
>   of sociological, psychological, anthropologi-
>   cal, etc. aspects of two or more cultural
>   groups, either within the same country or in
>   different countries.
>   *x* Comparison of cultures; Intercultural studies;
>   Transcultural studies
>   *xx* **Culture; Social sciences**

Cross-examination. *See* **Witnesses**

Crossword puzzles 793.73
>   *xx* **Puzzles; Word games**

Crowds 302.3
>   *See also* **Protests, demonstrations, etc.; Riots—
>   Control; Social psychology**
>   *x* Mobs
>   *xx* **Riots; Social psychology**

CRTs. *See* **Cathode ray tubes**

Crucifixion of Christ. *See* **Jesus Christ—
>   Crucifixion**

Crude oil. *See* **Petroleum**

Cruelty 179
>   *See also* **Atrocities**
>   *x* Brutality
>   *xx* **Ethics**

Cruelty to animals. *See* **Animal abuse**

Cruelty to children. *See* **Child abuse**

Crusades 909.07
>   *See also* **Chivalry**
>   *xx* **Chivalry; Church history—600-1500, Middle
>   Ages; Middle Ages—History**

Crustacea 565; 595.3
>   *See also* names of shellfish, e.g. **Crabs; Lobsters;**
>   etc.
>   *xx* **Invertebrates; Shellfish**

Cryobiology 574.19
>   *See also* **Cold—Physiological effect**
>   *x* Freezing; Low temperature biology
>   *xx* **Biology; Cold; Low temperatures**

Cryogenic internment. *See* **Cryonics**

Cryogenic surgery. *See* **Cryosurgery**

Cryogenics. *See* **Low temperatures**

Cryonics 621.5
>   *x* Burial; Cryogenic internment; Freezing of hu-
>   man bodies; Human cold storage

Cryosurgery 617
>   *x* Cryogenic surgery
>   *xx* **Cold—Therapeutic use; Surgery**

Cryotherapy. *See* **Cold—Therapeutic use**

Cryptography 652
>   *See also* **Ciphers**
>   *x* Secret writing
>   *xx* **Ciphers; Signs and symbols; Writing**

Crystal gazing. *See* **Divination**

Crystalline rocks. *See* **Rocks**

Crystallization. *See* **Crystallography**

Crystallography 548
>   *See also* **Mineralogy**
>   *x* Crystallization; Crystals
>   *xx* **Chemistry, Physical and theoretical;**

Crystallography—*Continued*
    Petrology; Rocks; Science
Crystals. *See* **Crystallography**
Cub Scouts. *See* **Boy Scouts**
Cuba 972.91
    xx **Islands**
Cuba—History 972.91
Cuba—History—1958-1959, Revolution 972.91
Cuba—History—1959- 972.91
Cuba—History—1961, Invasion 972.91
    x Bay of Pigs invasion; Operation Pluto; Pluto
        operation
Cube root 513
    xx **Arithmetic**
Cubic measurement. *See* **Volume (Cubic content)**
Cubism 709.04; 759.06
    See also **Postimpressionism (Art)**
    xx **Painting; Postimpressionism (Art)**
Cults 291.9
    See also **Ancestor worship; Sects**
    x Religious cults
    xx **Religions; Sects**
Cultural anthropology. *See* **Ethnology**
Cultural change. *See* **Social change**
Cultural exchange programs. *See* **Exchange of per-
        sons programs**
Cultural relations 306; 341.7
    See also **Exchange of persons programs**
    x Intercultural relations
    xx **Intellectual cooperation; International cooper-
        ation; International relations**
Culturally deprived. *See* **Socially handicapped**
Culturally deprived children. *See* **Socially handi-
        capped children**
Culturally handicapped. *See* **Socially handicapped**
Culturally handicapped children. *See* **Socially
        handicapped children**
Culture 306; 909
    Use for general discussions of refinement in
        manners, taste, etc. and the intellectual con-
        tent of civilization. Materials limited to the
        culture of individual nations are entered un-
        der names of countries with the subdivi-
        sions *Civilization* or *Social life and cus-
        toms.*
    See also

Acculturation	**Education**
Biculturalism	**Humanism**
Civilization	**Learning and scholarship**
Cross cultural studies	**Popular culture**

    x Intellectual life
    xx **Civilization; Education; Learning and scholar-
        ship**
Culture conflict 155.8; 306
    x Conflict of cultures; Cross cultural conflict;
        Culture shock; Future shock
    xx **Ethnic relations; Ethnopsychology; Race rela-
        tions**
Culture contact. *See* **Acculturation**
Culture, Popular. *See* **Popular culture**

Culture shock. *See* **Culture conflict**
Curates. *See* **Clergy**
Curiosities and wonders 001.9
   See also **Eccentrics and eccentricities; Monsters;**
      also subjects with the subdivision
      Miscellanea, e.g. **Medicine—Miscellanea;**
      etc.
   x Enigmas; Facts, Miscellaneous; Miscellaneous
      facts; Oddities; Trivia; Wonders
Currency. *See* **Money**
Currency devaluation. *See* **Monetary policy**
Current events 909.82
      Use for materials on the study and teaching of
      current events. Periodicals and yearbooks
      devoted to the events themselves are en-
      tered under **History—Periodicals; History—**
      Yearbooks.
   xx **History, Modern—Study and teaching**
Currents, Alternating. *See* **Electric currents, Alter-**
      nating
Currents, Electric. *See* **Electric currents**
Currents, Ocean. *See* **Ocean currents**
Curricula (Courses of study). *See* **Education—**
      Curricula; and types of education and
      schools with the subdivision *Curricula,* e.g.
      Library education—Curricula; Colleges and
      universities—Curricula; etc.
Curriculum materials centers. *See* **Instructional**
      materials centers
Curtains. *See* **Drapery**
Custody kidnapping. *See* **Kidnapping, Parental**
Custody of children. *See* **Child custody**
Custom duties. *See* **Tariff**
Customs, Social. *See* **Manners and customs;** and
      names of ethnic groups, countries, cities,
      etc. with the subdivision *Social life and cus-*
      toms, e.g. **Indians of North America—**
      Social life and customs; Jews—Social life
      and customs; United States—Social life and
      customs; etc.
Customs (Tariff). *See* **Tariff**
Cybernetics 001.53
   See also **Bionics; Computers; System analysis;**
      Systems engineering
   x Automatic control; Mechanical brains
   xx **Calculators; Communication; Electronics; Sys-**
      tem theory
Cycles. *See* **Periodicity**
Cycles, Business. *See* **Business cycles**
Cycles, Motor. *See* **Motorcycles**
Cycling. *See* **Bicycles and bicycling; Motorcycles;**
      Tricycles
Cyclones 551.5
      Materials on the cyclonic storms of the West In-
      dies are entered under **Hurricanes.** Storms
      of the China Seas and the Philippines are
      entered under **Typhoons.**
   xx **Hurricanes; Meteorology; Storms; Tornadoes;**
      Winds
Cyclopedias. *See* **Encyclopedias and dictionaries**

Cyclotron 539.7; 621.48

   x Atom smashing; Magnetic resonance accelerator

   xx **Atoms; Nuclear physics; Transmutation (Chemistry)**

Cytology. *See* **Cells**

Czechoslovakia 943.7

Czechoslovakia—History—1968- , Intervention 943.7

   x Russian intervention in Czechoslovakia; Soviet invasion of Czechoslovakia

D.D.T. (Insecticide) 668

   x DDT (Insecticide); Dichloro-diphenyltrichloroethane

   xx **Insecticides**

D Day. *See* **Normandy (France), Attack on, 1944**

D.N.A. *See* **DNA**

Daily readings (Spiritual exercises). *See* **Devotional calendars**

Dairies. *See* **Dairying**

Dairy cattle 636.2

   See also names of breeds of dairy cattle, e.g. **Holstein-Friesian cattle;** etc.

   x Milch cattle

   xx **Cattle; Dairying**

Dairy farming. *See* **Dairying**

Dairy products 637; 641.3

   See also **Dairying;** also names of dairy products, e.g. **Butter, Cheese, Milk,** etc.

   x Products, Dairy

   xx **Dairying**

Dairying (May subdiv. geog.) 636.2; 637

   Use for materials on the production and marketing of milk, usually cows' milk and its products and for general materials on the care of dairy cattle, their breeding, feeding, management, and milking.

   See also **Cattle; Dairy cattle; Dairy products; Milk**

   x Dairies; Dairy farming

   xx **Agriculture; Cattle; Dairy products; Home economics; Livestock**

Dams 627

   See also names of dams, e.g. **Hoover Dam (Ariz. and Nev.);** etc.

   xx **Civil engineering; Floods—Control; Hydraulic structures; Irrigation; Rivers; Water power; Water supply**

Dance music 781; 785.42

   See also **Jazz music; Music, Popular (Songs, etc.)**

   x Big band music

   xx **Dancing; Instrumental music; Music**

Dancers 793.3092; 920

   See also types of dancers, e.g. **Ballet dancers;** etc.

   xx **Entertainers**

Dancing (May subdiv. geog.) 793.3

   See also **Aerobics; Dance music;** also types of dances and dancing, e.g. **Ballet; Break dancing; Folk dancing; Modern dance; Tap danc-**

Dancing—*Continued*
ing; etc.
xx **Amusements; Etiquette; Performing arts**
Dancing, Aerobic. *See* **Aerobics**
Dancing—United States 793.3
See also **Folk dancing, American**
x United States—Dancing
Dangerous animals 591.6
See also **Animal attacks; Poisonous animals**
xx **Animals; Wildlife**
Dangerous materials. *See* **Hazardous substances**
Dangerous occupations. *See* **Occupations, Dangerous**
Danish language 439.8
May be subdivided like **English language.**
xx **Norwegian language; Scandinavian languages**
Danish literature 839.8
May use same subdivisions and names of literary forms as for **English literature.**
xx **Scandinavian literature**
Dark Ages. *See* **Middle Ages**
Darkroom technique in photography. *See* **Photography—Processing**
Darwinism. *See* **Evolution**
Data networks, Computer. *See* **Computer networks**
Data processing. *See* **Electronic data processing; Information storage and retrieval systems;** and subjects with the subdivision *Data processing,* e.g. **Banks and banking—Data processing;** etc.
Data storage and retrieval systems. *See* **Information storage and retrieval systems**
Data transmission systems 001.64; 621.38; *004.6; *621.39
See also **Computer networks; Information networks; Library information networks; Teletext systems; Video telephone**
x Transmission of data
xx **Electronic data processing; Telecommunication**
Date etiquette. *See* **Dating (Social customs)**
Dates, Historical. *See* **Chronology, Historical**
Dating, Radiocarbon. *See* **Radiocarbon dating**
Dating (Social customs) 306.7; 392
See also **Love**
x Courting; Courtship; Date etiquette
xx **Etiquette; Love; Manners and customs**
Daughters and fathers. *See* **Fathers and daughters**
Daughters and mothers. *See* **Mothers and daughters**
Day 529
See also **Night**
xx **Chronology; Night; Time**
Day care centers. *See* **Child care centers**
Day dreams. *See* **Fantasy**
Day nurseries. *See* **Child care centers**
Day of Atonement. *See* **Yom Kippur**
Days. *See* **Birthdays; Fasts and feasts; Festivals; Holidays;** and names of special days, e.g. **Christmas; Memorial Day;** etc.

DDT (Insecticide). *See* **D.D.T. (Insecticide)**
Dead Sea scrolls 221.4; 229; 296.1
 x Qumran texts
Dead, Worship of the. *See* **Ancestor worship**
Deaf 362.4
 See also **Hearing ear dogs**
 x Hearing impaired
 xx **Physically handicapped**
Deaf, Dogs for. *See* **Hearing ear dogs**
Deaf—Education 371.91
 x Education of the deaf
 xx **Education; Vocational education; Vocational
  guidance**
Deaf—Institutional care 362.4
 x Asylums; Charitable institutions; Homes (In-
  stitutions)
Deaf—Means of communication 419-/
 x Finger alphabet; Lip reading; Sign language
 xx **Nonverbal communication**
Deafness 362.4; 617.8
 See also **Ear; Hearing; Hearing aids**
 xx **Hearing**
Death 128; 236
 See also

Bereavement	**Longevity**
Brain death	**Mortality**
Future life	**Right to die**
Heaven	**Terminal care**
Hell	**Terminally ill**

 xx **Biology; Eschatology; Life; Mortality**
Death masks. *See* **Masks (Sculpture)**
Death, Mercy. *See* **Euthanasia**
Death notices. *See* **Obituaries**
Death penalty. *See* **Capital punishment**
Death rate. *See* **Mortality; Vital statistics**
Death, Right of. *See* **Right to die**
Death with dignity. *See* **Right to die**
Deaths, Registers of. *See* **Registers of births, etc.**
Debates and debating 808.53
 See also **Discussion groups; Parliamentary prac-
  tice; Radio addresses, debates, etc.**
 x Argumentation; Discussion; Speaking
 xx **Public speaking; Rhetoric**
Debtor and creditor 332.7; 346
 Use for economic and statistical materials about
  debt as well as for legal materials involving
  debtor and creditor.
 See also **Bankruptcy; Collecting of accounts;
  Credit**
 xx **Commercial law; Credit**
Debts, Public (May subdiv. geog.) **336.3**
 See also **Bonds; Deficit financing;** also names of
  wars with the subdivision *Finance,* e.g.
  World War, 1939-1945—Finance; etc.
 x National debts; Public debts; State debts; War
  debts
 xx **Bonds; Credit; Deficit financing; Economics;
  Finance; Loans**

Debts, Public—United States 336.73
  x United States—Debts, Public; United
      States—Public debts
Decalogue. *See* **Ten commandments**
Deceit. *See* **Fraud**
Decentralization of schools. *See* **Schools—
      Decentralization**
Deceptive advertising. *See* **Advertising, Fraudulent**
Decimal system 389; 513
  xx **Numeration; Weights and measures**
Decision making 153.8; 302.3; 658.4
  See also **Choice (Psychology); Critical thinking;
      Problem solving**
  xx **Choice (Psychology); Game theory; Problem
      solving**
Decks (Domestic architecture). *See* **Patios**
Declamations, Musical. *See* **Monologues with mu-
      sic**
Declaration of independence (U.S.). *See* **United
      States—Declaration of independence**
Decoration and ornament (May subdiv. geog. adjec-
      tive form, e.g. **Decoration and ornament,
      Mexican;** etc.) **745; 745.4**
  Use for materials dealing with the forms and
      styles of decoration in various fields of fine
      arts or applied art; the history of such styles
      of ornament, such as Empire, Louis XV,
      etc.; and with the various manifestations in
      different countries or periods, such as Chi-
      nese or Renaissance. Materials limited to
      the decoration of houses are entered under
      Interior design. Consider also **Decorative
      arts** and **Handicraft.**
  See also

Alphabets	**Ironwork**
Antiques	**Jewelry**
Art objects	**Leather work**
Arts and crafts movement	**Lettering**
Bronzes	**Metalwork**
Carpets	**Monograms**
China painting	**Mosaics**
Decoupage	**Mural painting and deco-**
Design	**ration**
Egg decoration	**Needlework**
Embroidery	**Painting**
Enamel and enameling	**Plants in art**
Flower arrangement	**Pottery**
Furniture	**Sculpture**
Garden ornaments and	**Show windows**
furniture	**Stencil work**
Gems	**Stucco**
Glass painting and stain-	**Table setting and decora-**
ing	**tion**
Holiday decorations	**Tapestry**
Illumination of books and	**Terra cotta**
manuscripts	**Textile design**
Illustration of books	**Wood carving**
Interior design	

  x Art, Decorative; Arts, Decorative; Decorative
      art; Decorative design; Decorative painting;

Decoration and ornament—*Continued*
　　　　Design, Decorative; Ornament; Painting,
　　　　Decorative
　　xx **Art; Decorative arts**
Decoration and ornament, American 745; 745.4
　　x American decoration and ornament; United
　　　　States—Decoration and ornament
Decoration and ornament, Architectural 729
　　x Architectural decoration and ornament; Ar-
　　　　chitecture—Decoration and ornament
　　xx **Architecture**
Decoration Day. *See* **Memorial Day**
Decoration, Interior. *See* **Interior design**
Decorations, Holiday. *See* **Holiday decorations**
Decorations of honor 355.1; 929.8
　　See also **Heraldry; Insignia; Medals;** also names
　　　　of medals
　　x Badges of honor; Emblems
　　xx **Heraldry; Insignia; Medals**
Decorative art. *See* **Decoration and ornament**
Decorative arts (May subdiv. geog.) **745**
　　Use for general materials on the various applied
　　　　art forms having some utilitarian as well as
　　　　decorative purpose, including furniture,
　　　　woodwork, silverware, glassware, ceramics,
　　　　needlework, the decoration of buildings, etc.
　　　　Consider also **Decoration and ornament** and
　　　　Handicraft.
　　See also

Antiques	**Glassware**
Art metalwork	**Interior design**
Art objects	**Jewelry**
Arts and crafts movement	**Lacquer and lacquering**
Calligraphy	**Leather work**
Ceramics	**Mosaics**
Costume	**Needlework**
Decoration and ornament	**Porcelain**
Decoupage	**Pottery**
Enamel and enameling	**Rugs**
Fabrics	**Silverware**
Folk art	**Tapestry**
Furniture	**Woodwork**

　　x Applied arts; Art industries and trade; Arts,
　　　　Applied; Arts, Decorative; Arts, Minor; Mi-
　　　　nor arts
　　xx **Art; Folk art**
Decorative arts—United States 680; 745
　　x United States—Decorative arts
Decorative design. *See* **Decoration and ornament**
Decorative metalwork. *See* **Art metalwork**
Decorative painting. *See* **Decoration and ornament**
Decoupage 745.54
　　xx **Decoration and ornament; Decorative arts; Pa-**
　　　　per crafts
Decoys (Hunting) 745.593; 799.2
　　x Bird decoys (Hunting)
　　xx **Hunting; Shooting**
Deduction (Logic). *See* **Logic**
Deep diving vehicles. *See* **Submersibles**
Deep sea diving. *See* **Diving, Submarine**

Deep sea drilling (Petroleum).   *See* **Oil well drilling, Submarine**
Deep sea engineering.   *See* **Ocean engineering**
Deep sea mining.   *See* **Ocean mining**
Deep sea technology.   *See* **Oceanography**
Deep sea vehicles.   *See* **Submersibles**
Deep submergence vehicles.   *See* **Submersibles**
Deer 599.73
   See also **Reindeer**
   xx **Game and game birds**
Defamation.   *See* **Libel and slander**
Defective speech.   *See* **Speech disorders**
Defective vision.   *See* **Vision disorders**
Defectors, Military.   *See* **Desertion, Military**
Defense, Civil.   *See* **Civil defense**
Defense (Law).   *See* **Actions and defenses**
Defense policy.   *See* **Military policy**
Defenses, Air.   *See* **Air defenses**
Defenses, National.   *See* **Industrial mobilization;**
          and names of countries with the subdivision
          Defenses, e.g. **United States—Defenses;**
          etc.
Defenses, Radar.   *See* **Radar defense networks**
Deficit financing (May subdiv. geog.) **336.3**
   See also **Debts, Public**
   x Compensatory spending; Deficit spending
   xx **Debts, Public; Finance**
Deficit spending.   *See* **Deficit financing**
Defoliants.   *See* **Herbicides**
Degrees, Academic 378
   x Academic degrees; College degrees; Doctors'
          degrees; Honorary degrees; University de-
          grees
   xx **Colleges and universities**
Degrees of latitude and longitude.   *See* **Geodesy;**
          Latitude; Longitude
Dehydrated foods.   *See* **Food, Dried**
Dehydrated milk.   *See* **Milk, Dried**
Deism 211
   See also **Atheism; Christianity; Free thought;**
          God; Positivism; Rationalism; Theism
   xx **Atheism; Christianity; God; Rationalism; Reli-**
          gion; Theism; Theology
Deities.   *See* **Gods and goddesses**
Dejection.   *See* **Depression, Mental**
Delinquency, Juvenile.   *See* **Juvenile delinquency**
Delinquents.   *See* **Criminals; Juvenile delinquency**
Delusions.   *See* **Hallucinations and illusions; Super-**
          stition; Witchcraft
Demineralization of salt water.   *See* **Sea water con-**
          version
Democracy 321.4; 321.8
   See also

Aristocracy	**Referendum**
Equality	**Representative government**
Federal government	**and representation**
Freedom	**Republics**
Middle classes	**Socialism**
Monarchy	**Suffrage**

   x Popular government; Self-government

Democracy—*Continued*

 xx **Aristocracy; Constitutional history; Constitutional law; Equality; Federal government; Monarchy; Political science; Representative government and representation; Republics**

Democratic Party (U.S.) 324.2736

 xx **Political parties**

Demoniac possession 133.4

 See also **Devil; Exorcism**

 xx **Devil; Exorcism**

Demonology 133.4

 See also **Apparitions; Charms; Devil; Exorcism; Occult sciences; Superstition; Witchcraft**

 x Evil spirits; Spirits

 xx **Apparitions; Devil; Exorcism; Ghosts; Occult sciences; Superstition; Witchcraft**

Demonstrations for Black civil rights—United States. *See* **Blacks—Civil rights**

Demonstrations (Protest). *See* **Protests, demonstrations, etc.**

Demountable houses. *See* **Prefabricated houses**

Denatured alcohol. *See* **Alcohol, Denatured**

Denominational schools. *See* **Church schools**

Denominations, Religious. *See* **Sects;** and names of particular denominations and sects, e.g. **Presbyterian Church;** etc.

Dentistry 617.6

 See also **Teeth**

 x Medicine, Dental

 xx **Teeth**

Deoxyribonucleic acid. *See* **DNA**

Department stores 658.8

 See also **Selling**

 x Stores

 xx **Business; Retail trade**

Dependencies. *See* **Colonies; Colonization**

Dependent children. *See* **Child welfare; Orphans**

Depression, Mental 157; 616.85

 x Dejection; Depressive psychoses; Melancholia; Mental depression; Mentally depressed

 xx **Neuroses; Psychology, Pathological**

Depressions, Economic 338.5

 x Business depressions; Economic depressions; Panics, Economic; Recessions, Economic

 xx **Business cycles; Economics**

Depressive psychoses. *See* **Depression, Mental**

Deprogramming. *See* **Brainwashing**

Derailments. *See* **Railroads—Accidents**

Dermatitis. *See* **Skin—Diseases**

Derricks. *See* **Cranes, derricks, etc.**

Desalination of water. *See* **Sea water conversion**

Desalting of water. *See* **Sea water conversion**

Descent. *See* **Genealogy; Heredity**

Description. *See* names of cities with the subdivision *Description,* e.g. **Chicago (Ill.)—Description;** etc.; names of modern countries, states, and regions with the subdivision *Description and travel,* e.g. **United States—Description and travel;** etc.; and names of ancient countries with the subdivi-

179

Description—*Continued*

sion *Description and geography,* e.g.
Greece—Description and geography; etc.

Descriptive geometry. *See* **Geometry, Descriptive**

Desegregated schools. *See* **School integration**

Desegregation in education. *See* **School integration**

Desert animals 591.52

See also names of desert animals, e.g. **Camels;** etc.

xx **Animals; Deserts; Wildlife**

Desert plants 581.5

See also names of desert plants, e.g. **Cactus;** etc.

xx **Botany—Ecology; Deserts; Plants**

Desertion. *See* **Desertion and nonsupport; Desertion, Military; Runaway adults**

Desertion and nonsupport 173; 306.8

See also **Child support; Runaway adults**

x Abandonment of family; Desertion; Nonsupport

xx **Divorce; Domestic relations**

Desertion, Military (May subdiv. geog.) **355.1**

See also **Amnesty; Military service, Compulsory—Draft resisters;** also names of wars with the subdivision *Desertions,* e.g. **World War, 1939-1945—Desertions;** etc.

x Army desertion; Defectors, Military; Desertion; Military desertion

xx **Military offenses; Military service, Compulsory—Draft resisters**

Desertion, Military—United States 355.1

x United States. Army—Desertions

Deserts 551.4

See also **Desert animals; Desert plants**

Design 745.4

Use for materials on the theory of design.

See also **Fashion design; Interior design: Pattern making; Textile design**

xx **Decoration and ornament; Pattern making**

Design, Architectural. *See* **Architecture—Details**

Design, Decorative. *See* **Decoration and ornament**

Design, Industrial 745.2

See also **Human engineering; Systems engineering**

x Art, Applied; Industrial design

Design, Interior. *See* **Interior design**

Design, System. *See* **System design**

Designed genetic change. *See* **Genetic engineering**

Designs, Architectural. *See* **Architecture—Designs and plans**

Designs, Floral. *See* **Flower arrangement**

Desoxyribonucleic acid. *See* **DNA**

Desserts 641.8

See also names of desserts, e.g. **Ice cream, ices, etc.;** etc.

xx **Caterers and catering; Cookery; Dinners and dining**

Destiny. *See* **Fate and fatalism**

Destitution. *See* **Poverty**

Destruction of Jews (1933-1945). *See* **Holocaust, Jewish (1933-1945)**

Details, Architectural. *See* **Architecture—Details**
Detective stories. *See* **Mystery and detective stories**
Detectives 351.74; 363.2; 920
    See also **Criminal investigation; Police; Secret service**
    xx **Criminal investigation; Police; Secret service**
Detergent pollution of rivers, lakes, etc. 363.7; 628.1
    x Water—Detergent pollution
    xx **Detergents, Synthetic; Water—Pollution**
Detergents, Synthetic 668
    See also **Detergent pollution of rivers, lakes, etc.**
    x Synthetic detergents
    xx **Cleaning compounds; Soap**
Determinism and indeterminism. *See* **Free will and determinism**
Deuterium oxide 546
    x Heavy water; Water—Heavy water
Devaluation of currency. *See* **Monetary policy**
Developing countries 330.9
    Use for comprehensive materials on those countries having relatively low per capita incomes in comparison with North American and Western European countries.
    This heading may be subdivided by those topical subdivisions used under countries, regions, etc. and may be used as a geographic subdivision, e.g **Education—Developing countries;** etc.
    See also **Economic assistance; States, New; Technical assistance**
    x Fourth World; Less developed countries; Third World; Underdeveloped areas
    xx **Economic assistance; Economic conditions; Industrialization; Technical assistance**
Developing countries—Commerce 338.91; 382
Development. *See* **Embryology; Evolution; Modernization**
Devices (Heraldry). *See* **Heraldry; Insignia; Symbolism**
Devil 235
    See also **Demoniac possession; Demonology**
    x Satan
    xx **Demoniac possession; Demonology; Folklore**
Devil's Triangle. *See* **Bermuda Triangle**
Devotion. *See* **Prayer; Worship**
Devotional calendars 242
    x Christian devotional calendars; Daily readings (Spiritual exercises); Devotional exercises (Daily readings)
    xx **Calendars; Devotional literature**
Devotional exercises 242; 248.3
    Use for general materials on acts of private prayer and private worship and for materials on religious practices other than the corporate worship of a congregation. Materials on the religious literature used as aids in devotional exercises are entered under **Devotional literature.**
    See also **Meditation; Prayer**
    x Devotions; Family devotions; Family prayers;

Devotional exercises—*Continued*
>   Theology, Devotional
>   *xx* **Prayer; Worship**

Devotional exercises (Daily readings). *See* **Devotional calendars**

Devotional literature 242
>   See note under **Devotional exercises.**
>   *See also* **Devotional calendars; Hymns; Liturgies; Meditations**
>   *xx* **Christian literature; Literature**

Devotions. *See* **Devotional exercises**

Dewey Decimal Classification. *See* **Classification, Dewey Decimal**

Diagnosis 616
>   *See also* **Body temperature; Pain; Pathology; Prenatal diagnosis**
>   *x* Symptoms
>   *xx* **Medicine—Practice; Pathology**

Diagrams, Statistical. *See* **Statistics—Graphic methods**

Dialectical materialism 335.4
>   *x* Historical materialism
>   *xx* **Communism; Socialism**

Dialectics. *See* **Logic**

Dialects. *See* names of languages with the subdivision *Dialects,* e.g. **English language— Dialects;** etc.

Diamonds 553
>   *xx* **Carbon; Precious stones**

Diaries. *See* **Autobiographies**

Dichloro-diphenyl-trichloroethane. *See* **D.D.T. (Insecticide)**

Dictators 321.9092; 920
>   *xx* **Heads of state; Kings, queens, rulers, etc.; Totalitarianism**

Dictionaries. *See* **Encyclopedias and dictionaries**

Dictionaries, Biographical. *See* **Biography— Dictionaries**

Dictionaries, Classical. *See* **Classical dictionaries**

Dictionaries, Multilingual. *See* **Polyglot dictionaries**

Dictionaries, Picture. *See* **Picture dictionaries**

Dictionaries, Polyglot. *See* **Polyglot dictionaries**

Dies (Metalworking) 621.9; 671.2
>   *xx* **Metalwork**

Diesel automobiles. *See* **Automobiles, Diesel**

Diesel engines 621.43
>   *xx* **Engines; Gas and oil engines**

Diet 613.2
>   *See also*

Beverages	**Menus**
Cookery	**Nutrition**
Digestion	**Reducing**
Eating customs	**School children—Food**
Food, Dietetic	**Vegetarianism**

>   also names of diets, e.g. **Salt free diet;** etc.
>
>   *x* Dietetics
>
>   *xx* **Cookery; Digestion; Health; Hygiene; Nutrition; Reducing**

Diet in disease 615; 615.8

> *See also* **Cookery for the sick; Diet therapy;** also
> names of diets, e.g. **Salt free diet;** etc.
> *x* Dieting
> *xx* **Therapeutics**

Diet—Therapeutic use. *See* **Diet therapy**

Diet therapy 615.8

> *See also* names of diseases with the subdivision
> *Diet therapy,* e.g. **Cancer—Diet therapy;**
> etc.; also names of food with the subdivi-
> sion *Therapeutic use,* e.g.
> **Corn—Therapeutic use;** etc.
> *x* Diet—Therapeutic use; Invalid cookery
> *xx* **Cookery for the sick; Diet in disease; Thera-**
> **peutics**

Dietary fiber. *See* **Food—Fiber content**

Dietetic food. *See* **Food, Dietetic**

Dietetics. *See* **Diet**

Dieting. *See* **Diet in disease; Reducing**

Diets, Reducing. *See* **Reducing**

Digestion 574.1; 612

> *See also* **Diet; Food; Indigestion; Nutrition**
> *xx* **Diet; Nutrition; Physiological chemistry;**
> **Physiology; Stomach**

Digital audio disc players. *See* **Compact disc play-**
ers

Digital circuits. *See* **Digital electronics**

Digital electronics 621.381; *005.72

> *x* Digital circuits
> *xx* **Electronics**

Dimension, Fourth. *See* **Fourth dimension**

Diners. *See* **Restaurants, bars, etc.**

Dinners and dining 642

> *See also* **Carving (Meat, etc.); Cookery; Desserts;**
> **Food; Menus**
> *x* Banquets; Eating; Gastronomy
> *xx* **Caterers and catering; Cookery; Entertaining;**
> **Etiquette; Food; Menus**

Dinosaurs 567.9

> *xx* **Prehistoric animals; Reptiles, Fossil**

Dioptrics. *See* **Refraction**

Diphtheria 616.9

> *xx* **Children—Diseases; Diseases**

Diplomacy 327.2; 341.3

> *See also* **Diplomatic and consular service; Diplo-**
> **mats; Treaties;** also names of countries with
> the subdivision *Foreign relations,* e.g.
> **United States—Foreign relations;** etc.
> *xx* **Diplomatic and consular service; International**
> **relations**

Diplomatic and consular service 341.3

> *See also* **Diplomacy; Diplomats;** also names of
> countries with the subdivision *Diplomatic*
> *and consular service,* e.g. **United States—**
> **Diplomatic and consular service;** etc.
> *x* Consulates; Embassies; Foreign service; Lega-
> tions
> *xx* **Diplomacy; Diplomats; International relations**

Diplomats 327.2092; 920

> *See also* **Diplomatic and consular service; States-**

Diplomats—*Continued*
    men
      x Ambassadors; Consuls; Ministers (Diplomatic
        agents)
    xx **Diplomacy; Diplomatic and consular service;**
        International relations; Politicians; States-
        men
Dipsomania. *See* **Alcoholism**
Diptera. *See* **Flies; Mosquitoes**
Direct access storage devices (Data processing). *See*
    Computer storage devices
Direct current machinery. *See* **Electric machine-**
    ry—Direct current
Direct legislation. *See* **Referendum**
Direct primaries. *See* **Primaries**
Direct selling 658.8
    See also **Mail-order business; Telemarketing**
    xx **Marketing; Retail trade**
Direct taxation. *See* **Income tax; Taxation**
Direction (Motion pictures). *See* **Motion pictures—**
    Production and direction
Direction sense 152.1; 796.5
    See also **Navigation**
    x Orientation; Orienteering; Sense of direction
    xx **Hiking**
Direction (Theater). *See* **Theater—Production and**
    direction
Directories
    Use for materials about directories and for bibli-
      ographies of directories.
    See also subjects and names of countries, cities,
      etc. with the subdivision *Directories,* e.g.
      Junior colleges—Directories; Physicians—
      Directories; United States—Directories; etc.
Directories—Telephone. *See* names of cities with
    the subdivision *Directories—Telephone,* e.g.
    Chicago (Ill.)—Directories—Telephone;
    etc.
Directors and producers. *See* specific medium
    phrase heading, e.g. **Motion picture produc-**
    ers and directors; etc.
Directory, French, 1795-1799. *See* **France—**
    History—1789-1799, Revolution
Dirigible balloons. *See* **Airships**
Disability insurance. *See* **Insurance, Accident; In-**
    surance, Health
Disability, Learning. *See* **Learning disabilities**
Disability, Reading. *See* **Reading disability**
Disabled. *See* **Handicapped**
Disadvantaged. *See* **Socially handicapped**
Disadvantaged children. *See* **Socially handicapped**
    children
Disarmament. *See* **Arms control**
Disaster preparedness. *See* **Disaster relief**
Disaster relief 363.3
    See also **Civil defense; Food relief**
    x Disaster preparedness; Emergency prepared-
      ness; Emergency relief
    xx **Charities; Civil defense; Public welfare**

Disasters 904

See also types of disasters, e.g. **Accidents; Fires; Natural disasters; Railroads—Accidents; Shipwrecks;** etc.

x Catastrophes

xx **Accidents**

Disc players, Compact. *See* **Compact disc players**

Disciples, Twelve. *See* **Apostles**

Discipline of children. *See* **School discipline**

Discography. *See* **Sound recordings;** and subjects and names of persons with the subdivision *Discography,* e.g.

Music—Discography; Shakespeare, William, 1564-1616—Discography; etc.

Discount stores 381; 658.8

x Stores

xx **Retail trade**

Discoverers. *See* **Discoveries (in geography); Explorers**

Discoveries (in geography) 910

See also

America—Exploration	**Northeast Passage**
Antarctic regions	**Northwest Passage**
Arctic regions	**Scientific expeditions**
Explorers	**Voyages and travels**

also names of countries with the subdivision *Description and travel,* e.g. **United States—Description and travel;** etc.

x Discoverers; Discoveries, Maritime; Explorations; Maritime discoveries; Navigators

xx **Adventure and adventurers; Explorers; Geography; History; Voyages and travels**

Discoveries (in science). *See* **Inventions; Patents; Science**

Discoveries, Maritime. *See* **Discoveries (in geography)**

Discrimination 177; 305

Use for general materials on discrimination by race, religion, sex, age, social status, or other factors. Reverse discrimination is subsumed under **Discrimination** and headings beginning with the word **Discrimination.**

See also **Age discrimination; Civil rights; Minorities; Race discrimination; Segregation; Sex discrimination; Toleration**

xx **Ethnic relations; Human relations; Minorities; Prejudices; Race relations; Segregation; Social problems; Social psychology; Toleration**

Discrimination, Age. *See* **Age discrimination**

Discrimination in education 370.19

Use same pattern for discrimination in other areas.

See also **Segregation in education**

x Education, Discrimination in

xx **Race discrimination; Segregation in education**

Discrimination in employment 331.1

See also **Affirmative action programs; Age and employment; Equal pay for equal work;** also names of groups of people with the subdivision *Employment,* e.g.

Discrimination in employment—*Continued*
        Blacks—Employment; Men—Employment; Women—Employment; etc.
  x E.E.O.; EEO; Employment discrimination; Equal employment opportunity; Equal opportunity in employment; Fair employment practice; Job discrimination; Right to work
Discrimination in housing 363.5
  x Fair housing; Housing, Discrimination in; Open housing; Segregation in housing
Discrimination in public accommodations 305
  x Public accommodations, Discrimination in; Segregation in public accommodations
Discrimination, Racial. *See* **Race discrimination**
Discrimination, Sex. *See* **Sex discrimination**
Discs, Optical. *See* **Optical storage devices**
Discs, Sound. *See* **Sound recordings**
Discs, Video. *See* **Videodiscs**
Discussion. *See* **Conversation; Debates and debating**
Discussion groups 374
  x Forums (Discussions); Great books program; Group discussion; Panel discussions
  xx **Debates and debating**
Disease germs. *See* **Bacteriology; Germ theory of disease**
Disease (Pathology). *See* **Pathology**
Diseases 614.4; 616
  See also **Epidemics; Health; Medicine—Practice; Mental illness; Pathology; Sick;** also names of diseases and groups of diseases, e.g. **AIDS (Disease); Diphtheria; Communicable diseases;** etc.; and subjects with the subdivision *Diseases,* e.g. **Animals—Diseases; Children—Diseases; Skin—Diseases;** etc.
  x Illness; Sickness
  xx **Health; Medicine; Sick**
Diseases and pests. *See* **Agricultural pests; Bacteriology, Agricultural; Fungi; Household pests; Insects, Injurious and beneficial; Parasites; Plants—Diseases;** and names of individual pests, e.g. **Locusts;** etc.; and names of crops, etc. with the subdivision *Diseases and pests,* e.g. **Fruit—Diseases and pests;** etc.
Diseases, Communicable. *See* **Communicable diseases**
Diseases, Contagious. *See* **Communicable diseases**
Diseases, Industrial. *See* **Occupational diseases**
Diseases, Infectious. *See* **Communicable diseases**
Diseases, Mental. *See* **Mental illness; Psychology, Pathological**
Diseases, Occupational. *See* **Occupational diseases**
Diseases of animals. *See* **Animals—Diseases**
Diseases of children. *See* **Children—Diseases**
Diseases of occupation. *See* **Occupational diseases**
Diseases of plants. *See* **Plants—Diseases**
Diseases of the blood. *See* **Blood—Diseases**
Diseases of women. *See* **Women—Diseases**
Diseases—Prevention. *See* **Medicine, Preventive**
Diseases, Tropical. *See* **Tropical medicine**

Dishes. *See* **Glassware; Porcelain; Pottery**
Dishonesty. *See* **Honesty**
Disinfection and disinfectants 614.4
>   *See also* **Antiseptics; Fumigation**
>   *x* Germicides
>   *xx* **Antiseptics; Bacteriology; Chemistry, Medical and pharmaceutical; Communicable diseases; Fumigation; Hygiene; Public health; Sanitation**

Disney World (Fla.). *See* **Walt Disney World (Fla.)**
Disobedience. *See* **Obedience**
Displaced persons. *See* **Refugees; Refugees, Political;** and names of wars with the subdivision *Refugees,* e.g. **World War, 1939-1945—Refugees;** etc.
Disposal of refuse. *See* **Refuse and refuse disposal**
Disputes, Labor. *See* **Labor disputes**
Dissent 322.4
>   *x* Nonconformity; Protest
>   *xx* **Conformity**

Dissertations, Academic 378
>   Use for materials about theses and dissertations.
>   *x* Academic dissertations; Doctoral theses; Theses
>   *xx* **Colleges and universities**

Distillation 641.2; 663
>   *See also* **Alcohol; Essences and essential oils; Liquors and liqueurs**
>   *x* Stills
>   *xx* **Alcohol; Liquors and liqueurs**

Distribution, Cooperative. *See* **Cooperation; Cooperative societies**
Distribution (Economics). *See* **Commerce; Marketing**
Distribution of animals and plants. *See* **Biogeography**
Distribution of wealth. *See* **Economics; Wealth**
District libraries. *See* **Regional libraries**
District nurses. *See* **Nurses**
District schools. *See* **Rural schools**
Districting (in city planning). *See* **Zoning**
Dividends. *See* **Securities; Stocks**
Divination 133.3
>   *See also*

Astrology	**Oracles**
Clairvoyance	**Palmistry**
Dreams	**Prophecies (Occult sciences)**
Fortune telling	
Occult sciences	**Superstition**

>   *x* Crystal gazing; Necromancy; Soothsaying
>   *xx* **Clairvoyance; Occult sciences; Oracles; Prophecies (Occult sciences); Supernatural; Superstition**

Divine healing. *See* **Christian Science; Miracles; Spiritual healing**
Diving 797.2
>   *See also* **Scuba diving; Skin diving**
>   *xx* **Swimming; Water sports**

Diving, Scuba. *See* **Scuba diving**
Diving, Skin. *See* **Skin diving**

Diving, Submarine 627
 See also **Scuba diving; Skin diving; Underwater
  exploration**
 x Deep sea diving; Submarine diving
 xx **Oceanography—Research; Underwater exploration**
Divinity of Christ. *See* **Jesus Christ—Divinity**
Division of powers. *See* **Separation of powers**
Divorce 173; 306.8; 346.01
 See also **Children of divorced parents; Desertion
  and nonsupport; Marriage; Marriage—
  Annulment; Remarriage**
 x Separation (Law)
 xx **Domestic relations; Family; Marriage; Marriage—Annulment; Men—Social condi-
  tions; Social problems; Women—Social
  conditions**
Divorce counseling. *See* **Divorce mediation**
Divorce mediation 362.8
 See also **Child custody; Child support**
 x Divorce counseling; Mediation, Divorce
 xx **Marriage counseling**
DNA 574.87
 See also **Recombinant DNA**
 x D.N.A.; Deoxyribonucleic acid; Desoxyri-
  bonucleic acid
 xx **Cells; Heredity; Nucleic acids**
DNA cloning. *See* **Clones and cloning; Molecular
  cloning**
DNA synthesizer. *See* **Genetic engineering, Auto-
  mated**
Docks 386; 387.1; 627
 See also **Harbors**
 xx **Harbors; Hydraulic structures; Marinas**
Doctoral theses. *See* **Dissertations, Academic**
Doctors. *See* **Physicians**
Doctors' degrees. *See* **Degrees, Academic**
Doctrinal theology. *See* **Theology, Doctrinal**
Doctrine of fairness (Broadcasting). *See* **Fairness
  doctrine (Broadcasting)**
Documentary films. *See* **Motion pictures, Docu-
  mentary**
Documentation 025
 See also

 Archives   **Information services**
 Bibliographic control   **Information storage and**
 Bibliography   **retrieval systems**
 Cataloging   **Library science**
 Classification—Books
  also subjects with the subdivison
   Documentation, e.g.
    Agriculture—Documentation; etc.
 xx **Information science; Information services**
Documents. *See* **Archives; Charters; Government
  publications**
Dog. *See* **Dogs**
Dog breeding. *See* **Dogs—Breeding**
Dog guides. *See* **Guide dogs**
Dogmatic theology. *See* **Theology, Doctrinal**

Dogs 599.74; 636.7
> *See also* classes of dogs, e.g. **Guide dogs; Hearing ear dogs;** etc.; also names of specific breeds, e.g. **Collies;** etc.
> *x* Dog
> *xx* **Pets**

Dogs—Breeding 636.7
> *x* Dog breeding
> *xx* **Breeding**

Dogs—Fiction E; Fic; S C
> *xx* **Animals—Fiction**

Dogs for the blind. *See* **Guide dogs**

Dogs for the deaf. *See* **Hearing ear dogs**

Dogs in literature 809
> *xx* **Animals in literature**

Dogs—Psychology 156
> *xx* **Animal intelligence; Psychology, Comparative**

Dogs—Training 636.7
> *xx* **Animals—Training**

Dogs—War use 355.4
> *x* War use of dogs
> *xx* **Animals—War use; Working animals**

Doll. *See* **Dolls**

Dollhouses 688.7
> *x* Miniature objects
> *xx* **Toys**

Dolls 688.7
> *x* Doll
> *xx* **Toys**

Domesday book 942.02
> *x* Doomsday book

Domestic animals 636
> Use for general materials on farm animals. Materials limited to animals as pets are entered under **Pets.** Materials on stock raising as an industry are entered under **Livestock.** Names of all animals are not included in this list but are to be added as needed.
> *See also* **Animal abuse; Livestock; Working animals;** also names of domestic animals, e.g. **Cats; Cattle; Pets; Poultry; Reindeer;** etc.
> *x* Animal industry; Animals, Domestic; Beasts; Farm animals
> *xx* **Agriculture; Animals; Breeding; Livestock; Pets; Zoology, Economic**

Domestic animals—Diseases. *See* **Animals— Diseases**

Domestic appliances. *See* **Household appliances, Electric; Household equipment and supplies**

Domestic architecture. *See* **Architecture, Domestic**

Domestic arts. *See* **Home economics**

Domestic education. *See* **Home instruction**

Domestic finance. *See* **Budgets, Household**

Domestic relations 306.8
> *See also* **Desertion and nonsupport; Divorce; Family; Marriage; Parent and child; Visitation rights (Domestic relations)**
> *x* Family relations
> *xx* **Family; Marriage**

Domestic violence. *See* **Family violence**

Domestic workers. *See* **Household employees**

Dominicans 271

    x Black Friars; Friars, Black; Friars Preachers; Jacobins (Dominicans); Mendicant orders; Preaching Friars; Saint Dominic, Order of; St. Dominic, Order of

    xx **Religious orders for men, Catholic**

Dominion of the sea. *See* **Sea power**

Dominions, British. *See* **Commonwealth of Nations**

Donation of organs, tissues, etc. 362.1

    See also **Transplantation of organs, tissues, etc.**

    x Anatomical gifts; Organ donation; Tissue donation

    xx **Gifts; Transplantation of organs, tissues, etc.**

Donations. *See* **Gifts**

Doomsday book. *See* **Domesday book**

Door to door selling. *See* **Peddlers and peddling**

Doors 729

    xx **Architecture—Details; Building; Carpentry**

Double employment. *See* **Supplementary employment**

Double stars. *See* **Stars**

Doubt. *See* **Belief and doubt**

Draft dodgers. *See* **Military service, Compulsory—Draft resisters**

Draft evaders. *See* **Military service, Compulsory—Draft resisters**

Draft, Military. *See* **Military service, Compulsory**

Draft resisters. *See* **Military service, Compulsory—Draft resisters**

Drafting, Automatic. *See* **Computer graphics**

Drafting, Mechanical. *See* **Mechanical drawing**

Dragons 398.2

    xx **Animals—Folklore; Animals, Mythical; Folklore; Monsters**

Drainage 631.6

    Use for materials on land drainage. Materials on house drainage are entered under **Drainage, House.**

    See also **Marshes; Sewerage**

    x Land drainage

    xx **Agricultural engineering; Civil engineering; Hydraulic engineering; Municipal engineering; Reclamation of land; Sanitary engineering; Sewerage; Soils**

Drainage, House 728

    See note under **Drainage.**

    See also **Plumbing; Sanitary engineering; Sewerage**

    x House drainage

    xx **Plumbing; Sanitation, Household**

Drama 808.2

    Use for general materials on drama. Materials on the history and criticism of drama as literature are entered under **Drama—History and criticism.** Materials on criticism of drama as presented on the stage are entered under **Dramatic criticism.** Materials on the presentation of plays are entered under **Acting; Amateur theater; Theater—Production and direction.** Materials on how to write plays are entered under **Drama—Technique.** Collections of plays are entered under **Drama—Collected works; American drama—Collected works; English drama—Collected works;** etc.

Drama—*Continued*
  See also

Acting	**Motion picture plays**
American drama	**Mysteries and miracle**
Ballet	**plays**
Children's plays	**One act plays**
College and school drama	**Opera**
Comedy	**Pantomimes**
Dramatic criticism	**Passion plays**
Dramatists	**Plots (Drama, fiction, etc.)**
English drama	**Puppets and puppet plays**
Folk drama	**Radio plays**
Indians of North Ameri-	**Religious drama**
ca—Drama	**Television plays**
Masks (Plays)	**Theater**
Morality plays	**Tragedy**

  also names of special subjects, historical events,
    and famous persons with the subdivision
    Drama, e.g. **Easter—Drama; United
    States—History—1861-1865, Civil War—
    Drama; Napoleon I, Emperor of the French,
    1769-1821—Drama;** etc.
  x Stage
  xx **Literature; Theater**
Drama—Collected works 808.82
  Use for collections of plays by several authors.
  See also **American drama—Collected works;
    Children's plays; College and school dra-
    ma—Collected works; English drama—
    Collected works**
  x Plays
Drama—History and criticism 809.2
  See also **American drama—History and criti-
    cism; English drama—History and criticism;**
    etc.
Drama in education 372.6
  See also **Acting; Amateur theater; College and
    school drama; Religious drama; Theater**
  xx **Acting; Amateur theater; College and school
    drama; School assembly programs**
Drama—Plots. *See* **Plots (Drama, fiction, etc.)**
Drama, Religious. *See* **Religious drama**
Drama—Technique 808.2
  See also **Motion picture plays—Technique; Ra-
    dio plays—Technique; Television plays—
    Technique**
  x Play writing; Playwriting
  xx **Authorship; Characters and characteristics in
    literature**
Dramatic art. *See* **Acting**
Dramatic criticism 792.9
  Use for materials on criticism of drama as pres-
    ented on the stage. Materials on criticism of
    drama as a literary form are entered under
    **Drama—History and criticism; American
    drama—History and criticism;** etc.
  x Theater criticism
  xx **Criticism; Drama; Theater**
Dramatic music. *See* **Opera; Operetta**
Dramatic plots. *See* **Plots (Drama, fiction, etc.)**

Dramatists (May subdiv. geog. adjective form, e.g.
Dramatists, American; etc.) **809.2; 920**
Use for materials dealing largely with the personal lives of several playwrights. Materials dealing with their literary work are entered under **Drama—History and criticism; English drama—History and criticism;** etc.
   x Playwrights; Writers
  xx **Authors; Drama; Poets**
Dramatists, American 809.2
   x American dramatists; United States—Dramatists
Drapery 684.3
   x Curtains
  xx **Interior design; Upholstery**
Draughts. *See* **Checkers**
Drawing (May subdiv. geog. adjective form, e.g.
Drawing, American; etc.) **741; 743**
  See also

Anatomy, Artistic	**Mechanical drawing**
Architectural drawing	**Painting**
Commercial art	**Pastel drawing**
Crayon drawing	**Pen drawing**
Figure drawing	**Pencil drawing**
Geometrical drawing	**Perspective**
Graphic methods	**Shades and shadows**
Illustration of books	**Topographical drawing**
Landscape drawing	

   x Drawings; Sketching
  xx **Art; Graphic arts; Illustration of books; Perspective**
Drawing, American 741.09; 941.9
   x American drawing; United States—Drawing
Drawing, Architectural. *See* **Architectural drawing**
Drawing, Automatic. *See* **Computer graphics**
Drawing, Computer. *See* **Computer art**
Drawing, Electronic. *See* **Computer art; Computer graphics**
Drawing materials. *See* **Artists' materials**
Drawings. *See* **Drawing**
Dreaming. *See* **Dreams**
Dreams 154.6
  See also **Fantasy; Psychoanalysis; Sleep**
   x Dreaming
  xx **Brain; Divination; Fortune telling; Mind and body; Psychical research; Psychoanalysis; Psychology, Physiological; Sleep; Subconsciousness; Superstition; Visions**
Dredging 627
  xx **Civil engineering; Hydraulic engineering**
Dress. *See* **Clothing and dress**
Dress accessories 646
  xx **Clothing and dress**
Dressing of ores. *See* **Ore dressing**
Dressmaking 646.4; 687
  See also **Needlework; Sewing; Tailoring**
   x Garment making
  xx **Clothing and dress; Fashion; Needlework; Sewing; Tailoring**

Dressmaking—Patterns 646.4; 687
   x Patterns for crafts
Dried flowers. *See* **Flowers, Drying**
Dried foods. *See* **Food, Dried**
Dried milk. *See* **Milk, Dried**
Drifting of continents. *See* **Continental drift**
Drill and minor tactics 355.5
   See also **Military art and science**
   x Military drill; Minor tactics
   xx **Military art and science**
Drill (Nonmilitary) 613.7
   x Marches (Exercises)
   xx **Physical education**
Drilling and boring 621.9
   Use for materials dealing with workshop opera-
      tions in metal, wood, etc. Materials relating
      to the operation of cutting holes in earth or
      rock are entered under **Boring.**
   x Boring (Metal, wood, etc.)
Drilling and boring (Earth and rocks). *See* **Boring**
Drilling, Oil well. *See* **Oil well drilling**
Drilling platforms 627
   x Artificial islands; Islands, Artificial; Offshore
      structures; Platforms, Drilling; Structures,
      Offshore
   xx **Ocean engineering; Oil well drilling, Subma-
      rine**
**Drinking age (May subdiv. geog.) 351.76; 363.4;
      613.8**
   x Age, Drinking; Minimum drinking age
   xx **Youth—Alcohol use**
Drinking and youth. *See* **Youth—Alcohol use**
**Drinking of alcoholic beverages (May subdiv. geog.)
      178; 351.76; 363.4; 394.1**
   Use for materials on drinking in its social as-
      pects and as a social problem.
   See also **Alcoholism; Drunk driving; Temper-
      ance;** also classes of persons and ethnic
      groups with the subdivision *Alcohol use,*
      e.g. **Youth—Alcohol use;** etc.
   x Alcohol consumption; Alcoholic beverage
      consumption; Consumption of alcoholic
      beverages; Drinking problem; Liquor prob-
      lem; Social drinking
   xx **Alcoholic beverages; Alcoholism; Temperance**
Drinking problem. *See* **Alcoholism; Drinking of al-
      coholic beverages**
Drinks. *See* **Alcoholic beverages; Beverages; Li-
      quors and liqueurs**
Driver education. *See* **Automobile drivers—
      Education**
Drivers, Automobile. *See* **Automobile drivers**
Driving under the influence of alcohol. *See* **Drunk
      driving**
Dromedaries. *See* **Camels**
Drop forging. *See* **Forging**
Dropouts 371.2
   x School dropouts; School withdrawals
   xx **Educational counseling; School attendance;
      Youth**

Droughts 551.57; 632
   See also **Dust storms; Rain and rainfall**
   xx **Meteorology; Rain and rainfall**
Drug abuse 613.8; 616.86
   Use for materials on the misuse of drugs in a
       broad sense. Materials limited to addiction
       to hard drugs such as opium, heroin, etc. are
       entered under **Narcotic habit.**
   See also **Drug addicts;** also classes of people with
       the subdivision *Drug use,* e.g.
       Criminals—Drug use; Youth—Drug use;
       etc.; also types of drug abuse, e.g.
       Alcoholism; Narcotic habit; etc.
   x Addiction to drugs; Drug addiction; Drug
       habit; Drug use; Drugs—Abuse; Drugs—
       Misuse
   xx **Crimes without victims; Substance abuse**
Drug abuse—Study and teaching. *See* **Drug educa-
       tion**
Drug addiction. *See* **Drug abuse; Narcotic habit**
Drug addicts 613.8; 616.8
   See also classes of people with the subdivision
       Drug use, e.g. **Criminals—Drug use;**
       Youth—Drug use; etc.
   x Addicts, Drug; Narcotic addicts
   xx **Drug abuse; Narcotic habit; Narcotics and
       crime**
Drug education 371.7; 613.8
   Use for materials on the study of drugs, includ-
       ing their source, abuse, chemical composi-
       tion, and social, physical, and personal ef-
       fects.
   x Drug abuse—Study and teaching
   xx **Health education**
Drug habit. *See* **Drug abuse; Narcotic habit**
Drug plants. *See* **Botany, Medical**
Drug pushers. *See* **Narcotic traffic**
Drug therapy. *See* **Chemotherapy**
Drug traffic. *See* **Narcotic traffic**
Drug use. *See* **Drug abuse;** and classes of people
       with the subdivision *Drug use,* e.g.
       Criminals—Drug use; Youth—Drug use;
       etc.
Drugs 615
   See also **Materia medica; Orphan drugs; Phar-
       macology; Poisons and poisoning;** also
       classes of people with the subdivision *Drug
       use,* e.g. **Criminals—Drug use; Youth—
       Drug use;** etc.; and names of groups of
       drugs, e.g. **Narcotics;** etc.; and names of in-
       dividual drugs
   x Pharmaceuticals
   xx **Chemistry, Medical and pharmaceutical; Ma-
       teria medica; Pharmacology; Pharmacy;
       Therapeutics**
Drugs—Abuse. *See* **Drug abuse**
Drugs—Adulteration and analysis 363.1
   xx **Consumer protection**
Drugs and criminals. *See* **Criminals—Drug use**
Drugs and teenagers. *See* **Youth—Drug use**

Drugs and youth. *See* **Youth—Drug use**
Drugs—Generic substitution 615
    x Generic drugs
    xx **Generic products**
Drugs—Misuse. *See* **Drug abuse**
Drugs, Nonprescription 615
    x Nonprescription drugs; Over-the-counter
        drugs; Patent medicines
Drugs, Orphan. *See* **Orphan drugs**
Drugs—Physiological effect 613.8
Drugs—Psychological aspects 615
    x Psychological aspects
    xx **Psychology, Applied**
Druids and Druidism 299
    xx **Celts; Religions**
Drum 789
    xx **Musical instruments; Percussion instruments**
Drum majoring 371.8; 785.06
    See also **Baton twirling**
    xx **Bands (Music); Baton twirling**
Drunk driving 363.1; 364.1
    x Driving under the influence of alcohol
    xx **Drinking of alcoholic beverages; Traffic acci-**
        dents
Drunkards. *See* **Alcoholics**
Drunkenness. *See* **Alcoholism; Temperance**
Dry cleaning 646.6; 667
    x Clothing and dress—Dry cleaning
    xx **Cleaning**
Dry farming 631.5
    x Farming, Dry
    xx **Agriculture; Irrigation**
Dry goods. *See* **Fabrics**
Dual employment. *See* **Supplementary employment**
Ducks 636.5
    xx **Poultry**
Ductless glands. *See* **Endocrine glands**
Dueling 179; 394
    x Fighting
    xx **Manners and customs; Martial arts**
Dumps, Toxic. *See* **Hazardous waste sites**
Dunes. *See* **Sand dunes**
Dungeons. *See* **Prisons**
Duplicate bridge. *See* **Bridge (Game)**
Duplicating processes. *See* **Copying processes and**
        machines
Dust, Radioactive. *See* **Radioactive fallout**
Dust storms 551.5
    xx **Droughts; Erosion; Storms**
Dusting and spraying. *See* **Spraying and dusting**
Duties. *See* **Tariff; Taxation**
Duty 170
    See also **Conscience**
    xx **Ethics; Human behavior**
Dwarf trees 582.16; 635.9
    See also names of dwarf trees, e.g. **Bonsai;** etc.
    xx **Trees**
Dwellings. *See* **Architecture, Domestic; Houses;**
        Housing; and classes of people with the
        subdivision *Housing,* e.g. **Physically handi-**

Dwellings—*Continued*
        capped—**Housing;** etc.
Dyes and dyeing   667; 746.6
    See also **Bleaching;** also types of dyeing, e.g.
        Batik; Tie dyeing; etc.
    xx **Bleaching; Chemistry, Technical; Cleaning;**
        Color; Pigments; Textile chemistry; Textile
        industry; Wool
Dying children.   *See* **Terminally ill children**
Dying patients.   *See* **Terminally ill**
Dynamics   531
    See also

Aerodynamics	**Motion**
Astrodynamics	**Physics**
Force and energy	**Quantum theory**
Hydrodynamics	**Statics**
Kinematics	**Thermodynamics**
Matter	

    x **Kinetics**
    xx **Force and energy; Mathematics; Mechanics;**
        Physics; Statics
Dynamite   662
    xx **Explosives**
Dynamos.   *See* **Electric generators**
Dyslexia   371.9; 616.85
    xx **Reading disability**
Dyspepsia.   *See* **Indigestion**
E.E.O.   *See* **Discrimination in employment**
E.R.A.'s.   *See* **Equal rights amendments**
E.S.P.   *See* **Extrasensory perception**
Eagles   598
    xx **Birds of prey**
Ear   611; 612
    See also **Hearing**
    xx **Deafness; Head; Hearing**
Early Christian literature.   *See* **Christian litera-**
        ture—30(ca.)-600, Early
Early warning system, Ballistic missile.   *See* **Ballis-**
        tic missile early warning system
Earth   525; 550
    Use for general materials on the whole planet.
        Materials limited to the structure and com-
        position of the earth and the physical
        changes which it has undergone and is still
        undergoing are entered under **Geology.**
    See also

Antarctic regions	**Ice age**
Arctic regions	**Latitude**
Atmosphere	**Longitude**
Creation	**Meteorology**
Earthquakes	**Ocean**
Geodesy	**Oceanography**
Geography	**Physical geography**
Geology	**Universe**
Geophysics	

    x **World**
    xx **Creation; Geology; Physical geography; Solar**
        system; Universe
Earth—Age   551.7
Earth—Chemical composition.   *See* **Geochemistry**

Earth—Crust 551.1
    See also **Plate tectonics**
Earth, Effect of man on. *See* **Man—Influence on nature**
Earth fills. *See* **Landfills**
Earth—Internal structure 551.1
Earth—Photographs from space 778.3
    xx **Space photography**
Earth sciences 550
    See also

Climate	**Geophysics**
Geochemistry	**Meteorology**
Geography	**Oceanography**
Geology	**Water**

    x Geoscience
    xx **Science**
Earth sheltered houses 690; 728
    x Houses, Earth sheltered; Houses, Underground; Underground houses
    xx **House construction; Houses; Underground architecture**
Earth—Space attack and defense. *See* **Space warfare**
Earthenware. *See* **Pottery**
Earthquakes (May subdiv. geog.) **551.2**
    See also subject headings for types of structures subject to earthquake forces with the subdivision *Earthquake effects,* e.g. **Buildings—Earthquake effects; Skyscrapers—Earthquake effects;** etc.
    x Seismography; Seismology
    xx **Earth; Geology; Natural disasters; Physical geography**
Earthquakes and building. *See* **Buildings—Earthquake effects**
Earthquakes—California 551.2
Earthquakes—United States 551.2
    x United States—Earthquakes
Earthwork. *See* **Soils (Engineering)**
Earthworks (Archeology). *See* **Excavations (Archeology)**
Earthworks (Art) 709.04
    x Landscape sculpture; Site oriented art
    xx **Art, Modern—1900-1999 (20th century)**
East. *See* **Asia**
East Africa. *See* **Africa, East**
East and West 306; 909
    Use for materials on both acculturation and cultural conflict between Asian and Occidental civilizations.
    See also **Acculturation; Civilization, Asian; Civilization, Occidental**
    xx **Acculturation**
East Asia 950
    Use for materials on East Asia including China, Japan, Korea, Taiwan, Hong Kong and Macao.
    x Asia, East; East (Far East); Far East; Orient
    xx **Asia**
East (Far East). *See* **East Asia**

East Germany. *See* **Germany (East)**
East Indians 954
   See also **Hindus**
   x Indians (of India)
   xx **Hindus**
East (Near East). *See* **Middle East**
Easter 263; 394.2
   x Ecclesiastical fasts and feasts; Religious festi-
       vals
   xx **Holy Week; Lent**
Easter carols. *See* **Carols**
Easter—Drama 808.82; 812; etc.
   xx **Drama**
Easter egg decoration. *See* **Egg decoration**
Eastern churches 281
   See also **Orthodox Eastern Church**
Eastern Empire. *See* **Byzantine Empire**
Eastern Europe 947
   x Europe, Eastern
Eastern Seaboard. *See* **Atlantic States**
Easy reading materials E
   x Beginning reading materials; Preprimers; Pre-
       school reading materials; Primers
   xx **Children's literature; Reading materials**
Eating. *See* **Dinners and dining**
Eating customs 394.1
   See also **Eating disorders; Table etiquette**
   x Food customs; Food habits
   xx **Diet; Human behavior; Nutrition**
Eating disorders 616.3; 616.85
   See also types of eating disorders, e.g. **Anorexia
       nervosa;** etc.
   x Appetite disorders; Ingestion disorders
   xx **Eating customs; Psychology, Pathological**
Eavesdropping 363.2
   See also **Wiretapping**
   x Bugging, Electronic; Electronic bugging; Elec-
       tronic eavesdropping; Electronic listening
       devices; Listening devices; Surveillance,
       Electronic
   xx **Criminal investigation; Privacy, Right of; Wi-
       retapping**
Eccentrics and eccentricities 920
   x Cranks
   xx **Curiosities and wonders; Personality**
Ecclesiastical antiquities. *See* **Christian antiquities**
Ecclesiastical architecture. *See* **Church architecture**
Ecclesiastical art. *See* **Christian art and symbolism**
Ecclesiastical biography. *See* **Christianity—
       Biography**
Ecclesiastical fasts and feasts. *See* **Fasts and feasts;**
       and names of special fasts and feasts, e.g.
       Easter; Lent; etc.
Ecclesiastical furniture. *See* **Church furniture**
Ecclesiastical history. *See* **Church history**
Ecclesiastical law 262.9
   See also **Tithes**
   x Canon law; Church law; Law, Ecclesiastical
   xx **Church—Government policy; Law**
Ecclesiastical rites and ceremonies. *See* **Funeral**

Ecclesiastical rites and ceremonies—*Continued*
    rites and ceremonies; Liturgies; Lord's Sup-
    per; Rites and ceremonies; Sacraments
Echo ranging. *See* **Sonar**
Eclipses, Lunar 523.3
    x Lunar eclipses; Moon—Eclipses
    xx **Astronomy**
Eclipses, Solar 523.7
    x Solar eclipses; Sun—Eclipses
    xx **Astronomy**
Ecology 574.5
    See also **Adaptation (Biology); Biogeography;**
    Botany—Ecology; Food chains (Ecology);
    also types of ecology, e.g. **Marine ecology;**
    etc.
    x Balance of nature; Biology—Ecology; Eco-
    systems
    xx **Environment**
Ecology, Human. *See* **Human ecology**
Ecology, Marine. *See* **Marine ecology**
Ecology, Social. *See* **Human ecology**
Economic aspects. *See* subjects with the subdivi-
    sion *Economic aspects,* e.g.
    Agriculture—Economic aspects; etc.
Economic assistance (May subdiv. geog. adjective
    form) **338.91**
    Use for general materials on international eco-
    nomic aid given in the form of gifts, loans,
    relief grants, or technical assistance. Materi-
    als limited to the latter are entered under
    Technical assistance.
    See also **Developing countries; Reconstruction**
    (1939-1951); Technical assistance; World
    War, 1939-1945—Civilian relief
    x Aid to developing areas; Assistance to devel-
    oping areas; Foreign aid program
    xx **Developing countries; Economic policy; Inter-**
    national cooperation; International eco-
    nomic relations; Reconstruction (1939-1951)
Economic assistance, American 338.973
    x American economic assistance; United
    States—Economic assistance
Economic assistance, Domestic 338.93-338.99
    See also **Community development; Government**
    lending; Grants-in-aid; Poverty; Public
    works; Subsidies; Unemployed
    x Anti-poverty programs; Antipoverty pro-
    grams; Poor relief
    xx **Economic policy; Grants-in-aid; Unemployed**
Economic botany. *See* **Botany, Economic**
Economic conditions 330.9
    Use for general materials on some or all of the
    following: natural resources, business, com-
    merce, industry, labor, manufactures, finan-
    cial conditions; and for the history of the
    economic development of several countries.
    See also **Business cycles; Developing countries;**
    Economic policy; Geography, Commercial;
    Labor supply; Natural resources; Quality of
    life; also classes of people and names of

Economic conditions—*Continued*

    countries, cities, areas, etc. with the subdivision *Economic conditions,* e.g.
    Blacks—Economic conditions; United States—Economic conditions; etc.

  x Business depressions; Economic development; Economic history; Stabilization in industry; World economics

  xx **Business; Economics; Geography, Commercial; Social conditions; Wealth**

Economic cycles. *See* **Business cycles**

Economic depressions. *See* **Depressions, Economic**

Economic development. *See* **Economic conditions**

Economic entomology. *See* **Insects, Injurious and beneficial**

Economic forecasting 338.5

  See also **Business forecasting; Employment forecasting**

  xx **Business cycles; Economics; Forecasting**

Economic geography. *See* **Geography, Commercial**

Economic geology. *See* **Geology, Economic**

Economic history. *See* **Economic conditions**

Economic mobilization. *See* **Industrial mobilization**

Economic planning. *See* **Economic policy**

Economic policy 338.9-338.91

  Use for materials on the policy of government towards economic problems.

  See also

Commercial policy	**policy**
Economic assistance	**International economic relations**
Economic assistance, Domestic	**Land reform**
Fiscal policy	**Municipal ownership**
Free trade and protection	**National security**
Government lending	**Sanctions (International law)**
Government ownership	
Human resources policy	**Social policy**
Industrial mobilization	**Subsidies**
Industrialization	**Tariff**
Industry—Government	**Technical assistance**

  also names of countries and states with the subdivision *Economic policy,* e.g. **United States—Economic policy; Ohio—Economic policy;** etc.; and names of countries with the subdivision *Commercial policy,* e.g. **United States—Commercial policy;** etc.

  x Economic planning; National planning; Planning, Economic; Planning, National; Welfare state; World economics

  xx **Economic conditions; Economics; Industry—Government policy; National security; Social policy**

Economic relations, Foreign. *See* **International economic relations**

Economic sanctions. *See* **Sanctions (International law)**

Economic zones (Maritime law). *See* **Territorial waters**

Economic zoology. *See* **Zoology, Economic**

Economics 330
See also

Balance of trade
Barter
Business
Capital
Capitalism
Christianity and econom-
   ics
Commerce
Consumption (Economics)
Cooperation
Cost of living
Credit
Debts, Public
Depressions, Economic
Economic conditions
Economic forecasting
Economic policy
Finance
Free trade and protection

Government ownership
Income
Industry
Labor
Land use
Money
Monopolies
Population
Prices
Profit
Property
Saving and thrift
Socialism
Statistics
Trusts, Industrial
Underground economy
Wages
Waste (Economics)
Wealth

    also subjects with the subdivision *Economic as-*
      pects, e.g. **Agriculture—Economic aspects;**
      etc.
  x Distribution of wealth; Political economy;
      Production
  xx **Social sciences**
Economics and Christianity. *See* **Christianity and**
    economics
Economics—History 330.1; 330.09
    Use for materials describing the development of
      economic theories. Materials on the eco-
      nomic conditions and development of coun-
      tries are entered under **Economic conditions.**
Economics, Medical. *See* **Medical economics**
Economics of war. *See* **War—Economic aspects**
Economy. *See* **Saving and thrift**
Economy, Underground. *See* **Underground econ-**
    omy
Ecosystems. *See* **Ecology**
Ectogenesis, Preimplantational. *See* **Fertilization in**
    vitro
Ecumenical councils. *See* **Councils and synods**
Ecumenical movement. *See* **Christian unity**
Eddas 839
  xx **Old Norse literature; Poetry; Scandinavian lit-**
    erature
Edible plants. *See* **Plants, Edible**
Editions. *See* **Bibliography—Editions**
Editors and editing. *See* **Journalism; Journalists;**
    Publishers and publishing
Education (May subdiv. geog.) **370**
    Subdivisions listed under this heading may be
      used under other education headings where
      applicable. All types of education are not in-
      cluded in this list but are to be added as
      needed.
    See also

Adult education
Area studies

Audiovisual education
Basic education

Education—*Continued*

Books and reading
Business education
Church and education
Classical education
Coeducation
Colleges and universities
Continuing education
Correspondence schools
 and courses
Culture
Educators
Evening and continuation
 schools
Fundamentalism and edu-
 cation
Home instruction
International education
Learning and scholarship
Learning, Psychology of
Libraries
Library education
Literacy
Mainstreaming in educa-
 tion
Military education
Moral education
Naval education
Physical education
Professional education
Religious education
Scholarships, fellowships,
 etc.
Schools
Socialization
Special education
Study, Method of
Teachers
Teaching
Technical education
Vocational education
World War, 1939-1945—
 Education and the war

also names of classes of people and social and
 ethnic groups with the subdivision
 Education, e.g. **Automobile drivers—
 Education; Blacks—Education; Deaf—
 Education; Mentally handicapped chil-
 dren—Education;** etc.; subjects with the
 subdivision *Study and teaching,* e.g.
 Science—Study and teaching; etc.; and
 headings beginning with the words
 Education and **Educational**

  x Instruction; Pedagogy
 xx **Civilization; Coeducation; Culture; Learning
   and scholarship; Schools; Teaching**
Education, Adult. *See* **Adult education**
Education—Aims and objectives 370.11
Education and church. *See* **Church and education**
Education and Fundamentalism. *See* **Fundamental-
   ism and education**
Education and radio. *See* **Radio in education**
Education and religion. *See* **Church and education**
Education and state. *See* **Education—Government
   policy**
Education and television. *See* **Television in educa-
   tion**
Education associations. *See* **Educational associa-
   tions**
Education at home. *See* **Home instruction**
Education—Automation. *See* **Computer assisted
   instruction**
Education, Bilingual 370.19; 371.97
  x Bilingual education
 xx **Bilingualism; Intercultural education**
Education, Business. *See* **Business education**
Education, Character. *See* **Moral education**
Education, Christian. *See* **Christian education**
Education, Classical. *See* **Classical education**
Education, Compulsory 379
  See also **Children—Employment; Evening and**

Education, Compulsory—*Continued*
    continuation schools; School attendance
    x Compulsory education; Compulsory school
        attendance
    xx **School attendance**
Education, Continuing. *See* **Continuing education**
Education—Curricula 375
    See also **Articulation (Education);** also types of
        education and schools with the subdivision
        Curricula, e.g. **Library education—
        Curricula; Colleges and universities—
        Curricula;** etc.
    x Core curriculum; Courses of study; Curricula
        (Courses of study); Schools—Curricula;
        Study, Courses of
Education—Data processing. *See* **Computer as-
        sisted instruction**
Education—Developing countries 370.9172
Education, Discrimination in. *See* **Discrimination
        in education**
Education, Elementary 372
    Use for general materials on education of chil-
        dren below the secondary school level.
    See also **Creative activities; Exceptional children;
        Kindergarten; Montessori method of educa-
        tion; Nursery schools; Readiness for school**
    x Children—Education; Education of children;
        Education, Primary; Elementary education;
        Grammar schools; Primary education
    xx **Children**
Education, Ethical. *See* **Moral education; Religious
        education**
Education—Experimental methods 371.3
    See also **Experimental schools;** also types of ex-
        perimental methods, e.g. **Nongraded
        schools; Open plan schools;** etc.
    x Activity schools; Experimental methods in ed-
        ucation; Progressive education; Teaching—
        Experimental methods
Education—Federal aid. *See* **Federal aid to educa-
        tion**
Education—Finance 379.1
    See also **Federal aid to education; State aid to ed-
        ucation**
    x School finance; School taxes; Tuition
    xx **Finance**
Education for librarianship. *See* **Library education**
Education—Government policy 379
    See also **Federal aid to education; Scholarships,
        fellowships, etc.; State aid to education**
    x Education and state; Educational policy; State
        and education
Education, Higher 378
    Use for general consideration of education above
        the secondary level, i.e. for materials on col-
        lege education, professional education, etc.
        Use for materials not specific enough to be
        entered under **Colleges and universities.**
    See also **Adult education; Classical education;
        Colleges and universities; Junior colleges;**

Education, Higher—*Continued*
    **Professional education; Technical education;
    University extension**
  x Higher education
  xx **Colleges and universities**
Education, Home. *See* **Home instruction**
Education, Industrial. *See* **Industrial arts educa-
    tion; Technical education**
Education—Integration. *See* **School integration**
Education, Intercultural. *See* **Intercultural educa-
    tion**
Education, International. *See* **International educa-
    tion**
Education, Medical. *See* **Medicine—Study and
    teaching**
Education, Military. *See* **Military education**
Education, Moral. *See* **Moral education**
Education, Multicultural. *See* **Intercultural educa-
    tion**
Education, Musical. *See* **Music—Study and teach-
    ing**
Education, Naval. *See* **Naval education**
Education, Nonformal. *See* **Experimental schools;
    Free universities**
Education of adults. *See* **Adult education**
Education of children. *See* **Education, Elementary**
Education of criminals. *See* **Prisoners—Education**
Education of men. *See* **Men—Education**
Education of prisoners. *See* **Prisoners—Education**
Education of the blind. *See* **Blind—Education**
Education of the deaf. *See* **Deaf—Education**
Education of veterans. *See* **Veterans—Education**
Education of women. *See* **Women—Education**
Education of workers. *See* **Labor—Education**
Education—Personnel service. *See* **Educational
    counseling**
Education, Physical. *See* **Physical education**
Education, Preschool 372
  See also **Kindergarten; Nursery schools; Readi-
    ness for school**
  x Children—Education; Infants—Education;
    Preschool education
  xx **Kindergarten; Nursery schools**
Education, Primary. *See* **Education, Elementary**
Education, Professional. *See* **Professional education**
Education, Religious. *See* **Religious education**
Education, Scientific. *See* **Science—Study and
    teaching**
Education, Secondary 373
  A more inclusive subject than **High schools.**
  See also **Adult education; Evening and continua-
    tion schools; High schools; Junior high
    schools; Private schools; Public schools**
  x High school education; Secondary education;
    Secondary schools
  xx **High schools**
Education, Segregation in. *See* **Segregation in edu-
    cation**
Education, Special. *See* **Special education**
Education—State aid. *See* **State aid to education**

Education—Statistics 370
Education—Study and teaching 370.7
Use for materials on the study and teaching of
education as a science. Materials limited to
the methods of training teachers are entered
under **Teachers—Training.** Materials on
the methods of teaching are entered under
Teaching.
See also **Teachers colleges; Teachers—Training**
x Pedagogy
Education, Technical. *See* **Technical education**
Education, Theological. *See* **Religious education;**
Theology—Study and teaching
Education—United States 370
x United States—Education
Education, Vocational. *See* **Vocational education**
Educational administration. *See* **Schools—**
Administration
Educational associations 370.6
See also **Parents' and teachers' associations**
x Education associations
xx **Societies; Teachers**
Educational consultants 370.7
xx **Consultants**
Educational counseling 371.4
Use for materials on the assistance given to students by schools, colleges, or universities in
the selection of a program of studies suited
to their abilities, interests, future plans, and
general circumstances. Materials on the assistance given to students in understanding
and coping with adjustment problems are
entered under **School counseling.** Consider
also **Vocational guidance.**
See also **Dropouts; School counseling; School**
psychologists; Vocational guidance
x Academic advising; Education—Personnel
service; Educational guidance; Guidance
counseling, Educational; Personnel service
in education; Student guidance; Students—
Counseling
xx **Counseling; School counseling; Vocational**
guidance
Educational films. *See* **Libraries and motion pic-**
tures; Motion pictures in education
Educational freedom. *See* **Academic freedom**
Educational guidance. *See* **Educational counseling**
Educational measurements. *See* **Educational tests**
and measurements
Educational policy. *See* **Education—Government**
policy
Educational psychology 370.15
See also

Apperception	**Memory**
Attention	**Mental tests**
Child psychology	**Perception**
Imagination	**Psychology, Applied**
Learning, Psychology of	**Thought and thinking**

x Psychology, Educational
xx **Child psychology; Psychology; Teaching**

Educational sociology 370.19
   x Social problems in education; Sociology, Educational
   xx **Sociology**
Educational surveys 370
   x School surveys; Surveys
   xx **Social surveys**
Educational television. *See* **Public television; Television in education**
Educational tests and measurements 371.2
   See also **Ability—Testing; Colleges and universities—Entrance examinations; Examinations; Grading and marking (Students); Mental tests**
   x Educational measurements; Tests
   xx **Mental tests**
Educators 370.92; 920
   See also **Teachers**
   x College teachers; Faculty (Education)
   xx **Education; Teachers**
EEO. *See* **Discrimination in employment**
Efficiency, Household. *See* **Home economics**
Efficiency, Industrial 658
   Use for materials dealing with specific means of increasing efficiency and output in business and industries. Such materials include time and motion studies, and the application of psychological principles.
   See also

Executive ability	**Motion study**
Factory management	**Office management**
Job analysis	**Personnel management**
Labor productivity	**Time study**

   x Industrial efficiency
   xx **Business; Cost accounting; Engineering; Executive ability; Factory management; Industrial management; Industry; Management; Personnel management**
Egg decoration 745.59
   x Easter egg decoration; Eggshell craft
   xx **Decoration and ornament; Handicraft**
Eggs 598; 636.5
   See also **Birds—Eggs and nests**
Eggshell craft. *See* **Egg decoration**
Egypt 962
Egypt—Antiquities 932
   x Egyptology
Egypt—History 932; 962
   See also **Sinai Campaign, 1956**
Egypt—History—1970- 962
Egyptology. *See* **Egypt—Antiquities**
Eight-hour day. *See* **Hours of labor**
Eighteenth century 909.7
   See note under **Nineteenth century.**
   See also **Enlightenment**
   x 1700-1799 (18th century)
Elderly (May subdiv. geog.) **155.67; 305.2**
   See also **Aging; Libraries and the elderly; Retirement income; Social work with the elderly**
   x Aged; Older people; Senior citizens

Elderly—*Continued*

    xx **Gerontology; Old age**

Elderly abuse 362.6

    x Abuse of the elderly; Battered elderly; Elderly—Mistreatment; Elderly neglect; Gramslamming; Parent abuse

    xx **Family violence**

Elderly and libraries. *See* **Libraries and the elderly**

Elderly—Care and hygiene 362.6; 618.97

    See also **Nursing homes**

Elderly—Counseling of 362.6

    xx **Counseling**

Elderly—Diseases 618.97

    x Geriatrics

Elderly—Home care 362.6

    xx **Home care services**

Elderly—Housing 362.6

    See also **Retirement communities**

    x Housing for the elderly

Elderly—Institutional care 362.6

    x Homes for the elderly; Old age homes

Elderly—Life skills guides 362.6; 646.7

    See also **Retirement**

    xx **Life skills; Retirement**

Elderly—Medical care 362.6; 618.97

    See also **Medicare**

    x Medical care for the elderly

    xx **Medical care**

Elderly—Mistreatment. *See* **Elderly abuse**

Elderly neglect. *See* **Elderly abuse**

Elderly—Recreation 790.1

    xx **Recreation**

Elderly—Societies 367; 790.1

Elderly—United States 305.2

    x United States—Elderly

Election (Theology). *See* **Predestination**

Electioneering. *See* **Politics, Practical**

Elections (May subdiv. geog.) **324.6**

    See also

Campaign funds	**Referendum**
Equal time rule (Broadcasting)	**Representative government and representation**
Presidents—United States—Election	**Suffrage**
	Voter registration
Primaries	

    x Ballot; Franchise; Polls, Election; Voting

    xx **Politics, Practical; Primaries; Proportional representation; Representative government and representation**

Elections—Finance. *See* **Campaign funds**

Elections, Primary. *See* **Primaries**

Elections—United States 324.9

    x United States—Elections

Elections—United States—Finance. *See* **Campaign funds—United States**

Electoral college. *See* **Presidents—United States—Election**

Electric apparatus and appliances 621.3028; 644

    See also names of electric apparatus and appliances, e.g. **Burglar alarms; Electric batteries;**

Electric apparatus and appliances—*Continued*
  Electric generators; Electric lamps; etc.
    x Apparatus, Electric; Appliances, Electric; Electric appliances
    xx **Electric engineering; Scientific apparatus and instruments**
Electric apparatus and appliances, Domestic. *See* **Household appliances, Electric**
Electric appliances. *See* **Electric apparatus and appliances; Household appliances, Electric**
Electric automobiles. *See* **Automobiles, Electric**
Electric batteries 621.31
    See also **Fuel cells; Solar batteries; Storage batteries**
    x Batteries, Electric; Cells, Electric
    xx **Electric apparatus and appliances; Electrochemistry; Storage batteries**
Electric circuits 621.319
    See also **Electronic circuits**
    x Circuits, Electric
Electric communication. *See* **Telecommunication**
Electric condensers. *See* **Condensers (Electricity)**
Electric conductors 621.319
    See also **Radio, Shortwave**
    x Conductors, Electric
Electric controllers 629.8
    x Automatic control
Electric currents 537.6; 621.31
    See also **Electric measurements; Electric transformers**
    x Currents, Electric
Electric currents, Alternating 537.6; 621.31
    x Alternating currents; Currents, Alternating
Electric distribution. *See* **Electric lines; Electric power distribution**
Electric engineering 621.3
    See also

Electric apparatus and appliances	**Electric railroads**
	Electricity in mining
Electric lighting	**Radio**
Electric machinery	**Telegraph**
Electric power distribution	**Telephone**

    xx **Engineering; Mechanical engineering**
Electric equipment of automobiles. *See* **Automobiles—Electric equipment**
Electric eye. *See* **Photoelectric cells**
Electric generators 621.31
    x Dynamos; Generators, Electric
    xx **Electric apparatus and appliances; Electric machinery**
Electric heating 621.39; 644; 697
    x Electricity in the home
    xx **Heating**
Electric household appliances. *See* **Household appliances, Electric**
Electric industries 338.4
    See also **Radio industry and trade**
    x Electric utilities; Industries, Electric
    xx **Public utilities**

Electric lamps 621.32; 645
> *See also* **Electric lighting**
> *x* Incandescent lamps
> *xx* **Electric apparatus and appliances; Electric lighting; Lamps**

Electric light. *See* **Electric lighting; Photometry; Phototherapy**

Electric lighting 621.32
> *See also* **Electric lamps**
> *x* Arc light; Electric light; Electricity in the home; Light, Electric
> *xx* **Electric engineering; Electric lamps; Electric wiring; Lighting**

Electric lighting, Fluorescent. *See* **Fluorescent lighting**

Electric lines 621.319
> Use for materials on general transmission systems.
> *See also* **Electric wiring**
> *x* Electric distribution; Electric power transmission; Electric transmission; Electricity—Distribution; Power transmission, Electric; Transmission of power
> *xx* **Electric power distribution**

Electric machinery 621.31
> Use for discussions of more than one kind or class of machines. Materials dealing with smaller machines and appliances are entered under **Electric apparatus and appliances.**
> *See also* **Electric generators; Electric motors; Electric transformers**
> *xx* **Electric engineering; Machinery**

Electric machinery—Alternating current 621.319
> *x* Alternating current machinery

Electric machinery—Direct current 621.319
> *x* Direct current machinery

Electric measurements 621.37
> *See also* **Electric meters; Electric testing**
> *x* Measurements, Electric
> *xx* **Electric currents; Electric testing; Weights and measures**

Electric meters 621.37
> *x* Meters, Electric
> *xx* **Electric measurements**

Electric motors 621.4
> *See also* **Electric transformers**
> *x* Induction motors; Motors
> *xx* **Electric machinery**

Electric power 621.31
> *xx* **Energy resources; Power (Mechanics)**

Electric power distribution 621.319
> *See also* **Electric lines; Electric wiring**
> *x* Electric distribution; Electric power transmission; Electric transmission; Electricity—Distribution; Power transmission, Electric; Rural electrification; Transmission of power
> *xx* **Electric engineering; Power transmission**

Electric power failures 621.319
  x Blackouts, Electric power; Brownouts; Electric
      power interruptions; Power blackouts;
      Power failures
Electric power in mining. *See* **Electricity in mining**
Electric power interruptions. *See* **Electric power
      failures**
Electric power plants 621.31
  See also **Hydroelectric power plants**
  x Electric utilities; Power plants, Electric
  xx **Power plants**
Electric power transmission. *See* **Electric lines;
      Electric power distribution**
Electric railroads 621.33; 625.1
  See also **Railroads—Electrification; Street rail-
      roads**
  x Interurban railroads; Railroads, Electric
  xx **Electric engineering; Public utilities; Rail-
      roads; Railroads—Electrification; Street
      railroads; Transportation**
Electric signs 621.32; 659.13
  See also **Neon tubes**
  x Signs (Advertising); Signs, Electric
  xx **Advertising; Signs and signboards**
Electric smelting. *See* **Electrometallurgy**
Electric switches. *See* **Electric switchgear**
Electric switchgear 621.31
  x Electric switches; Switches, Electric
Electric testing 621.37
  See also **Electric measurements**
  xx **Electric measurements**
Electric toys 688.7
  xx **Toys**
Electric transformers 621.31
  x Transformers, Electric
  xx **Electric currents; Electric machinery; Electric
      motors**
Electric transmission. *See* **Electric lines; Electric
      power distribution**
Electric utilities. *See* **Electric industries; Electric
      power plants; Public utilities**
Electric waves 537; 621.381
  See also **Electromagnetic waves; Microwaves;
      Radio, Shortwave**
  x Hertzian waves; Radio waves
  xx **Waves**
Electric welding 671.5
  x Arc welding; Resistance welding; Spot weld-
      ing; Welding, Electric
  xx **Welding**
Electric wiring 621.319
  See also **Electric lighting; Telegraph; Telephone**
  x Wiring, Electric
  xx **Electric lines; Electric power distribution**
Electricity 537; 621.3
  See also **Electrons; Lightning; Magnetism; Ra-
      dioactivity; Telegraph; Telephone; X rays**
  also headings beginning with **Electric** and
      Electro
  xx **Magnetism; Physics**

Electricity—Distribution. *See* **Electric lines; Electric power distribution**

Electricity in agriculture   631.3

Use same form for electricity in other endeavors, e.g. **Electricity in mining;** etc.

x Electricity on the farm; Rural electrification

xx **Agricultural engineering; Agricultural machinery**

Electricity in medicine. *See* **Electrotherapeutics**

Electricity in mining   622

See also **Mining engineering**

x Electric power in mining; Mining, Electric

xx **Electric engineering; Mining engineering**

Electricity in the home. *See* **Electric heating; Electric lighting; Household appliances, Electric**

Electricity, Medical. *See* **Electrotherapeutics**

Electricity on the farm. *See* **Electricity in agriculture**

Electrification of railroads. *See* **Railroads—Electrification**

Electrochemistry   541.3; 547.1; 660.2

See also **Electric batteries; Electrometallurgy; Electroplating; Electrotyping; Fuel cells**

xx **Chemistry, Physical and theoretical; Chemistry, Technical**

Electromagnetic waves   537

See also **Gamma rays; Heat; Infrared radiation; Light; Microwaves; Ultraviolet rays; X rays**

x Waves, Electromagnetic

xx **Electric waves; Radiation**

Electromagnetism   537; 621.3

See also **Masers**

xx **Magnetism**

Electromagnets   538

x Magnet winding

xx **Magnetism; Magnets**

Electrometallurgy   669

See also **Electroplating; Electrotyping**

x Electric smelting

xx **Electrochemistry; Electroplating; Electrotyping; Metallurgy; Smelting**

Electron microscope and microscopy   502.8; 535; 578

xx **Microscope and microscopy**

Electron tubes. *See* **Vacuum tubes**

Electronic apparatus and appliances   621.381

See also **Electronic toys;** also names of electronic apparatus and appliances, e.g. **Computers; Intercommunication systems; Video games;** etc.

x Apparatus, Electronic; Appliances, Electronic

xx **Electronics; Scientific apparatus and instruments**

Electronic art. *See* **Computer art; Video art**

Electronic brains. *See* **Artificial intelligence; Computers**

Electronic bugging. *See* **Eavesdropping**

Electronic bulletin boards. *See* **Computer bulletin boards**

Electronic calculating machines. *See* **Computers**

Electronic circuits   621.381
 xx **Electric circuits; Electronics**
Electronic computers. *See* **Computers**
Electronic cottage. *See* **Telecommuting**
Electronic data processing   001.64; *004
 See also

Computer assisted instruc-	Online data processing
tion	Optical data processing
Computer bulletin boards	**Programming (Computers)**
Computer graphics	**Programming languages**
Computer networks	**(Computers)**
Computer systems	System design
Data transmission systems	

    also subjects with the subdivision *Data process-
 ing,* e.g. **Banks and banking—Data processing;** etc.
 x Automatic data processing; Data processing
 xx **Computers; Information science; Information
 storage and retrieval systems**
Electronic drawing. *See* **Computer art; Computer
 graphics**
Electronic eavesdropping. *See* **Eavesdropping**
Electronic games. *See* **Electronic toys; Video games**
Electronic listening devices. *See* **Eavesdropping**
Electronic mail systems   383; 384.1; 384.6; *384.3
    Use for materials on the electronic transmission
 of letters, messages, etc. through a communications network. May include telex and
 facsimile transmission as well as communications using computers and computer terminals.
 See also **Computer bulletin boards**
 xx **Postal service; Teletext systems**
Electronic marketing. *See* **Telemarketing**
Electronic music   789.9
 x Music, Electronic; Synthesizer music; Tape recorder music
 xx **Music**
Electronic musical instruments. *See* **Musical instruments, Electronic**
Electronic publishing   070.5; 686.2
    Use for materials on the process of publishing in
 which data is entered on a word processor
 or computer terminal, submitted to an editor or publisher and made available online
 or offline.
 See also **Teletext systems**
 x Online publishing; Publishing, Electronic
 xx **Information services; Publishers and publishing; Telecommunication**
Electronic toys   688.7
 See also **Video games**
 x Electronic games; Games, Electronic
 xx **Electronic apparatus and appliances; Toys**
Electronics   537.5; 621.381
 See also

Amplifiers (Electronics)	appliances
Cybernetics	**Electronic circuits**
Digital electronics	High-fidelity sound sys-
Electronic apparatus and	tems

Electronics—*Continued*
> Microelectronics   Transistors
> Semiconductors
>> *xx* Electrons; Photoelectric cells; Vacuum tubes

Electrons 539.7
> *See also* Electronics
>> *xx* Atoms; Electricity; Neutrons; Particles (Nuclear physics); Physics; Protons; Radioactivity

Electroplating 671.7
> *See also* Electrometallurgy
>> *xx* Electrochemistry; Electrometallurgy; Metalwork

Electrotherapeutics 615.8
> *See also* Radiotherapy
>> *x* Electricity in medicine; Electricity, Medical; Medical electricity
>> *xx* Massage; Physical therapy; Therapeutics

Electrotyping 686.2
> *See also* Electrometallurgy
>> *xx* Electrochemistry; Electrometallurgy; Printing

Elementary education. *See* Education, Elementary

Elementary particles (Physics). *See* Particles (Nuclear physics)

Elementary school libraries. *See* School libraries (Elementary school)

Elements, Chemical. *See* Chemical elements

Elephants 569; 599.6
> *xx* Mammals

Elevators 621.8
> *x* Lifts
> *xx* Hoisting machinery

Elite (Social sciences) (May be subdiv. geog.) 305.5
> *xx* Leadership; Power (Social sciences); Social classes; Social groups

Elizabeth, Queen of Great Britain, 1926- 92
> *x* Rulers
> *xx* Kings, queens, rulers, etc.

Elk Mountain (Wyo.) 978.7
> *xx* Mountains

Elocution. *See* Public speaking

Elves. *See* Fairies

Emancipation. *See* Freedom

Emancipation of slaves. *See* Slavery; Slavery—United States

Emancipation of women. *See* Women—Civil rights

Embassies. *See* Diplomatic and consular service

Emblems. *See* Decorations of honor; Heraldry; Insignia; Mottoes; Seals (Numismatics); Symbolism

Embroidery 746.44
> *See also* types of embroidery, e.g. Beadwork; Crewelwork; Needlepoint; etc.
>> *xx* Decoration and ornament; Needlework; Sewing

Embryology 574.3; 612
> *See also* Cells; Fetus; Genetics; Protoplasm; Reproduction
>> *x* Development
>> *xx* Biology; Cells; Evolution; Protoplasm; Repro-

Embryology—*Continued*
            duction; Zoology
Emergencies.   *See* **Accidents; First aid**
Emergency assistance.   *See* **Helping behavior**
Emergency medicine   616
   xx **Medicine**
Emergency preparedness.   *See* **Disaster relief**
Emergency relief.   *See* **Disaster relief**
Emergency survival.   *See* **Survival skills**
Emigration.   *See* **Immigration and emigration**
Eminent domain   333.1; 343
      x Condemnation of land; Expropriation; Land,
            Condemnation of
      xx **Constitutional law; Land use; Property; Rail-
            roads; Real estate**
Emotional stress.   *See* **Stress (Psychology)**
Emotionally disturbed children   155.4
      See also **Juvenile delinquency; Mentally ill chil-
            dren**
      x Behavior problems (Children); Children,
            Emotionally disturbed; Maladjusted chil-
            dren; Problem children
   xx **Exceptional children**
Emotions   152.4
      See also

Attitude (Psychology)	**Laughter**
Bashfulness	**Love**
Belief and doubt	**Pain**
Fear	**Pleasure**
Horror	**Prejudices**
Joy and sorrow	**Sympathy**

      also names of other emotions
      x Feelings; Frustration; Passions
      xx **Psychology; Psychology, Physiological**
Emperors.   *See* **Kings, queens, rulers, etc.; Roman
            emperors;** and names of emperors, kings,
            etc.
Empiricism   146
      See also **Pragmatism**
      x Experience
      xx **Knowledge, Theory of; Philosophy; Pragma-
            tism; Reality**
Employee absenteeism.   *See* **Absenteeism (Labor)**
Employee benefits.   *See* **Nonwage payments**
Employee health services.   *See* **Occupational health
            services**
✷ **Employee morale   331.2; 658.3**
      See also **Job satisfaction**
      xx **Absenteeism (Labor); Morale; Personnel man-
            agement; Psychology, Applied; Work**
✷ **Employees   331.11; 920**
      See also classes of employees, e.g. **Office em-
            ployees;** etc.
Employees and officials.   *See* **Civil service;** and
            names of countries, cities, etc. and organiza-
            tions with the subdivision *Officials and em-
            ployees,* e.g. **Chicago (Ill.)—Officials and
            employees; United Nations—Officials and
            employees;** etc.
Employees, Clerical.   *See* **Office employees**

Employment security. *See* **Job security**

Employment, Supplementary. *See* **Supplementary employment**

Employment, Temporary. *See* **Temporary employment**

Enamel and enameling 738.4

    x Porcelain enamels

    xx **Decoration and ornament; Decorative arts**

Encounter groups. *See* **Group relations training**

Encyclicals, Papal 262.9

    x Papal encyclicals

Encyclopedias and dictionaries 030; 031; etc.; 403; 413; etc.

    See also **Classical dictionaries; Picture dictionaries; Polyglot dictionaries;** also names of languages and subjects with the subdivision *Dictionaries,* e.g. **English language—Dictionaries; Biography—Dictionaries; Chemistry—Dictionaries; English literature—Dictionaries; United States—Biography—Dictionaries;** etc.

    x Cyclopedias; Dictionaries; Glossaries; Subject dictionaries

    xx **Reference books**

End of the earth. *See* **End of the world**

End of the world 001.9; 236; 291.2; 525

    Use for materials on the end of the world from an eschatological point of view including Judgment Day, signs, fulfillments of prophecies, etc., an astronomical point of view, or discussions of other possible causes.

    x End of the earth; World, End of the

    xx **Eschatology**

Endangered animals. *See* **Rare animals**

Endangered plants. *See* **Rare plants**

Endangered species 574

    See also **Bison; Plant conservation; Rare animals; Rare plants; Wildlife conservation**

    x Threatened species; Vanishing species

    xx **Nature conservation; Rare animals; Rare plants**

Endocrine glands 616.4

    See also **Hormones**

    x Ductless glands; Glands, Ductless

    xx **Endocrinology; Hormones**

Endocrinology 616.4

    See also **Endocrine glands; Hormones**

Endowed charities. *See* **Charities; Endowments**

Endowments 361.6-361.7

    See also **Charities; Scholarships, fellowships, etc.**

    x Endowed charities; Foundations (Endowments); Philanthropy

    xx **Charities**

Endurance, Physical. *See* **Physical fitness**

Energy. *See* **Energy resources; Force and energy**

Energy and state. *See* **Energy resources—Government policy**

Energy, Biomass. *See* **Biomass energy**

Energy conservation 333.79

    See also **Energy consumption; Energy re-**

Energy conservation—*Continued*

> sources—**Government policy;** also types of energy conservation, e.g. **Recycling (Waste, etc.);** etc.
>
> *x* Conservation of energy; Conservation of power resources; Power resources conservation
>
> *xx* **Conservation of natural resources; Energy consumption; Energy resources**

Energy consumption 333.7-333.9

> *See also* **Energy conservation;** also subjects with the subdivision *Fuel consumption,* e.g. **Automobiles—Fuel consumption;** etc.
>
> *x* Consumption of energy
>
> *xx* **Energy conservation; Energy resources**

Energy conversion from waste. *See* **Waste products as fuel**

Energy conversion, Microbial. *See* **Biomass energy**

Energy development 333.79

> *x* Energy resources development; Power resources development

Energy policy. *See* **Energy resources—Government policy**

Energy resources 333.7-333.9

> Materials on the physics and engineering aspects of power are entered under **Power (Mechanics).**
>
> *See also*

Biomass energy	**Renewable energy resources**
Electric power	**sources**
Energy conservation	**Solar energy**
Energy consumption	**Water power**
Fuel	**Wind power**
Ocean energy resources	

> *x* Energy; Power resources; Power supply
>
> *xx* **Natural resources; Power (Mechanics)**

Energy resources development. *See* **Energy development**

Energy resources—Government policy 333.7-333.9; 351.82

> *x* Energy and state; Energy policy; State and energy
>
> *xx* **Energy conservation**

Energy resources, Ocean. *See* **Ocean energy resources**

Energy resources, Renewable. *See* **Renewable energy resources**

Energy technology. *See* **Power (Mechanics)**

Enforcement of law. *See* **Law enforcement**

Engineering 620

> All types of engineering are not included in this list but are to be added as needed.
>
> *See also*

Aeronautics	**Engineers**
Agricultural engineering	**Genetic engineering**
Building materials	**Highway engineering**
Chemical engineering	**Human engineering**
Civil engineering	**Hydraulic engineering**
Efficiency, Industrial	**Marine engineering**
Electric engineering	**Mechanical drawing**

Engineering—*Continued*

Mechanics
Military engineering
Mining engineering
Municipal engineering
Nuclear engineering
Ocean engineering
Railroad engineering
Reliability (Engineering)
Sanitary engineering
Steam engineering
Structural engineering
Systems engineering
Traffic engineering
Water supply engineering

  x Construction
  xx **Building; Industrial arts; Mechanics; Technology**

Engineering drawing. *See* **Mechanical drawing**
Engineering, Genetic. *See* **Genetic engineering**
Engineering instruments 620; 621.028
  x Instruments, Engineering
  xx **Scientific apparatus and instruments**
Engineering materials. *See* **Materials**
Engineering—Periodicals 620; 621.05
  xx **Periodicals**
Engineering, Structural. *See* **Structural engineering**
Engineering—Study and teaching 620; 621.07
  xx **Technical education**
Engineers 621.092; 920
  See also **Inventors**
  xx **Engineering**
Engines 621.4
  See also

Airplanes—Engines
Automobiles—Engines
Diesel engines
Farm engines
Fire engines
Fuel
Gas and oil engines
Heat engines
Marine engines
Pumping machinery
Solar engines
Steam engines
Turbines

  x Motors
  xx **Machinery; Mechanical engineering**
England 914.2; 942
  Use with the subdivisions *Description and travel;
    Industries; Intellectual life; Social life and
    customs* for works limited to England.
  xx **Great Britain**
England, Church of. *See* **Church of England**
England—History. *See* **Great Britain—History**
English as a foreign language. *See* **English as a second language**
English as a second language 428
  See also **English language—Conversations and
    phrases**
  x English as a foreign language; English for foreigners; English language as a second language; English language—Study and teaching, Foreign; English language—Texts for
    foreigners
English authors. *See* **Authors, English**
English composition. *See* **English language—
    Composition and exercises**
English drama 822
  See also **Morality plays; Mysteries and miracle
    plays**
  xx **Drama; English literature**

English drama—Collected works 822.08
    xx **Drama—Collected works**
English drama—History and criticism 822.09
    xx **Drama—History and criticism**
English essays 824.08
    Use for collections of literary essays by several
        authors.
    xx **English literature; Essays**
English fiction 823; Fic
    x Fiction, English
    xx **English literature; Fiction**
English fiction—History and criticism 823.09
English for foreigners. *See* **English as a second lan-**
    guage; English language—Conversations
    and phrases
English grammar. *See* **English language—**
    Grammar
English history. *See* **Great Britain—History**
English language 420
    Subdivisions used under this heading may be
        used under other languages unless otherwise
        specified.
    xx **Language and languages**
English language—0-1100. *See* **Anglo-Saxon lan-**
    guage
English language—Acronyms. *See* **Acronyms**
English language—Americanisms. *See* **American-**
    isms
English language—Antonyms *See* **English lan-**
    guage—Synonyms and antonyms
English language as a second language. *See* **English**
    as a second language
English language—Business English 808
    Business English is a unique subdivision and
        should not be used under other languages.
    See also **Business letters**
    x Business English
    xx **Business letters**
English language—Composition and exercises 808
    See also **Rhetoric**
    x Composition (Rhetoric); English composition
    xx **Rhetoric**
English language—Conversations and phrases 427;
    428
    x English for foreigners
    xx **English as a second language**
English language—Dialects 427
    See also **Americanisms**
    x Dialects
English language—Dictionaries 423
    Dictionaries of English and another language are
        assigned the heading **English language—**
        Dictionaries—[name of second language],
        i.e. **English language—Dictionaries—**
        French; etc.
    See also **English language—Terms and phrases**
    x Glossaries
    xx **Encyclopedias and dictionaries; English lan-**
    guage—Terms and phrases

English language—Dictionaries—French 443
> Use for English-French dictionaries. French-English dictionaries are entered under **French language—Dictionaries—English.** Use both headings for an English-French and French-English dictionary.
>
> *See also* **French language—Dictionaries—English**
>
> *xx* **French language—Dictionaries—English**

English language—Errors 428

English language—Etymology 422
> *x* Etymology

English language—Examinations, questions, etc. 420.76
> *xx* **Examinations**

English language—Foreign words and phrases 422
> *x* Foreign language phrases

English language—Grammar 425
> *See also* **English language—Usage**
>
> *x* English grammar
>
> *xx* **Grammar**

English language—History 420.9
> *xx* **History**

English language—Homonyms 423
> *x* Homonyms

English language—Idioms 427
> *See also* **English language—Provincialisms; English language—Usage**
>
> *x* Idioms
>
> *xx* **English language—Provincialisms**

English language—Jargon 427
> *x* Jargon

English language—Orthography. *See* **English language—Spelling**

English language—Phonetics. *See* **English language—Pronunciation**

English language—Phrases and terms. *See* **English language—Terms and phrases**

English language—Programmed instruction 420.7
> *x* Self-instruction
>
> *xx* **Programmed instruction**

English language—Pronunciation 421
> *x* English language—Phonetics; Phonology; Pronunciation
>
> *xx* **Phonetics**

English language—Provincialisms 427
> *See also* **English language—Idioms**
>
> *x* Localism; Provincialism
>
> *xx* **English language—Idioms**

English language—Punctuation. *See* **Punctuation**

English language—Reading materials. *See* **Reading materials**

English language—Rhetoric. *See* **Rhetoric**

English language—Rhyme 808.1
> *xx* **Rhyme**

English language—Slang 427
> *x* Slang

English language—Social aspects 420

English language—Spelling 421
> *See also* **Spellers; Spelling reform**

English language—Spelling—*Continued*
> *x* English language—Orthography; Orthography; Spelling

English language—Spelling reform. *See* **Spelling reform**

English language—Study and teaching 420.7

English language—Study and teaching, Foreign. *See* **English as a second language**

English language—Synonyms and antonyms 423
> *x* Antonyms; English language—Antonyms; Synonyms; Thesauri

English language—Terms and phrases 427
> Use for general lists of words and phrases which are applicable to certain situations (curious expressions, public speaking phrases, etc.) rather than to a specific subject. If the list is limited to a special field, use the name of the subject with the subdivision *Dictionaries,* e.g. **Chemistry—Dictionaries;** etc.
>
> *See also* **English language—Dictionaries**
> *x* English language—Phrases and terms
> *xx* **English language—Dictionaries**

English language—Texts for foreigners. *See* **English as a second language**

English language—Usage 428
> *xx* **English language—Grammar; English language—Idioms**

English language—Versification. *See* **Versification**

English letters 826
> *xx* **English literature; Letters**

English literature 820
> Subdivisions used under this heading may be used under other literatures.
>
> *See also*

Authors, English	**English prose literature**
English drama	**English wit and humor**
English essays	**Parodies**
English fiction	**Satire, English**
English letters	**Short stories**
English newspapers	**Speeches, addresses, etc.,**
English periodicals	**English**
English poetry	

> *xx* **Literature**

English literature—0-1100. *See* **Anglo-Saxon literature**

English literature—African authors. *See* **African literature (English)**

English literature—Bibliography 016.82

English literature—Bio-bibliography 016.82
> *x* Bio-bibliography
> *xx* **Authors, English**

English literature—Collected works 820.8
> Use for collections of poetry and prose by several authors. Collections of prose are entered under **English prose literature.** Collections of poetry are entered under **English poetry—Collected works.**
>
> *See also* **English poetry—Collected works; English prose literature**

English literature—Collected works—*Continued*
   x Collected works; Collections of literature
   xx **Literature—Collected works**
English literature—Criticism. *See* **English literature—History and criticism**
English literature—Dictionaries 820.3
   See also **English literature—Indexes**
   xx **Encyclopedias and dictionaries; English literature—Indexes**
**English literature—Examinations, questions, etc.
   820.76**
   xx **English literature—Study and teaching**
English literature—History and criticism 820.9
   x English literature—Criticism
   xx **Criticism; History**
English literature—Indexes 820
   See also **English literature—Dictionaries**
   xx **English literature—Dictionaries**
English literature—Outlines, syllabi, etc. 820.2
   See also **English literature—Study and teaching**
   x Outlines, syllabi, etc.
   xx **English literature—Study and teaching; Literature—Outlines, syllabi, etc.**
English literature—Study and teaching 820.7
   See also **English literature—Examinations, questions, etc.; English literature—Outlines, syllabi, etc.**
   xx **English literature—Outlines, syllabi, etc.**
English newspapers 072
   xx **English literature; Newspapers**
English orations. *See* **Speeches, addresses, etc., English**
English parodies. *See* **Parodies**
English periodicals 052
   xx **English literature; Periodicals**
English poetry 821
   xx **English literature; Poetry**
English poetry—Collected works 821.08
   xx **English literature—Collected works; Poetry—
   Collected works**
English poetry—History and criticism 821.09
   xx **Criticism; Poetry—History and criticism**
English prose literature 820.8; 828
   Use for collections of prose writings which may
   include several literary forms, such as es-
   says, fiction, orations, etc.
   x Prose literature, English
   xx **English literature; English literature—
   Collected works**
English satire. *See* **Satire, English**
English speeches. *See* **Speeches, addresses, etc., En-
   glish**
English wit and humor 827.08
   Use for collections of several authors. May be
   used also for materials about English wit
   and humor.
   xx **English literature; Wit and humor**
Engravers 760.92; 920
   See also **Etchers; Lithographers**
   xx **Artists**

Engraving (May subdiv. geog. adjective form, e.g.
              Engraving, American; etc.) 760; 765
      See also **Etching; Gems; Linoleum block print-**
            ing; Mezzotint engraving; Photoengraving;
            Wood engraving
      x Copper engraving; Engravings; Line engrav-
            ing; Steel engraving
      xx **Art; Etching; Graphic arts; Illustration of**
            books; Pictures
Engraving, American 760; 769
      x American engraving; United States—
            Engraving
Engravings. *See* **Engraving**
Enhanced radiation weapons. *See* **Neutron weapons**
Enigmas. *See* **Curiosities and wonders; Riddles**
Enlarging (Photography). *See* **Photography—**
            Enlarging
Enlightenment 190; 909.7; 940.2
      Use for materials on the philosophic movement
          of the 18th century marked by the question-
          ing of traditional doctrines and values, natu-
          ralistic and individualistic tendencies, and
          an emphasis on the empirical method in sci-
          ence and the free use of reason.
      xx **Eighteenth century; Philosophy, Modern; Ra-**
            tionalism
Enlistment. *See* **United States. Army—Recruiting,**
            enlistment, etc.; United States. Navy—
            Recruiting, enlistment, etc.
Ensembles (Mathematics). *See* **Set theory**
Ensigns. *See* **Flags**
Ensilage. *See* **Silage and silos**
Enteric fever. *See* **Typhoid fever**
Entertainers 791.092; 920
      See also names of types of entertainers, e.g.
            Actors and actresses; Clowns; Comedians;
            Dancers; etc.
Entertaining 395; 642
      Use for materials dealing with the art and skill
          of entertaining and hospitality.
      See also **Amusements; Business entertaining;**
            Dinners and dining; Games; Luncheons;
            Parties
      x Guests; Hospitality
      xx **Amusements; Etiquette; Home economics**
Entertainments. *See* **Amusements; Christmas enter-**
            tainments; Church entertainments; Skits
Entomology. *See* **Insects**
Entomology, Economic. *See* **Insects, Injurious and**
            beneficial
Entomology, Medical. *See* **Insects as carriers of**
            disease
Entozoa. *See* **Parasites**
Entrance examinations for colleges. *See* **Colleges**
            and universities—Entrance examinations
Entrance requirements for colleges and
          universities. *See* **Colleges and universi-**
          ties—Entrance requirements; and names of
          individual colleges and universities with the
          subdivision *Entrance requirements*

Entrepreneurs (May subdiv. geog.) **338; 339.2; 920**
　　xx **Business; Business people; Self-employed;**
　　　　Small business
Environment 304.2
　　See also **Ecology;** also subjects with the subdivi-
　　　　sion *Environmental aspects,* e.g. **Nuclear**
　　　　power plants—Environmental aspects; etc.
Environment and pesticides. *See* **Pesticides—**
　　　　Environmental aspects
Environment and state. *See* **Environment—**
　　　　Government policy
Environment—Government policy (May subdiv.
　　　　geog.) **304.2**
　　See also **Conservation of natural resources; Hu-**
　　　　man ecology; Man—Influence on nature;
　　　　Natural resources; Pollution
　　x Environment and state; Environmental pol-
　　　　icy; State and environment
　　xx **Human ecology; Man—Influence on nature**
Environment—Government policy—United States
　　　　304.2
　　x American environmental policy; United
　　　　States—Environmental policy
Environment, Space. *See* **Space environment**
Environmental aspects. *See* subjects with the sub-
　　　　division *Environmental aspects,* e.g.
　　　　Nuclear power plants—Environmental as-
　　　　pects; etc.
Environmental health 616.9
　　See also **Air—Pollution; Occupational health and**
　　　　safety; Pollution; Water—Pollution; also
　　　　subjects with the subdivision *Environmental*
　　　　aspects, e.g. **Nuclear power plants—**
　　　　Environmental aspects; etc.
　　x Health—Environmental aspects
　　xx **Man—Influence of environment; Public health**
Environmental policy. *See* **Environment—**
　　　　Government policy
Environmental pollution. *See* **Pollution**
Environmental radioactivity. *See* **Radioactive pol-**
　　　　lution
Enzymes 547.7; 574.1
　　See also **Fermentation**
Eolithic period. *See* **Stone Age**
Ephemerides. *See* **Nautical almanacs**
Epic poetry 808.1; 808.81; 811.08; etc.
　　See also **Romances**
　　xx **Poetry**
Epidemics 614.4
　　See also **Communicable diseases;** also names of
　　　　contagious diseases, e.g. **Smallpox;** etc.
　　x Pestilences
　　xx **Communicable diseases; Diseases; Public**
　　　　health
Epigrams 808.88; 818; etc.
　　See also **Proverbs; Quotations; Toasts**
　　x Sayings
　　xx **Proverbs; Wit and humor**
Epigraphy. *See* **Inscriptions**

Epilepsy 616.8

    xx **Nervous system—Diseases**

Episcopal Church 283

    Use for materials on the Episcopal Church in the United States after 1789. Materials on the Episcopal Church in the United States prior to 1789 are entered under **Church of England—United States.**

    See also **Church of England—United States**

    x Protestant Episcopal Church in the U.S.A.

    xx **Church of England—United States**

Epistemology. *See* **Knowledge, Theory of**

Epitaphs 929

    x Burial; Graves

    xx **Biography; Cemeteries; Inscriptions; Tombs**

Epithets. *See* **Names; Nicknames**

Epizoa. *See* **Parasites**

Equal employment opportunity. *See* **Discrimination in employment**

Equal opportunity in employment. *See* **Discrimination in employment**

Equal pay for equal work 331.13

    x Pay equity

    xx **Discrimination in employment; Wages; Women—Employment**

Equal rights amendments (May subdiv. geog.) **323.4; 342; 353.9**

    x Amendments, Equal rights; E.R.A.'s; ERAs

    xx **Constitutions; Sex discrimination**

Equal time rule (Broadcasting) 324.7; 384.54; 384.55

    Use for materials on the requirement that all qualified candidates for public office be granted equal broadcast time if one of the candidates is granted time.

    See also **Fairness doctrine (Broadcasting)**

    x Rule of equal time (Broadcasting)

    xx **Elections; Fairness doctrine (Broadcasting); Radio broadcasting; Television broadcasting; Television in politics**

Equality 323.42

    See also **Aristocracy; Democracy; Freedom; Individualism; Social classes; Socialism**

    x Inequality; Social equality

    xx **Democracy; Freedom; Socialism; Sociology**

Equations, Chemical. *See* **Chemical equations**

Equestrianism. *See* **Horseback riding**

Equipment and supplies. *See* appropriate subjects with the subdivision *Equipment and supplies,* e.g. **Sports—Equipment and supplies;** etc.

ERAs. *See* **Equal rights amendments**

Ergonomics. *See* **Human engineering**

Erosion 551.3

    See also **Dust storms; Soil conservation;** also types of erosion, e.g. **Soil erosion;** etc.

    xx **Soil conservation**

Erotic art 704.9

    x Art, Erotic; Art, Immoral; Immoral art; Sex in art

    xx **Erotica**

Erotic literature 704.9

 x Immoral literature; Literature, Erotic; Literature, Immoral

 xx **Erotica**

Erotica 704.9

 See also **Erotic art; Pornography;** also types of erotica, e.g. **Erotic art, Erotic literature;** etc.

 xx **Pornography**

Errors 001.9

 Use for materials on errors of judgment, errors of observation, scientific errors, popular misconceptions, etc. Errors in language are entered under names of languages with the subdivision *Errors,* e.g. **English language—Errors;** etc.

 See also **Superstition**

 x Fallacies; Mistakes

 xx **Superstition**

Ersatz products. *See* **Substitute products**

Eruptions. *See* **Geysers; Volcanoes**

Escape lifestyle. *See* **Counter culture**

Escapes 365; 904

 x Hostage escapes; Prison escapes

 xx **Adventure and adventurers; Prisons**

Eschatology 236; 291.2

 See also **Death; End of the world; Future life; Immortality; Millennium; Second Advent**

 x Intermediate state

 xx **Theology**

Eskimos. *See* **Inuit**

ESP. *See* **Extrasensory perception**

Esperanto 499

 xx **Language, Universal**

Espionage (May subdiv. geog. adjective form) **327.1; 355.3**

 See also **Spies**

 xx **Intelligence service; Secret service; Subversive activities**

Espionage, American 327.1; 355.3

 x American espionage

Esquimaux. *See* **Inuit**

Essay 808.4

 Use for materials on the appreciation of the essay and on writing the essay.

 xx **Literature**

Essays 808.84

 Use for collections of literary essays by authors of different nationalities. Collections of literary essays by American authors are entered under **American essays;** by English authors, under **English essays;** etc. Essays limited to a particular subject, by one or more authors, are entered under that subject. If it is not treated comprehensively, add the subdivision *Addresses and essays.*

 See also **American essays; English essays;** etc.; also general subjects with the subdivision *Addresses and essays,* e.g.

 Agriculture—Addresses and essays; United States—History—Addresses and essays;

Essays—*Continued*
> **World War, 1939-1945—Addresses and essays;** etc.
> *x* Collections of literature
> *xx* **Literature—Collected works**

Essences and essential oils 664; 668
> *See also* **Flavoring essences; Perfumes**
> *x* Aromatic plant products; Oils, Essential; Vegetable oils; Volatile oils
> *xx* **Distillation; Oils and fats**

Estate planning 332.024; 343.05
> *See also* **Inheritance and transfer tax; Insurance; Investments; Taxation**
> *xx* **Finance, Personal**

Estate tax. *See* **Inheritance and transfer tax**

Esthetics 111; 701
> *See also*

Art appreciation	**Rhythm**
Color	**Romanticism**
Criticism	**Sculpture**
Painting	**Values**
Poetry	

> *x* Aesthetics; Beauty; Taste (Esthetics)
> *xx* **Art**

Estimates. *See* appropriate technical subjects with the subdivision *Estimates,* e.g. **Building—Estimates;** etc.

Estrangement (Social psychology). *See* **Alienation (Social psychology)**

Etchers 760.92; 920
> *xx* **Artists; Engravers**

Etching 767
> *See also* **Engraving**
> *x* Etchings
> *xx* **Art; Engraving; Pictures**

Etchings. *See* **Etching**

Eternal life. *See* **Future life**

Eternal punishment. *See* **Hell**

Eternity 115
> Use for materials on the philosophical concept of eternity. Materials dealing with the character and form of a future life are entered under **Future life.**
> *See also* **Future life**
> *xx* **Future life**

Ethanol. *See* **Alcohol as fuel**

Ethical education. *See* **Moral education; Religious education**

Ethics (May subdiv. geog. adjective form, e.g. **Ethics, Japanese; Ethics, Jewish;** etc.) **170**
> *See also*

Charity	**Loyalty**
Conscience	**Moral education**
Cruelty	**Secularism**
Duty	**Sin**
Free will and determinism	**Social ethics**
Good and evil	**Spiritual life**
Honesty	**Stoics**
Human behavior	**Utilitarianism**
Joy and sorrow	**Values**
Justice	

227

Ethics—*Continued*

also types of ethics, e.g. **Business ethics; Christian ethics; Professional ethics; Work ethics;** etc.; and subjects with the subdivision *Moral and religious aspects,* e.g. **Birth control—Moral and religious aspects;** etc.

x Moral philosophy; Morality; Morals; Natural law; Philosophy, Moral

xx **Human behavior; Philosophy**

Ethics, American 170

x American ethics; United States—Ethics

Ethics, Biological. *See* **Bioethics**

Ethics, Business. *See* **Business ethics**

Ethics, Christian. *See* **Christian ethics**

Ethics, Legal. *See* **Legal ethics**

Ethics, Medical. *See* **Medical ethics**

Ethics, Political. *See* **Political ethics**

Ethics, Professional. *See* **Professional ethics**

Ethics, Sexual. *See* **Sexual ethics**

Ethics, Social. *See* **Social ethics**

Ethics, Work. *See* **Work ethics**

Ethiopian-Italian War, 1935-1936. *See* **Italo-Ethiopian War, 1935-1936**

Ethnic groups 305.8

Use for theoretical materials on groups of people who are bound together by common ties of ancestry and culture. Materials on several ethnic groups in a particular region or country are entered under **Ethnology** subdivided geographically. Materials on individual ethnic groups are entered unter the name of the group, e.g. **Mexican Americans;** etc.

See also **Ethnic relations; Minorities; Race relations**

x Groups, Ethnic

xx **Ethnology**

Ethnic psychology. *See* **Ethnopsychology**

Ethnic relations 305.8; 323.1

See also **Culture conflict; Discrimination; Intercultural education; Minorities; Race relations**

x Conflict, Ethnic; Relations among ethnic groups

xx **Acculturation; Ethnic groups; Ethnology; Minorities; Race relations; Social problems; Sociology**

Ethnography. *See* **Ethnology**

Ethnology (May subdiv. geog.) **572**

See note under **Ethnic groups.**

See also

Acculturation	**Folklore**
Anthropogeography	**Language and languages**
Anthropology	**Man, Nonliterate**
Anthropometry	**Man, Prehistoric**
Archeology	**Manners and customs**
Cannibalism	**Physical anthropology**
Civilization	**Race**
Costume	**Race relations**
Ethnic groups	**Sacrifice**
Ethnic relations	**Society, Nonliterate folk**
Ethnopsychology	**Totems and totemism**

Ethnology—*Continued*

also names of peoples, e.g. **Blacks; Teutonic peoples;** etc.; and names of countries with the subdivision *Social life and customs,* e.g. **United States—Social life and customs;** etc.

x Aborigines; Cultural anthropology; Ethnography; Geographical distribution of people; Native peoples; Races of people; Social anthropology

xx **Anthropology; Archeology; Civilization; Geography; History; Man; Science**

Ethnology—United States 572.973

See also **Americans;** also names of individual ethnic groups, e.g. **Hispanic Americans; Indians of North America; Mexican Americans;** etc.

x United States—Ethnology; United States—Peoples

Ethnopsychology 155.8

See also **Culture conflict; National characteristics; Social psychology;** also names of racial or ethnic groups with the subdivision *Psychology,* e.g. **Indians of North America—Psychology;** etc.

x Cross cultural psychology; Ethnic psychology; Folk psychology; National psychology; Psychology, Ethnic; Psychology, National; Psychology, Racial; Race psychology

xx **Anthropology; Ethnology; National characteristics; Psychology; Social psychology; Sociology**

Ethyl alcohol fuel. *See* **Alcohol as fuel**

Etiquette 395

See also **Courtesy; Dancing; Dating (Social customs); Dinners and dining; Entertaining; Letter writing; Manners and customs;** also types of etiquette as in phrases, e.g. **Table etiquette;** etc.; and names of countries with the subdivision *Social life and customs*

x Ceremonies; Manners; Politeness; Salutations

xx **Human behavior; Manners and customs**

Etymology. *See* names of languages with the subdivision *Etymology,* e.g. **English language—Etymology;** etc.

Eucharist. *See* **Lord's Supper**

Eugenics 573.2; 575.1

See also **Birth control; Heredity**

xx **Anthropology; Family; Genetics; Heredity; Population; Social problems**

Europe 914; 940

x Europe, Western; Western Europe

Europe, Central. *See* **Central Europe**

Europe, Eastern. *See* **Eastern Europe**

Europe—History 940

Europe—History—0-476 936; 937

Europe—History—476-1492 940.1; 940.2

See also **Holy Roman Empire; Hundred Years' War, 1339-1453; Middle Ages—History; Thirteenth century**

xx **Middle Ages—History**

Europe—History—1492-1789 940.2
> *See also* **Thirty Years' War, 1618-1648**
> *xx* **Reformation**

Europe—History—1789-1900 940.2
> *x* Europe—History—1800-1899 (19th century);
> Napoleonic Wars

Europe—History—1800-1899 (19th century). *See*
Europe—History—1789-1900

Europe—History—1900-1999 (20th century) 940.5

Europe—History—1914-1945 940.5
> *See also* **World War, 1914-1918; World War,
> 1939-1945**

Europe—History—1945- 940.55

Europe—Politics and government 940
> May be subdivided by period using the same
> subdivisions as under **Europe—History,**
> e.g. **Europe—Politics and government—
> 1789-1900.**
>
> *See also* **European federation**

Europe, Western. *See* **Europe**

European Common Market. *See* **European Economic Community**

European Economic Community 382.9
> *x* Common market; European Common Market

European federation 341.24; 940
> *x* Federation of Europe; Paneuropean federation; United States of Europe (proposed)
> *xx* **Europe—Politics and government; Federal
> government; International organization**

European War, 1914-1918. *See* **World War, 1914-1918**

European War, 1939-1945. *See* **World War, 1939-1945**

Euthanasia 174
> *See also* **Right to die**
> *x* Death, Mercy; Killing, Mercy; Mercy killing;
> Right to life
> *xx* **Homicide; Medical ethics; Right to die**

Evacuation of civilians. *See* names of wars with
the subdivision *Evacuation of civilians,* e.g.
World War, 1939-1945—Evacuation of civilians; etc.

Evaluation of literature. *See* **Books and reading;
Books and reading—Best books; Books—
Reviews; Criticism; Literature—History and
criticism**

Evangelism. *See* **Evangelistic work**

Evangelism and politics. *See* **Religion and politics**

Evangelistic healing. *See* **Spiritual healing**

Evangelistic work 253.7
> *See also* **Conversion; Missions, Christian; Revivals**
> *x* Evangelism; Revival (Religion)
> *xx* **Church work; Missions, Christian; Revivals**

Evening and continuation schools 374
> *See also* **Adult education**
> *x* Continuation schools; Evening schools; Night
> schools
> *xx* **Adult education; Continuing education; Education; Education, Compulsory; Education,**

Evening and continuation schools—*Continued*
Secondary; Public schools; Technical education

Evening schools. *See* **Evening and continuation schools**

Evergreens 585
xx **Landscape gardening; Shrubs; Trees**

Everyday living skills. *See* **Life skills**

Evidences of Christianity. *See* **Apologetics**

Evidences of the Bible. *See* **Bible—Evidences, authority, etc.**

Evil. *See* **Good and evil**

Evil spirits. *See* **Demonology**

Evolution 573.2; 575
See also

Adaptation (Biology)	ronment
Anatomy, Comparative	**Man—Origin**
Biology	**Mendel's law**
Creation	**Natural selection**
Embryology	**Religion and science**
Heredity	**Social change**
Life—Origin	**Variation (Biology)**
Man—Influence of envi-	

x Darwinism; Development; Mutation (Biology); Origin of species
xx **Biology; Creation; Genetics; Heredity; Man—Origin; Natural selection; Philosophy, Modern; Religion and science; Variation (Biology); Zoology**

Evolution—Study and teaching 573.2; 575
See also **Creation—Study and teaching**
xx **Creation—Study and teaching**

Ex-Catholic priests. *See* **Ex-priests**

Ex libris. *See* **Bookplates**

Ex-priests 253
x Catholic ex-priests; Ex-Catholic priests
xx **Catholic Church—Clergy; Priests**

Ex-service men. *See* **Veterans**

Examinations 371.2
Use for general materials, such as discussions of the value of examinations, statistics, history, etc. Materials discussing the requirements for examinations in particular branches of study, or compilations of questions and answers for such examinations, are entered under the subject with the subdivision *Examinations, questions, etc.,* e.g. **English language—Examinations, questions, etc.;** etc.

See also **Civil service—Examinations; Colleges and universities—Entrance examinations; Colleges and universities—Entrance requirements; Mental tests;** also particular branches of study with the subdivision *Examinations, questions, etc.,* e.g. **English language—Examinations, questions, etc.; Music—Examinations, questions, etc.;** etc.; and names of individual examinations, e.g. **Graduate record examination; Scholastic aptitude test;** etc.

Examinations—*Continued*

    x Achievement tests; Objective tests; Tests

    xx **Educational tests and measurements; Questions and answers; Teaching**

Excavation 624.1

    xx **Civil engineering; Tunnels**

Excavations (Archeology) (May subdiv. geog.) **930.1**

    See also **Mounds and mound builders**

    x Earthworks (Archeology); Ruins

    xx **Archeology; Cities and towns, Ruined, extinct, etc.; Mounds and mound builders**

Excavations (Archeology)—United States 973

    x United States—Excavations (Archeology)

Exceptional children 155.4

    See also **Brain damaged children; Emotionally disturbed children; Feral children; Gifted children; Handicapped children; Mainstreaming in education; Slow learning children**

    x Abnormal children; Children, Abnormal; Children, Exceptional

    xx **Children; Education, Elementary**

Exchange 332.4; 332.6

    See also **Commerce; Foreign exchange; Money; Stock exchange**

    xx **Commerce**

Exchange, Barter. *See* **Barter**

Exchange, Foreign. *See* **Foreign exchange**

Exchange of persons programs 370.19

    See also classes of persons participating in an exchange, e.g. **Teachers, Interchange of;** etc.

    x Cultural exchange programs; Interchange of visitors; Specialists exchange programs; Visitors' exchange programs

    xx **Cultural relations; International cooperation**

Exchange of prisoners of war. *See* **Prisoners of war**

Exchange of teachers. *See* **Teachers, Interchange of**

Exchange rates. *See* **Foreign exchange**

Executions. *See* **Capital punishment**

Executive ability 658.4

    See also **Efficiency, Industrial; Leadership**

    x Administrative ability

    xx **Ability; Efficiency, Industrial**

Executive departments. *See* names of countries, states, etc. with the subdivision *Executive departments,* e.g. **United States—Executive departments;** etc.

Executive departments—Reorganization. *See* names of countries, states, etc. with the subdivision *Executive departments—Reorganization,* e.g. **United States—Executive departments—Reorganization;** etc.

Executive investigations. *See* **Governmental investigations**

Executive power (May subdiv. geog.) **351.003; 353.03**

    Use for materials that discuss the duties, rights and abuses of the highest administrative authority of a country, often as compared or

Executive power—*Continued*
    contrasted with the legislative power.
    See also **Heads of state; Monarchy; Presidents;**
        Prime ministers; Separation of powers
    x Presidents—Powers and duties
    xx **Constitutional law; Political science; Presidents**
Executive power—United States 353.03
    x Presidents—Unites States—Power; United
        States—Executive power
Executors and administrators 346.05
    See also **Wills**
    x Administrators and executors
    xx **Inheritance and succession; Wills**
Exegesis, Biblical. *See* **Bible—Criticism, interpretation, etc.**
Exercise 613.7; 796.4
    See also **Bodybuilding; Gymnastics; Physical education; Physical fitness; Reducing;** also
    names of special exercises and physical activities, e.g. **Aerobics; Rowing; Weight lifting;** etc.
    xx **Health; Hygiene; Physical education**
Exercises, Aerobic. *See* **Aerobics**
Exercises, Reducing. *See* **Reducing**
Exhaustion. *See* **Fatigue**
Exhibitions
    See also **Craft shows; Fashion shows; Flower shows;** also subjects with the subdivision *Exhibitions,* e.g. **Art—Exhibitions; Printing—Exhibitions;** etc.; and names of exhibitions, e.g. **Expo '89 (Paris, France);** etc.
    x Exhibits; Expositions; Industrial exhibitions; International exhibitions; World's fairs
    xx **Fairs**
Exhibits. *See* **Exhibitions**
Exiles. *See* **Refugees**
Existentialism 142
    xx **Metaphysics; Phenomenology; Philosophy, Modern**
Exobiology. *See* **Life on other planets; Space biology**
Exorcism 133.4
    See also **Demoniac possession; Demonology; Witchcraft**
    xx **Demoniac possession; Demonology; Superstition**
Expanding universe. *See* **Universe**
Expeditions, Antarctic and Arctic. *See* **Antarctic regions; Arctic regions;** and names of expeditions, e.g. **Byrd Antarctic Expedition;** etc.
Expeditions, Scientific. *See* **Scientific expeditions**
Experience. *See* **Empiricism**
Experimental farms. *See* **Agricultural experiment stations**
Experimental films 791.43
    x Avant-garde films; Motion pictures, Experimental; Personal films; Underground films
    xx **Motion pictures**

Experimental methods in education. *See* **Education—Experimental methods**

Experimental psychology. *See* **Psychology, Physiological**

Experimental schools 371
> Use for materials on schools in which new teaching methods, organizations of subject matter, educational theories, personnel practices, etc. are tested.
> *See also* **Open plan schools**
> *x* Alternative schools; Education, Nonformal; Free schools; Project schools; Schools, Nonformal
> *xx* **Education—Experimental methods; Open plan schools**

Experimental theater 792
> *x* Avant-garde theater
> *xx* **Theater**

Experimental universities. *See* **Free universities**

Experiments, Scientific. *See* **Science—Experiments;** and particular branches of science with the subdivision *Experiments,* e.g. **Chemistry—Experiments,** etc.

Exploration, Space. *See* **Outer space—Exploration**

Exploration, Submarine. *See* **Underwater exploration**

Exploration, Underwater. *See* **Underwater exploration**

Explorations. *See* **America—Exploration; Discoveries (in geography); Explorers;** and names of countries with the subdivision *Exploring expeditions,* e.g. **United States—Exploring expeditions;** etc.

Explorer (Artificial satellite) 629.46
> *xx* **Artificial satellites**

Explorers 910.92; 920
> *See also* **America—Exploration; Discoveries (in geography); Travelers; United States—Description and travel; United States—Exploring expeditions; Voyages and travels;** also names of countries with the subdivisions *Description and travel* and *Exploring expeditions,* e.g. **United States—Exploring expeditons;** etc.; and names of individual explorers
> *x* Discoverers; Explorations; Navigators; Voyagers
> *xx* **Adventure and adventurers; America—Exploration; Discoveries (in geography); Heroes and heroines; Travelers; Voyages and travels**

Exploring expeditions. *See* names of countries with the subdivision *Exploring expeditions,* e.g. **United States—Exploring expeditions;** etc.; and names of expeditions, e.g. **Lewis and Clark Expedition (1804-1806);** etc.

Explosions 904
> *xx* **Accidents**

Explosives 623.4; 662
> *See also* types of explosives and explosive de-

234

Explosives—*Continued*
    vices, e.g. **Ammunition; Dynamite; Gunpow-
        der; Torpedoes;** etc.
xx **Chemistry**
Expo '89 (Paris, France) 607.4
    x Paris (France). World's Fair, 1989; World's
        Fair (1989: Paris, France)
xx **Exhibitions; Fairs**
Exports. *See* **Commerce; Tariff**
Expositions. *See* **Exhibitions**
Express highways 625.7
    x Freeways; Interstate highways; Limited access
        highways; Motorways; Parkways; Super-
        highways; Toll roads; Turnpikes (Modern)
xx **Roads; Traffic engineering**
Express service 380.5
    See also **Pony express**
xx **Railroads; Transportation**
Expressionism (Art) 759.06
    See also **Postimpressionism (Art)**
xx **Painting; Postimpressionism (Art)**
Expropriation. *See* **Eminent domain**
Extended care facilities. *See* **Long-term care facili-
        ties**
Extension work, Agricultural. *See* **Agricultural ex-
        tension work**
Extermination of Jews (1933-1945). *See* **Holocaust,
        Jewish (1933-1945)**
Extermination of pests. *See* **Pests—Control**
Extinct animals 560, 562-569
    See also **Prehistoric animals; Rare animals;** also
        names of extinct animals, e.g. **Mastodon;**
        etc.
    x Animals, Extinct
xx **Fossils; Prehistoric animals; Rare animals;
        Wildlife**
Extinct cities. *See* **Cities and towns, Ruined, ex-
        tinct, etc.**
Extinct plants. *See* **Plants, Fossil**
Extracurricular activities. *See* **Student activities**
Extragalactic nebulae. *See* **Galaxies**
Extramarital relationships. *See* **Adultery**
Extrasensory perception 133.8
    See also **Telepathy**
    x E.S.P.; ESP
xx **Clairvoyance; Psychical research**
Extraterrestrial bases 629.44
    See note under **Space colonies.**
    See also **Space colonies**
xx **Space colonies**
Extraterrestrial beings 574.999
    x Aliens from outer space; Interplanetary visi-
        tors
xx **Life on other planets**
Extraterrestrial communication. *See* **Interstellar
        communication**
Extraterrestrial environment. *See* **Space environ-
        ment**
Extraterrestrial life. *See* **Life on other planets;
        Space biology**

Extravehicular activity (Space flight) 629.45

    x Space vehicles—Extravehicular activity;
        Space walk; Walking in space

    xx **Space flight**

Extremism (Political science). *See* **Radicals and
    radicalism; Right and left (Political science)**

Extremities, Artificial. *See* **Artificial limbs**

Eye 611; 612

    See also **Optometry; Vision**

    xx **Face; Head; Optometry; Vision**

Eyeglasses 617.7; 681

    See also kinds of eyeglasses, e.g. **Contact lenses;**
        etc.

    x Spectacles

F.M. radio. *See* **Radio frequency modulation**

Fables 398.2

    Use for materials in which animals or inanimate
        objects speak and act like human beings.
        Also used for materials about fables.

    See also **Animals—Fiction; Folklore; Parables**

    x Tales

    xx **Allegories; Fiction; Folklore; Legends; Litera-**
        ture; Parables

Fabrics 677

    See also names and types of fabrics, e.g. **Linen;**
        Nylon; Synthetic fabrics; etc.

    x Cloth; Dry goods; Textiles

    xx **Decorative arts**

Fabrics, Synthetic. *See* **Synthetic fabrics**

Face 611; 612

    See also **Eye; Nose; Physiognomy**

    xx **Head; Physiognomy**

Facetiae. *See* **Anecdotes; Wit and humor**

Factories 725

    See also kinds of factories, e.g. **Mills and mill-**
        work; etc.; also headings beginning with the
        word **Factory**

    x Industrial plants; Mill and factory buildings;
        Plants, Industrial

    xx **Industrial buildings; Mills and millwork**

Factories—Management. *See* **Factory management**

Factories—Training departments. *See* **Employ-**
    ees—Training

Factory and trade waste. *See* **Industrial wastes**

Factory management 658.5

    Use for materials on the technical aspects of
        manufacturing processes. Materials on gen-
        eral principles of management of industries
        are entered under **Industrial management.**

    See also

Efficiency, Industrial	**Office management**
Job analysis	**Personnel management**
Management—Employee	**Supervisors**
participation	**Time study**
Motion study	

    x Factories—Management; Production engi-
        neering; Shop management

    xx **Efficiency, Industrial; Industrial management;**
        Management; Personnel management

Factory schools. *See* **Employees—Training**

Factory waste. *See* **Industrial wastes**
Factory workers. *See* **Labor**
Facts, Miscellaneous. *See* **Curiosities and wonders**
Faculty (Education). *See* **Colleges and universi-
ties—Faculty; Educators; Teachers**
Faience. *See* **Pottery**
Failure in business. *See* **Bankruptcy; Business fail-
ures**
Failure of banks. *See* **Bank failures**
Failures, Structural. *See* **Structural failures**
Fair employment practice. *See* **Discrimination in
employment**
Fair housing. *See* **Discrimination in housing**
Fair trade. *See* **Competition, Unfair**
Fair trade (Tariff). *See* **Free trade and protection**
Fair trial and free press. *See* **Freedom of the press
and fair trial**
Fair use (Copyright) 341.7
xx **Copyright**
Fairies 398
See also **Fairy tales**
x Elves; Gnomes; Goblins
xx **Folklore; Superstition**
Fairness doctrine (Broadcasting) 384.54; 384.55
Use for materials on the requirement that, if one
side of a controversial issue is aired, the
other side must have the same opportunity.
See also **Equal time rule (Broadcasting)**
x Doctrine of fairness (Broadcasting)
xx **Equal time rule (Broadcasting); Radio broadcasting; Television broadcasting; Television
in politics**
Fairs 607.4
See also **Exhibitions; Markets;** also names of
fairs, e.g. **Expo '89 (Paris, France);** etc.
x Bazaars; Trade fairs; World's fairs
xx **Markets**
Fairy tales 398.2
See also **Folklore**
x Children's stories; Stories; Tales
xx **Children's literature; Fairies; Fiction; Folklore; Legends; Literature**
Faith 234
Use for materials on religious belief and doubt.
Materials on belief and doubt from the
philosophical standpoint are entered under
Belief and doubt.
See also **Agnosticism; Atheism; Hope; Skepticism; Truth**
x Religious belief
xx **Religion; Salvation; Spiritual life; Theology**
Faith, Confessions of. *See* **Creeds**
Faith cure. *See* **Spiritual healing**
Faith healing. *See* **Spiritual healing**
Faith—Psychology 200.1; 234; 253.5
xx **Psychology, Religious**
Faithfulness. *See* **Loyalty**
Falconry 799.2
x Hawking
xx **Game and game birds; Hunting**

Fall. *See* **Autumn**
Fallacies. *See* **Errors; Logic**
Falling stars. *See* **Meteors**
Fallout, Radioactive. *See* **Radioactive fallout**
Fallout shelters. *See* **Air raid shelters**
False advertising. *See* **Advertising, Fraudulent**
Falsehood. *See* **Truthfulness and falsehood**
Families, Nonrelated. *See* **Shared housing**
Family 306.8
> Use for materials stressing the sociological con-
> cept and structure of the family. Materials
> stressing the everyday life, interaction, and
> relationships of family members are entered
> under **Family life.**

> *See also*

Brothers and sisters	**Family reunions**
Childlessness	**Home**
Clans	**Marriage**
Divorce	**Married women**
Domestic relations	**Parent and child**
Eugenics	**Single parent family**
Family life	**Widows**

> also names of members of the family, e.g.
> **Children; Fathers; Mothers;** etc.
> *xx* **Domestic relations; Family reunions; Home;
> Human relations; Marriage; Sociology**
Family budget. *See* **Budgets, Household**
Family devotions. *See* **Devotional exercises; Fami-
> ly—Religious life**
Family histories. *See* **Genealogy**
Family life 306.8
> See note under **Family.**
> *x* Family relations; Home life
> *xx* **Family**
Family life education 306.8; 362.8
> *See also* **Home economics; Human relations;
> Marriage counseling; Sex education**
> *xx* **Human relations**
Family names. *See* **Names, Personal**
Family planning. *See* **Birth control**
Family prayers. *See* **Devotional exercises; Family—
> Religious life**
Family relations. *See* **Domestic relations; Family
> life**
Family—Religious life 249
> *x* Family devotions; Family prayers; Family
> worship
> *xx* **Religious life**
Family reunions 306.8; 392
> *See also* **Family**
> *x* Reunions, Family
> *xx* **Family**
Family social work. *See* **Social case work**
Family trees. *See* **Genealogy**
Family violence 362.8
> *See also* **Child abuse; Elderly abuse; Husband
> abuse; Wife abuse**
> *x* Domestic violence; Household violence
> *xx* **Violence**
Family worship. *See* **Family—Religious life**

Famines (May subdiv. geog.) **904**
  xx **Food supply; Starvation**
Famines—United States 904
  x United States—Famines
Famous people. *See* **Celebrities**
Fanaticism 152.4; 200.1; 303
  See also **Asceticism**
  x Intolerance
Fancy dress. *See* **Costume**
Fans 391
  xx **Costume**
Fantastic fiction 808.3; Fic
  See also **Science fiction**
  xx **Fiction**
Fantasy 154.3
  See also **Hallucinations and illusions**
  x Day dreams
  xx **Dreams; Imagination**
Far East. *See* **East Asia**
Farm animals. *See* **Domestic animals; Livestock**
Farm buildings 631.2; 728
  See also names of specific farm buildings, e.g.
    Barns; etc.
  x Architecture, Rural; Buildings, Farm; Rural
    architecture
  xx **Architecture; Architecture, Domestic; Build-
    ings**
Farm corporations. *See* **Agribusiness**
Farm credit. *See* **Agricultural credit**
Farm crops. *See* **Farm produce**
Farm engines 631.3
  See also **Agricultural engineering; Tractors**
  xx **Agricultural machinery; Engines; Gas and oil
    engines; Steam engines**
Farm implements. *See* **Agricultural machinery**
Farm laborers. *See* **Agricultural laborers**
Farm life (May subdiv. geog.) **307.7; 630.1**
  See also **Country life; Ranch life; Sociology, Ru-
    ral**
  x Rural life
  xx **Country life; Farmers; Sociology, Rural**
Farm life—United States 307.7; 630.1
  x United States—Farm life
Farm machinery. *See* **Agricultural machinery**
Farm management 631
  See also **Agriculture—Economic aspects**
  xx **Agriculture—Economic aspects; Farms; Man-
    agement**
Farm mechanics. *See* **Agricultural engineering; Ag-
    ricultural machinery**
Farm produce 633
  See also names of farm products, e.g. **Hay;** etc.
  x Agricultural products; Crops; Farm crops
  xx **Food; Raw materials**
Farm produce—Marketing 338.1
  See also **Agriculture—Economic aspects**
  x Fruit—Marketing; Marketing of farm pro-
    duce; Vegetables—Marketing
  xx **Agriculture—Economic aspects; Marketing;
    Prices**

239

Farm tenancy   333.5
>   Use for materials on the economic and social aspects of farm tenancy. Materials dealing with the legal aspects are entered under **Landlord and tenant.**
>   *x* Agriculture—Tenant farming; Farming on shares; Sharecropping; Tenant farming
>   *xx* **Farms; Land tenure; Landlord and tenant**

Farmers   631.092
>   *See also* **Farm life**
>   *xx* **Agriculture; Country life**

Farmers' cooperatives.   *See* **Agriculture, Cooperative**

Farming.   *See* **Agriculture**

Farming corporations.   *See* **Agribusiness**

Farming, Dry.   *See* **Dry farming**

Farming on shares.   *See* **Farm tenancy**

Farms   631.2
>   *See also* **Farm management; Farm tenancy**
>   *xx* **Agriculture; Land use; Real estate**

Farms, Experimental.   *See* **Agricultural experiment stations**

Farriering.   *See* **Blacksmithing**

Fascism (May subdiv. geog.)   **320.5; 321.9; 355.6**
>   Use for materials on the political philosophy, movement or regime that advocates a centralized autocratic government, severe economic and social regimentation, and the exaltation of nation and race over the individual. Materials on fascism in Germany during the Nazi regime are entered under **National socialism.**
>   *See also* **National socialism**
>   *x* Authoritarianism; Neo-fascism; Neo-nazism
>   *xx* **National socialism; Totalitarianism**

Fascism—Germany   943.087
>   *See also* **National socialism**

Fascism—United States   973.9
>   *x* United States—Fascism

Fashion   391
>   Use for materials describing the prevailing mode or style of dress. Descriptive and historical materials on the costume of particular countries, periods, or peoples and materials on fancy dress and theatrical costumes are entered under **Costume.** Materials dealing with clothing from a practical standpoint, including the art of dress, are entered under **Clothing and dress.**
>   *See also* **Clothing and dress; Costume; Dressmaking; Tailoring**
>   *x* Style in dress
>   *xx* **Clothing and dress; Costume**

Fashion design   746.9
>   *x* Costume design
>   *xx* **Commercial art; Design**

Fashion models.   *See* **Models, Fashion**

Fashion shows   391.074; 659.1
>   *xx* **Exhibitions**

Fashionable society.   *See* **Upper classes**

Fast breeder reactors. *See* **Nuclear reactors**
Fast foods. *See* **Convenience foods**
Faster reading. *See* **Rapid reading**
Fasting 178
>   *See also* **Asceticism; Fasts and feasts; Hunger;
>   Hunger strikes; Starvation**
>   *x* Abstinence
>   *xx* **Hunger; Starvation**
Fasts and feasts 263; 394.2
>   Use for materials on religious fasts and feasts in
>   general and on Christian fasts and feasts.
>   May be subdivided by religion, e.g. **Fasts
>   and feasts—Judaism;** etc. Materials on sec-
>   ular festivals are entered under **Festivals.**
>   *See also* **Festivals; Holidays;** also names of indi-
>   vidual fasts and feasts
>   *x* Church festivals; Days; Ecclesiastical fasts and
>   feasts; Feasts; Fiestas; Holy days; Religious
>   festivals
>   *xx* **Fasting; Festivals; Holidays; Rites and cere-
>   monies**
Fasts and feasts—Judaism 296.4
>   *See also* names of individual fasts and feasts,
>   e.g. **Hanukkah; Passover; Yom Kippur;** etc.
>   *x* Festivals—Jews; Holidays, Jewish; Jewish
>   holidays; Jews—Festivals
>   *xx* **Judaism**
Fat. *See* **Oils and fats**
Fatally ill children. *See* **Terminally ill children**
Fatally ill patients. *See* **Terminally ill**
Fate and fatalism 149
>   *See also* **Free will and determinism; Predestina-
>   tion**
>   *x* Destiny; Fortune
>   *xx* **Philosophy**
Fathers 392
>   *xx* **Family; Homemakers; Men**
Fathers and daughters 306.8
>   *x* Daughters and fathers
>   *xx* **Girls; Parent and child**
Fathers and sons 305.3; 306.8
>   *x* Sons and fathers
>   *xx* **Boys; Parent and child**
Fatigue 612; 613.7
>   *See also* **Jet lag; Rest**
>   *x* Exhaustion; Weariness
>   *xx* **Physiology; Rest**
Fatness. *See* **Obesity**
Fats. *See* **Oils and fats**
Fauna. *See* **Animals; Zoology**
Fayence. *See* **Pottery**
Fear 152.4
>   *See also* **Horror; Phobias; Separation anxiety in
>   children**
>   *x* Anxiety
>   *xx* **Courage; Emotions; Nervous system—
>   Diseases; Neuroses**
Feast of Dedication. *See* **Hanukkah**
Feast of Lights. *See* **Hanukkah**
Feasts. *See* **Fasts and feasts**

Fecundity. *See* **Fertility**

Federal aid to education 379.1
> Use same pattern for federal aid to other subjects.
> *x* Education—Federal aid
> *xx* **Colleges and universities—Finance; Education—Finance; Education—Government policy; Grants-in-aid**

Federal aid to libraries 021.8
> *x* Libraries—Federal aid
> *xx* **Grants-in-aid; Libraries—Government policy; Library finance**

Federal budget. *See* **Budget—United States**

Federal-city relations
> *x* City-federal relations; Federal-municipal relations; Municipal-federal relations; Urban-federal relations
> *xx* **Federal government; Municipal government**

Federal courts. *See* **Courts—United States**

Federal government 351
> *See also* **Democracy; European federation; Federal-city relations; Federal-state relations; State governments**
> *x* Confederacies; Federalism
> *xx* **Constitutional law; Democracy; Political science; Republics; State governments**

Federal grants. *See* **Grants-in-aid**

Federal-Indian relations. *See* **Indians of North America—Government policy**

Federal libraries. *See* **Government libraries**

Federal-municipal relations. *See* **Federal-city relations**

Federal Reserve banks 332.1
> *xx* **Banks and banking**

Federal revenue sharing. *See* **Revenue sharing**

Federal spending policy. *See* **United States—Appropriations and expenditures**

Federal-state relations
> *x* State-federal relations
> *xx* **Federal government; State governments**

Federal-state tax relations. *See* **Intergovernmental tax relations**

Federalism. *See* **Federal government**

Federation, International. *See* **International organization**

Federation of Europe. *See* **European federation**

Feedback control systems 629.8
> *See also* **Servomechanisms**
> *xx* **Automation**

Feedback (Psychology) 153.1
> *See also* **Biofeedback training**
> *xx* **Learning, Psychology of**

Feeding behavior in animals. *See* **Animals—Food**

Feeds 633
> *See also* **Forage plants; Hay; Root crops; Silage and silos;** also names of feeds, e.g. **Oats;** etc.
> *x* Fodder
> *xx* **Grasses; Hay; Root crops**

Feeling. *See* **Perception; Touch**

Feelings. *See* **Emotions**

Feet. *See* **Foot**

Fellowships. *See* **Scholarships, fellowships, etc.**

Felony. *See* **Crime**

Female climacteric. *See* **Menopause**

Female role. *See* **Sex role**

Feminine psychology. *See* **Women—Psychology**

Feminism 305.4; 323.4

 See also **Women—Civil rights; Women's move-**
  ment

 x Women—Rights; Women's rights

 xx **Women—Civil rights; Women's movement**

Fencing 796.8

 x Fighting

 xx **Physical education**

Feral animals. *See* **Wildlife**

Feral children 155.4

 x Wild children; Wolf children

 xx **Exceptional children**

Fermentation 547; 663

 See also **Bacteriology; Wine and wine making;**
  Yeast

 xx **Bacteriology; Chemistry; Enzymes; Wine and**
  wine making

Ferns 587; 635.9

 xx **Plants**

Fertility 574.1; 591.1

 Use for general materials on fertility in animals,
  including humans. Materials limited to fertility in humans are entered under **Fertility,**
  Human.

 See also **Infertility**

 x Fecundity

 xx **Infertility; Reproduction**

Fertility control. *See* **Birth control**

Fertility, Human 304.6; 612; 616.6

 See note under **Fertility.**

 See also **Birth control; Childlessness; Infertility;**
  Population

 x Human fertility

 xx **Birth control; Birthrate; Population**

Fertilization in vitro 174; 574.1; 591.1

 x Ectogenesis, Preimplantational; Fertilization,
  Laboratory; Fertilization, Test tube; In
  vitro fertilization; Laboratory fertilization;
  Preimplantational ectogenesis; Test tube
  fertilization

 xx **Genetic engineering**

Fertilization in vitro, Human 174; 176; 612

 x Babies, Test tube; Human fertility in vitro; Infants, Test tube; Test tube babies

Fertilization, Laboratory. *See* **Fertilization in vitro**

Fertilization of plants 581.1

 x Plants—Fertilization; Pollination

 xx **Flowers; Insects; Plant breeding; Plant physi-**
  ology; Plants

Fertilization, Test tube. *See* **Fertilization in vitro**

Fertilizers and manures 631.8; 668

 See also **Compost; Lime; Nitrates; Phosphates;**
  Potash

Fertilizers and manures—*Continued*
    x Manures
    xx **Agricultural chemicals; Soils**
Festivals (May subdiv. geog.) **394.2**
    See note under **Fasts and feasts.**
    See also **Fasts and feasts; Holidays; Pageants;**
        also names of types of festivals, e.g. **Craft**
        shows; Music festivals; etc.
    x Carnivals; Days; Fiestas
    xx **Fasts and feasts; Manners and customs; Pag-**
        eants
Festivals—Jews. *See* **Fasts and feasts—Judaism**
Festivals—United States 394.2
    x United States—Festivals
Fetal death. *See* **Abortion**
Fetus 574.3; 612
    x Unborn child
    xx **Embryology; Reproduction**
Feudalism 321.3
    See also **Chivalry; Clans; Middle Ages; Peas-**
        antry
    x Fiefs; Vassals
    xx **Chivalry; Civilization, Medieval; Land tenure;**
        Land use; Middle Ages—History
Fever 616
    See also **Body temperature;** also names of fevers,
        e.g. **Malaria;** etc.
    xx **Body temperature; Medicine—Practice; Ther-**
        apeutics
Fiat money. *See* **Paper money**
Fiber content of food. *See* **Food—Fiber content**
Fiber glass. *See* **Glass fibers**
Fibers 677
    See also **Cotton; Flax; Hemp; Linen; Paper; Silk;**
        Wool
    x Textile fibers
    xx **Cotton; Hemp**
Fibers, Glass. *See* **Glass fibers**
Fiction 808.3
    Use for fiction as a literary form.
    See also

Allegories	**Plot-your-own stories**
American fiction	**Plots (Drama, fiction, etc.)**
Fables	**Romances**
Fairy tales	**Romanticism**
Folklore	**Short story**
Humorous stories	**United States—Fiction**
Legends	

        also **American fiction, English fiction;** etc. and
        persons, places and subjects with the subdi-
        vision *Fiction,* e.g. **Animals—Fiction; Slav-**
        ery—United States—Fiction; Napoleon I,
        Emperor of the French, 1769-1821—Fiction;
        United States—Fiction; etc.; and such
        phrase headings that do not lend themselves
        to subdivision, e.g. **Fantastic fiction; Histor-**
        ical fiction; Love stories; Mystery and detec-
        tive stories; Science fiction; etc.
    x Novels; Stories
    xx **Literature**

Fiction, American. *See* **American fiction**
Fiction, English. *See* **English fiction**
Fiction, Historical. *See* **Historical fiction**
Fiction—History and criticism 809.3
Fiction—Plots. *See* **Plots (Drama, fiction, etc.)**
Fiction—Technique 808.3
    x Technique
    xx **Authorship**
Fictitious animals. *See* **Animals, Mythical**
Fictitious names. *See* **Pseudonyms**
Fictitious places. *See* **Geographical myths**
Fiddle. *See* **Violin**
Fiefs. *See* **Feudalism; Land tenure**
Field athletics. *See* **Track athletics**
Field hockey 796.35
    x Hockey
Field hospitals. *See* **Hospitals, Military; Medicine, Military**
Field photography. *See* **Outdoor photography**
Field trips 069.1; 371.3
    x School excursions; School trips
Fiestas. *See* **Fasts and feasts; Festivals**
Fifth column. *See* **Subversive activities; World War, 1939-1945—Collaborationists**
Fighting. *See* **Battles; Boxing; Bullfights; Dueling; Fencing; Gladiators; Military art and science; Naval art and science; Self-defense; War**
Figure drawing 743
    See also **Figure painting**
    x Human figure in art
    xx **Anatomy, Artistic; Drawing; Figure painting**
Figure painting 757
    See also **Figure drawing; Portrait painting**
    x Human figure in art
    xx **Anatomy, Artistic; Figure drawing; Painting; Portrait painting**
Figure skating. *See* **Ice skating; Roller skating**
Files and filing 025.3; 651.5
    See also **Indexing**
    x Alphabetizing; Filing systems
    xx **Indexing; Office management**
Filing systems. *See* **Files and filing**
Filling stations. *See* **Automobiles—Service stations**
Fills (Earthwork). *See* **Landfills**
Film projectors. *See* **Projectors**
Filmography. *See* **Motion pictures;** and subjects and names of individuals with the subdivision *Filmography,* e.g.
    Animals—Filmography; Shakespeare, William, 1564-1616—Filmography; etc.
Films. *See* **Filmstrips; Microfilms; Motion pictures**
Filmstrips 371.3; 778.2
    See also **Slides (Photography)**
    x Films; Strip films
    xx **Audiovisual materials; Photography; Slides (Photography)**

Finance (May subdiv. geog.) **332; 336**
    See also

Bankruptcy	**Insurance**
Banks and banking	**Interest (Economics)**
Bonds	**Internal revenue**
Budget	**Investments**
Capital	**Metropolitan finance**
Church finance	**Monetary policy**
Commerce	**Money**
Credit	**Municipal finance**
Debts, Public	**Paper money**
Deficit financing	**Prices**
Finance, Personal	**Securities**
Fiscal policy	**Speculation**
Foreign exchange	**Stock exchange**
Government lending	**Tariff**
Income	**Taxation**
Income tax	**Wealth**
Inflation (Finance)	

    also subjects with the subdivision *Finance,* e.g.
        Education—Finance; etc.
    x Finance, Public; Funds; Public finance
    xx **Budget; Economics; Monetary policy**
Finance, Church. *See* **Church finance**
Finance, Household. *See* **Budgets, Household**
Finance, Municipal. *See* **Municipal finance**
Finance, Personal 332.024
    See also **Budgets, Household; Consumer credit;**
        Estate planning; Insurance; Investments;
        Saving and thrift
    x Budgets, Personal; Personal finance
    xx **Finance**
Finance, Public. *See* **Finance**
Finance—United States 336.73
    x United States—Finance
Financial accounting. *See* **Accounting**
Financiers. *See* **Capitalists and financiers**
Finding things. *See* **Lost and found possessions**
Fine arts. *See* **Arts**
Finger alphabet. *See* **Deaf—Means of communica-**
    tion
Finger games. *See* **Finger play**
Finger marks. *See* **Fingerprints**
Finger painting 751.4
    x Painting, Finger
    xx **Child artists; Painting**
Finger play 796.1
    x Finger games
    xx **Play**
Finger pressure therapy. *See* **Acupressure**
Finger prints. *See* **Fingerprints**
Fingerprints 363.2
    x Finger marks; Finger prints
    xx **Anthropometry; Criminal investigation; Crimi-**
        nals—Identification; Identification
Finishes and finishing. *See* **Lacquer and lacquering;**
    Paint; Painting, Industrial; Varnish and var-
    nishing; Wood finishing
Finno-Russian War, 1939-1940. *See* **Russo-Finnish**
    War, 1939-1940

Fire 536

See also **Combustion; Fires; Fuel; Heat; Heating**

xx **Chemistry; Combustion; Heat**

Fire balls. *See* **Meteors**

Fire bombs. *See* **Incendiary bombs**

Fire departments 628.9

x Fire stations

Fire engines 628.9

xx **Engines; Fire fighting**

Fire fighters 363.3092; 920

x Firemen and firewomen

Fire fighting 628.9

See also **Fire engines**

xx **Fire prevention; Fires**

Fire insurance. *See* **Insurance, Fire**

Fire prevention (May subdiv. geog.) **363.3**

See also **Fire fighting; Fireproofing;** also types of institutions, buildings, industries, and vehicles with the subdivision *Fires and fire prevention,* e.g. **Nuclear power plants—Fires and fire prevention;** etc.

x Prevention of fire

xx **Fires**

Fire stations. *See* **Fire departments**

Firearms 623.4; 739.7

See also **Gunpowder; Ordnance; Shooting;** also types of firearms, e.g. **Pistols; Rifles; Shotguns;** etc.

x Guns; Small arms, Weapons and weaponry

xx **Arms and armor; Shooting**

Firearms—Control. *See* **Firearms—Law and legislation**

Firearms industry and trade 338.4; 683.4

Use for materials on the small arms industry. Materials on heavy firearms are entered under **Ordnance.**

Firearms—Law and legislation 344

x Firearms—Control; Gun control; Guns—Control

Firemen and firewomen. *See* **Fire fighters**

Fireplaces 697; 749

See also **Chimneys**

xx **Architecture—Details; Heating; Space heaters**

Fireproofing 628.9; 693.8

xx **Fire prevention; Insurance, Fire**

Fires (May subdiv. geog.) **363.3; 904**

See also **Fire fighting; Fire prevention; Forest fires; Insurance, Fire;** also subjects with the subdivision *Fires and fire prevention,* e.g. **Nuclear power plants—Fires and fire prevention;** etc.

xx **Accidents; Disasters; Fire**

Fireworks 662

First aid 616.02

See also **Accidents; Artificial respiration; Bandages and bandaging; Cardiac resuscitation; Lifesaving**

x Emergencies; Injuries; Wounded, First aid to

xx **Accidents; Home accidents; Hospitals, Military; Lifesaving; Medicine, Military; Nurs-**

247

First aid—*Continued*

> ing; **Rescue work; Self-care, Health; Sick**

First editions. *See* **Bibliography—First editions**

First generation children. *See* **Children of immi-grants**

First ladies—United States. *See* **Presidents—United States—Spouses**

Fiscal policy (May subdiv. geog.) **336.3**

> *See also* **Monetary policy**
>
> *xx* **Economic policy; Finance; Monetary policy**

Fiscal policy—United States 336.73

> *x* United States—Fiscal policy

Fish. *See* **Fishes**

Fish as food 641.3

> *xx* **Fishes; Food; Seafood**

Fish culture 639.3

> *x* Fish hatcheries
>
> *xx* **Aquariums; Fishes**

Fish hatcheries. *See* **Fish culture**

Fisheries (May subdiv. geog.) **639.3**

> Use for materials on the fishing industry.
>
> *See also* **Fishes; Pearlfisheries; Whaling**
>
> *x* Fishing industry; Sea fisheries
>
> *xx* **Aquaculture; Fishes; Marine resources; Natu-ral resources**

Fisheries—United States 639.3

> *x* United States—Fisheries

Fishes (May subdiv. geog.) **597**

> Names of all fishes are not included in this list but are to be added as needed, e.g. **Salmon;** etc.
>
> *See also* **Aquariums; Fish as food; Fish culture; Fisheries; Fishing; Tropical fish;** also names of fishes, e.g. **Salmon;** etc.
>
> *x* Fish; Ichthyology
>
> *xx* **Fisheries; Marine animals; Vertebrates**

Fishes—Geographical distribution 597.09

> *x* Geographical distribution of animals and plants
>
> *xx* **Biogeography**

Fishes—Photography. *See* **Photography of fishes**

Fishes—United States 597.0973

> *x* United States—Fishes

Fishing (May subdiv. geog.) **799.1**

> Use for materials on fishing as a sport. Materials on fishing as an industry are entered under **Fisheries.**
>
> *See also* **Flies, Artificial;** also types of fishing, e.g. **Fly casting; Spear fishing; Trout fishing;** etc.
>
> *x* Angling
>
> *xx* **Fishes; Water sports**

Fishing—Equipment and supplies 799.1

> *x* Fishing tackle

Fishing flies. *See* **Flies, Artificial**

Fishing industry. *See* **Fisheries**

Fishing tackle. *See* **Fishing—Equipment and sup-plies**

Fishing—United States 799.1

> *x* United States—Fishing

Five-day work week. *See* **Hours of labor**
Flags (May subdiv. geog.) **929.9**
    See also **Signals and signaling**
    x Banners; Ensigns
    xx **Heraldry; Signals and signaling**
Flags—United States 929.9
    x American flag; United States—Flags
Flats. *See* **Apartment houses**
Flatware, Silver. *See* **Silverware**
Flavoring essences 664
    xx **Cookery; Essences and essential oils; Food**
Flax 633.5; 677
    See also **Linen**
    xx **Fibers; Linen; Yarn**
Flexible hours of labor. *See* **Hours of labor**
Flexiplace. *See* **Telecommuting**
Flexitime. *See* **Hours of labor**
Flies 595.77
    See also names of flies, e.g. **Fruit flies;** etc.
    x Diptera; Fly; House flies
    xx **Household pests; Insects as carriers of disease;**
        Pests
Flies, Artificial 688.7; 799.1
    See also **Fly casting**
    x Artificial flies; Fishing flies
    xx **Fishing**
Flight 629.132
    See also **Aeronautics**
    x Flying; Locomotion
    xx **Aeronautics**
Flight attendants. *See* **Airlines—Flight attendants**
Flight to the moon. *See* **Space flight to the moon**
Flight training. *See* **Aeronautics—Study and teach-**
      ing; Airplanes—Piloting
Flights around the world. *See* **Aeronautics—Flights**
Flint implements. *See* **Stone implements**
Floating hospitals. *See* **Hospital ships**
Floats (Parades). *See* **Parades**
Flood control. *See* **Floods—Control**
Flood prevention. *See* **Floods—Control**
Floods (May subdiv. geog. by countries, states, cities,
      etc. and by rivers) **551.4; 904**
    See also **Reclamation of land; Rivers**
    xx **Meteorology; Natural disasters; Rain and**
      rainfall; Rivers; Water
Floods and forests. *See* **Forest influences**
Floods—Control 627
    See also **Dams; Forest influences; Rivers**
    x Flood control; Flood prevention
    xx **Forest influences; Hydraulic engineering**
Floors 694; 721
    xx **Architecture—Details; Building; Carpentry**
Flora. *See* **Botany; Plants**
Floral decoration. *See* **Flower arrangement**
Floriculture. *See* **Flower gardening**
Florists' designs. *See* **Flower arrangement**
Flour 664
    See also **Grain; Wheat**
    x Breadstuffs
    xx **Wheat**

Flour mills 664
>   *x* Grist mills; Milling (Flour)
>   *xx* **Mills and millwork**

Flower arrangement 745.92
>   Use for materials on the artistic arrangement of flowers, including decoration of houses, churches, etc. with flowers.
>   *x* Designs, Floral; Floral decoration; Florists' designs; Flowers—Arrangement
>   *xx* **Decoration and ornament; Flowers; Table setting and decoration**

Flower gardening 635.9
>   Use for practical materials on the cultivation of flowering plants for either commercial or private purposes.
>   *See also*

Annuals (Plants)	**Perennials**
Bulbs	**Plant breeding**
Flowers	**Plant propagation**
Greenhouses	**Plants, Ornamental**
House plants	**Window gardening**

>   also names of flowers, e.g. **Roses;** etc.
>   *x* Floriculture
>   *xx* **Botany; Flowers; Gardening; Horticulture; Plants**

Flower painting and illustration 758
>   *x* Flowers in art
>   *xx* **Flowers; Painting; Plants in art**

Flower shows 635.9074
>   *x* Flowers—Exhibitions
>   *xx* **Exhibitions**

Flowers (May subdiv. geog.) **582**
>   Use for general materials on the botanical characteristics of flowers, guides for studying and classifying them or for the study of flowers from the artistic point of view. Materials limited to the cultivation of flowers are entered under **Flower gardening.**
>   Names of all flowers are not included in this list but are to be added as needed, in the plural form, e.g. **Roses;** etc.
>   *See also*

Annuals (Plants)	**Perennials**
Fertilization of plants	**Plants**
Flower arrangement	**State flowers**
Flower gardening	**Wild flowers**
Flower painting and illustration	**Window gardening**

>   also names of flowers, e.g. **Roses;** etc.
>   *xx* **Botany; Flower gardening; Plants**

Flowers—Arrangement. *See* **Flower arrangement**

Flowers, Artificial. *See* **Artificial flowers**

Flowers, Drying 745.92
>   *x* Dried flowers

Flowers—Exhibitions. *See* **Flower shows**

Flowers in art. *See* **Flower painting and illustration; Plants in art**

Flowers, State. *See* **State flowers**

Flowers—United States 582
>   *x* United States—Flowers

Flowers, Wild. *See* **Wild flowers**

Flu. *See* **Influenza**

Fluid mechanics 532; 620.1
>Use for materials on the branch of mechanics dealing with the properties of liquids or gases, either at rest or in motion.
>
>*See also* **Hydraulic engineering; Hydraulics; Hydrodynamics; Hydrostatics**
>
>*x* Hydromechanics
>*xx* **Mechanics**

Fluorescent lighting 621.32
>*x* Electric lighting, Fluorescent; Light, Electric
>*xx* **Lighting**

Fluoridation of water. *See* **Water—Fluoridation**

Flute 788
>*xx* **Wind instruments**

Fly. *See* **Flies**

Fly casting 799.1
>*xx* **Fishing; Flies, Artificial**

Flying. *See* **Flight**

Flying bombs. *See* **Guided missiles**

Flying saucers. *See* **Unidentified flying objects**

FM radio. *See* **Radio frequency modulation**

Fodder. *See* **Feeds**

Fog 551.57
>*xx* **Meteorology; Water**

Fog signals. *See* **Signals and signaling**

Foliage. *See* **Leaves**

Folk art (May subdiv. geog. or ethnic adjective form, e.g. **Folk art, Swedish;** etc.) **745**
>Use for general and historical materials on peasant and popular art in the fields of decorative arts, music, dancing, theater, etc.
>
>*See also* **Arts and crafts movement; Decorative arts; Handicraft**
>
>*x* Peasant art
>*xx* **Art; Art and society; Decorative arts; Handicraft**

Folk art, American 745
>*x* American folk art; United States—Folk art
>*xx* **Art, American**

Folk dancing (May subdiv. geog. or ethnic adjective form, e.g. **Folk dancing, Swedish;** etc.) **793.3**
>*See also* **Indians of North America—Dances; Square dancing**
>
>*x* National dances
>*xx* **Dancing; Folk music**

Folk dancing, American 793.3
>*x* American folk dancing; United States—Folk dancing
>*xx* **Dancing—United States**

Folk drama 808.82; 812; etc.
>*See also* **Puppets and puppet plays**
>
>*x* Folk plays
>*xx* **Drama**

Folk lore. *See* **Folklore**

Folk medicine 615.8
>*x* Folklore, Medical; Medical folklore
>*xx* **Medicine, Popular**

Folk music (May subdiv. geog.) **781.7**
  See also **Folk dancing**
  xx **Music**
Folk music—United States **781.773**
  See also **Country music**
  x American folk music; United States—Folk
    music
Folk plays. *See* **Folk drama**
Folk psychology. *See* **Ethnopsychology**
Folk society, Nonliterate. *See* **Society, Nonliterate
  folk**
Folk songs (May subdiv. geog. or ethnic adjective
    form, except for the U.S. and states and re-
    gions of the U.S. where the noun form is
    used, e.g. **Folk songs, French;** etc.; but **Folk
    songs—United States; Folk songs—Ohio;**
    etc.) **784.4**
  See note under **Ballads.**
  See also **Ballads; Carols; Folklore; National
    songs**
  xx **Ballads; Folklore; National songs; Songs; Vo-
    cal music**
Folk songs, African. *See* **Songs, African**
Folk songs, American. *See* **Folk songs—United
  States**
Folk songs, Black (African). *See* **Songs, African**
Folk songs, Black (American). *See* **Black songs**
Folk songs—United States **784.4**
  x American folk songs; Folk songs, American;
    United States—Folk songs
  xx **Songs, American**
Folk tales. *See* **Folklore**
Folklore (May subdiv. geog.) **398; 398.2**
  Use for general materials on folklore. May also
    be used as a form heading for a story or a
    collection of stories based on spoken rather
    than written traditions.
  See also

Chapbooks	**Legends**
Charms	**Monsters**
Devil	**Mythology**
Dragons	**Nursery rhymes**
Fables	**Proverbs**
Fairies	**Sagas**
Fairy tales	**Storytelling**
Folk songs	**Superstition**
Ghosts	**Tall tales**
Graffiti	**Tongue twisters**
Grail	**Witchcraft**
Halloween	

  also topics as themes in folklore and names of
    ethnic, national or occupational groups with
    the subdivision *Folklore,* e.g.
    **Animals—Folklore; Plants—Folklore;
    Weather—Folklore; Blacks—Folklore; Indi-
    ans of North America—Folklore; Inuit—
    Folklore; Jews—Folklore;** etc.
  x Folk lore; Folk tales; Tales; Traditions
  xx **Ethnology; Fables; Fairy tales; Fiction; Folk
    songs; Legends; Manners and customs; My-**

252

Folklore—*Continued*
    thology; Storytelling; Superstition
Folklore, Black. *See* **Blacks—Folklore**
Folklore, Inuit. *See* **Inuit—Folklore**
Folklore, Jewish. *See* **Jews—Folklore**
Folklore, Medical. *See* **Folk medicine**
Folklore—United States 398.2
    x United States—Folklore
Folkways. *See* **Manners and customs**
Food 641; 641.3; 664
    See also
Beverages	**Grain**
Convenience foods	**Markets**
Cookery	**Nutrition**
Dinners and dining	**Seafood**
Farm produce	**Vegetarianism**
Fish as food	**Vitamins**
Flavoring essences	

    also names of foods, e.g. **Bread; Fruit; Meat;
        Vegetables;** etc.; also types of food, e.g.
        **Animal food; Food, Artificial; Food, Dietetic;
        Food, Natural;** etc.; and subjects with the
        subdivision *Food,* e.g. **Animals—Food;
        School children—Food;** etc.
    x Gastronomy
    xx **Cookery; Digestion; Dinners and dining;
        Home economics; Hygiene; Nutrition**
Food additives 641.4; 664
    x Additives, Food
    xx **Food—Analysis; Food—Preservation**
Food adulteration and inspection 363.1
    See also **Food—Law and legislation; Meat in-
        spection; Milk supply**
    x Adulteration of food; Analysis of food; Food
        inspection; Inspection of food; Pure food
    xx **Consumer protection; Food—Law and legisla-
        tion; Public health**
Food—Analysis 543
    See also **Food additives; Food—Composition**
    x Analysis (Chemistry); Analysis of food; Chem-
        istry of food; Food chemistry
    xx **Chemistry, Technical; Food—Composition**
Food, Artificial 641.3; 664
    x Artificial food; Synthetic food
    xx **Food; Synthetic products**
Food assistance programs. *See* **Food relief**
Food, Canned. *See* **Canning and preserving**
Food chains (Ecology) 574.5
    xx **Animals—Food; Ecology**
Food chemistry. *See* **Food—Analysis; Food—
        Composition**
Food—Cholesterol content 641
    x Cholesterol content of food
    xx **Food—Composition**
Food—Composition 543
    See also **Food—Analysis;** also
        **Food—Cholesterol content; Food—Fiber
        content; Food—Sodium content;** and similar
        headings
    x Chemistry of food; Food chemistry

Food—Composition—*Continued*
  xx **Food—Analysis**
Food contamination 363.1
  x Contaminated food
Food—Control. *See* **Food supply**
Food, Cost of. *See* **Cost of living**
Food customs. *See* **Eating customs**
Food, Dehydrated. *See* **Food, Dried**
Food, Dietetic 641.3; 664
  x Dietetic food
  xx **Diet; Food**
Food, Dried 641.4; 664
  See also **Food, Freeze dried**
  x Dehydrated foods; Dried foods; Food, Dehy-
      drated
  xx **Food—Preservation**
Food—Fiber content 641
  x Dietary fiber; Fiber content of food; Roughage
  xx **Food—Composition**
Food for invalids. *See* **Cookery for the sick**
Food for school children. *See* **School children—**
      Food
Food, Freeze dried 641.4; 664
  x Freeze dried food
  xx **Food, Dried**
Food, Frozen 641.4; 664
  See also **Ice cream, ices, etc.**
  x Frozen food
  xx **Food—Preservation**
Food habits. *See* **Eating customs**
Food, Health. *See* **Food, Natural**
Food inspection. *See* **Food adulteration and inspec-**
      tion
Food—Labeling 641
  x Food labels
Food labels. *See* **Food—Labeling**
Food—Law and legislation 344
  See also **Food adulteration and inspection**
  x Food laws; Laws
  xx **Food adulteration and inspection; Law; Legis-**
      lation
Food laws. *See* **Food—Law and legislation**
Food, Natural 641.3
  See also **Cookery—Natural foods**
  x Food, Health; Health food; Natural food; Or-
      ganic food
  xx **Food**
Food plants. *See* **Plants, Edible**
Food poisoning 615.9
  xx **Poisons and poisoning**
Food—Preservation 641.4; 664
  See also **Canning and preserving; Cold storage;**
      Food additives; Food, Dried; Food, Frozen;
      also names of food with the subdivision
      Preservation, e.g. **Fruit—Preservation;** etc.
  x Preservation of food
  xx **Food supply**
Food relief (May subdiv. geog.) **363.8**
  See also types of food relief, e.g. **Meals on**
      wheels programs; etc.; also names of wars

Food relief—*Continued*
>   with the subdivisions *Civilian relief* or *Food supply,* e.g. **World War, 1939-1945— Civilian relief; World War, 1939-1945— Food supply;** etc.
>   *x* Food assistance programs
>   *xx* **Charities; Disaster relief; Public welfare; Unemployed**

Food service 642; 647
>   Use for materials on quantity preparation and service of food for outside the home.
>   *See also* **Caterers and catering; Restaurants, bars, etc.**
>   *x* Mass feeding; Volume feeding

Food—Sodium content 641
>   *x* Sodium content of food
>   *xx* **Food—Composition**

Food supply 338.1
>   *See also* **Aquaculture; Famines; Food— Preservation; Meat industry and trade**
>   *x* Food—Control

Foot 611
>   *x* Feet; Toes

Foot—Care and hygiene. *See* **Podiatry**

Football 796.332
>   *See also* **Soccer**
>   *xx* **College sports; Sports**

Football—Coaching 796.332
>   *xx* **Coaching (Athletics)**

Footwear. *See* **Shoes**

Forage plants 633.2
>   *See also* **Grasses; Pastures; Silage and silos; Soybean;** also names of specific forage plants, e.g. **Corn; Hay; Soybeans;** etc.
>   *xx* **Feeds; Grasses; Pastures; Plants**

Force and energy 531
>   *See also* **Dynamics; Mechanics; Motion; Quantum theory**
>   *x* Conservation of energy; Energy
>   *xx* **Dynamics; Mechanics; Motion; Power (Mechanics); Quantum theory**

Force pumps. *See* **Pumping machinery**

Forced indoctrination. *See* **Brainwashing**

Forced labor. *See* **Convict labor; Peonage; Slavery**

Ford automobile 629.2
>   *xx* **Automobiles**

Forecasting
>   *See also* types of forecasting, e.g. **Business forecasting; Economic forecasting; Weather forecasting;** etc.
>   *x* Future; Predictions

Foreign aid program. *See* **Economic assistance; Military assistance; Technical assistance**

Foreign area studies. *See* **Area studies**

Foreign automobiles. *See* **Automobiles, Foreign**

Foreign economic relations. *See* **International economic relations**

Foreign economic relations—United States. *See* **United States—Foreign economic relations**

Foreign exchange 332.4

    x Cambistry; Exchange, Foreign; Exchange
        rates; International exchange

  xx **Banks and banking; Exchange; Finance;**
      Money; Stock exchange

Foreign investments. *See* **Investments, Foreign**

Foreign language laboratories. *See* **Language labo-**
    ratories

Foreign language phrases. *See* **Languages, Mod-**
    ern—Conversations and phrases; and
    names of languages with the subdivision
    Conversations and phrases, e.g. **French lan-**
    guage—Conversations and phrases; etc.
    Materials on foreign words and phrases in-
    corporated into languages are entered under
    the names of languages with the subdivision
    Foreign words and phrases, e.g. **English lan-**
    guage—Foreign words and phrases; etc.

Foreign missions, Christian. *See* **Missions, Chris-**
    tian

Foreign opinion. *See* names of countries with the
    subdivision *Foreign opinion,* or *Foreign*
    opinion subdivided geog. adjective form,
    e.g. **United States—Foreign opinion; United**
    States—Foreign opinion, French; etc.

Foreign policy. *See* names of countries with the
    subdivision *Foreign relations,* e.g. **United**
    States—Foreign relations; etc.

Foreign population. *See* **Immigration and emigra-**
    tion; and names of countries with the sub-
    division *Immigration and emigration,* e.g.
    United States—Immigration and emigration;
    etc.; and names of countries, cities, etc. with
    the subdivision *Foreign population,* e.g.
    Chicago (Ill.)—Foreign population; United
    States—Foreign population; etc.

Foreign relations. *See* **International relations;** and
    names of countries with the subdivision
    Foreign relations, e.g. **United States—**
    Foreign relations; etc.

Foreign service. *See* **Diplomatic and consular ser-**
    vice

Foreign students. *See* **Students, Foreign**

Foreign study 370.19

    x Overseas study; Study abroad; Study, Foreign;
        Study overseas

Foreign trade. *See* **Commerce**

Foreigners. *See* **Aliens; Citizenship; Naturalization;**
    and names of countries, cities, etc. with the
    subdivision *Foreign population,* e.g. **United**
    States—Foreign population; etc.

Foremen and foreladies. *See* **Supervisors**

Forenames. *See* **Names, Personal**

Forensic medicine. *See* **Medical jurisprudence**

Foreordination. *See* **Predestination**

Forest animals 591.52

   See also **Jungle animals**

  xx **Animals; Wildlife**

Forest conservation. *See* **Forests and forestry**

Forest fires 634.9
   xx **Fires**
Forest influences 581.5
   See also **Botany—Ecology; Floods—Control;**
      Forests and forestry; Rain and rainfall
   x Climate and forests; Floods and forests; For-
      ests and climate; Forests and floods; Forests
      and rainfall; Forests and water supply;
      Rainfall and forests
   xx **Climate; Floods—Control; Rain and rainfall;**
      Water supply
Forest plants 581.52
   xx **Plants**
Forest products 634.9; 674
   See also **Gums and resins; Lumber and lumber-**
      ing; Rubber; Wood
   xx **Botany, Economic; Commercial products; Raw**
      materials
Forest reserves 719
   See also **Forests and forestry; National parks and**
      reserves; Wilderness areas
   x National forests; Public lands
   xx **National parks and reserves; Wildlife conser-**
      vation
Forestry. *See* **Forests and forestry**
Forests and climate. *See* **Forest influences**
Forests and floods. *See* **Forest influences**
Forests and forestry (May subdiv. geog.) 574.5;
      634.9
   Use for general materials on forests and on for-
      est conservation. Consider also **Jungles** or
      Rain forests.
   See also

Jungles	**Reforestation**
Lumber and lumbering	**Tree planting**
Pruning	**Trees**
Rain forests	**Wood**

   also headings beginning with the word **Forest**
   x Arboriculture; Conservation of forests; Forest
      conservation; Forestry; Preservation of for-
      ests; Timber; Woods
   xx **Agriculture; Forest influences; Forest reserves;**
      Natural resources; Trees; Wood
Forests and forestry—United States 574.5; 634.9
   x United States—Forests and forestry
Forests and rainfall. *See* **Forest influences**
Forests and water supply. *See* **Forest influences**
Forgery 332.9; 364.1
   See also **Counterfeits and counterfeiting**
   xx **Crime; Fraud; Impostors and imposture**
Forgery of works of art 751.5
   See also **Literary forgeries**
   x Art forgeries; Art objects, Forgery of
   xx **Art**
Forging 671.3; 682
   See also **Blacksmithing; Ironwork; Welding**
   x Drop forging
   xx **Blacksmithing; Ironwork**
Form, Musical. *See* **Musical form**
Formal gardens. *See* **Gardens**

Formosa. *See* **Taiwan**

Formula translation (Computer program language). *See* **FORTRAN (Computer program language)**

Fortification 623

> *See also* **Military engineering**; also names of countries with the subdivision *Defenses,* e.g. **United States—Defenses**; etc.
>
> *x* Forts
>
> *xx* **Military art and science; Military engineering**

FORTRAN (Computer program language) 001.64; *005.13

> *x* Formula translation (Computer program language)
>
> *xx* **Programming languages (Computers)**

Forts. *See* **Fortification**

Fortune. *See* **Fate and fatalism; Probabilities; Success; Wealth**

Fortune telling 133.3

> *See also* **Astrology; Clairvoyance; Dreams; Palmistry; Tarot**
>
> *xx* **Amusements; Clairvoyance; Divination; Occult sciences; Prophecies (Occult sciences); Superstition**

Fortunes. *See* **Income; Wealth**

Forums (Discussions). *See* **Discussion groups**

Fossil mammals. *See* **Mammals, Fossil**

Fossil plants. *See* **Plants, Fossil**

Fossil reptiles. *See* **Reptiles, Fossil**

Fossils 560

> *See also* **Extinct animals; Mammals, Fossil; Plants, Fossil; Prehistoric animals; Reptiles, Fossil**
>
> *x* Animals, Fossil; Paleontology
>
> *xx* **Geology, Stratigraphic; Natural history; Science; Zoology**

Foster grandparents 362.7

> *xx* **Voluntarism**

Foster home care 362.7

> *See also* **Adoption; Children—Institutional care; Group homes**
>
> *x* Child placing; Children—Placing out
>
> *xx* **Adoption; Child welfare; Children— Institutional care; Group homes**

Foundations 624.1

> *See also* **Basements; Compressed air; Concrete; Masonry; Soils (Engineering); Walls**
>
> *xx* **Architecture—Details; Building; Civil engineering; Masonry; Structural engineering; Walls**

Foundations (Endowments). *See* **Endowments**

Founding 671.2

> Use for materials on the melting and casting of metals.
>
> *See also* **Brass; Metalwork; Pattern making; Type and type founding**
>
> *x* Casting; Foundry practice; Iron founding; Molding (Metal); Moulding (Metal)
>
> *xx* **Metalwork; Pattern making**

Foundlings. *See* **Orphans**

Foundry practice. *See* **Founding**
Four-day work week. *See* **Hours of labor**
Four-H clubs. *See* **4-H clubs**
Fourth dimension 516; 530.1
     x Dimension, Fourth
     xx **Mathematics; Space and time**
Fourth of July 394.2
     x 4th of July; Anniversaries; Independence Day
        (United States); July Fourth
     xx **Holidays; United States—History—1775-**
        1783, Revolution
Fourth World. *See* **Developing countries**
Fractal geometry. *See* **Fractals**
Fractals 516
     Use for materials on shapes or mathematical
        sets that have fractional, i.e. irregular, di-
        mensions as opposed to the regular dimen-
        sions of Euclidean geometry.
     x Fractal geometry; Sets, Fractal; Sets of frac-
        tional dimension
     xx **Geometry; Mathematical models; Set theory;**
        Topology
Fractions 513
     xx **Arithmetic; Mathematics**
Fractures 617
     xx **Bones; Wounds and injuries**
Framing of pictures. *See* **Picture frames and fram-**
        ing
France 944
     May be subdivided like U.S. except for *History.*
France—History 944
France—History—0-1328 944
     See also **Celts**
France—History—1328-1589, House of Valois 944
     See also **Hundred Years' War, 1339-1453**
France—History—1589-1789, Bourbons 944
France—History—1789-1799, Revolution 944.04
     x Directory, French, 1795-1799; French Revolu-
        tion; Napoleonic Wars; Reign of Terror;
        Revolution, French; Terror, Reign of
     xx **Revolutions**
France—History—1799-1815 944.05
France—History—1815-1914 944.06-944.08
France—History—1914-1940 944.081
France—History—1940-1945, German occupation
        944.081
     x German occupation of France, 1940-1945
France—History—1945-1958 944.082
France—History—1958-1969 944.083
France—History—1969- 944.083
Franchise. *See* **Citizenship; Elections; Suffrage**
Franciscans 271
     x Friars, Gray; Friars, Minor; Gray Friars; Grey
        Friars; Mendicant orders; Minorites; Saint
        Francis, Order of; St. Francis, Order of
     xx **Religious orders for men, Catholic**
Fraternities and sororities 371.8
     x College fraternities; College sororities; Greek
        letter societies; Sororities
     xx **Colleges and universities; Secret societies; Stu-**

Fraternities and sororities—*Continued*
dents—Societies
Fraud 364.1
See also **Forgery; Impostors and imposture;**
Swindlers and swindling
x Deceit; Ripoffs
xx **Impostors and imposture; Swindlers and swin-**
dling
Fraud, Computer. *See* **Computer crimes**
Fraud, Credit card. *See* **Credit card crimes**
Frauds, Literary. *See* **Literary forgeries**
Fraudulent advertising. *See* **Advertising, Fraudu-**
lent
Freaks. *See* **Monsters**
Free agency. *See* **Free will and determinism**
Free coinage. *See* **Monetary policy**
Free diving. *See* **Scuba diving; Skin diving**
Free fall. *See* **Weightlessness**
Free love 306.7
xx **Sexual ethics**
Free material 371.3
x Giveaways
Free press. *See* **Freedom of the press**
Free press and fair trial. *See* **Freedom of the press**
and fair trial
Free schools. *See* **Experimental schools**
Free speech 323.44
See also **Freedom of information; Freedom of the**
press; Libel and slander
x Freedom of speech; Liberty of speech; Speech,
Liberty of
xx **Censorship; Civil rights; Freedom of assembly;**
Freedom of information; Intellectual free-
dom; Libel and slander
Free thought 211
See also **Agnosticism; Bible—Evidences, author-**
ity, etc.; Rationalism; Religious freedom;
Skepticism
xx **Deism; Freedom of conscience; God; Rational-**
ism
Free trade and protection 382.7
See also **Balance of trade; Tariff**
x Fair trade (Tariff); Protection; Tariff question—Free trade and protection
xx **Commerce; Commercial policy; Economic pol-**
icy; Economics; Tariff
Free universities 378
See also **Colleges and universities—Entrance re-**
quirements
x Alternative universities; Colleges and universities, Nonformal; Education, Nonformal;
Experimental universities; Nonformal colleges and universities; Open universities
xx **Colleges and universities**
Free verse 808.1
x Vers libre
xx **Poetry**
Free will and determinism 123
x Choice, Freedom of; Determinism and indeterminism; Free agency; Freedom of choice;

Free will and determinism—*Continued*
>Freedom of the will; Indeterminism; Liberty of the will; Will

>*xx* **Ethics; Fate and fatalism; Philosophy; Predestination; Sin**

Freebooters. *See* **Pirates**

Freedom 323.44
>Use for general or abstract materials on the power or condition of acting or choosing without compulsion or constraint.

>*See also*

Academic freedom	**Freedom of association**
Anarchism and anarchists	**Freedom of conscience**
Civil rights	**Freedom of movement**
Conformity	**Intellectual freedom**
Equality	**Religious freedom**
Freedom of assembly	**Slavery**

>*x* Civil liberty; Emancipation; Liberty; Natural law; Personal freedom

>*xx* **Civil rights; Democracy; Equality; Political science**

Freedom, Academic. *See* **Academic freedom**

Freedom marches—United States. *See* **Blacks—Civil rights**

Freedom of assembly 323.4
>*See also* **Free speech; Freedom of association; Public meetings; Riots**

>*x* Assembly, Right of; Right of assembly

>*xx* **Civil rights; Freedom**

Freedom of association 323.44
>*x* Association, Freedom of; Right of association

>*xx* **Civil rights; Freedom; Freedom of assembly**

Freedom of choice. *See* **Free will and determinism**

Freedom of conscience 323.44
>*See also* **Conscientious objectors; Free thought; Public opinion; Religious freedom**

>*x* Intolerance; Liberty of conscience

>*xx* **Church—Government policy; Conscience; Freedom; Religious freedom; Toleration**

Freedom of information 323.44
>*See also* **Censorship; Free speech; Freedom of the press; Press—Government policy**

>*x* Information, Freedom of; Right to know

>*xx* **Censorship; Civil rights; Free speech; Freedom of the press; Intellectual freedom**

Freedom of movement 323.44
>*x* Movement, Freedom of

>*xx* **Civil rights; Freedom**

Freedom of religion. *See* **Religious freedom**

Freedom of speech. *See* **Free speech**

Freedom of teaching. *See* **Academic freedom**

Freedom of the press 323.44
>*See also* **Books—Censorship; Freedom of information; Libel and slander; Press**

>*x* Free press; Liberty of the press; Press censorship

>*xx* **Censorship; Civil rights; Free speech; Freedom of information; Intellectual freedom; Journalism; Libel and slander; Newspapers; Periodicals; Press**

Freedom of the press and fair trial   323.42; 323.44; 342

  x Fair trial and free press; Free press and fair trial; Prejudicial publicity; Trial by publicity

  xx **Press**

Freedom of the will.   *See* **Free will and determinism**

Freedom of worship.   *See* **Religious freedom**

Freelancers.   *See* **Self-employed**

Freemasons   366

  x Masonic orders; Masons (Secret order)

  xx **Secret societies**

Freeways.   *See* **Express highways**

Freeze dried food.   *See* **Food, Freeze dried**

Freezing.   *See* **Cryobiology; Frost; Ice; Refrigeration and refrigerating machinery**

Freezing of human bodies.   *See* **Cryonics**

Freight and freightage   380.5; 385-388

  See also **Aeronautics, Commercial; Railroads— Rates; Trucking**

  xx **Maritime law; Materials handling; Railroads; Railroads—Rates; Transportation**

French and Indian War.   *See* **United States— History—1755-1763, French and Indian War**

French Canadian literature   810; 840; C810; C840

  May use same subdivisions and names of literary forms as for **English literature**.

  x Canadian literature, French; French literature—Canada

  xx **Canadian literature**

French Canadians   971

  xx **Canadians**

French Equatorial Africa.   *See* **Africa, French-speaking Equatorial**

French foreign opinion—United States.   *See* **United States—Foreign opinion, French**

French language   440

  May be subdivided like **English language**.

  xx **Romance languages**

French language—Conversations and phrases   448

  x Conversation in foreign languages; Foreign language phrases

French language—Dictionaries—English   443

  See note under **English language— Dictionaries—French**.

  See also **English language—Dictionaries— French**

  xx **English language—Dictionaries—French**

French language—Reading materials   448.6

French literature   840

  May use same subdivisions and names of literary forms as for **English literature**.

  xx **Literature; Romance literature**

French literature—Canada.   *See* **French Canadian literature**

French literature—West Indian authors.   *See* **West Indian literature (French)**

French poetry   841

  See also **Troubadours**

French Revolution. *See* **France—History—1789-
1799, Revolution**
French West Africa. *See* **Africa, French-speaking
West**
Frequency modulation, Radio. *See* **Radio fre-
quency modulation**
Fresco painting. *See* **Mural painting and decoration**
Freshwater animals 591.92
> *See also* **Aquariums; Marine animals;** also names
> of fresh water animals, e.g. **Beavers;** etc.
> *x* Animals, Aquatic; Animals, Freshwater;
> Aquatic animals; Water animals
> *xx* **Animals; Freshwater biology; Wildlife**
Freshwater aquaculture. *See* **Aquaculture**
Freshwater biology 574.92
> *See also* **Aquariums; Freshwater animals; Fresh-
> water plants; Marine biology**
> *xx* **Biology; Marine biology; Natural history**
Freshwater plants 581.92
> *See also* **Aquariums; Marine plants**
> *x* Aquatic plants; Water plants
> *xx* **Freshwater biology; Marine plants; Plants**
Friars, Black. *See* **Dominicans**
Friars, Gray. *See* **Franciscans**
Friars, Minor. *See* **Franciscans**
Friars Preachers. *See* **Dominicans**
Friends, Imaginary. *See* **Imaginary playmates**
Friends, Society of. *See* **Society of Friends**
Friendship 177
> *See also* **Imaginary playmates; Love**
> *x* Affection
> *xx* **Human behavior; Love; Social ethics**
Friesian cattle. *See* **Holstein-Friesian cattle**
Fringe benefits. *See* **Nonwage payments**
Frogmen and frogwomen. *See* **Skin diving**
Frogs 597.8
> *x* Tadpoles
> *xx* **Amphibians**
Frontier and pioneer life (May subdiv. geog. by state
and region) **978**
> *See also* **Cowhands; Indians of North America—
> Captivities; Overland journeys to the Pacific
> (U.S.); Ranch life**
> *x* Border life; Pioneer life
> *xx* **Adventure and adventurers**
Frontiers. *See* **Boundaries;** and names of countries
with the subdivision *Boundaries,* e.g.
United States—Boundaries; etc.
Frost 551.3; 551.5
> *See also* **Ice; Refrigeration and refrigerating ma-
> chinery**
> *x* Freezing
> *xx* **Meteorology; Water**
Frozen food. *See* **Food, Frozen**
Frozen stars. *See* **Black holes (Astronomy)**
Fruit 634; 641.3
> Names of all fruits are not included in this list
> but are to be added as needed, usually in the
> singular form, e.g. **Apple;** etc.
> *See also* **Fruit culture;** also types of fruit, e.g.

263

Fruit—*Continued*
>> **Berries; Citrus fruit;** etc.; and names of
>> fruits, e.g. **Apple;** etc.
> *xx* **Botany; Food**

Fruit—Canning. *See* **Fruit—Preservation**

Fruit culture 634
> *See also* **Berries; Grafting; Nurseries (Horticul-
> ture); Plant propagation; Pruning**
> *x* Arboriculture; Orchards
> *xx* **Agriculture; Fruit; Gardening; Horticulture;
> Trees**

Fruit—Diseases and pests 634
> *See also* **Spraying and dusting**
> *x* Diseases and pests
> *xx* **Agricultural pests; Bacteriology, Agricultural;
> Insects, Injurious and beneficial; Pests;
> Plants—Diseases**

Fruit flies 595.77
> *xx* **Flies**

Fruit—Marketing. *See* **Farm produce—Marketing**

Fruit—Preservation 641.4; 664
> *x* Fruit—Canning
> *xx* **Canning and preserving; Food—Preservation**

Frustration. *See* **Attitude (Psychology); Emotions**

Fuel 662; 665
> *See also* **Biomass energy; Heating;** also names of
> fuel, e.g. **Alcohol as fuel; Charcoal; Coal;
> Gas; Petroleum as fuel; Synthetic fuels;
> Wood;** etc.; and subjects with the subdivi-
> sion *Fuel consumption,* e.g.
> **Automobiles—Fuel consumption;** etc.
> *xx* **Combustion; Energy resources; Engines; Fire;
> Heating; Home economics; Smoke preven-
> tion**

Fuel cells 621.31
> *xx* **Electric batteries; Electrochemistry**

Fuel consumption. *See* subjects with the subdivi-
> sion *Fuel consumption,* e.g.
> **Automobiles—Fuel consumption;** etc.

Fuel, Liquid. *See* **Gasoline; Petroleum as fuel**

Fuel oil. *See* **Petroleum as fuel**

Fugue 781.4
> *xx* **Composition (Music); Counterpoint; Music—
> Theory; Musical form**

Fulfillment, Self. *See* **Self-realization**

Fumigation 614.4; 648
> *See also* **Disinfection and disinfectants**
> *xx* **Communicable diseases; Disinfection and dis-
> infectants; Insecticides**

Functional competencies. *See* **Life skills**

Fund raising 361.7
> *x* Community chests; Money raising

Fundamental education. *See* **Basic education**

Fundamental life skills. *See* **Life skills**

Fundamental theology. *See* **Apologetics**

Fundamentalism 273
> Use for materials on the conservative interpreta-
> tion of Christianity as opposed to Modern-
> ism.
> *See also* **Modernism**

Fundamentalism—*Continued*

    xx **Modernism**

Fundamentalism and education 377

    Use same form for fundamentalism and other subjects.

    See also **Christian education; Church schools; Creation—Study and teaching; Religion in the public schools**

    x Education and Fundamentalism

    xx **Christian education; Church and education; Church schools; Creation—Study and teaching; Education; Religion in the public schools**

Funding for the arts. *See* **Art patronage; Arts—Government policy**

Funds. *See* **Finance**

Funeral directors. *See* **Undertakers and undertaking**

Funeral rites and ceremonies 393

    See also **Cremation**

    x Burial; Ecclesiastical rites and ceremonies; Graves; Mortuary customs; Mourning customs

    xx **Archeology; Cremation; Manners and customs; Rites and ceremonies**

Fungi 589.2

    See also **Bacteriology; Molds (Botany); Mushrooms; Plants—Diseases**

    x Diseases and pests; Mycology

    xx **Agricultural pests; Molds (Botany); Mushrooms; Pests**

Fungicides 632; 668

    See also **Spraying and dusting**

    x Germicides

    xx **Pesticides; Spraying and dusting**

Funicular railroads. *See* **Cable railroads**

Funnies. *See* **Comic books, strips, etc.**

Fur 675; 685

    See also **Hides and skins**

    xx **Hides and skins**

Fur seals. *See* **Seals (Animals)**

Fur trade 338.3

    xx **Trapping**

Furbearing animals 639

    See also names of furbearing animals, e.g. **Beavers;** etc.

    xx **Animals; Wildlife; Zoology, Economic**

Furnaces 697

    See also **Blast furnaces; Smelting**

    xx **Heating; Smoke prevention**

Furniture (May subdiv. geog. adjective form, e.g. **Furniture, American;** etc.) **684.1; 749**

    See also

Built-in furniture	**supplies**
Cabinet work	**Schools—Equipment and**
Church furniture	**supplies**
Garden ornaments and	**Upholstery**
furniture	**Veneers and veneering**
Libraries—Equipment and	**Wood carving**

    also names of articles of furniture, e.g. **Chairs;**

Furniture—*Continued*
  Mirrors; etc.
  xx **Art objects; Decoration and ornament; Decorative arts; Home economics; Interior design; Manufactures; Upholstery; Woodwork**
Furniture, American 684.1; 749
  x American furniture; Colonial furniture (U.S.); Furniture, Colonial; United States—Furniture
Furniture, Built in. *See* **Built-in furniture**
Furniture, Colonial. *See* **Furniture, American**
Furniture finishing 684.1; 749
  x Furniture—Refinishing; Furniture—Restoration; Refinishing furniture
Furniture—Refinishing. *See* **Furniture finishing**
Furniture—Restoration. *See* **Furniture finishing**
Future. *See* **Forecasting**
Future life 236
  Use for materials dealing with the character and form of a future existence. Materials dealing with the question of the endless existence of the soul are entered under **Immortality.** Materials on the philosophical concept of eternity are entered under **Eternity.**
  See also **Eternity; Heaven; Hell; Immortality; Millennium; Soul; Spiritualism**
  x Afterlife; Eternal life; Future punishment; Hades; Intermediate state; Life after death; Life, Future; Resurrection; Retribution
  xx **Death; Eschatology; Eternity; Immortality**
Future punishment. *See* **Future life**
Future shock. *See* **Culture conflict**
Futurism (Art) 759.06
  See also **Kinetic sculpture; Postimpressionism (Art)**
  xx **Art; Painting; Postimpressionism (Art)**
G.I.'s. *See* **Soldiers—United States; Veterans—United States**
G.R.E. *See* **Graduate record examination**
Gaels. *See* **Celts**
Galaxies 523.1
  x Extragalactic nebulae; Nebulae, Extragalactic
  xx **Astronomy; Stars**
Gales. *See* **Winds**
Galleries, Art. *See* names of appropriate subjects with the subdivision *Museums,* e.g. **Art—Museums; World War, 1939-1945—Museums;** etc.; and names of galleries and museums
Gambling 175; 795
  See also **Probabilities;** also types of gambling, e.g. **Card games; Horse racing; Lotteries;** etc.
  x Betting; Gaming; Vice
  xx **Crimes without victims**
Game and game birds 636.6
  See also **Falconry; Game protection; Hunting; Shooting; Trapping;** also names of animals and birds, e.g. **Deer; Pheasants;** etc.
  x Wild fowl

Game and game birds—*Continued*
   xx **Animals; Birds; Hunting; Trapping; Wildlife**
Game preserves 333.95
   xx **Hunting; Wildlife conservation**
Game protection 333.95; 636.9
   See also **Birds—Protection**
   x Game wardens; Protection of game
   xx **Birds—Protection; Game and game birds;**
      Hunting; Wildlife conservation
Game theory 519.3
   See also **Decision making**
   x Games, Theory of; Theory of games
   xx **Mathematical models; Mathematics; Probabil-**
      ities
Game wardens. *See* **Game protection**
Games 793-796
   See also **Amusements; Children's parties; Indians**
      of North America—Games; Kindergarten;
      Play; Sports; also names of types of games
      and of individual games, e.g. **Ball games;**
      Card games; Chess; Indoor games; Olympic
      games; Singing games; Tennis; Video games;
      Word games; etc.
   x Pastimes
   xx **Amusements; Entertaining; Physical educa-**
      tion; Play; Recreation; Sports
Games, Electronic. *See* **Electronic toys; Video**
      games
Games, Olympic. *See* **Olympic games**
Games, Theory of. *See* **Game theory**
Games, Video. *See* **Video games**
Gaming. *See* **Gambling**
Gamma rays 537.5; 539.7
   xx **Electromagnetic waves; Radiation; X rays**
Gangs. *See* **Criminals; Juvenile delinquency**
Garage sales 381
   x Yard sales
   xx **Secondhand trade**
Garbage. *See* **Refuse and refuse disposal**
Garden design. *See* **Landscape gardening**
Garden furniture. *See* **Garden ornaments and furni-**
      ture
Garden ornaments and furniture 717
   See also **Sundials**
   x Garden furniture
   xx **Decoration and ornament; Furniture; Gardens;**
      Landscape architecture
Garden pests. *See* **Agricultural pests; Insects, Inju-**
      rious and beneficial; Plants—Diseases
Gardening 635; 635.9
   Use for practical materials on the practical as-
      pects of the cultivation of flowers, fruits,
      vegetables, etc.
   See also

Bulbs	**Greenhouses**
Climbing plants	**Grounds maintenance**
Flower gardening	**Horticulture**
Fruit culture	**Indoor gardening**
Gardens	**Insects, Injurious and ben-**
Grafting	**eficial**

Gardening—*Continued*

Landscape gardening
Nurseries (Horticulture)
Organiculture
Plant propagation
Plants

Plants, Cultivated
Pruning
Vegetable gardening
Weeds
Window gardening

   x Planting
   xx **Agriculture; Horticulture; Plants**

Gardening in space. *See* **Aeroponics**

Gardening in the shade 635
   x Gardens, Shade; Shade gardens; Shady gardens

Gardens (May subdiv. geog.) **635**
   Use for general materials about the history of gardens, various types of gardens, and designs of gardens. Materials limited to the cultivation of gardens are entered under **Gardening.** Materials limited to garden design are entered under **Landscape gardening.**
   See also **Botanical gardens; Garden ornaments and furniture; Rock gardens**
   x Formal gardens
   xx **Gardening**

Gardens, Miniature 635.9
   x Miniature gardens; Miniature objects; Tray gardens
   xx **Indoor gardening; Terrariums**

Gardens, Shade. *See* **Gardening in the shade**

Garment making. *See* **Dressmaking; Tailoring**

Garments. *See* **Clothing and dress**

Garments, Leather. *See* **Leather garments**

Gas 665.5-665.8
   See also **Coal tar products; Gases; Petroleum**
   x Coal gas; Illuminating gas
   xx **Coal tar products; Fuel; Public utilities**

Gas and oil engines 621.43
   See also **Carburetors; Diesel engines; Farm engines;** also subjects with the subdivision *Engines,* e.g. **Airplanes—Engines; Automobiles—Engines;** etc.
   x Gas engines; Gasoline engines; Internal-combustion engines; Oil engines; Petroleum engines
   xx **Engines**

Gas companies. *See* **Public utilities**

Gas engines. *See* **Gas and oil engines**

Gas, Natural. *See* **Natural gas**

Gas stations. *See* **Automobiles—Service stations**

Gas turbines 621.43
   xx **Turbines**

Gas warfare. *See* **Poisonous gases—War use**

Gases 530.4; 533
   See also **Pneumatics; Poisonous gases;** also names of gases, e.g. **Nitrogen;** etc.
   xx **Gas; Hydrostatics; Mechanics; Physics; Pneumatics**

Gases, Poisonous. *See* **Poisonous gases**

Gasification of coal. *See* **Coal gasification**

Gasohol 662
   xx **Alcohol as fuel**

Gasoline 665.5
    x Fuel, Liquid; Liquid fuel
    xx **Petroleum**
Gasoline engines. *See* **Gas and oil engines**
Gastronomy. *See* **Cookery; Dinners and dining;**
        Food; Menus
Gauchos. *See* **Cowhands**
Gay liberation movement 306.7
    xx **Homosexuality**
Gay lifestyle. *See* **Homosexuality**
Gay men 306.7
    x Gays, Men; Homosexuals, Male
Gay women 306.7
    x Gays, Women; Homosexuals, Female; Lesbi-
        ans
Gays, Men. *See* **Gay men**
Gays, Women. *See* **Gay women**
Gazetteers 910.3
    See also **Names, Geographical;** also names of
        countries, states, etc. with the subdivision
        Gazetteers, e.g. **United States—Gazetteers;**
        etc.
    xx **Names, Geographical**
Gearing 621.8
    See also **Automobiles—Transmission devices;**
        Mechanical movements
    x Bevel gearing; Cog wheels; Gears; Spiral gear-
        ing
    xx **Machinery; Mechanical movements; Power**
        transmission; Wheels
Gears. *See* **Gearing**
Geese 636.5
    x Goose
    xx **Poultry**
Gemini project 629.45
    x Project Gemini
    xx **Orbital rendezvous (Space flight); Space flight**
Gems 736
    Use for materials on cut and polished precious
        stones treated from the point of view of art
        or antiquity. Materials on uncut stones
        treated from the mineralogical point of view
        are entered under **Precious stones.** Materi-
        als on gems in which the emphasis is on the
        setting are entered under **Jewelry.**
    See also **Jewelry; Precious stones**
    x Jewels
    xx **Archeology; Art; Decoration and ornament;**
        Engraving; Jewelry; Mineralogy; Precious
        stones
Gemstones. *See* **Precious stones**
Gender identity. *See* **Sex role**
Gene machine. *See* **Genetic engineering, Auto-**
    mated
Gene splicing. *See* **Genetic engineering; Recombi-**
    nant DNA
Genealogy 929
    See also **Biography; Heraldry; Registers of**
        births, etc.; Wills; also names of families,
        e.g. **Lincoln family;** etc.

Genealogy—*Continued*
>   *x* Ancestry; Descent; Family histories; Family
>   trees; Pedigrees
>   *xx* **Biography; Heraldry; History**

Generals 355.3092; 920
>   *xx* **Military personnel**

Generation.   *See* **Reproduction**

Generation gap.   *See* **Conflict of generations**

Generative organs.   *See* **Reproductive system**

Generators, Electric.   *See* **Electric generators**

Generic drugs.   *See* **Drugs—Generic substitution**

Generic products 658.8
>   *See also* **Drugs—Generic substitution**
>   *x* Products, Generic
>   *xx* **Commercial products; Manufactures**

Genes.   *See* **Heredity**

Genetic aspects.   *See* names of diseases with the
>   subdivision *Genetic aspects,* e.g.
>   **Cancer—Genetic aspects;** etc.

Genetic code 574.87
>   *xx* **Molecular biology**

Genetic counseling 616; 618
>   *xx* **Medical genetics; Prenatal diagnosis**

Genetic engineering 574.87; 575
>   *See also* **Biotechnology; Clones and cloning; Fer-
>   tilization in vitro; Genetic engineering, Auto-
>   mated; Molecular cloning; Recombinant
>   DNA**
>   *x* Designed genetic change; Engineering, Ge-
>   netic; Gene splicing; Genetic intervention;
>   Genetic surgery; Splicing of genes
>   *xx* **Biotechnology; Engineering; Genetic recombi-
>   nation**

Genetic engineering, Automated 574.87; 575
>   *x* Automated genetic engineering; DNA synthe-
>   sizer; Gene machine
>   *xx* **Genetic engineering**

Genetic engineering—Government policy 363.9

Genetic engineering—Social aspects 363.9
>   *x* Social aspects

Genetic intervention.   *See* **Genetic engineering**

Genetic recombination 574.87
>   *See also* **Genetic engineering; Genetic transfor-
>   mation; Recombinant DNA**
>   *x* Recombination, Genetic
>   *xx* **Chromosomes**

Genetic surgery.   *See* **Genetic engineering**

Genetic transformation 574.87
>   *x* Transformation (Genetics)
>   *xx* **Genetic recombination**

Genetics 573.2; 575.1
>   Use for materials dealing with reproduction, he-
>   redity, evolution and variation.
>   *See also*

Adaptation (Biology)	**Evolution**
Behavior genetics	**Heredity**
Breeding	**Medical genetics**
Chromosomes	**Natural selection**
Eugenics	**Variation (Biology)**

>   *xx* **Biology; Breeding; Embryology; Life (Biol-**

Genetics—*Continued*
  ogy); **Mendel's law; Reproduction**
Genitalia. *See* **Reproductive system**
Genius 153.9
 See also **Creation (Literary, artistic, etc.); Gifted**
  children
 x Talent
 xx **Psychology**
Gentiles and Jews. *See* **Jews and Gentiles**
Geochemistry 551.9
 See also **Geothermal resources**
 x Chemical geology; Earth—Chemical composition; Geological chemistry
 xx **Chemistry; Earth sciences; Petrology; Physical**
  geography; Rocks
Geodesy 526
 See also **Latitude; Longitude; Surveying**
 x Degrees of latitude and longitude
 xx **Earth; Measurement; Surveying**
Geographical atlases. *See* **Atlases**
Geographical distribution of animals and
  plants. *See* **Biogeography;** and names of
  plants and animals with the subdivision
  Geographical distribution, e.g.
  Fishes—Geographical distribution; Plants—
  Geographical distribution; etc.
Geographical distribution of people. *See* **An-**
  thropogeography; Ethnology
Geographical myths 398.2
 x Cities, Imaginary; Fictitious places; Imaginary
  places; Islands, Imaginary; Places, Imaginary
 xx **Mythology**
Geographical names. *See* **Names, Geographical**
Geography 910
 Use for general materials, frequently school materials, which describe the surface of the
  earth with its various peoples, animals, natural products and industries. For travel materials limited to a particular place, use the
  subdivision *Description and travel* under regions, countries, etc.; and the subdivision
  Description under names of cities. Materials
  dealing with the physical features of the
  earth's surface and its atmosphere are entered under **Physical geography.**
 See also

Anthropogeography	**Ethnology**
Atlases	**Maps**
Biogeography	**Physical geography**
Boundaries	**Surveying**
Discoveries (in geography)	**Voyages and travels**

 also names of countries, states, etc. with the subdivisions *Description and travel* and
  Geography, e.g. **United States—Description**
  and travel; United States—Geography; etc.
 x Social studies
 xx **Earth; Earth sciences; World history**
Geography, Ancient 913
 Use for materials on the geography of the an-

Geography, Ancient—*Continued*
> cient world in general.
> *See also* names of countries of antiquity with the subdivison *Description and geography,* e.g. **Greece—Description and geography;** etc.
> *x* Ancient geography; Classical geography
> *xx* **Geography, Historical; History, Ancient**

Geography, Biblical.   *See* **Bible—Geography**

Geography, Commercial   330.9
> *See also* **Economic conditions; Trade routes**
> *x* Commercial geography; Economic geography; Geography, Economic; World economics
> *xx* **Commerce; Commercial products; Economic conditions**

Geography—Dictionaries   910.3
> Use for dictionaries of geographic terms. Materials listing names and descriptions of places are entered under **Gazetteers.**

Geography, Economic.   *See* **Geography, Commercial**

Geography, Historical   911
> Use for materials that discuss the extent of territory held by the states or nations at a given period of history. When limited to one country or region use the name of the place with the subdivision *Historical geography.* Under names of countries of antiquity use, instead, the subdivision *Description and geography.*
> *See also* **Geography, Ancient;** also names of modern countries or regions with the subdivision *Historical geography,* e.g. **United States—Historical geography;** etc.; and names of ancient countries with the subdivision *Description and geography,* e.g. **Greece—Description and geography;** etc.
> *x* Historical geography
> *xx* **History**

Geography, Historical—Maps.   *See* **Atlases, Historical**

Geography, Military.   *See* **Military geography**
Geography, Physical.   *See* **Physical geography**
Geography—Pictorial works.   *See* **Views**
Geography, Political.   *See* **Boundaries; Geopolitics**
Geography, Social.   *See* **Anthropogeography**
Geological chemistry.   *See* **Geochemistry**
Geological physics.   *See* **Geophysics**

Geologists   551.092; 920
> *xx* **Scientists**

Geology (May subdiv. geog.)   **550**
> See note under **Earth.**
> *See also*

Astrogeology	**Geysers**
Continental drift	**Glaciers**
Continental shelf	**Mineralogy**
Coral reefs and islands	**Mountains**
Creation	**Oceanography**
Earth	**Ore deposits**
Earthquakes	**Petrology**

Geology—*Continued*
>
> **Physical geography** **Submarine geology**
> **Rocks** **Volcanoes**
>
> *x* Geoscience
> *xx* **Creation; Earth; Earth sciences; Natural history; Petrology; Rocks; Science**

Geology, Dynamic. *See* **Geophysics**
Geology, Economic 553
> *See also*
>
> **Coal** **Petroleum—Geology**
> **Mines and mineral resources** **Quarries and quarrying**
> **sources** **Soils**
> **Natural gas** **Stone**
> **Ores**
>
> also names of other geological products, e.g.
> **Asbestos; Gypsum;** etc.
> *x* Economic geology

Geology, Historical. *See* **Geology, Stratigraphic**
Geology, Lunar. *See* **Lunar geology**
Geology—Maps 550.22
> *xx* **Maps**

Geology—Moon. *See* **Lunar geology**
Geology, Stratigraphic 551.7
> *See also* **Fossils**
> *x* Geology, Historical; Historical geology;
> Rocks—Age; Stratigraphic geology

Geology, Submarine. *See* **Submarine geology**
Geology—United States 557.3
> *x* United States—Geology

Geometrical drawing 516; 604.2
> *See also* **Geometry, Descriptive; Graphic methods; Mechanical drawing; Perspective**
> *x* Mathematical drawing; Plans
> *xx* **Drawing; Geometry; Mechanical drawing**

Geometry 516
> *See also* **Fractals; Geometrical drawing; Ratio and proportion; Topology; Trigonometry; Volume (Cubic content)**
> *x* Geometry, Plane; Geometry, Solid; Plane geometry; Solid geometry
> *xx* **Mathematics**

Geometry, Analytic 516.3
> *x* Analytical geometry

Geometry, Descriptive 516
> *See also* **Perspective**
> *x* Descriptive geometry
> *xx* **Geometrical drawing**

Geometry, Plane. *See* **Geometry**
Geometry, Projective 516
> *x* Projective geometry

Geometry, Solid. *See* **Geometry**
Geophysics 551
> *See also* **Auroras; Meteorology; Oceanography; Plate tectonics**
> *x* Geological physics; Geology, Dynamic; Physics, Terrestrial; Terrestrial physics
> *xx* **Earth; Earth sciences; Physical geography; Physics; Space sciences**

Geopolitics 320.1; 327.101
> *See also* **Anthropogeography; Boundaries; World**

Geopolitics—*Continued*
  politics
  x Geography, Political
  xx **Anthropogeography; Boundaries; International
    relations; Political science; World politics**
Geoscience. *See* **Earth sciences; Geology**
Geothermal resources 333.8
  See also names of geothermal resources, e.g.
    Geysers; etc.
  x Natural steam energy; Thermal waters
  xx **Geochemistry; Ocean energy resources; Re-
    newable energy resources**
Geriatrics. *See* **Elderly—Diseases**
Germ theory. *See* **Life—Origin**
Germ theory of disease 616
  See also **Bacteriology**
  x Bacilli; Disease germs; Germs; Microbes
  xx **Bacteriology; Communicable diseases**
Germ warfare. *See* **Biological warfare**
German Democratic Republic. *See* **Germany
  (East)**
German Federal Republic. *See* **Germany (West)**
German Hebrew. *See* **Yiddish language**
German language 430
  May be subdivided like **English language.**
German literature 830
  May use same subdivisions and names of liter-
    ary forms as for **English literature.**
German occupation of France, 1940-1945. *See*
  **France—History—1940-1945, German oc-
    cupation**
German occupation of Netherlands, 1940-1945. *See*
  **Netherlands—History—1940-1945, German
    occupation**
Germany 943
  Use for materials discussing the pre-World War
    II region and the country, as well as the
    post-World War II zones of occupation col-
    lectively or East Germany and West Ger-
    many together since 1949. Materials discuss-
    ing the eastern part of Germany before
    1949, the Russian occupation zone, or the
    German Democratic Republic are entered
    under **Germany (East).** Materials discussing
    the western part of Germany before 1949,
    the United States, British, and French occu-
    pation zones, or the German Federal Re-
    public are entered under **Germany (West).**
  May be subdivided like U.S. except for *History.*
  See also **Germany (East); Germany (West)**
Germany (Democratic Republic). *See* **Germany
  (East)**
Germany (East) 943.1
  See note under **Germany.**
  x East Germany; German Democratic Republic;
    Germany (Democratic Republic)
  xx **Germany**
Germany (Federal Republic). *See* **Germany (West)**
Germany—History 943

274

Germany—History—0-1517 943
  See also **Holy Roman Empire**
Germany—History—1517-1740 943
  See also **Thirty Years' War, 1618-1648**
Germany—History—1740-1815 943
  See also **Seven Years' War, 1756-1763**
Germany—History—1815-1866 943
Germany—History—1848-1849, Revolution 943
Germany—History—1866-1918 943.08
Germany—History—1918-1933 943.085
Germany—History—1933-1945 943.086
Germany—History—1945- 943.087
Germany (West) 943.087
  See note under **Germany.**
  x German Federal Republic; Germany (Federal
      Republic); West Germany
  xx **Germany**
Germicides. *See* **Disinfection and disinfectants;
      Fungicides**
Germination 581.1
  x Seeds—Germination
  xx **Plant physiology**
Germs. *See* **Bacteriology; Germ theory of disease;
      Microorganisms**
Gerontology 612
  See also **Aging; Elderly; Old age**
Gestalt psychology 150.19
  x Configuration (Psychology); Psychology,
      Structural; Structural psychology
  xx **Consciousness; Knowledge, Theory of; Percep-
      tion; Psychology; Senses and sensation**
Getting ready for bed. *See* **Bedtime**
Gettysburg (Pa.), Battle of, 1863 973.7
  xx **United States—History—1861-1865, Civil
      War—Campaigns; War**
Geysers 551.2
  x Eruptions; Thermal waters
  xx **Geology; Geothermal resources; Physical ge-
      ography; Water**
Ghost stories. *See* **Ghosts—Fiction**
Ghost towns
  See also **Cities and towns, Ruined, extinct, etc.**
  x Abandoned towns
  xx **Cities and towns, Ruined, extinct, etc.**
Ghosts 133.1
  See also **Apparitions; Demonology; Hallucina-
      tions and illusions; Psychical research; Spir-
      itualism; Superstition**
  x Haunted houses; Phantoms; Poltergeists;
      Specters; Spirits
  xx **Apparitions; Folklore; Hallucinations and illu-
      sions; Psychical research; Spiritualism; Su-
      perstition**
Ghosts—Fiction Fic; S C
  x Ghost stories
Giants 398.2
  xx **Animals, Mythical; Monsters**
Gift wrapping 745.54
  x Wrapping of gifts
  xx **Gifts; Packaging; Paper crafts**

Gifted children 155.4
> *See also* **Child artists; Child authors**
> *x* Bright children; Children, Gifted; Precocious children; Superior children; Talent
> *xx* **Exceptional children; Genius**

Gifts
> *See also* **Donation of organs, tissues, etc.; Gift wrapping**
> *x* Bequests; Donations; Philanthropy; Presents

Gipsies. *See* **Gypsies**

Girl Scouts (May subdiv. geog.) **369.463**
> *xx* **Girls' clubs; Scouts and scouting**

Girls 155.4; 305.2
> *See also* **Children; Fathers and daughters; Mothers and daughters; Young women; Youth**
> *xx* **Children; Women; Young women; Youth**

Girls' agricultural clubs. *See* **4-H clubs; Agriculture—Societies; Girls' clubs**

Girls' clubs 369.46
> *See also* **4-H clubs; Camp Fire Girls; Girl Scouts**
> *x* Girls' agricultural clubs; Girls—Societies and clubs
> *xx* **Clubs; Social settlements; Societies; Women—Societies**

Girls—Education 372-373; 376

Girls—Employment. *See* **Children—Employment; Women—Employment**

Girls—Societies and clubs. *See* **Girls' clubs**

GIs. *See* **Soldiers—United States; Veterans—United States**

Giveaways. *See* **Free material**

Glacial epoch. *See* **Ice age**

Glaciers 551.3
> *xx* **Geology; Ice; Physical geography; Water**

Gladiators 796.8; 920
> *x* Fighting

Gladness. *See* **Happiness**

Glands 611; 612

Glands, Ductless. *See* **Endocrine glands**

Glass 666
> *xx* **Ceramics; Windows**

Glass construction 693
> *xx* **Building materials**

Glass fibers 666
> *x* Fiber glass; Fibers, Glass; Glass, Spun; Spun glass

Glass manufacture 666
> *xx* **Ceramic industries**

Glass painting and staining 748.5
> *x* Glass, Stained; Painted glass; Stained glass; Windows, Stained glass
> *xx* **Decoration and ornament; Painting**

Glass, Spun. *See* **Glass fibers**

Glass, Stained. *See* **Glass painting and staining**

Glassware 642; 748.2
> *See also* **Vases**
> *x* Dishes
> *xx* **Decorative arts; Tableware; Vases**

Glazes 666; 738.1
> *xx* **Ceramics; Pottery**

Gliders (Aeronautics) 629.133
    x Aircraft; Sailplanes (Aeronautics)
    xx **Aeronautics; Airplanes**
Gliding and soaring 797.5
    x Air surfing; Hang gliding; Soaring flight
Global satellite communications systems. *See* **Artificial satellites in telecommunication**
Globes 912
Glossaries. *See* **Encyclopedias and dictionaries;** and names of languages or subjects with the subdivision *Dictionaries,* e.g. **English language—Dictionaries; Chemistry—Dictionaries;** etc.
Glue 668
    xx **Adhesives**
Gnomes. *See* **Fairies**
Gnosticism 299
    xx **Church history—30(ca.)-600, Early church; Philosophy; Religions**
Go karts. *See* **Karts and karting**
Goblins. *See* **Fairies**
God (May subdiv. by religion) **211; 212; 231**
    See also

Agnosticism	Mythology
Atheism	Natural theology
Creation	Rationalism
Deism	Religion
Free thought	Theism
Metaphysics	

    xx **Creation; Deism; Metaphysics; Philosophy; Religion; Theism**
God—Christianity 231
    Use same pattern for God in other religions.
    See also **Christianity; Holy Spirit; Jesus Christ; Providence and government of God; Theology; Trinity**
    xx **Christianity; Theology; Trinity**
Goddesses. *See* **Gods and goddesses**
Gods and goddesses 291; 292
    See also **Mythology; Religions**
    x Deities; Goddesses
    xx **Mythology; Religions**
Gold 332.4; 549, 553.4, 669
    See also **Coinage; Gold mines and mining; Goldwork; Money**
    x Bimetallism; Bullion
    xx **Coinage; Metals; Monetary policy; Money; Precious metals**
Gold articles. *See* **Goldwork**
Gold fish. *See* **Goldfish**
Gold mines and mining 622
    See also **Prospecting**
    xx **Gold**
Gold plate. *See* **Plate**
Gold rush. *See* **California—Gold discoveries**
Gold work. *See* **Goldwork**
Golden Gate Bridge (San Francisco, Calif.) 624; 979.4
    xx **Bridges**

Goldfish 597; 639.3

   x Gold fish

   xx **Aquariums**

Goldsmithing. *See* **Goldwork**

Goldwork 739.2

   See also **Jewelry; Plate**

   x Gold articles; Gold work; Goldsmithing

   xx **Art metalwork; Gold; Jewelry; Metalwork**

Golf courses 796.352

   xx **Grounds maintenance**

Good and evil 170; 216; 241

   See also **Sin**

   x Evil

   xx **Ethics; Suffering; Theology**

Good Friday 263

   See also **Jesus Christ—Crucifixion**

   xx **Holy Week; Jesus Christ—Crucifixion; Lent**

Good grooming. *See* **Grooming, Personal**

Good Neighbor Policy. *See* **Pan-Americanism**

Goose. *See* **Geese**

Gothic architecture. *See* **Architecture, Gothic**

Gothic fiction Fic; S C

   x Suspense fiction

Goths. *See* **Teutonic peoples**

Gout 616.3

   See also **Arthritis**

Government. *See* **Political science;** and names of countries, cities, etc. with the subdivision *Politics and government,* e.g. **United States—Politics and government;** etc.

Government and business. *See* **Industry—Government policy**

Government and the press. *See* **Press—Government policy**

Government buildings. *See* **Public buildings**

Government by commission. *See* **Municipal government by commission**

Government, Comparative. *See* **Comparative government**

Government documents. *See* **Government publications**

Government employees. *See* **Civil service;** and names of countries, cities, etc. with the subdivision *Officials and employees,* e.g. **United States—Officials and employees; Chicago (Ill.)—Officials and employees;** etc.

Government housing. *See* **Public housing**

Government investigations. *See* **Governmental investigations**

Government lending (May subdiv. geog.) 332.7; 351.82

   xx **Economic assistance, Domestic; Economic policy; Finance; Industry—Government policy; Loans**

Government libraries 027.5

   Use for materials on special libraries maintained by government funds.

   See also **National libraries; State libraries**

   x Federal libraries; Libraries, Governmental

Government libraries—*Continued*
   xx **Special libraries**
Government, Local. *See* **Local government**
Government, Mandatory. *See* **Mandates**
Government, Military. *See* **Military government**
Government, Municipal. *See* **Municipal government**
Government ownership 338.9
   See also **Municipal ownership; Railroads—Government policy**
   x Nationalization; Public ownership; Socialization of industry; State ownership
   xx **Corporations; Economic policy; Economics; Industry—Government policy; Political science; Socialism**
Government ownership of railroads. *See* **Railroads—Government policy**
Government policy. *See* subjects with the subdivision *Government policy,* e.g. **Homeless people—Government policy; Industry—Government policy;** etc.
Government procurement. *See* **Government purchasing**
Government publications 025.17
   See also names of countries, cities, etc. with the subdivision *Government publications,* e.g. **United States—Government publications;** etc.
   x Documents; Government documents; Official publications; Public documents
Government purchasing (May subdiv. geog.) **351.71; 352.1**
   See also **Buy national policy**
   x Government procurement; Procurement, Government; Public procurement; Purchasing, Government
   xx **Buying**
Government records—Preservation. *See* **Archives**
Government regulation of commerce. *See* **Commercial policy; Interstate commerce; Tariff**
Government regulation of industry. *See* **Industry—Government policy**
Government regulation of railroads. *See* **Interstate commerce; Railroads—Government policy**
Government reorganization. *See* **United States—Executive departments—Reorganization**
Government, Resistance to 322.4
   See also **Hunger strikes; Insurgency; Passive resistance; Revolutions**
   x Civil disobedience; Resistance to government
   xx **Insurgency; Political crimes and offenses; Political ethics; Political science; Revolutions**
Government service. *See* **Civil service**
Government spending policy. *See* **United States—Appropriations and expenditures**
Governmental investigations (May subdiv. geog.) **328; 351.9**
   Use for materials on investigations initiated by the legislative, executive and judicial branches of the government.

Governmental investigations—*Continued*

   x Congressional investigations; Executive investigations; Government investigations; Investigations, Governmental; Judicial investigations; Legislative investigations

   xx **Justice, Administration of**

Governmental investigations—United States 328.73; 353.009

   x United States—Governmental investigations

Governments in exile. *See* **World War, 1939-1945—Governments in exile**

Governors 351.092; 920

   xx **State governments**

Graal. *See* **Grail**

Grace (Theology) 234

   xx **Conversion; Salvation; Theology**

Grading and marking (Students) 371.2

   See also **Ability grouping in education; Mental tests; School reports**

   x Marking (Students); Students—Grading and marking

   xx **Educational tests and measurements; School reports**

Graduate record examination 378

   x G.R.E.; GRE

   xx **Colleges and universities—Entrance examinations; Scholastic aptitude test**

Graduates, College. *See* **College graduates**

Graduation. *See* **Commencements**

Graffiti 001.55

   xx **Folklore; Inscriptions**

Graft in politics. *See* **Corruption in politics**

Grafting 631.5

   xx **Botany; Fruit culture; Gardening; Plant propagation; Trees**

Grail 398.2

   See also **Arthurian romances**

   x Graal; Holy Grail

   xx **Arthurian romances; Folklore; Legends**

Grain 633.1

   See also names of cereal plants, e.g. **Corn; Wheat;** etc.

   x Breadstuffs; Cereals

   xx **Botany, Economic; Flour; Food**

Grammar 415

   See also **Language and languages; Philology, Comparative;** also names of languages with the subdivision *Grammar,* e.g. **English language—Grammar;** etc.

   xx **Language and languages**

Grammar schools. *See* **Education, Elementary; Public schools**

Gramslamming. *See* **Elderly abuse**

Grand opera. *See* **Opera**

Grange 334

   xx **Agriculture—Societies**

Granite 552

   xx **Petrology; Rocks**

Grants. *See* **Subsidies**

Grants-in-aid 338.9
Use for materials on grants of money made from
a central government to a local government.
See also **Economic assistance, Domestic; Federal
aid to education; Federal aid to libraries**
x Block grants; Federal grants
xx **Economic assistance, Domestic**
Grapes 634
See also **Wine and wine making**
x Vineyards
xx **Wine and wine making**
Graph theory 510; 511
x Graphs, Theory of; Theory of graphs
xx **Algebra; Mathematical analysis; Topology**
Graphic arts (May subdiv. geog. adjective form, e.g.
Graphic arts, French; etc.) **760**
See also types of graphic arts, e.g. **Drawing; Engraving; Painting; Printing; Prints;** etc.
x Art, Graphic; Arts, Graphic
xx **Art**
Graphic arts, American 769.973
x American graphic arts; United States—
Graphic arts
Graphic methods 001.4; 511
See also **Statistics—Graphic methods**
x Graphs
xx **Drawing; Geometrical drawing; Mechanical
drawing**
Graphics, Computer. *See* **Computer graphics**
Graphite 549; 553.2
x Black lead
xx **Carbon**
Graphology 137
See note under **Writing.**
xx **Handwriting; Writing**
Graphs. *See* **Graphic methods**
Graphs, Theory of. *See* **Graph theory**
Grasses 584; 633.2
See also **Feeds; Forage plants; Grasslands; Hay;
Pastures**
x Herbage
xx **Botany, Economic; Forage plants; Hay;
Lawns; Pastures**
Grasslands (May subdiv. geog.) **581.5**
xx **Grasses**
Graves. *See* **Cemeteries; Epitaphs; Funeral rites
and ceremonies; Mounds and mound build-
ers; Tombs**
Graveyard of the Atlantic. *See* **Bermuda Triangle**
Graveyards. *See* **Cemeteries**
Gravitation 521; 531
x Gravity
xx **Physics**
Gravity. *See* **Gravitation**
Gravity free state. *See* **Weightlessness**
Gray Friars. *See* **Franciscans**
GRE. *See* **Graduate record examination**
Grease. *See* **Lubrication and lubricants; Oils and
fats**
Great books program. *See* **Discussion groups**

Great Britain 941
> May be subdivided like U.S. except for *History*. For a list of subjects which may be used under either England or Great Britain, see **England.**

> *See also* **Commonwealth of Nations; England**

Great Britain—Colonies 325.41
> *xx* **Colonies; Commonwealth of Nations**

Great Britain—History 941
> *x* England—History; English history

Great Britain—History—0-1066 941.01
> *See also* **Anglo-Saxons; Celts**

Great Britain—History—1066-1154, Norman period 941.02
> *See also* **Hastings, (Essex, England), Battle of, 1066; Normans**

Great Britain—History—1154-1399, Plantagenets 941.03

Great Britain—History—1399-1485, Lancaster and York 941.04
> *See also* **Hundred Years' War, 1339-1453**

Great Britain—History—1455-1485, War of the Roses 941.04
> *x* Wars of the Roses, 1455-1485

Great Britain—History—1485-1603, Tudors 941.05
> *See also* **Armada, 1588**

Great Britain—History—1603-1714, Stuarts 941.06

Great Britain—History—1642-1660, Civil War and Commonwealth 941.06
> *x* Civil War—England; Commonwealth of England

Great Britain—History—1714-1837 941.07

Great Britain—History—1800-1899 (19th century) 941.08-941.081
> *x* Industrial revolution

Great Britain—History—1853-1856, Crimean War. *See* **Crimean War, 1853-1856**

Great Britain—History—1900-1999 (20th century) 941.082

Great Britain—History—1945-1952 941.085

Great Britain—History—1952- 941.085

Great Britain—Kings, queens, rulers, etc. 920; 941.092
> *xx* **Kings, queens, rulers, etc.**

Greece 949.5

Greece, Ancient. *See* **Greece—History—0-323**

Greece—Antiquities 938
> *xx* **Classical antiquities**

Greece—Biography 920; 938.092
> *x* Classical biography

Greece—Civilization. *See* **Civilization, Greek**

Greece—Description and geography 913.8
> Use for descriptive and geographic materials on ancient Greece instead of the subdivisions *Description and travel* and *Historical geography.*

> *x* Description; Historical geography
> *xx* **Geography, Ancient; Geography, Historical**

Greece—Description and travel 914.95
>Use for descriptive and geographic materials on modern Greece.

Greece—History 938; 949.5

Greece—History—0-323 938
>*x* Greece, Ancient

Greece—History—323-1453 949.5
>*x* Greece, Medieval

Greece—History—1453- 949.5
>*x* Greece, Modern

Greece—History—1967-1974 949.5

Greece—History—1974- 949.5

Greece, Medieval. *See* **Greece—History—323-1453**

Greece, Modern. *See* **Greece—History—1453-**

Greek antiquities. *See* **Classical antiquities**

Greek architecture. *See* **Architecture, Greek**

Greek art. *See* **Art, Greek**

Greek Church. *See* **Orthodox Eastern Church**

Greek civilization. *See* **Civilization, Greek; Hellenism**

Greek language 480
>May be subdivided like **English language.**
>*See also* **Hellenism**
>*x* Classical languages

Greek language, Modern 489
>May be subdivided like **English language.**
>*x* Romaic language

Greek letter societies. *See* **Fraternities and sororities; Secret societies**

Greek literature 880
>May use same subdivisions and names of literary forms as for **English literature.**
>*See also* **Classical literature; Hellenism**
>*xx* **Classical literature**

Greek literature, Modern 889
>*x* Neo-Greek literature; Romaic literature

Greek mythology. *See* **Mythology, Classical**

Greek philosophy. *See* **Philosophy, Ancient**

Greek sculpture. *See* **Sculpture, Greek**

Greenbacks. *See* **Paper money**

Greenhouses 631.3; 635.9
>*x* Hothouses
>*xx* **Flower gardening; Gardening; Horticulture**

Greenhouses, Window. *See* **Window gardening**

Greeting cards 741.68
>*x* Cards, Greeting; Christmas cards

Gregorian chant. *See* **Chants (Plain, Gregorian, etc.)**

Grey Friars. *See* **Franciscans**

Grief. *See* **Joy and sorrow**

Grievance procedures (Public administration). *See* **Ombudsman**

Grill cookery. *See* **Barbecue cookery**

Grinding and polishing 621.9
>*x* Buffing; Polishing

Grippe. *See* **Influenza**

Grist mills. *See* **Flour mills**

Grocery trade 338.4
>*See also* **Supermarkets**

Grooming, Personal 646.7
> *x* Beauty, Personal; Good grooming; Personal
>> appearance; Personal grooming
> *xx* **Hygiene**

Grottoes. *See* **Caves**

Ground cushion phenomena 629.3
> *See also* **Ground effect machines**
> *x* Air bearing lift
> *xx* **Aerodynamics; Pneumatics**

Ground effect machines 629.3
> *See also* **Helicopters; Vertically rising airplanes**
> *x* Air bearing vehicles; Air cushion vehicles;
>> Ground proximity machines; Hovercraft;
>> Surface effect machines
> *xx* **Ground cushion phenomena**

Ground proximity machines. *See* **Ground effect
machines**

Grounds maintenance 712
> Use for materials on maintenance of public, in-
>> dustrial, and institutional grounds and large
>> estates.
> *See also* **Golf courses; Roadside improvement**
> *xx* **Gardening**

Group discussion. *See* **Discussion groups**

Group dynamics. *See* **Social groups**

Group health. *See* **Insurance, Health**

Group homes 362-362.8
> Use for materials on planned housing for groups
>> of unrelated people needing supervision.
> *See also* **Foster home care; Halfway houses**
> *x* Community based residences; Group resi-
>> dences; Residential treatment centers
> *xx* **Foster home care; Institutional care; Social
>> work**

Group hospitalization. *See* **Insurance, Hospitalization**

Group insurance. *See* **Insurance, Group**

Group living. *See* **Collective settlements**

Group medical practice, Prepaid. *See* **Health maintenance organizations**

Group medical service. *See* **Insurance, Health**

Group problem solving. *See* **Problem solving,
Group**

Group relations training 616.89
> *x* Encounter groups; Sensitivity training; T
>> groups
> *xx* **Human relations**

Group residences. *See* **Group homes**

Group theory 510; 512
> *See also* **Algebra, Boolean**
> *x* Groups, Theory of
> *xx* **Algebra; Mathematics; Number theory**

Group travel. *See* **Travel**

Group values. *See* **Social values**

Group work, Social. *See* **Social group work**

Grouping by ability. *See* **Ability grouping in education**

Groups, Ethnic. *See* **Ethnic groups**

Groups, Social. *See* **Social groups**

Groups, Theory of. *See* **Group theory**

Growth 155.4; 574.3; 591.3; 612.6
   See also **Children—Growth; Plants—Growth**
   xx **Physiology**
Guaranteed annual income. *See* **Wages—Annual wage**
Guaranteed income. *See* **Wages—Annual wage**
Guerrilla warfare (May subdiv. geog. except U.S.) 355.4
   See also **World War, 1939-1945—Underground movements**
   x Unconventional warfare
   xx **Insurgency; Military art and science; Tactics; War**
Guerrillas 356
   See also **National liberation movements**
   x Partisans
   xx **National liberation movements**
Guests. *See* **Entertaining**
Guidance. *See* **Counseling**
Guidance counseling, Educational. *See* **Educational counseling**
Guidance counseling, School. *See* **School counseling**
Guidance, Vocational. *See* **Vocational guidance**
Guide dogs 636.7
   x Blind, Dogs for the; Dog guides; Dogs for the blind; Seeing eye dogs
   xx **Animals and the handicapped; Dogs**
Guide posts. *See* **Signs and signboards**
Guidebooks. *See* names of countries, states, etc. with the subdivision *Description and travel—Guidebooks,* e.g. **United States—Description and travel—Guidebooks**; etc.; and names of cities with the subdivision *Description—Guidebooks,* e.g. **Chicago (Ill.)—Description—Guidebooks**; etc.
Guided missiles 623.4
   See also types of missiles, e.g. **Antimissile missiles; Ballistic missiles**; etc.; also names of specific missiles, e.g. **Nike rocket**; etc.
   x Bombs, Flying; Flying bombs; Missiles, Guided
   xx **Bombs; Projectiles; Rocketry; Rockets (Aeronautics)**
Guitar 787.6
   xx **Stringed instruments**
Guitar music 787.6
   xx **Instrumental music**
Gulf States (U.S.) 976
   xx **United States**
Gums and resins 668
   x Resins; Rosin
   xx **Chemistry, Technical; Forest products; Plastics**
Gun control. *See* **Firearms—Law and legislation**
Gunning. *See* **Hunting; Shooting**
Gunpowder 623.4
   See also **Ammunition**
   x Powder, Smokeless; Smokeless powder
   xx **Ammunition; Explosives; Firearms**

Guns. *See* **Firearms; Ordnance; Rifles; Shotguns**
Guns—Control. *See* **Firearms—Law and legislation**
Gymnastics 796.4
  See also **Acrobats and acrobatics; Physical education**
  x Calisthenics
  xx **Acrobats and acrobatics; Athletics; Exercise; Physical education; Sports**
Gypsies 305.8
  x Gipsies; Romanies
Gypsum 553.6
  x Plaster of paris
  xx **Geology, Economic**
Gyroscope 629.135; 681
  xx **Aeronautical instruments**
H.B.O. *See* **Home Box Office**
H bomb. *See* **Hydrogen bomb**
H.M.O.'s. *See* **Health maintenance organizations**
Habit 152.3
  See also **Instinct; Narcotic habit; Tobacco habit**
  xx **Human behavior; Instinct; Psychology**
Habitations, Human. *See* **Architecture, Domestic; Houses; Housing**
Habitations of animals. *See* **Animals—Habitations**
Habits of animals. *See* **Animals—Habits and behavior**
Hades. *See* **Future life; Hell**
Hair and hairdressing 611; 646.7
  Includes materials on hairdressing and haircutting.
  See also **Wigs**
  x Coiffure; Hairdressing
  xx **Head**
Hairdressing. *See* **Hair and hairdressing**
Halftone process. *See* **Photoengraving**
Halfway houses 362.1-362.8
  Use for materials on centers for formerly institutionalized individuals, such as mental patients or drug addicts, that are designed to facilitate their readjustment to private life.
  xx **Correctional institutions; Group homes**
Halley's comet 523.6
  xx **Comets**
Hallmarks
  See also **Plate**
  x Marks on plate
  xx **Plate**
Halloween 394.2
  x All Hallows' Eve
  xx **Folklore**
Hallucinations and illusions 616.85; 616.89
  See also **Apparitions; Ghosts; Magic; Optical illusions; Personality disorders**
  x Delusions; Illusions
  xx **Apparitions; Fantasy; Ghosts; Personality disorders; Psychical research; Psychology, Pathological; Subconsciousness; Visions**
Ham radio stations. *See* **Amateur radio stations**
Hand shadows. *See* **Shadow pictures**

Hand weaving. *See* **Weaving**

Handbooks, manuals, etc. *See* general subjects with the subdivision *Handbooks, manuals, etc.,* e.g. **Photography—Handbooks, manuals, etc.;** etc.

Handedness. *See* **Left- and right-handedness**

Handguns. *See* **Pistols**

Handi-animals. *See* **Animals and the handicapped**

Handicapped 362.1-362.4

> *See also* **Mentally handicapped; Physically handicapped; Sick; Socially handicapped**
>
> *x* Disabled

Handicapped and animals. *See* **Animals and the handicapped**

Handicapped and architecture. *See* **Architecture and the handicapped**

Handicapped children 362.7

> *See also* **Brain damaged children; Hyperactive children; Mainstreaming in education; Mentally handicapped children; Physically handicapped children; Socially handicapped children**
>
> *x* Abnormal children; Children, Abnormal
>
> *xx* **Children; Exceptional children**

Handicraft 745.5; 746

> Use for materials on creative work done by hand, sometimes with the aid of simple tools or machines. Consider also **Decoration and ornament** and **Decorative arts.**
>
> *See also*

Arts and crafts movement	**Hobbies**
Craft shows	**Industrial arts**
Creative activities	**Industrial arts education**
Folk art	**Occupational therapy**

> also names of individual crafts, e.g. **Collage; Egg decoration; Leather work; Weaving;** etc.
>
> *x* Crafts (Arts)
>
> *xx* **Arts and crafts movement; Folk art; Hobbies; Occupational therapy**

Handling of materials. *See* **Materials handling**

Handwriting 652

> See note under **Writing.**
>
> *See also* **Calligraphy; Graphology; Writing**
>
> *x* Copybooks; Penmanship
>
> *xx* **Business education; Writing**

Hang gliding. *See* **Gliding and soaring**

Hanging. *See* **Capital punishment**

Hanukkah 296.4; 394.2

> *x* Chanukah; Feast of Dedication; Feast of Lights; Lights, Feast of; Maccabbees, Feast of the
>
> *xx* **Fasts and feasts—Judaism**

Happiness 158

> *See also* **Joy and sorrow; Pleasure**
>
> *x* Gladness
>
> *xx* **Joy and sorrow; Pleasure**

Harassment, Sexual. *See* **Sexual harassment**

Harbors (May subdiv. geog.) **386; 387.1; 627**

> *See also* **Docks; Marinas; Pilots and pilotage**
>
> *x* Ports

Harbors—*Continued*
    xx Civil engineering; Docks; Hydraulic struc-
        tures; Merchant marine; Navigation; Ship-
        ping; Transportation
Hard drugs. *See* Narcotics
Hares. *See* Rabbits
Harmony 781.3
    xx Composition (Music); Music; Music—Study
        and teaching; Music—Theory
Harry S. Truman Library 026
    xx Presidents—United States—Archives
Harvesting machinery 631.3; 631.5
    x Reapers
    xx Agricultural machinery
Hastings, (Essex, England), Battle of, 1066 941.02
    xx Great Britain—History—1066-1154, Norman
        period
Hats 391; 646.5; 687
    See also Millinery
    xx Clothing and dress; Costume; Millinery
Haunted houses. *See* Ghosts
Hawking. *See* Falconry
Hay 633.3; 664
    See also Feeds; Grasses; also names of hay
        crops, e.g. Alfalfa; etc.
    xx Farm produce; Feeds; Forage plants; Grasses
Hay fever 616.2
    xx Allergy
Hazardous materials. *See* Hazardous substances
Hazardous substances 604.7
    See also Hazardous wastes; Poisons and poison-
        ing
    x Dangerous materials; Hazardous materials;
        Inflammable substances; Toxic substances
    xx Materials; Occupational health and safety
Hazardous substances—Transportation 363.1
Hazardous waste disposal. *See* Hazardous wastes
Hazardous waste sites 363.1; 604.7; 628.3-628.4
    See also Love Canal Chemical Waste Landfill
        (Niagara Falls, N.Y.)
    x Chemical landfills; Dumps, Toxic; Toxic
        dumps
    xx Landfills
Hazardous wastes 604.7
    See also Pollution
    x Hazardous waste disposal; Wastes, Hazardous
    xx Hazardous substances; Industrial wastes; Pol-
        lution; Refuse and refuse disposal
HBO. *See* Home Box Office
Head 611; 612
    See also Brain; Ear; Eye; Face; Hair and hair-
        dressing; Nose; Phrenology
    xx Brain
Heads of state (May subdiv. geog.) 351.003; 920
    See also Dictators; Kings, queens, rulers, etc.;
        Presidents; Prime ministers
    x Rulers; State, Heads of
    xx Executive power; Statesmen
Healing, Mental. *See* Mental healing
Healing, Spiritual. *See* Spiritual healing
Health 613; 616
    Use for materials on physical, mental, and social
        well-being. Materials on personal body care
        are entered under Hygiene.

Health—*Continued*
> *See also*

Diet	Longevity
Diseases	Mental health
Exercise	Physical fitness
Health education	Rest
Holistic medicine	Self-care, Health
Hygiene	Sleep

> also parts of the body and people dependent on others with the subdivision *Care and hygiene,* e.g. **Children—Care and hygiene;** and classes of people with the subdivision *Health and hygiene,* e.g. **Women—Health and hygiene;** etc.
>
> *x* Personal health
>
> *xx* **Diseases; Holistic medicine; Hygiene; Medicine; Medicine, Preventive; Physiology**

Health and hygiene. *See* classes of people except those dependent upon others with the subdivision *Health and hygiene,* e.g.
> **Women—Health and hygiene;** etc.

Health boards 614.06
> *x* Boards of health; Public health boards
>
> *xx* **Public health**

Health care. *See* **Medical care**

Health care, Self. *See* **Self-care, Health**

Health clubs. *See* **Health resorts, spas, etc.**

Health counseling 362; 613.07
> *xx* **Counseling; Health education**

Health education 371.7; 613.07
> *See also* **Drug education; Health counseling; School hygiene**
>
> *x* Health—Study and teaching; Hygiene—Study and teaching
>
> *xx* **Children—Care and hygiene; Health; Physical education**

Health—Environmental aspects. *See* **Environmental health**

Health food. *See* **Food, Natural**

Health, Industrial. *See* **Occupational health and safety**

Health insurance. *See* **Insurance, Health**

Health maintenance organizations 368.3; 610.6
> *x* Comprehensive health care organizations; Group medical practice, Prepaid; H.M.O.'s; HMOs; Prepaid group medical practice
>
> *xx* **Insurance, Health; Medical care**

Health, Mental. *See* **Mental health**

Health of children. *See* **Children—Care and hygiene**

Health of infants. *See* **Infants—Care and hygiene**

Health, Public. *See* **Public health**

Health resorts, spas, etc. 613
> *See also* **Summer resorts; Winter resorts**
>
> *x* Health clubs; Physical fitness centers; Resorts; Sanatoriums; Spas; Watering places
>
> *xx* **Hydrotherapy; Medicine; Sick; Summer resorts; Travel; Winter resorts**

Health, Self-care. *See* **Self-care, Health**

Health—Study and teaching. *See* **Health education**

Healths, Drinking of. *See* **Toasts**
Hearing 617.8
  See also **Deafness; Ear**
  x Acoustics
  xx **Deafness; Ear; Senses and sensation; Sound**
Hearing aids 617.8
  See also **Hearing ear dogs**
  xx **Deafness**
Hearing ear dogs 636.7
  x Deaf, Dogs for; Dogs for the deaf
  xx **Animals and the handicapped; Deaf; Dogs;**
    Hearing aids
Hearing impaired. *See* **Deaf**
Heart 611; 612
  See also **Artificial heart; Blood—Circulation**
  xx **Anatomy, Human; Cardiovascular system;**
    Physiology
Heart attack. *See* **Heart—Diseases**
Heart—Diseases 616.1
  x Angina pectoris; Cardiac diseases; Coronary
    heart diseases; Heart attack
Heart—Diseases—Prevention 616.1
  xx **Medicine, Preventive**
Heart resuscitation. *See* **Cardiac resuscitation**
Heart—Surgery 617
  x Open heart surgery
  xx **Surgery**
Heart—Surgery—Nursing 610.73; 616.1
  xx **Nursing**
Heart—Transplantation 617
  xx **Transplantation of organs, tissues, etc.**
Heat 536
  See also **Combustion; Fire; Steam; Temperature;**
    Thermodynamics; Thermometers and ther-
    mometry
  xx **Combustion; Electromagnetic waves; Fire;**
    Temperature; Thermodynamics
Heat—Conduction 536
Heat engines 621.43
  See also **Steam engines; Thermodynamics**
  x Hot air engines
  xx **Engines; Thermodynamics**
Heat insulating materials. *See* **Insulation (Heat)**
Heat pumps 621.4
  xx **Pumping machinery; Thermodynamics**
Heat—Transmission 536
Heathenism. *See* **Paganism**
Heating 644; 697
  See also

Chimneys	**Oil burners**
Electric heating	**Radiant heating**
Fireplaces	**Solar heating**
Fuel	**Space heaters**
Furnaces	**Steam heating**
Hot air heating	**Stoves**
Hot water heating	**Ventilation**
Insulation (Heat)	

    also subjects with the subdivision *Heating and*
      ventilation, e.g. **Houses—Heating and venti-**
      lation; etc.

Heating—*Continued*
   xx **Fire; Fuel; Home economics; Ventilation**
Heaven 236
   See also **Angels**
   xx **Death; Future life**
Heavy water. *See* **Deuterium oxide**
Hebrew language 492.4
   May be subdivided like **English language.**
   See also **Yiddish language**
   x Jewish language; Jews—Language
Hebrew literature 892.4
   May use same subdivisions and names of literary forms as for **English literature.**
   See also **Bible; Cabala; Jewish literature; Talmud**
   x Jews—Literature
   xx **Jewish literature**
Hebrews. *See* **Jews**
Heirs. *See* **Inheritance and succession**
Helicopters 387.7; 629.133
   x Aircraft
   xx **Aeronautics; Airplanes; Ground effect machines**
Helicopters—Piloting 629.132; 629.133
   xx **Airplanes—Piloting**
Heliports 387.7
   xx **Airports**
Helium 546
   xx **Radioactivity**
Hell 236
   x Eternal punishment; Hades; Retribution
   xx **Death; Future life**
Hellenism 938; 939
   x Greek civilization
   xx **Civilization, Greek; Greek language; Greek literature; Humanism**
Helpfulness. *See* **Helping behavior**
Helping behavior 361-362
   See also **Counseling**
   x Assistance in emergencies; Emergency assistance; Helpfulness
   xx **Human behavior; Human relations**
Hemp 633.5; 677
   See also **Fibers; Rope**
   xx **Fibers; Linen; Rope**
Heraldry 929.6
   See also

Chivalry	**Knights and knighthood**
Decorations of honor	**Mottoes**
Flags	**Nobility**
Genealogy	**Seals (Numismatics)**
Insignia	

   x Arms, Coats of; Coats of arms; Crests; Devices (Heraldry); Emblems; Pedigrees
   xx **Archeology; Biography; Chivalry; Decorations of honor; Genealogy; Knights and knighthood; Nobility; Signs and symbols; Symbolism**
Herbage. *See* **Grasses**
Herbal medicine. *See* **Botany, Medical**

Herbals. *See* **Botany, Medical; Herbs; Materia medica**

Herbaria. *See* **Plants—Collection and preservation**

Herbicides 632; 668

> *See also* **Spraying and dusting;** also names of herbicides, e.g. **Agent Orange;** etc.
> *x* Defoliants; Weed killers; Weedicides
> *xx* **Agricultural chemicals; Pesticides; Spraying and dusting**

Herbs 635

> *x* Herbals

Herbs, Medical. *See* **Botany, Medical**

Hereditary diseases. *See* **Medical genetics**

Hereditary succession. *See* **Inheritance and succession**

Heredity 575.1

> *See also*

Blood groups	**Evolution**
Chromosomes	**Mendel's law**
DNA	**Natural selection**
Eugenics	**Variation (Biology)**

> *x* Ancestry; Descent; Genes; Inheritance (Biology)
> *xx* **Biology; Breeding; Children; Eugenics; Evolution; Genetics; Man; Mendel's law; Natural selection; Sociology**

Heredity of diseases. *See* **Medical genetics**

Hereford cattle 636.2

> *xx* **Beef cattle**

Hermeneutics, Biblical. *See* **Bible—Criticism, interpretation, etc.**

Hermetic art and philosophy. *See* **Alchemy; Astrology; Occult sciences**

Hermits 920

> *x* Recluses
> *xx* **Religious orders; Saints**

Heroes and heroines 920

> *See also* **Courage; Explorers; Martyrs; Mythology; Saints**
> *x* Heroines; Heroism
> *xx* **Adventure and adventurers; Courage; Mythology**

Heroines. *See* **Heroes and heroines; Women—Biography; Women in the Bible**

Heroism. *See* **Courage; Heroes and heroines**

Hertzian waves. *See* **Electric waves**

Hi-fi systems. *See* **High-fidelity sound systems**

Hibernation of animals. *See* **Animals—Hibernation**

Hidden treasure. *See* **Buried treasure**

Hides and skins 636.08

> *See also* **Fur; Leather; Tanning**
> *x* Animal products; Pelts; Skins
> *xx* **Fur; Leather; Tanning**

Hieroglyphics 411

> Use for materials on that form of picture writing which is distinguished by conventionalized pictures used chiefly to represent meanings that seem arbitrary and are seldom obvious, such as the pictographic styles used in an-

Hieroglyphics—*Continued*
cient Egypt, Crete, Central America, and
Mexico.
See also **Picture writing; Rosetta stone inscription**
xx **Inscriptions; Picture writing; Writing**
High blood pressure. *See* **Hypertension**
High-fidelity sound systems 621.389
See also **Stereophonic sound systems**
x Hi-fi systems
xx **Electronics; Sound—Recording and reproducing**
High-frequency radio. *See* **Radio, Shortwave**
High rise buildings. *See* **Skyscrapers**
High school education. *See* **Education, Secondary**
High school libraries. *See* **School libraries (High
school)**
High schools (May subdiv. geog.) **373.1**
See also **Commencements; Education, Secondary;
Junior high schools**
x Secondary schools
xx **Education, Secondary; Public schools**
High schools, Junior. *See* **Junior high schools**
High schools, Rural. *See* **Rural schools**
High society. *See* **Upper classes**
High speed aerodynamics. *See* **Aerodynamics, Supersonic**
High speed aeronautics 629.132
See also **Aerodynamics, Supersonic; Aerothermodynamics; Rocket planes; Rockets (Aeronautics)**
x Aeronautics, High speed
xx **Aeronautics**
High treason. *See* **Treason**
Higher criticism. *See* **Bible—Criticism, interpretation, etc.**
Higher education. *See* **Education, Higher**
Highjacking of airplanes. *See* **Hijacking of airplanes**
Highland clans. *See* **Clans**
Highland costume. *See* **Tartans**
Highway accidents. *See* **Traffic accidents**
Highway beautification. *See* **Roadside improvement**
Highway construction. *See* **Roads**
Highway engineering 625.7
See also **Roads; Traffic engineering**
x Road engineering
xx **Civil engineering; Engineering; Roads**
Highway transportation. *See* **Transportation, Highway**
Highwaymen. *See* **Robbers and outlaws**
Highways. *See* **Roads**
Hijacking of airplanes 364.1
Use same form for the hijacking of other modes
of transportation.
x Aeronautics, Commercial—Hijacking; Air piracy; Airlines—Hijacking; Airplane hijacking; Airplanes—Hijacking; Highjacking of
airplanes; Sky hijacking; Skyjacking
xx **Offenses against public safety**

Hiking   796.5

    See also **Direction sense;** also names of forms of hiking, e.g. **Backpacking; Walking;** etc.

    xx **Outdoor life; Walking**

Hillbilly music.   *See* **Country music**

Hindoos.   *See* **Hindus**

Hinduism   294.5

    See also **Brahmanism; Caste; Vedas; Yoga**

    xx **Brahmanism; Religions**

Hindus   572.954

    See also **East Indians**

    x Hindoos

    xx **East Indians**

Hippies (May subdiv. geog.)   **305.5**

    x Yippies

    xx **Bohemianism**

Hippies—United States   305.5

    x United States—Hippies

Hire-purchase plan.   *See* **Instalment plan**

Hispanic Americans   305.8

    Use for materials on United States citizens of Latin American descent. Materials on citizens of Latin American countries are entered under **Latin Americans.**

    See also names of groups of U.S. citizens from specific countries, e.g. **Mexican Americans;** etc.

    x Latinos (U.S.)

    xx **Ethnology—United States**

Hispano-American War, 1898.   *See* **United States—History—1898, War of 1898**

Histochemistry.   *See* **Physiological chemistry**

Historians (May subdiv. geog. adjective form)   **907.092; 920**

    See also **Archeologists**

    x Writers

    xx **Historiography; History**

Historians, American   907.092; 920

    x American historians; United States—Historians

Historic buildings (May subdiv. geog.)   **725-726; 728.09**

    See also **Literary landmarks;** also types of historic buildings, e.g. **Castles; Churches; Temples; Theaters;** etc.

    x Buildings, Historic; Historic houses; Houses, Historic

    xx **Architecture; Buildings; Historic sites; Monuments**

Historic buildings—Chicago (Ill.)   720.9773; 917.73

    x Chicago (Ill.)—Historic buildings

Historic buildings—United States   720.9; 725; 726

    x United States—Historic buildings

    xx **Architecture, Colonial**

Historic houses.   *See* **Historic buildings**

Historic sites (May subdiv. geog.)

    See also **Historic buildings**

    x Historical sites

    xx **Archeology; History**

Historical atlases.   *See* **Atlases, Historical**

Historical chronology. *See* **Chronology, Historical**
Historical dictionaries. *See* **History—Dictionaries**
Historical fiction   808.3; 809.3

> Use for materials about historical fiction. Historical novels are entered under the names of historical topics, events, and characters with the subdivision *Fiction.*
>
> *See also* names of historical events and characters with the subdivision *Fiction,* e.g. **Slavery—United States—Fiction; United States—History—1861-1865, Civil War—Fiction; Napoleon I, Emperor of the French, 1769-1821—Fiction;** etc.
>
> *x* Fiction, Historical
> *xx* **Fiction; History**

Historical geography. *See* **Atlases, Historical; Geography, Historical;** and names of modern countries or regions with the subdivision *Historical geography,* e.g. **United States—Historical geography;** etc.; and names of ancient countries with the subdivision *Description and geography,* e.g. **Greece—Description and geography;** etc.
Historical geology. *See* **Geology, Stratigraphic**
Historical materialism. *See* **Dialectical materialism**
Historical records—Preservation. *See* **Archives**
Historical sites. *See* **Historic sites**
Historical societies. *See* **History—Societies**
Historiography   907.2

> See note under **History.**
>
> *See also* **Historians;** also subjects with the subdivision *Historiography,* e.g. **Philosophy—Historiography; United States—History—Historiography;** etc.
>
> *x* History—Criticism; History—Historiography

History   900

> Use for general materials on history as a science. This includes the principles of history, the influence of various factors on history and the relation of the science of history to other subjects. Materials on the interpretation and meaning of history, the course of events and their resulting consequences, are entered under **History—Philosophy.** Materials limited to the study and criticism of sources of history, methods of historical research, and the writing of history are entered under **Historiography.**
>
> *See also*

Anthropogeography	**Geography, Historical**
Archeology	**Historians**
Biography	**Historic sites**
Chronology	**Historical fiction**
Church history	**Kings, queens, rulers, etc.**
Civilization	**Man**
Colonization	**Massacres**
Constitutional history	**Middle Ages—History**
Discoveries (in geography)	**Military history**
Ethnology	**Naval history**
Genealogy	**Numismatics**

History—*Continued*

Oral history	**Seals (Numismatics)**
Political science	**World history**

also headings beginning with the word **History;** and names of countries, states, etc. with the subdivisions *Antiquities; Foreign relations; History; Politics and government.* The history of a subject is entered under the name of the subject with the subdivision *History,* or, for literature, film, and music headings, *History and criticism,* e.g. **Art—History; English language—History; English literature—History and criticism; Music—History and criticism;** etc.

x Social studies

History, Ancient 930

See also **Archeology; Bible; Civilization, Ancient; Classical dictionaries; Geography, Ancient; Inscriptions; Numismatics;** also names of ancient peoples, e.g. **Hittites;** etc,; and names of countries of antiquity

x Ancient history

xx **World history**

History—Atlases. *See* **Atlases, Historical**

History, Biblical. *See* **Bible—History of biblical events**

History—Chronology. *See* **Chronology, Historical**

History, Church. *See* **Church history**

History, Constitutional. *See* **Constitutional history**

History—Criticism. *See* **Historiography**

History—Dictionaries 903

x Historical dictionaries

History—Historiography. *See* **Historiography**

History, Local. *See* names of countries, states, etc. with the subdivision *History, Local,* e.g. **United States—History, Local;** etc.

History, Medieval. *See* **Middle Ages—History**

History, Military. *See* **Military history;** and names of countries with the subdivision *History, Military,* e.g. **United States—History, Military;** etc.

History, Modern 909.08-909.83

Use for materials covering the period after 1453.

See also **Civilization, Modern; Reformation; Renaissance**

x Modern history

xx **Civilization, Modern; World history**

History, Modern—1800-1899 (19th century) 909.81

See also **Nineteenth century**

History, Modern—1900-1999 (20th century) 909.82

See also **Twentieth century; World War, 1914-1918; World War, 1939-1945**

History, Modern—Study and teaching 909.0807

See also **Current events**

History, Natural. *See* **Natural history**

History, Naval. *See* **Naval history;** and names of countries with the subdivision *History, Naval,* e.g. **United States—History, Naval;** etc.

History, Oral. *See* **Oral history**

History—Philosophy 901
　　See note under **History.**
　　See also **Civilization**
　　x Philosophy of history
　　xx **Philosophy**
History—Societies 906
　　See also **United States—History—Societies**
　　x Historical societies
History—Sources 900
　　Use only for documents, records and other
　　　　source materials upon which narrative his-
　　　　tory is based.
　　See also **Archives; Charters;** also names of coun-
　　　　tries, states, etc. with the subdivision
　　　　History—Sources, e.g. **United States—**
　　　　History—Sources; etc.; and names of peri-
　　　　ods of history and names of wars with the
　　　　subdivision *Sources,* e.g. **United States—**
　　　　History—1861-1865, Civil War—Sources;
　　　　World War, 1939-1945—Sources; etc.
History, Universal. *See* **World history**
Histrionics. *See* **Acting; Theater**
Hittites 939
　　xx **History, Ancient**
HMOs. *See* **Health maintenance organizations**
Hoaxes. *See* **Impostors and imposture**
Hobbies 790.1
　　See also **Collectors and collecting; Handicraft;**
　　　　also names of hobbies
　　x Avocations; Recreations
　　xx **Amusements; Handicraft; Leisure; Recreation**
Hoboes. *See* **Tramps**
Hockey. *See* **Field hockey; Ice hockey**
Hogs. *See* **Pigs**
Hoisting machinery 621.8
　　See also types of hoisting machinery, e.g.
　　　　Conveying machinery; Cranes, derricks, etc.;
　　　　Elevators; etc.
　　x Lifts
　　xx **Conveying machinery; Machinery**
Holiday decorations 394.2; 745.4
　　x Decorations, Holiday
　　xx **Decoration and ornament**
Holidays 394.2
　　See also **Fasts and feasts; Vacations;** also names
　　　　of holidays, e.g. **Fourth of July; Valentine's**
　　　　Day; etc.
　　x Anniversaries; Days; Legal holidays; National
　　　　holidays
　　xx **Fasts and feasts; Festivals; Manners and cus-**
　　　　toms; Vacations
Holidays, Jewish. *See* **Fasts and feasts—Judaism**
Holistic health. *See* **Holistic medicine**
Holistic medicine 150; 615
　　See also **Health; Mind and body; Self-care,**
　　　　Health
　　x Holistic health; Humanistic medicine;
　　　　Wholistic medicine
　　xx **Alternative medicine; Health; Medicine; Mind**
　　　　and body; Self-care, Health

Holland. *See* **Netherlands**

Holocaust, Jewish (1933-1945) 940.54; 943.086

> Use for materials on the period of persecution and extermination of European Jews by National Socialist, or Nazi, Germany which began with Adolf Hitler's rise to power in 1933.
>
> *See also* **World War, 1939-1945—Jews;** also names of concentration camps
>
> *x* Destruction of Jews (1933-1945); Extermination of Jews (1933-1945); Jewish holocaust (1933-1945)
>
> *xx* **Antisemitism; Jews—Persecutions; World War, 1939-1945—Jews**

Holography 774

> *x* Laser photography; Lensless photography; Photography, Laser; Photography, Lensless
>
> *xx* **Laser recording**

Holstein-Friesian cattle 636.2

> *x* Friesian cattle
>
> *xx* **Dairy cattle**

Holy days. *See* **Fasts and feasts**

Holy Ghost. *See* **Holy Spirit**

Holy Grail. *See* **Grail**

Holy Office. *See* **Inquisition**

Holy Roman Empire 943

> *xx* **Europe—History—476-1492; Germany—History—0-1517; Middle Ages—History**

Holy Scriptures. *See* **Bible**

Holy See. *See* **Papacy; Popes**

Holy Spirit 231

> *See also* **Trinity**
>
> *x* Holy Ghost; Spirit, Holy
>
> *xx* **God—Christianity; Theology; Trinity**

Holy Week 263

> *See also* **Easter; Good Friday**
>
> *xx* **Lent**

Home 306.8; 640

> *See also* **Family; Home economics; Marriage**
>
> *xx* **Family; Marriage**

Home accidents 363.1

> *See also* **First aid**
>
> *xx* **Accidents**

Home and school 371.1

> *See also* **Parent-teacher relationships; Parents' and teachers' associations**
>
> *x* School and home
>
> *xx* **Parent-teacher relationships; Parents' and teachers' associations**

Home Box Office 384.55

> *x* H.B.O.; HBO
>
> *xx* **Cable television; Subscription television**

Home business 650

> *See also* **Telecommuting**
>
> *x* At-home employment; Cottage industry; Home labor; Work at home; Working at home
>
> *xx* **Business; Self-employed; Small business**

Home buying. *See* **Houses—Buying and selling**

Home care services   361-362
> *See also* **Home nursing;** also classes of people
> with the subdivision *Home care,* e.g.
> **Elderly—Home care;** etc.
> *x* Home health care; Home medical care
> *xx* **Medical care**

Home computers   621.3819; *621.391
> *x* Household data processing; Personal comput-
> ers
> *xx* **Computers; Microcomputers; Minicomputers;**
> **Telecommuting**

Home construction.   *See* **House construction**

Home decoration.   *See* **Interior design**

Home delivered meals.   *See* **Meals on wheels pro-**
> **grams**

Home designs.   *See* **Architecture, Domestic—**
> **Designs and plans**

Home economics   640
> *See also*

Consumer education	**Household employees**
Cookery	**Household pests**
Cost of living	**Interior design**
Dairying	**Laundry**
Entertaining	**Mobile home living**
Food	**Sewing**
Fuel	**Shopping**
Furniture	**Storage in the home**
Heating	**Ventilation**
House cleaning	

> *x* Domestic arts; Efficiency, Household; Home-
> making; Household management; House-
> keeping
> *xx* **Family life education; Home**

Home economics—Accounting.   *See* **Budgets,**
> **Household**

Home economics—Equipment and supplies.   *See*
> **Household equipment and supplies**

Home education.   *See* **Correspondence schools and**
> **courses; Home instruction**

Home health care.   *See* **Home care services**

Home instruction   649
> *See also* **Child development; Child rearing; Par-**
> **enting; Tutors and tutoring**
> *x* Domestic education; Education at home; Edu-
> cation, Home; Home education; Home
> teaching; Instruction, Home; Teaching at
> home
> *xx* **Child development; Child rearing; Education;**
> **Parenting; Teaching**

Home labor.   *See* **Home business; Telecommuting**

Home life.   *See* **Family life**

Home loans.   *See* **Mortgages**

Home medical care.   *See* **Home care services**

Home missions, Christian.   *See* **Missions, Christian**

Home movies.   *See* **Amateur motion pictures**

Home nursing   649.8
> *See also* **Sick**
> *xx* **Home care services; Nursing; Sick**

Home purchase.   *See* **Houses—Buying and selling**

Home remodeling.   *See* **Houses—Remodeling**

Home repairing. *See* **Houses—Maintenance and repair**

Home sharing. *See* **Shared housing**

Home storage. *See* **Storage in the home**

Home study courses. *See* **Correspondence schools and courses**

Home teaching. *See* **Home instruction**

Home work (Employment). *See* **Telecommuting**

Homeless people 362
    See also **Refugees; Runaway adults; Runaway children; Tramps**
    x Homelessness
    xx **Poor; Social problems**

Homeless people—Government policy 362.5
    x Government policy

Homelessness. *See* **Homeless people**

Homemakers 306.8
    See also **Fathers; Mothers**
    x Househusbands; Housewives

Homemaking. *See* **Home economics**

Homeopathy 615.5
    xx **Medicine; Medicine—Practice**

Homes. *See* **Houses**

Homes for the elderly. *See* **Elderly—Institutional care**

Homes (Institutions). *See* **Charities; Institutional care; Orphanages;** and classes of people with the subdivision *Institutional care,* e.g. **Blind—Institutional care; Children—Institutional care; Deaf—Institutional care;** etc.

Homes, Mobile. *See* **Mobile homes**

Homework (Employment). *See* **Telecommuting**

Homicide 364.1
    See also **Euthanasia**

Homonyms. *See* names of languages with the subdivision *Homonyms,* e.g. **English language—Homonyms;** etc.

Homosexuality 306.7
    See also **Gay liberation movement; Lesbianism**
    x Gay lifestyle
    xx **Sexual behavior**

Homosexuals, Female. *See* **Gay women**

Homosexuals, Male. *See* **Gay men**

Honesty 179
    See also **Truthfulness and falsehood**
    x Dishonesty
    xx **Ethics; Human behavior; Truthfulness and falsehood**

Honey 638; 641.3
    See also **Bees**
    xx **Bees**

Honor system. *See* **Self-government (in education)**

Honorary degrees. *See* **Degrees, Academic**

Hooked rugs. *See* **Rugs, Hooked**

Hoover Dam (Ariz. and Nev.) 627
    x Boulder Dam (Ariz. and Nev.); Colorado River—Hoover Dam
    xx **Dams**

Hope 179; 241
  xx Faith
Hormones 574.19; 612
  See also Endocrine glands
  xx Endocrine glands; Endocrinology
Hornbooks 028.5; 372.4
Horology. *See* Clocks and watches; Sundials
Horoscopes 133.5
  xx Astrology
Horror 152.4
  xx Emotions; Fear
Horror—Fiction Fic
  x Horror stories
Horror stories. *See* Horror—Fiction
Horse. *See* Horses
Horse breeding. *See* Horses—Breeding
Horse racing 798.4
  x Racing
  xx Gambling
Horseback riding 798.2
  See also Rodeos
  x Equestrianism; Riding
Horsebreaking. *See* Horses—Training
Horses 599.72; 636.1
  See also Ponies
  x Horse
Horses—Breeding 636.1
  x Horse breeding
  xx Breeding
Horses—Diseases 636.089
Horses—Training 636.1
  x Horsebreaking
  xx Animals—Training
Horseshoeing. *See* Blacksmithing
Horticulture 635
  Use for materials on the scientific and economic
    aspects of the cultivation of flowers, fruits,
    vegetables, etc.
  See also

Aeroponics	Hydroponics
Flower gardening	Landscape gardening
Fruit culture	Organiculture
Gardening	Vegetable gardening
Greenhouses	

  xx Agriculture; Gardening; Plants
Hosiery 391; 687
  x Stockings
  xx Clothing and dress; Textile industry
Hospices 362.1
  xx Hospitals; Social medicine; Terminal care
Hospital libraries 027.6
  x Libraries, Hospital
  xx Libraries
Hospital ships 362.1; 623.8
  x Floating hospitals
  xx Hospitals; Ships
Hospitality. *See* Entertaining
Hospitalization insurance. *See* Insurance, Hospital-
    ization

Hospitals (May subdiv. geog.) **362.1**
    See also

Children's hospitals	**Long-term care facilities**
Hospices	**Medical centers**
Hospital ships	**Nursing**
Life support systems	**Nursing homes**
(Medical environment)	**Psychiatric hospitals**

    also names of hospitals
    x Infirmaries; Institutions, Charitable and phil-
        anthropic; Sanatoriums
    xx **Charities, Medical; Institutional care; Medical**
        centers; Medicine; Nursing; Public health;
        Public welfare; Sick
Hospitals, Military   355.7
    See also **First aid;** also names of wars with the
        subdivision *Medical care,* e.g. **World War,**
        1939-1945—Medical care; etc.
    x Field hospitals; Military hospitals; Veterans—
        Hospitals
    xx **Medicine, Military; Military art and science;**
        Veterans
Hospitals—United States   362.1
    x United States—Hospitals
Hostage escapes.   *See* **Escapes**
Hostage negotiation
    xx **Hostages**
Hostages (May subdiv. geog. adjective form)   **920**
    See also **Hostage negotiation**
    xx **Terrorism**
Hostages, American (May subdiv. geog. except U.S.)
    920
    x American hostages; United States—Hostages
Hostages, American—Iran
    See also **Iran hostage crisis, 1979-1981**
Hostels, Youth.   *See* **Youth hostels**
Hostesses, Airline.   *See* **Airlines—Flight attendants**
Hot air engines.   *See* **Heat engines**
Hot air heating   697
    x Warm air heating
    xx **Heating**
Hot water heating   697
    xx **Heating**
Hotels, motels, etc. (May subdiv. geog.)   **647; 728**
    x Auto courts; Bed and breakfast accommoda-
        tions; Boarding houses; Inns; Lodging
        houses; Motels; Motor courts; Rooming
        houses; Tourist accommodations
Hotels, motels, etc.—United States   647; 728
    x United States—Hotels, motels, etc.
Hothouses.   *See* **Greenhouses**
Hotlines (Telephone counseling)   **361; 362.2**
    See also **Crisis centers**
    x Crisis counseling; Crisis intervention tele-
        phone service; Peer counseling; Switch-
        board hotlines; Telephone counseling
    xx **Counseling; Crisis centers; Human relations;**
        Information services; Social work
Hours of labor   331.2
    See also **Children—Employment; Part-time em-**
        ployment

Hours of labor—*Continued*

    x Alternative work schedules; Compressed work week; Eight-hour day; Five-day work week; Flexible hours of labor; Flexitime; Four-day work week; Labor, Hours of; Overtime; Working day; Working hours

    xx **Children—Employment; Labor**

Hours (Time). *See* **Chronology**

House boats. *See* **Houseboats**

House buying. *See* **Houses—Buying and selling**

House cleaning 648

    xx **Cleaning; Home economics; Sanitation, Household**

House construction 690

    See also **Houses;** also special kinds of house construction, e.g. **Earth sheltered houses; Log cabins and houses; Prefabricated houses;** etc.

    x Building, House; Construction, House; Home construction; Residential construction

    xx **Architecture, Domestic; Building**

House decoration. *See* **Interior design**

House drainage. *See* **Drainage, House**

House flies. *See* **Flies**

House furnishing. *See* **Interior design**

House painting 698

    xx **Painting, Industrial**

House plans. *See* **Architecture, Domestic—Designs and plans**

House plants 635.9

    See also **Indoor gardening**

    xx **Flower gardening; Indoor gardening; Plants; Plants, Cultivated; Window gardening**

House purchase. *See* **Houses—Buying and selling**

House repairing. *See* **Houses—Maintenance and repair**

House sanitation. *See* **Sanitation, Household**

House selling. *See* **Houses—Buying and selling**

House trailers. *See* **Mobile homes; Travel trailers and campers**

Houseboats 728.7

    x House boats

    xx **Boats and boating**

Household appliances. *See* **Household equipment and supplies**

Household appliances, Electric 643-644

    See also names of specific appliances

    x Appliances, Electric; Domestic appliances; Electric apparatus and appliances, Domestic; Electric appliances; Electric household appliances; Electricity in the home; Labor saving devices, Household

    xx **Household equipment and supplies**

Household budget. *See* **Budgets, Household**

Household data processing. *See* **Home computers**

Household employees 640

    x Domestic workers; Housemaids; Servants

    xx **Home economics; Labor**

Household equipment and supplies 643; 683

    See also **Household appliances, Electric**

Household equipment and supplies—*Continued*
> *x* Cooking utensils; Domestic appliances; Home economics—Equipment and supplies; Household appliances; Implements, utensils, etc.; Kitchen utensils; Labor saving devices, Household; Utensils, Kitchen

Household finances. *See* **Budgets, Household; Cost of living**
Household management. *See* **Home economics**
Household moving. *See* **Moving, Household**
Household pests 648
> *See also* names of pests, e.g. **Flies;** etc.
> *x* Diseases and pests; Vermin
> *xx* **Home economics; Insects, Injurious and beneficial; Pests; Sanitation, Household**

Household sanitation. *See* **Sanitation, Household**
Household violence. *See* **Family violence**
Househusbands. *See* **Homemakers**
Housekeeping. *See* **Home economics**
Housemaids. *See* **Household employees**
Houses 728
> Use for general materials on houses.
> *See also* **Apartment houses; Building; Housing; Solar homes; Tenement houses;** also types of houses, e.g. **Earth sheltered houses; Log cabins and houses; Prefabricated houses;** etc.; and parts of the house, e.g. **Kitchens;** etc.
> *x* Cottages; Dwellings; Habitations, Human; Homes; Residences; Summer homes
> *xx* **Architecture, Domestic; House construction**

Houses—Buying and selling 333.33
> *x* Home buying; Home purchase; House buying; House purchase; House selling
> *xx* **Real estate business**

Houses, Earth sheltered. *See* **Earth sheltered houses**
Houses—Heating and ventilation 644; 697
> *xx* **Heating**

Houses, Historic. *See* **Historic buildings**
Houses, Log. *See* **Log cabins and houses**
Houses—Maintenance and repair 643
> *x* Home repairing; House repairing
> *xx* **Buildings—Maintenance and repair**

Houses of animals. *See* **Animals—Habitations**
Houses, Prefabricated. *See* **Prefabricated houses**
Houses—Remodeling 643
> *x* Home remodeling; Remodeling of houses

Houses, Underground. *See* **Earth sheltered houses**
Housewives. *See* **Homemakers**
Housing 363.5
> Use for materials on the social and economic aspects of the housing problem.
> *See also* **Apartment houses; City planning; Mobile homes; Public housing; Shared housing; Tenement houses; Timesharing (Real estate)** also subjects with the subdivision *Housing,* e.g. **Blacks—Housing; Physically handicapped—Housing;** etc.
> *x* Dwellings; Habitations, Human
> *xx* **City planning; Houses; Landlord and tenant;**

Housing—*Continued*
>> Social problems; Tenement houses; Welfare
>> work in industry

Housing, Black. *See* **Blacks—Housing**

Housing, Discrimination in. *See* **Discrimination in
housing**

Housing for the elderly. *See* **Elderly—Housing**

Housing for the physically handicapped. *See* **Physically handicapped—Housing**

Housing loans. *See* **Mortgages**

Housing projects, Government. *See* **Public housing**

Houston Astros (Baseball team) 796.357
>> *x* Astros (Baseball team); Houston (Tex.). Baseball Club (National League)
>> *xx* **Baseball clubs**

Houston (Tex.). Baseball Club (National
>> League). *See* **Houston Astros (Baseball
>> team)**

Hovercraft. *See* **Ground effect machines**

Hudson River (N.Y.)—Bridges. *See* **Bridges—
Hudson River (N.Y.)**

Huguenots 284
>> *See also* **Saint Bartholomew's Day, Massacre of,
>> 1572**
>> *xx* **Christianity; Reformation**

Hull House 361.4
>> *xx* **Social settlements**

Human anatomy. *See* **Anatomy, Human**

Human behavior 150; 302
>> *See also*

Aggressiveness (Psychology)	**Human relations**
	Justice
Behavior modification	**Life skills**
Behaviorism	**Lifestyles**
Cannibalism	**Love**
Charity	**Loyalty**
Courage	**Obedience**
Courtesy	**Patience**
Duty	**Patriotism**
Eating customs	**Self-respect**
Ethics	**Social adjustment**
Etiquette	**Spiritual life**
Friendship	**Sympathy**
Habit	**Temperance**
Helping behavior	**Truthfulness and falsehood**
Honesty	

>> *x* Behavior; Conduct of life; Morals; Personal conduct; Social behavior
>> *xx* **Character; Courtesy; Ethics; Human relations;
>> Life skills**

Human body. *See* **Anatomy, Human; Physiology**

Human cold storage. *See* **Cryonics**

Human ecology 304.2
>> *See also* **Anthropogeography; Environment—
>> Government policy; Man—Influence of environment; Man—Influence on nature; Population; Survival skills**
>> *x* Ecology, Human; Ecology, Social; Social ecology
>> *xx* **Environment—Government policy; Sociology**

305

Human engineering 620.8

Use for materials on engineering design as related to human anatomical, physiological and psychological capabilities and limitations.

See also **Life support systems (Space environment)**

x Biomechanics; Ergonomics

xx **Design, Industrial; Engineering; Industrial management; Machinery—Design; Psychology, Applied; Psychology, Physiological**

Human fertility. *See* **Fertility, Human**

Human fertility in vitro. *See* **Fertilization in vitro, Human**

Human figure in art. *See* **Anatomy, Artistic; Figure drawing; Figure painting**

Human life education. *See* **Sex education**

Human race. *See* **Anthropology; Man**

Human relations 158; 302

Use for materials that deal with the integration of people so that they can live and work together with psychological, social, and economic satisfaction.

See also

Conflict of generations	**Life skills**
Discrimination	**Personal space**
Family	**Personnel management**
Family life education	**Prejudices**
Group relations training	**Psychology, Applied**
Helping behavior	**Social adjustment**
Hotlines (Telephone counseling)	**Social values**
Human behavior	**Teacher-student relationships**
Intercultural education	**Toleration**
Interfaith relations	**Transactional analysis**

also interpersonal relations between individuals or groups of individuals, e.g. **Jews and Gentiles; Landlord and tenant; Parent and child;** etc.

x Interpersonal relations

xx **Family life education; Human behavior; Life skills; Psychology, Applied; Social psychology**

Human resource management. *See* **Personnel management**

Human resources 331.11

See also **Labor supply; Military service, Compulsory; Military service, Voluntary; Unemployment;** also names of wars with the subdivision *Human resources,* e.g. **World War, 1939-1945—Human resources;** etc.

x Man power; Manpower; Woman power

xx **Employment; Labor supply**

Human resources development. *See* **Human resources policy**

Human resources policy 331.11

See also **Labor supply; Occupational retraining; Occupational training; Vocational education**

x Human resources development; Manpower policy

Human resources policy—*Continued*
  xx **Economic policy; Labor supply**
Human rights. *See* **Civil rights**
Human survival skills. *See* **Survival skills**
Human values. *See* **Values**
Humanism 001.2; 144; 880
  Use for materials on culture founded on the
    study of the classics, sometimes narrowly
    for Greek and Roman scholarship.
  See also **Classical education; Hellenism; Human-
    ities; Learning and scholarship; Renaissance**
  xx **Classical education; Culture; Learning and
    scholarship; Literature; Philosophy; Renais-
    sance**
Humanism—1900-1999 (20th century) 144
  Use for materials on any intellectual, philosophi-
    cal or religious movement or system which
    is centered in people rather than in nature,
    the supernatural, or the absolute.
Humanistic medicine. *See* **Holistic medicine**
Humanitarians. *See* **Philanthropists**
Humanities 001.3
  See also **Classical education;** also such subjects
    as **Art; Literature; Music; Philosophy;** etc.
  xx **Classical education; Humanism**
Humanities and science. *See* **Science and the hu-
    manities**
Humanity, Religion of. *See* **Positivism**
Humans in space. *See* **Space flight**
Humidity 551.57
  x Air, Moisture of; Atmospheric humidity; Rel-
    ative humidity
  xx **Meteorology; Weather**
Humor. *See* **Wit and humor;** and names of wars
    with the subdivision *Humor, caricatures,
    etc.,* e.g. **World War, 1939-1945—Humor,
    caricatures, etc.;** etc.
Humorists 809.7; 920
  xx **Wit and humor**
Humorous pictures. *See* **Cartoons and caricatures;
    Comic books, strips, etc.**
Humorous poetry 808.81; 811.08; etc.
  See also **Limericks; Nonsense verses**
  xx **Poetry; Wit and humor**
Humorous stories 808.87; 817; etc.
  x Stories
  xx **Fiction; Wit and humor**
Hundred Years' War, 1339-1453 944
  x 100 years' war
  xx **Europe—History—476-1492; France—
    History—1328-1589, House of Valois;
    Great Britain—History—1399-1485, Lan-
    caster and York**
Hungary—History 943.9
Hungary—History—1956, Revolution 943.9
  xx **Revolutions**
Hunger 363.8
  See also **Fasting; Starvation**
  xx **Fasting; Starvation**

Hunger strikes 322; 323.4

    x Strikes, Hunger

    xx **Fasting; Government, Resistance to; Nonviolence; Passive resistance; Protests, demonstrations, etc.**

Hunting (May subdiv. geog.) 799.2

    See also **Decoys (Hunting); Game and game birds; Game preserves; Game protection;** also types of hunting, e.g. **Falconry; Shooting; Tracking and trailing; Trapping; Whaling;** etc.

    x Gunning

    xx **Game and game birds; Shooting; Trapping**

Hunting, Job. *See* **Job hunting**

Hunting—United States 799.2

    x United States—Hunting

Hurricanes (May subdiv. geog.) 551.5

    Use for storms originating in the region of the West Indies.

    See also **Cyclones; Storms; Typhoons**

    xx **Meteorology; Storms; Typhoons; Winds**

Husband abuse 362.8

    x Abuse of husbands; Battered husbands; Battered men; Husband battering; Husband beating

    xx **Family violence**

Husband battering. *See* **Husband abuse**

Husband beating. *See* **Husband abuse**

Husbands, Runaway. *See* **Runaway adults**

Hybridization. *See* **Plant breeding**

Hydraulic cement. *See* **Cement**

Hydraulic engineering 627

    See also

Boring	**Irrigation**
Drainage	**Pumping machinery**
Dredging	**Reclamation of land**
Floods—Control	**Rivers**
Hydraulic structures	**Turbines**
Hydraulics	**Water**
Hydrodynamics	**Water supply engineering**
Hydrostatics	**Wells**

    xx **Civil engineering; Engineering; Fluid mechanics; Hydraulics; Rivers; Water; Water power; Water supply engineering**

Hydraulic machinery 621.2

    See also **Turbines**

    xx **Machinery; Water power**

Hydraulic structures 627

    See also **Pipelines;** also types of hydraulic structures, e.g. **Aqueducts; Canals; Dams; Docks; Harbors; Reservoirs;** etc.

    xx **Hydraulic engineering; Structural engineering**

Hydraulics 621.2; 627

    Use for materials on technical applications of the theory of hydrodynamics.

    See also **Hydraulic engineering; Hydrodynamics; Hydrostatics; Water; Water power**

    x Water flow

    xx **Fluid mechanics; Hydraulic engineering; Liquids; Mechanics; Physics**

Hydrodynamics 532

> Use for materials on the theory of the motion and action of fluids. Materials on the experimental investigation and technical application of this theory are entered under **Hydraulics.**

See also **Hydrostatics; Viscosity; Waves**

xx **Dynamics; Fluid mechanics; Hydraulic engineering; Hydraulics; Liquids; Mechanics**

Hydroelectric power. *See* **Water power**

Hydroelectric power plants 621.31

x Power plants, Hydroelectric

xx **Electric power plants; Water power; Water resources development**

Hydrofoil boats 623.8

Hydrogen 546

xx **Chemical elements**

Hydrogen bomb 623.4

See also **Atomic bomb; Radioactive fallout**

x H bomb; Thermonuclear bomb

xx **Atomic bomb; Bombs; Nuclear warfare; Nuclear weapons**

Hydrogen nucleus. *See* **Protons**

Hydrology. *See* **Water**

Hydromechanics. *See* **Fluid mechanics**

Hydropathy. *See* **Hydrotherapy**

Hydrophobia. *See* **Rabies**

Hydroponics 631.5

x Agriculture, Soilless; Chemiculture; Plants—Soilless culture; Soilless agriculture; Water farming

xx **Horticulture**

Hydrostatics 532

See also **Gases**

xx **Fluid mechanics; Hydraulic engineering; Hydraulics; Hydrodynamics; Liquids; Mechanics; Physics; Statics**

Hydrotherapy 615.8

See also **Baths; Health resorts, spas, etc.**

x Hydropathy; Water cure

xx **Baths; Physical therapy; Therapeutics; Water**

Hygiene 613

See also

Air	**Health**
Baths	**Infants—Care and hygiene**
Children—Care and hygiene	**Mental health**
	Military health
Diet	**Physical education**
Disinfection and disinfectants	**Rest**
	Sanitation
Exercise	**School hygiene**
Food	**Sleep**
Grooming, Personal	**Ventilation**

x Body care; Personal cleanliness; Personal hygiene

xx **Cleanliness; Health; Medicine; Medicine, Preventive; Sanitation**

Hygiene, Industrial. *See* **Occupational health and safety**

Hygiene, Mental. *See* **Mental health**

Hygiene, Military. *See* **Military health**
Hygiene, Public. *See* **Public health**
Hygiene, School. *See* **School hygiene**
Hygiene, Sexual. *See* **Sexual hygiene**
Hygiene, Social. *See* **Prostitution; Public health;**
    Sexual hygiene; Venereal diseases
Hygiene—Study and teaching. *See* **Health educa-**
    tion
Hygiene, Tropical. *See* **Tropical medicine**
Hymenoptera. *See* **Ants; Bees; Wasps**
Hymnology. *See* **Hymns**
Hymns 245; 783.9
    See also **Carols; Church music; Religious poetry**
    x Hymnology; Psalmody
    xx **Church music; Devotional literature; Liturgies;**
        Poetry; Religious poetry; Songs; Vocal mu-
        sic
Hyperactive children 155.4
    See also **Hyperactivity**
    x Children, Hyperactive; Hyperkinetic children;
        Overactive children
    xx **Handicapped children; Hyperactivity**
Hyperactivity 152.3
    See also **Hyperactive children**
    x Hyperkinesia; Overactivity
    xx **Hyperactive children**
Hyperkinesia. *See* **Hyperactivity**
Hyperkinetic children. *See* **Hyperactive children**
Hypertension 574.1; 612
    x High blood pressure
    xx **Blood pressure**
Hypnotism 154.7
    See also **Mental suggestion; Mind and body; Per-**
        sonality disorders; Psychoanalysis; Subcon-
        sciousness; Therapeutics, Suggestive
    x Animal magnetism; Autosuggestion; Mesmer-
        ism
    xx **Clairvoyance; Mental healing; Mental sugges-**
        tion; Mind and body; Mind reading; Per-
        sonality disorders; Psychical research; Psy-
        choanalysis; Psychology, Physiological;
        Subconsciousness; Therapeutics, Suggestive
I.B.M. 7090 (Computer). *See* **IBM 7090 (Com-**
    puter)
I.C.B.M. *See* **Intercontinental ballistic missiles**
I.Q. tests. *See* **Mental tests**
I.R.A.'s (Pensions). *See* **Individual retirement ac-**
    counts
I.S.B.D. *See* **International Standard Bibliographic**
    Description
I.S.B.N. *See* **International Standard Book Numbers**
I.S.S.N. *See* **International Standard Serial Num-**
    bers
IBM 7090 (Computer) 621.3819; *621.391
    x I.B.M. 7090 (Computer)
    xx **Computers**
ICBM. *See* **Intercontinental ballistic missiles**
Ice 551.3
    See also **Glaciers; Icebergs**
    x Freezing

Ice—*Continued*
    xx **Cold; Frost; Physical geography; Water**
Ice age 551.7
    x Glacial epoch
    xx **Earth**
Ice boats. *See* **Iceboats**
Ice cream, ices, etc. 637; 641.8
    See also **Confectionery**
    x Ices
    xx **Desserts; Food, Frozen**
Ice hockey 796.96
    x Hockey
    xx **Winter sports**
Ice manufacture. *See* **Refrigeration and refrigerat-
    ing machinery**
Ice skating 796.91
    x Figure skating; Skating
    xx **Winter sports**
Ice sports. *See* **Winter sports**
Icebergs 551.3
    xx **Ice; Ocean; Physical geography**
Iceboats 623.8
    x Ice boats
    xx **Boats and boating**
Icelandic language 439
    xx **Scandinavian languages**
Icelandic language—0-1500. *See* **Old Norse lan-
    guage**
Icelandic literature 839
    See also **Old Norse literature**
    xx **Scandinavian literature**
Ices. *See* **Ice cream, ices, etc.**
Ichthyology. *See* **Fishes**
Iconography. *See* **Art; Christian art and symbolism;
    Portraits; Religious art and symbolism**
Ideal states. *See* **Utopias**
Idealism 141
    See also **Materialism; Realism; Transcendental-
    ism**
    xx **Materialism; Philosophy; Positivism; Realism;
    Transcendentalism**
Identification
    See also **Fingerprints**; also subjects with the sub-
    division *Identification,* e.g.
        **Airplanes—Identification; Criminals—
        Identification;** etc.
Identity. *See* **Individuality; Personality**
Idioms. *See* names of languages with the subdivi-
    sion *Idioms,* e.g. **English language—Idioms;**
    etc.
Illegal aliens. *See* **Aliens, Illegal**
Illegitimacy 346.01; 362.7
    x Bastardy; Children, Illegitimate
    xx **Social problems**
Illiteracy. *See* **Literacy**
Illiterate societies. *See* **Society, Nonliterate folk**
Illness. *See* **Diseases**
Illuminated manuscripts. *See* **Illumination of books
    and manuscripts**
Illuminating gas. *See* **Gas**

Illumination. *See* **Lighting**
Illumination of books and manuscripts 096; 745.6
> *See also* **Initials**
>> *x* Illuminated manuscripts; Manuscripts, Illumi-
>> nated; Miniatures (Illumination of books
>> and manuscripts); Ornamental alphabets
>> *xx* **Alphabets; Art; Art, Medieval; Books; Chris-
>> tian art and symbolism; Decoration and or-
>> nament; Illustration of books; Initials;
>> Manuscripts**

Illusions. *See* **Hallucinations and illusions; Optical
illusions**
Illustration of books 741.64
> *See also* **Caldecott Medal books; Drawing; En-
> graving; Illumination of books and manu-
> scripts; Photomechanical processes**
>> *x* Book illustration
>> *xx* **Art; Books; Color printing; Decoration and or-
>> nament; Drawing**

Illustrations. *See* subjects with the subdivision
Pictorial works, e.g. **Animals—Pictorial
works; United States—History—1861-1865,
Civil War—Pictorial works;** etc.
Illustrations, Humorous. *See* **Cartoons and carica-
tures**
Illustrators (May subdiv. geog. adjective form, e.g.
Illustrators, French; etc.) **741.6092; 920**
> *xx* **Artists**
Illustrators, American 741.6092; 920
>> *x* American illustrators; United States—
>> Illustrators

Images, National. *See* **National characteristics**
Imaginary animals. *See* **Animals, Mythical**
Imaginary friends. *See* **Imaginary playmates**
Imaginary places. *See* **Geographical myths**
Imaginary playmates 155.4; E
>> *x* Friends, Imaginary; Imaginary friends; Invisi-
>> ble playmates; Make-believe playmates;
>> Playmates, Imaginary
> *xx* **Friendship; Imagination; Play**
Imagination 153.3
> *See also* **Creation (Literary, artistic, etc.); Fan-
> tasy; Imaginary playmates**
> *xx* **Educational psychology; Intellect; Psychology**
Immersion, Baptismal. *See* **Baptism**
Immigrants. *See* **Immigration and emigration**
Immigration and emigration 325
> Use for materials on migration from one country
> to another. Materials on the movement of
> population within a country for permanent
> settlement are entered under **Migration, In-
> ternal.**
> *See also* **Aliens; Aliens, Illegal; Anthropogeogra-
> phy; Children of immigrants; Colonization;
> Naturalization; Refugees;** also names of
> countries with the subdivision *Immigration
> and emigration,* e.g. **United States—
> Immigration and emigration;** etc.; names of
> countries, cities, etc. with the subdivision
> *Foreign population,* e.g. **United States—**

Immigration and emigration—*Continued*
> **Foreign population;** etc.; and names of nationality groups, e.g. **Mexican Americans; Mexicans—United States;** etc.
> *x* Emigration; Foreign population; Immigrants; Migration; Population, Foreign
> *xx* **Colonies; Colonization; Race relations; Social problems; Sociology**

Immoral art. *See* **Erotic art**
Immoral literature. *See* **Erotic literature**
Immortality 129
> Use for materials dealing with the question of the endless existence of the soul. Materials dealing with the character and form of a future existence are entered under **Future life.**
> *See also* **Future life**
> *x* Life after death
> *xx* **Eschatology; Future life; Soul; Theology**

Immunity 574.2; 612
> *See also* **Allergy; Communicable diseases; Vaccination**
> *xx* **Bacteriology; Communicable diseases; Medicine, Preventive; Pathology; Vaccination**

Immunization. *See* **Vaccination**
Impeachments 351.9
> *See also* **Recall (Political science)**
> *xx* **Justice, Administration of**

Imperialism 325
> *See also* **Colonies; Colonization;** also names of countries with the subdivision *Foreign relations,* e.g. **United States—Foreign relations;** etc.
> *x* Colonialism
> *xx* **Political science**

Implements, utensils, etc. *See* **Agricultural machinery; Household equipment and supplies; Stone implements; Tools**
Imports. *See* **Commerce; Tariff**
Impostors and imposture 364.1
> *See also* **Counterfeits and counterfeiting; Forgery; Fraud; Quacks and quackery; Swindlers and swindling**
> *x* Charlatans; Hoaxes; Pretenders
> *xx* **Fraud; Swindlers and swindling**

Impregnation, Artificial. *See* **Artificial insemination**
Impressionism (Art) 759.05
> *See also* **Postimpressionism (Art)**
> *x* Neo-impressionism (Art)
> *xx* **Painting; Postimpressionism (Art)**

Imprisonment. *See* **Prisons**
In-service training. *See* **Employees—Training; Librarians—In-service training**
In vitro fertilization. *See* **Fertilization in vitro**
Inaudible sound. *See* **Ultrasonics**
Incandescent lamps. *See* **Electric lamps**
Incas 980.004
> *xx* **Indians of South America**
Incendiary bombs 623.4
> *x* Bombs, Incendiary; Fire bombs

Incendiary bombs—*Continued*

    xx **Bombs; Incendiary weapons**

Incendiary weapons 623.4

    See also **Incendiary bombs**

    xx **Chemical warfare**

Incest 157; 306.7

    See also **Child molesting**

    xx **Sex crimes**

Incineration. *See* **Cremation; Refuse and refuse disposal**

Income 339.2-339.4

    See also **Capital; Profit; Retirement income; Wages—Annual wage**

    x Fortunes

    xx **Economics; Finance; Profit; Property; Wealth**

Income tax 336.24

    See also **Tax credits**

    x Direct taxation; Payroll taxes; Taxation of income

    xx **Finance; Internal revenue; Taxation; Wealth**

Income, Untaxed. *See* **Underground economy**

Indentured servants. *See* **Contract labor**

Independence Day (United States). *See* **Fourth of July**

Independent schools. *See* **Private schools**

Independent study 371.3

    Use for materials on individual study that may be directed or assisted by instructional staff through periodic consultations.

    xx **Study, Method of; Tutors and tutoring**

Indeterminism. *See* **Free will and determinism**

Index librorum prohibitorum. *See* **Books—Censorship; Catholic literature**

Indexes

    See also **Subject headings;** also subjects with the subdivision *Indexes,* e.g. **Newspapers—Indexes; Periodicals—Indexes; Short stories—Indexes;** etc.

    xx **Bibliography**

Indexing 025.3

    See also **Cataloging; Files and filing**

    xx **Bibliographic control; Bibliography; Cataloging; Files and filing**

India rubber. *See* **Rubber**

Indian languages (North American). *See* **Indians of North America—Languages**

Indian literature (American). *See* **American literature—American Indian authors**

Indian literature (East Indian). *See* **Indic literature**

Indian literature (North American Indian). *See* **Indians of North America—Literature**

Indian reservations. *See* **Indians of North America—Reservations**

Indians 970.004

    Use for general materials on the Indians of the Western Hemisphere. Names of all peoples and linguistic families are not included in this list but are to be added as needed.

    May be subdivided topically like **Indians of North America.**

Indians—*Continued*

    See also **Indians of Central America; Indians of Mexico; Indians of North America; Indians of South America; Indians of the West Indies**

    x American Indians; Amerindians

Indians of Canada. *See* **Indians of North America—Canada**

Indians of Central America (May subdiv. geog. by countries or regions of Central America, e.g. **Indians of Central America—Guatemala;** etc.) **972.8004**

    May be subdivided topically like **Indians of North America.**

    See also **Mayas**

    x American Indians; Amerindians

    xx **Indians**

Indians (of India). *See* **East Indians**

Indians of Mexico (May subdiv. geog. by states of Mexico, e.g. **Indians of Mexico—Yucatan;** etc.) **972.004**

    May be subdivided topically like **Indians of North America.**

    See also **Aztecs; Mayas**

    x American Indians; Amerindians

    xx **Indians**

Indians of North America (May subdiv. geog. by Canada, its provinces or regions or by the United States, its states or regions, e.g. **Indians of North America—British Columbia; Indians of North America—Massachusetts;** etc.) **970.004**

    Names of all peoples and linguistic families are not included in this list but are to be added as needed, e.g. **Navajo Indians;** etc.

    Topical subdivisions used under this heading may also be used under names of peoples and linguistic families.

    See also **Cliff dwellers and cliff dwellings; Mounds and mound builders;** also names of peoples and linguistic families, e.g. **Navajo Indians;** etc.

    x American Indians; Amerindians; Native Americans; Native peoples; North American Indians; Pre-Columbian Americans; Precolumbian Americans

    xx **Ethnology—United States; Indians**

Indians of North America—Amusements. *See* **Indians of North America—Games; Indians of North America—Social life and customs**

Indians of North America—Antiquities 970.004

    See also **Mounds and mound builders**

    xx **Antiquities; United States—Antiquities**

Indians of North America—Art 709.01

    x Art, Indian

Indians of North America—Canada 971.004

    x Canadian Indians; Indians of Canada

Indians of North America—Captivities 970.004

    xx **Frontier and pioneer life**

315

Indians of North America—Children 305.2; 970.004
   xx **Children**
Indians of North America—Chronology 529;
      970.004
   xx **Chronology**
Indians of North America—Civilization and culture
      970.004
Indians of North America—Claims 970.004
   x Indians of North America—Land claims; In-
      dians of North America—Legal status,
      laws, etc.
Indians of North America—Costume and adornment
      970.004
Indians of North America—Customs. *See* **Indians**
      of North America—Social life and customs
Indians of North America—Dances 793.3; 970.004
   xx **Folk dancing; Indians of North America—**
      Religion; Indians of North America—Social
      life and customs
Indians of North America—Drama 812; 822; etc.
   xx **Drama**
Indians of North America—Economic conditions
      970.004
Indians of North America—Education 371.9;
      970.004
   x Indians of North America—Schools
Indians of North America—Ethnology 572.97
Indians of North America—Fiction Fic
Indians of North America—Folklore 398
      Use for materials about the folklore of North
      American Indians. Collections of North
      American Indian legends, myths, tales, etc.
      are entered under **Indians of North Ameri-**
      ca—Legends.
   See also **Indians of North America—Legends**
   x Indians of North America—Mythology
   xx **Folklore; Indians of North America—Legends**
Indians of North America—Games 790.1; 970.004
   x Indians of North America—Amusements; In-
      dians of North America—Recreations; In-
      dians of North America—Sports
   xx **Games; Indians of North America—Social life**
      and customs
Indians of North America—Government policy
      323.1; 970.004
   x Federal-Indian relations; Indians of North
      America—Legal status, laws, etc.
Indians of North America—History 970.004
   See also **Indians of North America—Wars**
Indians of North America—Industries 338.4; 680;
      970.004
Indians of North America—Land claims. *See* **Indi-**
      ans of North America—Claims
Indians of North America—Languages 497
   See also **Indians of North America—Sign lan-**
      guage; also names of individual languages,
      e.g. **Navajo language;** etc.
   x Indian languages (North American)

Indians of North America—Legal status, laws,
etc. *See* **Indians of North America—
Claims; Indians of North America—
Government policy**
Indians of North America—Legends 398.2
Use for collections of North American Indian
legends, myths, tales, etc. Materials about
the folklore of North American Indians are
entered under **Indians of North America—
Folklore.**
See also **Indians of North America—Folklore**
x Indians of North America—Mythology; Leg-
ends, Indian
xx **Indians of North America—Folklore**
Indians of North America—Literature 897
Use for literature written in the Indian lan-
guages. For literature written in the English
language use **American literature—American
Indian authors.**
x Indian literature (North American Indian)
xx **Literature**
Indians of North America—Missions, Christian 266
x Missions, Indian
Indians of North America—Music. *See* **Indians of
North America—Songs and music**
Indians of North America—Mythology. *See* **Indi-
ans of North America—Folklore; Indians of
North America—Legends; Indians of North
America—Religion**
Indians of North America—Names 929.4
Indians of North America—Origin 970.004
Indians of North America—Poetry 811; 821; etc.
xx **Poetry**
Indians of North America—Psychology 155.8
xx **Ethnopsychology**
Indians of North America—Recreations. *See* **Indi-
ans of North America—Games**
Indians of North America—Religion 299
See also **Indians of North America—Dances; To-
tems and totemism**
x Indians of North America—Mythology; My-
thology, Indian
xx **Mythology; Religion**
Indians of North America—Reservations 333.1
x Indian reservations; Reservations, Indian
Indians of North America—Rites and ceremonies 299
xx **Rites and ceremonies**
Indians of North America—Schools. *See* **Indians
of North America—Education**
**Indians of North America—Sign language 001.56;
419**
x Sign language
xx **Indians of North America—Languages**
Indians of North America—Silverwork 739.2
**Indians of North America—Social conditions
970.004**
xx **Social conditions**
**Indians of North America—Social life and customs
970.004**
See also **Indians of North America—Dances;**

Indians of North America—Social life and customs —*Continued*
    Indians of North America—Games
    x Customs, Social; Indians of North America—Amusements; Indians of North America—Customs; Social customs; Social life and customs
  xx **Manners and customs**
Indians of North America—Songs and music 784.7
    x Indians of North America—Music; Music, Indian
Indians of North America—Sports. *See* **Indians of North America—Games**
Indians of North America—Wars 970.004
    See also **Black Hawk War, 1832; King Philip's War, 1675-1676; Pontiac's Conspiracy, 1763-1765; United States—History—1689-1697, King William's War; United States—History—1755-1763, French and Indian War**
  xx **Indians of North America—History**
Indians of South America (May subdiv. by country, e.g. **Indians of South America—Peru;** etc.) **980.004**
    May be subdivided topically like **Indians of North America.**
    See also **Incas**
    x American Indians; Amerindians
  xx **Indians**
Indians of the West Indies 972.9004
    May be subdivided topically like **Indians of North America.**
    x American Indians; Amerindians
  xx **Indians**
Indic literature 891
    x Indian literature (East Indian)
Indigestion 616.3
    x Dyspepsia
  xx **Digestion**
Individual retirement accounts 332.024
    x I.R.A.'s (Pensions); IRAs (Pensions)
  xx **Pensions; Retirement income**
Individualism 141; 302.5; 330.1
    See also **Communism; Socialism**
  xx **Equality; Socialism; Sociology**
Individuality 155.2
    See also **Conformity; Personality; Self**
    x Identity
  xx **Conformity; Consciousness; Personality; Psychology**
Individualized instruction 371.3
    Use for materials on the adaptation of instruction to meet individual needs within the group.
  xx **Open plan schools; Slow learning children; Tutors and tutoring**
Indochina 959
    Use for area comprising Laos, Cambodia, and Vietnam.
Indoctrination, Forced. *See* **Brainwashing**

Indoor games 793
>*See also* **Amusements**
>*xx* **Amusements; Games**

Indoor gardening 635.9
>*See also* **Aquariums; Gardens, Miniature; House plants; Terrariums; Window gardening**
>*xx* **Gardening; House plants**

Induction coils 537.6; 621.319
>*See also* **Condensers (Electricity)**

Induction (Logic). *See* **Logic**

Induction motors. *See* **Electric motors**

Industrial alcohol. *See* **Alcohol, Denatured**

Industrial arbitration. *See* **Arbitration, Industrial**

Industrial arts 600
>*See also* **Engineering; Technology;** also names of specific industries, arts, trades, e.g. **Bookbinding; Printing; Shipbuilding;** etc.; and names of countries, cities, etc. with the subdivision *Industries,* e.g. **United States—Industries;** etc.
>*x* Arts, Useful; Mechanic arts; Trades; Useful arts
>*xx* **Handicraft; Technology**

Industrial arts education 607
>*See also* **Technical education**
>*x* Education, Industrial; Industrial education; Industrial schools; Manual training
>*xx* **Handicraft; Technical education; Vocational education**

Industrial arts shops. *See* **School shops**

Industrial buildings 725
>*See also* **Factories; Office buildings; Skyscrapers**
>*x* Buildings, Industrial
>*xx* **Architecture; Buildings**

Industrial chemistry. *See* **Chemical engineering; Chemical industries; Chemistry, Technical**

Industrial combinations. *See* **Trusts, Industrial**

Industrial conciliation. *See* **Arbitration, Industrial**

Industrial councils. *See* **Management—Employee participation**

Industrial design. *See* **Design, Industrial**

Industrial diseases. *See* **Occupational diseases**

Industrial disputes. *See* **Labor disputes**

Industrial drawing. *See* **Mechanical drawing**

Industrial education. *See* **Industrial arts education; Technical education**

Industrial efficiency. *See* **Efficiency, Industrial**

Industrial engineering. *See* **Industrial management**

Industrial exhibitions. *See* **Exhibitions**

Industrial health. *See* **Occupational health and safety**

Industrial insurance. *See* **Insurance, Industrial**

Industrial libraries. *See* **Corporate libraries**

Industrial management 658
>Use for general materials on the application of the principles of management to industries, including problems of production, marketing, financial control, office management, etc. Materials limited to the technical aspects of manufacturing processes are entered under **Factory management.**

Industrial management—*Continued*

　See also

Business	**Materials handling**
Buying	**Occupational health and**
Efficiency, Industrial	**safety**
Factory management	**Office management**
Human engineering	**Personnel management**
Industrial relations	**Production standards**
Job analysis	**Sales management**
Machinery	**Welfare work in industry**
Marketing	

　　x Business administration; Business enter-
　　　prises—Management; Corporations—
　　　Management; Industrial engineering; Indus-
　　　trial organization; Industry—Organization,
　　　control, etc.; Management, Industrial

　xx **Business; Industry; Management**

Industrial materials.　*See* **Materials**

Industrial mergers.　*See* **Conglomerate corporations;**
　　　Railroads—Consolidation; Trusts, Industrial

Industrial mobilization　355.2

　　Use for materials dealing with industrial and la-
　　　bor policies and programs for defense mobi-
　　　lization.

　See also **Munitions**

　　x Defenses, National; Economic mobilization;
　　　Industry and war; Mobilization, Industrial;
　　　National defenses

　xx **Armaments; Economic policy; Military art and**
　　　science; War—Economic aspects

Industrial organization.　*See* **Industrial management**

Industrial painting.　*See* **Painting, Industrial**

Industrial plants.　*See* **Factories**

Industrial psychology.　*See* **Psychology, Applied**

Industrial relations　331

　　Use for general materials on employer-employee
　　　relations. Materials on problems of person-
　　　nel and relations from the employer's point
　　　of view are entered under **Personnel man-**
　　　agement.

　See also

Arbitration, Industrial	**Management—Employee**
Collective bargaining	**participation**
Labor contract	**Personnel management**
Labor disputes	**Strikes and lockouts**
Labor unions	

　　x Capital and labor; Employer-employee rela-
　　　tions; Labor and capital; Labor-
　　　management relations; Labor relations

　xx **Industrial management; Labor**

Industrial revolution.　*See* **Great Britain—**
　　　History—1800-1899 (19th century); Indus-
　　　try—History

Industrial robots.　*See* **Robots, Industrial**

Industrial safety.　*See* **Occupational health and**
　　　safety

Industrial schools.　*See* **Industrial arts education;**
　　　Technical education

Industrial trusts.　*See* **Trusts, Industrial**

Industrial uses of space.　*See* **Space industrialization**

Industrial wastes 658.5

    See also **Hazardous wastes; Pollution; Refuse and refuse disposal; Waste products; Water—Pollution**

    x Factory and trade waste; Factory waste; Trade waste; Waste disposal

    xx **Refuse and refuse disposal; Waste products; Water—Pollution**

Industrial workers. *See* **Labor**

Industrialization 338

    Use for general materials only. Materials on the industrialization of individual countries, regions, etc. are entered under the name of country, city, etc. with the subdivision *Industries.*

    See also **Developing countries; Modernization; Space industrialization; Technical assistance**

    xx **Economic policy; Industry; Modernization; Technical assistance**

Industries. *See* **Industry;** and names of industries, e.g. **Steel industry and trade;** etc.; and names of countries, cities, etc. with the subdivision *Industries,* e.g. **United States—Industries;** etc.

Industries, Chemical. *See* **Chemical industries**

Industries, Electric. *See* **Electric industries**

Industry 338; 600

    Use for general materials on manufacturing and mechanical activities. Names of all individual industries are not included in this list but are to be added as needed, e.g. **Steel industry and trade;** etc.

    See also

Business failures	**Industrialization**
Business people	**Machinery in industry**
Efficiency, Industrial	**Manufactures**
Industrial management	**Steel industry and trade**

    x Industries; Production

    xx **Civilization; Economics**

Industry and state. *See* **Industry—Government policy**

Industry and war. *See* **Industrial mobilization; War—Economic aspects**

Industry—Government policy (May subdiv. geog.) **338; 351.82; 650**

    See also

Agriculture—Government policy	**Public interest**
Economic policy	**Public service commissions**
Government lending	**Railroads—Government policy**
Government ownership	**Subsidies**

    x Business and government; Government and business; Government policy; Government regulation of industry; Industry and state; Industry—Organization, control, etc.; Laissez faire; Socialization of industry; State and industry; State regulation of industry

    xx **Economic policy; Socialism**

**Industry—Government policy—United States 338;
  353.0082; 650**
  x United States—Industry—Government policy
Industry—History 609
  x Industrial revolution
Industry—Organization, control, etc. *See* **Indus-
  trial management; Industry—Government
  policy**
Inebriates. *See* **Alcoholics**
Inequality. *See* **Equality**
Infallibility of the Pope. *See* **Popes—Infallibility**
Infantile paralysis. *See* **Poliomyelitis**
Infants 155.4
  Use for materials about children in the earliest
    period of life, usually the first two years
    only.
  See also **Children**
  x Babies
  xx **Children**
Infants and strangers. *See* **Children and strangers**
Infants—Care and hygiene 649
  See also **Baby sitters**
  x Health of infants
  xx **Children—Care and hygiene; Hygiene; Nurs-
    ing**
Infants—Clothing 646; 649
Infants—Diseases 618.92
Infants—Education. *See* **Education, Preschool**
Infants—Nutrition 641.1; 649
  See also **Breast feeding**
Infants, Sale of. *See* **Adoption—Corrupt practices**
Infants, Test tube. *See* **Fertilization in vitro, Hu-
  man**
Infection and infectious diseases. *See* **Communica-
  ble diseases**
Infertility 616.6
  Use for materials on infertility in humans and in
    animals.
  See also **Fertility; Sterilization (Birth control)**
  x Sterility in animals; Sterility in humans
  xx **Childlessness; Fertility; Fertility, Human;
    Sterilization (Birth control)**
Infidelity, Marital. *See* **Adultery**
Infirmaries. *See* **Hospitals**
Inflammable substances. *See* **Hazardous substances**
Inflation (Finance) 332.4
  See also **Monetary policy; Paper money; Wage-
    price policy**
  xx **Finance; Monetary policy**
Influenza 616.2
  x Flu; Grippe
  xx **Cold (Disease)**
Information centers. *See* **Information services**
Information, Freedom of. *See* **Freedom of informa-
  tion**
Information networks 001.5; 001.53; *004.6
  See also **Computer networks;** also types of infor-
    mation networks, e.g. **Library information
    networks;** etc.
  x Automated information networks; Networks,

Information networks—*Continued*
　　　Information
　　xx　Data transmission systems; Information services; Information storage and retrieval systems

Information science　020
　　See also Documentation; Electronic data processing; Information services; Information storage and retrieval systems; Library science
　　xx　Communication

Information services　020
　　See also

Archives	retrieval systems
Business—Information	Libraries
services	Machine readable biblio-
Documentation	graphic data
Electronic publishing	Reference services (Li-
Hotlines (Telephone coun-	braries)
seling)	Research
Information networks	United Nations—
Information storage and	Information services

　　x　Information centers
　　xx　Documentation; Information science; Libraries; Research

Information storage and retrieval systems　025
　　See also Electronic data processing; Information networks; Libraries—Automation; Machine readable bibliographic data; Teletext systems
　　x　Automatic information retrieval; Computer-based information systems; Data processing; Data storage and retrieval systems; Punched card systems
　　xx　Bibliographic control; Bibliography; Computers; Documentation; Information science; Information services; Libraries—Automation

Infrared radiation　535
　　xx　Electromagnetic waves; Radiation

Ingestion disorders.　*See* **Eating disorders**

Inheritance and succession　346.05
　　See also Executors and administrators; Inheritance and transfer tax; Land tenure; Wills
　　x　Bequests; Heirs; Hereditary succession; Intestacy; Legacies; Succession, Intestate
　　xx　Parent and child; Wealth; Wills

Inheritance and transfer tax　343.05
　　x　Estate tax; Taxation of legacies; Transfer tax
　　xx　Estate planning; Inheritance and succession; Internal revenue; Taxation

Inheritance (Biology).　*See* **Heredity**

Initialisms.　*See* **Acronyms**

Initials　745.6
　　See also Alphabets; Illumination of books and manuscripts; Lettering; Monograms; Printing—Specimens; Type and type founding
　　xx　Alphabets; Illumination of books and manuscripts; Lettering; Monograms; Type and type founding

Initiative and referendum.　*See* **Referendum**

Injunctions 331.89
>*See also* Strikes and lockouts
>*xx* Constitutional law; Labor unions; Strikes and
>>lockouts

Injuries. *See* Accidents; First aid; Wounds and inju-
>ries

Injurious insects. *See* Insects, Injurious and benefi-
>cial

Injurious occupations. *See* Occupations, Dangerous

Ink drawing. *See* Pen drawing

Inland navigation 386
>*See also* Canals; Lakes; Rivers
>*x* Navigation, Inland
>*xx* Canals; Navigation; Rivers; Shipping; Trans-
>>portation; Water resources development;
>>Waterways

Inns. *See* Hotels, motels, etc.

Innuit. *See* Inuit

Inoculation. *See* Vaccination

Inorganic chemistry. *See* Chemistry, Inorganic

Input equipment (Computers). *See* Computer pe-
>ripherals

Inquisition (May subdiv. geog.) **272**
>*x* Holy Office
>*xx* Catholic Church; Church history—600-1500,
>>Middle Ages

Insane. *See* Mentally ill

Insane—Hospitals. *See* Mentally ill—Institutional
>care; Psychiatric hospitals

Insanity. *See* Mental illness—Jurisprudence

Inscriptions 417
>*See also* Brasses; Epitaphs; Graffiti; Hieroglyph-
>>ics; Seals (Numismatics)
>*x* Epigraphy
>*xx* Archeology; History, Ancient

Insecticides 668
>*See also* Fumigation; Insects, Injurious and bene-
>>ficial; Spraying and dusting; also names of
>>insecticides, e.g. D.D.T. (Insecticide); etc.
>*xx* Agricultural chemicals; Insects, Injurious and
>>beneficial; Pesticides; Spraying and dusting

Insecticides—Toxicology 668
>*xx* Poisons and poisoning

Insects 595.7
>*See also* Fertilization of plants; also names of in-
>>sects, e.g. Ants; Bees; Butterflies; Moths;
>>Wasps; etc.
>*x* Entomology
>*xx* Invertebrates

Insects as carriers of disease 614.4
>*See also* Flies; Mosquitoes
>*x* Entomology, Medical; Medical entomology
>*xx* Communicable diseases; Insects, Injurious and
>>beneficial

Insects, Destructive and useful. *See* Insects, Injuri-
>ous and beneficial

Insects, Injurious and beneficial 632
>*See also* Aeronautics in agriculture; Agricultural
>>pests; Household pests; Insecticides; Insects
>>as carriers of disease; also names of injuri-

Insects, Injurious and beneficial—*Continued*
ous and beneficial insects, e.g. **Locusts; Silkworms;** etc.; and names of crops, trees, etc. with the subdivision *Diseases and pests,* e.g. **Fruit—Diseases and pests;** etc.

 x Diseases and pests; Economic entomology; Entomology, Economic; Garden pests; Injurious insects; Insects, Destructive and useful

 xx **Agricultural pests; Gardening; Insecticides; Parasites; Pests; Zoology, Economic**

Insemination, Artificial. *See* **Artificial insemination**

Inservice training. *See* **Employees—Training; Librarians—In-service training**

Insignia 929

 See also **Decorations of honor; Medals;** also armies and navies and other appropriate subjects with the subdivision *Insignia* or *Medals, badges, decorations, etc.,* e.g. **Colleges and universities—Insignia; United States. Army—Insignia; United States. Army—Medals, badges, decorations, etc.; United States. Navy—Insignia; United States. Navy—Medals, badges, decorations, etc.;** etc.

 x Badges of honor; Devices (Heraldry); Emblems

 xx **Decorations of honor; Heraldry; Medals**

Insolvency. *See* **Bankruptcy**

Insomnia 616.8

 See also **Sleep**

 x Sleeplessness; Wakefulness

 xx **Sleep**

Inspection of food. *See* **Food adulteration and inspection**

Inspection of meat. *See* **Meat inspection**

Inspection of schools. *See* **School supervision; Schools—Administration**

Inspiration. *See* **Creation (Literary, artistic, etc.)**

Inspiration, Biblical. *See* **Bible—Inspiration**

Instalment plan 658.8

 x Hire-purchase plan

 xx **Business; Buying; Consumer credit; Credit**

Instinct 152.3; 156

 See also **Animal intelligence; Habit; Psychology, Comparative**

 x Animal instinct

 xx **Animal intelligence; Animals—Habits and behavior; Habit; Psychology; Psychology, Comparative**

Institutional care 361

 See also **Group homes; Hospitals; Nursing homes; Orphanages;** also classes of people with the subdivision *Institutional care,* e.g. **Blind—Institutional care; Children—Institutional care; Mentally ill—Institutional care;** etc.

 x Asylums; Benevolent institutions; Charitable institutions; Homes (Institutions)

 xx **Charities; Charities, Medical; Public welfare**

Institutions, Charitable and philanthropic. *See* **Charities; Hospitals**

Instruction. *See* **Education; Teaching**

Instruction, Home. *See* **Home instruction**

Instructional materials centers   021; 027.7-027.8

    See also **School libraries**

    x Audiovisual materials centers; Curriculum materials centers; Learning resource centers; Media centers (Education); Multimedia centers; School media centers

  xx **Libraries**

Instructional supervision. *See* **School supervision**

Instrument flying   629.132

  xx **Aeronautical instruments; Airplanes—Piloting**

Instrumental music   785

    See also **Musical instruments**; also types of instrumental music, e.g. **Band music; Chamber music; Dance music; Guitar music; Orchestral music; Piano music;** etc.

    x Music, Instrumental

  xx **Music; Musical instruments**

Instrumentation and orchestration   785

    See also **Musical instruments**

    x Orchestration

  xx **Bands (Music); Composition (Music); Music; Musical instruments; Orchestra**

Instruments, Aeronautical. *See* **Aeronautical instruments**

Instruments, Astronautical. *See* **Astronautical instruments**

Instruments, Astronomical. *See* **Astronomical instruments**

Instruments, Engineering. *See* **Engineering instruments**

Instruments, Measuring. *See* **Measuring instruments**

Instruments, Meteorological. *See* **Meteorological instruments**

Instruments, Musical. *See* **Musical instruments**

Instruments, Negotiable. *See* **Negotiable instruments**

Instruments, Scientific. *See* **Scientific apparatus and instruments**

Insulation (Heat)   693.8; 697

    x Heat insulating materials; Thermal insulation

  xx **Heating**

Insulation (Sound). *See* **Soundproofing**

Insults. *See* **Invective**

Insurance   368

    All types of insurance are not included in this list but are to be added as needed in inverted form, e.g. **Insurance, Automobile;** etc.

    See also **Saving and thrift**

    x Underwriting

  xx **Estate planning; Finance; Finance, Personal**

Insurance, Accident   368.3

    See also **Workers' compensation**

    x Accident insurance; Disability insurance; Insurance, Disability

Insurance, Accident—*Continued*

   xx **Insurance, Casualty**

Insurance, Automobile 368.2

   x Automobile insurance; No fault automobile insurance

Insurance, Casualty 368.5

   See also **Insurance, Accident**

   x Casualty insurance

Insurance, Disability. *See* **Insurance, Accident; Insurance, Health**

Insurance, Fire 368.1

   See also **Fireproofing**

   x Fire insurance

   xx **Fires**

Insurance, Group 368.3

   Includes group life insurance. Materials on group insurance in other fields are entered under the specific heading, e.g. **Insurance, Health;** etc.

   x Group insurance

   xx **Insurance, Life**

Insurance, Health 368.3

   See also **Health maintenance organizations; Insurance, Hospitalization; Workers' compensation**

   x Disability insurance; Group health; Group medical service; Health insurance; Insurance, Disability; Insurance, Sickness; Medical care, Prepaid; Medical service, Prepaid; Prepaid medical care; Sickness insurance; Socialized medicine

   xx **Social security**

Insurance, Hospitalization 368.3

   x Group hospitalization; Hospitalization insurance; Socialized medicine

   xx **Insurance, Health**

Insurance, Industrial 368.7-368.8

   Use for materials on insurance as carried on by companies whose agents collect the premiums from policy holders in small weekly payments.

   x Industrial insurance

   xx **Insurance, Life; Labor; Saving and thrift**

Insurance, Life 368.3

   See also **Annuities; Insurance, Group; Insurance, Industrial; Probabilities**

   x Life insurance

   xx **Annuities**

Insurance, Malpractice 368

   x Malpractice insurance

Insurance, Marine 368.2

   x Marine insurance

   xx **Commerce; Maritime law; Merchant marine; Shipping**

Insurance, Old age. *See* **Old age pensions**

Insurance, Sickness. *See* **Insurance, Health**

Insurance, Social. *See* **Social security**

Insurance, State and compulsory. *See* **Social security**

Insurance, Unemployment 368.4

  x Labor—Insurance; Payroll taxes; Unemployment insurance

  xx **Social security; Unemployed; Unemployment**

Insurance, Workers'. *See* **Social security**

Insurance, Workers' compensation. *See* **Workers' compensation**

Insurgency (May subdiv. geog. except U.S.) **322.4; 355.02**

  See also **Government, Resistance to; Guerrilla warfare; Internal security; Subversive activities; Terrorism**

  x Rebellions

  xx **Government, Resistance to; Internal security; Revolutions**

Integrated churches. *See* **Church and race relations**

Integrated schools. *See* **School integration**

Integration in education. *See* **Articulation (Education); School integration; Segregation in education**

Integration, Racial. *See* **Blacks—Integration; Race relations**

Intellect 153.4

  See also

Creation (Literary, artistic, etc.)	**Mental tests**
	Perception
Imagination	**Reason**
Knowledge, Theory of	**Reasoning**
Logic	**Senses and sensation**
Memory	**Thought and thinking**

  x Intelligence; Mind; Understanding

  xx **Knowledge, Theory of; Psychology; Reasoning; Thought and thinking**

Intellectual cooperation 370.19

  See also **Congresses and conventions; Cultural relations; International education**

  x Cooperation, Intellectual

  xx **International cooperation; International education**

Intellectual freedom 323.4

  See also **Academic freedom; Censorship; Free speech; Freedom of information; Freedom of the press**

  xx **Freedom**

Intellectual life. *See* **Culture; Learning and scholarship;** and particular classes of people and names of countries, cities, etc. with the subdivision *Intellectual life,* e.g.
  Blacks—Intellectual life; United States—Intellectual life; etc.

Intellectual property. *See* **Copyright; Inventions; Patents**

Intellectuals (May subdiv. geog.) **305.5**

  See also particular classes of people and names of countries, cities, etc. with the subdivision *Intellectual life,* e.g. **Blacks—Intellectual life; United States—Intellectual life;** etc.

  x Intelligentsia

  xx **Professions**

Intelligence. *See* **Intellect**

Intelligence agents. *See* **Spies**

Intelligence, Artificial. *See* **Artificial intelligence**

Intelligence of animals. *See* **Animal intelligence**

Intelligence service (May subdiv. geog.) **327; 355.3**

Use for materials on a government agency that is engaged in obtaining information, usually about an enemy, but sometimes about an ally or a neutral country, and also blocking the attempts by foreign agents to gain information about one's own national secrets. Some intelligence services are used for covert political action, such as aerial and space reconnaissance, electronic eavesdropping, and the employment of secret agents.

See also **Espionage; Secret service**

x Counterespionage; Counterintelligence

xx **Secret service**

Intelligence service—United States 355.3

x United States—Intelligence service

Intelligence tests. *See* **Mental tests**

Intelligentsia. *See* **Intellectuals**

Intemperance. *See* **Alcoholism; Temperance**

Inter-American relations. *See* **Pan-Americanism**

Interactive videotex systems. *See* **Teletext systems**

Interchange of teachers. *See* **Teachers, Interchange of**

Interchange of visitors. *See* **Exchange of persons programs**

Intercollegiate athletics. *See* **Athletics; College sports**

Intercommunication systems 621.38; 651.7

See also **Closed-circuit television; Microwave communication systems**

x Interoffice communication systems; Loud speakers

xx **Electronic apparatus and appliances; Sound—Recording and reproducing; Telecommunication**

Intercontinental ballistic missiles 623.4

See also names of specific ICBM missiles, e.g. **Atlas (Missile)**; etc.

x I.C.B.M.; ICBM

xx **Ballistic missiles**

Intercultural education 370.19

Use for materials dealing with the eradication of racial and religious prejudices by showing the nature and effects of race, creed and immigrant cultures.

See also **Education, Bilingual; International education**

x Education, Intercultural; Education, Multicultural; Multicultural education

xx **Acculturation; Ethnic relations; Human relations; International education; Race relations**

Intercultural relations. *See* **Cultural relations**

Intercultural studies. *See* **Cross cultural studies**

Interest centers approach to teaching. *See* **Open plan schools**

Interest (Economics) 332.8
   xx **Banks and banking; Business arithmetic; Capital; Finance; Loans**
Interest groups. *See* **Lobbying and lobbyists**
Interfaces, Computer. *See* **Computer interfaces**
Interfaith marriage. *See* **Intermarriage, Religious**
Interfaith relations 261; 262.2
   xx **Christian unity; Human relations**
Intergovernmental tax relations 336.1
   See also **Revenue sharing**
   x Federal-state tax relations; State-local tax relations; Tax relations, Intergovernmental; Tax sharing
   xx **Taxation**
Interior decoration. *See* **Interior design**
Interior design 747
   Use for materials on the art and techniques of planning and supervising the design and execution of architectural interiors and their furnishings.
   See also

Bedspreads	**Paper hanging**
Carpets	**Quilts**
Drapery	**Rugs**
Furniture	**Tapestry**
Mural painting and decoration	**Upholstery**
	Wallpaper

   x Arts, Decorative; Decoration, Interior; Design, Interior; Home decoration; House decoration; House furnishing; Interior decoration
   xx **Art; Decoration and ornament; Decorative arts; Design; Home economics**
Interlibrary loans. *See* **Library circulation**
Interlocking signals. *See* **Railroads—Signaling**
Intermarriage 306.8
   x Marriage, Mixed; Mixed marriage
   xx **Marriage**
Intermarriage, Religious 261.8; 306.8
   Use same form for other types of intermarriage.
   x Interfaith marriage
Intermediate state. *See* **Eschatology; Future life**
Internal-combustion engines. *See* **Gas and oil engines**
Internal revenue 336.1-336.2
   See also **Income tax; Inheritance and transfer tax**
   x Revenue, Internal
   xx **Finance; Taxation**
Internal revenue law 343.04-343.05
   x Law, Internal revenue
   xx **Law**
Internal security (May subdiv. geog.) **351.1**
   See also **Insurgency; Subversive activities**
   x Loyalty oaths; Security, Internal
   xx **Insurgency; Subversive activities**
Internal security—United States 363.2
   x United States—Internal security
International agencies 060
   See also names of individual agencies
   x Associations, International; International as-

International agencies—*Continued*
sociations; International organizations
xx **International cooperation**
International arbitration. *See* **Arbitration, International**
International associations. *See* **International agencies**
International business enterprises 382.1
See also **Investments, Foreign**
x Business enterprises, International; Business—International aspects; Corporations, International; Corporations, Multinational; Multinational corporations
xx **Commerce; Corporations; International economic relations**
International conferences. *See* **Congresses and conventions**
International cooperation 327
Use for general materials on international cooperative activities, with or without the participation of governments.
See also

Arbitration, International	**International education**
Congresses and conventions	**International organization**
Cultural relations	**International police**
Economic assistance	**League of Nations**
Exchange of persons programs	**Reconstruction (1939-1951)**
Intellectual cooperation	**Technical assistance**
International agencies	**United Nations**

also subjects with the subdivision *International cooperation,* e.g. **Astronautics—International cooperation;** etc.
x Cooperation, International
xx **Cooperation; International education; International law; International organization; International relations; Reconstruction (1939-1951)**
International copyright. *See* **Copyright**
International economic relations 382.1
See also **Balance of payments; Commercial policy; Economic assistance; International business enterprises; Sanctions (International law); Technical assistance**
x Economic relations, Foreign; Foreign economic relations
xx **Economic policy; International relations**
International education 370.19
Use for materials on education for international understanding, world citizenship, etc.
See also **Comparative librarianship; Intellectual cooperation; Intercultural education; International cooperation; Teachers, Interchange of**
x Education, International
xx **Education; Intellectual cooperation; Intercultural education; International cooperation**
International exchange. *See* **Foreign exchange**

International exhibitions. *See* **Exhibitions**

International federation. *See* **International organization**

International language. *See* **Language, Universal**

International law 341

> *See also*

Aliens	**Naturalization**
Arbitration, International	**Neutrality**
Asylum, Right of	**Pirates**
Boundaries	**Privateering**
International cooperation	**Refugees, Political**
International organization	**Salvage**
International relations	**Sanctions (International**
Intervention (International	**law)**
law)	**Slave trade**
Mandates	**Space law**
Maritime law	**Treaties**
Military law	**War**

> *x* Law, International; Law of nations; Nations, Law of; Natural law
>
> *xx* **International organization; International relations; Law; War**

International mediation. *See* **Arbitration, International**

International organization 341.2

> Use for materials on plans leading towards political organization of nations.
>
> *See also* **European federation; International cooperation; International law; International police; Mandates; World politics;** also names of specific organizations, e.g. **United Nations;** etc.
>
> *x* Federation, International; International federation; Organization, International; World government; World organization
>
> *xx* **Congresses and conventions; International cooperation; International law; International relations; Security, International; World politics**

International organizations. *See* **International agencies**

International police 341

> *x* Interpol; Police, International
>
> *xx* **International cooperation; International organization; International relations; Security, International**

International politics. *See* **World politics**

International relations 327

> Use for materials on the theory of international relations. Historical accounts are entered under **World politics; Europe—Politics and government;** etc. Materials limited to relations between two countries are entered under the name of one or both countries with the subdivision *Foreign relations.*
>
> *See also*

Arbitration, International	**Relations (Diplomatic)**
Arms control	**Cultural relations**
Boundaries	**Diplomacy**
Catholic Church—	**Diplomatic and consular**

International relations—*Continued*

service	**Monroe Doctrine**
Diplomats	**Munitions**
Geopolitics	**National security**
International cooperation	**Nationalism**
International economic re-	**Neutrality**
lations	**Peace**
International law	**Refugees, Political**
International organization	**Security, International**
International police	**Treaties**
Mandates	**World politics**

also names of countries with the subdivision
Foreign relations, e.g. **United States—**
Foreign relations; etc.

x Foreign relations

xx **International law; National security; World**
politics

International security. *See* **Security, International**

International space cooperation. *See* **Astronau-**
tics—International cooperation

International Standard Bibliographic Description
025.3

x I.S.B.D; ISBD

International Standard Book Numbers 070.5

x I.S.B.N.; ISBN

xx **Publishers' standard book numbers**

International Standard Serial Numbers 070.5

x I.S.S.N.; ISSN

International trade. *See* **Commerce**

Internationalism. *See* **Nationalism**

Internment camps. *See* **Concentration camps**

Interoffice communication systems *See* **Intercom-**
munication systems

Interpersonal relations. *See* **Human relations**

Interplanetary communication. *See* **Interstellar**
communication

Interplanetary visitors. *See* **Extraterrestrial beings**

Interplanetary voyages 629.45

See also **Outer space—Exploration; Rockets**
(Aeronautics); Space flight

x Interstellar travel; Outer space travel; People
in space; Space travel

xx **Astronautics; Space flight**

Interplanetary warfare. *See* **Space warfare**

Interpol. *See* **International police**

Interpreting and translating. *See* **Translating and**
interpreting

Interpretive dance. *See* **Modern dance**

Interracial adoption 362.7

x Adoption, Interracial

xx **Adoption; Race relations**

Interracial relations. *See* **Race relations**

Interscholastic sports. *See* **School sports**

Interstate commerce 381

See note under **Commerce.**

See also **Railroads—Government policy; Re-**
straint of trade

x Commerce, Interstate; Government regulation
of commerce; Government regulation of
railroads

Interstate commerce—*Continued*
   xx **Commerce; Railroads—Government policy;**
        Railroads—Rates; Restraint of trade;
        Trusts, Industrial
Interstate highways. *See* **Express highways**
Interstellar communication 621.38
   See also **Astronautics—Communication systems;**
        Radio astronomy
   x Extraterrestrial communication; Interplane-
        tary communication; Outer space—
        Communication; Space communication;
        Space telecommunication
   xx **Life on other planets; Telecommunication**
Interstellar travel. *See* **Interplanetary voyages**
Interstellar warfare. *See* **Space warfare**
Interurban railroads. *See* **Electric railroads; Street**
       railroads
Intervention (International law) 341.5
   See also **Monroe Doctrine; Neutrality**
   x Military intervention
   xx **International law; Neutrality; War**
Interviewing 158
   See also **Counseling; Psychology, Applied; Talk**
       shows
   xx **Applications for positions; Counseling; Psy-**
       chology, Applied; Social psychology
Interviewing (Journalism). *See* **Journalism; Report-**
       ers and reporting
Interviews, Parent-teacher. *See* **Parent-teacher con-**
       ferences
Intestacy. *See* **Inheritance and succession**
Intolerance. *See* **Fanaticism; Freedom of con-**
       science; Religious freedom; Toleration
Intoxicants. *See* **Alcohol; Alcoholic beverages; Li-**
       quors and liqueurs; Stimulants
Intoxication. *See* **Alcoholism; Narcotic habit; Tem-**
       perance
Intuition 153.4
   See also **Perception; Reality**
   xx **Knowledge, Theory of; Perception; Philoso-**
       phy; Psychology; Rationalism
Inuit 970.004
   x Eskimos; Esquimaux; Innuit
Inuit—Folklore 398.2
   x Folklore, Inuit
Invalid cookery. *See* **Cookery for the sick; Diet**
       therapy
Invalids. *See* **Physically handicapped; Sick**
Invasion of privacy. *See* **Privacy, Right of**
Invective 808.88
   x Abuse, Verbal; Insults; Verbal abuse
   xx **Satire**
Inventions 608
   See also **Creation (Literary, artistic, etc.); Inven-**
       tors; Patents
   x Discoveries (in science); Intellectual property
   xx **Civilization; Inventors; Machinery; Patents;**
       Technology
Inventors 608.092; 920
   See also **Inventions**

Inventors—*Continued*
 xx **Engineers; Inventions**
Inventory control 658.7
 x Stock control
 xx **Management; Retail trade**
Invertebrates 592
 See also **Corals; Crustacea; Insects; Mollusks;**
 Protozoa; Sponges; Worms
 xx **Zoology**
Investigations, Governmental. *See* **Governmental**
 investigations
Investment in real estate. *See* **Real estate invest-**
 ment
Investment trusts 332.63
 x Mutual funds
 xx **Banks and banking; Trust companies**
Investments 332.6
 See also

Annuities	**Savings and loan associations**
Bonds	**Securities**
Mortgages	**Speculation**
Real estate investment	**Stock exchange**
Saving and thrift	**Stocks**

 xx **Banks and banking; Capital; Estate planning;**
 Finance; Finance, Personal; Loans; Saving
 and thrift; Securities; Speculation; Stock ex-
 change; Stocks
Investments, Foreign 332.6
 x Foreign investments
 xx **International business enterprises**
Invisible playmates. *See* **Imaginary playmates**
IQ tests. *See* **Mental tests**
Iran 935; 955
 x Persia
Iran—Foreign relations—United States 327.55
 See also **Iran hostage crisis, 1979-1981**
Iran—History—1941-1979 955
Iran—History—1979- 955
Iran hostage crisis, 1979-1981 327.55; 327.73; 955
 x Iranian seizure of American embassy
 xx **Hostages, American—Iran; Iran—Foreign re-**
 lations—United States; United States—
 Foreign relations—Iran
Iranian seizure of American embassy. *See* **Iran**
 hostage crisis, 1979-1981
IRAs (Pensions). *See* **Individual retirement ac-**
 counts
Ireland—Unification. *See* **Irish unification question**
Irish unification question 941.5
 x Ireland—Unification; Reunification of Ireland
Iron 669; 672
 See also **Building, Iron and steel; Iron ores; Iron-**
 work
 xx **Steel**
Iron Age 930
 See also **Archeology; Bronze Age**
 x Prehistory
 xx **Archeology; Bronze Age**
Iron and steel building. *See* **Building, Iron and**

Iron and steel building—*Continued*
        steel
Iron curtain countries. *See* **Communist countries**
Iron founding. *See* **Founding**
Iron industry and trade 338.2
    See also **Steel industry and trade**
    xx **Ironwork; Steel industry and trade**
Iron ores 549
    xx **Iron; Ore deposits; Ores**
Ironing. *See* **Laundry**
Ironwork 669; 672
    See also **Blacksmithing; Forging; Iron industry**
        and trade; Metalwork; Steel industry and
        trade; Welding
    x Wrought iron work
    xx **Decoration and ornament; Forging; Iron; Met-**
        alwork
Irreversible coma. *See* **Brain death**
Irrigation (May subdiv. geog.) **333.91; 631.7**
    See also **Dams; Dry farming; Reclamation of**
        land; Water rights; Windmills
    xx **Agricultural engineering; Civil engineering;**
        Hydraulic engineering; Reclamation of land;
        Reservoirs; Soils; Water resources develop-
        ment; Water supply
Irrigation—United States 333.91; 631.7
    x United States—Irrigation
ISBD. *See* **International Standard Bibliographic**
    Description
ISBN. *See* **International Standard Book Numbers**
Islam 297
    Use for materials on the religion. Materials on
        the believers in this religion are entered un-
        der **Muslims.**
    See also **Bahaism; Koran; Mosques**
    x Islamism; Mohammedanism; Moslemism;
        Muhammedanism; Muslimism
    xx **Religions**
Islamic art. *See* **Art, Islamic**
Islamic countries 915.6; 956
    See also **Arab countries**
    x Muslim countries
Islamism. *See* **Islam**
Islands 551.4
    See also **Coral reefs and islands;** also names of
        islands and groups of islands, e.g. **Cuba; Is-**
        lands of the Pacific; etc.
Islands, Artificial. *See* **Drilling platforms**
Islands, Imaginary. *See* **Geographical myths**
Islands of the Pacific 993-996
    x Oceania; Pacific Islands; South Sea Islands
    xx **Islands**
Isotopes 539
    See also **Radioisotopes**
Israel 956.94
    xx **Middle East**
Israel-Arab relations. *See* **Jewish-Arab relations**
Israel-Arab War, 1948-1949 956
    x Arab-Israel War, 1948-1949
Israel-Arab War, 1956. *See* **Sinai Campaign, 1956**

Israel-Arab War, 1967 956

   x Arab-Israel War, 1967; Six Day War, 1967

Israel-Arab War, 1973 956

   x Arab-Israel War, 1973; Yom Kippur War,
      1973

Israel—Collective settlements. *See* **Collective set-
      tlements—Israel**

Israeli-Arab relations. *See* **Jewish-Arab relations**

Israeli intervention in Lebanon, 1982- . *See*
      **Lebanon—History—1982- , Israeli inter-
      vention**

Israelis 956.94

   xx **Jews**

Israelites. *See* **Jews**

ISSN. *See* **International Standard Serial Numbers**

Italo-Ethiopian War, 1935-1936 963

   x Ethiopian-Italian War, 1935-1936

Italy 945

   May be subdivided like U.S. except for *History.*

Italy—History 945

Italy—History—0-1559 945

Italy—History—1559-1789 945

Italy—History—1789-1815 945

Italy—History—1815-1914 945.09

Italy—History—1914-1945 945.091

Italy—History—1945-1976 945.092

Italy—History—1976- 945.092

Ivory 679

   x Animal products

Jacobins (Dominicans). *See* **Dominicans**

Jails. *See* **Prisons**

Japan 952

Japan—History 952

Japan—History—0-1868 952

Japan—History—1868-1945 952.03

**Japan—History—1945-1952, Allied occupation
      952.04**

   xx **Military occupation; World War, 1939-1945—
      Occupied territories**

Japan—History—1952- 952.04

Japanese color prints. *See* **Color prints, Japanese**

Japanese paper folding. *See* **Origami**

Japanese prints. *See* **Color prints, Japanese**

Jargon. *See* subjects with the subdivision *Jargon,*
      e.g. **English language—Jargon;** etc.

Jazz ensembles 785.06

Jazz music 781

   See also **Blues (Songs, etc.)**

   xx **Dance music; Music**

Jestbooks. *See* **Chapbooks**

Jesuits 271

   x Jesus, Society of; Society of Jesus

   xx **Religious orders for men, Catholic**

Jesus Christ 232

   See also **Atonement—Christianity; Christianity;
      Lord's Supper; Second Advent; Trinity**

   x Christ; Christology

   xx **Christianity; God—Christianity; Trinity**

Jesus Christ—Art 704.9

   See also **Bible—Pictorial works; Christian art**

Jesus Christ—Art—*Continued*
  and symbolism; Mary, Blessed Virgin,
  Saint—Art
 x Jesus Christ—Iconography; Jesus Christ in art
 xx **Christian art and symbolism; Mary, Blessed**
  Virgin, Saint—Art
Jesus Christ—Atonement. *See* **Atonement—**
  Christianity
Jesus Christ—Biography 232.9
 See also **Jesus Christ—Crucifixion; Jesus**
  Christ—Nativity
Jesus Christ—Birth. *See* **Jesus Christ—Nativity**
Jesus Christ—Crucifixion 232.9
 See also **Good Friday**
 x Crucifixion of Christ
 xx **Good Friday; Jesus Christ—Biography**
Jesus Christ—Divinity 232
 See also **Trinity; Unitarianism**
 x Divinity of Christ
 xx **Unitarianism**
Jesus Christ—Drama 808.82; 812; etc.
 See also **Passion plays**
Jesus Christ—Iconography. *See* **Jesus Christ—Art**
Jesus Christ in art. *See* **Jesus Christ—Art**
Jesus Christ—Last Supper. *See* **Lord's Supper**
Jesus Christ—Messiahship 232
Jesus Christ—Nativity 232.9
 See also **Christmas**
 x Jesus Christ—Birth; Nativity of Christ
 xx **Christmas; Jesus Christ—Biography**
Jesus Christ—Parables 232.9
 xx **Bible—Parables; Parables**
Jesus Christ—Prayers 232.9
 See also **Lord's prayer**
Jesus Christ—Prophecies 232
 xx **Bible—Prophecies**
Jesus Christ—Resurrection 232.9
 x Resurrection
Jesus Christ—Second Advent. *See* **Second Advent**
Jesus Christ—Sermon on the mount. *See* **Sermon**
  on the mount
Jesus Christ—Teachings 232.9
 x Teachings of Jesus
Jesus people 269
 xx **Youth—Religious life**
Jesus, Society of. *See* **Jesuits**
Jet lag 616.9
 xx **Aviation medicine; Biological rhythms; Fa-**
  tigue
Jet planes 629.133
 See also **Short take off and landing aircraft**
 x Airplanes, Jet propelled
Jet propulsion 621.43; 629.47
 See also **Rockets (Aeronautics)**
 xx **Airplanes—Engines; Rockets (Aeronautics)**
Jewelry 739.27
 See note under **Gems.**
 See also **Gems; Goldwork; Silverwork;** also
  names of specific jewelry
 x Costume jewelry; Jewels

Jewelry—*Continued*

    xx **Art metalwork; Decoration and ornament; Decorative arts; Gems; Goldwork; Metalwork; Silver; Silverwork**

Jewels. *See* **Gems; Jewelry; Precious stones**

Jewish-Arab relations 956

    See also **Lebanon—History—1982- , Israeli intervention**

    x Arab-Jewish relations; Israel-Arab relations; Israeli-Arab relations; Palestine problem, 1917-

    xx **Palestinian Arabs**

Jewish civilization. *See* **Jews—Civilization**

Jewish holidays. *See* **Fasts and feasts—Judaism**

Jewish holocaust (1933-1945). *See* **Holocaust, Jewish (1933-1945)**

Jewish language. *See* **Hebrew language; Yiddish language**

Jewish literature 839; 892.4

    See also **Bible; Cabala; Hebrew literature; Talmud; Yiddish literature**

    x Jews—Literature

    xx **Hebrew literature**

Jewish religion. *See* **Judaism**

Jews (May subdiv. geog.) **572.917; 909**

    See also **Israelis**

    x Hebrews; Israelites

    xx **Church history; Judaism**

Jews and Gentiles 305.6

    See also **Antisemitism**

    x Gentiles and Jews; Jews—Relations with Gentiles

    xx **Human relations**

Jews—Antiquities 933

Jews—Civilization 909

    x Civilization, Jewish; Jewish civilization

Jews—Colonization 325

    xx **Colonization**

Jews—Customs. *See* **Jews—Social life and customs**

Jews—Economic conditions 330.9

Jews—Festivals. *See* **Fasts and feasts—Judaism**

Jews—Folklore 398.2

    x Folklore, Jewish

Jews—Language. *See* **Hebrew language; Yiddish language**

Jews—Literature. *See* **Hebrew literature; Jewish literature**

Jews—Persecutions 909; 933

    See also **Holocaust, Jewish (1933-1945); World War, 1939-1945—Jews—Rescue**

    xx **Antisemitism; Persecution**

Jews—Political activity 909; 956.94

Jews—Relations with Gentiles. *See* **Jews and Gentiles**

Jews—Religion. *See* **Judaism**

Jews—Restoration 956.94

    Use for materials dealing with the belief that the Jews, in fulfillment of Biblical prophecy, would some day return to Palestine.

    See also **Zionism**

Jews—Restoration—*Continued*
   xx **Zionism**
Jews—Rites and ceremonies. *See* **Judaism—**
      Customs and practices
Jews—Ritual. *See* **Judaism—Liturgy**
Jews—Social conditions 305.8; 909
   Use for materials relating to social conditions of
      the Jews themselves. Materials on the rela-
      tion of the Jews to non-Jews are entered un-
      der **Jews and Gentiles.**
   xx **Social conditions**
Jews—Social life and customs 956.94
   x Customs, Social; Jews—Customs; Social cus-
      toms; Social life and customs
   xx **Manners and customs**
Job analysis 658.3
   See also **Motion study; Time study**
   x Personnel classification
   xx **Efficiency, Industrial; Factory management;**
      Industrial management; Occupations; Per-
      sonnel management; Wages
Job applications. *See* **Applications for positions**
Job discrimination. *See* **Discrimination in employ-**
      ment
Job hunting 331.1; 650.1
   See also **Applications for positions; Résumés**
      (Employment)
   x Hunting, Job; Job searching
   xx **Employment agencies; Vocational guidance**
Job performance standards. *See* **Performance stan-**
      dards
Job placement guidance. *See* **Vocational guidance**
Job résumés. *See* **Résumés (Employment)**
Job retraining. *See* **Occupational retraining**
Job satisfaction 658.3
   See also **Burn out (Psychology)**
   x Satisfaction in work; Work satisfaction
   xx **Attitude (Psychology); Employee morale; Per-**
      sonnel management; Work
Job searching. *See* **Job hunting**
Job security 658.3
   See also **Employees—Dismissal**
   x Employment security; Security, Job
   xx **Personnel management**
Job sharing 331.2; 658.3
   x Sharing of jobs
   xx **Part-time employment**
Job stress 658.3
   See also **Burn out (Psychology)**
   x Occupational stress; On the job stress; Organi-
      zational stress; Work stress
   xx **Stress (Physiology); Stress (Psychology)**
Job training. *See* **Occupational training**
Jobs. *See* **Employment agencies; Occupations; Pro-**
      fessions
Jogging 613.7; 796.4
   xx **Running**
Joint custody of children. *See* **Child custody**
Joke books. *See* **Jokes**

Jokes 808.7; 808.87; 817; etc.
  See also **Practical jokes**
  x Joke books
  xx **Wit and humor**
Journalism 070
  Use for materials dealing with writing for the periodical press and with the editing of this
  writing, or for materials on journalism as an
  occupation. Materials limited to the history,
  organization and management of newspapers are entered under **Newspapers.** Journalism in a particular field is entered under
  Journalism with adjective modifier, e.g.
  Journalism, Scientific; etc.
  See also

Broadcast journalism	**Newspapers**
College and school jour-	**Periodicals**
nalism	**Press**
Freedom of the press	**Reporters and reporting**
Libel and slander	

  x Editors and editing; Interviewing (Journalism); Writing (Authorship)
  xx **Authorship; Broadcast journalism; Literature;**
  Newspapers; Periodicals; Reporters and re-
  porting
Journalism—Objectivity 070.4
  x Slanted journalism
Journalism, Scientific 070.4
  x Scientific journalism
Journalistic photography. *See* **Photography, Jour-**
  nalistic
Journalists 070.92; 920
  x Columnists; Editors and editing; Writers
Journals. *See* **Periodicals**
Journals (Machinery). *See* **Bearings (Machinery)**
Journeys. *See* **Voyages and travels; Voyages around**
  the world; and names of countries, regions,
  etc. with the subdivision *Description and*
  travel, e.g. **United States—Description and**
  travel; etc.
Joy and sorrow 152.4
  See also **Happiness; Pleasure**
  x Affliction; Grief; Sorrow
  xx **Emotions; Ethics; Happiness; Suffering**
Judaeo-German. *See* **Yiddish language**
Judaism 296
  See also

Atonement—Judaism	**Rabbis**
Cabala	**Sabbath**
Fasts and feasts—Judaism	**Synagogues**
Jews	**Talmud**

  x Jewish religion; Jews—Religion
  xx **Religions**
Judaism—Customs and practices 296.4
  See also **Judaism—Liturgy**
  x Jews—Rites and ceremonies
  xx **Rites and ceremonies**
Judaism—Liturgy 296.4
  x Jews—Ritual
  xx **Judaism—Customs and practices; Liturgies**

Judges 347.092; 920

    See also **Courts; Women judges**

    x Chief justices

    xx **Courts; Lawyers**

Judicial investigations. *See* **Governmental investigations**

Judiciary. *See* **Courts**

Judo 796.8

    See also **Karate**

    xx **Physical education; Self-defense; Wrestling**

July Fourth. *See* **Fourth of July**

Jungle animals 591.52

    xx **Animals; Forest animals; Wildlife**

Jungles 634.9

    Use for materials on impenetrable thickets of second-growth vegetation replacing tropical rain forest that has been disturbed or degraded. Consider also **Rain forests.**

    x Selvas; Tropical jungles

    xx **Forests and forestry; Rain forests; Tropics**

Junior colleges 378

    x Community colleges

    xx **Colleges and universities; Education, Higher**

Junior colleges—Directories 378.025

    xx **Directories**

Junior high school libraries. *See* **School libraries (High school)**

Junior high schools 373.2

    x High schools, Junior; Secondary schools

    xx **Education, Secondary; High schools; Public schools**

Junk. *See* **Waste products**

Jurisprudence. *See* **Law**

Jurisprudence, Medical. *See* **Medical jurisprudence**

Jurists. *See* **Lawyers**

Jury 345; 347

    x Trial by jury

    xx **Courts; Criminal law**

Justice 340

    xx **Ethics; Human behavior; Law**

Justice, Administration of 350-353

    See also **Courts; Crime; Governmental investigations; Impeachments**

    x Administration of justice

    xx **Courts; Crime**

Juvenile courts 345

    See also **Probation**

    x Children's courts

    xx **Courts; Juvenile delinquency; Probation; Reformatories**

Juvenile delinquency 364.3

    See also **Child welfare; Juvenile courts; Prostitution, Juvenile; Reformatories; School violence; Youth—Drug use**

    x Children, Delinquent; Delinquency, Juvenile; Delinquents; Gangs

    xx **Child welfare; Crime; Emotionally disturbed children; Reformatories; Social problems**

Juvenile delinquency—Case studies 364.3092

    x Case studies

Juvenile literature. *See* **Children's literature**
Juvenile prostitution. *See* **Prostitution, Juvenile**
K.K.K. *See* **Ku Klux Klan (1865-1876); Ku Klux
Klan (1915-   )**
Kabbala. *See* **Cabala**
Kamuti. *See* **Bonsai**
Karate 796.8
xx **Judo; Self-defense**
Kart racing. *See* **Karts and karting**
Karts and karting 796.7
x Go karts; Kart racing
xx **Automobile racing**
Keramics. *See* **Ceramics**
Keyboards (Electronics) 001.64; 652; *004.7
x Computer keyboards; Word processor key-
boards
xx **Computer peripherals; Office equipment and
supplies**
Keyboards (Musical instruments) 786
xx **Organ; Piano**
Keys. *See* **Locks and keys**
Kibbutz. *See* **Collective settlements—Israel**
Kidnapping 364.1
x Abduction
xx **Criminal law; Offenses against the person**
Kidnapping, Parental 306.8; 364.1
x Child snatching by parents; Childnapping;
Custody kidnapping; Parental kidnapping
xx **Child custody**
Killing, Mercy. *See* **Euthanasia**
Kindergarten 372
See also **Creative activities; Education, Pre-
school; Montessori method of education**
xx **Children; Education, Elementary; Education,
Preschool; Games; Nursery schools;
Schools; Teaching**
Kinematics 531
See also **Mechanical movements; Mechanics;
Motion**
xx **Dynamics; Mechanics; Motion**
Kinetic art 701; 709.04
See also **Kinetic sculpture**
x Art in motion; Art, Kinetic
xx **Art, Abstract; Art, Modern—1900-1999 (20th
century)**
Kinetic sculpture 731; 735
See also **Mobiles (Sculpture)**
x Sculpture in motion; Sculpture, Kinetic
xx **Futurism (Art); Kinetic art**
Kinetics. *See* **Dynamics; Motion**
King Philip's War, 1675-1676 973.2
x United States—History—1675-1676, King
Philip's War
xx **Indians of North America—Wars; United
States—History—1600-1775, Colonial period**
King William's War, 1689-1697. *See* **United
States—History—1689-1697, King Wil-
liam's War**

Kings, queens, rulers, etc. 920

> *See also* **Courts and courtiers; Dictators; Presidents; Roman emperors;** also names of countries with the subdivision *Kings, queens, rulers, etc.,* e.g. **Great Britain—Kings, queens, rulers, etc.;** also names of individual kings, queens, and rulers, e.g. **Elizabeth II, Queen of Great Britain, 1926- ;** etc.
>
> *x* Emperors; Monarchs; Queens; Royalty; Rulers; Sovereigns
>
> *xx* **Courts and courtiers; Heads of state; History; Monarchy; Political science**

Kitchen gardens. *See* **Vegetable gardening**

Kitchen utensils. *See* **Household equipment and supplies**

Kitchens 643

> *xx* **Houses**

Kites 629.133; 796.1

> *xx* **Aeronautics**

Knighthood. *See* **Knights and knighthood**

Knights and knighthood 394; 940.1

> *See also* **Chivalry; Heraldry**
>
> *x* Knighthood
>
> *xx* **Chivalry; Heraldry; Middle Ages; Nobility**

Knights of the Round Table. *See* **Arthurian romances**

Knitting 746.43

Knots and splices 623.88

> *x* Splicing
>
> *xx* **Navigation; Rope**

Knowledge, Theory of 001.2-001.4; 121

> Use for materials dealing with the origin, nature, methods and limits of human knowledge.
>
> *See also*

Apperception	**Perception**
Belief and doubt	**Pragmatism**
Empiricism	**Rationalism**
Gestalt psychology	**Reality**
Intellect	**Senses and sensation**
Intuition	**Truth**

> *x* Cognition; Epistemology; Understanding
>
> *xx* **Apperception; Consciousness; Intellect; Logic; Metaphysics; Philosophy; Reality; Truth**

Kodak camera 771.3

> *xx* **Cameras**

Koran 297

> *x* Alkoran; Qur'an
>
> *xx* **Islam; Sacred books**

Korea 951.9

> Use for materials on Korea as a whole before 1948 when two separate republics were established.
>
> *See also* **Korea (North); Korea (South)**

Korea (Democratic People's Republic). *See* **Korea (North)**

Korea (North) 951.9

> Use for materials on the Democratic People's Republic of Korea, established in 1948.
>
> *x* Korea (Democratic People's Republic); North Korea

Korea (North)—*Continued*
  xx **Korea**
Korea (Republic). *See* **Korea (South)**
Korea (South) 951.9
  Use for materials on the Republic of Korea, established in 1948.
  x Korea (Republic); South Korea
  xx **Korea**
Korean War, 1950-1953 951.9
Ku Klux Klan (1865-1876) 322.4
  x K.K.K.
  xx **Reconstruction (1865-1876)**
Ku Klux Klan (1915-) 322.4
  x K.K.K.
Labor (May subdiv. geog.) **331**
  Use for materials on the human activity that provides the goods and services in an economy. These services are performed by workers for wages as distinguished from those rendered by entrepreneurs for profits. Also use for materials on the group of workers who perform these services for wages.
  See also

Absenteeism (Labor)	**Occupational diseases**
Apprentices	**Occupations**
Arbitration, Industrial	**Occupations, Dangerous**
Capitalism	**Open and closed shop**
Children—Employment	**Part-time employment**
Church and labor	**Peasantry**
Collective bargaining	**Peonage**
Communism	**Proletariat**
Contract labor	**Slavery**
Convict labor	**Socialism**
Cost of living	**Strikes and lockouts**
Employment	**Supplementary employ-**
Employment agencies	**ment**
Hours of labor	**Syndicalism**
Household employees	**Unemployed**
Industrial relations	**Wages**
Insurance, Industrial	**Welfare work in industry**
Labor unions	**Women—Employment**
Libraries and labor	**Work ethics**
Machinery in industry	**World War, 1939-1945—**
Men—Employment	**Human resources**
Middle classes	**Youth—Employment**
Migrant labor	

  also names of classes of laborers, e.g. **Agricultural laborers; Miners;** etc.; and headings beginning with the word **Labor.**
  x Blue collar workers; Factory workers; Industrial workers; Laborers; Manual workers; Skilled workers; Unskilled workers; Working classes
  xx **Economics; Social classes; Social conditions; Socialism; Sociology; Work**
Labor absenteeism. *See* **Absenteeism (Labor)**
Labor—Accidents 658.3
Labor and capital. *See* **Industrial relations**
Labor and libraries. *See* **Libraries and labor**
Labor and the church. *See* **Church and labor**

Labor arbitration. *See* **Arbitration, Industrial**
Labor (Childbirth). *See* **Childbirth**
Labor contract 331.1; 331.89
> Use for materials dealing with agreements be-
> tween employer and employee in which the
> latter agrees to perform work in return for
> compensation from the former.
> *See also* **Collective bargaining; Open and closed**
> **shop; Wages**
> *x* Collective labor agreements; Trade agree-
> ments (Labor)
> *xx* **Collective bargaining; Contracts; Industrial re-**
> **lations**
Labor disputes 331.89
> *See also* **Arbitration, Industrial; Collective bar-**
> **gaining; Strikes and lockouts**
> *x* Disputes, Labor; Industrial disputes
> *xx* **Industrial relations**
Labor—Education 331.2
> *x* Education of workers
Labor force. *See* **Labor supply**
Labor, Hours of. *See* **Hours of labor**
Labor—Housing 363.5
Labor—Insurance. *See* **Insurance, Unemployment;**
> **Old age pensions; Social security**
Labor-management relations. *See* **Industrial rela-**
> **tions**
Labor market. *See* **Labor supply**
Labor, Migratory. *See* **Migrant labor**
Labor negotiations. *See* **Arbitration, Industrial;**
> **Collective bargaining**
Labor organizations. *See* **Labor unions**
Labor output. *See* **Labor productivity**
Labor participation in management. *See* **Manage-**
> **ment—Employee participation**
Labor productivity 331.11
> *See also* **Machinery in industry; Production stan-**
> **dards;** also subjects with the subdivision
> *Labor productivity,* e.g. **Employees—Labor**
> **productivity;** etc.
> *x* Labor output; Productivity of labor
> *xx* **Efficiency, Industrial; Machinery in industry**
Labor relations. *See* **Industrial relations**
Labor saving devices, Household. *See* **Household**
> **appliances, Electric; Household equipment**
> **and supplies**
Labor supply 331.11
> *See also*

Children—Employment	**Unemployed**
Employment agencies	**Unemployment**
Employment forecasting	**Women—Employment**
Human resources	**World War, 1939-1945—**
Human resources policy	**Human resources**
Men—Employment	**Youth—Employment**
Occupational retraining	

> *x* Labor force; Labor market
> *xx* **Economic conditions; Employment; Employ-**
> **ment agencies; Employment forecasting;**
> **Human resources; Human resources policy;**
> **Unemployed**

Labor turnover 331.12
>*See also* **Employment agencies**
>*xx* **Personnel management**

Labor unions (May subdiv. geog.) **331.88**
>*See also* **Arbitration, Industrial; Collective bar-
>gaining; Injunctions; Open and closed shop;
>Sabotage; Strikes and lockouts; Syndicalism;**
>also names of types of unions and names of
>individual labor unions, e.g. **Librarians'
>unions; United Steelworkers of America;**
>etc.
>*x* Labor organizations; Organized labor; Trade
>unions; Unions, Labor
>*xx* **Collective bargaining; Cooperation; Industrial
>relations; Labor; Socialism; Societies;
>Strikes and lockouts**

Labor unions—United States 331.88
>*x* American labor unions; United States—Labor
>unions

Labor—United States 331.1
>*x* United States—Labor

Laboratories, Language. *See* **Language laboratories**
Laboratories, Space. *See* **Space stations**
Laboratory fertilization. *See* **Fertilization in vitro**
Laboratory manuals. *See* scientific and technical
>subjects with the subdivision *Laboratory
>manuals,* e.g. **Chemistry—Laboratory man-
>uals;** etc.
Laborers. *See* **Labor;** and names of classes of la-
>borers, e.g. **Agricultural laborers; Miners;**
>etc.

Lace and lace making 746.2
>*xx* **Crocheting; Needlework; Weaving**

Lacquer and lacquering 667
>*See also* **Varnish and varnishing**
>*x* Finishes and finishing
>*xx* **Decorative arts; Varnish and varnishing;
>Wood finishing**

Laissez faire. *See* **Industry—Government policy**
Laity 262
>May be subdivided by religious denomination.
>*See also* **Lay ministry**
>*x* Laymen
>*xx* **Lay ministry**

Laity—Catholic Church 262
>*x* Catholic laity

Lakes (May subdiv. geog. country and state) **551.48**
>*See also* names of lakes
>*xx* **Inland navigation; Physical geography; Water;
>Waterways**

Lakes—United States 551.48
>*x* United States—Lakes

Lamaze method of childbirth. *See* **Natural child-
>birth**
Lamps 621.32; 749
>*See also* **Electric lamps**
>*xx* **Lighting**

Land. *See* **Land use**
Land, Condemnation of. *See* **Eminent domain**
Land drainage. *See* **Drainage**

Land question. *See* **Land tenure**

Land, Reclamation of. *See* **Reclamation of land**

Land reform (May subdiv. geog.) **333.3**

> *See also* **Agriculture—Government policy; Land tenure**
>
> *x* Agrarian reform; Reform, Agrarian
>
> *xx* **Agriculture—Government policy; Economic policy; Land use; Social policy**

Land settlement (May subdiv. geog.) **325**

> *See also* **Colonization; Migration, Internal**
>
> *x* Resettlement; Settlement of land
>
> *xx* **Colonies; Migration, Internal**

Land settlement—United States 325.73

> *x* United States—Land settlement

Land surveying. *See* **Surveying**

Land tenure 333.3

> Use for general and historical discussions on systems of holding land.
>
> *See also* **Farm tenancy; Feudalism; Landlord and tenant; Peasantry; Real estate**
>
> *x* Agrarian question; Fiefs; Land question; Tenure of land
>
> *xx* **Agriculture; Agriculture—Economic aspects; Inheritance and succession; Land reform; Land use; Peasantry; Real estate**

Land use 333

> Use for general materials that cover such topics as types of land, the utilization, distribution and development of land and the economic factors which affect the value of land. Materials dealing only with ownership of land are entered under **Real estate.**
>
> *See also* **Eminent domain; Farms; Feudalism; Land reform; Land tenure; Real estate; Reclamation of land**
>
> *x* Land
>
> *xx* **Agriculture; Economics**

Landfills 363.1; 628.3-628.4

> Use for materials on places for waste disposal in which waste is buried in layers of earth in low ground.
>
> *See also* **Hazardous waste sites;** also names of landfills, e.g. **Love Canal Chemical Waste Landfill (Niagara Falls, N.Y.);** etc.
>
> *x* Earth fills; Fills (Earthwork); Sanitary landfills

Landlord and tenant 333.5

> Use for materials on the legal relationships between landlord and tenant.
>
> *See also* **Apartment houses; Farm tenancy; Housing**
>
> *x* Tenant and landlord
>
> *xx* **Commercial law; Human relations; Land tenure; Real estate**

Landmarks, Literary. *See* **Literary landmarks**

Landmarks, Preservation of. *See* **Natural monuments**

Landscape architecture 712

> *See also* **Garden ornaments and furniture; Landscape gardening; Landscape protection; Parks; Patios; Roadside improvement**

Landscape architecture—*Continued*

    x Landscape design

    xx **Landscape gardening; Landscape protection**

Landscape design. *See* **Landscape architecture**

Landscape drawing 743

    See also **Landscape painting**

    xx **Drawing; Landscape painting**

Landscape gardening 714-717

    See also **Evergreens; Landscape architecture;**
        Plants, Ornamental; Shrubs; Trees

    x Garden design; Planting

    xx **Gardening; Horticulture; Landscape architec-**
        ture; Shrubs; Trees

Landscape painting 758

    See also **Landscape drawing**

    xx **Landscape drawing; Painting**

Landscape protection 333.7-333.9

    See also **Landscape architecture; Natural monu-**
        ments; Regional planning

    x Beautification of landscape; Natural beauty
        conservation; Preservation of natural sce-
        nery; Protection of natural scenery; Scenery

    xx **Landscape architecture; Nature conservation;**
        Regional planning

Landscape sculpture. *See* **Earthworks (Art)**

Language and languages 400's

    Use for general materials on the history, philoso-
        phy, origin, etc. of language. Comparative
        studies of languages are entered under
        Philology, Comparative.

    See also

Bilingualism	**Semantics**
Conversation	**Sociolinguistics**
Grammar	**Speech**
Literature	**Translating and interpret-**
Philology, Comparative	**ing**
Phonetics	**Verbal learning**
Programming languages	**Voice**
(Computers)	**Writing**
Rhetoric	

    also names of languages or groups of cognate
        languages, e.g. **English language;** etc.; also
        classes of people with the subdivision
        Language, e.g. **Children—Language;** etc.

    x Comparative linguistics; Linguistics; Philology

    xx **Anthropology; Communication; Ethnology;**
        Grammar; Philology, Comparative; Speech

Language and languages—Comparative
        philology. *See* **Philology, Comparative**

Language and society. *See* **Sociolinguistics**

Language arts 400's

    See also **Creative writing; Literature; Reading;**
        Speech; Writing

    x Communication arts

    xx **Communication**

Language games. *See* **Literary recreations**

Language, International. *See* **Language, Universal**

Language laboratories 407

    See also **Languages, Modern—Study and teach-**
        ing

Language laboratories—*Continued*
> *x* Foreign language laboratories; Laboratories,
> Language
> *xx* **Languages, Modern—Study and teaching**

Language, Universal   401
> *See also* **Esperanto**
> *x* International language; Language, Interna-
> tional; Universal language; World language

Languages, Modern   400's
> Use for materials dealing collectively with living
> literary languages.
> May be subdivided like **English language.**
> *x* Modern languages

**Languages, Modern—Conversations and phrases
    438; 448; etc.**
> *x* Conversation in foreign languages; Foreign
> language phrases

Languages, Modern—Study and teaching   407
> *See also* **Language laboratories**
> *xx* **Language laboratories**

Lantern projection.   *See* **Projectors**
Lantern slides.   *See* **Slides (Photography)**
Large and small.   *See* **Size and shape**
Large print books   028
> *x* Books for sight saving; Books—Large print;
> Large type books; Sight saving books
> *xx* **Blind—Books and reading**

Large type books.   *See* **Large print books**
Laser-beam recording.   *See* **Laser recording**
Laser disc players.   *See* **Compact disc players**
Laser photography.   *See* **Holography**
Laser recording   621.36; 621.38
> *See also* **Holography; Optical storage devices**
> *x* Laser-beam recording; Recording, Laser
> *xx* **Lasers; Optical storage devices**

Lasers   535.5; 621.36
> *See also* **Laser recording**
> *x* Light amplification by stimulated emission of
> radiation; Masers, Optical; Optical masers
> *xx* **Light**

Lasers in aeronautics   629.13
> Use same form for lasers in other subjects.
> *xx* **Aeronautics**

Last Supper.   *See* **Lord's Supper**
Latchkey children   306.8; 640
> Use for materials on children who carry
> doorkeys to let themselves into the house on
> returning from school because the parents
> are at work.
> *xx* **Children of working parents**

Lathe work.   *See* **Lathes; Turning**
Lathes   621.9
> *See also* **Turning**
> *x* Lathe work
> *xx* **Turning; Woodworking machinery**

Latin America   980
> Use for materials discussing collectively the area
> and/or countries south of the Rio Grande,
> as well as all or parts of three or more of the
> regions that make up Latin America, i.e.

Latin America—*Continued*

Mexico, Central America, South America, and the West Indies. **Latin America** may also be used as the collective geographic heading and subdivision for the Spanish-speaking countries of Latin America.

See also **Pan-Americanism; South America;** also names of individual Latin American countries

x Spanish America

xx **America**

Latin America—Politics and government 980

x Politics

Latin American literature 860

Use for materials on French, Portuguese, and/or Spanish literature of Latin American countries.

May use same subdivisions and names of literary forms as for **English literature.**

See also **Brazilian literature**

x South American literature

xx **American literature; Spanish literature**

Latin Americans 920; 980

Use for materials on citizens of Latin American countries. Materials on United States citizens of Latin American descent are entered under **Hispanic Americans.**

Latin language 470

May be subdivided like **English language.**

See also **Romance languages**

x Classical languages

Latin literature 870

May use same subdivisions and names of literary forms as for **English literature.**

See also **Christian literature—30(ca.)-600, Early; Classical literature**

x Roman literature

xx **Classical literature**

Latinos (U.S.) *See* **Hispanic Americans**

Latitude 526; 527

x Degrees of latitude and longitude

xx **Earth; Geodesy; Nautical astronomy**

Latter-day Saints. *See* **Church of Jesus Christ of Latter-day Saints**

Laughter 152.4

See also **Wit and humor**

xx **Emotions**

Launching of satellites. *See* **Artificial satellites—Launching**

Laundry 648

x Ironing; Washing

xx **Cleaning; Home economics; Sanitation, Household**

Law (May subdiv. geog.) **340**

See also

Actions and defenses	**Legal ethics**
Courts	**Legislation**
Justice	**Medical jurisprudence**
Lawyers	**Police**

also special branches of law, e.g. **Administrative**

Law—*Continued*

> law; Commercial law; Constitutional law; Corporation law; Criminal law; Ecclesiastical law; Internal revenue law; International law; Maritime law; Military law; Space law; etc. For laws on special subjects see names of subjects with the subdivision *Law and legislation,* e.g. Automobiles—Law and legislation; Food—Law and legislation; etc.

> *x* Jurisprudence; Laws; Statutes
> *xx* Legislation; Political science

Law, Administrative. *See* Administrative law

Law, Business. *See* Commercial law

Law, Commercial. *See* Commercial law

Law, Constitutional. *See* Constitutional law

Law, Corporation. *See* Corporation law

Law, Criminal. *See* Criminal law

Law, Ecclesiastical. *See* Ecclesiastical law

Law enforcement 363.2

> *See also* Police
> *x* Enforcement of law

Law, Internal revenue. *See* Internal revenue law

Law, International. *See* International law

Law, Maritime. *See* Maritime law

Law, Military. *See* Military law

Law of nations. *See* International law

Law of the sea. *See* Maritime law

Law reform 340

> *x* Legal reform

Law, Space. *See* Space law

Law suits. *See* Actions and defenses

Law—United States 349.73

> *x* United States—Law

Law—Vocational guidance 340.023

> *xx* Professions; Vocational guidance

Lawn tennis. *See* Tennis

Lawns 716

> *See also* Grasses

Laws. *See* Law; Legislation; and subjects with the subdivision *Law and legislation,* e.g.

> Automobiles—Law and legislation; Food—Law and legislation; etc.

Lawyers 340.092; 920

> *See also* Judges; Legal ethics
> *x* Attorneys; Bar; Barristers; Jurists; Legal profession
> *xx* Law

Lay ministry 253

> *See also* Laity
> *x* Volunteers in church work
> *xx* Church work; Laity

Laymen. *See* Laity

Layout and typography. *See* Printing

Lead poisoning 615.9

> *xx* Occupational diseases; Poisons and poisoning

Leadership 158

> *See also* Elite (Social sciences)
> *xx* Ability; Executive ability; Social groups; Success

League of Nations 341.22
  xx **Arbitration, International; International coop-
      eration; Peace; World War, 1914-1918—
      Peace**
League of Nations—Mandatory system. *See* **Man-
      dates**
Learned societies. *See* **Societies**
Learning and scholarship 001.2
  See also **Culture; Education; Humanism; Profes-
      sional education; Research**
  x Intellectual life; Scholarship
  xx **Civilization; Culture; Education; Humanism;
      Research**
Learning, Art of. *See* **Study, Method of**
Learning center approach to teaching. *See* **Open
      plan schools**
Learning, Concept. *See* **Concept learning**
Learning disabilities 153.1; 370.15
  See also types of learning disabilities, e.g.
      Reading disability; etc.
  x Disability, Learning; Learning disorders
  xx **Learning, Psychology of; Slow learning chil-
      dren**
Learning disorders. *See* **Learning disabilities**
Learning, Psychology of 153.1
  See also **Behavior modification; Biofeedback
      training; Brainwashing; Concept learning;
      Feedback (Psychology); Learning disabili-
      ties; Verbal learning**
  x Psychology of learning
  xx **Animal intelligence; Child psychology; Educa-
      tion; Educational psychology; Memory**
Learning resource centers. *See* **Instructional materi-
      als centers**
Learning, Verbal. *See* **Verbal learning**
Lease and rental services 333.5
  x Lease services; Rental services
Lease services. *See* **Lease and rental services**
Leather 675
  See also **Hides and skins; Tanning**
  xx **Hides and skins; Tanning**
Leather garments 685
  x Clothing, Leather; Garments, Leather; Skin
      garments
  xx **Clothing and dress; Leather work**
Leather industry and trade 338.4
  See also **Bookbinding; Shoe industry**
Leather work 745.53
  See also **Leather garments**
  xx **Decoration and ornament; Decorative arts;
      Handicraft**
Leaves 581
  x Foliage
  xx **Botany; Trees**
Lebanon 915.692; 956.92
Lebanon—History 956.92
Lebanon—History—1975-1976, Civil War 956.92
**Lebanon—History—1982- , Israeli intervention
      956.92**
  x Israeli intervention in Lebanon, 1982-

Lebanon—History—1982- , Israeli
        intervention—*Continued*
    xx **Jewish-Arab relations**
Lectures and lecturing 808.5
        Use for general materials on the art of lecturing,
            effectiveness of the lecture method, an-
            nouncements of lectures, etc. Collections of
            lectures on several subjects are entered un-
            der **Speeches, addresses, etc.** Lectures on
            one topic are entered under that subject. If
            it is not treated comprehensively add the
            subdivision *Addresses and essays.*
        See also **Radio addresses, debates, etc.;** also gen-
            eral subjects with the subdivision *Addresses
            and essays,* e.g. **Agriculture—Addresses and
            essays; United States—History—Addresses
            and essays; World War, 1939-1945—
            Addresses and essays;** etc.
        x Addresses; Speaking
    xx **Public speaking; Rhetoric; Speeches, ad-
        dresses, etc.; Teaching**
Left and right E
        Use for mostly children's materials on left and
            right as indications of location or direction.
            Materials on political views or attitudes are
            entered under **Right and left (Political sci-
            ence).** Materials on the physical characteris-
            tics of favoring one hand or the other are
            entered under **Left- and right-handedness.**
        x Right and left
Left- and right-handedness 152.3
        See note under **Left and right.**
        x Handedness; Right- and left-handedness
    xx **Psychology, Physiological**
Left (Political science). *See* **Right and left (Political
        science)**
Legacies. *See* **Inheritance and succession; Wills**
Legal aid 362.5
        See also types of legal aid, e.g. **Legal assistance
            to the poor;** etc.
        x Charities, Legal
Legal assistance to the poor 362.5
        x Legal representative of the poor; Legal service
            for the poor; Poor—Legal assistance
    xx **Legal aid; Public welfare**
Legal ethics 340
        x Ethics, Legal
    xx **Law; Lawyers; Professional ethics**
Legal holidays. *See* **Holidays**
Legal medicine. *See* **Medical jurisprudence**
Legal profession. *See* **Lawyers**
Legal reform. *See* **Law reform**
Legal representative of the poor. *See* **Legal assis-
        tance to the poor**
Legal responsibility. *See* **Liability (Law)**
Legal service for the poor. *See* **Legal assistance to
        the poor**
Legal tender. *See* **Paper money**
Legations. *See* **Diplomatic and consular service**
Legends (May subdiv. geog. noun form, e.g.
            Legends—Ireland; etc., or, where country
            subdivision is not applicable, use ethnic or
            religious subdivision, adjective form, e.g.
            Legends, Jewish; etc.) **398.2**
        Use for tales coming down from the past, espe-
            cially those relating to actual events or per-
            sons. Collections of tales written between
            the eleventh and fourteenth centuries and
            dealing with the age of chivalry are entered
            under **Romances.**

Legends—*Continued*
> *See also*

Fables	**Mythology**
Fairy tales	**Romances**
Folklore	**Saints**
Grail	**Tall tales**

> *x* Stories; Tales; Traditions
> *xx* **Fiction; Folklore; Literature; Saints**

Legends, Celtic 398.2
> *x* Celtic legends

Legends, Indian. *See* **Indians of North America—
    Legends**

Legends, Norse 398.2
> *x* Norse legends

Legends—United States 398.2
> *x* United States—Legends

Legerdemain. *See* **Magic**

Legislation 328
> Use for materials on the theory of lawmaking
>   and descriptions of the preparation and en-
>   actment of laws.
>
> *See also* **Law; Legislative bodies; Parliamentary
>   practice;** also subjects with the subdivision
>   *Law and legislation,* e.g. **Automobiles—Law
>   and legislation; Food—Law and legislation;**
>   etc.
>
> *x* Laws
> *xx* **Constitutional law; Law; Political science**

Legislation, Direct. *See* **Referendum**

Legislative bodies 328
> Use for descriptions and histories of law making
>   bodies, discussions of one-house legislatures,
>   etc.
>
> *See also* **Parliamentary practice; Right and left
>   (Political science);** also names of individual
>   legislative bodies, e.g. **United States. Con-
>   gress;** etc.
>
> *x* Parliaments; Unicameral legislatures
> *xx* **Constitutional law; Legislation; Representative
>   government and representation**

Legislative investigations. *See* **Governmental inves-
    tigations**

Legislative reapportionment. *See* **Apportionment
    (Election law)**

Leisure 790.01
> *See also* **Hobbies; Recreation; Retirement; Time
>   management**

LEM. *See* **Lunar excursion module**

Lending. *See* **Loans**

Lending of library materials. *See* **Library circula-
    tion**

Lenses 535
> *See also* types of lenses, e.g. **Contact lenses;** etc.

Lensless photography. *See* **Holography**

Lent 263
> *See also* **Easter; Good Friday; Holy Week**
> *x* Ecclesiastical fasts and feasts

Lepidoptera. *See* **Butterflies; Moths**

Lesbianism 306.7
> *xx* **Homosexuality**

Lesbians. *See* **Gay women**
Less developed countries. *See* **Developing countries**
Letter writing 808.6
> Use for materials on composition, forms, and etiquette of correspondence. Materials limited to business correspondence are entered under **Business letters.** Collections of literary letters are entered under **Letters.**
>
> *See also* **Business letters**
>
> *x* Correspondence; Salutations
>
> *xx* **Etiquette; Rhetoric; Style, Literary**

Lettering 745.6
> *See also* **Alphabets; Initials; Monograms; Sign painting**
>
> *x* Ornamental alphabets
>
> *xx* **Alphabets; Decoration and ornament; Initials; Mechanical drawing; Painting, Industrial; Sign painting**

Letters 808.86
> See note under **Letter writing.**
>
> *See also* **American letters; English letters**
>
> *x* Correspondence
>
> *xx* **Literature—Collected works**

Letters of credit. *See* **Credit; Negotiable instruments**
Letters of marque. *See* **Privateering**
Letters of recommendation. *See* **Applications for positions**
Letters of the alphabet. *See* **Alphabet**
Leukemia 616.99
> *xx* **Blood—Diseases; Cancer**

Levant. *See* **Middle East**
Lewis and Clark Expedition (1804-1806) 973.4
> *x* Exploring expeditions
>
> *xx* **United States—Exploring expeditions; United States—History—1783-1809**

Liability (Law) 346
> *See also* **Malpractice**
>
> *x* Accountability; Legal responsibility; Responsibility, Legal
>
> *xx* **Contracts**

Liability, Professional. *See* **Malpractice**
Libel and slander 346.03
> *See also* **Free speech; Freedom of the press; Privacy, Right of**
>
> *x* Character assassination; Defamation; Slander (Law)
>
> *xx* **Free speech; Freedom of the press; Journalism**

Liberalism 320.5
> *See also* **Right and left (Political science)**
>
> *xx* **Right and left (Political science)**

Liberation movements, National. *See* **National liberation movements**
Liberation theology 261.8
> Use for materials on the Christian theological movement which argues for the total liberation of humanity and which supports causes of social justice.
>
> *x* Theology of liberation
>
> *xx* **Church and social problems; Sociology, Chris-**

Liberation theology—*Continued*
        tian; **Theology, Doctrinal**
Liberty. *See* **Freedom**
Liberty of conscience. *See* **Freedom of conscience**
Liberty of speech. *See* **Free speech**
Liberty of the press. *See* **Freedom of the press**
Liberty of the will. *See* **Free will and determinism**
Librarians 020.92; 920
    See also **Black librarians; Library technicians**
Librarians, Black. *See* **Black librarians**
Librarians—Collective bargaining. *See* **Collective**
        bargaining—Librarians
Librarians—Education. *See* **Library education**
Librarians—In-service training 023
    x In-service training; Inservice training
    xx **Library education**
Librarians—Professional ethics 174
    xx **Professional ethics**
Librarians—Rating 023
    xx **Performance standards**
Librarians—Recruiting 023
    xx **Recruiting of employees**
Librarians—Training. *See* **Library education**
Librarians' unions 331.88
    x Library unions
    xx **Labor unions**
Librarianship. *See* **Library science**
Librarianship, Comparative. *See* **Comparative li-**
        brarianship
Libraries (May subdiv. geog.) **027**
    See also special types of libraries, e.g. **Academic**
        libraries; Archives; Business libraries;
        Church libraries; Hospital libraries; Infor-
        mation services; Instructional materials cen-
        ters; Music libraries; Public libraries; School
        libraries; School libraries (High school);
        Special libraries; names of individual li-
        braries, e.g. **Library of Congress;** etc.; and
        headings beginning with the words **Libraries**
        and **Library.**
    xx **Archives; Books; Books and reading; Educa-**
        tion; Information services
Libraries—Acquisitions 025.2
    See also **Book selection**
    x Acquisitions (Libraries); Book buying (Li-
        braries); Libraries—Order department; Li-
        brary acquisitions
    xx **Libraries—Collection development; Library**
        technical processes
Libraries—Administration 025.1
    See also **Libraries—Trustees; Library finance**
    x Administration; Library administration; Li-
        brary policies
Libraries—Advertising. *See* **Advertising—Libraries**
Libraries and Blacks 027.6
    x Blacks and libraries; Library services to
        Blacks
    xx **Blacks; Reader services (Libraries)**
Libraries and children. *See* **Children's libraries**

Libraries and community   021
> Use same form for libraries and other subjects.
> *See also* **Public relations—Libraries**
> *x* Community and libraries

Libraries and labor   027.6
> *x* Labor and libraries; Library services to labor
> *xx* **Labor; Reader services (Libraries)**

Libraries and motion pictures   021
> *x* Educational films; Motion pictures and libraries
> *xx* **Library services; Motion pictures in education**

Libraries and pictures   021
> *xx* **Pictures**

Libraries and readers.   *See* **Reader services (Libraries)**

Libraries and schools   021
> *See also* **Children's libraries; Children's literature; Libraries and students; School libraries**
> *x* Schools and libraries
> *xx* **Children's libraries; Children's literature; School libraries; Schools**

Libraries and state.   *See* **Libraries—Government policy**

Libraries and students   027.62
> *x* Students and libraries
> *xx* **Libraries and schools**

Libraries and the elderly   027.6
> *x* Elderly and libraries; Library services to the elderly
> *xx* **Elderly; Reader services (Libraries)**

Libraries and young adults.   *See* **Young adults' library services**

Libraries—Automation   025.5
> *See also* **Information storage and retrieval systems; Machine readable bibliographic data;** also names of projects and systems, e.g. **MARC system;** etc.
> *x* Library automation
> *xx* **Automation; Information storage and retrieval systems**

Libraries—Boards of trustees.   *See* **Libraries—Trustees**

Libraries, Business.   *See* **Business libraries**

Libraries—Catalogs.   *See* **Library catalogs**

Libraries—Censorship   021.8

Libraries—Centralization   021.6
> *x* Library systems

Libraries, Children's.   *See* **Children's libraries**

Libraries, Church.   *See* **Church libraries**

Libraries—Circulation, loans.   *See* **Library circulation**

Libraries—Classification.   *See* **Classification—Books**

Libraries—Collection development   025.2
> *See also* **Book selection; Libraries—Acquisitions**
> *x* Collection development (Libraries)
> *xx* **Library technical processes**

Libraries—Collective bargaining.   *See* **Collective bargaining—Librarians**

Libraries, College.   *See* **Academic libraries**

Libraries, Company. *See* **Corporate libraries**
Libraries—Cooperation. *See* **Library cooperation**
Libraries, Corporate. *See* **Corporate libraries**
Libraries, County. *See* **County libraries**
Libraries—Equipment and supplies 022
    x Library equipment and supplies; Library sup-
        plies
   xx **Furniture**
Libraries—Federal aid. *See* **Federal aid to libraries**
Libraries—Finance. *See* **Library finance**
Libraries—Government policy 021.8; 351.85
    See also **Federal aid to libraries; State aid to li-**
        braries
    x Libraries and state
Libraries, Governmental. *See* **Government libraries**
Libraries, Hospital. *See* **Hospital libraries**
Libraries, Industrial. *See* **Corporate libraries**
Libraries—Law and legislation 344
    x Library laws; Library legislation
Libraries—Lighting 022
   xx **Lighting**
Libraries, Music. *See* **Music libraries**
Libraries, National. *See* **National libraries**
Libraries—Order department. *See* **Libraries—**
        Acquisitions
Libraries, Presidential. *See* **Presidents—United**
        States—Archives
Libraries, Public. *See* **Public libraries**
Libraries—Public relations. *See* **Public relations—**
        Libraries
Libraries, Regional. *See* **Regional libraries**
Libraries, School. *See* **School libraries**
Libraries, Special. *See* **Special libraries**
Libraries—Special collections 026
   May be subdivided by subject or form, e.g.
        Libraries—Special collections—Science fic-
        tion; Libraries—Special collections—
        Videotapes; etc.
    x Special collections in libraries
Libraries—Standards 020
Libraries, State. *See* **State libraries**
Libraries—State aid. *See* **State aid to libraries**
Libraries—Statistics 020
Libraries—Technical services. *See* **Library techni-**
    cal processes
Libraries—Trustees 021.8
    x Libraries—Boards of trustees; Library boards;
        Library trustees
   xx **Libraries—Administration**
Libraries—United States 027
    x United States—Libraries
Libraries, University. *See* **Academic libraries**
Libraries, Young adults'. *See* **Young adults' library**
    services
Library acquisitions. *See* **Libraries—Acquisitions**
Library administration. *See* **Libraries—**
    Administration
Library advertising. *See* **Advertising—Libraries**
Library architecture 727
    x Buildings, Library; Library buildings

Library architecture—*Continued*
  xx **Architecture**
Library assistants. *See* **Library technicians**
Library automation. *See* **Libraries—Automation**
Library boards. *See* **Libraries—Trustees**
Library buildings. *See* **Library architecture**
Library catalogs 017-019
  See also types of library catalogs, e.g. **Catalogs,**
    Book; Catalogs, Card; Catalogs, Classified;
    Catalogs, Online; Catalogs, Subject; Library
    catalogs on microfilm; etc.
  x Catalogs; Catalogs, Library; Libraries—
    Catalogs
Library catalogs on microfilm 025.3
  x Catalogs, COM; Catalogs on microfilm; COM
    catalogs
  xx **Library catalogs; Microfilms**
Library circulation 025.6
  x Book lending; Circulation of library materials;
    Interlibrary loans; Lending of library mate-
    rials; Libraries—Circulation, loans
  xx **Library services**
Library classification. *See* **Classification—Books**
Library clerks. *See* **Library technicians**
Library consortia. *See* **Library cooperation; Library**
    information networks
Library cooperation 021.6
  See also **Library information networks**
  x Consortia, Library; Cooperation, Library; Li-
    braries—Cooperation; Library consortia
Library education 020.7
  Use for materials on the education of librarians.
    Materials dealing with the instruction of
    readers in library use are entered under
    Library instruction.
  See also **Librarians—In-service training; Library**
    schools
  x Education for librarianship; Librarians—
    Education; Librarians—Training; Library
    science—Study and teaching
  xx **Education; Professional education**
Library education—Audiovisual aids 020.7
  xx **Audiovisual education; Audiovisual materials**
Library education—Curricula 020.7
  x Core curriculum; Courses of study; Curricula
    (Courses of study); Schools—Curricula;
    Study, Courses of
  xx **Education—Curricula**
Library equipment and supplies. *See* **Libraries—**
    Equipment and supplies
Library extension 021.6
  See also **Bookmobiles; County libraries**
Library finance 025.1
  See also **Federal aid to libraries; State aid to li-**
    braries
  x Libraries—Finance
  xx **Libraries—Administration**
Library information networks 021.6
  x Consortia, Library; Library consortia; Library
    networks; Library systems; Networks, Li-

Library information networks—*Continued*
    brary
    xx **Data transmission systems; Information networks; Library cooperation**
Library instruction 025.5
    Use for materials dealing with the instruction of readers in library use. Materials on the education of librarians are entered under **Library education.**
    x Library orientation; Library skills; Library user orientation
    xx **Reader services (Libraries)**
Library laws. *See* **Libraries—Law and legislation**
Library legislation. *See* **Libraries—Law and legislation**
Library materials. *See* **Library resources**
Library materials—Preservation. *See* **Library resources—Conservation and restoration**
Library networks. *See* **Library information networks**
Library of Congress 027.5; 027.6
    x United States. Library of Congress
    xx **Libraries**
Library orientation. *See* **Library instruction**
Library policies. *See* **Libraries—Administration**
Library processing. *See* **Library technical processes**
Library reference services. *See* **Reference services (Libraries)**
Library resources 021
    x Library materials
Library resources—Conservation and restoration 025.8
    x Books—Preservation; Conservation of works of art, books, etc.; Library materials—Preservation; Preservation of library resources
Library schools 020.7
    xx **Library education**
Library science 020
    Use for general materials on the knowledge and skill necessary for the organization and administration of libraries. Materials about services offered by libraries to patrons are entered under **Library services.**
    See also **Bibliography; Cataloging; Classification—Books; Comparative librarianship; Library services; Library surveys; Library technical processes**; also headings beginning with the words **Libraries** and **Library**
    x Librarianship
    xx **Bibliography; Documentation; Information science**
Library science—Study and teaching. *See* **Library education**
Library services 025.5
    See note under **Library science.**
    See also **Libraries and motion pictures; Library circulation; Reader services (Libraries)**
    xx **Library science**

361

Library services to Blacks. *See* **Libraries and Blacks**

Library services to children. *See* **Children's libraries**

Library services to labor. *See* **Libraries and labor**

Library services to the elderly. *See* **Libraries and the elderly**

Library services to young adults. *See* **Young adults' library services**

Library skills. *See* **Library instruction**

Library supplies. *See* **Libraries—Equipment and supplies**

Library surveys 020

   x Surveys

   xx **Library science**

Library systems. *See* **Libraries—Centralization; Library information networks**

Library technical processes 025

   Use for materials on the activities and processes concerned with the acquisition, organization, and preparation of library materials for use.

   See also **Cataloging; Classification—Books; Libraries—Acquisitions; Libraries—Collection development**

   x Centralized processing (Libraries); Libraries—Technical services; Library processing; Processing (Libraries); Technical services (Libraries)

   xx **Library science**

Library technicians 020.92; 920

   x Library assistants; Library clerks; Paraprofessional librarians

   xx **Librarians; Paraprofessions and paraprofessionals**

Library trustees. *See* **Libraries—Trustees**

Library unions. *See* **Librarians' unions**

Library user orientation. *See* **Library instruction**

Librettos 781.9

   See also **Operas—Stories, plots, etc.;** also musical forms with the subdivision *Librettos,* e.g. **Operas—Librettos;** etc.

Life 128

   See also **Death**

Life after death. *See* **Future life; Immortality**

Life (Biology) 574; 577

   See also **Biology; Genetics; Longevity; Middle age; Old age; Protoplasm; Reproduction**

   xx **Biology**

Life care communities. *See* **Retirement communities**

Life, Christian. *See* **Christian life**

Life expectancy. *See* **Longevity**

Life, Future. *See* **Future life**

Life histories. *See* **Biography;** and names of countries, cities, etc. and subjects with the subdivision *Biography,* e.g. **Musicians—Biography;** etc.

Life insurance. *See* **Insurance, Life**

Life on other planets 574.999
> See note under **Space biology**.
> *See also* **Extraterrestrial beings; Interstellar communication**
> *x* Astrobiology; Exobiology; Extraterrestrial life; Planets, Life on other
> *xx* **Astronomy; Planets; Space biology; Universe**

Life—Origin 113
> *x* Germ theory; Origin of life
> *xx* **Evolution**

Life quality. *See* **Quality of life**

Life saving. *See* **Lifesaving**

Life sciences 570
> *See also* **Agriculture; Biology; Medicine**
> *x* Biosciences
> *xx* **Science**

Life sciences ethics. *See* **Bioethics**

Life skills 158; 640
> Use for materials on skills needed by an individual to exist in modern society, including skills related to education, employment, finance, etc.
> *See also* **Human behavior; Human relations; Survival skills;** also types and groups of persons with the subdivision *Life skills guides,* e.g. **Elderly—Life skills guides;** etc.
> *x* Basic life skills; Competencies, Functional; Coping behavior; Everyday living skills; Functional competencies; Fundamental life skills; Personal life skills; Skills, Life
> *xx* **Human behavior; Human relations; Success**

Life span prolongation. *See* **Longevity**

Life, Spiritual. *See* **Spiritual life**

Life styles. *See* **Lifestyles**

Life support systems (Medical environment) 362.1
> *xx* **Hospitals; Terminal care**

Life support systems (Space environment) 629.47
> *See also* **Apollo project; Astronauts—Clothing; Space ships**
> *xx* **Human engineering; Space medicine**

Life support systems (Submarine environment) 627

Lifelong education. *See* **Adult education; Continuing education**

Lifesaving 363.1
> *See also* **First aid**
> *x* Life saving
> *xx* **First aid; Rescue work**

Lifestyles 306
> Use for the distinctive way of life or manner of living characteristic of an individual or groups of people.
> *See also* names of lifestyles, e.g. **Counter culture; Unmarried couples;** etc.
> *x* Alternative lifestyle; Life styles
> *xx* **Human behavior; Quality of life**

Lifts. *See* **Elevators; Hoisting machinery**

Light 535
> *See also*

Color	**Optics**
Lasers	**Phosphorescence**

Light—*Continued*

Photometry	Refraction
Radiation	Spectrum analysis
Radioactivity	X rays

    xx **Electromagnetic waves; Optics; Photometry; Physics; Radiation; Spectrum analysis; Vibration; Waves**

Light amplification by stimulated emission of radiation. *See* **Lasers**

Light and shade. *See* **Shades and shadows**

Light, Electric. *See* **Electric lighting; Fluorescent lighting; Photometry; Phototherapy**

Light production in animals. *See* **Bioluminescence**

Light ships. *See* **Lightships**

Light—Therapeutic use. *See* **Phototherapy**

Lighthouses 387.1; 623.89; 627
    See also **Lightships**
    xx **Navigation**

Lighting (May subdiv. geog.) 621.32
    See also **Candles; Electric lighting; Fluorescent lighting; Lamps;** also subjects with the subdivision *Lighting,* e.g. **Libraries—Lighting; Streets—Lighting;** etc.
    x Illumination

Lightning 551.5
    xx **Electricity; Meteorology; Thunderstorms**

Lights, Feast of. *See* **Hanukkah**

Lightships 623.89; 627
    x Light ships
    xx **Lighthouses**

Limbs, Artificial. *See* **Artificial limbs**

Lime 631.8; 666
    See also **Cement**
    xx **Fertilizers and manures**

Limericks 808.81; 811.08; etc.
    See also **Nonsense verses**
    x Rhymes
    xx **Humorous poetry; Nonsense verses**

Limitation of armament. *See* **Arms control**

Limited access highways. *See* **Express highways**

Lincoln, Abraham, 1809-1865 92
    xx **Presidents—United States**

Lincoln Day. *See* **Lincoln's Birthday**

Lincoln family 920; 929
    xx **Genealogy**

Lincoln's Birthday 394.2
    x Lincoln Day

Line engraving. *See* **Engraving**

Linear algebras. *See* **Algebras, Linear**

Linear system theory. *See* **System analysis**

Linen 677
    See also **Flax; Hemp**
    xx **Fabrics; Fibers; Flax**

Linguistics. *See* **Language and languages**

Linoleum block printing 761
    x Block printing
    xx **Color prints; Engraving**

Linotype 686.2
    xx **Printing; Type and type founding; Typesetting**

Lip reading. *See* **Deaf—Means of communication**

Liquefaction of coal. *See* **Coal liquefaction**
Liqueurs. *See* **Liquors and liqueurs**
Liquid fuel. *See* **Gasoline; Petroleum as fuel**
Liquids 532
> *See also* **Hydraulics; Hydrodynamics; Hydrostat-
> ics**
> *xx* **Mechanics; Physics**

Liquor industry 338.4
> *xx* **Alcohol**

Liquor problem. *See* **Alcoholism; Drinking of alcoholic beverages**
Liquors and liqueurs 663
> *See also* **Distillation;** also names of specific li-
> quors and liqueurs
> *x* Drinks; Intoxicants; Liqueurs; Spirits, Alco-
> holic
> *xx* **Alcohol; Alcoholic beverages; Beverages; Dis-
> tillation; Stimulants**

Listening 152.1
> *See also* **Attention**
> *xx* **Attention**

Listening devices. *See* **Eavesdropping**
Literacy (May subdiv. geog.) **379**
> *See also* **Computer literacy; Visual literacy**
> *x* Illiteracy
> *xx* **Education**

Literacy, Computer. *See* **Computer literacy**
Literacy, Visual. *See* **Visual literacy**
Literary awards. *See* **Literary prizes**
Literary characters. *See* **Characters and character-
istics in literature**
Literary criticism. *See* **Criticism; Literature—
History and criticism**
Literary forgeries 098
> *x* Frauds, Literary
> *xx* **Forgery of works of art**

Literary landmarks (May subdiv. geog.) **809; 810.9;
etc.**
> *x* Authors—Homes and haunts; Landmarks,
> Literary
> *xx* **Historic buildings; Literature—History and
> criticism**

Literary landmarks—United States 810.9
> *x* United States—Literary landmarks

Literary prizes 800
> *See also* names of awards, e.g. **Caldecott Medal
> books; Newbery Medal books;** etc.
> *x* Awards, Literary; Book awards; Book prizes;
> Literary awards; Literature—Prizes; Prizes,
> Literary
> *xx* **Rewards (Prizes, etc.)**

Literary property. *See* **Copyright**
Literary recreations 793.7
> *See also* **Charades; Plot-your-own stories; Rid-
> dles; Word games**
> *x* Language games; Recreations, Literary
> *xx* **Amusements**

Literary style. *See* **Style, Literary**
Literature 800's
> Use for materials on literature in general, not
> limited to history, philosophy, or any one
> aspect.

Literature—*Continued*
　　See also

Authorship	Humanism
Ballads	Indians of North Ameri-
Biography (as a literary	ca—Literature
form)	Journalism
Books	Legends
Catholic literature	Music and literature
Chapbooks	Parody
Children's literature	Plots (Drama, fiction, etc.)
Christian literature—	Poetry
30(ca.)-600, Early	Religious literature
Classical literature	Romanticism
Criticism	Sagas
Devotional literature	Satire
Drama	Short story
Essay	Style, Literary
Fables	Wit and humor
Fairy tales	World War, 1939-1945—
Fiction	Literature and the war

　　　　also names of literatures, e.g. **English literature;**
　　　　　　French literature; etc.; and subjects and
　　　　　　themes in literature, e.g. **Bible in literature;**
　　　　　　Blacks in literature; Characters and charac-
　　　　　　teristics in literature; Children in literature;
　　　　　　Realism in literature; Symbolism in litera-
　　　　　　ture; Women in literature; etc.
　　　x Belles-lettres
　　xx **Books; Books and reading; Humanities; Lan-**
　　　　guage and languages; Language arts
Literature and communism. *See* **Communism and**
　　　　literature
Literature and music. *See* **Music and literature**
Literature—Bio-bibliography 016.8
　　See also **Authors**
　　xx **Authors**
Literature, Classical. *See* **Classical literature**
Literature—Collected works 808.8
　　See also **Essays; Letters; Parodies; Quotations;**
　　　　Romances; Short stories; also names of liter-
　　　　atures and names of literary forms with the
　　　　subdivision *Collected works,* e.g. **English**
　　　　literature—Collected works; Poetry—
　　　　Collected works; etc.
　　x Literature—Selections
Literature, Comparative 809
　　x Comparative literature
　　xx **Philology, Comparative**
Literature—Competitions 800
　　x Competitions
　　xx **Contests; Rewards (Prizes, etc.)**
Literature—Criticism. *See* **Literature—History and**
　　　　criticism
Literature—Dictionaries 803
　　See also **Literature—Indexes**
　　xx **Literature—Indexes**
Literature, Erotic. *See* **Erotic literature**
Literature—Evaluation. *See* **Books and reading;**
　　　　Books and reading—Best books; Books—
　　　　Reviews; Criticism; Literature—History and

Literature—Evaluation—*Continued*
    criticism
Literature—History and criticism 809
    See also **Authors; Criticism; Literary landmarks**
    x Appraisal of books; Books—Appraisal; Evaluation of literature; Literary criticism; Literature—Criticism; Literature—Evaluation
    xx **Authors; Style, Literary**
Literature, Immoral. *See* **Erotic literature**
Literature—Indexes 800
    See also **Literature—Dictionaries**
    xx **Literature—Dictionaries**
Literature, Medieval 809
    May use same subdivisions as for **Literature.**
    See also **Christian literature—30(ca.)-600, Early**
    x Medieval literature
    xx **Middle Ages; Renaissance**
Literature—Outlines, syllabi, etc. 802
    See also **English literature—Outlines, syllabi, etc.**
Literature—Prizes. *See* **Literary prizes**
Literature—Selections. *See* **Literature—Collected works**
Literature—Stories, plots, etc. 808.8
    Use for collections of stories, plots, etc. Materials dealing with the construction and analysis of plots as a literary technique are entered under **Plots (Drama, fiction, etc.).**
Literature—Yearbooks 805
    x Annuals
    xx **Yearbooks**
Literatures of the Soviet Union. *See* **Soviet Union—Literatures**
Lithographers 763.092; 920
    xx **Engravers**
Lithography 686.2; 763; 764
    See also **Offset printing**
    xx **Color printing; Prints**
Lithoprinting. *See* **Offset printing**
Litigation. *See* **Actions and defenses**
Littering. *See* **Refuse and refuse disposal**
Little league baseball 796.357
    xx **Baseball**
Little theater movement 792
    x Community theater; Theater—Little theater movement
    xx **Amateur theater; Theater**
Liturgies 264
    Use for general materials on the forms of prayers, rituals, and ceremonies used in public worship, including the theological and historical study of liturgies.
    See also **Hymns; Mass;** also names of individual religions and denominations with the subdivision *Liturgy,* e.g. **Catholic Church—Liturgy; Judaism—Liturgy;** etc.
    x Church service books; Ecclesiastical rites and ceremonies; Ritual; Service books (Liturgy)
    xx **Church music; Devotional literature; Theology**
Live poliovirus vaccine. *See* **Poliomyelitis vaccine**

Livestock 636
   Use for materials on breeds of livestock and on
      stock raising as an industry. General de-
      scriptions of farm and other domestic ani-
      mals are entered under **Domestic animals.**
   See also **Dairying; Domestic animals; Livestock**
      judging; Veterinary medicine; also names of
      livestock, e.g. **Cattle; Sheep;** etc.
   x Animal husbandry; Animal industry; Farm
      animals; Stock and stock breeding; Stock
      raising
   xx **Domestic animals**
Livestock—Breeding 636.08
   xx **Breeding**
Livestock judging 636
   x Stock judging
   xx **Livestock**
Living, Cost of. *See* **Cost of living**
Living, Standard of. *See* **Standard of living**
Living together. *See* **Unmarried couples**
Living wills. *See* **Right to die**
Lizards 597.95
   xx **Reptiles**
Loan associations. *See* **Savings and loan associa-**
      tions
Loan funds, Student. *See* **Student loan funds**
Loans 332.7
   See also

Credit unions	**Mortgages**
Debts, Public	**Personal loans**
Government lending	**Savings and loan associa-**
Interest (Economics)	**tions**
Investments	

   x Borrowing money; Lending
   xx **Credit**
Loans, Personal. *See* **Personal loans**
Lobbying and lobbyists 328
   See also **Corruption in politics;** also names of
      special lobbying and pressure groups
   x Interest groups; Lobbyists; Pressure groups
   xx **Corruption in politics; Politics, Practical**
Lobbyists. *See* **Lobbying and lobbyists**
Lobsters 595.3
   xx **Crustacea; Shellfish**
Local government 352
   Use for materials about local government of dis-
      tricts, counties, townships, etc. Materials
      about county government only are entered
      under **County government;** materials about
      city government are entered under
      Municipal government.
   See also **Cities and towns; County government;**
      Metropolitan government; Municipal gov-
      ernment; Public administration; State-local
      relations; Villages
   x Government, Local; Town meeting; Township
      government
   xx **Administrative law; Community organization;**
      Political science; Villages
Local history. *See* names of countries, states, etc.

Local history—*Continued*
　　with the subdivision *History, Local,* e.g.
　　United States—History, Local; etc.
Local-state relations.　*See* **State-local relations**
Local traffic.　*See* **City traffic**
Local transit (May subdiv. geog.)　**388.4**
　　Use for materials on the transit systems of urban
　　areas, such as bus lines, subways, etc. and
　　for materials on general local transportation
　　in urban areas, including private transporta-
　　tion, streets, roads, etc. Consider also
　　Transportation.
　　See also **Buses; Street railroads; Subways**
　　x City transit; Mass transit; Municipal transit;
　　　Public transit; Rapid transit; Transit sys-
　　　tems; Urban transportation
　　xx **Traffic engineering; Transportation**
Localism.　*See* **Sectionalism (U.S.);** and names of
　　languages with the subdivision
　　Provincialisms, e.g. **English language—**
　　Provincialisms; etc.
Lockouts.　*See* **Strikes and lockouts**
Locks and keys　683
　　x Keys
　　xx **Burglary protection**
Locomotion.　*See* **Aeronautics; Animal locomotion;**
　　Automobiles; Boats and boating; Flight;
　　Navigation; Transportation; Walking
Locomotives　625.2
　　x Railroads—Rolling stock; Rolling stock
　　xx **Machinery; Steam engines**
Locomotives—Models　625.1
　　xx **Machinery—Models**
Locusts　595.7; 632
　　x Diseases and pests
　　xx **Insects, Injurious and beneficial**
Locusts, Seventeen-year.　*See* **Cicadas**
Lodging houses.　*See* **Hotels, motels, etc.**
Log cabins and houses　728
　　x Cabins; Houses, Log
　　xx **House construction; Houses**
Logarithms　512.9
　　See also **Slide rule**
　　xx **Algebra; Mathematics—Tables, etc.; Trigo-**
　　　nometry—Tables, etc.
Logging.　*See* **Lumber and lumbering**
Logic　160
　　See also **Critical thinking; Knowledge, Theory of;**
　　　Probabilities; Reasoning; Thought and
　　　thinking
　　x Argumentation; Deduction (Logic); Dialectics;
　　　Fallacies; Induction (Logic)
　　xx **Intellect; Philosophy; Reasoning; Science—**
　　　Methodology; Thought and thinking
Logic, Symbolic and mathematical　511.3
　　See also **Algebra, Boolean; Set theory**
　　xx **Mathematics; Set theory**
Long distance running.　*See* **Marathon running**
Long distance swimming.　*See* **Marathon swimming**
Long life.　*See* **Longevity**

Long-term care facilities 362.1

  See also **Nursing homes**

  x Extended care facilities

  xx **Hospitals; Medical care**

Longevity 613

  See also **Aging; Middle age; Old age**

  x Life expectancy; Life span prolongation; Long
      life

  xx **Death; Health; Life (Biology); Middle age;
      Old age**

Longitude 526; 527

  See also **Time**

  x Degrees of latitude and longitude

  xx **Earth; Geodesy; Nautical astronomy**

Looking glasses. *See* **Mirrors**

Looms 677; 746

  xx **Weaving**

Loran 621.3841

  xx **Navigation**

Lord's Day. *See* **Sabbath**

Lord's prayer 226; 242

  xx **Jesus Christ—Prayers**

Lord's Supper 232.9; 264

  See also **Mass**

  x Communion; Ecclesiastical rites and ceremo-
      nies; Eucharist; Jesus Christ—Last Supper;
      Last Supper

  xx **Jesus Christ; Mass; Sacraments**

Losing things. *See* **Lost and found possessions**

Lost and found possessions E; Fic

  x Finding things; Losing things; Lost pets;
      Possesions, Lost and found

Lost children. *See* **Missing children**

Lost pets. *See* **Lost and found possessions**

Lotteries 336.1

  xx **Gambling**

Loud speakers. *See* **Intercommunication systems**

Louisiana Purchase 973.4; 976.3

  xx **United States—History—1783-1809**

Love 152.4; 306.7

  See also **Dating (Social customs); Friendship;
      Marriage**

  x Affection

  xx **Dating (Social customs); Emotions; Friend-
      ship; Human behavior**

**Love Canal Chemical Waste Landfill (Niagara Falls,
      N.Y.) 363.7**

  xx **Hazardous waste sites; Landfills**

Love poetry 808.1; 811; etc.

  x Poetry of love

  xx **Poetry**

Love stories 808.3

  x Romance novels; Romances (Love stories);
      Romantic fiction; Romantic stories

  xx **Fiction**

Love stories—Technique 808.3

  x Technique

  xx **Authorship**

Love (Theology) 231

  xx **Charity; Theology, Doctrinal**

Low income housing. *See* **Public housing**
Low sodium diet. *See* **Salt free diet**
Low temperature biology. *See* **Cryobiology**
Low temperatures 536; 621.5
>   *See also* **Cold; Cryobiology**
>   *x* Cryogenics; Temperatures, Low
>   *xx* **Cold; Temperature**

Loyalists, American. *See* **American Loyalists**
Loyalty 172
>   *See also* **Patriotism**
>   *x* Faithfulness
>   *xx* **Ethics; Human behavior**

Loyalty oaths. *See* **Internal security**
Lubrication and lubricants 621.8
>   *See also* **Bearings (Machinery); Oils and fats**
>   *x* Grease
>   *xx* **Bearings (Machinery); Machinery; Oils and fats**

Lullabies 784.6
>   *x* Cradle songs; Slumber songs
>   *xx* **Bedtime; Children's poetry; Children's songs; Songs**

Lumber and lumbering 634.9; 674
>   Use for materials on cut timber, its preparation for construction and building purposes, and uses of various kinds of lumber.
>   *x* Logging; Timber
>   *xx* **Forest products; Forests and forestry; Trees; Wood**

Luminescence. *See* **Phosphorescence**
Luminescence, Animal. *See* **Bioluminescence**
Lunar bases 629.45
>   *x* Moon bases

Lunar cars. *See* **Moon cars**
Lunar eclipses. *See* **Eclipses, Lunar**
Lunar excursion module 629.45
>   *x* LEM; Lunar module
>   *xx* **Space vehicles**

Lunar expeditions. *See* **Space flight to the moon**
Lunar exploration. *See* **Moon—Exploration**
Lunar geology 559.9
>   *See also* **Lunar petrology; Lunar soil**
>   *x* Geology, Lunar; Geology—Moon; Moon—Geology
>   *xx* **Astrogeology**

Lunar module. *See* **Lunar excursion module**
Lunar petrology 552; 552.0999
>   *x* Lunar rocks; Moon rocks; Rocks, Moon
>   *xx* **Lunar geology; Petrology**

Lunar photography 778.3
>   *See also* **Moon—Photographs**
>   *x* Moon photography
>   *xx* **Space photography**

Lunar probes 629.43
>   *See also* names of space projects, e.g. **Mariner project;** etc.
>   *x* Moon probes
>   *xx* **Space probes**

Lunar rocks. *See* **Lunar petrology**
Lunar rover vehicles. *See* **Moon cars**

Lunar soil   631.4
See also **Moon—Surface**
x Moon soil; Soils, Lunar
xx **Lunar geology; Moon—Surface**
Lunar surface.   See **Moon—Surface**
Lunar surface radio communication.   See **Radio in astronautics**
Lunar surface vehicles.   See **Moon cars**
Lunch rooms.   See **Restaurants, bars, etc.**
Luncheons   642
xx **Caterers and catering; Cookery; Entertaining; Menus**
Lungs   611; 612
See also **Respiration**
Lungs—Diseases   616.2
See also names of lung diseases, e.g. **Pneumonia; Tuberculosis;** etc.
Lying.   See **Truthfulness and falsehood**
Lymphatic system   612; 616.4
xx **Physiology**
Lynching   364.1
See also **Vigilance committees**
xx **Crime**
Lyricists   784.092; 920
x Songwriters
xx **Poets**
M.I.A.'s.   See **Missing in action**
Maccabbees, Feast of the.   See **Hanukkah**
Machine design.   See **Machinery—Design**
Machine intelligence.   See **Artificial intelligence**
Machine language.   See **Programming languages (Computers)**
Machine readable bibliographic data   025.3
See also names of projects or systems, e.g. **MARC system;** etc.
x Bibliographic data in machine readable form; Cataloging data in machine readable form; Computer stored cataloging data
xx **Cataloging; Information services; Information storage and retrieval systems; Libraries— Automation**
Machine readable catalog system.   See **MARC system**
Machine shop practice   670.42
x Shop practice
Machine shops   670.42
x Shops, Machine
Machine tools   621.9
See also names of machine tools, e.g. **Planing machines;** etc.
xx **Machinery; Milling machines; Tools**
Machine translating.   See **Translating and interpreting**
Machinery   621.8-621.9
See also

Agricultural machinery	**Engines**
Bearings (Machinery)	**Gearing**
Belts and belting	**Hoisting machinery**
Conveying machinery	**Hydraulic machinery**
Electric machinery	**Inventions**

Machinery—*Continued*

Locomotives **Milling machines**
Lubrication and lubricants **Patents**
Machine tools **Power transmission**
Mechanical drawing **Steam engines**
Mechanics **Woodworking machinery**
Metalworking machinery

x Machines

xx **Industrial management; Manufactures; Mechanical engineering; Mechanics; Mills and millwork; Power (Mechanics); Power transmission; Technology; Tools**

Machinery, Automatic. *See* **Automation**

Machinery—Design 621.8

See also **Human engineering; Machinery—Models**

x Machine design

Machinery—Drawing. *See* **Mechanical drawing**

Machinery in industry 338

Use for materials on the social and economic aspects of mechanization in the industrial world, the machine age, etc.

See also **Automation; Labor productivity; Robots, Industrial**

xx **Industry; Labor; Labor productivity; Technology and civilization**

Machinery—Models 621.8-621.9

See also **Airplanes—Models; Automobiles—Models; Locomotives—Models; Motorboats—Models; Railroads—Models; Ships—Models**

x Mechanical models; Models, Mechanical

xx **Machinery—Design**

Machines. *See* **Machinery**

Madonna. *See* **Mary, Blessed Virgin, Saint**

Magazines. *See* **Periodicals**

Magic 793.8

Use for materials dealing with modern ("Parlor") magic, legerdemain, etc., as entertainment. Materials on the supernatural not connected with magic tricks are entered under **Occult sciences.**

See also **Card tricks; Occult sciences; Symbolism of numbers; Tricks**

x Conjuring; Legerdemain; Magic tricks; Sleight of hand

xx **Amusements; Hallucinations and illusions; Occult sciences; Tricks**

Magic tricks. *See* **Magic**

Magna Carta 342; 942.03

Magnet schools 370.19; 371.9

Use for materials on schools offering special courses not available in the regular school curriculum and designed to attract students without reference to the usual attendance zone rules. Magnet schools are often used as an aid to voluntary school desegregation.

x Schools, Magnet

xx **Public schools; School integration**

Magnet winding. *See* **Electromagnets**

Magnetic needle. *See* **Compass**
Magnetic recorders and recording 621.389; 789.9
>   Use for general materials on audio, computer, and video recording on a magnetizable medium.
>   *See also* **Videotape recorders and recording**
>   *x* Cassette recorders and recording; Recorders, Tape; Tape recorders
>   *xx* **Sound—Recording and reproducing**

Magnetic resonance accelerator. *See* **Cyclotron**
Magnetism 538
>   *See also* **Compass; Electricity; Electromagnetism; Electromagnets; Magnets**
>   *xx* **Electricity; Physics**

Magnets 538
>   *See also* **Electromagnets**
>   *xx* **Magnetism**

Mail-order business 658.8; 659.13
>   *xx* **Advertising; Business; Direct selling; Selling**

Mail service. *See* **Postal service**
Mainstreaming in education 371.9
>   *See also* **Special education**
>   *xx* **Education; Exceptional children; Handicapped children; Special education**

Maintenance and repair. *See* **Buildings—Maintenance and repair;** and names of machines, instruments, etc. with the subdivision *Maintenance and repair,* e.g. **Automobiles—Maintenace and repair;** etc.

Maize. *See* **Corn**
Make-believe playmates. *See* **Imaginary playmates**
Makeup (Cosmetics). *See* **Cosmetics**
Makeup, Theatrical 791.43; 791.45; 792
>   *x* Theatrical makeup
>   *xx* **Amateur theater; Costume**

Making-choices stories. *See* **Plot-your-own stories**
Maladjusted children. *See* **Emotionally disturbed children**
Maladjustment (Psychology). *See* **Adjustment (Psychology)**
Malaria 616.9
>   *x* Ague
>   *xx* **Fever**

Male climacteric. *See* **Climacteric, Male**
Male role. *See* **Sex role**
Malfeasance in office. *See* **Misconduct in office**
Malignant tumors. *See* **Cancer**
Malls, Shopping. *See* **Shopping centers and malls**
Malnutrition 616.3
>   *See also* **Starvation**
>   *xx* **Nutrition; Starvation**

Malpractice 346.03
>   *See also* names of professional people with the subdivision *Malpractice,* e.g. **Physicians—Malpractice;** etc.
>   *x* Liability, Professional; Professional liability; Professions—Tort liability; Tort liability of professions
>   *xx* **Liability (Law)**

Malpractice insurance. *See* **Insurance, Malpractice**

Mammals 599

  See also groups of mammals, e.g. **Carnivores;**
      Mammals, Marine; Primates; etc.; also
      names of mammals, e.g. **Bats; Elephants;**
      etc.

  xx **Animals; Vertebrates; Zoology**

Mammals, Fossil 569

  See also names of extinct animals, e.g.
      Mastodon; etc.

  x Fossil mammals

  xx **Fossils**

Mammals, Marine 599.5

  See also names of marine mammals, e.g. **Seals**
      (Animals); Whales; etc.

  x Marine mammals

  xx **Mammals; Marine animals**

Man 572; 573

  Use this heading only in its generic meaning.

  See also **Anthropology; Anthropometry; Cre-**
      ation; Ethnology; Heredity

  x Human race

  xx **Anthropology; Creation; History**

Man—Antiquity. *See* **Man—Origin**

Man—Color 572; 573

  xx **Color**

Man in space. *See* **Space flight**

Man—Influence of environment 304.2; 573

  See also **Environmental health; Survival skills;**
      Weightlessness

  x Acclimatization; Altitude, Influence of

  xx **Adaptation (Biology); Anthropogeography;**
      Evolution; Human ecology

Man—Influence on nature 304.2; 574.5

  See also **Environment—Government policy; Pol-**
      lution

  x Earth, Effect of man on; Nature, Effect of man
      on

  xx **Environment—Government policy; Human**
      ecology

Man, Nonliterate 306

  x Nonliterate man; Preliterate man; Primitive
      man

  xx **Ethnology; Society, Nonliterate folk**

Man—Origin 573.2

  See also **Anatomy, Comparative; Evolution; Man,**
      Prehistoric

  x Antiquity of man; Man—Antiquity; Origin of
      man

  xx **Anatomy, Comparative; Evolution; Man, Pre-**
      historic; Physical anthropology; Religion
      and science

Man power. *See* **Human resources**

Man, Prehistoric 572; 573

  See also **Bronze Age; Cave dwellers; Man—**
      Origin; also names of prehistoric people, e.g.
      Cro-Magnons; etc.; and names of countries,
      cities, etc. with the subdivision *Antiquities,*
      e.g. **United States—Antiquities;** etc.

  x Prehistoric man

  xx **Antiquities; Archeology; Civilization, Ancient;**

Man, Prehistoric—*Continued*
      Ethnology; Man—Origin; Stone Age
Man (Theology) 218; 233
    See also **Soul**
    xx **Theology**
Management 658
    Use for general materials on the principles of
      management in factories, industries, shops,
      etc. Materials on the application of such
      principles are entered under the specific
      headings such as those listed below. Add
      others as needed.
    See also

Crisis management	**Office management**
Efficiency, Industrial	**Personnel management**
Factory management	**Sales management**
Farm management	**Telecommuting**
Industrial management	**Time management**
Inventory control	

    also subjects with the subdivision *Management,*
      e.g. **Natural resources—Management;** etc.;
      types of industries, industrial plants and
      processes, names of government agencies,
      special activities, etc.; and types of institu-
      tions and names of individual institutions
      with the subdivision *Administration,* e.g.
      Libraries—Administration; Schools—
      Administration; etc.
    x Administration; Management, Scientific; Or-
      ganization and management; Scientific
      management
Management—Employee participation 331.89; 658.3
    See also **Collective bargaining**
    x Consultative management; Employees' repre-
      sentation in management; Industrial coun-
      cils; Labor participation in management;
      Participative management; Workers' partic-
      ipation in management; Workshop councils
    xx **Collective bargaining; Factory management;**
      Industrial relations; Personnel management
Management, Industrial. *See* **Industrial manage-**
    ment
Management, Sales. *See* **Sales management**
Management, Scientific. *See* **Management**
Managers. *See* **Supervisors**
Mandates 321
    x Government, Mandatory; League of Na-
      tions—Mandatory system
    xx **International law; International organization;**
      International relations; World War, 1914-
      1918—Territorial questions
Manikins (Fashion models). *See* **Models, Fashion**
Manned space flight. *See* **Space flight**
Manned space flight—Rescue work. *See* **Space res-**
    cue operations
Manned undersea research stations. *See* **Undersea**
    research stations
Mannequins (Fashion models). *See* **Models, Fash-**
    ion
Manners. *See* **Courtesy; Etiquette**

Manners and customs 390

See also

Bohemianism	Folklore
Caste	Funeral rites and ceremo-
Chivalry	nies
Clothing and dress	Holidays
Costume	Marriage customs and
Courts and courtiers	rites
Dating (Social customs)	Popular culture
Dueling	Rites and ceremonies
Etiquette	Social classes
Festivals	Travel

also names of ethnic groups, countries, cities, etc. with the subdivision *Social life and customs,* e.g. **Indians of North America—Social life and customs; Jews—Social life and customs; United States—Social life and customs;** etc.

x Ceremonies; Customs, Social; Folkways; Social customs; Social life and customs; Traditions

xx **Civilization; Ethnology; Etiquette; Rites and ceremonies**

Manpower. *See* **Human resources**

Manpower policy. *See* **Human resources policy**

Manslaughter. *See* **Murder**

Manual training. *See* **Industrial arts education**

Manual workers. *See* **Labor**

Manufactures 338.4; 670

See also

Brand name products	Patents
Generic products	Prices
Machinery	Trademarks
Mills and millwork	Waste products

also names of articles manufactured, e.g. **Furniture;** etc.; and names of industries, e.g. **Paper making and trade;** etc.; also names of countries, cities, etc. with the subdivision *Industries,* e.g. **Chicago (Ill.)—Industries;** etc.

x Consumer goods; Consumer products

xx **Business; Commercial products; Industry; Technology**

Manufactures—Defects. *See* **Product recall**

Manufactures recall. *See* **Product recall**

Manufacturing in space. *See* **Space industrialization**

Manures. *See* **Fertilizers and manures**

Manuscripts 091

See also **Autographs; Charters; Illumination of books and manuscripts**

xx **Archives; Autographs; Bibliography; Books; Charters**

Manuscripts, Illuminated. *See* **Illumination of books and manuscripts**

Manuscripts—Prices. *See* **Books—Prices**

Map drawing 526.8

See also **Topographical drawing**

x Cartography; Chartography; Plans

xx **Topographical drawing**

Maple sugar 641.3; 664
  xx **Sugar**
Maps 912
  Use for general materials about maps and their
    history. Materials on the methods of map
    making and the mapping of areas are en-
    tered under **Map drawing.** Geographical at-
    lases of world coverage are entered under
    Atlases.
  See also **Atlases; Automobiles—Road guides;**
    Charts; also types of maps, e.g. **Road maps;**
    etc.; also subjects with the subdivision
    Maps, e.g. **Geology—Maps;** etc.; and
    names of countries, cities, etc. with the sub-
    division *Maps,* e.g. **United States—Maps;**
    Chicago (Ill.)—Maps; etc.
  x Cartography; Chartography; Plans
  xx **Charts; Geography**
Maps, Historical. *See* **Atlases, Historical**
Maps, Military. *See* **Military geography**
Maps, Road. *See* **Road maps**
Marathon running 796.4
  x Long distance running
  xx **Running**
Marathon swimming 797.2
  x Long distance swimming
  xx **Swimming**
Marble 553.5
  xx **Petrology; Stone**
MARC project. *See* **MARC system**
MARC system 025
  x Machine readable catalog system; MARC
    project; Project MARC
  xx **Bibliographic control; Libraries—Automation;**
    Machine readable bibliographic data
Marches (Demonstrations). *See* **Protests, demon-**
    strations, etc.
Marches (Exercises). *See* **Drill (Nonmilitary)**
Marches for Black civil rights—United States. *See*
    Blacks—Civil rights
Marches (Music) 785.1
  xx **Military music**
Margarine 641.3; 664
  x Butter, Artificial; Oleomargarine
  xx **Butter**
Mariculture. *See* **Aquaculture**
Marinas 387.1
  See also **Docks**
  x Yacht basins
  xx **Boats and boating; Harbors; Yachts and**
    yachting
Marine animals 591.92
  See also **Corals; Fishes; Mammals, Marine**
  x Animals, Aquatic; Animals, Marine; Animals,
    Sea; Aquatic animals; Marine fauna; Ma-
    rine zoology; Sea animals; Water animals
  xx **Animals; Freshwater animals; Marine biology;**
    Wildlife
Marine aquaculture. *See* **Aquaculture**

Marine aquariums 639.3

> *See also* names of specific marine aquariums,
> e.g. **Marineland (Fla.);** etc.

> *x* Aquariums, Saltwater; Oceanariums; Salt wa-
> ter aquariums; Sea water aquariums

> *xx* **Aquariums**

Marine architecture. *See* **Naval architecture; Shipbuilding**

Marine biology 574.92

> *See also* **Freshwater biology; Marine animals;
> Marine ecology; Marine plants; Marine re-
> sources; Ocean bottom; Photography, Sub-
> marine**

> *x* Biological oceanography; Biology, Marine;
> Ocean life

> *xx* **Biology; Freshwater biology; Natural history;
> Oceanography; Underwater exploration**

Marine disasters. *See* **Shipwrecks**

Marine ecology 574.5

> *x* Biological oceanography; Ecology, Marine

> *xx* **Ecology; Marine biology**

Marine engineering 623.8

> Use for materials on engineering as applied to
> ships and their machinery.

> *x* Naval engineering

> *xx* **Civil engineering; Engineering; Mechanical
> engineering; Naval architecture; Naval art
> and science; Steam navigation**

Marine engines 623.8

> *xx* **Engines; Shipbuilding; Steam engines**

Marine fauna. *See* **Marine animals**

Marine flora. *See* **Marine plants**

Marine geology. *See* **Submarine geology**

Marine insurance. *See* **Insurance, Marine**

Marine law. *See* **Maritime law**

Marine mammals. *See* **Mammals, Marine**

Marine mineral resources 553

> *See also* **Ocean mining**

> *x* Mineral resources, Marine; Ocean mineral re-
> sources

> *xx* **Marine resources; Mines and mineral re-
> sources; Ocean bottom; Ocean energy re-
> sources**

Marine painting 758

> *x* Sea in art; Seascapes; Ships in art

> *xx* **Painting**

Marine plants 581.92

> *See also* **Algae; Freshwater plants**

> *x* Aquatic plants; Marine flora; Water plants

> *xx* **Freshwater plants; Marine biology**

Marine pollution 363.7

> *See also* types of water pollution, e.g. **Oil pollu-
> tion of rivers, harbors, etc.; Oil spills;** etc.

> *x* Ocean pollution; Offshore water pollution;
> Sea pollution

> *xx* **Pollution**

Marine resources 333.91; 574.92

> *See also* **Aquaculture; Fisheries; Marine mineral
> resources; Ocean energy resources; Ocean
> engineering; Seafood**

Marine resources—*Continued*
    x Ocean—Economic aspects; Ocean resources;
        Resources, Marine; Sea resources
    xx **Commercial products; Marine biology; Natu-**
        ral resources; Oceanography
Marine transportation. *See* **Shipping**
Marine zoology. *See* **Marine animals**
Marineland (Fla.) 639.3
    xx **Marine aquariums**
Mariner project 629.43
    x Project Mariner
    xx **Lunar probes; Space probes**
Mariners. *See* **Sailors**
Mariner's compass. *See* **Compass**
Marionettes. *See* **Puppets and puppet plays**
Marital counseling. *See* **Marriage counseling**
Marital infidelity. *See* **Adultery**
Maritime discoveries. *See* **Discoveries (in geogra-**
       phy)
Maritime law   341; 343
    See also **Commercial law; Freight and freightage;**
        Insurance, Marine; Merchant marine; Pi-
        rates; Salvage; Territorial waters
    x Law, Maritime; Law of the sea; Marine law;
        Merchant marine—Law and legislation;
        Naval law; Navigation—Law and legisla-
        tion; Sea laws
    xx **Commercial law; International law; Law;**
        Shipping; Territorial waters
Market gardening. *See* **Vegetable gardening**
Market surveys 658.8
    See also **Public opinion polls**
    xx **Public opinion polls**
Marketing   380.1; 658.8
    Use for materials on the principles and methods
        involved in the distribution of merchandise
        from producer to consumer.
    See also **Direct selling; Sales management; Tele-**
        marketing; also subjects with the subdivi-
        sion *Marketing,* e.g. **Farm produce—**
        Marketing; etc.
    x Distribution (Economics); Merchandising
    xx **Advertising; Business; Industrial management;**
        Selling
Marketing (Home economics). *See* **Shopping**
Marketing of farm produce. *See* **Farm produce—**
       Marketing
Markets (May subdiv. geog.) **380.1; 658.8**
    See also **Fairs**
    xx **Business; Cities and towns; Commerce; Fairs;**
        Food
Marking (Students). *See* **Grading and marking**
       (Students)
Marks on plate. *See* **Hallmarks**
Marks, Potters'. *See* **Pottery—Marks**
Marriage   173; 306.8
    See also

Celibacy	**Domestic relations**
Childlessness	**Family**
Divorce	**Home**

Marriage—*Continued*

    Intermarriage   **Married women**
    Marriage contracts   **Remarriage**
    Marriage counseling   **Weddings**

    x Matrimony
    xx **Divorce; Domestic relations; Family; Home;**
        Love; Sacraments

Marriage—Annulment 306.8
    See also **Divorce**
    x Annulment of marriage
    xx **Divorce**

Marriage contracts 306.8; 346.01
    x Antenuptial contracts; Premarital contracts;
        Prenuptial contracts
    xx **Marriage**

Marriage counseling 362.8
    See also **Divorce mediation**
    x Marital counseling; Premarital counseling
    xx **Counseling; Family life education; Marriage**

Marriage customs and rites 392
    x Bridal customs
    xx **Manners and customs; Rites and ceremonies;**
        Weddings

Marriage, Mixed. *See* **Intermarriage**

Marriage, Open ended. *See* **Unmarried couples**

Marriage registers. *See* **Registers of births, etc.**

Marriage statistics. *See* **Vital statistics**

Married women 305.4; 306.8
    See also **Widows; Wife abuse**
    x Wives
    xx **Family; Marriage; Women**

Mars (Planet) 523.4
    See also **Mars probes**

Mars (Planet)—Exploration 629.43

Mars (Planet)—Geology 559.9
    xx **Astrogeology**

Mars (Planet)—Photographs 778.3

Mars probes 629.43
    x Martian probes
    xx **Mars (Planet); Space probes**

Marshall Plan. *See* **Reconstruction (1939-1951)**

Marshes 333.91; 551.4
    See also **Swamp animals**
    x Bogs; Swamps
    xx **Drainage; Reclamation of land**

Martial arts 796.8
    See also **Archery; Dueling; Self-defense**
    xx **Athletics; Self-defense**

Martian probes. *See* **Mars probes**

Martyrs 272.092; 920
    See also **Persecution; Saints**
    xx **Church history; Heroes and heroines; Persecu-**
        tion; Saints

Marxism. *See* **Communism; Socialism**

Mary, Blessed Virgin, Saint 232.91
    x Madonna; Virgin Mary

Mary, Blessed Virgin, Saint—Art 704.9
    See also **Jesus Christ—Art**
    xx **Christian art and symbolism; Jesus Christ—**
        Art

Masculine psychology.   *See* **Men—Psychology**
Masers 621.381
    x Microwave amplification by stimulated emission of radiation
    xx **Amplifiers (Electronics); Electromagnetism; Microwaves**
Masers, Optical.   *See* **Lasers**
Masks (Facial) 391
Masks (Plays) 808.82; 809.2; etc.
    x Masques (Plays)
    xx **Drama; Pageants; Theater**
Masks (Sculpture) 731
    x Death masks
    xx **Sculpture**
Masonic orders.   *See* **Freemasons**
Masonry 693
    See also

Bricklaying	**Foundations**
Bridges	**Plaster and plastering**
Cement	**Stonecutting**
Concrete	**Walls**

    xx **Bricklaying; Building; Civil engineering; Foundations; Stone; Walls**
Masons (Secret order).   *See* **Freemasons**
Masques (Plays).   *See* **Masks (Plays)**
Mass 264
    See also **Lord's Supper**
    xx **Liturgies; Lord's Supper**
Mass communication.   *See* **Communication; Mass media; Telecommunication**
Mass feeding.   *See* **Food service**
Mass media 302.2
    See also **Motion pictures; Newspapers; Periodicals; Popular culture; Radio broadcasting; Television broadcasting**
    x Mass communication; Media
    xx **Communication**
Mass psychology.   *See* **Social psychology**
Mass spectra.   *See* **Mass spectrometry**
Mass spectrometry 543; 547.3
    x Mass spectra; Mass spectrum analysis
    xx **Spectrum analysis**
Mass spectrum analysis.   *See* **Mass spectrometry**
Mass transit.   *See* **Local transit**
Massacres (May subdiv. geog.) **179; 900**
    See also names of individual massacres, e.g. **Saint Bartholomew's Day, Massacre of, 1572;** etc.
    xx **Atrocities; History; Persecution**
Massage 615.8
    See also **Acupressure; Chiropractic; Electrotherapeutics; Osteopathy**
    xx **Medicine—Practice; Osteopathy; Physical therapy**
Mastodon 569
    xx **Extinct animals; Mammals, Fossil**
Materia medica 615
    See also **Anesthetics; Drugs; Pharmacology; Pharmacy; Poisons and poisoning; Therapeutics;** also names of classes of drugs and

Materia medica—*Continued*
    individual drugs, e.g. **Narcotics;** etc.
  x Herbals; Pharmacopoeias
  xx **Chemistry, Medical and pharmaceutical;**
     Drugs; Medicine; Pharmacy; Therapeutics

Materialism 146
  See also **Idealism; Realism**
  xx **Idealism; Philosophy; Positivism; Realism**

Materials 620.1
  Use for comprehensive discussions on materials
    of enginnering and industry.
  See also **Strength of materials;** also types of ma-
    terials, e.g. **Building materials; Hazardous**
    substances; Raw materials; etc.
  x Engineering materials; Industrial materials;
    Strategic materials

Materials handling 380.5; 658.7
  See also **Conveying machinery; Freight and**
    freightage; Trucks
  x Handling of materials; Mechanical handling
  xx **Industrial management; Trucks**

Materials, Strength of. *See* **Strength of materials**

Maternity. *See* **Mothers**

Mathematical analysis 515
  See also **Algebra; Algebras, Linear; Calculus;**
    Graph theory; Programming (Computers)
  x Analysis (Mathematics)

Mathematical drawing. *See* **Geometrical drawing;**
  Mechanical drawing

Mathematical models 511
  See also **Fractals; Game theory; Programming**
    (Computers); System analysis; also subjects
    with the subdivision *Mathematical models,*
    e.g. **Pollution—Mathematical models;** etc.
  x Models, Mathematical

Mathematical recreations 793.7
  See also **Number games**
  x Recreations, Mathematical
  xx **Amusements; Puzzles; Scientific recreations**

Mathematical sets. *See* **Set theory**

Mathematicians 510.92; 920
  xx **Scientists**

Mathematics 510
  See also

Algebra	**Geometry**
Arithmetic	**Group theory**
Binary system (Mathemat-	**Logic, Symbolic and math-**
ics)	**ematical**
Biomathematics	**Measurement**
Calculus	**Number theory**
Dynamics	**Numerals**
Fourth dimension	**Numeration**
Fractions	**Set theory**
Game theory	**Trigonometry**

  also subjects with the subdivision *Mathematics,*
    e.g. **Astronomy—Mathematics;** etc.

  xx **Science**

Mathematics—Computer assisted instruction

  xx **Computer assisted instruction**

Mathematics—Tables, etc. 510.21
  See also **Logarithms; Trigonometry—Tables, etc.**
  x Ready reckoners
Matrimony. *See* **Marriage**
Matter 530; 530.4
  xx **Dynamics; Physics**
Mausoleums. *See* **Tombs**
Maxims. *See* **Proverbs**
Mayas 970.004; 972
  xx **Indians of Central America; Indians of Mexico**
Meal planning. *See* **Menus; Nutrition**
Meals for astronauts. *See* **Astronauts—Food**
Meals for school children. *See* **School children—Food**
Meals on wheels programs 363.8
  Use for materials on programs that deliver meals to the homebound.
  x Home delivered meals
  xx **Food relief**
Measurement 389; 530.8
  See also **Geodesy; Measuring instruments; Surveying; Volume (Cubic content); Weights and measures;** also subjects with the subdivision *Measurement,* e.g.
    Air—Pollution—Measurement; etc.
  x Mensuration; Metrology
  xx **Mathematics; Weights and measures**
Measurements, Electric. *See* **Electric measurements**
Measures. *See* **Weights and measures**
Measuring instruments 389; 681
  See also **Slide rule**
  x Instruments, Measuring
  xx **Measurement; Weights and measures**
Meat 641.3; 664
  See also names of meat, e.g. **Beef;** etc.
  xx **Food**
Meat-eating animals. *See* **Carnivores**
Meat industry and trade 338.1
  See also **Cold storage; Meat inspection**
  x Packing industry; Stockyards
  xx **Food supply**
Meat inspection 363.1
  x Inspection of meat
  xx **Food adulteration and inspection; Meat industry and trade; Public health**
Mechanic arts. *See* **Industrial arts**
Mechanical brains. *See* **Computers; Cybernetics**
Mechanical drawing 604.2
  See also **Architectural drawing; Geometrical drawing; Graphic methods; Lettering**
  x Drafting, Mechanical; Engineering drawing; Industrial drawing; Machinery—Drawing; Mathematical drawing; Plans; Structural drafting
  xx **Drawing; Engineering; Geometrical drawing; Machinery; Pattern making**
Mechanical engineering 620.1
  See note under **Mechanics, Applied.**

Mechanical engineering—*Continued*
    See also

Electric engineering	**Power (Mechanics)**
Engines	**Power transmission**
Machinery	**Robotics**
Marine engineering	**Steam engineering**
Mechanical movements	

    xx **Civil engineering; Steam engineering**
Mechanical handling. *See* **Materials handling**
Mechanical models. *See* **Machinery—Models**
Mechanical movements 531
    See also **Gearing; Robots**
    x Mechanisms (Machinery)
    xx **Gearing; Kinematics; Mechanical engineering;**
        Mechanics; Motion
Mechanical musical instruments. *See* **Musical instruments, Mechanical**
Mechanical painting. *See* **Painting, Industrial**
Mechanical speech recognition. *See* **Automatic speech recognition**
Mechanical stokers. *See* **Stokers, Mechanical**
Mechanical translating. *See* **Translating and interpreting**
Mechanics 531
    See also

Dynamics	**Mechanical movements**
Engineering	**Motion**
Fluid mechanics	**Power (Mechanics)**
Force and energy	**Statics**
Gases	**Steam engines**
Hydraulics	**Strains and stresses**
Hydrodynamics	**Strength of materials**
Hydrostatics	**Vibration**
Kinematics	**Viscosity**
Liquids	**Wave mechanics**
Machinery	

    xx **Engineering; Force and energy; Kinematics;**
        Machinery; Motion; Physics
Mechanics, Applied 621
    Use for materials on the application of the principles of mechanics to engineering structure other than machinery. Materials on the application of the principles of mechanics to the design, construction and operation of machinery are entered under **Mechanical engineering.**
    x Applied mechanics
Mechanics (Persons) 920
Mechanisms (Machinery). *See* **Mechanical movements**
Medallions. *See* **Medals**
Medals 355.1; 737
    See also **Decorations of honor; Insignia; Numismatics;** also names of military services and other appropriate subjects with the subdivision *Medals, badges, decorations, etc.,* e.g. **United States. Army—Medals, badges, decorations, etc.; United States. Navy—Medals, badges, decorations, etc.;** etc.; and names of specific medals

Medals—*Continued*
    x Badges of honor; Medallions
    xx **Decorations of honor; Insignia; Numismatics**
Media. *See* **Mass media**
Media centers (Education). *See* **Instructional materials centers**
Mediation. *See* **Arbitration and award**
Mediation, Divorce. *See* **Divorce mediation**
Mediation, Industrial. *See* **Arbitration, Industrial**
Mediation, International. *See* **Arbitration, International**
Medicaid 368.4
    x Medical care for the poor; Medical care, State
    xx **Poor—Medical care**
Medical botany. *See* **Botany, Medical**
Medical care 362.1
    See also **Charities, Medical; Health maintenance organizations; Home care services; Long-term care facilities; Occupational health services; Self-care, Health; Sports medicine;** also classes of peoples with the subdivision *Medical care,* e.g. **Elderly—Medical care;** etc.
    x Health care; Medical service
    xx **Public health**
Medical care—Costs 362.1
    x Cost of medical care; Costs; Medical service, Cost of; Medicine—Cost of medical care
    xx **Medical economics**
Medical care for the elderly. *See* **Elderly—Medical care; Medicare**
Medical care for the poor. *See* **Medicaid; Poor—Medical care**
Medical care—Moral and religious aspects. *See* **Medical ethics**
Medical care, Prepaid. *See* **Insurance, Health**
Medical care—Social aspects. *See* **Social medicine**
Medical care, State. *See* **Medicaid; Medicare**
Medical centers 362.1
    See also **Hospitals; Medicine—Study and teaching**
    xx **Hospitals**
Medical charities. *See* **Charities, Medical**
Medical chemistry. *See* **Chemistry, Medical and pharmaceutical**
Medical colleges. *See* **Medicine—Study and teaching**
Medical economics 338.4
    Use for comprehensive materials on the economic aspects of medical service from the point of view of both the practitioner and the public. Materials on special aspects of medical economics are entered under specific headings, e.g. **Medical care—Costs;** etc.
    See also **Medical care—Costs**
    x Economics, Medical
Medical education. *See* **Medicine—Study and teaching**
Medical electricity. *See* **Electrotherapeutics**

Medical entomology. *See* **Insects as carriers of disease**

Medical ethics 174
    See also **Euthanasia; Physicians—Malpractice; Social medicine**
    x Ethics, Medical; Medical care—Moral and religious aspects; Medicine—Moral and religious aspects
    xx **Bioethics; Professional ethics; Social medicine**
Medical folklore. *See* **Folk medicine**

Medical genetics 611; 616
    See also **Genetic counseling;** also names of diseases with the subdivision *Genetic aspects,* e.g. **Cancer—Genetic aspects;** etc.
    x Clinical genetics; Congenital diseases; Hereditary diseases; Heredity of diseases
    xx **Genetics; Pathology**

Medical jurisprudence 614
    Use for materials dealing with the application of medical knowledge to questions of law. Materials that include laws, or discussion of those laws which affect medicine and the medical profession, are entered under **Medicine—Law and legislation.**
    See also **Medicine—Law and legislation; Murder; Poisons and poisoning; Suicide;** also subjects with the subdivision *Jurisprudence,* e.g. **Mental illness—Jurisprudence;** etc.
    x Forensic medicine; Jurisprudence, Medical; Legal medicine; Medicine, Legal
    xx **Criminal investigation; Criminal law; Law; Medicine—Law and legislation; Medicine, State**

Medical law and legislation. *See* **Medicine—Law and legislation**

Medical malpractice. *See* names of groups of people in the medical field with the subdivision *Malpractice,* e.g. **Physicians—Malpractice;** etc.

Medical missions. *See* **Missions, Medical**
Medical photography. *See* **Photography, Medical**
Medical profession. *See* **Medicine; Physicians; Surgeons**
Medical research. *See* **Medicine—Research**
Medical self-care. *See* **Self-care, Health**
Medical service. *See* **Medical care**
Medical service, Cost of. *See* **Medical care—Costs**
Medical service, Prepaid. *See* **Insurance, Health**
Medical sociology. *See* **Social medicine**

Medical technologists 610.69
    xx **Allied health personnel**

Medical technology 610.28
    xx **Medicine**

Medical transplantation. *See* **Transplantation of organs, tissues, etc.**

Medicare 368.4
    x Medical care for the elderly; Medical care, State
    xx **Elderly—Medical care**

Medicinal plants. *See* **Botany, Medical**

Medicine 610
    All types of medicine are not included in this list but are to be added as needed.

Medicine—*Continued*

See also

Acupuncture
Alternative medicine
Anatomy
Aviation medicine
Bacteriology
Botany, Medical
Chemistry, Medical and pharmaceutical
Chiropractic
Diseases
Emergency medicine
Health
Health resorts, spas, etc.
Holistic medicine
Homeopathy
Hospitals
Hygiene
Materia medica
Medical technology
Mind and body
Missions, Medical
Nursing
Osteopathy
Pathology
Pharmacology
Pharmacy
Physiology
Quacks and quackery
Self-care, Health
Sports medicine
Submarine medicine
Surgery
Tropical medicine

also headings beginning with the word **Medical**
x Medical profession
xx **Life sciences; Pathology; Therapeutics**

Medicine and religion 615.8
See also **Christian Science; Mental healing; Spiritual healing**
x Religion and medicine

Medicine, Atomic. *See* **Nuclear medicine**

Medicine, Aviation. *See* **Aviation medicine**

Medicine—Biography 610.69; 920

Medicine—Cost of medical care. *See* **Medical care—Costs**

Medicine, Dental. *See* **Dentistry; Teeth—Diseases**

Medicine—Law and legislation 344
See note under **Medical jurisprudence.**
See also **Medical jurisprudence; Physicians—Malpractice; Right to die**
x Medical law and legislation
xx **Medical jurisprudence**

Medicine, Legal. *See* **Medical jurisprudence**

Medicine, Military 616.9
See also **Armies—Medical care; First aid; Hospitals, Military; Military health;** also names of wars with the subdivision *Medical care,* e.g. **World War, 1939-1945—Medical care;** etc.
x Field hospitals; Military medicine
xx **Armies—Medical care; Military health**

Medicine—Miscellanea 610.2
x Miscellanea
xx **Curiosities and wonders**

Medicine—Moral and religious aspects. *See* **Medical ethics**

Medicine, Nuclear. *See* **Nuclear medicine**

Medicine, Pediatric. *See* **Children—Diseases**

Medicine—Physiological effect. *See* **Pharmacology**

Medicine, Popular 616.02
Use for medical books written for the layman.
See also **Folk medicine**

Medicine—Practice 616
> *See also*
> | | |
> |---|---|
> | **Childbirth** | **Massage** |
> | **Children—Diseases** | **Nursing** |
> | **Communicable diseases** | **Osteopathy** |
> | **Diagnosis** | **Therapeutics** |
> | **Homeopathy** | |
>
> also names of diseases and groups of diseases, e.g. **Fever; Smallpox; Nervous system— Diseases;** etc.
>
> *xx* **Diseases**

Medicine, Preventive 616
> *See also* **Health; Hygiene; Immunity; Pathology;** also names of diseases with the subdivision *Prevention,* e.g.
> > **Heart—Diseases—Prevention;** etc.
>
> *x* Diseases—Prevention; Preventive medicine
> *xx* **Pathology; Public health**

Medicine, Psychosomatic 616.08
> *x* Psychosomatic medicine
> *xx* **Mind and body; Neuroses; Psychoanalysis; Psychology, Pathological**

Medicine—Research 610.7
> *x* Medical research
> *xx* **Research**

Medicine, Social. *See* **Social medicine**

Medicine—Social aspects. *See* **Social medicine**

Medicine, Socialized. *See* **Medicine, State**

Medicine, State 614
> Use for general materials on the relations of the state to medicine, public health, medical legislation, examinations of physicians by state boards, etc.
>
> *See also* **Charities, Medical; Medical jurisprudence; Public health**
> *x* Medicine, Socialized; National health service; Socialized medicine; State medicine

Medicine—Study and teaching 610.7
> *x* Education, Medical; Medical colleges; Medical education
> *xx* **Medical centers; Professional education; Schools; Vocational education**

Medicine, Submarine. *See* **Submarine medicine**

Medicine, Tropical. *See* **Tropical medicine**

Medicine—United States 610
> *x* United States—Medicine

Medicine, Veterinary. *See* **Veterinary medicine**

Medieval architecture. *See* **Architecture, Medieval**

Medieval art. *See* **Art, Medieval**

Medieval civilization. *See* **Civilization, Medieval**

Medieval history. *See* **Middle Ages—History**

Medieval literature. *See* **Literature, Medieval**

Medieval philosophy. *See* **Philosophy, Medieval**

Meditation 291.4; 296.7
> Use for materials on the act or process of meditating.
>
> *See also* **Transcendental meditation**
> *xx* **Devotional exercises; Spiritual life**

Meditations 242; 291.4; 296.7
> Use as a form heading for actual discourses writ-

Meditations—*Continued*
>ten to express the author's reflections or to
>serve as a guide to contemplation.

 xx **Devotional literature; Prayers**
Meetings, Public.   *See* **Public meetings**
Melancholia.   *See* **Depression, Mental**
Memoirs.   *See* **Autobiographies; Biography**
Memorial Day   394.2
 x Days; Decoration Day; National holidays
 xx **School assembly programs**
Memory   153.1
 See also **Attention; Learning, Psychology of**
 x Mnemonics
 xx **Brain; Educational psychology; Intellect; Psy-
    chology; Psychology; Psychology, Physiological;
    Thought and thinking**
Men   305.3
 See also **Boys; Fathers; Single men; Young men**
Men—Biography   920
 xx **Biography**
Men—Civil rights   305.3
 See also **Men's liberation movement**
 xx **Civil rights; Sex discrimination**
Men—Clothing.   *See* **Men's clothing**
Men—Clubs.   *See* **Men—Societies**
Men—Diseases   614.4; 616
Men—Education   370
 See also **Coeducation**
 x Education of men
 xx **Coeducation**
Men—Employment   331.11
 xx **Discrimination in employment; Labor; Labor
    supply**
Men in business.   *See* **Businessmen**
Men—Psychology   150; 155.3
 x Masculine psychology
Men, Single.   *See* **Single men**
Men—Social conditions   305.3
 See also **Divorce; Men—Societies; Men's libera-
    tion movement**
 xx **Social problems**
Men—Societies   367
 See also **Boys' clubs**
 x Men—Clubs; Men's clubs; Men's organiza-
    tions
 xx **Clubs; Men—Social conditions; Societies**
Mendel's law   575.1
 See also **Genetics; Heredity**
 xx **Breeding; Evolution; Heredity; Variation (Bi-
    ology)**
Mendicancy.   *See* **Begging**
Mendicant orders.   *See* **Dominicans; Franciscans**
Mennonites   289.7
 See also **Amish**
 xx **Baptists**
Menopause   618.1
 x Change of life in women; Climacteric, Female;
    Female climacteric
Men's clothing   646; 687
 x Clothing, Men's; Men—Clothing

Men's clothing—*Continued*
    xx **Clothing and dress**
Men's clubs. *See* **Men—Societies**
Men's liberation movement 323.4
    xx **Men—Civil rights; Men—Social conditions**
Men's organizations. *See* **Men—Societies**
Menstruation 612
    xx **Reproduction**
Mensuration. *See* **Measurement**
Mental arithmetic. *See* **Arithmetic, Mental**
Mental deficiency. *See* **Mental retardation**
Mental depression. *See* **Depression, Mental**
Mental diseases. *See* **Mental illness; Psychology,**
    Pathological
Mental healing 615.8
    Use for materials on psychic or psychological
        means to treat illness. Materials on the use
        of faith, prayer, or religious means to treat
        illness are entered under **Spiritual healing.**
    See also

Christian Science	**Psychotherapy**
Hypnotism	**Spiritual healing**
Mental suggestion	**Subconsciousness**
Mind and body	**Therapeutics, Suggestive**

    x Healing, Mental; Mind cure; Psychic healing
    xx **Christian Science; Medicine and religion;**
        Mental suggestion; Mind and body; Psycho-
        therapy; Spiritual healing; Subconscious-
        ness; Therapeutics, Suggestive
Mental health 362.2
    See also

Burn out (Psychology)	**Occupational therapy**
Mental illness	**Psychology, Pathological**
Mental retardation	**Psychology, Physiological**
Mind and body	**Worry**

    x Health, Mental; Hygiene, Mental; Mental hy
        giene
    xx **Health; Hygiene; Mental illness; Mind and**
        body
Mental hospitals. *See* **Mentally ill—Institutional**
    care; Psychiatric hospitals
Mental hygiene. *See* **Mental health**
Mental illness 362.2; 616.8
    See note under **Psychiatry.**
    See also **Mental health; Mental retardation;** also
        names of specific illnesses
    x Diseases, Mental; Mental diseases; Psychoses
    xx **Diseases; Mental health; Psychiatry; Psychol-**
        ogy, Pathological
Mental illness—Jurisprudence 344
    Use for materials on the legal aspects of mental
        disorders.
    x Insanity
    xx **Medical jurisprudence**
Mental institutions. *See* **Mentally ill—Institutional**
    care
Mental philosophy. *See* **Philosophy; Psychology**
Mental retardation 157; 362.3
    x Mental deficiency
    xx **Mental health; Mental illness**

Mental suggestion 131; 154.7; 615.8
  See also **Brainwashing; Hypnotism; Mental healing; Therapeutics, Suggestive**
  x Autosuggestion; Suggestion, Mental
  xx **Hypnotism; Mental healing; Mind and body; Psychical research; Subconsciousness; Therapeutics, Suggestive**
Mental telepathy. *See* **Telepathy**
Mental tests 153.9; 371.2
  See also **Ability—Testing; Educational tests and measurements**
  x I.Q. tests; Intelligence tests; IQ tests; Objective tests; Psychological tests; Tests
  xx **Child psychology; Educational psychology; Educational tests and measurements; Examinations; Grading and marking (Students); Intellect; Psychology, Physiological**
Mentally depressed. *See* **Depression, Mental**
Mentally deranged. *See* **Mentally ill**
Mentally handicapped 362.2; 362.3
  x Mentally retarded
  xx **Handicapped**
Mentally handicapped children 155.4; 362.2-362.3
  See also **Slow learning children**
  x Children, Retarded; Mentally retarded children; Retarded children
  xx **Child psychiatry; Handicapped children; Mentally ill children; Slow learning children**
Mentally handicapped children—Education 371.92
  xx **Education; Special education**
Mentally ill 616.8
  x Insane; Mentally deranged; Psychotics
  xx **Psychiatry**
Mentally ill children 155.4; 616.8
  See also **Mentally handicapped children**
  x Psychotic children
  xx **Child psychiatry; Emotionally disturbed children**
Mentally ill—Institutional care 362.2
  See also **Psychiatric hospitals**
  x Asylums; Charitable institutions; Insane—Hospitals; Mental hospitals; Mental institutions
  xx **Institutional care**
Mentally retarded. *See* **Mentally handicapped**
Mentally retarded children. *See* **Mentally handicapped children**
Menus 642
  See also **Caterers and catering; Dinners and dining; Luncheons**
  x Bills of fare; Gastronomy; Meal planning
  xx **Caterers and catering; Cookery; Diet; Dinners and dining**
Menus for space flight. *See* **Astronauts—Food**
Mercantile law. *See* **Commercial law**
Mercantile marine. *See* **Merchant marine**
Mercenary soldiers 355.3
  xx **Military personnel; Soldiers**
Merchandise. *See* **Commercial products**

Merchandising. *See* **Marketing; Retail trade**
Merchant marine 387.5
>*See also* **Harbors; Insurance, Marine; Shipping**
>*x* Mercantile marine
>*xx* **Maritime law; Sailors; Shipping; Ships; Transportation**
Merchant marine—Law and legislation. *See* **Maritime law**
Merchant marine—United States 387.5
>*x* United States—Merchant marine
Merchants 920
>*xx* **Business; Commerce**
Mercury 546
>*x* Quicksilver
Mercy killing. *See* **Euthanasia**
Mergers, Conglomerate. *See* **Conglomerate corporations**
Mergers, Corporate. *See* **Conglomerate corporations**
Mergers, Industrial. *See* **Railroads—Consolidation; Trusts, Industrial**
Mermaids and mermen 398.2
>*xx* **Animals, Mythical**
Mesmerism. *See* **Hypnotism**
Messages to Congress. *See* **Presidents—United States—Messages**
Messiness. *See* **Cleanliness**
Metabolism 574.1
>*See also* **Nutrition**
>*xx* **Biochemistry; Nutrition; Physiological chemistry**
Metal work. *See* **Metalwork**
Metallography 669
>Use for materials on the science of metal structures and alloys, especially the study of such structures visually, with the microscope. Materials dealing with the science and art of extracting metals from their ores, refining and preparing them for use, are entered under **Metallurgy.**
>*x* Analysis, Microscopic; Micrographic analysis; Microscopic analysis
>*xx* **Metals; Microscope and microscopy**
Metallurgy 669
>See note under **Metallography.**
>*See also* **Alloys; Chemical engineering; Chemistry, Technical; Electrometallurgy; Metals; Smelting**
>*xx* **Alloys; Chemical engineering; Ores; Smelting**
Metals 546; 549
>*See also* **Alloys; Metallography; Mineralogy; Precious metals; Solder and soldering;** also names of metals, e.g. **Gold;** etc.
>*xx* **Chemistry, Inorganic; Metallurgy; Ores**
Metals, Transmutation of. *See* **Alchemy; Transmutation (Chemistry)**
Metalwork 671; 739
>*See also*

Architectural metalwork	**Bronzes**
Art metalwork	**Copperwork**

Metalwork—*Continued*
    Dies (Metalworking)
    Electroplating
    Founding
    Goldwork
    Ironwork
    Jewelry
    Plate metalwork
    Sheet metalwork
    Silverwork
    Solder and soldering
    Steel
    Tinwork
    Welding

    x Metal work
    xx Decoration and ornament; Founding; Ironwork
Metalwork, Architectural. *See* Architectural metal-
    work
Metalwork, Art. *See* Art metalwork
Metalworking machinery 621.9
    xx Machinery
Metamorphic rocks. *See* Rocks
Metaphysics 110
    See also Existentialism; God; Knowledge, Theory
        of; Universe
    xx God; Philosophy
Meteorites 523.5
    xx Astronomy; Meteors
Meteorological instruments 551.5
    See also names of meteorological instruments,
        e.g. Barometer; Thermometers and ther-
        mometry; etc.
    x Instruments, Meteorological
    xx Scientific apparatus and instruments
Meteorological observatories. *See* Meteorology—
        Observatories
Meteorological satellites 629.46
    See also names of satellites, e.g. Tiros (Meteoro-
        logical satellite); etc.
    x Weather satellites
    xx Artificial satellites
Meteorology 551.5
    See note under Climate.
    See also
    Air
    Atmosphere
    Auroras
    Climate
    Clouds
    Cyclones
    Droughts
    Floods
    Fog
    Frost
    Humidity
    Hurricanes
    Lightning
    Rain and rainfall
    Rainbow
    Seasons
    Snow
    Solar radiation
    Storms
    Sunspots
    Thunderstorms
    Tornadoes
    Weather
    Weather—Folklore
    Weather forecasting
    Winds
    xx Atmosphere; Climate; Earth; Earth sciences;
        Geophysics; Physical geography; Rain and
        rainfall; Science; Storms; Weather
Meteorology in aeronautics 629.132
    x Aeronautics, Meteorology in
    xx Aeronautics; Weather forecasting
Meteorology—Observatories 551.5028
    x Meteorological observatories; Observatories,
        Meteorological; Weather stations

Meteorology—Tables, etc. 551.5

Meteors 523.5

See also **Meteorites**

x Falling stars; Fire balls; Shooting stars; Stars, Falling

xx **Astronomy; Solar system; Stars**

Meter. See **Musical meter and rhythm; Versification**

Meters, Electric. See **Electric meters**

Method of study. See **Study, Method of**

Methodology. See special subjects with the subdivision *Methodology,* e.g.

Science—Methodology; etc.

Metric system 389

xx **Weights and measures**

Metrical romances. See **Romances**

Metrology. See **Measurement; Weights and measures**

Metropolitan areas 307.7

See also **Cities and towns; Urban renewal;** also names of metropolitan areas, e.g. **Chicago metropolitan area (Ill.);** etc.

x Suburban areas; Urban areas

Metropolitan finance 336

xx **Finance; Municipal finance**

Metropolitan government 352

See also **Municipal government;** also names of metropolitan areas with the subdivision *Politics and government,* e.g. **Chicago metropolitan area (Ill.)—Politics and government;** etc.

xx **Local government; Municipal government**

Metropolitan planning. See **Regional planning**

Mexican Americans 305.8

Use for materials on American citizens of Mexican descent. Materials on noncitizens from Mexico are entered under

Mexicans—United States. Use these same patterns for other ethnic groups in the U.S. and other countries.

x Chicanos

xx **Ethnology—United States; Hispanic Americans; Immigration and emigration; Minorities; United States—Foreign population; United States—Immigration and emigration**

Mexican literature 860

May use same subdivisions and names of literary forms as for **English literature.**

Mexican War, 1845-1848. See **United States—History—1845-1848, War with Mexico**

Mexicans (May subdiv. geog.) 920; 972

Mexicans—United States 305.8

See note under **Mexican Americans.**

xx **Aliens; Immigration and emigration; Minorities; United States—Foreign population; United States—Immigration and emigration**

Mexico—Presidents. See **Presidents—Mexico**

Mezzotint engraving 766

xx **Engraving**

MIAs. See **Missing in action**

Mice 599.32; 636.08

   x Mouse

Microbes. *See* **Bacteriology; Germ theory of disease; Microorganisms; Viruses**

Microbial energy conversion. *See* **Biomass energy**

Microbiology 576

   See also **Bacteriology; Biotechnology; Microorganisms; Microscope and microscopy;** also subjects with the subdivision *Microbiology,* e.g. **Air—Microbiology;** etc.

   xx **Biology; Microorganisms; Microscope and microscopy**

Microchemistry 543-545; 547

   xx **Chemistry; Microscope and microscopy**

Microcomputers 621.381; *004.16; *621.391

   Use for materials on small, usually desk-top-sized computers whose central processing units may consist of a single integrated circuit type chip. Most microcomputers include a keyboard terminal and disk drives for floppy disks; some may include a video display terminal and a printer. Consider also **Minicomputers.**

   See also **Home computers; Microprocessors**

   xx **Computers**

Microelectronics 621.381

   x Microminiature electronic equipment; Microminiaturization (Electronics)

   xx **Electronics; Semiconductors**

Microfilming. *See* **Microphotography**

Microfilms 686.4

   See also **Library catalogs on microfilm**

   x Films

   xx **Microforms**

Microforms 001.55; 686.4

   See also types of microforms, e.g. **Microfilms;** etc.

   x Micropublications

   xx **Microphotography**

Micrographic analysis. *See* **Metallography; Microscope and microscopy**

Microminiature electronic equipment. *See* **Microelectronics**

Microminiaturization (Electronics). *See* **Microelectronics**

Microorganisms 576

   See also **Bacteriology; Microbiology; Microscope and microscopy; Protozoa; Viruses**

   x Germs; Microbes; Microscopic organisms

   xx **Bacteriology; Microbiology**

Microphotography 686.4

   Use for materials dealing with the photographing of objects of any size upon a microscopic or very small scale.

   See also **Microforms**

   x Microfilming

   xx **Photography**

Microprocessors 001.64; *004.16

   Use for materials on the central processing units of microcomputers.

Microprocessors—*Continued*
    xx **Microcomputers**
Micropublications. *See* **Microforms**
Microscope and microscopy 502.8; 535; 578
    See also **Electron microscope and microscopy;**
        Metallography; Microbiology; Microchem-
        istry
    x Analysis, Microscopic; Micrographic analysis;
        Microscopic analysis
    xx **Microbiology; Microorganisms**
Microscopic analysis. *See* **Metallography; Micro-**
        scope and microscopy
Microscopic organisms. *See* **Microorganisms**
Microwave amplification by stimulated emission of
    radiation. *See* **Masers**
Microwave communication systems 621.381
    See also **Closed-circuit television**
    xx **Intercommunication systems; Radio, Short-**
        wave; Telecommunication; Television
Microwave cookery 641.5; 641.7
    x Cookery, Microwave
    xx **Cookery**
Microwaves 537.5
    See also **Masers**
    xx **Electric waves; Electromagnetic waves; Radio,**
        Shortwave
Mid-career changes. *See* **Career changes**
Middle age 305.2
    See also **Age and employment; Aging; Longevity;**
        Old age
    x Age
    xx **Life (Biology); Longevity**
Middle Ages 909.07
    See also

Architecture, Medieval	**Knights and knighthood**
Art, Medieval	**Literature, Medieval**
Chivalry	**Philosophy, Medieval**
Church history—600-	**Renaissance**
1500, Middle Ages	**Thirteenth century**
Civilization, Medieval	

    x Dark Ages
    xx **Civilization, Medieval; Feudalism; Renais-**
        sance
Middle Ages—History 909.07; 940.1
    See also **Civilization, Medieval; Crusades; Eu-**
        rope—History—476-1492; Feudalism; Holy
        Roman Empire; Monasticism
    x History, Medieval; Medieval history
    xx **Europe—History—476-1492; History; World**
        history
Middle Atlantic States. *See* **Atlantic States**
Middle classes 305.5; 323.3
    x Bourgeoisie; Middle-income class
    xx **Democracy; Labor; Social classes**
Middle East 956
    See also **Arab countries; Israel**
    x East (Near East); Levant; Near East; Orient
    xx **Asia**
Middle East—Strategic aspects
    xx **Military geography; Strategy**

Middle-income class. *See* **Middle classes**
Middle West 977
> *See also* **Old Northwest**
> *x* Central States; Midwest; North Central States
> *xx* **Mississippi River Valley; Old Northwest;**
>   **United States**
Midwest. *See* **Middle West**
Midwifery. *See* **Childbirth**
Migrant labor 331.5-331.6
> Use for materials dealing with casual or seasonal
>   workers who move from place to place in
>   search of employment. Materials on the
>   movement of population within a country
>   for permanent settlement are entered under
>   **Migration, Internal.**
> *x* Labor, Migratory; Migratory workers
> *xx* **Agricultural laborers; Labor**
Migration. *See* **Immigration and emigration**
Migration, Internal 304.8
> See note under **Migrant labor.**
> *See also* **Land settlement**
> *xx* **Colonization; Land settlement; Population**
Migration of animals. *See* **Animals—Migration**
Migration of birds. *See* **Birds—Migration**
Migratory workers. *See* **Migrant labor**
Milch cattle. *See* **Dairy cattle**
Military aeronautics. *See* **Aeronautics, Military**
Military aid. *See* **Military assistance**
Military air bases. *See* **Air bases**
Military airplanes. *See* **Airplanes, Military**
Military art and science 355
> *See also*

Aeronautics, Military	**Guerrilla warfare**
Armaments	**Hospitals, Military**
Armed forces	**Industrial mobilization** .
Armies	**Military personnel**
Arms and armor	**Naval art and science**
Arms control	**Ordnance**
Battles	**Poisonous gases—War use**
Biological warfare	**Psychological warfare**
Camouflage (Military sci-	**Signals and signaling**
ence)	**Spies**
Camps (Military)	**Strategy**
Chemical warfare	**Tactics**
Civil defense	**Transportation, Military**
Drill and minor tactics	**War**
Fortification	

> also headings beginning with the word **Military**
> *x* Army; Fighting; Military power; Military sci-
>   ence
> *xx* **Armies; Drill and minor tactics; Military per-**
>   **sonnel; Naval art and science; Strategy;**
>   **War**
Military art and science—Study and teaching. *See*
>   **Military education**
Military assistance (May subdiv. geog. adjective
>   form) **355**
> *x* Arms aid; Arms sales; Foreign aid program;
>   Military aid; Mutual defense assistance pro-
>   gram

Military assistance, American 355
    x American military assistance
Military atrocities. *See* names of wars with the sub-
    division *Atrocities,* e.g. **World War, 1939-
    1945—Atrocities;** etc.; and names of spe-
    cific atrocities
Military biography. *See* names of armies and na-
    vies with the subdivision *Biography,* e.g.
    **United States. Army—Biography; United
    States. Navy—Biography;** etc.
Military camps. *See* **Camps (Military)**
Military costume. *See* **Uniforms, Military**
Military courts. *See* **Courts martial and courts of
    inquiry**
Military crimes. *See* **Military offenses**
Military desertion. *See* **Desertion, Military**
Military draft. *See* **Military service, Compulsory**
Military drill. *See* **Drill and minor tactics**
Military education 355.1; 355.5
    See also **Military training camps;** also names of
      military schools, e.g. **United States Military
      Academy;** etc.
    x Army schools; Education, Military; Military
      art and science—Study and teaching; Mili-
      tary training; Schools, Military
  xx **Education**
Military engineering 623
    See also **Fortification;** also names of wars with
      the subdivision *Engineering and construc-
      tion,* e.g. **World War, 1939-1945—
      Engineering and construction;** etc.
  xx **Civil engineering; Engineering; Fortification**
Military forces. *See* **Armies; Navies;** and names of
    countries with the subdivision *Armed forces,*
    e.g. **United States—Armed forces;** etc.
Military geography 355.4
    See also areas of the world with the subdivision
      Strategic aspects, e.g. **Middle East—
      Strategic aspects;** etc.
    x Geography, Military; Maps, Military
Military government (May subdiv. geog.) **341.6;
    355.4**
    x Government, Military
  xx **Military occupation; Public administration**
Military health 613.6
    See also **Armies—Medical care; Medicine, Mili-
      tary;** also names of wars with the subdivi-
      sion *Health aspects* or *Medical care,* e.g.
      **World War, 1939-1945—Health aspects;
      World War, 1939-1945—Medical care;** etc.
    x Hygiene, Military; Soldiers—Hygiene
  xx **Armies—Medical care; Hygiene; Medicine,
    Military; Sanitation**
Military history 355
    See also **Battles; Military policy; Naval history;**
      also names of countries with the subhead
      Army or the subdivision *History, Military,*
      e.g. **United States. Army; United States—
      History, Military;** and names of wars, bat-
      tles, sieges, etc.

Military history—*Continued*
> *x* History, Military; Wars
> *xx* **History; Naval history**

Military hospitals. *See* **Hospitals, Military**

Military intervention. *See* **Intervention (International law)**

Military law 343
> *See also* **Courts martial and courts of inquiry; Military offenses; Military service, Compulsory; Veterans—Law and legislation**
> *x* Articles of war; Law, Military; War, Articles of
> *xx* **Courts martial and courts of inquiry; International law; Law; War**

Military life. *See* **Military personnel;** and names of countries with the subdivision *Armed forces* or the subheads *Army, Navy,* etc. with the subdivision *Military life,* e.g. **United States—Armed forces—Military life; United States. Army—Military life;** etc.

Military medicine. *See* **Medicine, Military**

Military motorization. *See* **Transportation, Military**

Military music 785.1
> *See also* **Band music; Marches (Music);** also names of wars with the subdivision *Songs and music,* e.g. **World War, 1939-1945—Songs and music;** etc.
> *x* Music, Military
> *xx* **Music**

Military occupation 341.6; 355.4
> *See also* **Military government; World War, 1939-1945—Occupied territories;** also names of occupied countries with the subdivision *History—1940-1945, German occupation; History—1945-   , Allied occupation,* e.g. **Netherlands—History—1940-1945, German occupation; Japan—History—1945-1952, Allied occupation;** etc.
> *x* Occupation, Military; Occupied territory

Military offenses (May subdiv. geog.) **355.1**
> *See also* names of military offenses, e.g. **Desertion, Military;** etc.
> *x* Crimes, Military; Military crimes; Naval offenses; Offenses, Military
> *xx* **Criminal law; Military law**

Military offenses—United States 355.1
> *x* United States. Army—Crimes and misdemeanors; United States—Military offenses

Military pensions. *See* **Pensions, Military**

Military personnel 355.1-355.3
> *See also*

Armies	**Navies**
Generals	**Sailors**
Mercenary soldiers	**Soldiers**
Military art and science	**Veterans**

> also names of countries with the subdivision *Armed forces* or the subheads *Army, Navy,* etc. with the subdivision *Military life,* e.g. **United States—Armed forces—Military life;**

Military personnel—*Continued*
 United States. Army—Military life; etc.
 x Military life; Servicemen; Servicewomen
 xx **Armed forces; Military art and science; Veterans; War**
Military personnel missing in action. *See* **Missing in action**
Military personnel—United States 355.1-355.3
 x United States—Military personnel
Military policy 355
 See also **National security;** also names of countries with the subdivision *Military policy,* e.g. **United States—Military policy;** etc.
 x Defense policy
 xx **Military history; National security**
Military posts 355.7
 x Army posts
Military power. *See* **Armies; Arms control; Military art and science; Navies; Sea power**
Military science. *See* **Military art and science**
Military service, Compulsory 355.2
 x Compulsory military service; Conscription, Military; Draft, Military; Military draft; Military training, Universal; Selective service; Service, Compulsory military
 xx **Armies; Human resources; Military law**
Military service, Compulsory—Draft resisters 355.2
 See also **Conscientious objectors; Desertion, Military;** also names of wars with the subdivision *Draft resisters,* e.g. **World War, 1939-1945—Draft resisters;** etc.
 x Draft dodgers; Draft evaders; Draft resisters
 xx **Conscientious objectors; Desertion, Military**
Military service, Voluntary 355.2
 x Volunteer military service
 xx **Armed forces; Human resources**
Military signaling. *See* **Signals and signaling**
Military strategy. *See* **Strategy**
Military tactics. *See* **Tactics**
Military training. *See* **Military education**
Military training camps 355.7
 x Students' military training camps; Training camps, Military
 xx **Military education**
Military training, Universal. *See* **Military service, Compulsory**
Military transportation. *See* **Transportation, Military**
Military uniforms. *See* **Uniforms, Military**
Military vehicles. *See* **Vehicles, Military**
Militia. *See* names of countries and states with the subdivision *Militia,* e.g. **United States—Militia;** etc.
Milk 637; 641.3
 See also **Butter; Cheese**
 xx **Dairy products; Dairying**
Milk—Analysis 543; 637
Milk, Dried 637
 x Dehydrated milk; Dried milk; Powdered milk

Milk supply   338.1
> *xx*   Food adulteration and inspection; Public
>   health

Mill and factory buildings.   *See*   **Factories**

Millennialism.   *See*   **Millennium**

Millennium   236
> *See also* **Second Advent**
> *x*   Millennialism
> *xx*   **Eschatology; Future life; Second Advent**

Millikan rays.   *See*   **Cosmic rays**

Millinery   646.5; 687
> *See also* **Hats**
> *xx*   **Costume; Hats**

Milling (Flour).   *See*   **Flour mills**

Milling machines   621.9
> *See also* **Machine tools**
> *xx*   **Machinery**

Millionaires   920
> *See also* **Wealth**
> *xx*   **Capitalists and financiers; Wealth**

Mills and millwork   670.42
> *See also* **Factories; Machinery;** also names of
>   types of mills, e.g. **Flour mills;** etc.
> *xx*   **Factories; Manufactures; Technology**

Mime   792.3
> *See also* **Pantomimes**
> *xx*   **Acting; Pantomimes**

Mind.   *See*   **Intellect; Psychology**

Mind and body   150
> *See also*

Biofeedback training	**Personality disorders**
Consciousness	**Phrenology**
Dreams	**Psychoanalysis**
Holistic medicine	**Psychology, Pathological**
Hypnotism	**Psychology, Physiological**
Medicine, Psychosomatic	**Sleep**
Mental healing	**Spiritual healing**
Mental health	**Subconsciousness**
Mental suggestion	**Temperament**
Nervous system	

> *x*   Body and mind; Mind cure
> *xx*   **Brain; Holistic medicine; Hypnotism; Medi-
>   cine; Mental healing; Mental health; Phi-
>   losophy; Phrenology; Psychical research;
>   Psychoanalysis; Psychology, Physiological;
>   Subconsciousness**

Mind control.   *See*   **Brainwashing**

Mind cure.   *See*   **Christian Science; Mental healing;
       Mind and body**

Mind reading   133.8
> *See also* **Clairvoyance; Hypnotism; Telepathy**
> *xx*   **Clairvoyance; Psychical research; Telepathy**

Mine surveying   622.028
> *xx*   **Mining engineering; Prospecting; Surveying**

Mineral industries.   *See*   **Mines and mineral re-
       sources**

Mineral lands.   *See*   **Mines and mineral resources**

Mineral resources.   *See*   **Mines and mineral re-
       sources**

Mineral resources, Marine. *See* **Marine mineral resources**

Mineralogy 549

> *See also* **Gems; Petrology; Phosphorescence; Precious stones;** also names of minerals, e.g. **Quartz;** etc.
>
> *x* Minerals
>
> *xx* **Crystallography; Geology; Metals; Mines and mineral resources; Natural history; Ores; Petrology; Rocks; Science**

Minerals. *See* **Mineralogy; Mines and mineral resources;** and names of minerals, e.g. **Quartz;** etc.

Miners 622.092; 920

> *See also* types of miners, e.g. **Coal miners;** etc.
>
> *x* Laborers
>
> *xx* **Labor**

Mines and mineral resources (May subdiv. geog.) **338.2; 622**

> Use for general descriptive materials and for technical and economic materials on mining, metallurgy and minerals of economic value.
>
> *See also* **Marine mineral resources; Mineralogy; Mining engineering; Precious metals; Prospecting;** also specific types of mines and mining, e.g. **Coal mines and mining;** etc.
>
> *x* Mineral industries; Mineral lands; Mineral resources; Minerals; Mining
>
> *xx* **Geology, Economic; Natural resources; Ores; Raw materials**

Mines and mineral resources—United States 338.2; 622

> *x* United States—Mines and mineral resources

Mingles housing. *See* **Shared housing**

Miniature computers. *See* **Minicomputers**

Miniature gardens. *See* **Gardens, Miniature**

Miniature objects. *See* names of miniature objects, e.g. **Dollhouses; Gardens, Miniature; Models and model making; Toys;** etc.; and names of objects with the subdivision *Models,* e.g. **Airplanes—Models;** etc.

Miniature painting 757

> *See also* **Portrait painting**
>
> *x* Miniatures (Portraits)
>
> *xx* **Painting; Portrait painting**

Miniatures (Illumination of books and manuscripts). *See* **Illumination of books and manuscripts**

Miniatures (Portraits). *See* **Miniature painting**

Minibikes 629.2

> *xx* **Bicycles and bicycling; Motorcycles**

Minicomputers 621.3819; *004.16; *621.391

> Use for materials on computers larger than microcomputers, but smaller than mainframes. Consider also **Microcomputers.**
>
> *See also* **Home computers**
>
> *x* Miniature computers
>
> *xx* **Computers**

Minimum drinking age. *See* **Drinking age**

Minimum wage. *See* **Wages—Minimum wage**

Mining. *See* **Mines and mineral resources; Mining engineering**

Mining, Electric. *See* **Electricity in mining**

Mining engineering 622

See also **Boring; Electricity in mining; Mine surveying; Ocean mining**

x Mining

xx **Civil engineering; Coal mines and mining; Electricity in mining; Engineering; Mines and mineral resources**

Mining, Ocean. *See* **Ocean mining**

Ministers (Diplomatic agents). *See* **Diplomats**

Ministers of state. *See* **Cabinet officers**

Ministers of the gospel. *See* **Clergy**

Ministry (May subdiv. by religion or denomination) **253-254**

x Clergy—Office

Ministry, Christian 253-254

x Christian ministry

Minor arts. *See* **Decorative arts**

Minor tactics. *See* **Drill and minor tactics**

Minorites. *See* **Franciscans**

Minorities 305.8; 323.1

See also **Discrimination; Ethnic relations; Nationalism; Race relations; Segregation;** also names of peoples living within a country, state, or city dominated by another nationality, e.g. **Mexican Americans; Mexicans— United States;** etc.; and names of countries with the subdivisions *Foreign population* and *Race relations,* e.g. **United States— Foreign population; United States—Race relations;** etc.

x Minority groups

xx **Discrimination; Ethnic groups; Ethnic relations; Nationalism; Segregation**

Minorities in broadcasting 384.5; 791.4

Use same form for minorities in other subjects.

xx **Broadcasting**

Minority groups. *See* **Minorities**

Minstrels 791.092; 920

See also **Black minstrels; Troubadours**

xx **Poets**

Minstrels, Black. *See* **Black minstrels**

Mints 332.4

See also **Coinage**

xx **Coinage; Money**

Miracle plays. *See* **Mysteries and miracle plays**

Miracles 231

See also **Supernatural**

x Divine healing

xx **Apparitions; Shrines; Spiritual healing; Supernatural**

Miracles—Christianity 231.7

x Bible—Miracles

xx **Bible—Evidences, authority, etc.; Christianity; Church history**

Mirrors 748.8

x Looking glasses

Mirrors—*Continued*
　　xx **Furniture**
Miscarriage 618.3
　　x Abortion, Spontaneous; Spontaneous abortion
Miscellanea.　*See* subjects with the subdivision
　　　　Miscellanea, e.g. **Medicine—Miscellanea;**
　　　　etc.
Miscellaneous facts.　*See* **Curiosities and wonders**
Misconduct in office 351.9
　　See also **Corruption in politics; Police—Corrupt**
　　　　practices; also names of specific incidents
　　　　and offenses, e.g. **Watergate Affair, 1972-**
　　　　1974; etc.
　　x Malfeasance in office; Official misconduct
　　xx **Conflict of interests; Corruption in politics;**
　　　　Criminal law
Misdemeanors (Law).　*See* **Criminal law**
Misleading advertising.　*See* **Advertising, Fraudu-**
　　　　lent
Missiles, Ballistic.　*See* **Ballistic missiles**
Missiles, Guided.　*See* **Guided missiles**
Missing children 363.2
　　See also **Runaway children**
　　x Lost children
　　xx **Children; Criminal investigation; Missing per-**
　　　　sons
Missing in action
　　See also names of wars with the subdivision
　　　　Missing in action, e.g. **World War, 1939-**
　　　　1945—Missing in action; etc.
　　x M.I.A.'s; MIAs; Military personnel missing in
　　　　action
　　xx **Prisoners of war; Soldiers**
Missing persons (May subdiv. geog.) **363.2**
　　See also **Missing children**
　　xx **Criminal investigation**
Missionaries, Christian 920
　　xx **Missions, Christian**
Missions, Christian 266
　　See also **Evangelistic work; Missionaries, Chris-**
　　　　tian; Salvation Army; also names of
　　　　churches, denominations, religious orders,
　　　　etc. with the subdivision *Missions,* e.g.
　　　　Catholic Church—Missions; etc.
　　x Christian missions; Foreign missions, Chris-
　　　　tian; Home missions, Christian
　　xx **Christianity; Church history; Church work;**
　　　　Evangelistic work
Missions, Indian.　*See* **Indians of North America—**
　　　　Missions, Christian
Missions, Medical 362.1-362.4
　　x Medical missions
　　xx **Medicine**
Mississippi River Valley 917.7; 977
　　See also **Middle West**
　　x Mississippi Valley
　　xx **United States**
Mississippi River Valley—History 977
　　x New France—History
Mississippi Valley.　*See* **Mississippi River Valley**

Mistakes. *See* **Errors**

Mixed marriage. *See* **Intermarriage**

Mnemonics. *See* **Memory**

Mobile home living 728.7
> *See also* **Van life**
> *xx* **Home economics; Mobile homes**

Mobile home parks 647
> *xx* **Trailer parks**

Mobile homes 647; 728.7
> *See also* **Mobile home living**
> *x* Homes, Mobile; House trailers; Motor homes;
>> Trailers, Home
> *xx* **Housing; Travel trailers and campers**

Mobiles (Sculpture) 731
> *xx* **Kinetic sculpture; Sculpture**

Mobilization, Industrial. *See* **Industrial mobilization**

Mobs. *See* **Crowds; Riots**

Model airplanes. *See* **Airplanes—Models**

Model cars. *See* **Automobiles—Models**

Modeling 731.4; 738.1
> *See also* **Sculpture—Technique; Soap sculpture**
> *x* Clay modeling
> *xx* **Clay; Sculpture; Sculpture—Technique**

Models. *See* **Models and model making;** and
> names of objects with the subdivision
> *Models,* e.g. **Airplanes—Models;** etc.

Models and model making 688
> *See also* names of objects with the subdivision
>> *Models,* e.g. **Airplanes—Models; Ships—
>> Models;** etc.
> *x* Miniature objects; Models

Models, Fashion 659.1
> *x* Fashion models; Manikins (Fashion models);
>> Mannequins (Fashion models); Style mani-
>> kins

Models, Mathematical. *See* **Mathematical models**

Models, Mechanical. *See* **Machinery—Models**

Modern architecture. *See* **Architecture, Modern**

Modern art. *See* **Art, Modern**

Modern civilization. *See* **Civilization, Modern**

Modern dance 793.3
> *x* Interpretive dance
> *xx* **Dancing**

Modern history. *See* **History, Modern**

Modern languages. *See* **Languages, Modern**

Modern painting. *See* **Painting, Modern**

Modern philosophy. *See* **Philosophy, Modern**

Modern sculpture. *See* **Sculpture, Modern**

Modernism 230
> Use for materials on the movement in the Prot-
> estant churches that applies modern critical
> methods to biblical study and the history of
> dogma, and emphasizes the spiritual and
> ethical side of Christianity rather than his-
> toric dogmas and creeds.
> *See also* **Fundamentalism**
> *xx* **Fundamentalism**

Modernization 303.4
> Use for materials on the process of change in a

Modernization—*Continued*

society or social institution in which the most recent styles, ideas, or usages are acquired or adapted.

See also **Industrialization**

x Development

xx **Industrialization; Social change**

Mohammedan art. *See* **Art, Islamic**

Mohammedanism. *See* **Islam**

Mohammedans. *See* **Muslims**

Mold (Botany). *See* **Molds (Botany)**

Molding (Metal). *See* **Founding**

Molds (Botany) 589.2

See also **Fungi**

x Mold (Botany)

xx **Fungi**

Molecular biochemistry. *See* **Molecular biology**

Molecular biology 574.8

See also **Genetic code**

x Biology, Molecular; Molecular biochemistry; Molecular biophysics

xx **Biochemistry; Biophysics**

Molecular biophysics. *See* **Molecular biology**

Molecular cloning 174; 574.87

x Cloning, Molecular; DNA cloning

xx **Clones and cloning; Genetic engineering**

Molecular physiology. *See* **Biophysics**

Molecules 539; 541

xx **Chemistry, Physical and theoretical**

Molesting of children. *See* **Child molesting**

Mollusks 594

See also **Shells**

xx **Invertebrates; Shellfish; Shells**

Monarchs. *See* **Kings, queens, rulers, etc.**

Monarchy 321.6; 321.8

See also **Democracy; Kings, queens, rulers, etc.**

x Sovereigns

xx **Constitutional history; Constitutional law; Democracy; Executive power; Political science**

Monasteries (May subdiv. geog.) **255; 271; 726**

See also **Abbeys; Convents; Monasticism**

x Cloisters

xx **Abbeys; Convents; Monasticism**

Monastic orders. *See* **Religious orders**

Monasticism 255; 271

See also **Monasteries; Religious life; Religious orders**

xx **Civilization, Medieval; Middle Ages—History; Monasteries**

Monetary policy (May subdiv. geog.) **332.4**

See also **Finance; Fiscal policy; Gold; Inflation (Finance); Money; Silver**

x Bimetallism; Currency devaluation; Devaluation of currency; Free coinage

xx **Coinage; Finance; Fiscal policy; Inflation (Finance); Money**

Monetary policy—United States 332.4

x United States—Monetary policy

Money 332.4; 332.5

Use for materials on currency as a medium of exchange or measure of value.

Money—*Continued*
   See also

Banks and banking	**Foreign exchange**
Barter	**Gold**
Capital	**Mints**
Coinage	**Monetary policy**
Coins	**Paper money**
Counterfeits and counter-	**Silver**
feiting	**Wealth**
Credit	

   x Bullion; Currency; Specie; Standard of value
   xx **Banks and banking; Coinage; Economics; Exchange; Finance; Gold; Monetary policy; Silver; Wealth**

Money, Paper. *See* **Paper money**

Money raising. *See* **Fund raising**

Moneymaking projects for children 331.3
   x Children's moneymaking projects
   xx **Children—Employment**

Monkeys 599.8
   xx **Animals; Primates**

Monkeys—Habits and behavior 599.8
   xx **Animals—Habits and behavior**

Monks 255; 271
   xx **Religious orders for men**

Monograms 745.6
   See also **Initials**
   x Ciphers (Lettering)
   xx **Alphabets; Decoration and ornament; Initials; Lettering**

Monologues with music 808.5
   x Declamations, Musical; Narration with music; Recitations with music

Monoplanes. *See* **Airplanes**

Monopolies 338.8
   See also **Capitalism; Competition; Corporation law; Railroads—Consolidation; Restraint of trade; Trusts, Industrial**
   xx **Capital; Commerce; Competition; Economics; Restraint of trade; Trusts, Industrial**

Monorail railroads 385; 625.1
   x Railroads, Single rail; Single rail railroads
   xx **Railroads**

Monroe Doctrine 327.73
   xx **International relations; Intervention (International law); Pan-Americanism; United States—Foreign relations**

Monsters 398; 616.07
   See also **Dragons; Giants**
   x Freaks; Monstrosities
   xx **Animals—Folklore; Curiosities and wonders; Folklore**

Monstrosities. *See* **Monsters**

Montessori method of education 371.33; 372.1
   xx **Education, Elementary; Kindergarten; Teaching**

Months 529
   See also names of individual months
   xx **Calendars; Chronology**

Monumental brasses. *See* **Brasses**

Monuments (May subdiv. geog.) 725-726; 730
  See also **Historic buildings; Obelisks; Pyramids;
    Tombs**
  x Statues
  xx **Architecture; Sculpture**
Monuments, Natural. *See* **Natural monuments**
Moon 523.3
  See also **Tides**
  xx **Astronomy; Solar system**
Moon bases. *See* **Lunar bases**
Moon cars 629.2
  x Lunar cars; Lunar rover vehicles; Lunar sur-
    face vehicles
Moon—Eclipses. *See* **Eclipses, Lunar**
Moon—Exploration 629.45
  x Lunar exploration
  xx **Space flight to the moon**
Moon—Geology. *See* **Lunar geology**
Moon (in religion, folklore, etc.). *See* **Moon wor-
    ship**
Moon—Maps 523.3
Moon—Photographs 523.3
  xx **Lunar photography**
Moon—Photographs from space 523.3
  xx **Space photography**
Moon photography. *See* **Lunar photography**
Moon probes. *See* **Lunar probes**
Moon rocks. *See* **Lunar petrology**
Moon soil. *See* **Lunar soil**
Moon—Surface 523.3
  See also **Lunar soil**
  x Lunar surface
  xx **Lunar soil**
Moon, Voyages to. *See* **Space flight to the moon**
Moon worship 291.2
  x Moon (in religion, folklore, etc.)
  xx **Religion**
Moonlighting. *See* **Supplementary employment**
Moors 572.964; 909
  xx **Arabs**
Moral and religious aspects. *See* subjects with the
    subdivision *Moral and religious aspects,*
      e.g. **Birth control—Moral and religious as-
      pects;** etc.
Moral conditions 900
  See also names of countries, cities, etc. with the
    subdivision *Moral conditions,* e.g. **United
    States—Moral conditions;** etc.
  x Morals
  xx **Social conditions**
Moral education 370.11
  See also **Religious education**
  x Character education; Education, Character;
    Education, Ethical; Education, Moral; Ethi-
    cal education
  xx **Education; Ethics; Religious education**
Moral philosophy. *See* **Ethics**
Moral theology, Christian. *See* **Christian ethics**
Morale 152.4
  See also **Psychological warfare;** also types of mo-

Morale—*Continued*
　　　　rale, e.g. **Employee morale;** etc.
　　xx **Courage**
Moralities.　*See* **Morality plays**
Morality.　*See* **Ethics**
Morality plays　808.2; 808.82; 812; 812.08; etc.
　　See also **Mysteries and miracle plays**
　　x Moralities
　　xx **Drama; English drama; Mysteries and miracle
　　　　plays; Religious drama; Theater**
Morals.　*See* **Ethics; Human behavior; Moral condi-
　　　　tions**
Moravians　284
　　x United Brethren
Mormon Church.　*See* **Church of Jesus Christ of
　　　　Latter-day Saints**
Mormons　289.3
　　See also **Church of Jesus Christ of Latter-day
　　　　Saints**
Morphology.　*See* **Anatomy; Anatomy, Compara-
　　　　tive; Biology; Botany—Anatomy**
Morse code.　*See* **Cipher and telegraph codes**
Mortality　312; 614
　　See also **Death**
　　x Burial statistics; Death rate; Mortuary statis-
　　　　tics
　　xx **Death; Population; Vital statistics**
Mortar　666; 691
　　xx **Adhesives; Plaster and plastering**
Mortgage loans.　*See* **Mortgages**
Mortgages　332.7; 332.63
　　See also **Agricultural credit**
　　x Chattel mortgages; Home loans; Housing
　　　　loans; Mortgage loans
　　xx **Commercial law; Contracts; Credit; Invest-
　　　　ments; Loans; Personal loans; Real estate;
　　　　Securities**
Morticians.　*See* **Undertakers and undertaking**
Mortuary customs.　*See* **Cremation; Funeral rites
　　　　and ceremonies**
Mortuary statistics.　*See* **Mortality; Vital statistics**
Mosaics　729; 738.5; 748.5
　　See also **Mural painting and decoration**
　　xx **Decoration and ornament; Decorative arts;
　　　　Mural painting and decoration**
Moslem art.　*See* **Art, Islamic**
Moslemism.　*See* **Islam**
Moslems.　*See* **Muslims**
Mosques　726
　　xx **Architecture; Architecture, Asian; Church ar-
　　　　chitecture; Islam; Temples**
Mosquitoes　595.77
　　x Diptera
　　xx **Insects as carriers of disease**
Mosquitoes—Control　595.77; 614.4
　　xx **Pests—Control**
Mosses　588
　　xx **Plants**
Motels.　*See* **Hotels, motels, etc.**

Mothers 306.8
>*See also* **Adolescent mothers; Surrogate mothers**
>*x* Maternity
>*xx* **Family; Homemakers; Women**

Mothers and daughters 305.4; 306.8
>*x* Daughters and mothers
>*xx* **Girls; Parent and child**

Mothers and sons 306.8
>*x* Sons and mothers
>*xx* **Boys; Parent and child**

Mothers' pensions 362.8
>*See also* **Child welfare**
>*xx* **Child welfare; Pensions**

Mothers, Unmarried. *See* **Unmarried mothers**

Moths 595.78
>*See also* **Butterflies; Caterpillars; Silkworms**
>*x* Cocoons; Lepidoptera
>*xx* **Butterflies; Insects**

Motion 531
>*See also* **Force and energy; Kinematics; Mechanical movements; Mechanics; Speed**
>*x* Kinetics
>*xx* **Dynamics; Force and energy; Kinematics; Mechanics**

Motion picture actors and actresses. *See* **Actors and actresses**

Motion picture cameras 778.5
>*x* Movie cameras
>*xx* **Cameras; Motion picture photography**

Motion picture cartoons 741.5; 791.43
>*See also* **Animation (Cinematography)**
>*x* Animated cartoons
>*xx* **Animation (Cinematography); Cartoons and caricatures**

Motion picture direction. *See* **Motion pictures—Production and direction**

Motion picture industry 338.4; 791.43
>*See also* **Women in the motion picture industry**

Motion picture photography 778.5
>*See also* **Amateur motion pictures; Motion picture cameras**
>*x* Cinematography; Photography—Motion pictures
>*xx* **Photography**

Motion picture plays 808.2; 808.82; 812; 812.08; etc.
>Use as a form heading for actual screen scripts.
>*x* Photoplays; Scenarios; Screen plays
>*xx* **Drama**

Motion picture plays—Technique 808.2
>*x* Motion pictures—Play writing; Play writing; Playwriting
>*xx* **Drama—Technique**

Motion picture producers and directors 791.43
>*x* Directors and producers; Producers and directors

Motion picture production. *See* **Motion pictures—Production and direction**

Motion picture projectors. *See* **Projectors**

Motion pictures 791.43
>*See also* **Animals in motion pictures; Blacks in**

411

Motion pictures—*Continued*

    motion pictures; Experimental films; Sound—Recording and reproducing; Video-tapes; Women in motion pictures; World War, 1939-1945—Motion pictures and the war; also names of individual motion pictures

    x Cinema; Filmography; Films; Movies; Moving pictures; Talking pictures

    xx **Amusements; Audiovisual materials; Mass media; Theater**

Motion pictures, Amateur. *See* **Amateur motion pictures**

Motion pictures and children 649; 791.43

    Use for materials dealing with the effect of motion pictures on children and youth.

    Use same form for motion pictures and other subjects.

    See also **Television and children**

    x Children and motion pictures

    xx **Children; Television and children**

Motion pictures and libraries. *See* **Libraries and motion pictures**

Motion pictures—Biography 791.43092; 920

Motion pictures—Catalogs 016.79143

    x Catalogs

Motion pictures—Censorship 791.43

    xx **Censorship**

Motion pictures, Documentary 791.43

    x Documentary films

Motion pictures, Experimental. *See* **Experimental films**

Motion pictures in education 371.3; 791.43

    Use same form for motion pictures in other subjects.

    See also **Libraries and motion pictures**

    x Educational films

    xx **Audiovisual education; Teaching—Aids and devices**

Motion pictures—Moral and religious aspects 791.43

Motion pictures—Play writing. *See* **Motion picture plays—Technique**

Motion pictures—Production and direction 791.43

    x Direction (Motion pictures); Motion picture direction; Motion picture production

    xx **Theater—Production and direction**

Motion pictures, Silent 791.43

    x Silent films; Silent motion pictures

Motion study 658.5

    See also **Time study**

    xx **Efficiency, Industrial; Factory management; Job analysis; Personnel management; Production standards; Time study**

Motivation (Psychology) 153.8

    See also **Burn out (Psychology); Wishes**

    xx **Psychology**

Motor boats. *See* **Motorboats**

Motor buses. *See* **Buses**

Motor cars. *See* **Automobiles**

Motor coordination. *See* **Movement education**
Motor courts. *See* **Hotels, motels, etc.**
Motor cycles. *See* **Motorcycles**
Motor homes. *See* **Mobile homes**
Motor trucks. *See* **Trucks**
Motorboat racing. *See* **Boat racing**
Motorboats 623.8
   x Motor boats; Outboard motorboats; Power
      boats
   xx **Boats and boating**
Motorboats—Models 623.8
   xx **Machinery—Models**
Motorcycles 629.2
   See also **Minibikes;** also specific makes and
      models of motorcycles
   x Cycles, Motor; Cycling; Motor cycles; Motor-
      cycling
   xx **Bicycles and bicycling**
Motorcycling. *See* **Motorcycles**
Motoring. *See* **Automobiles—Touring**
Motorization, Military. *See* **Transportation, Mili-**
      tary
Motors. *See* **Electric motors; Engines**
Motorways. *See* **Express highways**
Mottoes 808.88; 818; etc.
   x Emblems
   xx **Heraldry**
Moulding (Metal). *See* **Founding**
Mounds and mound builders 970.004
   See also **Excavations (Archeology)**
   x Barrows; Burial; Graves
   xx **Archeology; Cliff dwellers and cliff dwellings;**
      Excavations (Archeology); Indians of North
      America; Indians of North America—
      Antiquities; Tombs
Mountain animals. *See* **Alpine animals**
Mountain climbing. *See* **Mountaineering**
Mountain plants. *See* **Alpine plants**
Mountaineering 796.5
   x Mountain climbing; Rock climbing
   xx **Mountains; Outdoor life**
Mountains (May subdiv. geog.) 551.4
   Names of all mountain ranges and mountains
      are not included in this list but are to be
      added as needed, e.g. **Rocky Mountains; Elk**
      Mountain (Wyo.); etc.
   See also **Mountaineering; Volcanoes;** also names
      of mountain ranges, e.g. **Rocky Mountains;**
      etc.; and names of mountains, e.g. **Elk**
      Mountain (Wyo.); etc.
   xx **Geology; Physical geography**
Mourning customs. *See* **Funeral rites and ceremo-**
      nies
Mouse. *See* **Mice**
Movable books. *See* **Toy and movable books**
Movement education 152.3; 153.7; 372.8
   x Creative movement; Motor coordination
   xx **Physical education**
Movement, Freedom of. *See* **Freedom of movement**
Movements of animals. *See* **Animal locomotion**

413

Movie cameras. *See* **Motion picture cameras**
Movies. *See* **Motion pictures**
Moving, Household 648
   x Household moving
Moving pictures. *See* **Motion pictures**
Muhammedanism. *See* **Islam**
Muhammedans. *See* **Muslims**
Multiage grouping. *See* **Nongraded schools**
Multicultural education. *See* **Intercultural education**
Multilingual dictionaries. *See* **Polyglot dictionaries**
Multilingual glossaries, phrase books, etc. *See* **Polyglot dictionaries**
Multimedia centers. *See* **Instructional materials centers**
Multimedia materials. *See* **Audiovisual materials**
Multinational corporations. *See* **International business enterprises**
Multiple birth. *See* **Birth, Multiple**
Multiple plot stories. *See* **Plot-your-own stories**
Multiplication 513
   xx **Arithmetic**
Mummies 393
   x Burial
   xx **Archeology**
Municipal administration. *See* **Municipal government**
Municipal art. *See* **Art, Municipal**
Municipal employees. *See* **Civil service; Municipal government;** and names of cities with the subdivision *Officials and employees,* e.g. **Chicago (Ill.)—Officials and employees;** etc.
Municipal engineering 628
   See also **Drainage; Refuse and refuse disposal; Sanitary engineering; Sewerage; Street cleaning; Water supply**
   xx **Engineering; Public works; Sanitary engineering**
Municipal-federal relations. *See* **Federal-city relations**
Municipal finance 352.1
   See also **Metropolitan finance**
   x Finance, Municipal
   xx **Finance; Municipal government**
Municipal government (May subdiv. geog.) **352**
   Use for materials on the government of cities in general and, when subdivided by country, for general consideration of municipal government of countries, or regions. Materials on the government of individual cities, towns, or areas are entered under the name of the city, town, or area with the subdivision *Politics and government.*
   See also **Cities and towns; Federal-city relations; Metropolitan government; Municipal finance; Public administration; State-local relations;** also names of cities with the subdivision *Politics and government,* e.g. **Chicago (Ill.)—Politics and government;** etc.

Municipal government—*Continued*
    x City government; Government, Municipal; Municipal administration; Municipal employees; Municipalities
    xx **Local government; Metropolitan government; Political science**
Municipal government by city manager 352
    x City manager; Commission government with city manager
Municipal government by commission 352
    x Commission government; Government by commission
Municipal government—United States 352
    x United States—Municipal government
Municipal improvements. *See* **Art, Municipal; Cities and towns—Civic improvement;** and names of cities with the subdivision *Public works,* e.g. **Chicago (Ill.)—Public works;** etc.
Municipal ownership 338.9; 352
    x Public ownership
    xx **Corporations; Economic policy; Government ownership**
Municipal planning. *See* **City planning**
Municipal transit. *See* **Local transit**
Municipalities. *See* **Cities and towns; Municipal government**
Munitions 338.4; 623.4
    See note under **Armaments.**
    See also **Arms race; Space weapons;** also names of wars with the subdivision *Equipment and supplies,* e.g. **World War, 1939-1945—Equipment and supplies;** etc.
    x Arms sales
    xx **Armaments; Industrial mobilization; International relations; War; War—Economic aspects**
Muppets. *See* **Puppets and puppet plays**
Mural painting and decoration 729; 751.7
    See also **Cave drawings; Mosaics; Rock drawings, paintings, and engravings**
    x Fresco painting; Wall decoration; Wall painting
    xx **Decoration and ornament; Interior design; Mosaics; Painting; Walls**
Murder 364.1
    See also **Assassination; Capital punishment; Trials (Murder)**
    x Manslaughter
    xx **Assassination; Crime; Criminal law; Medical jurisprudence; Offenses against the person**
Murder trials. *See* **Trials (Murder)**
Muscles 611; 612
    xx **Musculoskeletal system; Physiology**
Muscular system. *See* **Musculoskeletal system**
Musculoskeletal system 612
    See also **Bones; Muscles**
    x Muscular system
    xx **Anatomy; Physiology**

Museums (May subdiv. geog.) **069**

    See also appropriate subjects, names of wars
      and corporate bodies with the subdivision
      Museums, e.g. **Art—Museums; World War,
      1939-1945—Museums;** etc; and names of
      galleries and museums

Museums and schools 069; 371.074

    x Schools and museums
    xx **Schools**

Museums—United States 708.73

    x United States—Museums

Mushrooms 598.2

    See also **Fungi**
    x Toadstools
    xx **Fungi**

Music (May subdiv. geog. adjective form, e.g. **Music,
    American;** etc.) **780**

    All types of music are not included in this list
      but are to be added as needed for vocal or
      instrumental, classical or popular, solo or
      group music.

    See also

Chamber music	**Jazz music**
Church music	**Military music**
Composition (Music)	**Musicians**
Concerts	**Orchestral music**
Dance music	**Organ music**
Electronic music	**Piano music**
Folk music	**Radio and music**
Harmony	**Rock music**
Instrumental music	**Romanticism**
Instrumentation and or-	**Sound**
chestration	**Vocal music**

    also subjects with the subdivision *Songs and
      music,* e.g. **Aeronautics—Songs and music;
      Cowhands—Songs and music;** etc.; and
      headings beginning with the words **Music**
      and **Musical**
    xx **Humanities**

Music—Acoustics and physics 781

    See also **Sound**
    x Acoustics
    xx **Music—Theory; Physics; Sound**

Music, American 780.973

    See also **Black songs; Spirituals (Songs)**
    x American music; United States—Music

Music—Analysis, appreciation 780.1

    x Appreciation of music; Music appreciation;
      Musical appreciation

Music and literature 780

    x Literature and music; Music and poetry; Po-
      etry and music
    xx **Literature**

Music and poetry. *See* **Music and literature**

Music and radio. *See* **Radio and music**

Music—Anecdotes, facetiae, satire, etc. 780

    xx **Anecdotes; Wit and humor**

Music appreciation. *See* **Music—Analysis, appreci-
    ation**

Music, Black. *See* **Black music**

Music box 789
  xx **Musical instruments, Mechanical**
Music—Cataloging. *See* **Cataloging—Music**
Music, Choral. *See* **Choral music**
Music—Composition. *See* **Composition (Music)**
Music conductors. *See* **Conductors (Music)**
Music—Discography 789.9
  x Discography
Music, Dramatic. *See* **Opera; Operetta**
Music, Electronic. *See* **Electronic music**
Music—Examinations, questions, etc. 780.7
  xx **Examinations; Questions and answers**
Music festivals 780.73; 780.79
  x Musical festivals
  xx **Concerts; Festivals**
Music—History and criticism 780.9
  x Musical criticism
  xx **Criticism; History**
Music, Indian. *See* **Indians of North America—
    Songs and music**
Music, Influence of. *See* **Music—Psychological as-
    pects**
Music—Instruction and study. *See* **Music—Study
    and teaching**
Music, Instrumental. *See* **Instrumental music**
Music libraries 026
  x Libraries, Music
  xx **Libraries; Special libraries**
Music, Military. *See* **Military music**
Music—Notation. *See* **Musical notation**
Music, Popular (Songs, etc.) 784.5
  See also names of types of popular music, e.g.
      **Blues (Songs, etc.); Country music; Rock
      music;** etc.
  x Popular music; Popular songs; Songs, Popular
  xx **Dance music; Songs**
**Music, Popular (Songs, etc.)—Writing and publish-
    ing 784.5**
  x Song writing
  xx **Composition (Music)**
Music—Psychological aspects 781
  x Music, Influence of; Psychology of music
  xx **Psychology**
Music, Rock. *See* **Rock music**
Music, Sacred. *See* **Church music**
Music—Study and teaching 780.7
  See also **Composition (Music); Conducting; Har-
      mony; Musical form**
  x Education, Musical; Music—Instruction and
      study; Musical education; Musical instruc-
      tion; School music
Music—Theory 781
  See also **Composition (Music); Counterpoint;
      Fugue; Harmony; Music—Acoustics and
      physics; Musical form; Musical meter and
      rhythm**
Music videos 778.59
  x Videos, Music
  xx **Television programs**
Music, Vocal. *See* **Vocal music**

Musical ability 780.7
   x Musical talent; Talent
   xx **Ability**
Musical accompaniment 781.6
   x Accompaniment, Musical
   xx **Composition (Music)**
Musical appreciation. *See* **Music—Analysis, appreciation**
Musical comedies. *See* **Musical revues, comedies, etc.**
Musical composition. *See* **Composition (Music)**
Musical criticism. *See* **Music—History and criticism**
Musical education. *See* **Music—Study and teaching**
Musical festivals. *See* **Music festivals**
Musical form 781
   See also names of specific types of musical forms, e.g. **Concerto; Fugue; Opera; Operetta; Sonata; Symphony;** etc. Add names of musical forms as needed for the music itself, e.g. **Concertos; Suites;** etc.
   x Form, Musical
   xx **Music—Study and teaching; Music—Theory**
Musical instruction. *See* **Music—Study and teaching**
Musical instruments 781.91
   See also **Instrumental music; Instrumentation and orchestration; Orchestra; Tuning;** also groups of instruments, e.g. **Percussion instruments; Stringed instruments; Wind instruments;** etc.; and names of specific musical instruments, e.g. **Drum; Organ;** etc.
   x Instruments, Musical
   xx **Instrumental music; Instrumentation and orchestration**
Musical instruments, Electronic 789.9
   See also **Synthesizer (Musical instrument)**
   x Electronic musical instruments
Musical instruments, Mechanical 789
   See also names of instruments, e.g. **Music box;** etc.
   x Mechanical musical instruments
Musical meter and rhythm 781.6
   x Meter
   xx **Music—Theory; Rhythm**
Musical notation 781
   x Music—Notation; Notation, Music
Musical revues, comedies, etc. 782.81
   x Musical comedies; Musicals
   xx **Operas; Operetta**
Musical talent. *See* **Musical ability**
Musicals. *See* **Musical revues, comedies, etc.**
Musicians (May subdiv. geog. adjective form)
       780.92; 920
   See also types of musicians, e.g. **Composers; Conductors (Music); Organists; Pianists; Singers; Violinists, violoncellists, etc.;** etc.; and names of musicians
   xx **Music**

Musicians, American 780.92; 920
    x American musicians; United States—
        Musicians
Musicians—Biography 780.92; 920
    xx **Biography**
Musicians, Black. *See* **Black musicians**
Musicians—Portraits 780.2
    xx **Portraits**
Muslim countries. *See* **Islamic countries**
Muslimism. *See* **Islam**
Muslims (May subdiv. geog.) **297**
    x Mohammedans; Moslems; Muhammedans;
        Mussulmans
Muslims, Black. *See* **Black Muslims**
Muslims—United States 297
    See also **Black Muslims**
    x United States—Muslims
Mussulmans. *See* **Muslims**
Mutation (Biology). *See* **Evolution; Variation (Biol-
        ogy)**
Mutual defense assistance program. *See* **Military
        assistance**
Mutual funds. *See* **Investment trusts**
Mycology. *See* **Fungi**
Myotherapy. *See* **Acupressure**
Mysteries and miracle plays 808.2; 808.82; 812; etc.
    See also **Morality plays**
    x Bible plays; Miracle plays
    xx **Bible—Drama; Drama; English drama; Mo-
        rality plays; Pageants; Passion plays; Reli-
        gious drama; Theater**
**Mystery and detective stories 808.83; 813; etc.; Fic;
    S C**
    May be used for single novels as well as for col-
        lections of stories.
    x Detective stories; Stories
    xx **Fiction**
Mysticism 149; 248.2
    See also **Cabala; Religious art and symbolism;
        Spiritual life; Symbolism of numbers; Theos-
        ophy**
    xx **Philosophy; Religion; Theology**
Mythical animals. *See* **Animals, Mythical**
Mythology (May use ethnic or geog. subdiv. adjective
        form) **291.1**
    See also

Animals, Mythical	**Heroes and heroines**
Art and mythology	**Indians of North Ameri-**
Folklore	**ca—Religion**
Geographical myths	**Symbolism**
Gods and goddesses	**Totems and totemism**

    x Myths
    xx **Creation; Folklore; God; Gods and goddesses;
        Heroes and heroines; Legends; Religion;
        Religions**
Mythology, Classical 292
    x Classical mythology; Greek mythology; Ro-
        man mythology
    xx **Classical antiquities**
Mythology in art. *See* **Art and mythology**

Mythology, Indian. *See* **Indians of North America—Religion**

Myths. *See* **Mythology**

N.A.T.O. *See* **North Atlantic Treaty Organization**

Names 929.4

> *See also* types of names, e.g. **Code names; Names, Geographical; Names, Personal; Pseudonyms;** etc.
>
> *x* Epithets; Nomenclature; Proper names; Terminology

Names, Fictitious. *See* **Pseudonyms**

Names, Geographical (May subdiv. geog.) **910**

> *See also* **Gazetteers**
>
> *x* Geographical names; Place names
>
> *xx* **Gazetteers; Names**

Names, Geographical—United States 917.3

> *x* United States—Geographical names; United States—Names, Geographical

Names, Personal (May subdiv. geog. or by ethnic adjective, e.g. **Names, Personal—United States; Names, Personal—Scottish;** etc.) **929.4**

> *See also* **Nicknames; Pseudonyms**
>
> *x* Christian names; Family names; Forenames; Personal names; Surnames
>
> *xx* **Names**

Names, Personal—Scottish 929.4

> *x* Scottish personal names

Names, Personal—United States 929.4

> *x* American personal names; United States—Names, Personal; United States—Personal names

Names—Pronunciation 421

> *x* Pronunciation

Napoleon I, Emperor of the French, 1769-1821—Drama 812; 822; etc.

> *xx* **Drama**

Napoleon I, Emperor of the French, 1769-1821—Fiction 813; 823; etc.

> *xx* **Fiction; Historical fiction**

Napoleonic Wars. *See* **Europe—History—1789-1900; France—History—1789-1799, Revolution**

Narcotic addicts. *See* **Drug addicts**

Narcotic habit 362.2; 613.8; 616.8

> See note under **Drug abuse.**
>
> *See also* **Drug addicts;** also classes of people with the subdivision *Drug use,* e.g. **Criminals—Drug use; Youth—Drug use;** etc.
>
> *x* Addiction to drugs; Drug addiction; Drug habit; Intoxication
>
> *xx* **Drug abuse; Habit; Temperance**

Narcotic traffic 364.1

> *x* Drug pushers; Drug traffic

Narcotics 615

> *See also* **Stimulants;** also names of specific narcotics, e.g. **Opium;** etc.
>
> *x* Hard drugs; Opiates; Soporifics
>
> *xx* **Drugs; Materia medica; Stimulants;**

Narcotics—*Continued*
> Therapeutics

Narcotics and crime   364.1
> *See also* **Drug addicts**
> *x* Crime and narcotics

Narration with music.   *See* **Monologues with music**

Nation of Islam.   *See* **Black Muslims**

National anthems.   *See* **National songs**

National book week   021.7
> *x* Book week, National
> *xx* **Books and reading**

National characteristics (May subdiv. geog. adjective form)
> *See also* **Ethnopsychology**
> *x* Characteristics, National; Images, National; National images; National psychology; Psychology, National
> *xx* **Anthropology; Ethnopsychology; Nationalism; Social psychology**

National characteristics, American   155.8; 973
> *x* American characteristics; American national characteristics; United States—National characteristics

National consciousness.   *See* **Nationalism**

National dances.   *See* **Folk dancing**

National debts.   *See* **Debts, Public**

National defenses.   *See* **Industrial mobilization;** and names of countries with the subdivision *Defenses,* e.g. **United States—Defenses;** etc.

National forests.   *See* **Forest reserves**

National Guard (U.S.).   *See* **United States. National Guard**

National health service.   *See* **Medicine, State**

National holidays.   *See* **Holidays;** and names of national holidays, e.g. **Memorial Day;** etc.

National hymns.   *See* **National songs**

National images.   *See* **National characteristics**

National interest.   *See* **Public interest**

National liberation movements (May subdiv. geog. except U.S.)   **320.5**
> *See also* **Guerrillas;** also names of specific groups
> *x* Liberation movements, National
> *xx* **Colonies; Guerrillas; Nationalism; Revolutions**

National libraries   027.5
> Use for materials on libraries, maintained by government funds, that serve the nation as a whole, particularly in the function of collection and preservation of a nation's publications.
> *x* Libraries, National
> *xx* **Government libraries**

National monuments.   *See* **National parks and reserves; Natural monuments**

National parks and reserves (May subdiv. geog.)   **719**
> *See also* **Forest reserves; Natural monuments; Wilderness areas;** also names of national parks, e.g. **Yosemite National Park (Calif.);** etc.

National parks and reserves—*Continued*

 x National monuments; Public lands

 xx **Conservation of natural resources; Forest reserves; Parks; Wildlife conservation**

National parks and reserves—**United States** 719; 973

 x United States—National parks and reserves

National planning. *See* **Economic policy; Social policy;** and names of countries with the subdivision *Economic policy* or *Social policy,* e.g. **United States—Economic policy; United States—Social policy;** etc.; and appropriate topical subjects with the subdivision *Government policy,* e.g. **Environment—Government policy;** etc.

National psychology. *See* **Ethnopsychology; National characteristics**

National resources. *See* **Natural resources;** and names of countries with the subdivision *Economic conditions,* e.g. **United States—Economic conditions;** etc.

National security 350; 355

 See also **Economic policy; International relations; Military policy;** also names of countries with the subdivision *National security,* e.g. **United States—National security;** etc.

 xx **Economic policy; International relations; Military policy**

National socialism 320.5; 335.6

 Use for materials limited to fascism in Germany during the Nazi regime.

 See also **Fascism; Socialism**

 x Nazism

 xx **Fascism; Fascism—Germany; Socialism; Totalitarianism; World War, 1939-1945—Causes**

National songs (May subdiv. geog. adjective form) **784.7**

 See also **Folk songs; Patriotic poetry; War songs**

 x Anthems, National; National anthems; National hymns; Patriotic songs; Songs, National

 xx **Folk songs; Songs**

National songs, American **784.7**

 x American national songs; United States—National songs

 xx **Songs, American**

Nationalism 320.5

 See also **Minorities; National characteristics; National liberation movements; Patriotism**

 x Internationalism; National consciousness; Regionalism

 xx **International relations; Minorities; Patriotism; Political science**

Nationalism, Black. *See* **Black nationalism**

Nationalist China. *See* **Taiwan**

Nationality (Citizenship). *See* **Citizenship**

Nationalization. *See* **Government ownership**

Nationalization of railroads. *See* **Railroads—Government policy**

Nations, Law of. *See* **International law**

Native Americans. *See* **Indians of North America**

Native peoples. *See* **Ethnology; Indians of North America**

Nativity of Christ. *See* **Jesus Christ—Nativity**

NATO. *See* **North Atlantic Treaty Organization**

Natural beauty conservation. *See* **Landscape protection**

Natural Bridge (Va.) 975.5
    xx **Natural monuments**

Natural childbirth 618.4
    x Childbirth, Natural; Lamaze method of childbirth
    xx **Childbirth**

Natural disasters (May subdiv. geog.) **904**
    See also names of natural disasters, e.g.
        Earthquakes; Floods; etc.
    xx **Disasters**

Natural disasters—United States 904
    x United States—Natural disasters

Natural food. *See* **Food, Natural**

Natural food cookery. *See* **Cookery—Natural foods**

Natural gas 665.5; 665.7
    See also **Boring**
    x Gas, Natural
    xx **Geology, Economic; Wells**

Natural history (May subdiv. geog.) **500**
    Use for popular materials describing animals, plants, minerals and nature in general. Guides on the detailed study of birds, flowers, etc. are entered under **Nature study.**
    See also

Aquariums	**Freshwater biology**
Biogeography	**Geology**
Biology	**Marine biology**
Botany	**Mineralogy**
Fossils	**Zoology**

    x Animal lore; History, Natural
    xx **Animals; Biology; Science; Zoology**

Natural history, Biblical. *See* **Bible—Natural history**

Natural history—Outdoor guides. *See* **Nature study**

Natural history—United States 500
    x United States—Natural history

Natural law. *See* **Civil rights; Ethics; Freedom; International law**

Natural monuments (May subdiv. geog.) **719**
    Use for general materials on natural objects of historic or scientific interest such as caves, cliffs, and natural bridges, and for those created as national monuments by presidential proclamation.
    See also **Wilderness areas;** also names of natural monuments, e.g. **Natural Bridge (Va.);** etc.
    x Landmarks, Preservation of; Monuments, Natural; National monuments; Preservation of natural scenery; Protection of natural

Natural monuments—*Continued*
>> scenery
>> *xx* **Landscape protection; National parks and re-**
>>> **serves; Nature conservation**

Natural monuments—United States 973
>> *x* United States—Natural monuments

Natural parents. *See* **Birthparents**

Natural pesticides 668
>> *xx* **Pesticides**

Natural religion. *See* **Natural theology**

Natural resources (May subdiv. geog.) 333; 333.1-
>>> 333.5
>> *See also* **Conservation of natural resources; Fish-**
>>> **eries; Reclamation of land; Soil conserva-**
>>> **tion;** also names of natural resources, e.g.
>>> **Energy resources; Forests and forestry; Ma-**
>>> **rine resources; Mines and mineral resources;**
>>> etc.
>> *x* National resources; Resources, Natural
>> *xx* **Economic conditions; Environment—**
>>> **Government policy; Wildlife conservation**

Natural resources—Management 333
>> *xx* **Management**

Natural resources—United States 333
>> *See also* **United States—Economic conditions**
>> *x* United States—Natural resources

Natural selection 575.01
>> *See also* **Evolution; Heredity**
>> *x* Selection, Natural; Survival of the fittest
>> *xx* **Evolution; Genetics; Heredity; Variation (Biol-**
>>> **ogy)**

Natural steam energy. *See* **Geothermal resources**

Natural theology 210
>> Use for materials dealing with the knowledge of
>>> God's existence obtained by observing the
>>> visible processes of nature.
>> *See also* **Creation; Religion and science**
>> *x* Natural religion; Theology, Natural
>> *xx* **Apologetics; God; Religion; Religion and sci-**
>>> **ence; Theology**

Natural therapy. *See* **Naturopathy**

Naturalism in literature. *See* **Realism in literature**

Naturalists 500.92; 920
>> *See also* names of types of naturalists, e.g.
>>> **Biologists; Botanists;** etc.
>> *xx* **Scientists**

Naturalization 323.6
>> *See also* **Aliens; Citizenship**
>> *x* Foreigners
>> *xx* **Aliens; Americanization; Citizenship; Immi-**
>>> **gration and emigration; International law;**
>>> **Suffrage**

Nature conservation 333.7
>> *See also* **Endangered species; Landscape protec-**
>>> **tion; Natural monuments; Plant conserva-**
>>> **tion; Wildlife conservation**
>> *x* Conservation of nature; Nature protection;
>>> Preservation of natural scenery; Protection
>>> of natural scenery
>> *xx* **Conservation of natural resources**

Nature, Effect of man on. *See* **Man—Influence on nature**

Nature in literature 809
> *See also* **Animals in literature; Birds in literature; Nature in poetry**

Nature in poetry 809.1
> *x* Nature poetry; Poetry of nature
> *xx* **Nature in literature; Poetry**

Nature photography 778.9
> *See also* **Outdoor photography; Photography of animals; Photography of birds; Photography of fishes; Photography of plants**
> *x* Photography of nature
> *xx* **Nature study; Outdoor photography; Photography**

Nature poetry. *See* **Nature in poetry**

Nature protection. *See* **Nature conservation**

Nature study (May subdiv. geog.) **372.3; 507**
> See note under **Natural history.**
> *See also* **Animals—Habits and behavior; Botany; Nature photography; Zoology**
> *x* Natural history—Outdoor guides
> *xx* **Animals—Habits and behavior; Outdoor life; Science—Study and teaching**

Nature study—United States 509
> *x* United States—Nature study

Naturopathy 615.5
> *x* Natural therapy
> *xx* **Chiropractic; Therapeutics**

Nautical almanacs 528
> *x* Ephemerides
> *xx* **Almanacs; Navigation**

Nautical astronomy 527
> *See also* **Latitude; Longitude; Navigation**
> *x* Astronomy, Nautical
> *xx* **Astronomy; Navigation**

Navaho Indians. *See* **Navajo Indians**

Navaho language. *See* **Navajo language**

Navajo Indians 970.004
> *x* Navaho Indians
> *xx* **Indians of North America**

Navajo language 497
> *x* Navaho language
> *xx* **Indians of North America—Languages**

Naval administration. *See* **Naval art and science;** and names of countries with the subhead *Navy,* e.g. **United States. Navy;** etc.

Naval aeronautics. *See* **Aeronautics, Military**

Naval air bases. *See* **Air bases**

Naval airplanes. *See* **Airplanes, Military**

Naval architecture 623.8
> *See also* **Boatbuilding; Marine engineering; Shipbuilding; Ships; Steamboats; Warships**
> *x* Architecture, Naval; Marine architecture
> *xx* **Architecture; Shipbuilding**

Naval art and science 359
> *See also*

Camouflage (Military science)	**Military art and science**
	Navies
Marine engineering	**Navigation**

425

Naval art and science—*Continued*
Navy yards and naval sta-   Signals and signaling
  tions   Strategy
Privateering   Submarine warfare
Sailors   Submarines
Sea power   Torpedoes
Shipbuilding   Warships
   x Fighting; Naval administration; Naval sci-
     ence; Naval warfare; Navy
  xx **Military art and science; Navies; Navigation;**
     Strategy; War
Naval art and science—Study and teaching. *See*
    Naval education
Naval bases. *See* **Navy yards and naval stations**
Naval battles 359.4; 904
  See also **Battles; Naval history;** also names of
    countries with the subdivision *History, Na-*
    val, e.g. **United States—History, Naval;**
    etc.; names of wars with the subdivision
    Naval operations, e.g. **World War, 1939-**
    1945—Naval operations; etc.; and names of
    naval battles
  x Naval warfare
  xx **Battles; Sea power**
Naval biography. *See* names of navies with the
     subdivision *Biography,* e.g. **United States.**
    Navy—Biography; etc.
Naval education 359.5
  x Education, Naval; Naval art and science—
    Study and teaching; Naval schools
  xx **Education**
Naval engineering. *See* **Marine engineering**
Naval history 359.409
  See also **Military history; Pirates; Privateering;**
    Sea power; also names of countries with the
    subhead *Navy* or the subdivision *History,*
    Naval, e.g. **United States. Navy; United**
    States—History, Naval, etc.
  x History, Naval; Wars
  xx **History; Military history; Naval battles; Sea**
    power
Naval law. *See* **Maritime law**
Naval offenses. *See* **Military offenses**
Naval pensions. *See* **Pensions, Military**
Naval personnel. *See* **Sailors**
Naval power. *See* **Sea power**
Naval schools. *See* **Naval education**
Naval science. *See* **Naval art and science**
Naval shipyards. *See* **Navy yards and naval sta-**
    tions
Naval signaling. *See* **Signals and signaling**
Naval strategy. *See* **Strategy**
Naval uniforms. *See* **Uniforms, Military**
Naval warfare. *See* **Naval art and science; Naval**
    battles; Submarine warfare; and names of
    wars with the subdivision *Naval operations,*
    e.g. **World War, 1939-1945—Naval opera-**
    tions; etc.
Navies 359.3
  See also **Armies; Arms control; Naval art and**

Navies—*Continued*

science; Sailors; Sea power; Warships; also
names of countries with the subhead *Navy,*
e.g. **United States. Navy;** etc.

x Military forces; Military power; Navy

xx **Armaments; Armed forces; Armies; Military
personnel; Naval art and science; Sea
power; Ships; War; Warships**

Navigation   527; 623.89

See also

Compass	**Pilot guides**
Harbors	**Pilots and pilotage**
Inland navigation	**Radar**
Knots and splices	**Sailing**
Lighthouses	**Shipwrecks**
Loran	**Signals and signaling**
Nautical almanacs	**Steam navigation**
Nautical astronomy	**Tides**
Naval art and science	**Winds**
Ocean currents	

x Locomotion; Seamanship

xx **Direction sense; Nautical astronomy; Naval
art and science; Oceanography; Pilots and
pilotage; Sailing; Ships; Steam navigation**

Navigation, Aerial. *See* **Navigation (Aeronautics)**

Navigation (Aeronautics)   629.132

See also **Airplanes—Piloting; Radio in aeronautics**

x Aerial navigation; Aeronautics—Navigation;
Air navigation; Navigation, Aerial

xx **Aeronautics**

Navigation (Astronautics)   629.45

See also **Astronautical instruments; Space flight;
Space vehicles—Piloting**

x Astronavigation; Space navigation

xx **Astrodynamics; Astronautics; Space flight**

Navigation, Inland. *See* **Inland navigation**

Navigation—Law and legislation. *See* **Maritime
law**

Navigation, Steam. *See* **Steam navigation**

Navigators. *See* **Discoveries (in geography); Explorers; Sailors**

Navy. *See* **Naval art and science; Navies; Sea
power;** and names of countries with the
subhead *Navy,* e.g. **United States. Navy;**
etc.

Navy Sealab project. *See* **Sealab project**

Navy yards and naval stations   359.7

x Naval bases; Naval shipyards

xx **Naval art and science**

Nazism. *See* **National socialism**

Near East. *See* **Middle East**

Neatness. *See* **Cleanliness**

Nebulae, Extragalactic. *See* **Galaxies**

Necrologies. *See* **Obituaries**

Necromancy. *See* **Divination; Witchcraft**

Needlepoint   746.2

x Canvas embroidery

xx **Embroidery; Needlework**

Needlework 746.4

    See also types of needlework, e.g. **Dressmaking; Embroidery; Lace and lace making; Needlepoint; Sewing; Tapestry;** etc.

    xx **Decoration and ornament; Decorative arts; Dressmaking; Sewing**

Negotiable instruments 332.4; 332.7

    See also **Bonds**

    x Bills and notes; Bills of credit; Commercial paper; Instruments, Negotiable; Letters of credit

    xx **Banks and banking; Commercial law; Contracts; Credit**

Negritude. *See* **Blacks—Race identity**

Negroes. *See* **Blacks**

Neighborhood. *See* **Community life**

Neighborhood centers. *See* **Social settlements**

Neighborhood development. *See* **Community development**

Neighborhood schools. *See* **Schools**

Neo-fascism. *See* **Fascism**

Neo-Greek literature. *See* **Greek literature, Modern**

Neo-impressionism (Art). *See* **Impressionism (Art)**

Neo-Latin languages. *See* **Romance languages**

Neo-nazism. *See* **Fascism**

Neolithic period. *See* **Stone Age**

Neon tubes 621.32

    xx **Electric signs**

Nero, Emperor of Rome, 37-68 92

    x Emperors

    xx **Roman emperors**

Nerves 611; 612

    See also **Nervous system**

    xx **Nervous system**

Nerves—Diseases. *See* **Nervous system—Diseases**

Nervous breakdown. *See* **Neurasthenia**

Nervous exhaustion. *See* **Neurasthenia**

Nervous prostration. *See* **Neurasthenia**

Nervous system 611; 612

    See also **Brain; Nerves; Psychology, Pathological; Psychology, Physiological**

    x Neurology

    xx **Anatomy; Brain; Mind and body; Nerves; Physiology**

Nervous system—Diseases 616.8

    See also **Epilepsy; Fear; Neurasthenia; Worry**

    x Nerves—Diseases; Neuropathology

    xx **Medicine—Practice; Therapeutics**

Nests. *See* **Birds—Eggs and nests**

Netherlands 949.2

    x Holland

Netherlands—History 949.2

Netherlands—History—1940-1945, German occupation 949.2

    x German occupation of Netherlands, 1940-1945

    xx **Military occupation; World War, 1939-1945—Occupied territories**

Network theory. *See* **System analysis**

Networks, Computer. *See* **Computer networks**

Networks, Information. *See* **Information networks**
Networks, Library. *See* **Library information networks**
Neurasthenia 616.8
 x Nervous breakdown; Nervous exhaustion; Nervous prostration
 xx **Nervous system—Diseases**
Neurology. *See* **Nervous system**
Neuropathology. *See* **Nervous system—Diseases**
Neuroses 616.8
 See also **Depression, Mental; Fear; Medicine, Psychosomatic; Phobias**
 xx **Psychology, Pathological**
Neutrality 327.1; 341.6
 See also **Intervention (International law);** also names of countries with the subdivision *Neutrality,* e.g. **United States—Neutrality;** etc.
 x Nonalignment
 xx **International law; International relations; Intervention (International law); Privateering; Security, International**
Neutron bombs 623.4
 xx **Bombs; Neutron weapons**
Neutron weapons 623.4
 See also **Neutron bombs**
 x Enhanced radiation weapons; Weapons, Enhanced radiation; Weapons, Neutron
 xx **Nuclear weapons**
Neutrons 539.7
 See also **Atoms; Electrons; Protons**
 xx **Particles (Nuclear physics); Quantum theory**
New birth (Theology). *See* **Regeneration (Theology)**
New England 974
 xx **United States**
New France—History. *See* **Canada—History—0-1763 (New France); Mississippi River Valley—History**
New left. *See* **Right and left (Political science)**
New nations. *See* **States, New**
New Testament. *See* **Bible. N.T.**
New words. *See* **Words, New**
Newbery Medal books 028.5
 xx **Children's literature; Literary prizes**
News agencies 070.4
 x News services; Wire agencies
 xx **Press**
News broadcasting. *See* **Broadcast journalism**
News photography. *See* **Photography, Journalistic**
News services. *See* **News agencies**
Newspaper advertising 659.13
 Use for materials discussing advertising in newspapers. Materials discussing advertising of newspapers are entered under **Advertising—Newspapers.**
 x Advertising, Newspaper
 xx **Newspapers**
Newspaper clippings. *See* **Clippings (Books, newspapers, etc.)**

Newspaper work. *See* **Reporters and reporting**
Newspapers 070
    See note under **Journalism.**
    See also **Clippings (Books, newspapers, etc.);**
        Freedom of the press; Journalism; Newspa-
        per advertising; Periodicals; Press; Reporters
        and reporting; also **American newspapers;**
        English newspapers; etc.; and names of in-
        dividual newspapers
    xx **Journalism; Mass media; Periodicals; Press;**
        Serial publications
Newspapers—Advertising. *See* **Advertising—**
      Newspapers
Newspapers—Indexes 070.1
    xx **Indexes**
Nicene Creed 238
    xx **Creeds**
Nicknames 929.4
    x Epithets; Sobriquets; Soubriquets
    xx **Names, Personal**
Night 529
    See also **Bedtime; Day**
    xx **Chronology; Day; Time**
Night schools. *See* **Evening and continuation**
      schools
Nike rocket 623.4
    xx **Guided missiles**
Nineteenth century 909.81
    Use for general materials covering progress and
      development during this period in one or in
      several countries.
    x 1800-1899 (19th century)
    xx **History, Modern—1800-1899 (19th century)**
Nitrates 546; 661
    xx **Fertilizers and manures**
Nitrogen 546; 665
    xx **Gases**
No fault automobile insurance. *See* **Insurance, Au-**
      tomobile
Nobel prizes 800
    xx **Rewards (Prizes, etc.)**
Nobility 305.5; 929.7
    See also **Aristocracy; Heraldry; Knights and**
      knighthood
    x Baronage; Peerage
    xx **Aristocracy; Heraldry; Social classes**
Noise 534
    See also subjects with the subdivision *Noise,*
      e.g. **Airplanes—Noise;** etc.
    xx **Public health; Sound**
Noise pollution 363.7
    See also subjects with the subdivision *Noise,*
      e.g. **Airplanes—Noise;** etc.
    xx **Pollution**
Nomads 304.2; 306
    x Pastoral peoples
    xx **Society, Nonliterate folk**
Nomenclature. *See* **Names;** and scientific and
      technical subjects with the subdivision

Nomenclature—*Continued*
Terminology, e.g. **Botany—Terminology; etc.**
Nomination of presidents. *See* **Presidents—United States—Nomination**
Non-proliferation of nuclear weapons. *See* **Arms control**
Non-victim crimes. *See* **Crimes without victims**
Non-wage payments. *See* **Nonwage payments**
Nonalignment. *See* **Neutrality**
Nonbook materials. *See* **Audiovisual materials**
Noncitizens. *See* **Aliens**
Nonconformity. *See* **Conformity; Counter culture; Dissent**
Nondenominational churches. *See* **Community churches**
Nonfamily households. *See* **Shared housing**
Nonformal colleges and universities. *See* **Free universities**
Nonfossil fuels. *See* **Synthetic fuels**
Nongraded schools 371.2
  x Multiage grouping; Schools, Nongraded; Schools, Ungraded; Ungraded schools
  xx **Ability grouping in education; Education— Experimental methods**
Noninstitutional churches 289.9
  x Avant-garde churches; Churches, Avant-garde; Churches, Noninstitutional
Nonlinguistic communication. *See* **Nonverbal communication**
Nonliterate folk society. *See* **Society, Nonliterate folk**
Nonliterate man. *See* **Man, Nonliterate**
Nonmarital relations. *See* **Unmarried couples**
Nonnationals. *See* **Aliens**
Nonnutritive sweeteners. *See* **Sugar substitutes**
Nonobjective art. *See* **Art, Abstract**
Nonprescription drugs. *See* **Drugs, Nonprescription**
Nonprint materials. *See* **Audiovisual materials**
Nonprofitable drugs. *See* **Orphan drugs**
Nonpublic schools. *See* **Church schools; Private schools**
Nonrelated families. *See* **Shared housing**
Nonsense verses 808.81; 811; 821; etc.
  See also **Limericks; Tongue twisters**
  x Rhymes
  xx **Children's poetry; Humorous poetry; Limericks; Poetry—Collected works; Wit and humor**
Nonsupport. *See* **Desertion and nonsupport**
Nonverbal communication 001.56
  See also **Deaf—Means of communication; Personal space;** also types of nonverbal communication, e.g. **Body language;** etc.
  x Nonlinguistic communication
  xx **Communication**
Nonvictim crimes. *See* **Crimes without victims**
Nonviolence 172; 322.4
  See also **Hunger strikes; Pacifism; Passive resistance**
  xx **Pacifism; Passive resistance**

Nonviolent noncooperation. *See* **Passive resistance**

Nonwage payments 331.25

> *x* Employee benefits; Fringe benefits; Non-wage payments
>
> *xx* **Wages**

Nonword stories. *See* **Stories without words**

Nordic peoples. *See* **Teutonic peoples**

Normal schools. *See* **Teachers colleges**

Normandy (France), Attack on, 1944 940.54

> *x* D Day

Normans 941.02

> *See also* **Vikings**
>
> *xx* **Great Britain—History—1066-1154, Norman period; Vikings**

Norse languages. *See* **Old Norse language; Scandinavian languages**

Norse legends. *See* **Legends, Norse**

Norse literature. *See* **Old Norse literature; Scandinavian literature**

Norsemen. *See* **Vikings**

North Africa. *See* **Africa, North**

North America 970

> *See also* **Pacific Northwest**
>
> *xx* **America**

North America—Exploration. *See* **America—Exploration**

North American Indians. *See* **Indians of North America**

North Atlantic Treaty Organization 341.24

> *x* N.A.T.O.; NATO

North Central States. *See* **Middle West**

North Korea. *See* **Korea (North)**

North Pole 998

> *See also* **Arctic regions**
>
> *x* Polar expeditions
>
> *xx* **Arctic regions; Polar regions**

Northeast Passage 998

> *xx* **Arctic regions; Discoveries (in geography); Voyages and travels**

Northern lights. *See* **Auroras**

Northmen. *See* **Vikings**

Northwest, Canadian 971.2

> *x* Canada, Northwest; Canadian Northwest
>
> *xx* **Canada**

Northwest coast of North America

> *x* Northwest, Pacific coast; Pacific Northwest coast

Northwest, Old. *See* **Old Northwest**

Northwest, Pacific. *See* **Pacific Northwest**

Northwest, Pacific coast. *See* **Northwest coast of North America**

Northwest Passage 971.9

> *xx* **America—Exploration; Arctic regions; Discoveries (in geography); Voyages and travels**

Northwest Territory. *See* **Old Northwest**

Norwegian language 439.8

> May be subdivided like **English language.**
>
> *See also* **Danish language**
>
> *xx* **Scandinavian languages**

Norwegian language—0-1350. *See* **Old Norse**

Norwegian language—0-1350—*Continued*
    language
Norwegian literature 839.8
    May use same subdivisions and names of literary forms as for **English literature.**
    xx **Scandinavian literature**
Nose 611; 612
    xx **Face; Head; Smell**
Notation, Music. *See* **Musical notation**
Novelists (May subdiv. geog. adjective form) **809.3; 920**
    xx **Authors**
Novelists, American 809.3; 920
    x American novelists; United States—Novelists
Novels. *See* **Fiction**
Novels—Plots. *See* **Plots (Drama, fiction, etc.)**
Nuclear energy 539.7; 621.48
    See also **Atomic bomb; Nuclear engineering; Nuclear industry; Nuclear propulsion; Nuclear reactors**
    x Atomic energy; Atomic power; Nuclear power
    xx **Atomic theory; Nuclear physics**
Nuclear engineering 621.48
    See also **Nuclear reactors; Radioisotopes**
    xx **Engineering; Nuclear energy; Nuclear physics**
Nuclear freeze movement. *See* **Antinuclear movement**
Nuclear industry 621.48
    x Atomic industry
    xx **Nuclear energy**
Nuclear medicine 616.9
    x Atomic medicine; Medicine, Atomic; Medicine, Nuclear
    xx **Radiation—Physiological effect**
Nuclear particles. *See* **Particles (Nuclear physics)**
Nuclear physics 539.7
    See also

Chemistry, Physical and theoretical	**Nuclear reactors**
	Particles (Nuclear physics)
Cosmic rays	**Radioactivity**
Cyclotron	**Radiobiology**
Nuclear energy	**Transmutation (Chemistry)**
Nuclear engineering	

    x Atomic nuclei; Physics, Nuclear
    xx **Atoms; Chemistry, Physical and theoretical; Physics; Radioactivity**
Nuclear pollution. *See* **Radioactive pollution**
Nuclear power. *See* **Nuclear energy**
Nuclear power plants 621.48
    See also **Antinuclear movement**
    x Atomic power plants; Power plants, Atomic
    xx **Antinuclear movement; Power plants**
Nuclear power plants—Environmental aspects 333.79; 621.48
    x Environmental aspects
    xx **Environment; Environmental health**
Nuclear power plants—Fires and fire prevention 363.3; 621.48
    xx **Fire prevention; Fires**

Nuclear power plants—Security measures   621.48
>   *x* Security measures
>   *xx* **Burglary protection**

Nuclear propulsion   621.48; 629.47
>   *See also* **Nuclear reactors;** also specific applica-
>   tions, e.g. **Nuclear submarines;** etc.
>   *x* Atomic powered vehicles
>   *xx* **Nuclear energy**

Nuclear reactors   621.48
>   *x* Atomic piles; Breeder reactors; Fast breeder
>   reactors; Reactors (Nuclear physics)
>   *xx* **Nuclear energy; Nuclear engineering; Nuclear
>   physics; Nuclear propulsion**

Nuclear submarines   623.8
>   *x* Atomic submarines; Submarines, Nuclear
>   *xx* **Nuclear propulsion; Submarines**

Nuclear test ban.   *See* **Arms control**

Nuclear warfare   355
>   *See also* **Atomic bomb; Hydrogen bomb; Nuclear
>   weapons**
>   *x* Atomic warfare

Nuclear weapons   355.8; 623.4
>   *See also* **Antinuclear movement; Hydrogen bomb;**
>   also names of nuclear weapons, e.g. **Atomic
>   bomb; Ballistic missiles; Neutron weapons;**
>   etc.
>   *x* Atomic weapons; Weapons, Atomic; Weap-
>   ons, Nuclear
>   *xx* **Nuclear warfare; Ordnance**

Nuclear weapons and disarmament.   *See* **Arms control**

Nucleic acids   547.7; 574.87
>   *See also* **DNA; Ribonucleic acid**
>   *x* Polynucleotides

Nucleons.   *See* **Particles (Nuclear physics)**

Nudity in the performing arts   790.2
>   *xx* **Performing arts**

Number concept   119; 155.4; 372.7
>   See note under **Numeration.**
>   *xx* **Apperception; Psychology**

Number games   793.7
>   *xx* **Arithmetic—Study and teaching; Counting;
>   Mathematical recreations**

Number symbolism.   *See* **Symbolism of numbers**

Number systems.   *See* **Numeration**

Number theory   510.1
>   *See also* **Group theory; Numeration**
>   *x* Numbers, Theory of; Theory of numbers
>   *xx* **Algebra; Mathematics; Set theory**

Numbers, Theory of.   *See* **Number theory**

Numerals   513
>   *See also* **Symbolism of numbers;** also names of
>   individual numbers, e.g. **Three (The num-
>   ber);** etc.
>   *xx* **Mathematics**

Numeration   513
>   Use for materials on systems of numeration and
>   for the theory of numeration. Works on the
>   psychology of numeration are entered under
>   **Number concept.** Materials on counting, in-

Numeration—*Continued*

cluding counting books, are entered under **Counting.**

See also **Counting**; also systems of numeration, e.g. **Binary system (Mathematics); Decimal system**; etc.

x Number systems

xx **Arithmetic; Counting; Mathematics; Number theory**

Numerology. *See* **Symbolism of numbers**

Numismatics 737

Use for materials on coins, paper money, medals, and tokens considered as works of art, as historical specimens, or as aids to the study of history, archeology, etc.

See also **Coins; Medals; Seals (Numismatics)**

xx **Archeology; Coins; History; History, Ancient; Medals**

Nunneries. *See* **Convents**

Nuns 255; 271

x Sisters (in religious orders, congregations, etc.)

xx **Religious orders for women**

Nurse clinicians. *See* **Nurse practitioners**

Nurse practitioners 610.73092; 920

x Nurse clinicians

xx **Allied health personnel; Nurses**

Nurseries, Day. *See* **Child care centers**

Nurseries (Horticulture) 635

See also **Plant propagation**

xx **Fruit culture; Gardening; Trees**

Nursery rhymes 398

x Poetry for children; Rhymes

xx **Children's poetry; Children's songs; Folklore**

Nursery schools 372

See also **Child care centers; Education, Preschool; Kindergarten**

xx **Child care centers; Education, Elementary; Education, Preschool**

Nurses 610.7606; 920

See also types of nurses, e.g. **Nurse practitioners; Practical nurses; School nurses**; etc.

x District nurses; Trained nurses

Nursing 610.73; 649,8

See also **Children—Care and hygiene; Cookery for the sick; First aid; Hospitals; Infants— Care and hygiene; Sick**; also types of nursing, e.g. **Home nursing; Practical nursing**; etc.; and diseases and medical procedures with the subdivision *Nursing,* e.g. **Cancer—Nursing; Heart—Surgery— Nursing**; etc.

xx **Children—Care and hygiene; Hospitals; Medicine; Medicine—Practice; Sick; Therapeutics**

Nursing homes 362.1

xx **Elderly—Care and hygiene; Hospitals; Institutional care; Long-term care facilities**

Nursing (Infant feeding). *See* **Breast feeding**

Nutrition 641.1

See also **Diet; Digestion; Eating customs; Food;**

Nutrition—*Continued*
> **Malnutrition; Metabolism; Vitamins;** also
> subjects with the subdivision *Nutrition,* e.g.
> **Astronauts—Nutrition; Children—Nutrition;**
> **Plants—Nutrition;** etc.

   x Meal planning

   xx **Diet; Digestion; Food; Metabolism; Physiol-**
      ogy; Self-care, Health; Therapeutics

Nuts 634
> Names of all nuts are not included in this list
> but are to be added as needed, in the singu-
> lar form, e.g. **Pecan;** etc.

   See also names of nuts, e.g. **Pecan;** etc.

   xx **Trees**

Nylon 677

   xx **Fabrics; Synthetic fabrics**

Oak 582.16

   xx **Trees; Wood**

Oats 633.1

   xx **Feeds**

Obedience 179

   x Disobedience

   xx **Human behavior**

Obelisks 721

   xx **Archeology; Architecture; Monuments; Pyra-**
      mids

Obesity 613.2; 616.3

   x Corpulence; Fatness; Overweight

Obesity—Control. *See* **Reducing**

Obituaries 920

   x Death notices; Necrologies

   xx **Biography**

Objective tests. *See* **Examinations; Mental tests**

Obscene materials. *See* **Pornography**

Obscenity (Law) 345

   See also **Pornography**

Observatories, Astronomical. *See* **Astronomical ob-**
      servatories

Observatories, Meteorological. *See* Meteorology—
      Observatories

Obstetrics. *See* **Childbirth**

Occidental civilization. *See* **Civilization, Occidental**

Occult sciences 133

   See also

Alchemy	**Oracles**
Astrology	**Palmistry**
Cabala	**Prophecies (Occult sci-**
Clairvoyance	**ences)**
Demonology	**Spiritualism**
Divination	**Superstition**
Fortune telling	**Witchcraft**
Magic	

   x Hermetic art and philosophy; Sorcery

   xx **Astrology; Demonology; Divination; Magic;**
      Supernatural; Superstition; Witchcraft

Occupation, Military. *See* **Military occupation**

Occupational diseases 616.9

   See also **Lead poisoning; Occupational health**
      services; Occupations, Dangerous; Workers'
      compensation

Occupational diseases—*Continued*

    x Diseases, Industrial; Diseases, Occupational; Diseases of occupation; Industrial diseases; Occupations—Diseases and hygiene

    xx **Labor; Occupational health and safety; Occupations, Dangerous; Public health**

Occupational forecasting. *See* **Employment forecasting**

Occupational guidance. *See* **Vocational guidance**

Occupational health and safety 363.1; 658.3

    See also **Burn out (Psychology); Hazardous substances; Occupational diseases; Occupations, Dangerous**

    x Health, Industrial; Hygiene, Industrial; Industrial health; Industrial safety; Safety, Industrial

    xx **Environmental health; Industrial management; Public health**

Occupational health services 362.1; 658.3

    Use for materials on health services for employees, usually provided at the place of work.

    x Employee health services

    xx **Medical care; Occupational diseases**

Occupational retraining 331.25

    See note under **Occupational training.**

    x Job retraining; Retraining, Occupational

    xx **Employees—Training; Human resources policy; Labor supply; Occupational training; Technical education; Unemployed; Vocational education**

Occupational stress. *See* **Job stress**

Occupational therapy 615.8

    See also **Handicraft**

    xx **Handicraft; Mental health; Physical therapy; Physically handicapped—Rehabilitation; Therapeutics**

Occupational training 331.7; 331.25

    Use for materials on teaching people a skill after formal education. Materials on teaching a skill during the educational process are entered under **Vocational education.** Materials discussing on-the-job training are entered under **Employees—Training.** Materials on retraining are entered under **Occupational retraining.**

    See also **Employees—Training; Occupational retraining**

    x Job training; Training, Occupational; Training, Vocational; Vocational training

    xx **Human resources policy; Technical education; Vocational education**

Occupations 331.7

    Use for descriptions and lists of occupations.

    See also **Job analysis; Paraprofessions and paraprofessionals; Professions; Vocational guidance;** also names of countries, cities, etc. with the subdivision *Occupations,* e.g. **United States—Occupations; Chicago (Ill.)—Occupations;** etc.; and names of occupations

Occupations—*Continued*
>   *x* Careers; Jobs; Trades; Vocations
>   *xx* **Business; Labor; Professions; Vocational guid-
>   ance**

Occupations, Dangerous 331.7
>   *See also* **Occupational diseases**
>   *x* Dangerous occupations; Injurious occupations
>   *xx* **Accidents; Labor; Occupational diseases; Oc-
>   cupational health and safety**

Occupations—Diseases and hygiene. *See* **Occupational diseases**

Occupied territory. *See* **Military occupation**

Ocean 551.46
>   *See also* **Icebergs; Oceanography; Seashore;
>   Storms;** also names of oceans and seas, e.g.
>   **Atlantic Ocean;** etc.
>   *x* Oceans; Sea
>   *xx* **Earth; Physical geography; Water**

Ocean bottom 551.46
>   *See also* **Marine mineral resources**
>   *x* Ocean floor; Sea bed
>   *xx* **Marine biology; Oceanography; Submarine
>   geology**

Ocean cables. *See* **Cables, Submarine**

Ocean currents 551.47
>   *x* Currents, Ocean
>   *xx* **Navigation; Oceanography; Physical geogra-
>   phy**

Ocean—Economic aspects. *See* **Marine resources;
Shipping**

Ocean energy resources 333.91
>   *See also* **Geothermal resources; Marine mineral
>   resources**
>   *x* Energy resources, Ocean
>   *xx* **Energy resources; Marine resources; Ocean
>   engineering**

Ocean engineering 627
>   Use for materials on engineering beneath the
>   surface of the ocean.
>   *See also* **Drilling platforms; Ocean energy re-
>   sources; Ocean mining**
>   *x* Deep sea engineering; Submarine engineering;
>   Undersea engineering
>   *xx* **Engineering; Marine resources; Oceanography**

Ocean farming. *See* **Aquaculture**

Ocean floor. *See* **Ocean bottom**

Ocean life. *See* **Marine biology**

Ocean mineral resources. *See* **Marine mineral resources**

Ocean mining 622
>   *x* Deep sea mining; Mining, Ocean
>   *xx* **Marine mineral resources; Mining engineer-
>   ing; Ocean engineering**

Ocean pollution. *See* **Marine pollution**

Ocean resources. *See* **Marine resources**

Ocean routes. *See* **Trade routes**

Ocean transportation. *See* **Shipping**

Ocean travel 910.4
>   *See also* **Steamboats; Yachts and yachting**
>   *x* Sea travel

Ocean travel—*Continued*
    xx **Transportation; Travel; Voyages and travels**
Ocean waves 551.47
    x Sea waves; Surf; Tidal waves
    xx **Oceanography; Waves**
Oceanariums. *See* **Marine aquariums**
Oceanauts. *See* **Aquanauts**
Oceania. *See* **Islands of the Pacific**
Oceanographic research. *See* **Oceanography—Research**
Oceanographic submersibles. *See* **Submersibles**
Oceanography (May subdiv. geog. area, e.g.
        Oceanography—Atlantic Ocean; etc.)
        551.46-551.47
    See also

Marine biology	**Ocean engineering**
Marine resources	**Ocean waves**
Navigation	**Submarine geology**
Ocean bottom	**Tides**
Ocean currents	

    x Deep sea technology; Oceanology; Undersea
        technology
    xx **Earth; Earth sciences; Geology; Geophysics;**
        Ocean
Oceanography—Computer programs 551.46-551.47
    xx **Computer programs**
Oceanography—Research 551.46-551.47
    See also **Bathyscaphe; Diving, Submarine; Skin**
        diving; Submersibles; Undersea research sta-
        tions; Underwater exploration
    x Oceanographic research
Oceanology. *See* **Oceanography**
Oceans. *See* **Ocean**
Oddities. *See* **Curiosities and wonders**
Offenses against public safety 364.1
    See also names of specific offenses, e.g.
        Hijacking of airplanes; Riots; Sabotage; etc.
    x Crimes against public safety; Public safety,
        Crimes against
    xx **Criminal law**
Offenses against the person 364.1
    See also names of specific offenses, e.g.
        Assassination; Kidnapping; Murder; Rape;
        etc.
    x Crimes against the person; Persons, Crimes
        against
    xx **Criminal law**
Offenses, Military. *See* **Military offenses**
Office buildings (May subdiv. geog.) **725**
    See also **Skyscrapers**
    x Buildings, Office
    xx **Industrial buildings**
Office employees 331.7; 651.3
    See also **Office practice; Sales personnel**
    x Clerical employees; Clerks; Commercial em-
        ployees; Employees, Clerical
    xx **Employees; Office practice; Sales personnel**
Office equipment and supplies 651
    See also types of office equipment and supplies,
        e.g. **Calculators; Keyboards (Electronics);**

Office equipment and supplies—*Continued*
         Typewriters; etc.
    x Business machines; Office machines; Office
        supplies
    xx **Bookkeeping; Office management**
Office machines. *See* **Office equipment and sup-**
        plies
Office management 651.3
    See also **Files and filing; Office equipment and**
        supplies; Office practice; Personnel manage-
        ment; Secretaries; Word processing
    x Office procedures
    xx **Business; Efficiency, Industrial; Factory man-**
        agement; Industrial management; Manage-
        ment; Personnel management
Office practice 651.3
    See also **Office employees; Shorthand; Typewrit-**
        ing; Word processing
    x Secretarial practice
    xx **Office employees; Office management**
Office procedures. *See* **Office management**
Office supplies. *See* **Office equipment and supplies**
Office, Tenure of. *See* **Civil service**
Office work—Training. *See* **Business education**
Official misconduct. *See* **Misconduct in office**
Official publications. *See* **Government publications;**
        and names of countries, cities, etc. with the
        subdivision *Government publications,* e.g.
        United States—Government publications;
        etc.
Officials. *See* **Civil service;** and names of coun-
        tries, cities, etc. and corporate bodies with
        the subdivision *Officials and employees,* e.g.
        United States—Officials and employees;
        Chicago (Ill.)—Officials and employees;
        United Nations—Officials and employees;
        etc.
Offset printing 686.2
    x Lithoprinting; Printing, Offset
    xx **Lithography; Printing**
Offshore oil well drilling. *See* **Oil well drilling,**
        Submarine
Offshore structures. *See* **Drilling platforms**
Offshore water pollution. *See* **Marine pollution**
Ohio 977.1
    Subdivisions have been given under this subject
        to serve as a guide to the subdivisions that
        may be used under the name of any state of
        the United States or province of Canada.
        The subdivisions under **United States** may
        be consulted as a guide for formulating
        other references that may be needed.
Ohio—Antiquities 977.1
Ohio—Bibliography 016.9771
Ohio—Bio-bibliography 016.9771
Ohio—Biography 920
Ohio—Biography—Dictionaries 920
Ohio—Biography—Portraits 920
Ohio—Boundaries 977.1
Ohio—Census 317.71

Ohio—Church history 277.71
Ohio—Civilization 977.1
Ohio—Climate 551.69771
Ohio—Commerce 381
Ohio—Constitutional history 342.771
Ohio—Description and travel 917.71
Ohio—Description and travel—Guidebooks 917.71
Ohio—Description and travel—Views 917.71
Ohio—Directories 977.1025
    Use for lists of names and addresses. Lists of
       names without addresses are entered under
      Ohio—Registers.
    See also **Ohio—Registers**
    xx **Ohio—Registers**
Ohio—Economic conditions 330.9771
Ohio—Economic policy 338.9771
    x State planning
    xx **Economic policy**
Ohio—Executive departments 353.03
Ohio—Foreign population 325.771
Ohio—Galleries and museums 708.171
Ohio—Gazetteers 910.3
Ohio—Government publications 015.771
Ohio—Historic buildings 725; 977.1
Ohio—History 977.1
Ohio—History, Local 977.1
Ohio—History—Societies 977.106
Ohio—History—Sources 977.1
Ohio—Industries 338.9771
    x Ohio—Manufactures
Ohio—Intellectual life 977.1
Ohio—Manufactures. *See* **Ohio—Industries**
Ohio—Maps 912
Ohio—Militia 355.3; 363.2
Ohio—Moral conditions 977.1
Ohio—Occupations 331.7
Ohio—Officials and employees 351.1
Ohio—Politics and government 977.1
    xx **State governments**
Ohio—Population 317.71
Ohio—Public buildings 725
Ohio—Public lands 333.1
Ohio—Public works 351.86
Ohio—Race relations 305.8
Ohio—Registers 929.4
    Use for lists of names without addresses. Lists of
      names that include addresses are entered
      under **Ohio—Directories.**
    See also **Ohio—Directories**
    xx **Ohio—Directories**
Ohio—Religion 277.71
Ohio—Rural conditions 307.7
    x Rural conditions
Ohio—Social conditions 977.1
Ohio—Social life and customs 977.1
Ohio—Social policy 361.6; 977.1
    x State planning
Ohio—Statistics 317.71
Oil. *See* **Oils and fats; Petroleum**

Oil burners 697
    xx **Heating; Petroleum as fuel**
Oil engines. *See* **Gas and oil engines**
Oil fuel. *See* **Petroleum as fuel**
Oil painting. *See* **Painting**
Oil pollution of rivers, harbors, etc. 363.7
    x Rivers—Pollution
    xx **Marine pollution; Oil pollution of water; Oil**
        spills
Oil pollution of water 363.7
    See also **Oil pollution of rivers, harbors, etc.**
    x Petroleum pollution of water; Water—Oil pol-
        lution
    xx **Oil spills; Water—Pollution**
Oil spills 363.7
    See also **Oil pollution of rivers, harbors, etc.; Oil**
        pollution of water
    xx **Marine pollution**
Oil well drilling 622
    See also **Oil wells—Blowouts**
    x Drilling, Oil well; Petroleum—Well boring;
        Well drilling, Oil
Oil well drilling, Submarine 622
    See also **Drilling platforms**
    x Deep sea drilling (Petroleum); Offshore oil
        well drilling; Submarine oil well drilling;
        Underwater drill (Petroleum)
Oil wells 622
Oil wells—Blowouts 622
    x Blowouts, Oil well
    xx **Oil well drilling**
Oils and fats 665
    See also **Essences and essential oils; Lubrication**
        and lubricants; Petroleum
    x Animal oils; Fat; Fats; Grease; Oil; Vegetable
        oils
    xx **Coal tar products; Lubrication and lubricants**
Oils, Essential. *See* **Essences and essential oils**
Old age 305.2
    See also **Age and employment; Aging; Elderly;**
        Longevity; Retirement
    x Age
    xx **Gerontology; Life (Biology); Longevity; Mid-**
        dle age; Physiology
Old age homes. *See* **Elderly—Institutional care**
Old age pensions 331.25; 368.4
    x Insurance, Old age; Labor—Insurance
    xx **Pensions; Retirement income; Saving and**
        thrift; Social security
Old English language. *See* **Anglo-Saxon language**
Old English literature. *See* **Anglo-Saxon literature**
Old Icelandic language. *See* **Old Norse language**
Old Norse language 439
    See also **Scandinavian languages**
    x Icelandic language—0-1500; Norse languages;
        Norwegian language—0-1350; Old Icelandic
        language; Old Norwegian language
    xx **Scandinavian languages**
Old Norse literature 839
    See also **Eddas; Sagas; Scandinavian literature**

Old Norse literature—*Continued*
>   *x* Norse literature
>   *xx* **Icelandic literature; Scandinavian literature**

Old Northwest 977
>   Use for materials on the region between the Ohio and Mississippi rivers and the Great Lakes.
>   *See also* **Middle West**
>   *x* Northwest, Old; Northwest Territory
>   *xx* **Middle West; United States**

Old Norwegian language. *See* **Old Norse language**

Old Southwest 976
>   Use for materials on the section which comprised the southwestern part of the United States before the cessions of land from Mexico following the Mexican War. It included Louisiana, Texas, Arkansas, Tennessee, Kentucky and Missouri.
>   *x* Southwest, Old
>   *xx* **United States**

Old Testament. *See* **Bible. O.T.**

Older people. *See* **Elderly**

Oleomargarine. *See* **Margarine**

Olympic games 796.4; 796.9
>   *See also* **Special Olympics**
>   *x* Games, Olympic
>   *xx* **Athletics; Contests; Games; Sports**

Olympics, Special. *See* **Special Olympics**

Ombudsman (May subdiv. geog.) **328; 342**
>   *x* Citizen's defender; Grievance procedures (Public administration)
>   *xx* **Administrative law; Public interest**

On the job stress. *See* **Job stress**

One act plays 808.82; 812; 812.08; etc.
>   *x* Plays; Short plays
>   *xx* **Amateur theater; Drama**

One parent family. *See* **Single parent family**

Online catalogs. *See* **Catalogs, Online**

Online data processing 001.6; *004
>   *See also* **Computer bulletin boards**
>   *xx* **Electronic data processing**

Online publishing. *See* **Electronic publishing**

Online reference services. *See* **Reference services (Libraries)**

Opaque projectors. *See* **Projectors**

Open and closed shop 331.88
>   *x* Closed shop; Right to work; Union shop
>   *xx* **Labor; Labor contract; Labor unions**

Open classroom approach to teaching. *See* **Open plan schools**

Open education. *See* **Open plan schools**

Open ended marriage. *See* **Unmarried couples**

Open heart surgery. *See* **Heart—Surgery**

Open housing. *See* **Discrimination in housing**

Open plan schools 371.3
>   Use for materials on schools without interior walls.
>   *See also* **Experimental schools; Individualized instruction**
>   *x* Interest centers approach to teaching; Learn-

Open plan schools—*Continued*
ing center approach to teaching; Open class-
room approach to teaching; Open education
xx **Education—Experimental methods; Experimental schools**
Open universities. *See* **Free universities**
Opera 782.1
See also **Ballet; Operetta**
x Comic opera; Dramatic music; Grand opera;
Music, Dramatic
xx **Drama; Musical form; Theater**
Opera houses. *See* **Theaters**
Operas 782.1
See also **Musical revues, comedies, etc.**
xx **Vocal music**
Operas—Librettos 782.1
xx **Librettos**
Operas—Stories, plots, etc. 782.1
x Stories
xx **Librettos; Plots (Drama, fiction, etc.)**
Operation Pluto. *See* **Cuba—History—1961, Inva-
sion**
Operations research 658.5
See also **Systems engineering**
xx **Research; System theory; Systems engineering**
Operations, Surgical. *See* **Surgery**
Operetta 782.81
See also **Musical revues, comedies, etc.**
x Comic opera; Dramatic music; Music, Dra-
matic
xx **Musical form; Opera; Vocal music**
Opiates. *See* **Narcotics**
Opinion polls. *See* **Public opinion polls**
Opinion, Public. *See* **Public opinion**
Opium 615
xx **Narcotics**
Opium—Physiological effect 613.8
x Physiological effect
xx **Pharmacology**
**Optical data processing 651.8; *006.4; *621.36;
*621.399**
x Visual data processing
xx **Bionics; Electronic data processing**
Optical discs. *See* **Optical storage devices**
Optical illusions 152.1
x Illusions
xx **Hallucinations and illusions; Psychology,
Physiological; Vision**
Optical masers. *See* **Lasers**
Optical storage devices 621.38; *004.56; *621.397
Use for materials on data storage devices in
which data (audio, digital, or video) are optically encoded and that permit playing back
through a mechanical system or a laser system.
See also **Laser recording; Videodiscs**
x Discs, Optical; Optical discs
xx **Computer storage devices; Laser recording;
Optics**

Optics   535; 621.36
   See also

Color	**Radiation**
Light	**Refraction**
Optical storage devices	**Space optics**
Perspective	**Spectrum analysis**
Phosphorescence	**Vision**
Photometry	

   xx **Light; Photometry; Physics**

Optometry   617.7
   See also **Eye**
   xx **Eye**

Oracles   133.3
   See also **Divination**
   xx **Divination; Occult sciences; Prophecies (Occult sciences)**

Oral arithmetic.   *See* **Arithmetic, Mental**

Oral history   900
   Use for materials on recording the oral recollections of events by persons. Use appropriate subject headings for the content of the recollections.
   x History, Oral
   xx **History**

Orange   634
   xx **Citrus fruit**

Orations.   *See* **Speeches, addresses, etc.**

Oratorios   782.8
   xx **Church music; Vocal music**

Oratory.   *See* **Public speaking**

Orbital laboratories.   *See* **Space stations**

Orbital rendezvous (Space flight)   629.45
   See also names of projects, e.g. **Apollo project; Gemini project;** etc.; also names of space ships
   x Rendezvous in space; Space orbital rendezvous
   xx **Space flight; Space ships; Space stations**

Orbiting vehicles.   *See* **Artificial satellites; Space stations**

Orchards.   *See* **Fruit culture**

Orchestra   785.06
   See also **Bands (Music); Conducting; Conductors (Music); Instrumentation and orchestration; Orchestral music;** also names of types of orchestras
   xx **Bands (Music); Conducting; Musical instruments**

Orchestral music   785
   See also types of orchestral music, e.g. **Chamber music; Concertos; Quintets; Sonatas; String orchestra music; Suites; Symphonies;** etc.
   xx **Instrumental music; Music; Orchestra**

Orchestration.   *See* **Instrumentation and orchestration**

Orders, Architectural.   *See* **Architecture—Orders**

Orders, Monastic.   *See* **Religious orders**

Ordination   262
   xx **Rites and ceremonies; Sacraments**

Ordination of men   262

Ordination of women 262
Ordnance 355.8; 623.4

> *See also* names of general and specific military ordnance, e.g. **Bombs; Nuclear weapons; Projectiles;** etc.; also names of armies with the subdivision *Ordnance and ordnance stores,* e.g. **United States. Army—Ordnance and ordnance stores;** etc.
>
> *x* Cannon; Guns
> *xx* **Armaments; Arms and armor; Artillery; Fire-arms; Military art and science; Projectiles**

Ore deposits 553

> *See also* **Ores;** also names of ores, e.g. **Iron ores;** etc.
>
> *xx* **Geology; Ores**

Ore dressing 622

> *x* Dressing of ores
> *xx* **Smelting**

Oregon country. *See* **Pacific Northwest**
Oregon Trail 987

> *xx* **Overland journeys to the Pacific (U.S.); United States**

Ores 553

> *See also* **Metallurgy; Metals; Mineralogy; Mines and mineral resources; Ore deposits;** also names of ores, e.g. **Iron ores;** etc.
>
> *xx* **Geology, Economic; Ore deposits**

Organ 786.5

> *See also* **Keyboards (Musical instruments)**
> *x* Pipe organ
> *xx* **Musical instruments**

Organ donation. *See* **Donation of organs, tissues, etc.**
Organ music 786.8

> *xx* **Church music; Music**

Organ preservation (Anatomy). *See* **Preservation of organs, tissues, etc.**
Organ transplantation. *See* **Transplantation of organs, tissues, etc.**
Organic chemistry. *See* **Chemistry, Organic**
Organic farming. *See* **Organiculture**
Organic food. *See* **Food, Natural**
Organic gardening. *See* **Organiculture**
Organic waste as fuel. *See* **Waste products as fuel**
Organiculture 631.5

> *x* Organic farming; Organic gardening
> *xx* **Agriculture; Gardening; Horticulture**

Organists 780.92; 920

> *xx* **Musicians**

Organization and management. *See* **Management**
Organization, International. *See* **International organization**
Organizational stress. *See* **Job stress**
Organizations. *See* **Associations**
Organized crime 364.1

> *See also* types of organized crime, e.g. **Racketeering;** etc.
>
> *x* Crime syndicates
> *xx* **Crime**

Organized labor. *See* **Labor unions**

Organs (Anatomy)—Preservation. *See* **Preservation of organs, tissues, etc.**
Organs, Artificial. *See* **Artificial organs**
Orient. *See* **Asia; East Asia; Middle East**
Oriental architecture. *See* **Architecture, Asian**
Oriental art. *See* **Art, Asian**
Oriental civilization. *See* **Civilization, Asian**
Oriental rugs. *See* **Rugs, Oriental**
Orientation. *See* **Direction sense**
Orienteering. *See* **Direction sense**
Origami 745.54
> *x* Japanese paper folding; Paper folding, Japanese
> *xx* **Paper crafts**
Origin of life. *See* **Life—Origin**
Origin of man. *See* **Man—Origin**
Origin of species. *See* **Evolution**
Ornament. *See* **Decoration and ornament**
Ornamental alphabets. *See* **Illumination of books and manuscripts; Lettering**
Ornamental plants. *See* **Plants, Ornamental**
Ornithology. *See* **Birds**
Orphan drugs 615
> Use for materials on drugs which appear to be useful for the treatment of rare disorders but due to their limited commercial value have difficulty in finding funding for research and marketing.
> *x* Drugs, Orphan; Nonprofitable drugs
> *xx* **Drugs**
Orphanages (May subdiv. geog.) **362.7**
> *See also* **Child welfare**
> *x* Charitable institutions; Homes (Institutions)
> *xx* **Charities; Child welfare; Children—Institutional care; Institutional care; Public welfare**
Orphans 362.7
> *See also* **Abandoned children; Children, Adopted**
> *x* Dependent children; Foundlings
> *xx* **Abandoned children; Children; Children, Adopted**
Orthodox Eastern Church 281.9
> *x* Greek Church
> *xx* **Eastern churches**
Orthodox Eastern Church, Russian 281.9
> *x* Russian Church
Orthography. *See* **Spelling reform;** and names of languages with the subdivision *Spelling,* e.g. **English language—Spelling;** etc.
Orthopedic surgery. *See* **Orthopedics**
Orthopedics 617
> *See also* **Physically handicapped**
> *x* Orthopedic surgery; Surgery, Orthopedic
> *xx* **Physically handicapped; Surgery**
Osteology. *See* **Bones**
Osteopathy 615.5
> *See also* **Chiropractic; Massage**
> *xx* **Massage; Medicine; Medicine—Practice**
Ostrogoths. *See* **Teutonic peoples**
Outboard motorboats. *See* **Motorboats**

Outdoor cookery 641.5; 641.7
> *See also* **Barbecue cookery**
> *x* Camp cooking; Cookery, Outdoor
> *xx* **Camping; Cookery**

Outdoor education. *See* **Outdoor life**

Outdoor life 796.5
> *See also* types of outdoor education, life and ac-
> tivities, e.g. **Camping; Country life; Hiking;
> Mountaineering; Nature study; Sports; Wil-
> derness survival;** etc.
> *x* Outdoor education; Rural life
> *xx* **Camping; Country life; Sports**

Outdoor photography 778.7
> *See also* **Nature photography**
> *x* Field photography; Photography, Outdoor
> *xx* **Nature photography**

Outdoor recreation 796
> *See also* **Parks; Recreational vehicles;** also types
> of outdoor recreation, e.g. **Camping;** etc.
> *xx* **Recreation**

Outdoor survival. *See* **Wilderness survival**

Outer space 523.1
> *See also* **Space environment; Space warfare**
> *x* Space, Outer
> *xx* **Astronautics; Astronomy; Space sciences**

Outer space and civilization. *See* **Astronautics and
> civilization**

Outer space—Colonies. *See* **Space colonies**

Outer space—Communication. *See* **Interstellar
> communication**

Outer space—Exploration 629.4
> *See also* **Space probes**
> *x* Exploration, Space; Space exploration (As-
> tronautics); Space research
> *xx* **Interplanetary voyages; Space flight**

Outer space travel. *See* **Interplanetary voyages**

Outlaws. *See* **Robbers and outlaws**

Outlines, syllabi, etc. *See* general subjects with the
> subdivision *Outlines, syllabi, etc.,* e.g.
> **English literature—Outlines, syllabi, etc.;**
> etc.

Output equipment (Computers). *See* **Computer pe-
> ripherals**

Output standards. *See* **Production standards**

Over-the-counter drugs. *See* **Drugs, Nonprescrip-
> tion**

Overactive children. *See* **Hyperactive children**

Overactivity. *See* **Hyperactivity**

Overland journeys to the Pacific (U.S.) 978
> Use for materials on the pioneers' crossing of the
> continent toward the Pacific by foot, horse-
> back, wagon, etc.
> *See also* **Oregon Trail**
> *x* Transcontinental journeys (U.S.); Travels
> *xx* **Frontier and pioneer life; Voyages and travels**

Overseas study. *See* **Foreign study**

Overtime. *See* **Hours of labor; Wages**

Overweight. *See* **Obesity**

Overweight—Control. *See* **Reducing**

Ownership. *See* **Property**

Oxyacetylene welding. *See* **Welding**
Oxygen 546; 547
> *See also* **Ozone**
Oysters, Pearl. *See* **Pearlfisheries**
Ozone 665
> *xx* **Oxygen**
P.O.W.'s. *See* **Prisoners of war**
P.T.A.'s. *See* **Parents' and teachers' associations**
Pacific cable. *See* **Cables, Submarine**
Pacific Islands. *See* **Islands of the Pacific**
Pacific Northwest 979.5
> Use for materials on the old Oregon country, comprising the present states of Oregon, Washington and Idaho, parts of Montana and Wyoming, and the province of British Columbia.
> *x* Northwest, Pacific; Oregon country
> *xx* **North America; West (U.S.)**
Pacific Northwest coast. *See* **Northwest coast of North America**
Pacific States 979
> *xx* **West (U.S.)**
Pacifism 341.7
> *See also* **Conscientious objectors; Nonviolence**
> *x* Peace movements
> *xx* **Conscientious objectors; Nonviolence; Peace; War and religion**
Pack transportation. *See* **Backpacking**
Packaged houses. *See* **Prefabricated houses**
Packaging 658.5; 658.7; 658.8
> *See also* types of packaging and packaging materials, e.g. **Aluminum foil; Gift wrapping;** etc.
> *xx* **Advertising; Retail trade**
Packing industry. *See* **Meat industry and trade**
Paganism 291
> *x* Heathenism
> *xx* **Christianity and other religions; Religions**
Pageants 394, 791
> *See also* **Festivals; Masks (Plays); Mysteries and miracle plays**
> *xx* **Acting; Festivals**
Pain 152.1; 612
> *See also* **Anesthetics; Pleasure; Suffering**
> *xx* **Diagnosis; Emotions; Pleasure; Psychology, Physiological; Senses and sensation; Suffering**
Paint 645; 667
> *See also* **Corrosion and anticorrosives; Pigments**
> *x* Finishes and finishing
> *xx* **Corrosion and anticorrosives; Painting, Industrial; Pigments**
Painted glass. *See* **Glass painting and staining**
Painters (May subdiv. geog. adjective form) **709.2; 920**
> *See also* **Artists;** also names of individual painters
> *xx* **Artists**
Painters, American 709.2; 920
> *x* American painters; United States—Painters
Painters' materials. *See* **Artists' materials**
Painting (May subdiv. geog. adjective form) **750; 751**
> Names of all types of painting are not included in this list but are to be added as needed.

Painting—*Continued*
    See also

Animal painting and illus-	**Impressionism (Art)**
tration	**Landscape painting**
China painting	**Marine painting**
Color	**Miniature painting**
Composition (Art)	**Mural painting and deco-**
Cubism	**ration**
Expressionism (Art)	**Perspective**
Figure painting	**Portrait painting**
Finger painting	**Postimpressionism (Art)**
Flower painting and illus-	**Preraphaelitism**
tration	**Scene painting**
Futurism (Art)	**Stencil work**
Glass painting and stain-	**Textile painting**
ing	**Watercolor painting**

    x Oil painting; Paintings
   xx **Art; Composition (Art); Decoration and orna-**
       ment; Drawing; Esthetics; Graphic arts; Pic-
       tures
Painting, Abstract. *See* **Art, Abstract**
Painting, American 759.13
    x American painting; United States—Painting
Painting books. *See* **Coloring books**
Painting—Collected works 759
    x Collections of art, painting, etc.
Painting—Color reproductions. *See* **Color prints**
Painting—Conservation and restoration 751.6
    x Conservation of works of art, books, etc.;
       Preservation of works of art; Restoration of
       works of art
Painting, Decorative. *See* **Decoration and ornament**
Painting, Dutch 759.492
Painting, Finger. *See* **Finger painting**
Painting, Industrial 698
    See also **House painting; Lettering; Paint; Sign**
       painting; Varnish and varnishing; Wood fin-
       ishing
    x Finishes and finishing; Industrial painting;
       Mechanical painting; Painting, Mechanical
Painting, Mechanical. *See* **Painting, Industrial**
Painting, Modern 759.06
    x Modern painting
Painting, Modern—1800-1899 (19th century)
       759.05
Painting, Modern—1900-1999 (20th century)
       759.06
Painting, Religious. *See* **Religious art and symbol-**
       ism
Painting, Romanesque 759.02
    x Romanesque painting
   xx **Art, Romanesque**
Painting—Technique 751.4
    x Technique
Paintings. *See* **Painting**
Pair system. *See* **Binary system (Mathematics)**
Palaces (May subdiv. geog.) **728.8**
   xx **Architecture**
Paleobiogeography. *See* **Biogeography**
Paleobotany. *See* **Plants, Fossil**

Paleolithic period. *See* **Stone Age**
Paleontology. *See* **Fossils**
Palestine problem, 1917- . *See* **Jewish-Arab relations**
Palestinian Arabs 303.6; 572.95694
    See also **Jewish-Arab relations**
    x Arabs—Palestine
Palmistry 133.6
    xx **Divination; Fortune telling; Occult sciences**
Palsy, Cerebral. *See* **Cerebral palsy**
Pamphlets 025.17
    See also **Chapbooks**
Pan-Africanism 320.5; 327
    x African relations
    xx **Africa**
Pan-Americanism 320.5; 327
    Use for materials on the theory and policy of co-operation and mutual cultural understanding among the countries of America.
    See also **America—Politics and government; Monroe Doctrine**
    x Good Neighbor Policy; Inter-American relations
    xx **America—Politics and government; Latin America**
Panama Canal 972.87
    xx **Canals**
Panarabism 320.5
    xx **Arab countries—Politics and government**
Panel discussions. *See* **Discussion groups**
Panel heating. *See* **Radiant heating**
Paneuropean federation. *See* **European federation**
Panics, Economic. *See* **Depressions, Economic**
Pantomimes 792.3
    See also **Mime; Shadow pantomimes and plays**
    xx **Acting; Amateur theater; Ballet; Drama; Mime; Theater**
Papacy 262
    See also **Popes**
    x Holy See
    xx **Catholic Church; Church history; Popes**
Papal encyclicals. *See* **Encyclicals, Papal**
Paper 676
    xx **Fibers**
Paper bound books. *See* **Paperback books**
Paper crafts 731; 736; 745.54
    See also **Gift wrapping;** also names of paper crafts, e.g. **Decoupage; Origami;** etc.
    x Paper folding; Paper sculpture; Paper work; Papier-maché
Paper folding. *See* **Paper crafts**
Paper folding, Japanese. *See* **Origami**
Paper hanging 698
    See also **Wallpaper**
    xx **Interior design; Wallpaper**
Paper making and trade 338.4; 676
    See also **Book industries and trade**
    xx **Book industries and trade; Chemical industries; Manufactures**

Paper money 332.4

  x Bills of credit; Fiat money; Greenbacks; Legal tender; Money, Paper

  xx **Finance; Inflation (Finance); Money**

Paper sculpture. *See* **Paper crafts**

Paper work. *See* **Paper crafts**

Paperback books 070.5

  x Books, Paperback; Paper bound books

  xx **Bibliography—Editions; Books; Publishers and publishing**

Papier-maché. *See* **Paper crafts**

Parables 226

  See also **Allegories; Bible—Parables; Fables; Jesus Christ—Parables**

  xx **Allegories; Fables**

Parachute troops 356

  See also names of armies with the subdivision *Parachute troops,* e.g. **United States. Army—Parachute troops;** etc.

  x Paratroops

  xx **Aeronautics, Military; Parachutes**

Parachutes 623; 629.134

  See also **Parachute troops**

  xx **Aeronautics**

Parades 791

  x Floats (Parades); Processions

Paralysis, Anterior spinal. *See* **Poliomyelitis**

Paralysis, Cerebral. *See* **Cerebral palsy**

Paralysis, Infantile. *See* **Poliomyelitis**

Paralysis, Spastic. *See* **Cerebral palsy**

Paramedical personnel. *See* **Allied health personnel**

Paranormal phenomena. *See* **Psychical research**

Paraprofessional librarians. *See* **Library technicians**

Paraprofessions and paraprofessionals 331.7

  See also names of paraprofessions and paraprofessional personnel, e.g. **Library technicians;** etc.

  xx **Occupations; Professions; Vocational guidance**

Parapsychology. *See* **Psychical research**

Parasites 574.5; 581.5; 591.52

  See also **Bacteriology; Insects, Injurious and beneficial**

  x Animal parasites; Diseases and pests; Entozoa; Epizoa

  xx **Pests**

Parasols. *See* **Umbrellas and parasols**

Paratroops. *See* **Parachute troops**

Parcel post. *See* **Postal service**

Pardon 364.6

  See also **Amnesty**

  xx **Amnesty; Criminal justice, Administration of; Parole**

Parent abuse. *See* **Elderly abuse**

Parent and child 306.8

  Use for materials on the psychological and social interaction between parents and their minor children. Materials on the skills, attributes and attitudes needed for parenthood are entered under **Parenting.** Materials on the principles and techniques of raising children are entered under **Child rearing.**

Parent and child—*Continued*
 See also

Child abuse	**Conflict of generations**
Child custody	**Fathers and daughters**
Child rearing	**Fathers and sons**
Children of divorced par-	**Inheritance and succession**
ents	**Mothers and daughters**
Children of working par-	**Mothers and sons**
ents	**Parenting**

 x Child and parent
 xx **Children and adults; Conflict of generations; Domestic relations; Family; Human relations**
Parent-teacher conferences 371.1
 x Conferences, Parent-teacher; Interviews, Parent-teacher; Teacher-parent conferences
 xx **Parent-teacher relationships**
Parent-teacher relationships 370.19
 See also **Home and school; Parent-teacher conferences; Parents' and teachers' associations**
 x Parents and teachers; Teacher-parent relationships; Teachers and parents
 xx **Home and school**
Parental behavior. *See* **Parenting**
Parental custody. *See* **Child custody**
Parental kidnapping. *See* **Kidnapping, Parental**
Parenting 306.8
 See note under **Parent and child.**
 See also **Child rearing; Home instruction**
 x Parental behavior
 xx **Child rearing; Home instruction; Parent and child**
Parenting, Part-time 306.8; 649
 See also **Children of divorced parents; Single parent family**
 x Part-time parenting
 xx **Children of divorced parents**
Parents and teachers. *See* **Parent-teacher relationships**
Parents' and teachers' associations 370.19
 See also **Home and school**
 x P.T.A.'s; PTAs
 xx **Community and school; Educational associations; Home and school; Parent-teacher relationships; Societies**
Parents, Biological. *See* **Birthparents**
Parents, Single. *See* **Single parent family**
Parents without partners. *See* **Single parent family**
Paris (France). World's Fair, 1989. *See* **Expo '89 (Paris, France)**
Parish libraries. *See* **Church libraries**
Parish registers. *See* **Registers of births, etc.**
Parks (May subdiv. geog.) **719**
 See also **Amusement parks; Botanical gardens; National parks and reserves; Playgrounds; Zoos**
 xx **Cities and towns; Landscape architecture; Outdoor recreation; Playgrounds**
Parks—United States 719; 973
 x United States—Parks

Parkways. *See* **Express highways**

Parliamentary government. *See* **Representative government and representation**

Parliamentary practice 060.4

    x Rules of order

    xx **Debates and debating; Legislation; Legislative bodies; Public meetings**

Parliaments. *See* **Legislative bodies**

Parochial schools. *See* **Church schools**

Parodies 808.87

    See also names of prominent authors with the subdivision *Parodies, travesties, etc.,* e.g. **Shakespeare, William, 1564-1616— Parodies, travesties, etc.;** etc.

    x English parodies; Travesties

    xx **English literature; Literature—Collected works**

Parody 808.7

    Use for materials about parody. Collections of parodies are entered under **Parodies.**

    x Comic literature

    xx **Literature; Poetry; Satire; Wit and humor**

Parole 364.6

    See also **Pardon; Probation**

    xx **Crime; Criminal justice, Administration of; Probation; Social case work**

Part-time employment 331.2

    See also **Job sharing; Supplementary employment**

    x Alternative work schedules; Employment, Part-time

    xx **Employment; Hours of labor; Labor**

Part-time parenting. *See* **Parenting, Part-time**

Participative management. *See* **Management— Employee participation**

Particles (Nuclear physics) 539.7

    See also names of particles, e.g. **Electrons; Neutrons; Protons; Quarks;** etc.

    x Elementary particles (Physics); Nuclear particles; Nucleons

    xx **Nuclear physics**

Parties 793.2

    See also types of parties, e.g. **Children's parties; Showers (Parties);** etc.

    xx **Entertaining**

Parties, Political. *See* **Political parties**

Partisans. *See* **Guerrillas**

Passion plays 792.1

    See also **Mysteries and miracle plays**

    xx **Drama; Jesus Christ—Drama; Religious drama; Theater**

Passions. *See* **Emotions**

Passive resistance 172; 322.4

    See also **Boycott; Hunger strikes; Nonviolence**

    x Civil disobedience; Nonviolent noncooperation

    xx **Government, Resistance to; Nonviolence**

Passover 296.4; 394.2

    x Pesach

    xx **Fasts and feasts—Judaism**

Pastel drawing 741.2
>*See also* **Crayon drawing**
>*xx* **Crayon drawing; Drawing; Portrait painting**

Pastimes. *See* **Amusements; Games; Recreation**

Pastoral peoples. *See* **Nomads**

Pastoral psychiatry. *See* **Psychology, Pastoral**

Pastoral psychology. *See* **Psychology, Pastoral**

Pastoral theology. *See* **Pastoral work**

Pastoral work 253
>*See also* **Church work; Clergy; Preaching; Psychology, Pastoral**
>*x* Pastoral theology; Theology, Pastoral

Pastors. *See* **Clergy; Priests**

Pastry 641.8
>*xx* **Baking; Cookery**

Pastures 333.73-333.74
>*See also* **Forage plants; Grasses**
>*xx* **Agriculture; Cattle; Forage plants; Grasses**

Patchwork quilts. *See* **Quilts**

Patent medicines. *See* **Drugs, Nonprescription**

Patents 608
>*See also* **Inventions; Trademarks**
>*x* Discoveries (in science); Intellectual property
>*xx* **Inventions; Machinery; Manufactures; Trademarks**

Pathological botany. *See* **Plants—Diseases**

Pathological chemistry. *See* **Chemistry, Medical and pharmaceutical; Physiological chemistry**

Pathological psychology. *See* **Psychology, Pathological**

Pathology 616.07
>*See also*

Bacteriology	**Medicine**
Diagnosis	**Medicine, Preventive**
Immunity	**Physiological chemistry**
Medical genetics	**Therapeutics**

>*x* Disease (Pathology)
>*xx* **Diagnosis; Diseases; Medicine; Medicine, Preventive**

Pathology, Vegetable. *See* **Plants—Diseases**

Patience 152.4; 179
>*xx* **Human behavior**

Patience (Game). *See* **Solitaire (Game)**

Patients. *See* **Sick**

Patios 721; 729
>*x* Decks (Domestic architecture)
>*xx* **Landscape architecture**

Patriotic poetry 808.81; 811; etc.
>*xx* **National songs; Poetry—Collected works**

Patriotic songs. *See* **National songs**

Patriotism 172
>*See also* **Nationalism**
>*xx* **Citizenship; Human behavior; Loyalty; Nationalism**

Patronage of the arts. *See* **Art patronage**

Pattern making 671.2
>*See also* **Design; Founding; Mechanical drawing**
>*xx* **Design; Founding**

Patterns for crafts. *See* appropriate subjects with the subdivision *Patterns,* e.g.

Patterns for crafts—*Continued*
> **Dressmaking—Patterns;** etc.

Pauperism. *See* **Poverty**

Pavements 625.8
> *See also* **Asphalt; Roads; Streets**
> *xx* **Cement; Concrete; Roads; Streets**

Pay equity. *See* **Equal pay for equal work**

Pay television, Cable. *See* **Cable television**

Pay television, Subscription. *See* **Subscription television**

Payroll taxes. *See* **Income tax; Insurance, Unemployment**

Peace 172; 327.1; 341.7
> *See also* **Arbitration, International; Arms control; League of Nations; Pacifism; Security, International; War;** also names of wars with the subdivision *Peace,* e.g. **World War, 1939-1945—Peace;** etc.
> *xx* **Arbitration, International; Arms control; International relations; Reconstruction (1914-1939); Security, International; War**

Peace keeping forces. *See* **United Nations—Armed forces**

Peace movements. *See* **Pacifism**

Pearl Harbor (Oahu, Hawaii), Attack on, 1941 940.54
> *xx* **World War, 1939-1945; World War, 1939-1945—Campaigns**

Pearlfisheries 338.3; 639.3
> *x* Oysters, Pearl
> *xx* **Fisheries**

Peasant art. *See* **Folk art**

Peasantry 305.5; 307.7
> *See also* **Agricultural laborers; Land tenure; Sociology, Rural**
> *x* Rural life
> *xx* **Agricultural laborers; Feudalism; Labor; Land tenure; Sociology, Rural**

Pecan 634
> *xx* **Nuts**

Pedagogy. *See* **Education; Education—Study and teaching; Teaching**

Peddlers and peddling 658.8
> *x* Door to door selling
> *xx* **Sales personnel; Selling**

Pediatric psychiatry. *See* **Child psychiatry**

Pediatrics. *See* **Children—Care and hygiene; Children—Diseases**

Pedigrees. *See* **Genealogy; Heraldry**

Peer counseling. *See* **Counseling; Hotlines (Telephone counseling)**

Peer group influence. *See* **Peer pressure**

Peer pressure 303.3; 364.2
> *x* Peer group influence
> *xx* **Socialization**

Peerage. *See* **Nobility**

Pelts. *See* **Hides and skins**

Pen drawing 741.2
> *x* Ink drawing
> *xx* **Drawing**

Percussion instruments—*Continued*
   Drum; etc.
 xx **Musical instruments**
Perennials 635.9
 xx **Flower gardening; Flowers**
Performance standards 658.5
 See also subjects and classes of people with the
   subdivision *Rating,* e.g. **Bonds—Rating;**
   Employees—Rating; Librarians—Rating;
   etc.
 x Job performance standards; Rating; Work performance standards
Performing arts 790.2
 See also **Centers for the performing arts; Nudity**
   in the performing arts; Theater; also art
   forms performed on stage or screen, e.g.
   Ballet; Dancing; etc.
 x Show business
Perfumes 391; 668
 xx **Cosmetics; Essences and essential oils**
Periodic law 541
 xx **Chemical elements; Chemistry, Physical and**
   theoretical
Periodicals 050
 See also **Chapbooks; Freedom of the press; Jour-**
   nalism; Newspapers; also **American periodi-**
   cals; English periodicals; Press; etc.; and
   general subjects with the subdivision
   Periodicals, e.g. **Engineering—Periodicals;**
   etc.; and names of individual periodicals
 x Journals; Magazines
 xx **Journalism; Mass media; Newspapers; Press;**
   Serial publications
Periodicals—Indexes 050
 xx **Indexes**
Periodicity 574.1
 See also **Biological rhythms; Rhythm; Time**
 x Cycles
 xx **Rhythm; Time**
Permanent education. *See* **Continuing education**
Persecution 272
 See also **Jews—Persecutions; Martyrs; Massa-**
   cres; Religious freedom
 x Christians—Persecutions
 xx **Atrocities; Church history; Martyrs; Religious**
   freedom
Persia. *See* **Iran**
Persian rugs. *See* **Rugs, Oriental**
Personal actions (Law). *See* **Actions and defenses**
Personal appearance. *See* **Grooming, Personal**
Personal cleanliness. *See* **Hygiene**
Personal computers. *See* **Home computers**
Personal conduct. *See* **Human behavior**
Personal development. *See* **Personality; Success**
Personal films. *See* **Amateur motion pictures; Ex-**
   perimental films
Personal finance. *See* **Finance, Personal**
Personal freedom. *See* **Freedom**
Personal grooming. *See* **Grooming, Personal**
Personal health. *See* **Health**

Personal hygiene. *See* **Hygiene**
Personal life skills. *See* **Life skills**
Personal loans 332.7
>   Use for materials on loans to individuals for per-
>   sonal rather than business uses.
>   *See also* **Banks and banking, Cooperative; Credit
>   unions; Mortgages; Savings and loan associ-
>   ations**
>   *x* Consumer loans; Loans, Personal; Small loans
>   *xx* **Consumer credit; Loans**
Personal names. *See* **Names, Personal**
Personal narratives. *See* **Autobiographies; Biogra-
>   phy;** and subjects with the subdivision
>   *Biography* or *Correspondence,* and names
>   of events and wars with the subdivision
>   *Personal narratives,* e.g. **World War, 1939-
>   1945—Personal narratives;** etc.
Personal space 153.6; 302.2
>   Use for materials on the sense of physical space
>   required for psychological comfort.
>   *x* Space, Personal
>   *xx* **Human relations; Nonverbal communication;
>   Space and time**
Personal time management. *See* **Time management**
Personality 155.2
>   *See also* **Character; Eccentrics and eccentricities;
>   Individuality; Self; Soul**
>   *x* Identity; Personal development
>   *xx* **Consciousness; Individuality; Psychology; Soul**
Personality disorders 157; 616.8
>   *See also* **Hallucinations and illusions; Hypnotism**
>   *xx* **Hallucinations and illusions; Hypnotism;
>   Mind and body; Psychical research; Psy-
>   chology, Pathological; Subconsciousness**
Personnel administration. *See* **Personnel manage-
>   ment**
Personnel classification. *See* **Job analysis**
Personnel management 658.3
>   Use for materials dealing with problems of per-
>   sonnel in factories, business, etc., hiring and
>   dismissing employees, and general questions
>   of the relationship between officials and em-
>   ployees.
>   *See also*

Absenteeism (Labor)	**Job analysis**
Affirmative action pro-	**Job satisfaction**
grams	**Job security**
Applications for positions	**Labor turnover**
Counseling	**Management—Employee**
Efficiency, Industrial	**participation**
Employee morale	**Motion study**
Employees—Dismissal	**Office management**
Employees—Training	**Recruiting of employees**
Employment agencies	**Supervisors**
Factory management	**Time study**

>   *x* Employment management; Human resource
>   management; Personnel administration; Su-
>   pervision of employees
>   *xx* **Efficiency, Industrial; Factory management;
>   Human relations; Industrial management;**

Personnel management—*Continued*
    Industrial relations; Management; Office management
Personnel service in education. *See* **Educational counseling**
Persons, Crimes against. *See* **Offenses against the person**
Persons, Single. *See* **Single people**
Perspective 701
    See also **Drawing**
    x Architectural perspective
    xx **Drawing; Geometrical drawing; Geometry, Descriptive; Optics; Painting**
Persuasion (Rhetoric). *See* **Public speaking; Rhetoric**
Pesach. *See* **Passover**
Pest control. *See* **Pests—Control**
Pesticide pollution. *See* **Pesticides—Environmental aspects**
Pesticides 668
    See also **Fungicides; Herbicides; Insecticides; Natural pesticides**
    xx **Agricultural chemicals; Pests—Control; Poisons and poisoning**
Pesticides and wildlife 574.5
    x Wildlife and pesticides
    xx **Pesticides—Environmental aspects; Wildlife conservation**
Pesticides—Environmental aspects 574.5-574.6; 632
    See also **Pesticides and wildlife**
    x Environment and pesticides; Pesticide pollution
    xx **Pollution**
Pestilences. *See* **Epidemics**
Pests 574.6; 632
    Use for materials on detrimental or annoying plants or animals.
    See also types of pests, e.g. **Agricultural pests; Fungi; Household pests; Insects, Injurious and beneficial; Parasites;** etc.; also names of crops, trees, etc. with the subdivision *Diseases and pests,* e.g. **Fruit—Diseases and pests;** etc.; and names of pests, e.g. **Flies;** etc.
    x Vermin
    xx **Zoology, Economic**
Pests—Biological control 574.5
    x Agricultural pests—Biological control; Biological control of pests
Pests—Control 632
    See also **Pesticides;** also names of specific pests with the subdivision *Control,* e.g. **Mosquitoes—Control;** etc.
    x Control; Extermination of pests; Pest control; Pests—Extermination
    xx **Agricultural pests; Zoology, Economic**
Pests—Extermination. *See* **Pests—Control**
Pet-facilitated psychotherapy. *See* **Pet therapy**
Pet therapy 158; 362.2; 615.5
    x Animal-facilitated therapy; Animals, Visiting;

Pet therapy—*Continued*

    Companion-animal partnership; Pet-facilitated psychotherapy; Visiting animals

  xx **Animals and the handicapped; Therapeutics**

Petrochemicals 661

  x Petroleum chemicals

  xx **Chemicals**

Petroglyphs. *See* **Rock drawings, paintings, and engravings**

Petroleum (May subdiv. geog.) **665**

  See also **Boring; Coal tar products; Gasoline**

  x Coal oil; Crude oil; Oil

  xx **Gas; Oils and fats; Wells**

Petroleum as fuel 665

  See also **Oil burners**

  x Fuel, Liquid; Fuel oil; Liquid fuel; Oil fuel

  xx **Fuel**

Petroleum chemicals. *See* **Petrochemicals**

Petroleum engines. *See* **Gas and oil engines**

Petroleum—Geology 553.2

  xx **Geology, Economic; Prospecting**

Petroleum industry and trade 338.2

Petroleum—Pipelines 338.2; 665.5028

  x Pipelines, Petroleum

Petroleum pollution of water. *See* **Oil pollution of water**

Petroleum—United States 665

  x United States—Petroleum

Petroleum—Well boring. *See* **Oil well drilling**

Petrology 552

  See also **Crystallography; Geochemistry; Geology; Lunar petrology; Mineralogy; Rocks; Stone**

  also varieties of rocks, e.g. **Granite; Marble;** etc.

  xx **Geology; Mineralogy; Rocks; Science; Stone**

Pets 636.08

  See also **Domestic animals;** also names of animals, e.g. **Cats; Dogs;** etc.

  xx **Animals; Domestic animals**

Pewter 673

  xx **Alloys; Plate; Tin**

Phantoms. *See* **Apparitions; Ghosts**

Pharmaceutical chemistry. *See* **Chemistry, Medical and pharmaceutical**

Pharmaceuticals. *See* **Drugs**

Pharmacodynamics. *See* **Pharmacology**

Pharmacology 615

  Use for materials on the action and properties of drugs in general. Materials on the action of specific drugs are entered under the name of the drug with the subdivision *Physiological effect,* e.g. **Opium—Physiological effect;** etc.

  See also **Chemotherapy; Drugs; Opium—Physiological effect; Pharmacy**

  x Medicine—Physiological effect; Pharmacodynamics

  xx **Drugs; Materia medica; Medicine; Pharmacy; Physiological chemistry**

Pharmacopoeias. *See* **Materia medica**

Pharmacotherapy. *See* **Chemotherapy**
Pharmacy 615
    Use for materials on the art or practice of pre-
        paring, preserving, and dispensing drugs.
    See also **Botany, Medical; Chemistry, Medical**
        and pharmaceutical; Drugs; Materia medica;
        Pharmacology
    xx **Chemistry; Chemistry, Medical and pharma-**
        ceutical; Materia medica; Medicine; Phar-
        macology
Pheasants 598; 636.5
    xx **Game and game birds**
Phenomenology 142
    See also **Existentialism**
    xx **Philosophy, Modern**
Philanthropists 361.7092; 920
    x Altruists; Humanitarians
Philanthropy. *See* **Charities; Charity organization;**
        Endowments; Gifts; Social work
Philately. *See* **Postage stamps—Collectors and col-**
        lecting
Philology. *See* **Language and languages; Philology,**
        Comparative
Philology, Comparative 410
    Use for comparative studies of languages. Gen-
        eral materials on the history, philosophy, or-
        igin, etc. of languages are entered under
        Language and languages.
    See also **Language and languages; Literature,**
        Comparative
    x Comparative linguistics; Comparative philol-
        ogy; Language and languages—
        Comparative philology; Philology
    xx **Grammar; Language and languages**
Philosophers (May subdiv. geog. adjective form)
        180.92; 190.92; 920
Philosophers, American 191.092; 920
    x American philosophers; United States—
        Philosophers
Philosophers' stone. *See* **Alchemy**
Philosophy (May subdiv. geog. adjective form) **100**
    See also

Belief and doubt	**Mind and body**
Empiricism	**Mysticism**
Ethics	**Positivism**
Fate and fatalism	**Pragmatism**
Free will and determinism	**Psychology**
Gnosticism	**Rationalism**
God	**Realism**
Humanism	**Reality**
Idealism	**Skepticism**
Intuition	**Soul**
Knowledge, Theory of	**Theism**
Logic	**Transcendentalism**
Materialism	**Truth**
Metaphysics	**Universe**

    also subjects with the subdivision *Philosophy,*
        e.g. **History—Philosophy;** etc.
    x Mental philosophy
    xx **Humanities**

Philosophy, American 191
    x American philosophy; United States—
        Philosophy
Philosophy, Ancient 180
    See also **Stoics**
    x Ancient philosophy; Greek philosophy; Phi-
        losophy, Greek; Philosophy, Roman; Ro-
        man philosophy
Philosophy and religion 210
    See also **Religion—Philosophy**
    x Religion and philosophy
    xx **Religion—Philosophy**
Philosophy, Greek. *See* **Philosophy, Ancient**
Philosophy, Hindu 181
    See also **Yoga**
Philosophy—Historiography 107
    xx **Historiography**
Philosophy, Medieval 189
    x Medieval philosophy
    xx **Middle Ages**
Philosophy, Modern 190
    See also **Enlightenment; Evolution; Existential-**
        ism; Phenomenology
    x Modern philosophy
Philosophy, Moral. *See* **Ethics**
Philosophy of history. *See* **History—Philosophy**
Philosophy of religion. *See* **Religion—Philosophy**
Philosophy, Roman. *See* **Philosophy, Ancient**
Phobias 157; 616.85
    xx **Fear; Neuroses**
Phonetic spelling. *See* **Spelling reform**
Phonetics 414
    See also **Speech; Voice;** also names of languages
        with the subdivision *Pronunciation,* e.g.
        English language—Pronunciation; etc.
    x Phonics; Phonology
    xx **Language and languages; Sound; Speech;**
        Voice
Phonics. *See* **Phonetics**
Phonodiscs. *See* **Sound recordings**
Phonograph 789.9
    See also **Compact disc players; Sound—**
        Recording and reproducing
Phonograph records. *See* **Sound recordings**
Phonology. *See* **Phonetics;** and names of languages
    with the subdivision *Pronunciation,* e.g.
    English language—Pronunciation; etc.
Phonorecords. *See* **Sound recordings**
Phosphates 546; 631.8
    xx **Fertilizers and manures**
Phosphorescence 535; 574.19
    See also **Bioluminescence**
    x Luminescence
    xx **Light; Mineralogy; Optics; Radiation; Radio-**
        activity
Photocopying machines. *See* **Copying processes**
    and machines
Photoelectric cells 537.5; 621.3815
    See also **Electronics**
    x Electric eye

Photoengraving 686.2
 See also **Photomechanical processes**
 x Halftone process
 xx **Engraving; Photomechanical processes**
Photographic chemistry 771
 Use for materials on the chemical processes em-
  ployed in photography.
 See also **Photography—Processing**
 x Chemistry, Photographic
 xx **Chemistry**
Photographic film. *See* **Photography—Film**
Photographic slides. *See* **Slides (Photography)**
Photographic supplies. *See* **Photography—
  Equipment and supplies**
Photography 770
 See also

Astronomical photography	**Nature photography**
Cameras	**Photomechanical pro-**
Color photography	**cesses**
Filmstrips	**Slides (Photography)**
Microphotography	**Space photography**
Motion picture photogra-	**Telephotography**
phy	

Photography, Aerial 778.3
 Use for materials on photography from airplanes, balloons, high buildings, etc.
 See also **Remote sensing**
 x Aerial photography
Photography, Artistic 778
 x Artistic photography; Photography—Esthetics
 xx **Art**
Photography, Astronomical. *See* **Astronomical pho-
  tography**
Photography, Color. *See* **Color photography**
Photography, Commercial 778
 x Commercial photography
Photography—Darkroom technique. *See* **Photogra-
  phy—Processing**
Photography—Developing and developers 771
 xx **Photography—Processing**
Photography—Enlarging 770.28
 x Enlarging (Photography)
Photography—Equipment and supplies 771
 See also **Cameras**
 x Photographic supplies
Photography—Esthetics. *See* **Photography, Artistic**
Photography—Film 771
 x Photographic film
Photography—Handbooks, manuals, etc. 770.2
 x Handbooks, manuals, etc.
Photography in astronautics. *See* **Space photogra-
  phy**
Photography, Journalistic 070.4
 x Journalistic photography; News photography;
  Photojournalism
Photography, Laser. *See* **Holography**
Photography, Lensless. *See* **Holography**
Photography—Lighting 770.2
Photography, Medical 621.36; 778.3
 x Medical photography

Photography, Medical—*Continued*

    xx **Photography—Scientific applications**

Photography—Motion pictures. *See* **Motion picture photography**

Photography of animals 778.9

    Use for materials on the technique and accounts of photographing animals. Materials consisting of photographs and pictures of animals are entered under **Animals—Pictorial works**.

    See also **Animal painting and illustration; Animals—Pictorial works**

    x Animal photography; Animals—Photography

    xx **Animal painting and illustration; Animals—Pictorial works; Nature photography**

Photography of birds 778.9

    Use same form for photography of other subjects.

    x Bird photography; Birds—Photography

    xx **Nature photography**

Photography of fishes 778.9

    x Fishes—Photography

    xx **Nature photography**

Photography of nature. *See* **Nature photography**

Photography of plants 778.9

    x Plants—Photography

    xx **Nature photography**

Photography, Outdoor. *See* **Outdoor photography**

Photography—Portraits 778.9

    xx **Portraits**

Photography—Printing processes 772-773

    xx **Photography—Processing**

Photography—Processing 770.28

    See also names of special techniques, e.g. **Photography—Developing and developers; Photography—Printing processes;** etc.

    x Darkroom technique in photography; Photography—Darkroom technique

    xx **Photographic chemistry**

Photography—Retouching 770.28

    x Retouching (Photography)

Photography—Scientific applications 778.3

    See also specific applications, e.g. **Photography, Medical;** etc.

Photography, Space. *See* **Space photography**

Photography, Stereoscopic 778.4

    x Stereophotography

Photography, Submarine 778.7

    x Submarine photography; Underwater photography

    xx **Marine biology**

Photojournalism. *See* **Photography, Journalistic**

Photomechanical processes 686.2

    See also types of photomechanical processes, e.g. **Photoengraving;** etc.

    xx **Illustration of books; Photoengraving; Photography**

Photometry 535

    See also **Color; Light; Optics**

    x Electric light; Light, Electric

    xx **Light; Optics**

Photoplays.   *See* **Motion picture plays**
Photosynthesis 581.1
  xx **Plants**
Phototherapy 615.8
  See also **Radiotherapy; Ultraviolet rays**
  x Electric light; Light, Electric; Light—
    Therapeutic use
  xx **Physical therapy; Radiotherapy; Therapeutics**
Photovoltaic power generation 621.3815
  See also **Solar batteries**
  x Solar cells
  xx **Solar energy**
Phrenology 139
  See also **Mind and body; Physiognomy**
  xx **Brain; Head; Mind and body; Physiognomy;
    Psychology**
Physical anthropology 573
  See also **Man—Origin**
  x Anthropology, Physical; Biological anthropol-
    ogy; Somatology
  xx **Anthropology; Ethnology**
Physical chemistry.   *See* **Chemistry, Physical and
    theoretical**
Physical culture.   *See* **Physical education**
Physical education 613.7
  See also

Athletics	**Health education**
Coaching (Athletics)	**Movement education**
Drill (Nonmilitary)	**Physical fitness**
Exercise	**Posture**
Games	**Sports**
Gymnastics	

    also names of kinds of exercises, e.g. **Fencing;
      Judo;** etc.
  x Calisthenics; Education, Physical; Physical
    culture; Physical training
  xx **Athletics; Education; Exercise; Gymnastics;
    Hygiene; Sports**
Physical education—Medical aspects.   *See* **Sports
    medicine**
Physical fitness 613.7
  See also **Bodybuilding**
  x Endurance, Physical; Physical stamina; Stam-
    ina, Physical
  xx **Exercise; Health; Physical education; Self-
    care, Health**
Physical fitness centers.   *See* **Health resorts, spas,
    etc.**
Physical geography (May subdiv. geog.) **551**
  See note under **Geography.**
  See also

Climate	**Lakes**
Earth	**Meteorology**
Earthquakes	**Mountains**
Geochemistry	**Ocean**
Geophysics	**Ocean currents**
Geysers	**Rivers**
Glaciers	**Tides**
Ice	**Volcanoes**
Icebergs	**Winds**

Physical geography—*Continued*
   x Geography, Physical; Physiography
   xx **Earth; Geography; Geology**
Physical geography—United States 551
   x United States—Physical geography
Physical stamina. *See* **Physical fitness**
Physical therapy 615.8
   Use for general materials on the treatment of
      disability, injury or disease through exercise,
      heat, water, body manipulation, massage,
      etc.
   See also types of therapy, e.g. **Baths; Electroth-
      erapeutics; Hydrotherapy; Massage; Occu-
      pational therapy; Phototherapy; Radiother-
      apy;** etc.
   x Physiotherapy
   xx **Therapeutics**
Physical training. *See* **Physical education**
Physically handicapped 362.4
   See also **Orthopedics;** also names of the physi-
      cally handicapped, e.g. **Blind; Deaf;** etc.
   x Crippled people; Invalids; Soldiers, Disabled;
      War cripples
   xx **Handicapped; Orthopedics**
Physically handicapped children 155.4; 362.4; 362.7
   x Children, Crippled; Crippled children
   xx **Handicapped children**
Physically handicapped—Housing 362.4
   x Dwellings; Housing for the physically handi-
      capped
   xx **Housing**
Physically handicapped—Rehabilitation 362.4
   See also **Occupational therapy**
   x Rehabilitation
Physicians 610.69; 920
   See also **Women physicians;** also names of spe-
      cialists, e.g. **Radiologists; Surgeons;** etc.
   x Doctors; Medical profession
   xx **Surgeons**
Physicians—Directories 610.69025
   xx **Directories**
Physicians—Malpractice 346.03
   x Medical malpractice; Physicians Tort liabil
      ity
   xx **Malpractice; Medical ethics; Medicine—Law
      and legislation**
Physicians—Tort liability. *See* **Physicians—
      Malpractice**
Physicists 920
   xx **Scientists**
Physics 530
   See also

Astrophysics	**Geophysics**
Biophysics	**Gravitation**
Chemistry, Physical and	**Hydraulics**
theoretical	**Hydrostatics**
Dynamics	**Light**
Electricity	**Liquids**
Electrons	**Magnetism**
Gases	**Matter**

Physics—*Continued*

Mechanics	**Radiation**
Music—Acoustics and physics	**Radioactivity**
	Relativity (Physics)
Nuclear physics	**Solids**
Optics	**Sound**
Pneumatics	**Statics**
Quantum theory	**Thermodynamics**

    xx **Dynamics; Science**

Physics, Astronomical. *See* **Astrophysics**

Physics, Biological. *See* **Biophysics**

Physics, Nuclear. *See* **Nuclear physics**

Physics, Terrestrial. *See* **Geophysics**

Physiognomy 138

    See also **Face; Phrenology**

    xx **Face; Phrenology; Psychology**

Physiography. *See* **Physical geography**

Physiological chemistry 574.19; 612

    See also

Biochemistry	**Metabolism**
Chemistry, Medical and pharmaceutical	**Pharmacology**
	Poisons and poisoning
Chemistry, Organic	**Proteins**
Digestion	**Vitamins**

    x Animal chemistry; Chemistry, Animal; Chemistry, Pathological; Chemistry, Physiological; Histochemistry; Pathological chemistry

    xx **Biochemistry; Chemistry; Pathology; Physiology**

Physiological effect. *See* appropriate subjects with the subdivision *Physiological effect,* e.g. **Alcohol—Physiological effect; Opium—Physiological effect;** etc.

Physiological psychology. *See* **Psychology, Physiological**

Physiological stress. *See* **Stress (Physiology)**

Physiology 612

    See also

Anatomy	**Muscles**
Blood	**Musculoskeletal system**
Body temperature	**Nervous system**
Bones	**Nutrition**
Cells	**Old age**
Digestion	**Physiological chemistry**
Fatigue	**Psychology, Physiological**
Growth	**Reproduction**
Health	**Respiration**
Lymphatic system	**Senses and sensation**

    also names of organs of the body, e.g. **Heart;** etc.

    x Body, Human; Human body

    xx **Anatomy; Biology; Medicine; Science**

Physiology, Comparative 574.1

    x Comparative physiology

    xx **Zoology**

Physiology, Molecular. *See* **Biophysics**

Physiology of plants. *See* **Plant physiology**

Physiotherapy. *See* **Physical therapy**

Physique. *See* **Bodybuilding**

Phytogeography. *See* **Plants—Geographical**

Phytogeography—*Continued*
> **distribution**

Pianists 780.92; 920
> *xx* **Musicians**

Piano 786.2
> *See also* **Keyboards (Musical instruments)**

Piano music 786.4
> *xx* **Instrumental music; Music**

Piano—Tuning 786.2
> *xx* **Tuning**

Picketing. *See* **Strikes and lockouts**

Pickling. *See* **Canning and preserving**

Pickup campers. *See* **Travel trailers and campers**

Pictographs. *See* **Picture writing**

Pictorial works. *See* **Pictures;** and subjects with
> the subdivision *Pictorial works,* e.g.
> **Animals—Pictorial works; United States—
> History—1861-1865, Civil War—Pictorial
> works;** etc.

Picture books for children E
> *See also* **Coloring books; Stories without words;
> Toy and movable books**
> *xx* **Children's literature**

Picture books for children, Wordless. *See* **Stories
> without words**

Picture dictionaries 423.1; 433.1; etc.
> *x* Dictionaries, Picture; Word books
> *xx* **Encyclopedias and dictionaries**

Picture frames and framing 749
> *x* Framing of pictures

Picture galleries. *See* **Art—Museums**

Picture posters. *See* **Posters**

Picture telephone. *See* **Video telephone**

Picture writing 411
> Use for materials on the recording of events or
> the expression of messages by pictures rep-
> resenting actions or facts.
> *See also* **Cave drawings; Hieroglyphics; Rock
> drawings, paintings, and engravings**
> *x* Pictographs
> *xx* **Hieroglyphics; Writing**

Pictures 025.17; 759; 769; 779
> Use for general materials on the study and use of
> pictures; also for miscellaneous collections
> of pictures.
> *See also* **Cartoons and caricatures; Engraving;
> Etching; Libraries and pictures; Painting;
> Portraits;** also subjects with the subdivision
> *Pictorial works,* e.g. **Animals—Pictorial
> works; United States—History—1861-1865,
> Civil War—Pictorial works;** etc.; also
> names of countries, states, etc. with the sub-
> division *Description and travel—Views,* e.g.
> **United States—Description and travel—
> Views;** etc.; and names of cities with the
> subdivision *Description—Views,* e.g.
> **Chicago (Ill.)—Description—Views,** etc.
> *x* Pictorial works
> *xx* **Art**

Pictures, Humorous. *See* **Cartoons and caricatures**

Pigments 667; 751.2
    See also **Dyes and dyeing; Paint**
  xx **Paint**
Pigs 636.4
  x Hogs; Swine
Pilgrims and pilgrimages 248.4
    See also **Saints; Shrines**
  xx **Shrines; Voyages and travels**
Pilgrims (New England colonists) 974.4
  xx **Puritans; United States—History—1600-**
      1775, Colonial period
Pilot guides 623.88
  x Coast pilot guides
  xx **Navigation; Pilots and pilotage**
Piloting (Aeronautics). *See* types of aircraft with
      the subdivision *Piloting,* e.g.
      Airplanes—Piloting; etc.
Piloting (Astronautics). *See* **Space vehicles—**
      Piloting
Piloting (Ships). *See* **Pilots and pilotage**
Pilots, Airplane. *See* **Air pilots**
Pilots and pilotage 623.88
    See also **Navigation; Pilot guides**
  x Piloting (Ships); Pilots, Ship; Ship pilots
  xx **Harbors; Navigation; Sailors**
Pilots, Ship. *See* **Pilots and pilotage**
Ping-pong 796.34
  x Table tennis
Pioneer life. *See* **Frontier and pioneer life**
Pipe fitting 696
    See also **Plumbing**
  x Steam fitting
  xx **Plumbing**
Pipe lines. *See* **Pipelines**
Pipe organ. *See* **Organ**
Pipelines 621.8
    See also special subjects with the subdivision
      Pipelines, e.g. **Petroleum—Pipelines;** etc.
  x Pipe lines
  xx **Hydraulic structures; Transportation**
Pipelines, Petroleum. *See* **Petroleum—Pipelines**
Pipes, Tobacco. *See* **Tobacco pipes**
Pirates 364.1; 910.4
    See also **Privateering; United States—History—**
      1801-1805, Tripolitan War
  x Barbary corsairs; Buccaneers; Corsairs; Free-
     booters
  xx **Criminals; International law; Maritime law;**
     Naval history
Pistols 683
  x Handguns
  xx **Firearms**
Pity. *See* **Sympathy**
Place names. *See* **Names, Geographical**
Places, Imaginary. *See* **Geographical myths**
Places of retirement. *See* **Retirement communities**
Plague 616.9
  x Black death; Bubonic plague
Plain chant. *See* **Chants (Plain, Gregorian, etc.)**
Plainsong. *See* **Chants (Plain, Gregorian, etc.)**

Plane geometry. *See* **Geometry**

Plane trigonometry. *See* **Trigonometry**

Planetariums 523.0074

  xx **Astronomy**

Planets 523.4

  See also **Life on other planets; Solar system;
    Stars;** also names of planets, e.g. **Saturn
    (Planet);** etc.

  xx **Astronomy; Solar system; Stars**

Planets, Life on other. *See* **Life on other planets**

Planing machines 621.9

  xx **Machine tools**

Planned parenthood. *See* **Birth control**

Planning, City. *See* **City planning**

Planning, Economic. *See* **Economic policy;** and
    names of countries, states, etc. with the sub-
    division *Economic policy,* e.g. **United
    States—Economic policy;** etc.

Planning, National. *See* **Economic policy; Social
    policy;** and names of countries with the
    subdivision *Economic policy* or *Social pol-
    icy,* e.g. **United States—Economic policy;
    United States—Social policy;** etc.; and ap-
    propriate topical subjects with the subdivi-
    sion *Government policy,* e.g.
    Environment—Government policy; etc.

Planning, Regional. *See* **Regional planning**

Plans. *See* **Architectural drawing; Geometrical
    drawing; Map drawing; Maps; Mechanical
    drawing**

Plant anatomy. *See* **Botany—Anatomy**

Plant breeding 581.1; 631.5

  Use for materials on that form of plant propaga-
    tion that aims to improve plants, as by se-
    lection after controlled mating, etc.

  See also **Fertilization of plants; Plant propaga-
    tion**

  x Hybridization

  xx **Agriculture; Breeding; Flower gardening;
    Plant propagation**

Plant chemistry. *See* **Botanical chemistry; Plants—
    Analysis**

Plant conservation 639.9

  See also **Rare plants**

  x Conservation of plants; Plants—
    Conservation; Protection of plants; Wild
    flowers—Conservation

  xx **Botany, Economic; Conservation of natural re-
    sources; Endangered species; Nature conser-
    vation; Rare plants**

Plant diseases. *See* **Plants—Diseases**

Plant distribution. *See* **Plants—Geographical dis-
    tribution**

Plant introduction 581.5

  x Acclimatization

  xx **Botany, Economic**

Plant lore. *See* **Plants—Folklore**

Plant names, Popular 581

  See note under **Botany—Terminology.**

  See also **Botany—Terminology; Plants—**

471

Plant names, Popular—*Continued*
  Folklore
  x Botany—Nomenclature
  xx **Botany—Terminology**
Plant names, Scientific. *See* **Botany—Terminology**
Plant nutrition. *See* **Plants—Nutrition**
Plant pathology. *See* **Plants—Diseases**
Plant physiology 581.1
  See also **Fertilization of plants; Germination;**
    Plants—Growth; Plants—Nutrition
  x Botany—Physiology; Physiology of plants
  xx **Botany**
Plant propagation 581.1; 631.5
  Use for materials on the continuance or multi-
    plication of plants by successive production.
    Materials dealing with methods adopted to
    secure new and improved varieties are en-
    tered under **Plant breeding.**
  See also **Grafting; Plant breeding; Seeds**
  x Plants—Propagation; Propagation of plants
  xx **Flower gardening; Fruit culture; Gardening;**
    Nurseries (Horticulture); Plant breeding
Plantation life 307.7
Planting. *See* **Agriculture; Gardening; Landscape**
    gardening; Tree planting
Plants 581
  See also **Fertilization of plants; Flower garden-**
    ing; Forest plants; Gardening; Horticulture;
    Photosynthesis; Rare plants; also names of
    types of plants, e.g. **Alpine plants; Climbing**
    plants; Desert plants; Flowers; Forage
    plants; Freshwater plants; House plants;
    etc.; also names of individual plants, e.g.
    Ferns; Mosses; etc.; and headings beginning
    with the words **Plant** and **Plants**
  x Flora; Vegetable kingdom
  xx **Botany; Flowers; Gardening; Trees**
Plants—Analysis 581.19
  x Plant chemistry; Plants—Chemical analysis
  xx **Botanical chemistry**
Plants—Anatomy. *See* **Botany—Anatomy**
Plants—Chemical analysis. *See* **Plants—Analysis**
Plants—Collection and preservation 579
  x Botanical specimens—Collection and preser-
    vation; Herbaria; Preservation of botanical
    specimens; Specimens, Preservation of
  xx **Collectors and collecting**
Plants—Conservation. *See* **Plant conservation**
Plants, Cultivated (May subdiv. geog.) **631.5**
  See also **Annuals (Plants); House plants; Plants,**
    Edible; Plants, Ornamental
  xx **Gardening**
Plants, Cultivated—United States 631.5
  x United States—Plants, Cultivated
Plants—Diseases 581.2; 632
  See also names of crops, etc. with the subdivi-
    sion *Diseases and pests,* e.g.
    Fruit—Diseases and pests; etc.
  x Botany—Pathology; Diseases and pests; Dis-
    eases of plants; Garden pests; Pathological

472

Plants—Diseases—*Continued*
        botany; Pathology, Vegetable; Plant diseases; Plant pathology; Vegetable pathology
  xx **Agricultural pests; Fungi**
Plants—Ecology. *See* **Botany—Ecology**
Plants, Edible 581.6
  x Edible plants; Food plants; Plants, Useful
  xx **Botany, Economic; Plants, Cultivated**
Plants—Effect of poisons on 581.2
  See note under **Poisons and poisoning.**
  xx **Poisons and poisoning**
Plants, Extinct. *See* **Plants, Fossil**
Plants—Fertilization. *See* **Fertilization of plants**
Plants—Folklore 398
  x Plant lore
  xx **Folklore; Plant names, Popular**
Plants, Fossil 561
  x Botany, Fossil; Extinct plants; Fossil plants; Paleobotany; Plants, Extinct
  xx **Botany; Fossils**
Plants—Geographical distribution 581.9
  x Geographical distribution of animals and plants; Phytogeography; Plant distribution
  xx **Biogeography**
Plants—Growth 581.3
  xx **Growth; Plant physiology**
Plants in art 704.9
  See also **Flower painting and illustration**
  x Flowers in art; Trees in art
  xx **Decoration and ornament**
Plants, Industrial. *See* **Factories**
Plants, Medicinal. *See* **Botany, Medical**
Plants—Nutrition 581.1; 631.5
  x Plant nutrition
  xx **Nutrition; Plant physiology**
Plants, Ornamental 635.9; 715
  x Ornamental plants
  xx **Flower gardening; Landscape gardening; Plants, Cultivated; Shrubs**
Plants—Photography. *See* **Photography of plants**
Plants, Poisonous. *See* **Poisonous plants**
Plants—Propagation. *See* **Plant propagation**
Plants—Soilless culture. *See* **Aeroponics; Hydroponics**
Plants, Useful. *See* **Botany, Economic; Plants, Edible**
Plaster and plastering 693
  See also **Cement; Concrete; Mortar; Stucco**
  x Plastering
  xx **Masonry**
Plaster casts 731.4
  x Casting; Casts, Plaster
  xx **Sculpture**
Plaster of paris. *See* **Gypsum**
Plastering. *See* **Plaster and plastering**
Plastic materials. *See* **Plastics**
Plastic surgery. *See* **Surgery, Plastic**
Plastics 668.4
  See also **Chemistry, Organic—Synthesis; Gums and resins; Rubber, Artificial; Synthetic**

Plastics—*Continued*
> **products;** also names of specific plastics
> *x* Plastic materials
> *xx* **Chemistry, Organic—Synthesis; Polymers and polymerization; Synthetic products**

Plate 739.2
> *See also* **Hallmarks; Pewter; Sheffield plate**
> *x* Gold plate
> *xx* **Goldwork; Hallmarks; Silverwork**

Plate metalwork 671.8
> *xx* **Metalwork; Sheet metalwork**

Plate tectonics 551.1
> *See also* **Continental drift; Submarine geology**
> *xx* **Continental drift; Earth—Crust; Geophysics; Submarine geology**

Platforms, Drilling. *See* **Drilling platforms**

Play 790
> *See also* **Amusements; Finger play; Games; Imaginary playmates; Recreation; Sports**
> *xx* **Amusements; Children; Games; Recreation**

Play centers. *See* **Community centers; Playgrounds**

Play direction (Theater). *See* **Theater—Production and direction**

Play production. *See* **Amateur theater; Theater—Production and direction**

Play writing. *See* **Drama—Technique; Motion picture plays—Technique; Radio plays—Technique; Television plays—Technique**

Players, Compact disc. *See* **Compact disc players**

Playgrounds 796.06
> *See also* **Community centers; Parks; Summer schools**
> *x* Play centers; Public playgrounds; School playgrounds
> *xx* **Child welfare; Children; Community centers; Parks; Recreation; Social settlements**

Playhouses. *See* **Theaters**

Playing cards. *See* **Card games**

Playmates, Imaginary. *See* **Imaginary playmates**

Plays. *See* **Drama—Collected works; One act plays**

Plays, Bible. *See* **Bible—Drama**

Plays, Christmas. *See* **Christmas—Drama**

Plays, College. *See* **College and school drama—Collected works**

Plays for children. *See* **Children's plays**

Playwrights. *See* **Dramatists**

Playwriting. *See* **Drama—Technique; Motion picture plays—Technique; Radio plays—Technique; Television plays—Technique**

Pleasure 152.4
> *See also* **Happiness; Pain**
> *xx* **Emotions; Happiness; Joy and sorrow; Pain; Senses and sensation**

Plot-your-own stories E; Fic
> *x* Choose-your-own story plots; Making-choices stories; Multiple plot stories; Which-way stories
> *xx* **Children's literature; Fiction; Literary recreations**

474

Plots (Drama, fiction, etc.) 808
Use for materials dealing with the construction
and analysis of plots as a literary technique.
Collections of plots are entered under
Literature—Stories, plots, etc.
See also literary or musical forms with the sub-
division *Stories, plots, etc.,* e.g.
**Ballets—Stories, plots, etc.; Operas—
Stories, plots, etc.;** etc.
x Drama—Plots; Dramatic plots; Fiction—
Plots; Novels—Plots; Scenarios
xx **Authorship; Characters and characteristics in
literature; Drama; Fiction; Literature**
Plows 631.3
xx **Agricultural machinery**
Plumbing 696
See also **Drainage, House; Pipe fitting; Sanitary
engineering; Sanitation, Household; Sewer-
age; Solder and soldering**
xx **Drainage, House; Pipe fitting; Sanitation,
Household**
Pluto operation. *See* **Cuba—History—1961, Inva-
sion**
Plywood 674
xx **Wood**
Pneumatic transmission. *See* **Compressed air**
Pneumatics 533; 621.5
See also **Aerodynamics; Compressed air; Gases;
Ground cushion phenomena; Sound**
xx **Gases; Physics**
Pneumonia 616.2
xx **Lungs—Diseases**
Pocket calculators. *See* **Calculators**
Podiatry 617
x Chiropody; Foot—Care and hygiene
Poetics 808.1
Use for materials on the art and technique of po-
etry. General materials on the appreciation,
philosophy, etc. of poetry are entered under
Poetry.
See also **Rhyme; Rhythm; Versification**
x Poetry—Technique
Poetry 808.1
See note under **Poetics.**
Names of all types of poetry are not included in
this list but are to be added as needed.
See also

American poetry	**Free verse**
Ballads	**Humorous poetry**
Children's poetry	**Hymns**
Eddas	**Love poetry**
English poetry	**Nature in poetry**
Epic poetry	**Parody**

also subjects with the subdivision *Poetry,* e.g.
**Animals—Poetry; Bunker Hill (Boston,
Mass.), Battle of, 1775—Poetry; Chicago
(Ill.)—Poetry; Indians of North America—
Poetry; Shakespeare, William, 1564-1616—
Poetry;** etc.
x Poetry—Philosophy

Poetry—*Continued*
> *xx* **Esthetics; Literature; Versification**
Poetry and music. *See* **Music and literature**
Poetry—Collected works 808.81; 811.08; etc.
> *See also*

American poetry—	Patriotic poetry
Collected works	Religious poetry
Children's poetry	School verse
Christmas—Poetry	Sea poetry
English poetry—Collected	Songs
works	War poetry
Nonsense verses	

> *x* Collections of literature; Poetry—Selections;
> Rhymes
> *xx* **Literature—Collected works**
Poetry for children. *See* **Children's poetry; Nursery rhymes**
Poetry—History and criticism 809.1
> *See also* **American poetry—History and criticism;
> English poetry—History and criticism;** etc.
Poetry of love. *See* **Love poetry**
Poetry of nature. *See* **Nature in poetry**
Poetry—Philosophy. *See* **Poetry**
Poetry—Selections. *See* **Poetry—Collected works**
Poetry—Technique. *See* **Poetics**
Poets (May subdiv. geog. adjective form) **809.1; 920**
> Use for materials dealing with the personal lives
> of several poets. Materials about their liter-
> ary productions are entered under
> **Poetry—History and criticism; English poet-
> ry—History and criticism;** etc.
> *See also* **Dramatists; Lyricists; Minstrels; Trou-
> badours**
> *xx* **Authors**
Poets, American 809.1; 920
> *x* American poets; United States—Poets
Point Four program. *See* **Reconstruction (1939-
> 1951)**
Poison ivy 583
> *xx* **Poisonous plants**
Poisonous animals 591.6
> *See also* names of poisonous animals, e.g.
> **Rattlesnakes;** etc.
> *xx* **Animals; Dangerous animals; Poisons and poi-
> soning; Zoology**
Poisonous gases 363.1; 363.7
> *x* Asphyxiating gases; Gases, Poisonous
> *xx* **Gases; Poisons and poisoning**
Poisonous gases—War use 623.4
> *See also* **World War, 1914-1918—Gas warfare**
> *x* Gas warfare
> *xx* **Air defenses; Chemical warfare; Military art
> and science**
Poisonous plants 581.6
> *See also* names of poisonous plants, e.g. **Poison
> ivy;** etc.
> *x* Plants, Poisonous
> *xx* **Botany, Economic; Chemistry, Medical and
> pharmaceutical; Poisons and poisoning**
Poisonous substances. *See* **Poisons and poisoning**

Poisons and poisoning 615.9

> Materials on the poisonous effect of chemical substances on man and animals are entered under the names of substances with the subdivision *Toxicology,* e.g. **Insecticides—Toxicology;** etc. The headings **Arsenic poisoning** and **Lead poisoning** are exceptions. Materials on the effect of poisons on plants are entered under **Plants—Effect of poisons on.**
>
> *See also* **Food poisoning; Lead poisoning; Pesticides; Plants—Effect of poisons on; Poisonous animals; Poisonous gases; Poisonous plants;** also subjects with the subdivision *Toxicology,* e.g. **Insecticides—Toxicology;** etc.
>
> *x* Poisonous substances; Toxic substances; Toxicology
>
> *xx* **Accidents; Chemistry; Chemistry, Medical and pharmaceutical; Criminal law; Drugs; Hazardous substances; Materia medica; Medical jurisprudence; Physiological chemistry**

Polar expeditions. *See* **Antarctic regions; Arctic regions; North Pole; Polar regions; Scientific expeditions; South Pole**

Polar lights. *See* **Auroras**

Polar regions 998

> Use for materials dealing with both the Antarctic and Arctic regions.
>
> *See also* **Antarctic regions; Arctic regions; North Pole; South Pole**
>
> *x* Polar expeditions

Police (May subdiv. geog.) **363.2**

> *See also* **Animals in police work; Crime; Criminal investigation; Detectives; Secret service**
>
> *x* Police officers; Policemen; Policewomen; Women police
>
> *xx* **Crime; Criminal investigation; Detectives; Law; Law enforcement**

Police brutality. *See* **Police—Complaints against**

Police—Complaints against 363.2

> *x* Complaints against police; Police brutality

Police—Corrupt practices 363.2

> *x* Corruption, Police; Police corruption
>
> *xx* **Misconduct in office**

Police corruption. *See* **Police—Corrupt practices**

Police, International. *See* **International police**

Police officers. *See* **Police**

Police, State 352.2

> *x* State police

Police—United States 363.2

> *x* United States—Police

Policemen. *See* **Police**

Policewomen. *See* **Police**

Polio. *See* **Poliomyelitis**

Poliomyelitis 616.8

> *x* Infantile paralysis; Paralysis, Anterior spinal; Paralysis, Infantile; Polio; Spinal paralysis, Anterior

Poliomyelitis vaccine 614.4; 615

> *x* Live poliovirus vaccine; Sabin vaccine; Salk vaccine

Polishing.   *See* **Grinding and polishing**
Politeness.   *See* **Courtesy; Etiquette**
Political assessments.   *See* **Campaign funds**
Political asylum.   *See* **Asylum, Right of**
Political behavior.   *See* **Political psychology**
Political boundaries.   *See* **Boundaries**
Political conventions   324.5
   See also **Political parties; Primaries**
   x Conventions, Political
   xx **Political parties; Political science**
Political corruption.   *See* **Corruption in politics**
Political crimes and offenses   364.1
   See also

Anarchism and anarchists	**Government, Resistance to**
Assassination	**Political prisoners**
Concentration camps	**Terrorism**
Corruption in politics	**Treason**

   x Crimes, Political; Sedition
   xx **Political ethics; Subversive activities**
Political economy.   *See* **Economics**
Political ethics   172
   See also **Citizenship; Conflict of interests; Corruption in politics; Government, Resistance to; Political crimes and offenses**
   x Ethics, Political
   xx **Political science; Social ethics**
Political geography.   *See* **Boundaries**
Political participation.   *See* **Politics, Practical;** and classes of people with the subdivision *Political activity,* e.g. **College students—Political activity; Women—Political activity;** etc.
Political parties (May subdiv. geog.) **324.2**
   See also **Political conventions; Politics, Practical; Right and left (Political science);** also names of parties, e.g. **Democratic Party (U.S.); Republican Party (U.S.);** etc.
   x Parties, Political
   xx **Political conventions; Political science**
Political parties—Finance.   *See* **Campaign funds**
Political prisoners   365
   x Prisoners, Political
   xx **Political crimes and offenses; Prisoners**
Political psychology   302
   See also **Propaganda; Public opinion**
   x Political behavior; Politics, Practical—Psychological aspects; Psychology, Political
   xx **Political science; Psychology; Social psychology**
Political refugees.   *See* **Refugees, Political**
Political scandals.   *See* **Corruption in politics**
Political science   320
   Use for materials on the discipline of political science. Materials dealing with political processes in general, such as electioneering, political machines, etc., are entered under **Politics, Practical.** Materials on the political processes of particular regions, countries, cities, etc. are entered under the place

Political science—*Continued*

    names with the subdivision *Politics and govern-
ment,* e.g. **United States—Politics and government;** etc.

    See also

Anarchism and anarchists	**Municipal government**
Aristocracy	**Nationalism**
Bureaucracy	**Political conventions**
Citizenship	**Political ethics**
Civil rights	**Political parties**
Civil service	**Political psychology**
Communism	**Politics, Practical**
Comparative government	**Power (Social sciences)**
Constitutional history	**Public administration**
Constitutional law	**Representative government**
Constitutions	**and representation**
Constitutions, State	**Republics**
Democracy	**Revolutions**
Executive power	**Right and left (Political**
Federal government	**science)**
Freedom	**Separation of powers**
Geopolitics	**Socialism**
Government ownership	**State governments**
Government, Resistance to	**State rights**
Imperialism	**State, The**
Kings, queens, rulers, etc.	**Suffrage**
Law	**Taxation**
Legislation	**Utopias**
Local government	**World politics**
Monarchy	

    also names of countries, cities, etc. with the sub-
division *Politics and government,* e.g.
      United States—Politics and government;
      etc.

  x Administration; Civics; Civil government;
    Commonwealth, The; Government; Politics

  xx **Constitutional history; Constitutional law;
    History; Social sciences; State, The**

Political violence. *See* **Terrorism**

Politicians (May subdiv. geog.) **324.2092; 920; 923**

    See also **Diplomats; Statesmen; Women politi-
cians**

  xx **Statesmen**

Politicians, American. *See* **Politicians—United
States**

Politicians—United States 324.2092; 920

  x American politicians; Politicians, American;
    United States—Politicians

Politics. *See* **Political science; Politics, Practical;**
and names of continents, areas, countries,
states, counties, and cities with the subdivision *Politics and government,* e.g.
    **Asia—Politics and government; Latin Amer-
ica—Politics and government; United
States—Politics and government; Chicago
(Ill.) —Politics and government;** etc.

Politics and business. *See* **Business and politics**

Politics and Christianity. *See* **Christianity and politics**

Politics and religion. *See* **Religion and politics**

Politics and students. *See* **Students—Political activity**

Politics—Corrupt practices. *See* **Corruption in politics**

Politics, Practical 324.2; 324.7

Use for materials dealing with practical politics in general, such as electioneering, political machines, etc. Materials on the science of politics are entered under **Political science.**

See also

Business and politics	**Elections**
Campaign funds	**Lobbying and lobbyists**
Campaign literature	**Primaries**
Corruption in politics	**Television in politics**

also names of countries, cities, etc. with the subdivision *Politics and government,* e.g. **United States—Politics and government;** etc.; also classes of people with the subdivision *Political activity,* e.g. **College students—Political activity; Women—Political activity;** etc.; and headings beginning with the word **Political**

x Campaigns, Political; Electioneering; Political participation; Politics; Practical politics

xx **Political parties; Political science**

Politics, Practical—Psychological aspects. *See* **Political psychology**

Pollination. *See* **Fertilization of plants**

Polls, Election. *See* **Elections**

Polls, Public opinion. *See* **Public opinion polls**

Pollution 304.2; 363.7

See also types of pollution, e.g. **Air—Pollution; Hazardous wastes; Marine pollution; Noise pollution; Pesticides—Environmental aspects; Radioactive pollution; Water—Pollution;** etc.

x Contamination of environment; Environmental pollution

xx **Environment—Government policy; Environmental health; Hazardous wastes; Industrial wastes; Man—Influence on nature; Public health; Sanitary engineering; Sanitation**

Pollution control devices (Motor vehicles). *See* **Automobiles—Pollution control devices**

Pollution—Mathematical models 304.2

xx **Mathematical models**

Pollution of air. *See* **Air—Pollution**

Pollution of water. *See* **Water—Pollution**

Pollution, Radioactive. *See* **Radioactive pollution**

Poltergeists. *See* **Ghosts**

Polyglot dictionaries 413

x Dictionaries, Multilingual; Dictionaries, Polyglot; Multilingual dictionaries; Multilingual glossaries, phrase books, etc.; Polyglot glossaries, phrase books, etc.

xx **Encyclopedias and dictionaries**

Polyglot glossaries, phrase books, etc. *See* **Polyglot dictionaries**

Polymers and polymerization 541.3; 547.7; 668.9

See also types of polymers, e.g. **Plastics;** etc.

xx **Chemistry, Organic—Synthesis; Chemistry, Physical and theoretical**

Polynucleotides. *See* **Nucleic acids**

Ponds 551.48

   xx **Water**

Ponies 636.1

   xx **Horses**

Pontiac's Conspiracy, 1763-1765 973.2

   xx **Indians of North America—Wars; United States—History—1600-1775, Colonial period; United States—History—1755-1763, French and Indian War**

Pony express 383

   xx **Express service; Postal service**

Poor (May subdiv. geog.) **305.5; 362.5**

   See also **Homeless people; Unemployed**

   xx **Poverty; Public welfare**

Poor—Legal assistance. *See* **Legal assistance to the poor**

Poor—Medical care 362.6; 368.4

   See also **Medicaid**

   x Medical care for the poor

Poor relief. *See* **Charities; Economic assistance, Domestic; Public welfare**

Pop-up books. *See* **Toy and movable books**

Popes 262; 920

   See also **Papacy**

   x Holy See

   xx **Church history; Papacy**

Popes—Infallibility 262

   x Infallibility of the Pope

Popes—Temporal power 262

   See also **Church—Government policy**

   x Temporal power of the Pope

   xx **Church—Government policy; Church history—600-1500, Middle Ages**

Popes—Voyages and travels 262

   xx **Voyages and travels**

Popular culture 306

   Use for materials on literature, art, and music, etc. produced for the general public.

   See also names of countries, cities, etc. with the subdivision *Popular culture,* c.g. **United States—Popular culture;** etc.

   x Culture, Popular

   xx **Civilization; Communication; Culture; Manners and customs; Mass media; Recreation**

Popular government. *See* **Democracy**

Popular music. *See* **Music, Popular (Songs, etc.)**

Popular songs. *See* **Music, Popular (Songs, etc.)**

Popularity 158

Population 304.6

   See also **Birth control; Birthrate; Census; Eugenics; Fertility, Human; Migration, Internal; Mortality;** also names of countries, cities, etc. with the subdivision *Population,* e.g. **United States—Population; Chicago (Ill.)—Population;** etc.

   xx **Birth rate; Economics; Fertility, Human; Human ecology; Sociology; Vital statistics**

Population, Foreign. *See* **Immigration and emigration;** and names of countries with the sub-

Population, Foreign—*Continued*
    division *Immigration and emigration,* e.g.
    United States—Immigration and emigration;
    etc.; and names of countries, cities, etc. with
    the subdivision *Foreign population,* e.g.
    United States—Foreign population; Chicago
    (Ill.)—Foreign population; etc.
Porcelain 738.2
    See note under **Ceramics.**
    See also **China painting;** also names of varieties
        of porcelain
    x China (Porcelain); Chinaware; Dishes
    xx **Decorative arts; Pottery**
Porcelain enamels. *See* **Enamel and enameling**
Porcelain painting. *See* **China painting**
Pornography 176
    See also **Erotica**
    x Obscene materials
    xx **Erotica; Obscenity (Law)**
Portrait painting 757
    See also **Crayon drawing; Figure painting; Min-**
        iature painting; Pastel drawing
    xx **Figure painting; Miniature painting; Painting**
Portraits 704.9; 757; 778.9
    See also **Cartoons and caricatures; Photogra-**
        phy—Portraits; also headings for collective
        and individual biography and classes of peo-
        ple with the subdivision *Portraits,* e.g.
        United States—Biography—Portraits; Mu-
        sicians—Portraits; Shakespeare, William,
        1564-1616—Portraits; etc.
    x Iconography
    xx **Art; Biography; Pictures**
Ports. *See* **Harbors**
Portuguese literature 869
    See also **Brazilian literature**
    xx **Brazilian literature**
Position analysis. *See* **Topology**
Positivism 146
    See also **Agnosticism; Idealism; Materialism;**
        Pragmatism; Realism
    x Humanity, Religion of; Religion of humanity
    xx **Agnosticism; Deism; Philosophy; Rationalism;**
        Realism
Possesions, Lost and found. *See* **Lost and found**
    possessions
Post-impressionism. *See* **Postimpressionism (Art)**
Post office. *See* **Postal service**
Postage stamps 383; 769.56
    x Stamps, Postage
Postage stamps—Collectors and collecting 769.56
    x Collectibles; Collections of objects; Philately
    xx **Collectors and collecting**
Postal delivery code. *See* **Zip code**
Postal service (May subdiv. geog.) **383**
    See also **Air mail service; Electronic mail sys-**
        tems; Pony express; Zip code
    x Mail service; Parcel post; Post office
    xx **Communication; Transportation**

Postal service—United States 383

    x United States—Mail; United States—Postal
        service

Posters 741.67

    See also **Signs and signboards**

    x Advertising, Pictorial; Picture posters

    xx **Advertising; Commercial art; Signs and sign-**
        boards

Postimpressionism (Art) 709.03

    See also **Cubism; Expressionism (Art); Futurism**
        (Art); Impressionism (Art); Surrealism

    x Post-impressionism

    xx **Art, Modern—1800-1899 (19th century); Cub-**
        ism; Expressionism (Art); Futurism (Art);
        Impressionism (Art); Painting

Posture 613.7

    xx **Physical education**

Potash 631.8; 668

    xx **Fertilizers and manures**

Potatoes 633; 635

    xx **Vegetables**

Potters 738.092; 920

    xx **Artists**

Pottery (May subdiv. geog. adjective form, e.g.
        Pottery, Chinese; etc.) **666; 738**

    See note under **Ceramics.**

    See also **Glazes; Porcelain; Terra cotta; Tiles;**
        Vases

    x Crockery; Dishes; Earthenware; Faience; Fay
        ence; Stoneware

    xx **Archeology; Art objects; Ceramics; Clay in-**
        dustries; Decoration and ornament; Decora-
        tive arts; Tableware; Vases

Pottery, American 738

    x American pottery; United States—Pottery

Pottery—Marks 738

    x Marks, Potters'

Poultry 636.5

    See also names of domesticated birds, e.g.
        Ducks; Geese; Turkeys; etc.

    xx **Domestic animals**

Poverty 305.5; 362.5

    See also **Charities; Poor; Public welfare; Subsis-**
        tence economy; also names of countries with
        the subdivisions *Economic conditions* and
        Social conditions, e.g. **United States—**
        Economic conditions; United States—Social
        conditions; etc.

    x Destitution; Pauperism

    xx **Economic assistance, Domestic; Subsistence**
        economy; Wealth

Powder, Smokeless. *See* **Gunpowder**

Powdered milk. *See* **Milk, Dried**

Power blackouts. *See* **Electric power failures**

Power boats. *See* **Motorboats**

Power failures. *See* **Electric power failures**

Power (Mechanics) 531; 621

    See note under **Energy resources.**

Power (Mechanics)—*Continued*
   See also

Compressed air	**Power transmission**
Electric power	**Steam**
Energy resources	**Water power**
Force and energy	**Wind power**
Machinery	

   x Energy technology
   xx **Mechanical engineering; Mechanics; Steam engineering**
Power plants 621.4
   See also types of power plants, e.g. **Electric power plants; Nuclear power plants; Steam power plants;** etc.
   x Power stations
Power plants, Atomic. *See* **Nuclear power plants**
Power plants, Electric. *See* **Electric power plants**
Power plants, Hydroelectric. *See* **Hydroelectric power plants**
Power plants, Steam. *See* **Steam power plants**
Power politics. *See* **Balance of power; World politics—1945-1965; World politics—1965-**
Power resources. *See* **Energy resources**
Power resources conservation. *See* **Energy conservation**
Power resources development. *See* **Energy development**
Power (Social sciences) 303.3
   See also **Elite (Social sciences)**
   xx **Political science**
Power stations. *See* **Power plants**
Power supply. *See* **Energy resources**
Power tools 621.9
   xx **Tools**
Power transmission 621.8
   See also **Belts and belting; Cables; Electric power distribution; Gearing; Machinery**
   x Transmission of power
   xx **Belts and belting; Machinery; Mechanical engineering; Power (Mechanics)**
Power transmission, Electric. *See* **Electric lines; Electric power distribution**
Powerlifting. *See* **Weight lifting**
Powers, Separation of. *See* **Separation of powers**
POWs. *See* **Prisoners of war**
Practical jokes
   x Pranks
   xx **Jokes; Wit and humor**
Practical nurses 610.73
   xx **Nurses**
Practical nursing 610.73; 649.8
   xx **Nursing**
Practical politics. *See* **Politics, Practical**
Practice teaching. *See* **Student teaching**
Pragmatism 144
   See also **Empiricism; Reality; Truth; Utilitarianism**
   xx **Empiricism; Knowledge, Theory of; Philosophy; Positivism; Realism; Reality; Truth; Utilitarianism**

Pranks. *See* **Practical jokes**
Prayer 242
 See also **Devotional exercises; Prayers**
 x Devotion
 xx **Devotional exercises; Prayers; Worship**
Prayers 242; 264
 See also **Meditations; Prayer**
 x Collects; Theology, Devotional
 xx **Prayer**
Prayers in the public schools. *See* **Religion in the public schools**
Pre-Columbian Americans. *See* **Indians of North America**
Preachers. *See* **Clergy**
Preaching 251
 See also **Sermons**
 x Speaking
 xx **Pastoral work; Public speaking; Rhetoric; Sermons**
Preaching Friars. *See* **Dominicans**
Precious metals 549; 553.8
 See also **Gold; Silver**
 xx **Metals; Mines and mineral resources**
Precious stones 549; 553.8
 Use for mineralogical and technological materials on uncut stones. Materials on cut and polished precious stones treated from the point of view of art or antiquity are entered under **Gems.** Materials on gems in which the emphasis is on the setting are entered under **Jewelry.**
 See also **Gems;** also names of precious stones, e.g. **Diamonds;** etc.
 x Gemstones; Jewels; Stones, Precious
 xx **Gems; Mineralogy**
Precocious children. *See* **Gifted children**
Precolumbian Americans. *See* **Indians of North America**
Predestination 234
 See also **Free will and determinism**
 x Election (Theology); Foreordination
 xx **Calvinism; Fate and fatalism; Theology**
Predictions. *See* **Forecasting; Prophecies (Occult sciences)**
Prefabricated houses 693; 728
 x Demountable houses; Houses, Prefabricated; Packaged houses
 xx **Architecture, Domestic; Buildings, Prefabricated; House construction; Houses**
Pregnancy 612; 618.2
 See also **Childbirth; Prenatal care**
 xx **Childbirth; Reproduction**
Pregnancy, Adolescent 612; 618.2
 See also **Adolescent mothers**
 x Adolescent pregnancy; Pregnancy, Teenage; Teenage pregnancy
 xx **Adolescent mothers**
Pregnancy, Teenage. *See* **Pregnancy, Adolescent**
Pregnancy, Termination of. *See* **Abortion**

Prehistoric animals 560
　　See also **Dinosaurs; Extinct animals**
　　x Animals, Prehistoric
　　xx **Animals; Extinct animals; Fossils**
Prehistoric art. *See* **Art, Prehistoric**
Prehistoric man. *See* **Man, Prehistoric**
Prehistory. *See* **Archeology; Bronze Age; Iron Age;
　　Stone Age;** and names of countries, cities,
　　etc. with the subdivision *Antiquities,* e.g.
　　United States—Antiquities; etc.
Preimplantational ectogenesis. *See* **Fertilization in
　　vitro**
Prejudices 152.4; 177; 303.3
　　See also **Discrimination;** also types of prejudice,
　　e.g. **Antisemitism; Racism; Sexism;** etc.
　　x Antipathies; Bias (Psychology); Bigotry
　　xx **Attitude (Psychology); Emotions; Human rela-
　　tions; Race awareness**
Prejudicial publicity. *See* **Freedom of the press and
　　fair trial**
Preliterate man. *See* **Man, Nonliterate**
Preliterate society. *See* **Society, Nonliterate folk**
Premarital contracts. *See* **Marriage contracts**
Premarital counseling. *See* **Marriage counseling**
Premiers. *See* **Prime ministers**
Prenatal care 618.2
　　xx **Pregnancy**
Prenatal diagnosis 618.3
　　See also **Amniocentesis; Genetic counseling**
　　xx **Diagnosis**
Prenuptial contracts. *See* **Marriage contracts**
Prepaid group medical practice. *See* **Health main-
　　tenance organizations**
Prepaid medical care. *See* **Insurance, Health**
Preprimers. *See* **Easy reading materials**
Preraphaelitism 759.2; 759.05
　　xx **Painting**
Presbyterian Church 285
　　x Church denominations; Denominations, Reli-
　　gious; Religious denominations
Preschool children. *See* **Children**
Preschool education. *See* **Education, Preschool**
Preschool reading materials. *See* **Easy reading ma-
　　terials**
Presents. *See* **Gifts**
Preservation of antiquities. *See* **Antiquities—
　　Collection and preservation**
Preservation of botanical specimens. *See* **Plants—
　　Collection and preservation**
Preservation of buildings. *See* **Architecture—
　　Conservation and restoration**
Preservation of food. *See* **Food—Preservation**
Preservation of forests. *See* **Forests and forestry**
Preservation of historical records. *See* **Archives**
Preservation of library resources. *See* **Library re-
　　sources—Conservation and restoration**
Preservation of natural resources. *See* **Conservation
　　of natural resources**
Preservation of natural scenery. *See* **Landscape
　　protection; Natural monuments; Nature**

Preservation of natural scenery—*Continued*
    conservation; Wilderness areas
Preservation of organs, tissues, etc. 617
    See also **Transplantation of organs, tissues, etc.**
    x Organ preservation (Anatomy); Organs (Anatomy)—Preservation
Preservation of wildlife. *See* **Wildlife conservation**
Preservation of wood. *See* **Wood—Preservation**
Preservation of works of art. *See* subjects with the subdivision *Conservation and restoration,* e.g. **Painting—Conservation and restoration;** etc.
Preservation of zoological specimens. *See* **Zoological specimens—Collection and preservation**
Preserving. *See* **Canning and preserving**
Presidential aides. *See* **Presidents—United States—Staff**
Presidential campaigns—United States. *See* **Presidents—United States—Election**
Presidential libraries. *See* **Presidents—United States—Archives**
Presidents (May subdiv. geog.) **351.003; 920**
    See also **Executive power; Presidents—United States; Vice-presidents;** also names of presidents
    xx **Executive power; Heads of state; Kings, queens, rulers, etc.**
Presidents—Mexico 351.003; 920
    x Mexico—Presidents
Presidents—Powers and duties. *See* **Executive power**
Presidents—United States 353.03; 920
    When applicable, the following subdivisions may be used under names of presidents, prime ministers, and other rulers.
    See also names of presidents, e.g. **Lincoln, Abraham, 1809-1865;** etc.
    x United States—Presidents
    xx **Presidents**
Presidents—United States—Addresses and essays 353.03
    See also **Presidents—United States—Inaugural addresses**
Presidents—United States—Appointment 353.03
Presidents—United States—Archives 026
    See also names of libraries, e.g. **Harry S. Truman Library;** etc.
    x Libraries, Presidential; Presidential libraries; Presidents—United States—Libraries
Presidents—United States—Assassination 364.1
    xx **Assassination**
Presidents—United States—Children 920
Presidents—United States—Election (May subdiv. by date) **324.973**
    x Campaigns, Presidential—United States; Electoral college; Presidential campaigns—United States
    xx **Elections**
Presidents—United States—Family 920
Presidents—United States—Fathers 920

Presidents—United States—Succession 342; 353.03
  x Presidents—United States—Inability
Presidents—United States—Tombs 393
Presidents—United States—Voyages and travels
    353.03; 910
Presidents' wives—United States. *See* **Presidents—
    United States—Spouses**
Press 070
  See also **Broadcast journalism; Freedom of the
    press; Freedom of the press and fair trial;
    News agencies; Newspapers; Periodicals;
    Underground press**
  xx **Freedom of the press; Journalism; Newspa-
    pers; Periodicals; Propaganda; Public opin-
    ion; Publicity**
Press and government. *See* **Press—Government
    policy**
Press censorship. *See* **Freedom of the press**
Press clippings. *See* **Clippings (Books, newspapers,
    etc.)**
Press—Government policy 323.44
  x Government and the press; Press and govern-
    ment
  xx **Freedom of information; Reporters and report-
    ing**
Press, Underground. *See* **Underground press**
Press working of metal. *See* **Sheet metalwork**
Pressure groups. *See* **Lobbying and lobbyists**
Pressure suits. *See* **Astronauts—Clothing**
Pretenders. *See* **Impostors and imposture**
Prevention of accidents. *See* **Accidents—
    Prevention**
Prevention of crime. *See* **Crime prevention**
Prevention of cruelty to animals. *See* **Animal abuse**
Prevention of fire. *See* **Fire prevention**
Prevention of smoke. *See* **Smoke prevention**
Preventive medicine. *See* **Medicine, Preventive**
Price controls. *See* **Wage-price policy**
Price indexes, Consumer. *See* **Consumer price in-
    dexes**
Price-wage policy. *See* **Wage-price policy**
Prices 338.5
  See also **Consumer price indexes; Cost of living;
    Farm produce—Marketing; Wage-price pol-
    icy; Wages;** also subjects with the subdivi-
    sion *Prices,* e.g. **Art—Prices; Books—
    Prices;** etc.
  xx **Commerce; Consumption (Economics); Cost of
    living; Economics; Finance; Manufactures;
    Wages**
Priests 253; 253.092; 920
  See also **Ex-priests;** also names of church de-
    nominations with the subdivision *Clergy,*
    e.g. **Catholic Church—Clergy;** etc.
  x Pastors
  xx **Clergy**
Primaries 324.5
  See also **Elections**
  x Direct primaries; Elections, Primary
  xx **Elections; Political conventions; Politics, Prac-**

Primaries—*Continued*
　　tical; **Representative government and representation**
Primary education.　*See* **Education, Elementary**
Primates 599.8
　See also names of individual primates, e.g.
　　Monkeys; etc.
　xx **Animals; Mammals**
Primates—Habits and behavior 599.8
　xx **Animals—Habits and behavior**
Prime ministers (May subdiv. geog.)　**351.003; 920**
　x Premiers
　xx **Cabinet officers; Executive power; Heads of state**
Prime ministers—Great Britain 351.003; 920
Primers.　*See* **Easy reading materials**
Primitive Christianity.　*See* **Church history—**
　　30(ca.)-600, Early church
Primitive man.　*See* **Man, Nonliterate**
Primitive society.　*See* **Society, Nonliterate folk**
Princes and princesses 920
　x Royalty
Printing 686.2
　See also

Advertising layout and typography	**Linotype**
	Offset printing
Books	**Proofreading**
Color printing	**Type and type founding**
Electrotyping	**Typesetting**

　x Layout and typography; Typography
　xx **Bibliography; Book industries and trade;**
　　Books; Graphic arts; Industrial arts; Publishers and publishing; Typesetting
Printing—Exhibitions 686.2074
　See also **Book industries and trade—Exhibitions**
　x Books—Exhibitions
　xx **Book industries and trade—Exhibitions; Exhibitions**
Printing, Offset.　*See* **Offset printing**
Printing—Specimens 686.2
　See also **Type and type founding**
　x Type specimens
　xx **Advertising; Initials; Type and type founding**
Printing—Style manuals 686.02
　See also **Authorship—Handbooks, manuals, etc.**
　x Style manuals
　xx **Authorship—Handbooks, manuals, etc.**
Printing, Textile.　*See* **Textile printing**
Prints (May subdiv. geog. adjective form)　**769**
　See also **Lithography**
　xx **Graphic arts**
Prints, American 769
　x American prints; United States—Prints
Prison escapes.　*See* **Escapes**
Prison labor.　*See* **Convict labor**
Prison reform 365
　x Penal reform
Prison schools.　*See* **Prisoners—Education**
Prisoners 365
　See also **Political prisoners**

Prisoners—*Continued*

   x Convicts

   xx **Criminals; Prisons**

Prisoners—Education 365

   x Education of criminals; Education of prison-
      ers; Prison schools

   xx **Adult education; Prisons**

Prisoners of war (May subdiv. geog. adjective form)
      341.6

   See also **Concentration camps; Missing in action;**
      also names of wars with the subdivision
      Prisoners and prisons, e.g. **World War,**
      1939-1945—Prisoners and prisons; etc.

   x Exchange of prisoners of war; P.O.W.'s;
      POWs

   xx **Concentration camps**

Prisoners of war, American 341.6

   x American prisoners of war

Prisoners, Political. *See* **Political prisoners**

Prisons (May subdiv. geog.) **365**

   See also

Convict labor	**Prisoners**
Crime	**Prisoners—Education**
Criminal law	**Probation**
Escapes	**Reformatories**
Penal colonies	

   also names of prisons

   x Dungeons; Imprisonment; Jails; Penal institu-
      tions; Penitentiaries; Penology

   xx **Convict labor; Correctional institutions;**
      Crime; Criminal justice, Administration of;
      Punishment

Prisons—United States 365

   x United States—Prisons

Privacy, Right of 323.44

   See also **Computer crimes; Eavesdropping; Wi**
      retapping

   x Invasion of privacy; Right of privacy

   xx **Computer crimes; Libel and slander**

Private funding of the arts. *See* **Art patronage**

Private schools 371; 372; 373.2

   See also **Church schools; Public schools, En-**
      dowed (Great Britain)

   x Boarding schools; Independent schools; Non-
      public schools; Secondary schools

   xx **Education, Secondary**

Private theater. *See* **Amateur theater**

Privateering 341

   See also **Neutrality**

   x Letters of marque

   xx **International law; Naval art and science; Na-**
      val history; Pirates

Prize fighting. *See* **Boxing**

Prizes, Literary. *See* **Literary prizes**

Prizes (Rewards). *See* **Rewards (Prizes, etc.)**

Pro-choice movement. *See* **Abortion—Moral and**
      religious aspects

Pro-life movement. *See* **Abortion—Moral and reli-**
      gious aspects

Probabilities 519.2

    See also **Average; Game theory; Reliability (Engineering); Sampling (Statistics)**

    x Certainty; Fortune; Statistical inference

    xx **Algebra; Gambling; Insurance, Life; Logic; Statistics**

Probation 364.6

    See also **Juvenile courts; Parole**

    x Reform of criminals; Suspended sentence

    xx **Criminal law; Juvenile courts; Parole; Prisons; Punishment; Reformatories; Social case work**

Probes, Space. *See* **Space probes**

Problem children. *See* **Emotionally disturbed children**

Problem solving 510.76

    See also **Crisis management; Critical thinking; Decision making**

    x Solution achievement

    xx **Decision making**

Problem solving, Group 153.4

    x Brain storming; Group problem solving; Think tanks

    xx **Social groups**

Problems, exercises, etc. *See* subjects with the subdivision *Problems, exercises, etc.,* e.g. **Chemistry—Problems, exercises, etc.;** etc.

Processing (Libraries). *See* **Library technical processes**

Processions. *See* **Parades**

Procurement, Government. *See* **Government purchasing**

Producers and directors. *See* **Motion picture producers and directors**

Product recall 658.5

    x Commercial products recall; Manufactures—Defects; Manufactures recall; Recall of products

    xx **Consumer protection**

Production. *See* **Economics; Industry**

Production engineering. *See* **Factory management**

Production standards 658.5

    See also **Motion study; Time study;** also subjects with the subdivision *Production standards,* e.g. **Employees—Production standards;** etc.

    x Output standards; Standards of output; Time production standards; Work standards

    xx **Industrial management; Labor productivity**

Productivity of labor. *See* **Labor productivity**

Products, Brand name. *See* **Brand name products**

Products, Commercial. *See* **Commercial products**

Products, Dairy. *See* **Dairy products**

Products, Generic. *See* **Generic products**

Products, Waste. *See* **Waste products**

Professional associations. *See* **Trade and professional associations**

Professional education 378

    See also **Colleges and universities; Library education; Technical education; Vocational education;** also names of professions with the

Professional education—*Continued*
 subdivision *Study and teaching,* e.g.
 Medicine—Study and teaching; etc.
 x Education, Professional
 xx **Education; Education, Higher; Learning and scholarship; Technical education; Vocational education**
Professional ethics 174
 See also **Business ethics; Legal ethics; Medical ethics;** also names of professions with the subdivision *Professional ethics,* e.g.
 Librarians—Professional ethics; etc.
 x Ethics, Professional
 xx **Ethics**
Professional liability. *See* **Malpractice**
Professional sports 796
 See also names of specific sports
 xx **Sports**
Professions 331.7
 See also **College graduates; Intellectuals; Occupations; Paraprofessions and paraprofessionals; Vocational guidance;** also names of professions with the subdivision *Vocational guidance,* e.g. **Law—Vocational guidance;** etc.
 x Careers; Jobs; Vocations
 xx **Occupations; Self-employed; Vocational guidance**
Professions—Tort liability. *See* **Malpractice**
Professors. *See* **Teachers**
Profit 332.024; 336.02
 See also **Capitalism; Income**
 xx **Business; Capital; Economics; Income; Wealth**
Profit sharing 658.3
 See also **Cooperation**
 xx **Commerce; Cooperation; Wages**
Programmed instruction 371.3
 See also **Computer assisted instruction; Teaching machines;** also subjects with the subdivision *Programmed instruction,* e.g. **English language—Programmed instruction;** etc.
 x Programmed textbooks
 xx **Teaching—Aids and devices**
Programmed textbooks. *See* **Programmed instruction**
Programming (Computers) 001.64; *005.1
 See also **Computer programs; Computer software; Programming languages (Computers);** also subjects with the subdivision *Computer programs,* e.g. **Oceanography—Computer programs;** etc.
 x Computer programming; Computers—Programming
 xx **Computer software; Electronic data processing; Mathematical analysis; Mathematical models**
Programming languages (Computers) 001.64; *005.13
 See also specific languages, e.g. **FORTRAN (Computer program language);** etc.

493

Programming languages (Computers)—*Continued*
> *x* Autocodes; Automatic programming languages; Computer program languages; Machine language
> *xx* **Computer software; Electronic data processing; Language and languages; Programming (Computers)**

Programs, Computer. *See* **Computer programs**
Programs, Radio. *See* **Radio programs**
Programs, School assembly. *See* **School assembly programs**
Programs, Television. *See* **Television programs**
Progress 303.4
> *See also* **Civilization; Science and civilization; Social change; War and civilization**
> *xx* **Civilization**

Progressive education. *See* **Education— Experimental methods**
Prohibited books. *See* **Books—Censorship**
Prohibition 344
> Use for materials dealing with the legal prohibition of liquor traffic and liquor manufacture.
> *See also* **Temperance**
> *xx* **Temperance**

Project Apollo. *See* **Apollo project**
Project Gemini. *See* **Gemini project**
Project MARC. *See* **MARC system**
Project Mariner. *See* **Mariner project**
Project method in teaching 371.3
> *xx* **Teaching**

Project schools. *See* **Experimental schools**
Project Sealab. *See* **Sealab project**
Project Telstar. *See* **Telstar project**
Projectiles 623.4
> *See also* **Ammunition; Bombs; Guided missiles; Ordnance; Rockets (Aeronautics)**
> *x* Bullets; Shells (Projectiles)
> *xx* **Ordnance**

Projective geometry. *See* **Geometry, Projective**
Projectors 778.2
> *x* Film projectors; Lantern projection; Motion picture projectors; Opaque projectors; Slide projectors

Proletariat 305.5; 323.3
> *xx* **Labor; Socialism**

Proliferation of arms. *See* **Arms race**
Pronunciation. *See* **Names—Pronunciation;** and names of languages with the subdivision *Pronunciation,* e.g. **English language— Pronunciation;** etc.
Proofreading 070.5; 686.2
> *xx* **Printing**

Propaganda (May subdiv. geog. adjective form) **303.3; 327.1**
> *See also* **Advertising; Press; Psychological warfare; World War, 1939-1945—Propaganda**
> *xx* **Advertising; Political psychology; Public opinion; Publicity**

494

Propaganda, American 301.15
  x American propaganda; United States—
    Propaganda
Propagation of plants. *See* **Plant propagation**
Propellers, Aerial 629.134
  x Airplanes—Propellers
  xx **Airplanes**
Proper names. *See* **Names**
Property 330.1
  See also **Eminent domain; Income; Real estate;**
    Wealth
  x Ownership
  xx **Economics; Wealth**
Property, Literary. *See* **Copyright**
Property, Real. *See* **Real estate**
Prophecies (Bible). *See* **Bible—Prophecies**
Prophecies (Occult sciences) 133.3
  See also **Astrology; Divination; Fortune telling;**
    Oracles
  x Predictions
  xx **Divination; Occult sciences; Supernatural**
Prophets 221.9; 920
Proportion (Architecture). *See* **Architecture—**
    Composition, proportion, etc.
Proportional representation 328
  See also **Elections**
  x Representation, Proportional; Voting, Cumu-
    lative
  xx **Constitutional law; Representative government**
    and representation
Prose literature, American. *See* **American prose lit-**
    erature
Prose literature, English. *See* **English prose litera-**
    ture
Prosody. *See* **Versification**
Prospecting 622
  See also **Mine surveying; Petroleum—Geology**
  xx **Gold mines and mining; Mines and mineral**
    resources; Silver mines and mining
Prosthesis. *See* **Artificial limbs; Artificial organs;**
    Transplantation of organs, tissues, etc.
Prostitution 176; 306.7; 363.4; 364.3
  See also **Venereal diseases**
  x Hygiene, Social; Social hygiene; Vice
  xx **Crime; Sexual ethics; Sexual hygiene; Social**
    problems; Women—Social conditions
Prostitution, Juvenile 176; 306.7; 362.7; 363.4; 364.3
  x Adolescent prostitution; Child prostitution;
    Children and prostitution; Juvenile prosti-
    tution; Teenage prostitution
  xx **Child abuse; Juvenile delinquency**
Protection. *See* **Free trade and protection**
Protection against burglary. *See* **Burglary protec-**
    tion
Protection of animals. *See* **Animal abuse**
Protection of birds. *See* **Birds—Protection**
Protection of children. *See* **Child welfare**
Protection of game. *See* **Game protection**
Protection of natural scenery. *See* **Landscape pro-**
    tection; Natural monuments; Nature conser-

Protection of natural scenery—*Continued*
   vation; Wilderness areas
Protection of plants.   *See*   **Plant conservation**
Protection of wildlife.   *See*   **Wildlife conservation**
Proteins 547.7
   xx **Physiological chemistry**
Protest.   *See* **Dissent**
Protest marches and rallies.   *See* **Protests, demon-
      strations, etc.**
Protest movements (War).   *See* names of wars with
      the subdivision *Protests, demonstrations,
      etc.,* e.g. **World War, 1939-1945—Protests,
      demonstrations, etc.;** etc.
Protestant churches 280
   See also **Protestantism**
   xx **Church history; Protestantism**
Protestant Episcopal Church in the U.S.A.   *See*
      Episcopal Church
Protestant Reformation.   *See* **Reformation**
Protestantism 280
   See also **Protestant churches; Reformation**
   xx **Christianity; Church history; Protestant
      churches; Reformation**
Protests, demonstrations, etc. (May subdiv. geog.)
      322.4; 361.2
   Use for materials on public gatherings, marches,
      etc., organized for nonviolent protest even
      though incidental disturbances or rioting
      may occur.
   See also **Hunger strikes; Riots; Youth movement;**
      also wars with the subdivision *Protests,
      demonstrations, etc.,* e.g. **World War, 1939-
      1945—Protests, demonstrations, etc.;** etc.
   x Demonstrations (Protest); Marches (Demon-
      strations); Protest marches and rallies; Pub-
      lic demonstrations; Rallies (Protest)
   xx **Crowds; Public meetings; Riots**
Protests, demonstrations, etc.—Chicago (Ill.) 322.4
   x Chicago (Ill.)—Protests, demonstrations, etc.
**Protests, demonstrations, etc.—United States 322.4;
      361.2**
   x United States—Protests, demonstrations, etc.
Protons 539.7
   See also **Atoms; Electrons**
   x Hydrogen nucleus
   xx **Neutrons; Particles (Nuclear physics)**
Protoplasm 574.8
   See also **Cells; Embryology**
   xx **Biology; Cells; Embryology; Life (Biology)**
Protozoa 593
   xx **Cells; Invertebrates; Microorganisms**
Proverbs 398
   See also **Epigrams**
   x Adages; Maxims; Sayings
   xx **Epigrams; Folklore; Quotations**
Providence and government of God 214; 231
   xx **God—Christianity; Theology**
Provincialism.   *See* **Sectionalism (U.S.);** and names
      of languages with the subdivision
      Provincialisms, e.g. **English language—**

Provincialism—*Continued*
> **Provincialisms;** etc.

Pruning 631.5
> *xx* **Forests and forestry; Fruit culture; Gardening; Trees**

Psalmody. *See* **Church music; Hymns**

Pseudonyms 929.4
> *x* Anonyms; Fictitious names; Names, Fictitious; Pen names
> *xx* **Authors; Names; Names, Personal**

Psychiatric hospitals 362.2
> *x* Insane—Hospitals; Mental hospitals
> *xx* **Hospitals; Mentally ill—Institutional care**

Psychiatrists 920; 926
> *x* Psychopathologists
> *xx* **Psychologists**

Psychiatry 616.89
> Use for materials on clinical aspects of mental disorders, including therapy. Popular materials and materials on regional or social aspects of mental disorders are entered under **Mental illness.** Systematic descriptions of mental disorders are entered under **Psychology, Pathological.**
> *See also* **Adolescent psychiatry; Child psychiatry; Mental illness; Mentally ill; Psychology, Pathological; Psychotherapy**
> *xx* **Psychology, Pathological**

Psychiatry, Adolescent. *See* **Adolescent psychiatry**

Psychiatry, Child. *See* **Child psychiatry**

Psychic healing. *See* **Mental healing**

Psychical research 133
> Use for materials on investigations of phenomena that appear to be contrary to physical laws and beyond the normal sense perceptions.
> *See also*

Apparitions	**Mental suggestion**
Clairvoyance	**Mind and body**
Dreams	**Mind reading**
Extrasensory perception	**Personality disorders**
Ghosts	**Psychokinesis**
Hallucinations and illusions	**Spiritualism**
	Subconsciousness
Hypnotism	**Telepathy**

> *x* Paranormal phenomena; Parapsychology
> *xx* **Ghosts; Psychology; Research; Spiritualism; Supernatural**

Psychoanalysis 616.89
> *See also*

Dreams	**Psychology**
Hypnotism	**Psychology, Pathological**
Medicine, Psychosomatic	**Psychology, Physiological**
Mind and body	**Subconsciousness**

> *xx* **Dreams; Hypnotism; Mind and body; Psychology; Psychology, Pathological; Psychology, Physiological; Subconsciousness**

Psychogenetics. *See* **Behavior genetics**

Psychokinesis 133.8
> *x* Telekinesis

Psychokinesis—*Continued*

    xx **Psychical research; Spiritualism**

Psychological aspects. *See* topical subjects with the subdivision *Psychological aspects,* e.g. **Drugs—Psychological aspects; World War, 1939-1945—Psychological aspects;** etc.

Psychological stress. *See* **Stress (Psychology)**

Psychological tests. *See* **Mental tests**

Psychological warfare 355.3

    Use for materials dealing with the methods used to undermine the morale of the civilian population and the military forces of an enemy country.

    See also **Brainwashing;** also names of wars with the subdivision *Psychological aspects,* e.g. **World War, 1939-1945—Psychological aspects;** etc.

    x Cold war; War of nerves

    xx **Military art and science; Morale; Propaganda; Psychology, Applied; War**

Psychologists 150.92; 920

    See also **Psychiatrists**

Psychologists, School. *See* **School psychologists**

Psychology 150

    See also

Adjustment (Psychology)	**Instinct**
Adolescent psychology	**Intellect**
Aggressiveness (Psychology)	**Intuition**
Apperception	**Memory**
Assertiveness (Psychology)	**Motivation (Psychology)**
Attention	**Number concept**
Attitude (Psychology)	**Perception**
Behavior genetics	**Personality**
Behaviorism	**Phrenology**
Child psychology	**Physiognomy**
Choice (Psychology)	**Political psychology**
Consciousness	**Psychical research**
Educational psychology	**Psychoanalysis**
Emotions	**Reasoning**
Ethnopsychology	**Senses and sensation**
Genius	**Social psychology**
Gestalt psychology	**Stress (Psychology)**
Habit	**Subconsciousness**
Imagination	**Temperament**
Individuality	**Thought and thinking**
	Values

    also subdivision *Biography—Psychology* under names of individual literary authors, e.g. **Shakespeare, William, 1564-1616—Biography—Psychology;** also subdivision *Psychology* under titles of individual sacred works, and under religions, religious topics, names of animals, classes of persons, ethnic groups, and names of other individual persons, e.g. **Christianity—Psychology; Faith—Psychology; Dogs—Psychology; Indians of North America—Psychology;** etc.; and the subdivision *Psychological aspects* under topical subjects for works that discuss the influence of particular situations, condi-

Psychology—*Continued*

tions, activities, environments, or objects on the mental condition or personality of the individual, e.g. **Color—Psychological aspects; Music— Psychological aspects;** etc.

x Mental philosophy; Mind

xx **Brain; Philosophy; Psychoanalysis; Soul**

Psychology, Abnormal. *See* **Psychology, Pathological**

Psychology, Adolescent. *See* **Adolescent psychology**

Psychology, Applied 158

See also

Behavior modification	**Human relations**
Counseling	**Interviewing**
Employee morale	**Psychological warfare**
Human engineering	**Psychology, Pastoral**

also subjects with the subdivision *Psychological aspects,* e.g. **Drugs—Psychological aspects;** etc.

x Applied psychology; Industrial psychology; Psychology, Industrial; Psychology, Practical

xx **Educational psychology; Human relations; Interviewing; Psychology, Religious; Public relations; Social psychology**

Psychology, Biblical. *See* **Bible—Psychology**

Psychology, Child. *See* **Child psychology**

Psychology, Comparative 156

See also **Animal intelligence; Instinct; Sociobiology;** also names of animals with the subdivision *Psychology,* e.g.

Dogs—Psychology; etc.

x Animal psychology; Comparative psychology

xx **Animal intelligence; Instinct; Zoology**

Psychology, Criminal. *See* **Criminal psychology**

Psychology, Educational. *See* **Educational psychology**

Psychology, Ethnic. *See* **Ethnopsychology**

Psychology, Experimental. *See* **Psychology, Physiological**

Psychology, Industrial. *See* **Psychology, Applied**

Psychology, Medical. *See* **Psychology, Pathological**

Psychology, National. *See* **Ethnopsychology; National characteristics**

Psychology of color. *See* **Color—Psychological aspects**

Psychology of learning. *See* **Learning, Psychology of**

Psychology of music. *See* **Music—Psychological aspects**

Psychology, Pastoral 253.5

Use for materials on the application of psychology and psychiatry by the clergy to the spiritual problems of individuals.

x Pastoral psychiatry; Pastoral psychology

xx **Christian ethics; Church work; Pastoral work; Psychology, Applied; Psychology, Religious; Therapeutics, Suggestive**

Psychology, Pathological 157

See note under **Psychiatry.**

Psychology, Pathological—*Continued*

See also

Criminal psychology	Mental illness
Depression, Mental	Neuroses
Eating disorders	Personality disorders
Hallucinations and illu-	Psychiatry
sions	Psychoanalysis
Medicine, Psychosomatic	Subconsciousness

    x Abnormal psychology; Diseases, Mental;
       Mental diseases; Pathological psychology;
       Psychology, Abnormal; Psychology, Medi-
       cal; Psychopathology; Psychopathy

   xx **Criminal psychology; Mental health; Mind
       and body; Nervous system; Psychiatry; Psy-
       choanalysis**

Psychology, Physiological 152

See also

Behaviorism	Mental tests
Color sense	Mind and body
Dreams	Optical illusions
Emotions	Pain
Human engineering	Psychoanalysis
Hypnotism	Senses and sensation
Left- and right-handedness	Sleep
Memory	Temperament

    x Experimental psychology; Physiological psy-
       chology; Psychology, Experimental; Psycho-
       physics

   xx **Mental health; Mind and body; Nervous sys-
       tem; Physiology; Psychoanalysis**

Psychology, Political. *See* **Political psychology**
Psychology, Practical. *See* **Psychology, Applied**
Psychology, Racial. *See* **Ethnopsychology**

Psychology, Religious 200.1; 253.5

    See also **Psychology, Applied; Psychology, Pasto-
       ral;** also titles of individual sacred works
       and names of religions or religious topics
       with the subdivision *Psychology,* e.g.
       **Christianity—Psychology; Faith—
       Psychology;** etc.

    x Religious psychology

   xx **Religion**

Psychology, Social. *See* **Social psychology**
Psychology, Structural. *See* **Gestalt psychology**
Psychopathologists. *See* **Psychiatrists**
Psychopathology. *See* **Psychology, Pathological**
Psychopathy. *See* **Psychology, Pathological**
Psychophysics. *See* **Psychology, Physiological**
Psychoses. *See* **Mental illness**
Psychosomatic medicine. *See* **Medicine, Psychoso-
       matic**

Psychotherapy 616.89

    See also **Biofeedback training; Mental healing;
       Therapeutics, Suggestive**

   xx **Mental healing; Psychiatry; Therapeutics,
       Suggestive**

Psychotic children. *See* **Mentally ill children**
Psychotics. *See* **Mentally ill**
PTAs. *See* **Parents' and teachers' associations**

Public accommodations, Discrimination in. *See*
    Discrimination in public accommodations
Public administration 350
    Use for general materials on the principles and
    techniques involved in the conduct of public
    business. Materials limited to the govern-
    mental process of a particular country, state,
    etc. are entered under the name of the area
    with the subdivision *Politics and govern-
    ment.*

    See also **Administrative law; Bureaucracy; Civil
    service; Military government;** also names of
    countries, cities, etc. with the subdivision
    Politics and government, e.g. **United
    States—Politics and government;** etc.
    x Administration
    xx **Administrative law; Local government; Munic-
      ipal government; Political science**
Public assistance. *See* **Public welfare**
Public buildings 725

    See also names of countries, cities, etc. with the
    subdivision *Public buildings,* e.g. **United
    States—Public buildings; Chicago (Ill.)—
    Public buildings;** etc.
    x Buildings, Public; Government buildings
    xx **Architecture; Art, Municipal; Public works**
Public charities. *See* **Public welfare**
Public debts. *See* **Debts, Public**
Public demonstrations. *See* **Protests, demonstra-
    tions, etc.**
Public documents. *See* **Government publications**
Public figures. *See* **Celebrities**
Public finance. *See* **Finance**
Public health (May subdiv. geog.) **614**

    See also

Cemeteries	**Milk supply**
Charities, Medical	**Noise**
Communicable diseases	**Occupational diseases**
Community health services	**Occupational health and**
Cremation	**safety**
Disinfection and disinfec-	**Pollution**
tants	**Refuse and refuse disposal**
Environmental health	**Sanitary engineering**
Epidemics	**Sanitation**
Food adulteration and in-	**School hygiene**
spection	**Sewage disposal**
Health boards	**Social medicine**
Hospitals	**Street cleaning**
Meat inspection	**Vaccination**
Medical care	**Water—Pollution**
Medicine, Preventive	**Water supply**

    x Health, Public; Hygiene, Public; Hygiene, So-
      cial; Social hygiene
    xx **Medicine, State; Sanitation; Social problems**
Public health boards. *See* **Health boards**
Public health—United States 614
    x United States—Public health
Public housing (May subdiv. geog.) **363.5**
    x Government housing; Housing projects, Gov-

Public housing—*Continued*
  ernment; Low income housing
 xx **Housing**
Public interest 172; 320.01; 344
 See also **Ombudsman; Whistle blowing**
 x National interest
 xx **Industry—Government policy; State, The**
Public lands. *See* **Forest reserves; National parks**
  and reserves; and names of countries,
  states, etc. with the subdivision *Public*
  lands, e.g. **United States—Public lands;**
  etc.
Public libraries (May subdiv. geog.) 027.4
 See also **County libraries; Regional libraries**
 x Libraries, Public
 xx **Libraries**
Public meetings 302.3
 See also **Parliamentary practice; Protests, dem-**
  onstrations, etc.
 x Meetings, Public
 xx **Freedom of assembly**
Public opinion 303.3
 See also **Attitude (Psychology); Press; Propa-**
  ganda; Public relations; Publicity; also subjects with the subdivision *Public opinion,*
  e.g. **World War, 1939-1945—Public opinion;**
  etc.; and names of countries with the subdivision *Foreign opinion,* e.g. **United States—**
  Foreign opinion; etc.
 x Opinion, Public
 xx **Attitude (Psychology); Freedom of conscience;**
  Political psychology; Public relations
Public opinion polls 303.3
 See also **Market surveys**
 x Opinion polls; Polls, Public opinion; Straw
  votes
 xx **Market surveys**
Public ownership. *See* **Government ownership; Mu-**
  nicipal ownership
Public playgrounds. *See* **Playgrounds**
Public procurement. *See* **Government purchasing**
Public records—Preservation. *See* **Archives**
Public relations 659.2
 May be subdivided by topic, e.g. **Public rela-**
  tions—Libraries; etc.
 See also **Advertising; Business entertaining; Psy-**
  chology, Applied; Public opinion; Publicity
 xx **Advertising; Public opinion; Publicity**
Public relations—Libraries 021.7
 x Libraries—Public relations
 xx **Libraries and community**
Public safety, Crimes against. *See* **Offenses against**
  public safety
Public schools (May subdiv. geog.) 371; 372; 373.2
 Use for materials on preschool, elementary, and
  secondary schools supported by state and local government. Materials on British pri-
  vately endowed schools known as "public
  schools" are entered under **Public schools,**
  Endowed (Great Britain).

Public schools—*Continued*

    See also **Evening and continuation schools; High schools; Junior high schools; Magnet schools; Rural schools; Schools; Summer schools;** also headings beginning with the word **School**

    x Common schools; Grammar schools; Secondary schools

  xx **Education, Secondary; Schools**

Public schools and religion. *See* **Religion in the public schools**

Public schools, Endowed (Great Britain) 373.2; 373.42

    See note under **Public schools.**

  xx **Private schools**

Public schools—United States 379.73

    x United States—Public schools

Public service commissions 350

    Use for materials on bodies appointed to regulate or control public utilities.

    x Public utility commissions

  xx **Corporation law; Corporations; Industry—Government policy**

Public service corporations. *See* **Public utilities**

Public shelters. *See* **Air raid shelters**

Public speaking 808.5

    See also **Acting; Debates and debating; Lectures and lecturing; Preaching; Voice**

    x Elocution; Oratory; Persuasion (Rhetoric); Speaking

  xx **Voice**

Public television 384.55

    Use for materials on non-commercial television, publicly owned and operated, that presents educational, cultural, and public service programs.

    x Educational television; Television, Public

  xx **Television**

Public transit. *See* **Local transit**

Public utilities 343; 351.8; 363.6

    See also

Corporation law	**Railroads—Government**
Corporations	**policy**
Electric industries	**Street railroads**
Electric railroads	**Telegraph**
Gas	**Telephone**
Railroads	**Water supply**

    x Electric utilities; Gas companies; Public service corporations; Utilities, Public

  xx **Corporation law; Corporations**

Public utility commissions. *See* **Public service commissions**

Public welfare 361.6

    Use for materials on tax-supported welfare activities. Materials on privately supported welfare activities are entered under **Charities.** Materials on the methods employed in welfare work, public or private, are entered under **Social work.**

Public welfare—*Continued*
 See also

Charities
Child welfare
Children's hospitals
Disaster relief
Food relief
Hospitals
Institutional care

Legal assistance to the
 poor
Orphanages
Poor
Social medicine
Unemployed

  x Charities, Public; Poor relief; Public assistance; Public charities; Relief, Public; Social
   welfare; Welfare state; Welfare work
 xx **Charities; Poverty; Social work**
Public works 351.8
  See also **Municipal engineering; Public buildings;**
   also names of countries, cities, etc. with the
   subdivision *Public works,* e.g. **United
   States—Public works; Chicago (Ill.)—Public
   works;** etc.
 xx **Civil engineering; Economic assistance, Domestic**
Public worship 264
  x Church attendance
 xx **Worship**
Publicity 659.2
  See also **Advertising; Press; Propaganda; Public
   relations**
 xx **Advertising; Public opinion; Public relations**
Publishers and authors. *See* **Authors and publishers**
Publishers and publishing 070.5
  See also

Authors and publishers
Book industries and trade
Books
Booksellers and booksel-
 ling
Catalogs, Publishers'
Copyright

Electronic publishing
Paperback books
Printing
Publishers' standard book
 numbers
Serial publications

  x Book trade; Editors and editing; Publishing
 xx **Book industries and trade; Books; Booksellers
   and bookselling; Copyright**
Publishers' catalogs. *See* **Catalogs, Publishers'**
Publishers' standard book numbers 070.5
  See also **International Standard Book Numbers**
  x Book numbers, Publishers' standard; Standard
   book numbers
 xx **Publishers and publishing**
Publishing. *See* **Publishers and publishing**
Publishing, Electronic. *See* **Electronic publishing**
Pugilism. *See* **Boxing**
Pulmonary resuscitation. *See* **Artificial respiration**
Pulsars 521; 523
  x Pulsating radio sources
 xx **Stars**
Pulsating radio sources. *See* **Pulsars**
Pumping iron. *See* **Weight lifting**
Pumping machinery 621.2; 621.6
  See also types of pumping machinery, e.g. **Heat
   pumps;** etc.

Pumping machinery—*Continued*

    x Force pumps; Pumps; Steam pumps

    xx **Engines; Hydraulic engineering**

Pumps. *See* **Pumping machinery**

Punch and Judy. *See* **Puppets and puppet plays**

Punched card systems. *See* **Information storage and retrieval systems**

Punctuation 421

    x English language—Punctuation

    xx **Rhetoric**

Punishment 364.6

    See also **Capital punishment; Crime; Criminal law; Penal colonies; Prisons; Probation; Reformatories**

    x Penology

    xx **Crime; Criminal justice, Administration of; Criminal law**

Punishment in schools. *See* **School discipline**

Puns and punning 817; 818

    xx **Wit and humor**

Pupil-teacher relationships. *See* **Teacher-student relationships**

Puppets and puppet plays 791.5

    See also **Shadow pantomimes and plays**

    x Marionettes; Muppets; Punch and Judy

    xx **Drama; Folk drama; Theater**

Purchase tax. *See* **Sales tax**

Purchasing. *See* **Buying; Shopping**

Purchasing, Government. *See* **Government purchasing**

Pure food. *See* **Food adulteration and inspection**

Purification of water. *See* **Water—Purification**

Puritans 285; 920

    See also **Calvinism; Church of England—United States; Congregationalism; Pilgrims (New England colonists)**

    xx **Calvinism; Church of England—United States; Congregationalism; United States—History—1600-1775, Colonial period**

Puzzles 793.7

    See also **Crossword puzzles; Mathematical recreations; Riddles**

    xx **Amusements; Riddles**

Pyramids 722

    See also **Obelisks**

    xx **Archeology; Architecture, Ancient; Monuments**

Quacks and quackery 615.8

    xx **Impostors and imposture; Medicine; Swindlers and swindling**

Quakers. *See* **Society of Friends**

Qualitative analysis. *See* **Chemistry, Analytic**

Quality. *See* subjects with the subdivision *Quality,* e.g. **Air—Quality;** etc.

Quality control 519.8; 658.5

    See also specific industries with the subdivision *Quality control,* e.g. **Steel industry and trade—Quality control;** etc.; also subjects with the subdivision *Quality,* e.g. **Air—Quality;** etc.

Quality control—*Continued*
  xx **Reliability (Engineering); Sampling (Statistics)**
Quality of life 303.3
  Use for materials on the combination of objective standards and subjective attitudes, by which individuals and groups assess their life situations.
  See also **Lifestyles; Social values; Standard of living**
  x Life quality
  xx **Economic conditions; Social conditions; Social values**
Quantitative analysis. *See* **Chemistry, Analytic**
Quantity cookery. *See* **Cookery, Quantity**
Quantum mechanics. *See* **Quantum theory**
Quantum theory 530.1
  See also

Atomic theory	**Radiation**
Chemistry, Physical and theoretical	**Relativity (Physics)**
	Thermodynamics
Force and energy	**Wave mechanics**
Neutrons	

  x Quantum mechanics
  xx **Atomic theory; Chemistry, Physical and theoretical; Dynamics; Force and energy; Physics; Radiation; Relativity (Physics); Thermodynamics**
Quarantine. *See* **Communicable diseases**
Quarks 539.7
  xx **Particles (Nuclear physics)**
Quarries and quarrying 622
  See also **Stone**
  x Stone quarries
  xx **Geology, Economic; Stone**
Quartz 549
  x Minerals; Rock crystal
  xx **Mineralogy**
Quasars 521; 523
  x Quasi-stellar radio sources
  xx **Astronomy; Radio astronomy**
Quasi-stellar radio sources. *See* **Quasars**
Québec (Province) 971.4
Québec (Province)—History 971.4
Québec (Province)—History—Autonomy and independence movements 971.4
  x Québec (Province)—Separatist movement; Separatist movement in Québec (Province)
  xx **Canada—English-French relations**
Québec (Province)—Separatist movement. *See* **Québec (Province)—History—Autonomy and independence movements**
Queens. *See* **Kings, queens, rulers, etc.**
Queries. *See* **Questions and answers**
Questions and answers 793.7
  Use for informal quizzes of miscellany. Questions and answers on a particular subject are entered under the subject with the subdivision *Miscellanea,* e.g.
  Medicine—Miscellanea; etc. Examination

Questions and answers—*Continued*
> questions on a particular subject are entered under the subject with the subdivision *Examinations, questions, etc.,* e.g.
> **Music—Examinations, questions, etc.;** etc.
> *See also* **Examinations;** also subjects with the subdivision *Examinations, questions, etc.,* e.g. **Music—Examinations, questions, etc.;** etc.
> *x* Answers to questions; Queries; Quizzes

Quicksilver. *See* **Mercury**
Quilting 746.46
Quilts 746.46
> *x* Coverlets; Patchwork quilts
> *xx* **Interior design**

Quintets 785.7
> *xx* **Orchestral music**

Quislings. *See* **World War, 1939-1945—Collaborationists**
Quizzes. *See* **Questions and answers**
Qumran texts. *See* **Dead Sea scrolls**
Quotations 080; 808.8
> *See also* **Proverbs;** also subjects and names of people with the subdivision *Quotations,* e.g. **Presidents—United States—Quotations;** etc.
> *x* Sayings
> *xx* **Epigrams; Literature—Collected works**

Qur'an. *See* **Koran**
R.N.A. *See* **Ribonucleic acid**
R.V.'s. *See* **Recreational vehicles**
Rabbis 296.6
> *xx* **Clergy; Judaism**

Rabbits 599.32; 636
> *x* Hares

Rabies 616.9; 636.089
> *x* Hydrophobia

Race 572
> *xx* **Ethnology**

Race awareness 305.8
> *See also* **Blacks—Race identity; Prejudices; Racism**
> *xx* **Race relations**

Race discrimination 305.8
> Use for materials on the restriction or denial of rights, privileges, or choice because of race. Materials on prejudicial attitudes about particular groups because of their race are entered under **Racism.**
> *See also* types of discrimination, e.g. **Discrimination in education;** etc.
> *x* Discrimination, Racial; Racial discrimination
> *xx* **Discrimination; Race relations; Racism; Social problems**

Race identity. *See* names of races with the subdivision *Race identity,* e.g. **Blacks—Race identity;** etc.
Race prejudice. *See* **Racism**
Race problems. *See* **Race relations**
Race psychology. *See* **Ethnopsychology**
Race relations 305.8
> Use for materials on the contact and interaction between racial groups.

Race relations—*Continued*
  See also
  Acculturation   **Intercultural education**
  Culture conflict   **Interracial adoption**
  Discrimination   **Race awareness**
  Ethnic relations   **Race discrimination**
  Immigration and emigra- Racism
      tion

  also names of countries, cities, etc. with the sub-
      division *Race relations,* e.g. **United
      States—Race relations; Chicago (Ill.)—Race
      relations; South Africa—Race relations;** etc.
  x Integration, Racial; Interracial relations; Race
      problems
  xx **Ethnic groups; Ethnic relations; Ethnology;
      Minorities; Social problems; Sociology**
Race relations and the church. *See* **Church and
      race relations**
Races of people. *See* **Ethnology**
Racial balance in schools. *See* **Busing (School inte-
      gration); School integration; Segregation in
      education**
Racial bias. *See* **Racism**
Racial discrimination. *See* **Race discrimination**
Racial identity. *See* names of races with the subdi-
      vision *Race identity,* e.g. **Blacks—Race
      identity;** etc.
Racing. *See* names of types of racing, e.g.
      **Automobile racing; Bicycle racing; Boat rac-
      ing; Horse racing; Soap box derbies;** etc.
Racism 305.8; 320.5
  See note under **Race discrimination.**
  See also **Race discrimination**
  x Race prejudice; Racial bias
  xx **Attitude (Psychology); Prejudices; Race
      awareness; Race relations**
Racketeering 364.1
  x Crime syndicates
  xx **Crime; Organized crime**
Radar 621.3848
  xx **Navigation; Radio; Remote sensing**
Radar defense networks 623.7
  See also **Ballistic missile early warning system**
  x Defenses, Radar
  xx **Air defenses**
Radiant heating 697
  x Panel heating
  xx **Heating**
Radiation 539.2
  See also
  Cosmic rays   **Radioactivity**
  Electromagnetic waves **Radium**
  Gamma rays   **Sound**
  Infrared radiation   **Spectrum analysis**
  Light   **Ultraviolet rays**
  Phosphorescence   **X rays**
  Quantum theory
  xx **Light; Optics; Physics; Quantum theory;
      Waves**
Radiation biology. *See* **Radiobiology**

Radiation—Physiological effect 612
> *See also* **Atomic bomb—Physiological effect; Nuclear medicine**
> *xx* **Atomic bomb—Physiological effect**

Radiation—Safety measures 612

Radiation, Solar. *See* **Solar radiation**

Radiation therapy. *See* **Radiotherapy**

Radicals and radicalism 320.5
> *x* Extremism (Political science)
> *xx* **Revolutions; Right and left (Political science)**

Radio 621.3841
> *See also* **Radar; Sound—Recording and reproducing**
> *x* Wireless
> *xx* **Electric engineering; Telecommunication**

Radio addresses, debates, etc. 384.54; 808.5; 808.85
> *x* Radio lectures
> *xx* **Debates and debating; Lectures and lecturing; Radio broadcasting; Radio scripts**

Radio advertising 659.14
> *x* Advertising, Radio; Commercials, Radio; Radio commercials
> *xx* **Advertising; Radio broadcasting; Radio industry and trade**

Radio and music 782.8
> Use same form for radio and other subjects.
> *x* Music and radio
> *xx* **Music**

Radio apparatus industry. *See* **Radio industry and trade**

Radio astronomy 522
> *See also* names of celestial radio sources, e.g.
> **Quasars;** etc.
> *xx* **Astronomy; Interstellar communication**

Radio authorship 808.2
> *See also* **Radio plays—Technique; Radio scripts**
> *x* Radio script writing; Radio writing
> *xx* **Authorship; Radio broadcasting; Radio scripts**

Radio broadcasting 384.54
> *See also* **Equal time rule (Broadcasting); Fairness doctrine (Broadcasting); Radio addresses, debates, etc.; Radio advertising; Radio authorship; Radio programs; Television broadcasting**
> *xx* **Broadcasting; Mass media**

Radio chemistry. *See* **Radiochemistry**

Radio commercials. *See* **Radio advertising**

Radio drama. *See* **Radio plays**

Radio—Equipment and supplies 621.3841
> *See also* **Amplifiers, Vacuum tube; Radio—Receivers and reception**
> *xx* **Radio industry and trade**

Radio frequency modulation 621.3841
> *See also* **Radio, Shortwave**
> *x* F.M. radio; FM radio; Frequency modulation, Radio

Radio in aeronautics 629.135
> Use same form for radio in other subjects.
> *x* Aeronautics, Radio in
> *xx* **Aeronautics; Navigation (Aeronautics)**

Radio in astronautics 629.4
> *x* Lunar surface radio communication
> *xx* **Astronautics—Communication systems**

Radio in education 371.3
> *x* Education and radio
> *xx* **Audiovisual education; Teaching—Aids and devices**

Radio industry and trade 338.4
> *See also* **Radio advertising; Radio—Equipment and supplies**
> *x* Radio apparatus industry
> *xx* **Electric industries**

Radio journalism. *See* **Broadcast journalism**

Radio lectures. *See* **Radio addresses, debates, etc.**

Radio news. *See* **Broadcast journalism**

Radio operators 621.3841

Radio plays 808.82; 812; 812.08; etc.
> Use for individual radio plays, for collections of plays, and for works about them. Works on how to write radio plays are entered under **Radio plays—Technique.**
> *x* Radio drama; Scenarios
> *xx* **Drama; Radio programs; Radio scripts**

Radio plays—Technique 808.2
> *See also* **Television plays—Technique**
> *x* Play writing; Playwriting
> *xx* **Drama—Technique; Radio authorship; Television plays—Technique**

Radio programs 384.54
> *See also* types of programs and specific programs, e.g. **Radio plays; Talk shows;** etc.
> *x* Programs, Radio
> *xx* **Radio broadcasting**

Radio—Receivers and reception 621.3841
> *x* Radio reception; Radios
> *xx* **Radio—Equipment and supplies**

Radio reception. *See* **Radio—Receivers and reception**

Radio—Repairing 621.3841
> *x* Radio servicing
> *xx* **Repairing**

Radio script writing. *See* **Radio authorship**

Radio scripts 808.82
> *See also* **Radio addresses, debates, etc.; Radio authorship; Radio plays; Television scripts**
> *xx* **Radio authorship; Television scripts**

Radio servicing. *See* **Radio—Repairing**

Radio, Shortwave 621.3841
> *See also* **Amateur radio stations; Citizens band radio; Microwave communication systems; Microwaves**
> *x* High-frequency radio; Shortwave radio; U. H.F. radio; UHF radio; Ultrahigh frequency radio
> *xx* **Electric conductors; Electric waves; Radio frequency modulation**

Radio stations 384.54
> *See also* names of radio stations

Radio stations, Amateur. *See* **Amateur radio stations**

Radio waves. *See* **Electric waves**
Radio writing. *See* **Radio authorship**
Radioactive fallout 539.7
    x Dust, Radioactive; Fallout, Radioactive
    xx **Atomic bomb; Hydrogen bomb; Radioactive**
        pollution
Radioactive isotopes. *See* **Radioisotopes**
Radioactive pollution 363.1; 363.7; 621.48
    See also **Radioactive fallout**
    x Environmental radioactivity; Nuclear pollu-
        tion; Pollution, Radioactive
    xx **Pollution; Radioactivity**
Radioactive substances. *See* **Radioactivity**
Radioactivity 539.7
    See also

Cosmic rays	**Radiochemistry**
Electrons	**Radiotherapy**
Helium	**Radium**
Nuclear physics	**Transmutation (Chemis-**
Phosphorescence	**try)**
Radioactive pollution	**Uranium**
Radiobiology	**X rays**

    x Radioactive substances
    xx **Electricity; Light; Nuclear physics; Physics;**
        Radiation; Radium
Radiobiology 574.19
    x Radiation biology
    xx **Biology; Biophysics; Nuclear physics; Radio-**
        activity
Radiocarbon dating 539.7
    x Carbon 14 dating; Dating, Radiocarbon
    xx **Archeology**
Radiochemistry 541.3
    x Radio chemistry
    xx **Chemistry, Physical and theoretical; Radioac-**
        tivity
Radiography. *See* **X rays**
Radioisotopes 621.48
    x Radioactive isotopes
    xx **Isotopes; Nuclear engineering**
Radiologists 920
    x Roentgenologists
    xx **Physicians; Radiotherapy; X rays**
Radios. *See* **Radio—Receivers and reception**
Radiotherapy 615.8
    See also **Phototherapy; Radiologists; Radium;**
        Ultraviolet rays; X rays
    x Radiation therapy
    xx **Electrotherapeutics; Phototherapy; Physical**
        therapy; Radioactivity; Radium; Therapeu-
        tics; X rays
Radium 546; 547; 661
    See also **Radioactivity; Radiotherapy**
    xx **Radiation; Radioactivity; Radiotherapy**
Railroad accidents. *See* **Railroads—Accidents**
Railroad construction. *See* **Railroad engineering**
Railroad engineering 625.1
    x Railroad construction
    xx **Civil engineering; Engineering; Railroads**
Railroad fares. *See* **Railroads—Rates**

Railroad mergers. *See* **Railroads—Consolidation**
Railroad rates. *See* **Railroads—Rates**
Railroad workers. *See* **Railroads—Employees**
Railroads (May subdiv. geog.) **385; 625.1**
   See also

Electric railroads	**Monorail railroads**
Eminent domain	**Railroad engineering**
Express service	**Street railroads**
Freight and freightage	**Subways**

   also names of individual railroads
   x Railways; Trains, Railroad
   xx **Public utilities; Transportation**
Railroads—Accidents 363.1
   See also **Railroads—Safety appliances; Railroads—Signaling**
   x Collisions, Railroad; Derailments; Railroad accidents; Train wrecks; Wrecks
   xx **Accidents; Disasters**
Railroads and state. *See* **Railroads—Government policy**
Railroads, Cable. *See* **Cable railroads**
Railroads—Consolidation 338.8
   x Industrial mergers; Mergers, Industrial; Railroad mergers
   xx **Monopolies; Trusts, Industrial**
Railroads, Electric. *See* **Electric railroads**
Railroads—Electrification 621.33
   See also **Electric railroads**
   x Electrification of railroads
   xx **Electric railroads**
Railroads—Employees 385.023; 625.1023
   x Railroad workers
Railroads—Fares. *See* **Railroads—Rates**
Railroads—Finance 385
   See also **Railroads—Rates; Railroads—Statistics**
   x Capitalization (Finance)
Railroads—Government ownership. *See* **Railroads—Government policy**
Railroads—Government policy 351.87
   See also **Interstate commerce; Railroads—Rates**
   x Government ownership of railroads; Government regulation of railroads; Nationalization of railroads; Railroads and state; Railroads—Government ownership; Railroads, Nationalization of; State and railroads; State ownership of railroads
   xx **Government ownership; Industry—Government policy; Interstate commerce; Public utilities**
Railroads—Models 625.1
   xx **Machinery—Models**
Railroads, Nationalization of. *See* **Railroads—Government policy**
Railroads—Rates 385
   See also **Freight and freightage; Interstate commerce**
   x Railroad fares; Railroad rates; Railroads—Fares; Rebates (Railroads)
   xx **Freight and freightage; Railroads—Finance; Railroads—Government policy**

Railroads—Rolling stock. *See* **Locomotives**
Railroads—Safety appliances 625.1
  See also **Brakes; Railroads—Signaling**
  xx **Accidents—Prevention; Railroads—Accidents;
    Safety appliances**
Railroads—Signaling 625.1
  x Block signal systems; Interlocking signals
  xx **Railroads—Accidents; Railroads—Safety ap-
    pliances; Signals and signaling**
Railroads, Single rail. *See* **Monorail railroads**
Railroads—Statistics 385
  xx **Railroads—Finance**
Railroads, Street. *See* **Street railroads**
Railroads, Underground. *See* **Subways**
Railways. *See* **Railroads**
Rain, Acid. *See* **Acid rain**
Rain and rainfall 551.57
  See also **Acid rain; Droughts; Floods; Forest in-
    fluences; Meteorology; Snow; Storms**
  x Rainfall
  xx **Climate; Droughts; Forest influences; Meteo-
    rology; Storms; Water; Weather**
Rain forests (May subdiv. geog.) **634.9**
    Use for materials on forests of broad-leaved,
      mainly evergreen trees found in continually
      moist climates in the tropics, subtropics,
      and some parts of the temperate zones.
      Consider also **Jungles.**
  See also **Jungles**
  x Tropical rain forests
  xx **Forests and forestry**
Rain making. *See* **Weather—Control**
Rainbow 551.5
  See also **Refraction**
  xx **Meteorology**
Rainfall. *See* **Rain and rainfall**
Rainfall and forests. *See* **Forest influences**
Rallies (Protest). *See* **Protests, demonstrations, etc.**
Ranch life 307.7; 630.1
  See also **Cowhands**
  xx **Farm life; Frontier and pioneer life**
Random access memories (Data processing). *See*
    Computer storage devices
Random access storage devices (Data
    processing). *See* **Computer storage devices**
Random sampling. *See* **Sampling (Statistics)**
Rank. *See* **Social classes**
—**Rape 364.1**
  x Assault, Criminal; Criminal assault
  xx **Offenses against the person; Sex crimes**
Rapid reading 372.4
  x Accelerated reading; Faster reading; Speed
    reading
  xx **Reading—Remedial teaching**
Rapid transit. *See* **Local transit**
Rare animals 591
  See also **Endangered species; Extinct animals;
    Wildlife conservation;** also names of specific
    animals, e.g. **Bison;** etc.
  x Animals, Rare; Endangered animals; Threat-

Rare animals—*Continued*
  ened animals; Vanishing animals
 xx **Animals; Endangered species; Extinct animals; Wildlife; Wildlife conservation**
Rare books 090
 x Book rarities; Books, Rare
 xx **Bibliography—Editions**
Rare plants 581
 See also **Endangered species; Plant conservation**
 x Endangered plants; Threatened plants
 xx **Endangered species; Plant conservation; Plants**
Rating. *See* **Performance standards;** and subjects and classes of people with the subdivision *Rating,* e.g. **Bonds—Rating; Employees—Rating;** etc.
Ratio and proportion 513
 xx **Arithmetic; Geometry**
Rationalism 149; 211
 See also

Agnosticism	**Intuition**
Atheism	**Positivism**
Belief and doubt	**Realism**
Deism	**Reason**
Enlightenment	**Skepticism**
Free thought	**Theism**

 xx **Agnosticism; Atheism; Belief and doubt; Deism; Free thought; God; Knowledge, Theory of; Philosophy; Realism; Religion; Secularism**
Rattlesnakes 597.96
 xx **Poisonous animals; Snakes**
Raw materials 333
 See also **Farm produce; Forest products; Mines and mineral resources**
 xx **Commercial products; Materials**
Rayon 677
 x Acetate silk; Artificial silk; Silk, Artificial
 xx **Synthetic fabrics; Synthetic products**
Rays, Roentgen. *See* **X rays**
Rays, Ultra-violet. *See* **Ultraviolet rays**
Reaction (Political science). *See* **Right and left (Political science)**
Reactions, Chemical. *See* **Chemical reactions**
Reactors (Nuclear physics). *See* **Nuclear reactors**
Reader services (Libraries) 025.5
 Use for materials on that part of library service devoted to the provision of assistance, advice, etc. to library users. Reader services are usually in tandem with technical services.
 Materials on library services for specific types of library users or on services for users involved in specific activities are entered under specific headings, e.g. **Libraries and the elderly.**
 See also **Libraries and Blacks; Libraries and labor; Libraries and the elderly; Library instruction; Reference services (Libraries)**
 x Libraries and readers

Reader services (Libraries)—*Continued*

   xx **Library services**

Readers. *See* **Reading materials**

Readiness for school 372

   Use for materials on the prerequisite abilities, such as degree of psychosocial maturity, previous experience, cognition, physical abilities, etc., to learning in a school setting.

   x Readiness skills (Education); School readiness

   xx **Education, Elementary; Education, Preschool**

Readiness skills (Education). *See* **Readiness for school**

Reading 372.4

   Use for materials on methods of teaching reading, and general materials on the art of reading. Materials on teaching slow readers are entered under **Reading—Remedial teaching.** Materials on the cultural or informational aspects of reading and general discussions of books are entered under **Books and reading.**

   See also **Books and reading**

   x Children's reading; Reading—Study and teaching

   xx **Language arts**

Reading clinics. *See* **Reading—Remedial teaching**

Reading disability 371.9

   See also names of specific reading disabilities, e.g. **Dyslexia;** etc.

   x Disability, Reading; Reading retardation; Retarded readers

   xx **Learning disabilities**

Reading interests. *See* **Books and reading**

Reading materials 372.4

   Use for materials in English. For readers in other languages, use the language with the subdivision *Reading materials,* e.g. **French language—Reading materials;** etc.

   See also **Easy reading materials; Readings and recitations**

   x English language—Reading materials; Readers

   xx **Children's literature**

Reading—Remedial teaching 372.4

   See also **Rapid reading**

   x Reading clinics; Remedial reading

Reading retardation. *See* **Reading disability**

Reading—Study and teaching. *See* **Reading**

Readings and recitations 808.85

   x Recitations and readings; Speakers (Recitation books)

   xx **Reading materials; School assembly programs**

Ready reckoners. *See* **Mathematics—Tables, etc.**

Real estate 333.3

   Use for general materials on real property in the legal sense, i.e., ownership of land and buildings as opposed to personal property. Materials limited to the buying and selling of real property are entered under **Real estate business.** General materials on land without the ownership aspects are entered under **Land use.** Materials on the assess-

Real estate—*Continued*
>> ment of property are entered under
Taxation.

>> *See also* **Eminent domain; Farms; Land tenure;**
Landlord and tenant; Mortgages; Real estate
business

> *x* Property, Real; Real property; Realty

> *xx* **Land tenure; Land use; Property**

Real estate business 333.33
> See note under **Real estate.**

> *See also* **Houses—Buying and selling**

> *xx* **Business; Real estate**

Real estate investment 332.63
> *x* Investment in real estate; Real property in-
vestment

> *xx* **Investments; Speculation**

Real estate investment—Taxation 343.05
> *xx* **Taxation**

Real estate timesharing. *See* **Timesharing (Real es-**
tate)

Real property. *See* **Real estate**

Real property investment. *See* **Real estate invest-**
ment

Realism 149
> *See also* **Idealism; Materialism; Positivism; Prag-**
matism; Rationalism

> *xx* **Idealism; Materialism; Philosophy; Positiv-**
ism; Rationalism

Realism in literature 809
> *See also* **Romanticism**

> *x* Naturalism in literature

> *xx* **Literature; Romanticism**

Reality 111
> *See also* **Empiricism; Knowledge, Theory of;**
Pragmatism

> *xx* **Intuition; Knowledge, Theory of; Philosophy;**
Pragmatism; Truth

Realty. *See* **Real estate**

Reapers. *See* **Harvesting machinery**

Reapportionment (Election law). *See* **Apportion-**
ment (Election law)

Reason 160
> *See also* **Reasoning**

> *xx* **Intellect; Rationalism**

Reasoning 153.4; 160
> *See also* **Critical thinking; Intellect; Logic**

> *xx* **Intellect; Logic; Psychology; Reason; Thought**
and thinking

Rebates (Railroads). *See* **Railroads—Rates**

Rebellions. *See* **Insurgency; Revolutions**

Rebels (Social psychology). *See* **Alienation (Social**
psychology)

Rebirth. *See* **Reincarnation**

Rebuses. *See* **Riddles**

Recall of products. *See* **Product recall**

Recall (Political science) 324.6
> *xx* **Impeachments; Representative government**
and representation

Recessions, Economic. *See* **Depressions, Economic**

Recipes. *See* **Cookery**

Reciprocity. *See* **Commercial policy**

Recitations and readings. *See* **Readings and recita-tions**

Recitations with music. *See* **Monologues with mu-sic**

Reclamation of land   627; 631.6

　　Use for general materials on reclamation, includ-ing drainage and irrigation.

　　See also **Drainage; Irrigation; Marshes; Sand dunes**

　　x Clearing of land; Land, Reclamation of

　　xx **Agriculture; Civil engineering; Floods; Hy-draulic engineering; Irrigation; Land use; Natural resources; Soils**

Recluses. *See* **Hermits**

Recombinant DNA   574.87

　　x Gene splicing

　　xx **DNA; Genetic engineering; Genetic recombi-nation**

Recombination, Genetic. *See* **Genetic recombina-tion**

Recommendations for positions. *See* **Applications for positions**

Reconnaissance, Aerial. *See* **Aerial reconnaissance**

Reconstruction (1865-1876)   973.8

　　See also **Ku Klux Klan (1865-1876)**

　　x Carpetbag rule; United States—History—1861-1865, Civil War—Reconstruction

　　xx **United States—History—1865-1898**

Reconstruction (1914-1939)   940.3

　　See also **Peace; Veterans—Education; Veter-ans—Employment; World War, 1914-1918—Economic aspects**

　　x World War, 1914-1918—Reconstruction

Reconstruction (1939-1951) (May subdiv. geog. ex-cept U.S.) **940.53**

　　See also **Economic assistance; International coop-eration; Veterans—Education; Veterans—Employment; World War, 1939-1945—Civilian relief; World War, 1939-1945—Economic aspects; World War, 1939-1945—Reparations**

　　x Marshall Plan; Point Four program; World War, 1939-1945—Reconstruction

　　xx **Economic assistance; International coopera-tion; World War, 1939-1945—Economic as-pects**

Recorders, Tape. *See* **Magnetic recorders and re-cording**

Recording, Laser. *See* **Laser recording**

Recordings, Sound. *See* **Sound recordings**

Records of births, etc. *See* **Registers of births, etc.; Vital statistics**

Records, Phonograph. *See* **Sound recordings**

Records—Preservation. *See* **Archives**

Recovery of space vehicles. *See* **Space vehicles—Recovery**

Recovery of waste products. *See* **Recycling (Waste, etc.); Salvage (Waste, etc.)**

Recreation (May subdiv. geog.) **790**

　　Use for materials on the psychological and social aspects of recreation and for materials on organized recreational projects.

Recreation—*Continued*
> *See also*

Amusements	**Play**
Community centers	**Playgrounds**
Games	**Popular culture**
Hobbies	**Sports**
Outdoor recreation	**Vacations**

> also classes of people with the subdivision
> *Recreation,* e.g. **Elderly—Recreation;** etc.
> *x* Pastimes; Relaxation
> *xx* **Amusements; Leisure; Play**

Recreation centers. *See* **Community centers**

Recreational vehicles 629.2
> *See also* types of recreational vehicles, e.g.
> **Travel trailers and campers;** etc.
> *x* R.V.'s; RVs; Vehicles, Recreational
> *xx* **Outdoor recreation; Vehicles**

Recreations. *See* **Hobbies**

Recreations, Literary. *See* **Literary recreations**

Recreations, Mathematical. *See* **Mathematical recreations**

Recreations, Scientific. *See* **Scientific recreations**

Recruiting and enlistment. *See* names of armies
> and navies with the subdivision *Recruiting,*
> *enlistment, etc.,* e.g. **United States. Army—**
> **Recruiting, enlistment, etc.; United States.**
> **Navy—Recruiting, enlistment, etc.;** etc.

Recruiting of employees 658.3
> *See also* **Employment agencies;** also names of oc-
> cupations and professions with the subdivi-
> sion *Recruiting,* e.g.
> **Librarians—Recruiting;** etc.
> *xx* **Personnel management**

Rectors. *See* **Clergy**

Recurrent education. *See* **Continuing education**

Recycling (Waste, etc.) 604.6
> Use for materials on the processing of waste pa-
> per, cans, bottles, etc. Materials on the recy-
> cling or reuse of specific waste products are
> entered under the products with the subdivi-
> sion *Recycling.* Materials on reclaiming and
> reusing equipment or parts are entered un-
> der **Salvage (Waste, etc.).**
> *See also* **Refuse and refuse disposal; Salvage**
> **(Waste, etc.); Waste products;** also subjects
> with the subdivision *Recycling,* e.g.
> **Aluminum—Recycling;** etc.
> *x* Conversion of waste products; Recovery of
> waste products; Reuse of waste; Utilization
> of waste; Waste products—Recycling;
> Waste reclamation
> *xx* **Energy conservation; Refuse and refuse dis-**
> **posal; Salvage (Waste, etc.); Waste products**

Red 535.6; 752
> *xx* **Color**

Redemption. *See* **Salvation**

Reducing 613.2
> *See also* **Diet**
> *x* Body weight control; Dieting; Diets, Reduc-
> ing; Exercises, Reducing; Obesity—Control;

Reducing—*Continued*

　Overweight—Control; Weight control

　xx **Diet; Exercise**

Reference books 010-016; 028.7

　See also **Books and reading—Best books; Encyclopedias and dictionaries**

　xx **Books and reading**

Reference services (Libraries) 025.5

　Use for materials on activities designed to make information available to library users; includes direct personal assistance.

　x Library reference services; Online reference services; Reference work (Libraries)

　xx **Information services; Reader services (Libraries)**

Reference work (Libraries).　*See* **Reference services (Libraries)**

Referendum 328

　x Direct legislation; Initiative and referendum; Legislation, Direct

　xx **Constitutional law; Democracy; Elections; Representative government and representation**

Refinishing furniture.　*See* **Furniture finishing**

Reforestation 634.9

　See also **Tree planting**

　xx **Forests and forestry; Tree planting**

Reform, Agrarian.　*See* **Land reform**

Reform of criminals.　*See* **Criminals; Probation; Reformatories**

Reform schools.　*See* **Reformatories**

Reform, Social.　*See* **Social problems**

Reformation 270.6

　See also **Calvinism; Europe—History 1492-1789; Protestantism; Sixteenth century;** also names of religious sects, e.g. **Huguenots;** etc.

　x Anti-Reformation; Antireformation; Church history—1517-1648, Reformation; Counter-Reformation; Counterreformation; Protestant Reformation

　xx **Christianity; Church history; History, Modern; Protestantism; Sixteenth century**

Reformatories 365

　See also **Juvenile courts; Juvenile delinquency; Probation**

　x Penal institutions; Penology; Reform of criminals; Reform schools

　xx **Children—Institutional care; Correctional institutions; Crime; Juvenile delinquency; Prisons; Punishment**

Reformers 920

　Use for materials about political, social, religious, etc. reformers.

Refraction 535

　x Dioptrics

　xx **Light; Optics; Rainbow**

Refrigeration and refrigerating machinery 621.5

　See also **Air conditioning; Cold storage**

　x Cooling appliances; Freezing; Ice manufacture

Refrigeration and refrigerating
        machinery—*Continued*
  xx **Air conditioning; Cold storage; Frost**
Refugees (May subdiv. geog. adjective form, or by
        ethnic groups) **325; 341.4**
  x Displaced persons; Exiles
  xx **Aliens; Homeless people; Immigration and**
      emigration
Refugees, American 325.73
  x American refugees; United States—Refugees
Refugees, Political 341.4
  See also names of wars with the subdivision
      Refugees, e.g. **World War, 1939-1945—**
      Refugees; etc.
  x Displaced persons; Political refugees
  xx **Asylum, Right of; International law; Interna-**
      tional relations
Refuges, Wildlife. *See* **Wildlife refuges**
Refuse and refuse disposal 628.4
  See also

Hazardous wastes	**Sewage disposal**
Industrial wastes	**Street cleaning**
Recycling (Waste, etc.)	**Waste products**
Salvage (Waste, etc.)	**Water—Pollution**

  x Disposal of refuse; Garbage; Incineration; Lit-
      tering; Solid waste disposal; Waste disposal
  xx **Industrial wastes; Municipal engineering;**
      Public health; Recycling (Waste, etc.); Sal-
      vage (Waste, etc.); Sanitary engineering;
      Sanitation; Sewage disposal; Street clean-
      ing; Waste products; Water—Pollution
Regattas. *See* **Rowing; Yachts and yachting**
Regeneration (Christianity) 234; 248.2
  x Born again Christians; Christian new birth;
      Christian regeneration
  xx **Regeneration (Theology)**
Regeneration (Theology) 234
  See also **Conversion; Regeneration (Christianity);**
      Salvation
  x New birth (Theology)
  xx **Baptism; Conversion; Salvation; Theology,**
      Doctrinal
Regional libraries 027.4
  Use for materials on public libraries serving a
      group of communities, several counties, or
      other regions.
  See also **County libraries**
  x District libraries; Libraries, Regional
  xx **Public libraries**
Regional planning (May subdiv. geog.) **711**
  See also **City planning; Landscape protection;**
      Social surveys
  x County planning; Metropolitan planning;
      Planning, Regional; State planning
  xx **Landscape protection**
Regionalism. *See* **Nationalism; Sectionalism (U.S.)**
Registers of births, etc. 929
  See also **Vital statistics; Wills**
  x Birth records; Births, Registers of; Burial sta-
      tistics; Deaths, Registers of; Marriage regis-

Registers of births, etc.—*Continued*
      ters; Parish registers; Records of births, etc.;
      Vital records
  xx **Genealogy; Vital statistics**
Registers of persons. *See* names of countries, cities,
      etc. and names of colleges, universities, etc.
      with the subdivision *Registers,* e.g. **United
      States—Registers; United States. Military
      Academy—Registers;** etc.
Registration of voters. *See* **Voter registration**
Rehabilitation. *See* groups of people with the sub-
      division *Rehabilitation,* e.g. **Physically
      handicapped—Rehabilitation;** etc.
Reign of Terror. *See* **France—History—1789-1799,
      Revolution**
Reincarnation 129
  See also **Soul**
  x Rebirth
  xx **Soul; Theosophy**
Reindeer 599.73; 636.2
  xx **Deer; Domestic animals**
Reinforced concrete. *See* **Concrete, Reinforced**
Relations among ethnic groups. *See* **Ethnic rela-
      tions**
Relative humidity. *See* **Humidity**
Relativity (Physics) 530.1
  See also **Quantum theory; Space and time**
  xx **Physics; Quantum theory**
Relaxation. *See* **Recreation; Rest**
Reliability (Engineering)
Reliability engineering. **620**
  See also **Quality control; Structural failures**
  x Reliability engineering; Reliability of equip-
      ment; Systems reliability *See* **Reliability
      (Engineering)**
  xx **Engineering; Probabilities; Systems engineer-
      ing**
Reliability of equipment. *See* **Reliability (Engi-
      neering)**
Relief, Public. *See* **Public welfare**
Religion 200
  See also

Agnosticism	**Religions**
Ancestor worship	**Religious awakening**
Atheism	**Revelation**
Belief and doubt	**Sacrifice**
Deism	**Skepticism**
Faith	**Spiritual life**
God	**Sun worship**
Moon worship	**Supernatural**
Mysticism	**Superstition**
Mythology	**Theism**
Natural theology	**Theology**
Psychology, Religious	**Worship**
Rationalism	

      also names of peoples, ethnic groups, countries,
      states, etc. with the subdivision *Religion,*
      e.g. **Indians of North America—Religion;
      Blacks—Religion; United States—Religion;**
      etc.; and headings beginning with the words

Religion—*Continued*

　　Religion and Religious
　　xx God; Religions; Theology
Religion and art.　*See* Art and religion
Religion and astronautics　215
　　x Astronautics and religion
　　xx Astronautics and civilization; Religion and sci-
　　　ence
Religion and communism.　*See* Communism and
　　religion
Religion and education.　*See* Church and education
Religion and literature.　*See* Religion in literature
Religion and medicine.　*See* Medicine and religion
Religion and philosophy.　*See* Philosophy and reli-
　　gion
Religion and politics　261.7
　　See also Christianity and politics
　　x Evangelism and politics; Politics and religion
Religion and science　215
　　See also Bible and science; Creation; Evolution;
　　　Man—Origin; Natural theology; Religion
　　　and astronautics
　　x Science and religion
　　xx Apologetics; Evolution; Natural theology; The-
　　　ology
Religion and social problems.　*See* Church and so-
　　cial problems
Religion and state.　*See* Church—Government pol-
　　icy
Religion and war.　*See* War and religion
Religion in literature　809
　　See also Bible in literature
　　x Religion and literature
　　xx Bible in literature
Religion in the public schools　377
　　See also Fundamentalism and education
　　x Bible in the schools; Prayers in the public
　　　schools; Public schools and religion;
　　　Schools—Prayers
　　xx Church and education; Church—Government
　　　policy; Fundamentalism and education; Re-
　　　ligious education
Religion of humanity.　*See* Positivism
Religion—Philosophy　200.1
　　See also Philosophy and religion
　　x Philosophy of religion
　　xx Philosophy and religion
Religion—Study and teaching.　*See* Religious edu-
　　cation; Theology—Study and teaching
Religions　200
　　All religions are not included in this list but are
　　　to be added as needed.
　　See also

Bahaism	Gnosticism
Brahmanism	Gods and goddesses
Buddhism	Hinduism
Christianity	Islam
Confucianism	Judaism
Cults	Mythology
Druids and Druidism	Paganism

Religions—*Continued*

  Religion   **Taoism**
  Sects   **Theosophy**
  Shinto

  x Comparative religion

  xx **Civilization; Gods and goddesses; Religion**

Religions—Biography 200.92; 920

  See also names of religions with the subdivision *Biography,* e.g. **Christianity—Biography;** etc.

  x Religious biography

  xx **Biography**

Religious art. *See* **Art, Medieval; Church architecture; Religious art and symbolism**

Religious art and symbolism 704.9

  See also **Art and religion; Christian art and symbolism**

  x Iconography; Painting, Religious; Religious art; Religious painting; Religious symbolism; Sacred art; Sculpture, Religious

  xx **Archeology; Art; Art and religion; Mysticism; Symbolism**

Religious awakening 200; 269

  Use for materials on a renewal of interest in religion.

  x Awakening, Religious

  xx **Religion**

Religious belief. *See* **Faith**

Religious biography. *See* **Christianity—Biography; Religions—Biography**

Religious ceremonies. *See* **Rites and ceremonies**

Religious cults. *See* **Cults**

Religious denominations. *See* **Sects;** and names of particular denominations and sects, e.g. **Presbyterian Church;** etc.

Religious drama 808.82; 812; etc.

  See also **Bible—Drama; Christmas—Drama; Morality plays; Mysteries and miracle plays; Passion plays**

  x Drama, Religious

  xx **Drama; Drama in education; Religious literature**

Religious education 268; 377

  See note under **Church and education.**

  See also **Christian education; Moral education; Religion in the public schools; Sunday schools; Theology—Study and teaching**

  x Education, Ethical; Education, Religious; Education, Theological; Ethical education; Religion—Study and teaching

  xx **Education; Moral education; Theology—Study and teaching**

Religious festivals. *See* **Fasts and feasts;** and names of festivals, e.g. **Christmas; Easter;** etc.

Religious freedom 261.7; 323.44

  See also **Church—Government policy; Freedom of conscience; Persecution**

  x Freedom of religion; Freedom of worship; Intolerance; Religious liberty

Religious freedom—*Continued*

    xx **Church—Government policy; Civil rights;
Free thought; Freedom; Freedom of conscience; Persecution; Toleration**

Religious history. *See* **Church history**

Religious liberty. *See* **Religious freedom**

Religious life 248

    See also classes of people with the subdivision
Religious life, e.g. **Family—Religious life;**
etc.

    xx **Monasticism; Religious orders**

Religious life (Christian). *See* **Christian life**

Religious literature 800

    See also **Bible as literature; Christian literature;
Religious drama; Religious poetry; Sacred
books;** also names of religious and denominational literatures, e.g. **Catholic literature;
Christian literature—30(ca.)-600, Early;**
etc.

    xx **Bible as literature; Literature**

Religious music. *See* **Church music**

Religious orders 255; 271

    See also **Asceticism; Celibacy; Hermits; Religious
life**

    x Monastic orders; Orders, Monastic

    xx **Monasticism**

Religious orders for men (May subdiv. by religion or
denomination) **255; 271**

    See also **Monks**

Religious orders for men, Catholic 271

    See also names of specific orders, e.g.
Dominicans; Franciscans; Jesuits; etc.

Religious orders for women (May subdiv. by religion
or denomination) **255; 271**

    See also **Nuns**

    x Sisterhoods

    xx **Convents**

Religious orders for women, Catholic 271

    See also names of specific orders

Religious painting. *See* **Religious art and symbolism**

Religious poetry 808.81; 811; etc.

    See also **Carols; Hymns**

    xx **Hymns; Poetry—Collected works; Religious
literature**

Religious psychology. *See* **Psychology, Religious**

Religious symbolism. *See* **Religious art and symbolism**

Remarriage 306.8

    xx **Divorce; Marriage; Widows**

Remedial reading. *See* **Reading—Remedial teaching**

Remodeling of buildings. *See* **Buildings—
Remodeling**

Remodeling of houses. *See* **Houses—Remodeling**

Remote sensing 621.36

    See also **Aerial reconnaissance; Radar; Space optics**

    x Sensing, Remote; Terrain sensing, Remote

    xx **Photography, Aerial; Space optics**

Renaissance 940.2

> *See also* **Architecture, Renaissance; Art, Renaissance; Civilization, Medieval; Humanism; Literature, Medieval; Middle Ages; Sixteenth century**
>
> *x* Revival of letters
>
> *xx* **Civilization, Modern; History, Modern; Humanism; Middle Ages**

Rendezvous in space. *See* **Orbital rendezvous (Space flight)**

Renewable energy resources 333.79

> *See also* **Geothermal resources;** also names of renewable resources, e.g. **Solar energy; Water power; Wind power;** etc.
>
> *x* Alternate energy resources; Alternative energy resources; Energy resources, Renewable
>
> *xx* **Energy resources**

Rental services. *See* **Lease and rental services**

Reorganization of administrative agencies. *See* **United States—Executive departments—Reorganization**

Repairing 620

> *See also* **Buildings—Maintenance and repair;** also names of machines, instruments, etc. that require maintenance with the subdivision *Maintenance and repair,* e.g. **Automobiles—Maintenance and repair;** and names of subjects that need no maintenance with the subdivision *Repairing,* e.g. **Radio—Repairing;** etc.

Reparations (World War, 1939-1945). *See* **World War, 1939-1945—Reparations**

Report writing 808

> *x* Reports—Preparation
>
> *xx* **Authorship**

Reporters and reporting 070.4

> *See also* **Journalism; Press—Government policy**
>
> *x* Interviewing (Journalism); Newspaper work
>
> *xx* **Journalism; Newspapers**

Reports—Preparation. *See* **Report writing**

Representation. *See* **Representative government and representation**

Representation, Proportional. *See* **Proportional representation**

Representative government and representation 321.8

> *See also*
>
> | | |
> |---|---|
> | **Apportionment (Election law)** | **Proportional representation** |
> | **Constitutions** | **Recall (Political science)** |
> | **Democracy** | **Referendum** |
> | **Elections** | **Republics** |
> | **Legislative bodies** | **Suffrage** |
> | **Primaries** | |
>
> *x* Parliamentary government; Representation; Self-government
>
> *xx* **Constitutional history; Constitutional law; Democracy; Elections; Political science; Republics; Suffrage**

Representatives—United States. *See* **United States. Congress. House**

Reprints. *See* **Bibliography—Editions**
Reproduction 574.1; 612
   See also
   Artificial insemination   Genetics
   Cells   Menstruation
   Embryology   Pregnancy
   Fertility   Reproductive system
   Fetus   Sex (Biology)
      x Generation
      xx **Biology; Embryology; Life (Biology); Physiol-**
         ogy; Reproductive system; Sex (Biology)
Reproduction processes. *See* **Copying processes**
   and machines
Reproductive organs. *See* **Reproductive system**
Reproductive system 612
   See also **Reproduction; Transsexuality**
      x Generative organs; Genitalia; Reproductive
         organs; Sex organs
      xx **Reproduction; Sex (Biology)**
Reprography. *See* **Copying processes and machines**
Reptiles 597.9
   See also **Crocodiles; Lizards; Snakes; Turtles**
      xx **Vertebrates**
Reptiles, Fossil 567.9
   See also names of fossil reptiles, e.g. **Dinosaurs;**
      etc.
      x Fossil reptiles
      xx **Fossils**
Republic of China, 1949-. *See* **Taiwan**
Republic of South Africa. *See* **South Africa**
Republican Party (U.S.) 324.2734
      xx **Political parties**
Republics 321.8
   See also **Democracy; Federal government; Repre-**
      sentative government and representation
      x Commonwealth, The
      xx **Constitutional history; Constitutional law; De-**
         mocracy; Political science; Representative
         government and representation
Rescue of Jews, 1939-1945. *See* **World War, 1939-**
      1945—Jews—Rescue
Rescue operations, Space. *See* **Space rescue opera-**
      tions
Rescue work 363.1
   See also **First aid; Lifesaving; Space rescue oper-**
      ations
      x Search and rescue operations
      xx **Civil defense**
Research 001.4
   See also **Information services; Learning and**
      scholarship; Operations research; Psychical
      research; also subjects with the subdivision
      Research, e.g. **Agriculture—Research; Med-**
      icine—Research; etc.
      xx **Information services; Learning and scholar-**
         ship
Reservations, Indian. *See* **Indians of North Ameri-**
      ca—Reservations
Reservoirs 627; 628.1
   See also **Irrigation; Water supply**

Reservoirs—*Continued*
   xx **Hydraulic structures; Water supply**
Resettlement. *See* **Land settlement**
Residences. *See* **Architecture, Domestic; Houses**
Residential construction. *See* **House construction**
Residential security. *See* **Burglary protection**
Residential treatment centers. *See* **Group homes**
Resins. *See* **Gums and resins**
Resistance of materials. *See* **Strength of materials**
Resistance to government. *See* **Government, Resis-
     tance to**
Resistance welding. *See* **Electric welding**
Resorts. *See* types of resorts, e.g. **Health resorts,
     spas, etc.; Summer resorts; Winter resorts;**
     etc.
Resource management. *See* **Conservation of natural
     resources**
Resources, Marine. *See* **Marine resources**
Resources, Natural. *See* **Natural resources**
Respiration 612

   See also **Aerobics; Respiratory system**
   x Breathing
   xx **Lungs; Physiology; Singing; Voice**
Respiration, Artificial. *See* **Artificial respiration**
Respiratory organs. *See* **Respiratory system**
Respiratory system 574.4; 612
   x Respiratory organs
   xx **Respiration**
Responsibility, Legal. *See* **Liability (Law)**
Rest 613.7

   See also **Fatigue; Sleep**
   x Relaxation
   xx **Fatigue; Health; Hygiene**
Restaurants, bars, etc. (May subdiv. geog.) **647**

   See also **Coffee houses**
   x Bars and restaurants; Cafeterias; Diners;
     Lunch rooms; Saloons; Taverns; Tea
     rooms; Tearooms
   xx **Food service**
Restoration of automobiles. *See* **Automobiles—
     Restoration**
Restoration of buildings. *See* **Architecture—
     Conservation and restoration**
Restoration of works of art. *See* subjects with the
     subdivision *Conservation and restoration,*
     e.g. **Painting—Conservation and restoration;**
     etc.
Restraint of trade 338.6

   See also **Competition, Unfair; Interstate com-
     merce; Monopolies; Trusts, Industrial**
   x Combinations in restraint of trade; Restrictive
     trade practices; Trade, Restraint of
   xx **Commerce; Commercial law; Competition, Un-
     fair; Interstate commerce; Monopolies;
     Trusts, Industrial**
Restrictive trade practices. *See* **Restraint of trade**
Résumés (Employment) 331.1
   x Job résumés
   xx **Applications for positions; Job hunting**

Resurrection. *See* **Future life; Jesus Christ—
Resurrection**
Resuscitation, Heart. *See* **Cardiac resuscitation**
Resuscitation, Pulmonary. *See* **Artificial respira-
tion**
Retail sales tax. *See* **Sales tax**
Retail trade 658.8
> *See also*

Advertising	**Packaging**
Chain stores	**Sales personnel**
Department stores	**Selling**
Direct selling	**Shopping centers and**
Discount stores	**malls**
Inventory control	**Supermarkets**

> *x* Merchandising; Stores
> *xx* **Commerce**

Retarded children. *See* **Mentally handicapped chil-
dren; Slow learning children**
Retarded readers. *See* **Reading disability**
Retirement 305.2
> *See also* **Elderly—Life skills guides**
> *xx* **Elderly—Life skills guides; Leisure; Old age**

Retirement communities 307.7
> *x* Life care communities; Places of retirement;
> Retirement places
> *xx* **Elderly—Housing**

Retirement income 351.5; 368.4
> *See also* **Annuities; Individual retirement ac-
> counts; Old age pensions; Pensions**
> *xx* **Elderly; Income**

Retirement places. *See* **Retirement communities**
Retouching (Photography). *See* **Photography—
Retouching**
Retraining, Occupational. *See* **Occupational re-
training**
Retribution. *See* **Future life; Hell**
Reunification of Ireland. *See* **Irish unification ques-
tion**
Reunions, Family. *See* **Family reunions**
Reusable space vehicles. *See* **Space shuttles**
Reuse of waste. *See* **Recycling (Waste, etc.); Sal-
vage (Waste, etc.)**
Revelation 231
> *xx* **Religion; Supernatural; Theology**

Revenue. *See* **Tariff; Taxation**
Revenue, Internal. *See* **Internal revenue**
Revenue sharing 336; 336.1; 336.2
> Use for materials on the practice of returning a
> percentage of federal tax money to state and
> local governments for locally directed and
> controlled public service programs.
> *x* Federal revenue sharing; Tax sharing
> *xx* **Intergovernmental tax relations**

Reviews. *See* subjects with the subdivision
Reviews, e.g. **Books—Reviews;** etc.
Revival of letters. *See* **Renaissance**
Revival (Religion). *See* **Evangelistic work; Revivals**
Revivals 269
> *See also* **Evangelistic work**
> *x* Revival (Religion)

528

Revivals—*Continued*
  xx **Christian life; Church history; Church work;**
      Evangelistic work
Revolution, American. *See* **United States—**
      History—1775-1783, Revolution
Revolution, French. *See* **France—History—1789-**
      1799, Revolution
Revolution, Russian. *See* **Soviet Union—History—**
      1917-1921, Revolution
Revolutions 303.6
  See also **Government, Resistance to; Insurgency;**
      National liberation movements; Radicals and
      radicalism; Terrorism; also names of coun-
      tries with the subdivision *History—[dates],*
      Revolution, e.g.
      France—History—1789-1799, Revolution;
      Hungary—History—1956, Revolution; So-
      viet Union—History—1917-1921, Revolu-
      tion; United States—History—1775-1783,
      Revolution; etc.
  x Coups d'état; Rebellions; Sedition
  xx **Government, Resistance to; Political science**
Rewards (Prizes, etc.) 001.4
  See also **Contests; Literary prizes; Literature—**
      Competitions; also names of awards and
      prizes, e.g. **Nobel prizes;** etc.
  x Awards; Competitions; Prizes (Rewards)
  xx **Contests**
Rh factor. *See* **Blood groups**
Rhetoric 808
  See also

Criticism	**Preaching**
Debates and debating	**Punctuation**
Lectures and lecturing	**Satire**
Letter writing	**Style, Literary**

      also names of languages with the subdivision
      Composition and exercises, e.g. **English lan-**
      guage—Composition and exercises; etc.
  x Composition (Rhetoric); English language—
      Rhetoric; Persuasion (Rhetoric); Speaking
  xx **English language—Composition and exercises;**
      Language and languages; Style, Literary
Rheumatism 616.7
  See also **Arthritis**
Rhyme 808.1
  See also **Rhythm; Stories in rhyme;** also names
      of languages with the subdivision *Rhyme,*
      e.g. **English language—Rhyme;** etc.
  xx **Poetics; Versification**
Rhymes. *See* **Limericks; Nonsense verses; Nursery**
      rhymes; Poetry—Collected works
Rhythm 808.1
  See also **Musical meter and rhythm; Periodicity;**
      Versification
  xx **Esthetics; Periodicity; Poetics; Rhyme**
Ribonucleic acid 574.87
  x R.N.A.; Ribose nucleic acid; RNA
  xx **Nucleic acids**
Ribose nucleic acid. *See* **Ribonucleic acid**
Riches. *See* **Wealth**

Riddles 398; 793.7

    See also **Charades; Puzzles**

    x Conundrums; Enigmas; Rebuses

    xx **Amusements; Literary recreations; Puzzles**

Ride sharing. *See* **Car pools**

Riding. *See* **Horseback riding**

Rifles 799

    x Carbines; Guns

    xx **Arms and armor; Firearms**

Right and left. *See* **Left and right**

Right- and left-handedness. *See* **Left- and right-handedness**

Right and left (Political science) 320.5

    Use for general materials on political views or attitudes, i.e. conservative, traditional, liberal, radical, etc. Materials on the physical characteristics of favoring one hand or the other are entered under **Left- and right-handedness.** Materials on left and right as indications of location or direction are entered under **Left and right.**

    See also **Conservatism; Liberalism; Radicals and radicalism**

    x Extremism (Political science); Left (Political science); New left; Reaction (Political science); Right (Political science)

    xx **Conservatism; Legislative bodies; Liberalism; Political parties; Political science**

Right of assembly. *See* **Freedom of assembly**

Right of association. *See* **Freedom of association**

Right of asylum. *See* **Asylum, Right of**

Right of privacy. *See* **Privacy, Right of**

Right (Political science). *See* **Right and left (Political science)**

Right to choose movement. *See* **Abortion—Moral and religious aspects**

Right to die 174

    See also **Euthanasia; Suicide**

    x Death, Right of; Death with dignity; Living wills; Wills, Living

    xx **Death; Euthanasia; Medicine—Law and legislation; Suicide**

Right to know. *See* **Freedom of information**

Right to life. *See* **Euthanasia**

Right to life movement. *See* **Abortion—Moral and religious aspects**

Right to work. *See* **Discrimination in employment; Open and closed shop**

Rights, Civil. *See* **Civil rights**

Rights of women. *See* **Women—Civil rights**

Riot control. *See* **Riots—Control**

Riots (May subdiv. geog.) **303.6**

    See also **Crowds; Protests, demonstrations, etc.;** also names of institutions with the subdivision *Riots;* also names of specific riots

    x Civil disorders; Mobs

    xx **Crime; Freedom of assembly; Offenses against public safety; Protests, demonstrations, etc.**

Riots—Control 303.6

    x Riot control

Riots—Control—*Continued*
  xx **Crowds**
Ripoffs. *See* **Fraud**
Rites and ceremonies (May subdiv. geog.) **390**
    See also

Baptism	**Marriage customs and**
Fasts and feasts	**rites**
Funeral rites and ceremo-	**Ordination**
nies	**Sacraments**
Manners and customs	**Secret societies**

    also classes of people and ethnic groups with the
        subdivision *Rites and ceremonies,* e.g.
        Indians of North America—Rites and cere-
        monies; etc.; also names of individual reli-
        gions and denominations with the subdivi-
        sions *Liturgy* and *Customs and practices,*
        e.g. **Catholic Church—Liturgy; Judaism—**
        Customs and practices; etc.
    x Ceremonies; Ecclesiastical rites and ceremo-
        nies; Religious ceremonies; Ritual; Tradi-
        tions
  xx **Manners and customs**
Ritual. *See* **Liturgies; Rites and ceremonies**
River animals. *See* **Stream animals**
Rivers 551.48
    See also

Dams	**Stream animals**
Floods	**Water—Pollution**
Hydraulic engineering	**Water power**
Inland navigation	**Water rights**

    also names of rivers
  xx **Civil engineering; Floods; Floods—Control;**
        Hydraulic engineering; Inland navigation;
        Physical geography; Water; Waterways
Rivers—Pollution. *See* **Oil pollution of rivers, har-**
        bors, etc., Water—Pollution
RNA. *See* **Ribonucleic acid**
Road construction. *See* **Roads**
Road engineering. *See* **Highway engineering**
Road maps 910.2
    See also **Automobiles—Road guides;** also names
        of countries, areas, states, cities, etc. with
        the subdivision *Maps,* e.g. **United States—**
        Maps; Chicago (Ill.)—Maps; etc.
    x Maps, Road; Roads—Maps
  xx **Automobiles—Road guides; Maps**
Road signs. *See* **Signs and signboards**
Roads 388.1; 625.7
    See also **Express highways; Highway engineer-**
        ing; Pavements; Roadside improvement;
        Soils (Engineering); Street cleaning; Streets
    x Construction of roads; Highway construction;
        Highways; Road construction; Thorough-
        fares
  xx **Civil engineering; Highway engineering; Pave-**
        ments; Streets; Transportation
Roads—Maps. *See* **Road maps**
Roadside improvement 713
    x Highway beautification
  xx **Grounds maintenance; Landscape architecture;**

Roadside improvement—*Continued*
  Roads
Robbers and outlaws 364.3
  x Bandits; Brigands; Burglars; Highwaymen;
    Outlaws; Thieves
  xx **Criminals**
Robins 598.8
  xx **Birds**
Robotics 629.8
  Use for materials on the construction, mainte-
    nance, and automatic operation of robots.
  See also **Robots; Robots, Industrial**
  xx **Mechanical engineering**
Robots 629.8
  Use for materials on completety self-controlled
    electronic, electric, or mechanical devices
    that perform functions ordinarily ascribed
    to human beings or that operate with what
    appears to be almost human intelligence.
  x Androids; Automata
  xx **Mechanical movements; Robotics**
Robots, Industrial 629.8
  x Industrial robots; Working robots
  xx **Machinery in industry; Robotics**
Rochdale system. *See* **Cooperation**
Rock and roll music. *See* **Rock music**
Rock climbing. *See* **Mountaineering**
Rock crystal. *See* **Quartz**
**Rock drawings, paintings, and engravings 411; 743;
    759.01**
  See also **Cave drawings**
  x Petroglyphs; Rock engravings; Rock paintings
  xx **Archeology; Art; Art, Prehistoric; Cave draw-
    ings; Mural painting and decoration; Picture
    writing**
Rock engravings. *See* **Rock drawings, paintings,
    and engravings**
Rock gardens 635.9
  xx **Gardens**
Rock music 780.42; 784.5
  x Music, Rock; Rock and roll music
  xx **Music; Music, Popular (Songs, etc.)**
Rock paintings. *See* **Rock drawings, paintings, and
    engravings**
Rock tombs. *See* **Tombs**
Rocket airplanes. *See* **Rocket planes**
Rocket flight. *See* **Space flight**
Rocket planes 629.133
  See also names of rocket planes, e.g. **X-15
    (Rocket aircraft);** etc.
  x Airplanes, Rocket propelled; Rocket airplanes
  xx **High speed aeronautics; Space ships**
Rocketry 621.43
  See also **Ballistic missiles; Guided missiles;
    Rockets (Aeronautics); Space ships; Space
    vehicles**
  xx **Aeronautics; Astronautics**
Rockets (Aeronautics) 629.133
  See also **Artificial satellites—Launching; Guided
    missiles; Jet propulsion;** also names of types

Rockets (Aeronautics)—*Continued*
  of rockets, e.g. **Ballistic missiles; Guided
  missiles ;** etc.; and names of specific rockets
 x Aerial rockets
 xx **Aeronautics; High speed aeronautics; Interplanetary voyages; Jet propulsion; Projectiles; Rocketry**
Rocks 552
 See also **Crystallography; Geochemistry; Geology; Mineralogy; Petrology; Stone;** also varieties of rock, e.g. **Granite;** etc.
 x Crystalline rocks; Metamorphic rocks
 xx **Geology; Petrology; Stone**
Rocks—Age. *See* **Geology, Stratigraphic**
Rocks, Moon. *See* **Lunar petrology**
Rocky Mountains 978
 xx **Mountains**
Rodeos 791
 xx **Cowhands; Horseback riding; Sports**
Roentgen rays. *See* **X rays**
Roentgenologists. *See* **Radiologists**
Role conflict 302; 302.5
 Use for materials on the conflict within one per-
  son who is being called upon to fulfil two or
  more competing roles.
 See also **Sex role**
 xx **Social conflict; Social role**
Role playing 302
 xx **Social role**
Role, Social. *See* **Social role**
Roller skating 796.2
 x Figure skating; Skating
Rolling stock. *See* **Locomotives**
Romaic language. *See* **Greek language, Modern**
Romaic literature. *See* **Greek literature, Modern**
Roman antiquities. *See* **Classical antiquities;
  Rome—Antiquities**
Roman architecture. *See* **Architecture, Roman**
Roman art. *See* **Art, Roman**
Roman Catholic Church. *See* **Catholic Church**
Roman emperors 920
 See also names of Roman emperors, e.g. **Nero,
  Emperor of Rome, 37-68;** etc.
 x Emperors; Sovereigns
 xx **Kings, queens, rulers, etc.**
Roman Empire. *See* **Rome**
Roman literature. *See* **Latin literature**
Roman mythology. *See* **Mythology, Classical**
Roman philosophy. *See* **Philosophy, Ancient**
Romance languages 440
 See also names of languages belonging to the
  Romance group, e.g. **French language;** etc.
 x Neo-Latin languages
 xx **Latin language**
Romance literature 840
 See also names of literatures belonging to the
  Romance group, e.g. **French literature;** etc.
Romance novels. *See* **Love stories**
Romances 840
 Use for collections of medieval tales dealing

Romances—*Continued*

with the age of chivalry; they may be either metrical or prose versions and may or may not have a factual basis.

See also **Arthurian romances;** also names of historic persons with the subdivision *Romances*

x Chivalry—Romances; Metrical romances; Stories

xx **Chivalry; Epic poetry; Fiction; Legends; Literature—Collected works**

Romances (Love stories). *See* **Love stories**

Romanesque architecture. *See* **Architecture, Romanesque**

Romanesque art. *See* **Art, Romanesque**

Romanesque painting. *See* **Painting, Romanesque**

Romanies. *See* **Gypsies**

Romantic fiction. *See* **Love stories**

Romantic stories. *See* **Love stories**

Romanticism 141; 809

See also **Realism in literature**

xx **Esthetics; Fiction; Literature; Music; Realism in literature**

Rome 937

Use for materials about the Roman Empire. Materials dealing with the modern city of Rome are entered under **Rome (Italy).**

x Roman Empire

Rome—Antiquities 937

x Roman antiquities; Ruins

Rome—Biography 920

x Classical biography

Rome—Description and geography 913.37

Use for descriptive and geographic materials on ancient Rome instead of the subdivisions *Description and travel* and *Historical geography.*

Rome—History 937

Rome (Italy) 945

See note under **Rome.**

Rome (Italy)—Description 914.5

Rome (Italy)—History 945

Roofs 695

xx **Architecture—Details; Building; Building, Iron and steel; Carpentry**

Rooming houses. *See* **Hotels, motels, etc.**

Root crops 633

See also **Feeds**

xx **Feeds; Vegetables**

Rope 623.88; 677

See also **Cables; Hemp; Knots and splices**

xx **Hemp**

Roses 635.9

xx **Flower gardening; Flowers**

Rosetta stone inscription 493

xx **Hieroglyphics**

Rosin. *See* **Gums and resins**

Rotating memory devices (Data processing). *See* **Computer storage devices**

Rotation of crops. *See* **Crop rotation**

Roughage. *See* **Food—Fiber content**
Round stage. *See* **Arena theater**
Routes of trade. *See* **Trade routes**
Rowing 797.1
    x Regattas; Sculling
    xx **Athletics; Boats and boating; College sports;**
        Exercise; Water sports
Royalty. *See* **Kings, queens, rulers, etc.; Princes**
    and princesses
Rubber 678
    x India rubber
    xx **Forest products**
Rubber, Artificial 678
    x Artificial rubber; Synthetic rubber
    xx **Plastics; Synthetic products**
Rubber sheet geometry. *See* **Topology**
Rubber tires. *See* **Tires**
Rugs 645; 677; 746.7
    Use for materials on one-piece floor coverings,
        such as woven fabrics, animal skins, etc.
        Consider also **Carpets.**
    See also **Carpets**
    xx **Carpets; Decorative arts; Interior design**
Rugs, Hooked 746.7
    x Hooked rugs
Rugs, Oriental 746.7
    Use for materials on handwoven or hand-
        knotted one-piece rugs or carpets made in
        the Orient.
    x Oriental rugs; Persian rugs
Ruins. *See* **Archeology; Cities and towns, Ruined,**
    extinct, etc.; Excavations (Archeology); and
    names of countries, cities, etc. with the sub-
    division *Antiquities,* e.g.
    Rome—Antiquities; etc.
Rule of equal time (Broadcasting). *See* **Equal time**
    rule (Broadcasting)
Rulers. *See* **Heads of state; Kings, queens, rulers,**
    etc.; and names of individual rulers
Rules of order. *See* **Parliamentary practice**
Runaway adults 173; 306.8
    x Adults, Runaway; Desertion; Husbands, Run-
        away; Wives, Runaway
    xx **Desertion and nonsupport; Homeless people**
Runaway children 362.7
    x Children, Runaway; Runaway teenagers;
        Teenagers, Runaway; Youth, Runaway
    xx **Children; Homeless people; Missing children;**
        Youth
Runaway teenagers. *See* **Runaway children**
Running 796.4
    See also **Jogging; Marathon running**
    xx **Track athletics**
Rural architecture. *See* **Architecture, Domestic;**
    Farm buildings
Rural churches 254
    x Church work, Rural; Churches, Country;
        Churches, Rural; Country churches
    xx **Church work**
Rural conditions. *See* names of countries, states,

Rural conditions—*Continued*
        etc. with the subdivision *Rural conditions,*
        e.g. **United States—Rural conditions;**
        Ohio—Rural conditions; etc.
Rural credit. *See* **Agricultural credit**
Rural electrification. *See* **Electric power distribu-**
        tion; Electricity in agriculture
Rural high schools. *See* **Rural schools**
Rural life. *See* **Country life; Farm life; Outdoor life;**
        Peasantry
Rural schools 371
    x Country schools; District schools; High
        schools, Rural; Rural high schools
    xx **Public schools; Schools**
Rural sociology. *See* **Sociology, Rural**
Russia. *See* **Soviet Union**
Russian artificial satellites. *See* **Artificial satellites,**
        Russian
Russian Church. *See* **Orthodox Eastern Church,**
        Russian
Russian communism. *See* **Communism—Soviet**
        Union
Russian intervention in Czechoslovakia. *See*
        Czechoslovakia—History—1968- , Inter-
        vention
Russian literature 891.7
    Use for materials discussing literature in the
        Russian language which is the principal
        state and cultural language of the Soviet
        Union. Materials discussing several of the
        literatures of the Soviet Union are entered
        under **Soviet Union—Literatures.**
    May use same subdivisions and names of liter-
        ary forms as for **English literature.**
Russian revolution. *See* **Soviet Union—History—**
        1917-1921, Revolution
Russian satellite countries. *See* **Communist coun-**
        tries
Russians (May subdiv. geog.) **920; 947**
    Use for materials on the citizens of the Soviet
        Union and also for the dominant Slavic-
        speaking Great Russian ethnic group of the
        Soviet Union.
    xx **Soviet Union**
Russo-Finnish War, 1939-1940 948.97
    x Finno-Russian War, 1939-1940; Soviet
        Union—History—1939-1940, War with
        Finland
Russo-Turkish War, 1853-1856. *See* **Crimean War,**
        1853-1856
Rust. *See* **Corrosion and anticorrosives**
Rustless coatings. *See* **Corrosion and anticorrosives**
RVs. *See* **Recreational vehicles**
S.A.T. *See* **Scholastic aptitude test**
S.S.T.'s. *See* **Supersonic transport planes**
Sabbath 263; 296.4
    x Lord's Day
    xx **Judaism**
Sabin vaccine. *See* **Poliomyelitis vaccine**

Sabotage 331.89; 364.1
  xx **Labor unions; Offenses against public safety; Strikes and lockouts; Subversive activities; Terrorism**
Sacraments 234; 265
  See also **Baptism; Lord's Supper; Marriage; Ordination**
  x Ecclesiastical rites and ceremonies
  xx **Rites and ceremonies; Theology**
Sacred art. *See* **Christian art and symbolism; Religious art and symbolism**
Sacred books 291.8
  See also names of sacred books, e.g. **Bible; Koran; Vedas;** etc.
  x Books, Sacred
  xx **Religious literature**
Sacred music. *See* **Church music**
Sacred numbers. *See* **Symbolism of numbers**
Sacrifice 291.3
  See also **Atonement—Christianity**
  xx **Ethnology; Religion; Theology; Worship**
Safety appliances 363.1; 620.8
  See also **Accidents—Prevention;** also subjects with the subdivision *Safety appliances,* e.g. **Railroads—Safety appliances;** etc.
  x Safety devices; Safety equipment
  xx **Accidents—Prevention**
Safety devices. *See* **Safety appliances**
Safety education 371.7
  See also **Accidents—Prevention**
  xx **Accidents—Prevention**
Safety equipment. *See* **Safety appliances**
Safety, Industrial. *See* **Occupational health and safety**
Safety measures. *See* **Accidents—Prevention,** and subjects with the subdivision *Safety measures,* e.g. **Aeronautics—Safety measures;** etc.
Sagas 398.2; 839
  xx **Folklore; Literature; Old Norse literature; Scandinavian literature**
Sailboarding. *See* **Windsurfing**
Sailing 623.88; 797.1
  See also **Boats and boating; Navigation; Windsurfing; Yachts and yachting**
  xx **Boats and boating; Navigation; Ships; Water sports; Yachts and yachting**
Sailors 623.88092; 920
  See also **Merchant marine; Pilots and pilotage; Seafaring life;** also names of navies, e.g. **United States. Navy;** etc.
  x Mariners; Naval personnel; Navigators; Sailors' life; Sea life; Seamen
  xx **Military personnel; Naval art and science; Navies; Seafaring life; Voyages and travels**
Sailors' life. *See* **Sailors; Seafaring life**
Sailors' song. *See* **Sea songs**
Sailplanes (Aeronautics). *See* **Gliders (Aeronautics)**

Saint Bartholomew's Day, Massacre of, 1572 940.2; 944

    xx **Huguenots; Massacres**

Saint Dominic, Order of. *See* **Dominicans**

Saint Francis, Order of. *See* **Franciscans**

Saint Valentine's Day. *See* **Valentine's Day**

Saints 920

    See also **Hermits; Legends; Martyrs; Shrines;** also names of saints of different religions, e.g. **Christian saints;** etc.; and names of individual saints

    xx **Heroes and heroines; Legends; Martyrs; Pilgrims and pilgrimages; Shrines**

Salads 641.8

    xx **Cookery**

Salamanders 597.6

    xx **Amphibians**

Sale of infants. *See* **Adoption—Corrupt practices**

Sales, Auction. *See* **Auctions**

Sales management 658.8

    x Management, Sales

    xx **Industrial management; Management; Marketing; Selling**

Sales personnel 658.85

    See also **Booksellers and bookselling; Office employees; Peddlers and peddling**

    x Agents, Sales; Clerks (Retail trade); Salesmen; Saleswomen; Traveling sales personnel

    xx **Office employees; Retail trade**

Sales tax 336.2

    x Purchase tax; Retail sales tax; Taxation of sales

    xx **Taxation**

Salesmanship. *See* **Selling**

Salesmen. *See* **Sales personnel**

Saleswomen. *See* **Sales personnel**

Saline water. *See* **Sea water**

Salk vaccine. *See* **Poliomyelitis vaccine**

Salmon 597

    xx **Fishes**

Saloons. *See* **Restaurants, bars, etc.**

Salt free diet 613.2

    x Low sodium diet

    xx **Cookery for the sick; Diet; Diet in disease**

Salt water. *See* **Sea water**

Salt water aquariums. *See* **Marine aquariums**

Salutations. *See* **Etiquette; Letter writing**

Salvage 387.5; 627.7

    See also **Shipwrecks; Skin diving**

    xx **International law; Maritime law; Shipwrecks**

Salvage (Waste, etc.) 604.6

    See note under **Recycling (Waste, etc.).**

    See also **Recycling (Waste, etc.); Refuse and refuse disposal; Waste products; Waste products as fuel**

    x Conversion of waste products; Recovery of waste products; Reuse of waste; Solid waste disposal; Utilization of waste; Waste products—Recycling; Waste reclamation

    xx **Recycling (Waste, etc.); Refuse and refuse dis-**

Salvage (Waste, etc.)—*Continued*
posal; **Waste products**
Salvation 234
See also **Atonement—Christianity; Faith; Grace
(Theology); Regeneration (Theology); Sanctification; Sin**
x Redemption
xx **Regeneration (Theology)**
Salvation Army 267
xx **Missions, Christian**
Sampling (Statistics) 519.5
See also **Quality control**
x Random sampling
xx **Probabilities; Statistics**
Sanatoriums. *See* **Health resorts, spas, etc.; Hospitals**
Sanctification 234
xx **Salvation; Spiritual life; Theology**
Sanctions (International law) 341.5
x Economic sanctions
xx **Economic policy; International economic relations; International law**
Sanctuaries, Wildlife. *See* **Wildlife refuges**
Sanctuary (Law). *See* **Asylum, Right of**
Sanctuary movement (Refugee aid) 261
Use for materials on the network of religious
congregations, cities, etc., in the United
States that shelters refugees.
xx **Church and social problems; Social movements**
Sand dunes 551.3
x Dunes
xx **Reclamation of land; Seashore**
Sandwiches 641.8
xx **Cookery**
Sanitary affairs. *See* **Sanitary engineering; Sanita-
tion**
Sanitary engineering 628
See also

Drainage	**Sewerage**
Municipal engineering	**Soils—Bacteriology**
Pollution	**Street cleaning**
Refuse and refuse disposal	**Water supply**
Sanitation	

x Sanitary affairs
xx **Building; Civil engineering; Drainage, House;
Engineering; Municipal engineering;
Plumbing; Public health; Sanitation**
Sanitary landfills. *See* **Landfills**
Sanitation 363.7
See also

Cemeteries	**School hygiene**
Cremation	**United States—History—**
Disinfection and disinfec-	**1861-1865, Civil War—**
tants	**Health aspects**
Hygiene	**Ventilation**
Military health	**Water—Purification**
Pollution	**Water supply**
Public health	**World War, 1939-1945—**
Refuse and refuse disposal	**Health aspects**
Sanitary engineering	

Sanitation—*Continued*

 x Sanitary affairs

 xx **Cleanliness; Hygiene; Public health; Sanitary engineering**

Sanitation, Household 648

 See also **Drainage, House; House cleaning; Household pests; Laundry; Plumbing; Ventilation**

 x House sanitation; Household sanitation

 xx **Plumbing**

Santa Claus 394.2

 xx **Christmas**

SAT. *See* **Scholastic aptitude test**

Satan. *See* **Devil**

Satellite communication systems. *See* **Artificial satellites in telecommunication**

Satellites, Artificial. *See* **Artificial satellites**

Satire (May subdiv. geog. adjective form, e.g. **Satire, English;** etc.) **808.7; 808.87**

 See also **Invective; Parody**

 x Comic literature

 xx **Literature; Rhetoric; Wit and humor**

Satire, American 817

 x American satire

 xx **American literature**

Satire, English 827

 x English satire

 xx **English literature**

Satisfaction in work. *See* **Job satisfaction**

Saturn (Planet) 523.4

 xx **Planets; Solar system**

Saucers, Flying. *See* **Unidentified flying objects**

Saving and thrift 332.024

 See also **Cost of living; Insurance, Industrial; Investments; Old age pensions; Savings and loan associations**

 x Economy; Thrift

 xx **Cost of living; Economics; Finance, Personal; Insurance; Investments; Success**

Savings and loan associations 332.3

 x Building and loan associations; Cooperative building associations; Loan associations

 xx **Banks and banking; Cooperation; Cooperative societies; Investments; Loans; Personal loans; Saving and thrift**

Savings banks. *See* **Banks and banking**

Saws 621.9

 xx **Carpentry—Tools; Tools**

Saxons. *See* **Anglo-Saxons; Teutonic peoples**

Sayings. *See* **Epigrams; Proverbs; Quotations**

Scandinavian civilization. *See* **Civilization, Scandinavian**

Scandinavian languages 439.7-439.8

 See also **Danish language; Icelandic language; Norwegian language; Old Norse language; Swedish language**

 x Norse languages

 xx **Old Norse language**

Scandinavian literature 839.7-839.8

 See also **Danish literature; Eddas; Icelandic liter-**

Scandinavian literature—*Continued*
    ature; Norwegian literature; Old Norse liter-
    ature; Sagas; Swedish literature
  x Norse literature
  xx **Old Norse literature**
Scandinavians 920; 948
  Use for materials on the people of Scandinavia
    since the 10th century. Materials on the
    early Scandinavians are entered under
    Vikings.
  See also **Vikings**
Scenarios. *See* **Motion picture plays; Plots (Drama,
    fiction, etc.); Radio plays; Television plays**
Scene painting 751.7
  xx **Painting; Theaters—Stage setting and scenery**
Scenery. *See* **Landscape protection; Views;** and
    names of countries, states, etc. with the sub-
    division *Description and travel—Views,* e.g.
    **United States—Description and travel—
    Views;** etc.; and names of cities with the
    subdivision *Description—Views,* e.g.
    Chicago (Ill.)—Description—Views; etc.
Scenery (Stage). *See* **Theaters—Stage setting and
    scenery**
Scepticism. *See* **Skepticism**
Scholarship. *See* **Learning and scholarship**
Scholarships, fellowships, etc. 371.2; 378
  See also **Student loan funds**
  x Fellowships; Student aid
  xx **Colleges and universities; Education; Educa-
    tion—Government policy; Endowments;
    Student loan funds**
Scholastic aptitude test 378
  See also **Graduate record examination**
  x S.A.T.; SAT
  xx **Colleges and universities—Entrance examina-
    tions; Examinations**
School administration and organization. *See*
    Schools—Administration
School age mothers. *See* **Adolescent mothers**
School and community. *See* **Community and school**
School and home. *See* **Home and school**
School architecture. *See* **School buildings**
School assembly programs 372; 373
  Use for general materials on school entertain-
    ments, literary and otherwise, assembly pro-
    grams, etc. Collections of prose and poetry
    for public speaking are entered under
    Readings and recitations.
  See also **Commencements; Drama in education;
    Readings and recitations;** also names of days
    observed, e.g. **Memorial Day;** etc.
  x Assembly programs, School; Programs,
    School assembly; School entertainments;
    Schools—Exercises and recreations;
    Schools—Opening exercises
  xx **Student activities**
School attendance 371.2
  See also **Children—Employment; Dropouts; Edu-
    cation, Compulsory**

School attendance—*Continued*

 x Absence from school; Absenteeism (School); Attendance, School; Compulsory school attendance; School enrollment; Truancy (Schools)

 xx **Education, Compulsory**

School boards 379.1

 x Boards of education

 xx **Schools—Administration**

School books. *See* **Textbooks**

School buildings 727

 x Buildings, School; School architecture; School houses; Schoolhouses

 xx **Architecture; Buildings; Schools**

School buildings as recreation centers. *See* **Community centers**

School busing. *See* **Busing (School integration); School children—Transportation**

School children 370.19

 xx **Children; Students**

School children—Food 371.7

 x Food for school children; Meals for school children; School lunches

 xx **Children—Care and hygiene; Diet; Food**

School children—Transportation 371.8

 See also **Busing (School integration)**

 x School busing

 xx **Transportation**

School clubs. *See* **Students—Societies**

School counseling 371.4

 Use for materials on the assistance given to students by schools, colleges, or universities in understanding and coping with adjustment problems. Materials on the assistance given to students in the selection of a program of studies are entered under **Educational counseling.**

 See also **Educational counseling**

 x Guidance counseling, School

 xx **Counseling; Educational counseling**

School desegregation. *See* **School integration**

School discipline 371.5

 See also **Classroom management; Self-government (in education)**

 x Discipline of children; Punishment in schools

 xx **Schools—Administration; Teaching**

School drama. *See* **College and school drama**

School dropouts. *See* **Dropouts**

School enrollment. *See* **School attendance**

School entertainments. *See* **School assembly programs**

School excursions. *See* **Field trips**

School finance. *See* **Education—Finance**

School furniture. *See* **Schools—Equipment and supplies**

School houses. *See* **School buildings**

School hygiene 371.7

 x Children—Health; Hygiene, School

 xx **Children—Care and hygiene; Health education; Hygiene; Public health; Sanitation**

School inspection. *See* **School supervision; Schools—Administration**

School integration   370.19

  See also **Busing (School integration); Magnet schools; Segregation in education**

  x Desegregated schools; Desegregation in education; Education—Integration; Integrated schools; Integration in education; Racial balance in schools; School desegregation

  xx **Blacks—Education; Blacks—Integration; Segregation in education**

School journalism. *See* **College and school journalism**

School libraries   027.8

  See also **Children's libraries; Children's literature; Libraries and schools; School libraries (Elementary school); School libraries (High school)**

  x Libraries, School

  xx **Instructional materials centers; Libraries; Libraries and schools**

School libraries (Elementary school)   027.8

  See also **Children's libraries**

  x Elementary school libraries

  xx **Children's libraries; School libraries**

School libraries (High school)   027.8

  See also **Young adults' library services**

  x High school libraries; Junior high school libraries; Secondary school libraries

  xx **School libraries; Young adults' library services**

School life. *See* **Students**

School lunches. *See* **School children—Food**

School management. *See* **Schools—Administration**

School media centers. *See* **Instructional materials centers**

School music. *See* **Music—Study and teaching; School songbooks; Singing**

School newspapers. *See* **College and school journalism**

School nurses   371.7

  xx **Children—Care and hygiene; Nurses**

School organization. *See* **Schools—Administration**

School playgrounds. *See* **Playgrounds**

School plays. *See* **Children's plays; College and school drama—Collected works**

School principals. *See* **School superintendents and principals**

School psychologists   371.4

  x Psychologists, School

  xx **Educational counseling**

School readiness. *See* **Readiness for school**

School reports   371.2

  See also **Grading and marking (Students)**

  xx **Grading and marking (Students)**

School shops   373.2

  x Industrial arts shops

  xx **Technical education**

School songbooks   784.6

  See also **Children's songs**

  x School music; Songbooks, School

School songbooks—*Continued*
  xx **Singing; Songbooks; Songs**
School sports 371.8
  See also **Coaching (Athletics); College sports**
  x Interscholastic sports
  xx **Sports; Student activities**
School stories 808.83; 813; etc.; Fic
  x Stories
School superintendents and principals 371.2
  See also **School supervision**
  x School principals; Superintendents of schools
  xx **School supervision; Schools—Administration; Teachers; Teaching**
School supervision 371.1
  Use for materials on the supervision of instruction. Materials on the administrative duties of an educator are entered under **Schools—Administration.**
  See also **School superintendents and principals**
  x Inspection of schools; Instructional supervision; School inspection; Supervision of schools
  xx **School superintendents and principals; Schools—Administration; Teaching**
School surveys. *See* **Educational surveys**
School taxes. *See* **Education—Finance**
School teaching. *See* **Teaching**
School trips. *See* **Field trips**
School vandalism. *See* **School violence**
School verse 808.81; 811; etc.
  xx **Poetry—Collected works**
School violence 371.5
  x School vandalism; Student violence
  xx **Juvenile delinquency; Violence**
School withdrawals. *See* **Dropouts**
Schoolgirl mothers. *See* **Adolescent mothers**
Schoolhouses. *See* **School buildings**
Schools (May subdiv. geog.) **371**
  See also **Education; Libraries and schools; Museums and schools; School buildings; Summer schools; Summer schools, Religious;** also types of schools, e.g. **Church schools; Colleges and universities; Kindergarten; Public schools; Rural schools;** etc.; also subjects with the subdivision *Study and teaching,* e.g. **Medicine—Study and teaching;** etc.; headings beginning with the word **School;** and names of individual schools
  x Community schools; Neighborhood schools
  xx **Education; Public schools**
Schools—Administration 371.2
  See note under **School supervision.**
  See also

Articulation (Education)	**Schools—Centralization**
School boards	**Schools—Decentralization**
School discipline	**Self-government (in education)**
School superintendents and principals	**Teaching**
School supervision	

  x Educational administration; Inspection of

544

Schools—Administration—*Continued*
        schools; School administration and organi-
        zation; School inspection; School manage-
        ment; School organization; Schools—
        Management and organization
Schools and libraries. *See* **Libraries and schools**
Schools and museums. *See* **Museums and schools**
Schools as social centers. *See* **Community centers**
Schools—Centralization 379.1
  x Centralization of schools; Consolidation of
    schools
  xx **Schools—Administration**
Schools, Commercial. *See* **Business education**
Schools—Curricula. *See* **Education—Curricula;**
      and types of education and schools with the
      subdivision *Curricula,* e.g. **Library educa-**
      tion—Curricula; Colleges and universities—
      Curricula; etc.
Schools—Decentralization 379.1
  x Decentralization of schools
  xx **Schools—Administration**
Schools—Equipment and supplies 371.6
  x School furniture
  xx **Furniture**
Schools—Exercises and recreations. *See* **School as-**
    sembly programs
Schools, Magnet. *See* **Magnet schools**
Schools—Management and organization. *See*
    Schools—Administration
Schools, Military. *See* **Military education**
Schools, Nonformal. *See* **Experimental schools**
Schools, Nongraded. *See* **Nongraded schools**
Schools—Opening exercises. *See* **School assembly**
    programs
Schools, Parochial. *See* **Church schools**
Schools—Prayers. *See* **Religion in the public**
    schools
Schools, Ungraded. *See* **Nongraded schools**
Schools—United States 371
  x United States—Schools
Science (May subdiv. geog.) **500**
  See also

Astronomy	**Life sciences**
Bacteriology	**Mathematics**
Biology	**Meteorology**
Botany	**Mineralogy**
Chemistry	**Natural history**
Crystallography	**Petrology**
Earth sciences	**Physics**
Ethnology	**Physiology**
Fossils	**Space sciences**
Geology	**Zoology**

  also headings beginning with the word **Scientific**
  x Discoveries (in science)
Science and civilization 303.4
  x Civilization and science; Science and society
  xx **Civilization; Progress**
Science and religion. *See* **Religion and science**
Science and society. *See* **Science and civilization**
Science and space. *See* **Space sciences**

Science and state. *See* **Science—Government policy**
Science and the Bible. *See* **Bible and science**
Science and the humanities 001.3
    x Humanities and science
Science—Exhibitions 507.4
    x Science fairs
Science—Experiments 507
    See also particular branches of science with the
        subdivision *Experiments,* e.g.
        Chemistry—Experiments; etc.
    x Experiments, Scientific; Scientific experiments
Science fairs. *See* **Science—Exhibitions**
Science fiction 808.83; 813; etc.; Fic
    x Stories
    xx **Fantastic fiction; Fiction**
Science—Government policy 351.85
    x Science and state; Science policy; State and
        science
Science—Methodology 501
    See also **Logic**
    x Methodology; Scientific method
Science policy. *See* **Science—Government policy**
Science—Societies 506
    x Scientific societies
Science—Study and teaching 507
    See also **Nature study**
    x Education, Scientific; Scientific education
    xx **Education; Teaching**
Science—United States 509
    x American science; United States—Science
Scientific apparatus and instruments 502.8
    See also names of groups of instruments, e.g.
        Aeronautical instruments; Astronomical in-
        struments; Chemical apparatus; Electric ap-
        paratus and appliances; Electronic apparatus
        and appliances; Engineering instruments;
        Meteorological instruments; etc.; also
        names of specific instruments
    x Apparatus, Scientific; Instruments, Scientific;
        Scientific instruments
Scientific education. *See* **Science—Study and**
    teaching
Scientific expeditions 508
    See also names of regions explored, e.g.
        Antarctic regions; Arctic regions; etc.; and
        names of expeditions
    x Expeditions, Scientific; Polar expeditions;
        Travels
    xx **Discoveries (in geography); Voyages and trav-**
    els
Scientific experiments. *See* **Science—Experiments;**
    and particular branches of science with the
    subdivision *Experiments,* e.g.
    Chemistry—Experiments; etc.
Scientific instruments. *See* **Scientific apparatus and**
    instruments
Scientific journalism. *See* **Journalism, Scientific**
Scientific management. *See* **Management**
Scientific method. *See* special subjects with the
    subdivision *Methodology,* e.g.

Scientific method—*Continued*
 Science—Methodology; etc.
Scientific recreations 793.8
 See also **Mathematical recreations**
 x Recreations, Scientific
 xx **Amusements**
Scientific societies. *See* **Science—Societies**
Scientific writing. *See* **Technical writing**
Scientists 500.92; 920
 See also types of scientists, e.g. **Astronomers;**
 Chemists; Geologists; Mathematicians; Nat-
 uralists; Physicists; etc.; and names of indi-
 vidual scientists
Scottish clans. *See* **Clans**
Scottish tartans. *See* **Tartans**
Scouts and scouting 369.4
 See also **Boy Scouts; Girl Scouts**
Screen plays. *See* **Motion picture plays**
Screen printing. *See* **Silk screen printing**
Scriptures, Holy. *See* **Bible**
Scuba diving 797.2
 Use for materials on free diving with the aid of
 self-contained underwater breathing appara-
 tus.
 x Diving, Scuba; Free diving
 xx **Diving; Diving, Submarine; Skin diving**
Sculling. *See* **Rowing**
Sculptors (May subdiv. geog. adjective form, e.g.
 Sculptors, French; etc.) **730.92; 920**
 xx **Artists**
Sculptors, American 730.92; 920
 x American sculptors; United States—Sculptors
Sculpture (May subdiv. geog. adjective form, e.g.
 Sculpture, African; etc.) **730-735**
 See also types of sculpture, e.g. **Brasses;**
 Bronzes; Masks (Sculpture); Mobiles
 (Sculpture); Modeling; Monuments; Plaster
 casts; Soap sculpture; Wood carving; etc.
 x Statues
 xx **Art; Decoration and ornament; Esthetics**
Sculpture, American 730.973
 x American sculpture; United States—Sculpture
Sculpture, Greek 730.938; 730.9495
 x Greek sculpture
Sculpture in motion. *See* **Kinetic sculpture**
Sculpture, Kinetic. *See* **Kinetic sculpture**
Sculpture, Modern 735
 x Modern sculpture
Sculpture, Modern—1900-1999 (20th century) 735
Sculpture, Religious. *See* **Religious art and symbol-**
 ism
Sculpture—Technique 731.4
 See also **Modeling**
 xx **Modeling**
Sea. *See* **Ocean**
Sea animals. *See* **Marine animals**
Sea bed. *See* **Ocean bottom**
Sea farming. *See* **Aquaculture**
Sea fisheries. *See* **Fisheries**
Sea food. *See* **Seafood**

Sea in art. *See* **Marine painting**
Sea laboratories. *See* **Undersea research stations**
Sea laws. *See* **Maritime law**
Sea life. *See* **Sailors; Seafaring life;** and names of
       countries with the subhead *Navy,* e.g.
       United States. Navy; etc.
Sea lions. *See* **Seals (Animals)**
Sea mosses. *See* **Algae**
Sea poetry 808.81; 811; etc.
    See also **Sea songs**
    xx **Poetry—Collected works**
Sea pollution. *See* **Marine pollution**
Sea power 359
    See also **Arms control; Naval battles; Naval his-**
       tory; Navies; Warships; also names of coun-
       tries with the subhead *Navy* or the subdivi-
       sion *History, Naval,* e.g. **United States.**
       Navy; United States—History, Naval; etc.
    x Dominion of the sea; Military power; Naval
       power; Navy
    xx **Arms control; Naval art and science; Naval**
       history; Navies
Sea resources. *See* **Marine resources**
Sea routes. *See* **Trade routes**
Sea shells. *See* **Shells**
Sea-shore. *See* **Seashore**
Sea songs 784.7
    x Chanties; Sailors' song
    xx **Sea poetry; Songs**
Sea stories 808.83; 813; etc.
    x Stories
    xx **Adventure and adventurers**
Sea transportation. *See* **Shipping**
Sea travel. *See* **Ocean travel**
Sea water 551.4
    x Saline water; Salt water
    xx **Water**
Sea water aquariums. *See* **Marine aquariums**
Sea water conversion 628.1
    x Conversion of saline water; Demineralization
       of salt water; Desalination of water; Desalt-
       ing of water
    xx **Water—Purification**
Sea waves. *See* **Ocean waves**
Seafaring life 910.4
    See also **Sailors**
    x Sailors' life; Sea life
    xx **Adventure and adventurers; Sailors; Voyages**
       and travels
Seafood 597; 641.3
    See also **Fish as food;** also names of fish, shell-
       fish, etc. used as food
    x Sea food
    xx **Food; Marine resources**
Sealab project 551.46
    x Navy Sealab project; Project Sealab; United
       States. Navy—Sealab project
    xx **Undersea research stations**
Seals (Animals) 599.74
    x Fur seals; Sea lions

Seals (Animals)—*Continued*

   xx **Mammals, Marine**

Seals (Numismatics) 737

   x Emblems; Signets

   xx **Heraldry; History; Inscriptions; Numismatics**

Seamanship. *See* **Navigation**

Seamen. *See* **Sailors**

Search and rescue operations. *See* **Rescue work**

Seascapes. *See* **Marine painting**

Seashore 551.4

   See also **Beaches; Sand dunes**

   x Sea-shore

   xx **Ocean**

Seasons 525

   See also names of the seasons, e.g. **Autumn;** etc.

   xx **Astronomy; Climate; Meteorology**

Seaweeds. *See* **Algae**

Secession. *See* **State rights; United States—**
      History—1861-1865, Civil War—Causes

Second Advent 232

   See also **Millennium**

   x Jesus Christ—Second Advent; Second coming
      of Christ

   xx **Eschatology; Jesus Christ; Millennium**

Second coming of Christ. *See* **Second Advent**

Second hand trade. *See* **Secondhand trade**

Second job. *See* **Supplementary employment**

Secondary education. *See* **Education, Secondary**

Secondary employment. *See* **Supplementary employment**

Secondary school libraries. *See* **School libraries
      (High school)**

Secondary schools. *See* **Education, Secondary;
      High schools; Junior high schools; Private
      schools; Public schools**

Secondhand trade 381

   See also types of secondhand trade, e.g. **Garage
      sales;** etc.

   x Second hand trade; Used merchandise

   xx **Selling**

Secret service (May subdiv. geog.) **327.1; 355.3**

   Use for materials on a governmental service of a
      secret nature.

   See also **Detectives; Espionage; Intelligence service; Spies;** also names of wars with the subdivision *Secret service,* e.g. **World War,
      1939-1945—Secret service;** etc.

   xx **Detectives; Intelligence service; Police; Spies**

Secret service—United States 355.3

   x United States—Secret service

Secret societies 366; 371.8

   See also **Fraternities and sororities;** also names
      of secret societies, e.g. **Freemasons;** etc.

   x Greek letter societies

   xx **Rites and ceremonies; Societies**

Secret writing. *See* **Cryptography**

Secretarial practice. *See* **Office practice**

Secretaries 651.3

   xx **Business education; Office management**

Sectionalism (U.S.) 917.3; 973
>   *x* Localism; Provincialism; Regionalism

Sects 280-289
>   *See also* **Cults;** also names of churches and sects
>   *x* Church denominations; Denominations, Religious; Religious denominations
>   *xx* **Church history; Cults; Religions**

Secularism 211
>   *See also* **Atheism; Rationalism**
>   *xx* **Ethics; Theology; Utilitarianism**

Securities 332.6
>   *See also* types of securities, e.g. **Bonds; Investments; Mortgages; Stocks;** etc.
>   *x* Capitalization (Finance); Dividends
>   *xx* **Finance; Investments; Speculation; Stock exchange**

Securities exchange. *See* **Stock exchange**

Security, Internal. *See* **Internal security**

Security, International 327.1; 341.7
>   *See also* **Arbitration, International; Arms control; International organization; International police; Neutrality; Peace**
>   *x* Collective security; International security
>   *xx* **Arms control; International relations; Peace**

Security, Job. *See* **Job security**

Security measures. *See* subjects with the subdivision *Security measures,* e.g. **Nuclear power plants—Security measures;** etc.

Security, Social. *See* **Social security**

Sedition. *See* **Political crimes and offenses; Revolutions**

Seeds 582
>   *xx* **Botany; Plant propagation**

Seeds—Germination. *See* **Germination**

Seeing eye dogs. *See* **Guide dogs**

Segregation 305
>   *See also* **Discrimination; Minorities;** also names of groups of people with the subdivision *Segregation,* e.g. **Blacks—Segregation;** etc.
>   *x* Apartheid
>   *xx* **Discrimination; Minorities**

Segregation in education 370.19
>   *See also* **Busing (School integration); Discrimination in education; School integration**
>   *x* Education, Segregation in; Integration in education; Racial balance in schools
>   *xx* **Blacks—Education; Blacks—Segregation; Discrimination in education; School integration**

Segregation in housing. *See* **Discrimination in housing**

Segregation in public accommodations. *See* **Discrimination in public accommodations**

Seismography. *See* **Earthquakes**

Seismology. *See* **Earthquakes**

Selection, Artificial. *See* **Breeding**

Selection, Natural. *See* **Natural selection**

Selective service. *See* **Military service, Compulsory**

Self 126; 155.2
>   *xx* **Consciousness; Individuality; Personality**

Self-awareness. *See* **Self-perception**

Self-care, Health 613; 616

    See also **First aid; Holistic medicine; Nutrition; Physical fitness**

    x Health care, Self; Health, Self-care; Medical self-care; Self-care, Medical; Self health care; Self-help medical care

    xx **Alternative medicine; Health; Holistic medicine; Medical care; Medicine**

Self-care, Medical. *See* **Self-care, Health**

Self-concept. *See* **Self-perception**

Self-consciousness 155.2

Self-control 153.8

Self-defense 613.6; 796.8

    See also **Boxing; Judo; Karate; Martial arts**

    x Fighting

    xx **Martial arts**

Self-employed 331.12

    See also **Entrepreneurs; Home business; Professions; Small business**

    x Freelancers

Self-employed women 331.4

    x Women, Self-employed

    xx **Women—Employment**

Self-esteem. *See* **Self-respect**

Self-fulfillment. *See* **Self-realization**

Self-government. *See* **Democracy; Representative government and representation**

Self-government (in education) 371.5

    x Honor system; Student councils; Student government; Student self-government

    xx **School discipline; Schools—Administration**

Self health care. *See* **Self-care, Health**

Self-help medical care. *See* **Self-care, Health**

Self-instruction. *See* **Correspondence schools and courses;** and names of subjects with the subdivision *Programmed instruction,* e.g. **English language—Programmed instruction;** etc.

Self-love (Psychology). *See* **Self-respect**

Self-perception 155.2

    x Self-awareness; Self-concept

Self-realization 155.2; 158

    See also **Success**

    x Fulfillment, Self; Self-fulfillment

    xx **Success**

Self-respect 155.2; 179

    x Self-esteem; Self-love (Psychology)

    xx **Human behavior**

Self-starvation. *See* **Anorexia nervosa**

Selling 658.85

    See also **Advertising; Booksellers and bookselling; Mail-order business; Marketing; Peddlers and peddling; Sales management; Secondhand trade**

    x Salesmanship

    xx **Advertising; Business; Department stores; Retail trade**

Selling of infants. *See* **Adoption—Corrupt practices**

Selvas. *See* **Jungles**

Semantics 149; 412

    Use for materials on the historical and psychological study of meanings in language and changes in those meanings.

    See also **Semiotics; Words, New**

    xx **Language and languages; Semiotics**

Semiconductors 621.3815

    See also **Microelectronics; Transistors**

    xx **Electronics**

Semiotics 001.51; 302.2; 401

    Use for materials on the study of signs and symbols, especially the relationship between written and spoken signs (words, phrases, utterances) and whatever it is they stand for.

    See also **Semantics; Signs and symbols; Visual literacy**

    xx **Semantics; Signs and symbols**

Semitic peoples 572.9

    xx **Anthropology**

Senators—United States. *See* **United States. Congress. Senate**

Senescence. *See* **Aging**

Senior citizens. *See* **Elderly**

Sense of direction. *See* **Direction sense**

Senses and sensation 152.1; 612

    See also

Color sense	**Smell**
Gestalt psychology	**Taste**
Hearing	**Touch**
Pain	**Vision**
Pleasure	

    xx **Intellect; Knowledge, Theory of; Physiology; Psychology; Psychology, Physiological**

Sensing, Remote. *See* **Remote sensing**

Sensitivity training. *See* **Group relations training**

Separation anxiety in children 155.4

    xx **Adolescent psychology; Child psychology; Fear; Stress (Psychology)**

Separation (Law). *See* **Divorce**

Separation of powers (May subdiv. geog.) 342; 351

    x Division of powers; Powers, Separation of

    xx **Constitutional law; Executive power; Political science**

Separation of powers—United States 342

    x United States—Separation of powers

Separatism, Black. *See* **Black nationalism**

Separatist movement in Québec (Province). *See* **Québec (Province)—History—Autonomy and independence movements**

Sepulchers. *See* **Tombs**

Sepulchral brasses. *See* **Brasses**

Serial publications 050

    Use for general materials on publications in any medium issued in successive parts bearing numerical or chronological designations and intended to be continued indefinitely.

    See also **Books; Newspapers; Periodicals; Yearbooks**

    xx **Bibliography; Books; Publishers and publishing**

Serigraphy. *See* **Silk screen printing**
Sermon on the mount 226
    x Jesus Christ—Sermon on the mount
Sermons 251; 252
    See also **Preaching**
    xx **Preaching**
Serpents. *See* **Snakes**
Servants. *See* **Household employees**
Service books (Liturgy). *See* **Liturgies**
Service, Compulsory military. *See* **Military service,**
    Compulsory
Service stations, Automobile. *See* **Automobiles—**
    Service stations
Servicemen. *See* **Military personnel**
Servicewomen. *See* **Military personnel**
Servitude. *See* **Peonage; Slavery**
Servomechanisms 629.8
    x Automatic control
    xx **Automation; Feedback control systems**
Set theory 511.3
    See also **Algebra, Boolean; Arithmetic; Fractals;**
    Logic, Symbolic and mathematical; Number
    theory; Topology
    x Aggregates; Classes (Mathematics); Ensembles
    (Mathematics); Mathematical sets; Sets
    (Mathematics)
    xx **Logic, Symbolic and mathematical; Mathe-**
    matics
Sets, Fractal. *See* **Fractals**
Sets (Mathematics). *See* **Set theory**
Sets of fractional dimension. *See* **Fractals**
Settlement of land. *See* **Land settlement**
Settlements, Social. *See* **Social settlements**
Seven Years' War, 1756-1763 940.2
    xx **Germany—History—1740-1815**
Seventeen-year locusts. *See* **Cicadas**
Seventeenth century 909.08
    See note under **Nineteenth century.**
    x 1600-1699 (17th century)
Sewage disposal 628.3; 628.4
    See also **Refuse and refuse disposal; Water—**
    Pollution
    x Waste disposal
    xx **Public health; Refuse and refuse disposal; Wa-**
    ter—Pollution
Sewerage 628
    See also **Drainage**
    x Sewers
    xx **Drainage; Drainage, House; Municipal engi-**
    neering; Plumbing; Sanitary engineering
Sewers. *See* **Sewerage**
Sewing 646.2; 646.4
    See also **Dressmaking; Embroidery; Needlework**
    xx **Dressmaking; Home economics; Needlework**
Sex bias. *See* **Sexism**
Sex (Biology) 574.1; 574.3; 612
    Use for materials on the physiological traits that
    distinguish the males and females of a spe-
    cies.
    See also **Androgyny; Reproduction; Reproductive**

Sex—*Continued*

> **system;** also headings beginning with the word **Sexual**
>
> *xx* **Biology; Reproduction**

Sex change. *See* **Transsexuality**

Sex crimes 364.1

> *See also* names of sex crimes, e.g. **Child molesting; Incest; Rape;** etc.
>
> *x* Crimes, Sex; Sexual crimes
>
> *xx* **Crime; Sexual behavior**

Sex customs. *See* **Sexual behavior**

Sex differences (Psychology) 155.3

> *See also* **Androgyny; Sex discrimination; Sex role; Sexual behavior**
>
> *xx* **Androgyny; Sex discrimination; Sexual behavior**

Sex discrimination 305.3; 305.4

> Use for materials on the restriction or denial of rights, privileges, or choice because of one's sex. Materials on prejudicial attitudes toward people because of their sex are entered under **Sexism.**
>
> *See also* **Equal rights amendments; Men—Civil rights; Sex differences (Psychology); Women—Civil rights**
>
> *x* Discrimination, Sex
>
> *xx* **Discrimination; Sex differences (Psychology); Sexism**

Sex education 612; 649

> *See also* **Sexual hygiene**
>
> *x* Human life education; Sex instruction
>
> *xx* **Family life education; Sexual hygiene**

Sex in art. *See* **Erotic art**

Sex instruction. *See* **Sex education**

Sex organs. *See* **Reproductive system**

Sex (Psychology). *See* **Sexual behavior**

Sex role 305.3; 305.4

> Use for materials on the patterns of attitudes and behavior that are regarded as appropriate to one sex rather than the other.
>
> *See also* **Androgyny; Sexism; Transsexuality**
>
> *x* Female role; Gender identity; Male role
>
> *xx* **Androgyny; Role conflict; Sex differences (Psychology); Social role**

Sexism 305.3; 305.4

> See note under **Sex discrimination.**
>
> *See also* **Sex discrimination**
>
> *x* Sex bias
>
> *xx* **Attitude (Psychology); Prejudices; Sex role; Sexual behavior**

Sexual behavior 155.3

> *See also* **Androgyny; Homosexuality; Sex crimes; Sex differences (Psychology); Sexism; Sexual ethics; Sexual harassment;** also people and animals with the subdivision *Sexual behavior,* e.g. **College students—Sexual behavior;** etc.
>
> *x* Sex customs; Sex (Psychology); Sexuality
>
> *xx* **Sex differences (Psychology); Sexual ethics**

Sexual crimes. *See* **Sex crimes**

Sexual ethics 176
    See also

Adultery	**Prostitution**
Artificial insemination,	**Sexual behavior**
Human	**Sexual hygiene**
Birth control	**Unmarried couples**
Free love	

    x Ethics, Sexual
    xx **Sexual behavior; Social ethics**
Sexual harassment 331.13; 344; 370.19
    Use for materials on unsolicited and unwelcome
        sexual behavior that interferes with study,
        work or everyday activities and creates an
        intimidating or offensive environment.
    See also types of sexual harassment, e.g. **Child
        molesting;** etc.
    x Harassment, Sexual
    xx **Sexual behavior**
Sexual hygiene 613.9
    See also **Birth control; Prostitution; Sex educa-
        tion; Venereal diseases**
    x Hygiene, Sexual; Hygiene, Social; Social hy-
        giene
    xx **Sex education; Sexual ethics**)
Sexuality. *See* **Sexual behavior**
Shade gardens. *See* **Gardening in the shade**
Shades and shadows 741.2
    x Light and shade; Shadows
    xx **Drawing**
Shadow pantomimes and plays 791.5
    xx **Amateur theater; Pantomimes; Puppets and
        puppet plays; Shadow pictures; Theater**
Shadow pictures 793
    See also **Shadow pantomimes and plays**
    x Hand shadows; Shadowplay
    xx **Amusements**
Shadowplay. *See* **Shadow pictures**
Shadows. *See* **Shades and shadows**
Shady gardens. *See* **Gardening in the shade**
Shaft sinking. *See* **Boring**
Shakers 289
Shakespeare in fiction, drama, poetry, etc. *See*
           **Shakespeare, William, 1564-1616—Drama;
           Shakespeare, William, 1564-1616—Fiction;
           Shakespeare, William, 1564-1616—Poetry**
Shakespeare, William, 1564-1616 822.3
    When applicable, the following subdivisions
        may be used for other voluminous authors,
        e.g. **Dante; Goethe;** etc. The following sub-
        jects are to be used for materials about
        Shakespeare and about his writings. The
        texts of his plays, etc. are not given subject
        headings.
**Shakespeare, William, 1564-1616—Adaptations
    822.3**
    x Shakespeare, William, 1564-1616—
        Paraphrases
**Shakespeare, William, 1564-1616—Anniversaries
    822.3**

Shakespeare, William, 1564-1616—Authorship
822.3
x Bacon-Shakespeare controversy
Shakespeare, William, 1564-1616—Bibliography
016.8223
xx **Bibliography**
Shakespeare, William, 1564-1616—Biography 92; B
**Shakespeare, William, 1564-1616—Biography—
Psychology 92; B**
Shakespeare, William, 1564-1616—Characters
822.3
xx **Characters and characteristics in literature**
Shakespeare, William, 1564-1616—Collected works
822.3
x Collections of literature
Shakespeare, William, 1564-1616—Comedies 822.3
Use for criticism, etc. of the comedies, not for
the texts of the plays.
Shakespeare, William, 1564-1616—Concordances
822.303
x Concordances; Shakespeare, William, 1564-
1616—Indexes
xx **Shakespeare, William, 1564-1616—
Dictionaries**
**Shakespeare, William, 1564-1616—Contemporary
England 822.3; 942**
**Shakespeare, William, 1564-1616—Criticism, inter-
pretation, etc. 822.3**
Use for criticism of the plays in general; criti-
cism of the comedies is entered under
**Shakespeare, William, 1564-1616—
Comedies;** criticism of the tragedies under
**Shakespeare, William, 1564-1616—
Tragedies;** criticism of an individual play is
entered under **Shakespeare, William, 1564-
1616,** followed by the title of the play.
xx **Criticism**
Shakespeare, William, 1564-1616—Dictionaries
822.303
See also **Shakespeare, William, 1564-1616—
Concordances**
x Shakespeare, William, 1564-1616—Indexes
Shakespeare, William, 1564-1616—Discography
789.9; 822.3
x Discography
**Shakespeare, William, 1564-1616—Drama 812;
822; etc.**
x Shakespeare in fiction, drama, poetry, etc.
**Shakespeare, William, 1564-1616—Dramatic pro-
duction 822.3**
x Shakespeare, William, 1564-1616—Stage setting and scenery
**Shakespeare, William, 1564-1616—Fiction 813;
823; etc.; Fic**
x Shakespeare in fiction, drama, poetry, etc.
Shakespeare, William, 1564-1616—Filmography
822.3
x Filmography

Shakespeare, William, 1564-1616—Histories 822.3
  Use for criticism, etc. of the histories, not for the
      texts of the plays.
Shakespeare, William, 1564-1616—Indexes. *See*
      **Shakespeare, William, 1564-1616—
      Concordances; Shakespeare, William, 1564-
      1616—Dictionaries**
**Shakespeare, William, 1564-1616—Knowledge
      822.3**
  Use for materials on Shakespeare's knowledge or
      treatment of specific subjects.
  May be subdivided by subject, e.g. **Shakespeare,
      William, 1564-1616—Knowledge—Animals;**
      etc.
Shakespeare, William, 1564-1616—Music. *See*
      **Shakespeare, William, 1564-1616—Songs
      and music**
Shakespeare, William,
      1564-1616—Paraphrases. *See* **Shake-
      speare, William, 1564-1616—Adaptations**
**Shakespeare, William, 1564-1616—Parodies, traves-
      ties, etc. 822.3**
  xx **Parodies**
**Shakespeare, William, 1564-1616—Poetry 811; 821;
      etc.**
  x Shakespeare in fiction, drama, poetry, etc.
  xx **Poetry**
**Shakespeare, William, 1564-1616—Portraits
      822.3022**
  xx **Portraits**
**Shakespeare, William, 1564-1616—Quotations
      822.3**
**Shakespeare, William, 1564-1616—Religion and eth-
      ics 822.3**
**Shakespeare, William, 1564-1616—Songs and music
      822.3**
  x Shakespeare, William, 1564-1616—Music
Shakespeare, William, 1564-1616—Sonnets 822.3
**Shakespeare, William, 1564-1616—Stage history
      792; 822.3**
  xx **Theater**
Shakespeare, William, 1564-1616—Stage setting and
      scenery. *See* **Shakespeare, William, 1564-
      1616—Dramatic production**
Shakespeare, William, 1564-1616—Style. *See*
      **Shakespeare, William, 1564-1616—
      Technique**
**Shakespeare, William, 1564-1616—Technique
      822.3**
  x Shakespeare, William, 1564-1616—Style
Shakespeare, William, 1564-1616—Tragedies 822.3
  Use for criticism, etc. of the tragedies, not for
      the texts of the plays
Shape. *See* **Size and shape**
Sharecropping. *See* **Farm tenancy**
Shared custody. *See* **Child custody**
Shared housing 363.5
  Use for materials on individuals who share
      housing because of economic necessity,
      loneliness, etc.

Shared housing—*Continued*

    See also **Unmarried couples**

    x Families, Nonrelated; Home sharing; Mingles housing; Nonfamily households; Non-related families

  xx **Housing**

Shares of stock.   *See* **Stocks**

Sharing of jobs.   *See* **Job sharing**

Sheep 599.73; 636.3

  xx **Livestock**

Sheet metalwork 671.8

    See also **Plate metalwork**

    x Press working of metal

  xx **Metalwork**

Sheffield plate 739.2

  xx **Plate**

Shellfish 594; 641.3

    See also **Crabs; Crustacea; Lobsters; Mollusks**

Shells 564; 594

    See also **Mollusks**

    x Conchology; Sea shells

  xx **Mollusks**

Shells (Projectiles).   *See* **Projectiles**

Shelterbelts.   *See* **Windbreaks**

Shelters, Air raid.   *See* **Air raid shelters**

Shelters, Animal.   *See* **Animal shelters**

Shinto 299

  xx **Religions**

Ship building.   *See* **Shipbuilding**

Ship models.   *See* **Ships—Models**

Ship pilots.   *See* **Pilots and pilotage**

Shipbuilding 623.8

    See also **Boatbuilding; Marine engines; Naval architecture; Ships; Ships—Models; Steamboats**

    x Architecture, Naval; Marine architecture; Ship building; Ships—Construction

  xx **Boatbuilding; Industrial arts; Naval architecture; Naval art and science**

Shipping (May subdiv. geog.) **386; 387**

    See also **Harbors; Inland navigation; Insurance, Marine; Maritime law; Merchant marine; Territorial waters**

    x Marine transportation; Ocean—Economic aspects; Ocean transportation; Sea transportation; Water transportation

  xx **Merchant marine; Transportation**

Shipping—United States 386; 387

    x United States—Shipping

Ships 387.2; 623.8

    See also **Boats and boating; Hospital ships; Merchant marine; Navies; Navigation; Sailing;** also types of ships and vessels, e.g. **Clipper ships; Steamboats; Submarines; Warships; Yachts and yachting;** etc.; and names of individual ships

    x Vessels (Ships)

  xx **Boats and boating; Naval architecture; Shipbuilding**

Ships—Construction.   *See* **Shipbuilding**

Ships in art. *See* **Marine painting**
Ships—Models 623.8
    x Ship models
    xx **Machinery—Models; Models and model mak-
        ing; Shipbuilding**
Shipwrecks 910.4
    See also **Salvage; Survival (after airplane acci-
        dents, shipwrecks, etc.);** also names of
        wrecked ships
    x Marine disasters; Wrecks
    xx **Accidents; Adventure and adventurers; Disas-
        ters; Navigation; Salvage; Voyages and trav-
        els**
Shoe industry 338.4; 685
    xx **Leather industry and trade; Shoes**
Shoes 391; 646
    See also **Shoe industry**
    x Boots; Footwear
    xx **Clothing and dress**
Shooting 799.3
    Use for materials on the use of firearms. Materi-
        als on shooting game are entered under
        Hunting.
    See also **Archery; Decoys (Hunting); Firearms;
        Hunting**
    x Gunning
    xx **Firearms; Game and game birds; Hunting**
Shooting stars. *See* **Meteors**
Shop management. *See* **Factory management**
Shop practice. *See* **Machine shop practice**
Shop windows. *See* **Show windows**
Shoppers' guides. *See* **Consumer education; Shop-
    ping**
Shopping 640.73
    Use for materials on buying by the consumer.
        Materials on buying by government agencies
        and by commercial and industrial enter-
        prises are entered under **Buying.**
    See also **Buying; Consumer education; Consum-
        ers**
    x Buyers' guides; Marketing (Home economics);
        Purchasing; Shoppers' guides
    xx **Buying; Consumer education; Home economics**
Shopping centers and malls 658.8
    x Malls, Shopping; Shopping malls
    xx **Retail trade**
Shopping malls. *See* **Shopping centers and malls**
Shops, Machine. *See* **Machine shops**
Short plays. *See* **One act plays**
Short stories 808.83; 813; etc.; Fic
    May be used for collections of short stories by
        one author as well as for collections by sev-
        eral authors. Materials on the technique of
        writing short stories are entered under **Short
        story.**
    x Collections of literature; Stories
    xx **English literature; Literature—Collected
        works**
Short stories—Indexes 808.83
    xx **Indexes**

Short story 808.3
>Use for materials on the technique of short story writing. Collections of stories are entered under **Short stories.**
>
>*See also* **Storytelling**
>
>*xx* **Authorship; Fiction; Literature; Storytelling**

Short take off and landing aircraft 629.133
>*x* STOL aircraft
>
>*xx* **Jet planes**

Shorthand 653
>*See also* **Abbreviations**
>
>*x* Stenography
>
>*xx* **Abbreviations; Business education; Office practice; Writing**

Shortwave radio. *See* **Radio, Shortwave**

Shotguns 799
>*x* Guns
>
>*xx* **Firearms**

Show business. *See* **Performing arts**

Show windows 659.1
>*x* Shop windows; Window dressing
>
>*xx* **Advertising; Decoration and ornament; Windows**

Showers (Parties) 793.2
>*xx* **Parties**

Shows, Craft. *See* **Craft shows**

Shrines (May subdiv. geog.) **291.3; 726**
>*See also* **Miracles; Pilgrims and pilgrimages; Saints; Tombs**
>
>*xx* **Pilgrims and pilgrimages; Saints**

Shrubs 582.1; 635.9
>*See also* **Evergreens; Landscape gardening; Plants, Ornamental**
>
>*xx* **Botany; Landscape gardening; Trees**

Shuttles, Space. *See* **Space shuttles**

Shyness. *See* **Bashfulness**

Siblings. *See* **Brothers and sisters**

Sick 362.1
>*See also*

Cookery for the sick	**Home nursing**
Diseases	**Hospitals**
First aid	**Nursing**
Health resorts, spas, etc.	**Terminally ill**

>*x* Invalids; Patients
>
>*xx* **Diseases; Handicapped; Home nursing; Nursing**

Sickness. *See* **Diseases**

Sickness insurance. *See* **Insurance, Health**

Sidereal system. *See* **Stars**

Sieges. *See* **Battles**

Sight. *See* **Vision**

Sight saving books. *See* **Large print books**

Sign boards. *See* **Signs and signboards**

Sign language. *See* **Deaf—Means of communication; Indians of North America—Sign language**

Sign painting 667
>*See also* **Alphabets; Lettering; Signs and signboards**
>
>*xx* **Advertising; Lettering; Painting, Industrial;**

Sign painting—*Continued*
        Signs and signboards
Signals and signaling 384
    See also **Flags; Railroads—Signaling; Sonar**
     x Coastal signals; Fog signals; Military signaling;
        Naval signaling
    xx **Communication; Flags; Military art and sci-**
        ence; Naval art and science; Navigation;
        Signs and symbols
Signboards. *See* **Signs and signboards**
Signets. *See* **Seals (Numismatics)**
Signs (Advertising). *See* **Electric signs; Signs and**
     signboards
Signs and signboards 659.13
    See also **Electric signs; Posters; Sign painting**
     x Billboards; Guide posts; Road signs; Sign
        boards; Signboards; Signs (Advertising)
    xx **Advertising; Posters; Sign painting**
Signs and symbols 001.56
    See also **Abbreviations; Ciphers; Cryptography;**
      Heraldry; Semiotics; Signals and signaling;
      Symbolism
     x Symbols
    xx **Abbreviations; Semiotics; Symbolism**
Signs, Electric. *See* **Electric signs**
Silage and silos 631.2
     x Ensilage; Silos
    xx **Feeds; Forage plants**
Silent films. *See* **Motion pictures, Silent**
Silent motion pictures. *See* **Motion pictures, Silent**
Silk 677
    See also **Silkworms**
    xx **Fibers**
Silk, Artificial. *See* **Rayon**
Silk screen printing 764
     x Screen printing; Serigraphy
    xx **Color printing; Stencil work; Textile printing**
Silkworms 638
     x Cocoons
    xx **Insects, Injurious and beneficial; Moths; Silk**
Silos. *See* **Silage and silos**
Silver 332.4; 669
    See also **Coinage; Jewelry; Money; Silverware;**
      Silverwork
     x Bimetallism; Bullion
    xx **Coinage; Monetary policy; Money; Precious**
      metals
Silver articles. *See* **Silverwork**
Silver mines and mining 622
    See also **Prospecting**
Silver work. *See* **Silverwork**
Silversmithing. *See* **Silverwork**
Silverware 642; 739.2
     x Flatware, Silver
    xx **Decorative arts; Silver; Silverwork; Tableware**
Silverwork 739.2
    See also **Jewelry; Plate; Silverware**
     x Silver articles; Silver work; Silversmithing
    xx **Art metalwork; Jewelry; Metalwork; Silver**

Sin   170; 231; 241
>   *See also* **Free will and determinism**
>   *xx* **Christian ethics; Ethics; Good and evil; Salva-
>   tion; Theology**

Sinai Campaign, 1956   956
>   *x* Anglo-French intervention in Egypt, 1956;
>   Arab-Israel War, 1956; Israel-Arab War,
>   1956
>   *xx* **Egypt—History**

Singers   780.92; 784.092; 920
>   *xx* **Musicians**

Singing   784.9
>   *See also* **Choirs (Music); Respiration; School
>   songbooks; Vocal music; Voice**
>   *x* School music; Vocal culture; Voice culture
>   *xx* **Choirs (Music); Vocal music; Voice**

Singing games   796.1
>   *xx* **Games**

Singing societies.   *See* **Choral societies**

Single men   155.6; 305.3
>   *x* Men, Single; Unmarried men
>   *xx* **Men; Single people**

Single parent family   306.8
>   *See also* **Children of divorced parents; Unmarried
>   mothers; Widows**
>   *x* One parent family; Parents, Single; Parents
>   without partners
>   *xx* **Family; Parenting, Part-time; Widows**

Single people   155.6; 305.3; 305.4
>   *See also* **Single men; Single women; Unmarried
>   couples**
>   *x* People, Single; Persons, Single; Unmarried
>   people

Single rail railroads.   *See* **Monorail railroads**

Single women   155.6; 305.4
>   *See also* **Unmarried mothers; Widows**
>   *x* Unmarried women; Women, Single
>   *xx* **Single people; Women**

Sirius   523.8
>   *xx* **Stars**

Sisterhoods.   *See* **Religious orders for women**

Sisters and brothers.   *See* **Brothers and sisters**

Sisters (in religious orders, congregations, etc.).   *See*
>   **Nuns**

Sit-down strikes.   *See* **Strikes and lockouts**

Site oriented art.   *See* **Earthworks (Art)**

Six Day War, 1967.   *See* **Israel-Arab War, 1967**

Sixteenth century   909.08
>   See note under **Nineteenth century.**
>   *See also* **Reformation**
>   *x* 1500-1599 (16th century)
>   *xx* **Reformation; Renaissance**

Size and shape   516
>   *x* Large and small; Shape; Small and large
>   *xx* **Concepts; Perception**

Skating.   *See* **Ice skating; Roller skating**

Skeletal remains.   *See* **Anthropometry**

Skeleton   591.4; 611
>   Use for materials on the human or animal skele-
>   ton.

Skeleton—*Continued*
> *See also* **Bones**
> *xx* **Bones**

Skepticism 149; 211
> *See also* **Agnosticism; Belief and doubt; Truth**
> *x* Scepticism; Unbelief
> *xx* **Agnosticism; Atheism; Belief and doubt;**
>   **Faith; Free thought; Philosophy; Rational-**
>   **ism; Religion; Truth**

Sketching. *See* **Drawing**

Skiing, Snow. *See* **Skis and skiing**

Skiing, Water. *See* **Water skiing**

Skilled workers. *See* **Labor**

Skills, Life. *See* **Life skills**

Skin 611; 612

Skin—Diseases 616.5
> *See also* names of skin diseases, e.g. **Acne;** etc.
> *x* Dermatitis
> *xx* **Diseases**

Skin diving 797.2
> Use for free diving with masks, fins, and snor-
> kel.
> *See also* **Scuba diving; Undersea research sta-**
>   **tions; Underwater exploration**
> *x* Diving, Skin; Free diving; Frogmen and frog-
>   women; Snorkeling; Underwater swimming
> *xx* **Diving; Diving, Submarine; Oceanography—**
>   **Research; Salvage; Underwater exploration;**
>   **Water sports**

Skin garments. *See* **Leather garments**

Skins. *See* **Hides and skins**

Skis and skiing 796.9
> *See also* **Water skiing**
> *x* Skiing, Snow
> *xx* **Winter sports**

Skits 791
> *x* Entertainments

Sky diving. *See* **Skydiving**

Sky hijacking. *See* **Hijacking of airplanes**

Sky laboratories. *See* **Space stations**

Skydiving 797.5
> *x* Sky diving
> *xx* **Aeronautical sports**

Skyjacking. *See* **Hijacking of airplanes**

Skyscrapers 690; 725
> *x* High rise buildings
> *xx* **Architecture; Building, Iron and steel; Indus-**
>   **trial buildings; Office buildings**

Skyscrapers—Earthquake effects 690; 725
> *xx* **Earthquakes**

Slander (Law). *See* **Libel and slander**

Slang. *See* subjects with the subdivision *Slang,* e.g.
>   **English language—Slang;** etc.

Slanted journalism. *See* **Journalism—Objectivity**

Slave trade 380.1
> *xx* **International law; Slavery; Slavery—United**
>   **States**

Slavery (May subdiv. geog.) **326; 331.6**
> *See also* **Peonage; Slave trade**
> *x* Abolition of slavery; Antislavery; Compulsory

Slavery—*Continued*

    labor; Emancipation of slaves; Forced labor; Servitude

  xx **Contract labor; Freedom; Labor; Sociology**

Slavery—United States 305.8; 326

  See also **Abolitionists; Blacks; Slave trade; Southern States—History; State rights; Underground railroad**

  x Emancipation of slaves

  xx **Blacks; Underground railroad; United States—History—1861-1865, Civil War**

Slavery—United States—Fiction Fic

  x Stories

  xx **Fiction; Historical fiction**

Sleds and sledding 796.9

  xx **Winter sports**

Sleep 154.6; 613.7

  See also **Bedtime; Dreams; Insomnia**

  xx **Brain; Dreams; Health; Hygiene; Insomnia; Mind and body; Psychology, Physiological; Rest; Subconsciousness**

Sleeplessness. *See* **Insomnia**

Sleight of hand. *See* **Magic**

Slide projectors. *See* **Projectors**

Slide rule 510.28

  xx **Calculators; Logarithms; Measuring instruments**

Slides (Photography) 778.2

  See also **Filmstrips**

  x Color slides; Lantern slides; Photographic slides

  xx **Filmstrips; Photography**

Slow learning children 155.4

  Use for materials on children who have between average and mentally deficient intelligence and whose social behavior is less than age level standards.

  See also **Individualized instruction; Learning disabilities; Mentally handicapped children**

  x Children, Retarded; Retarded children

  xx **Exceptional children; Mentally handicapped children**

Slum clearance. *See* **Urban renewal**

Slumber songs. *See* **Lullabies**

Small and large. *See* **Size and shape**

Small arms. *See* **Firearms**

Small business 338.6

  Use for materials on small independent enterprises as contrasted with "big business".

  See also **Entrepreneurs; Home business**

  x Business, Small

  xx **Business; Self-employed**

Small loans. *See* **Personal loans**

Smallpox 616.9

  See also **Vaccination**

  xx **Communicable diseases; Epidemics; Medicine—Practice; Therapeutics; Vaccination**

Smell 152.1

  See also **Nose**

  xx **Senses and sensation**

Smelting 669
> *See also* **Blast furnaces; Electrometallurgy; Metallurgy; Ore dressing**
> *xx* **Furnaces; Metallurgy**

Smoke prevention 363.7; 628.5
> *See also* **Fuel; Furnaces**
> *x* Prevention of smoke

Smoke stacks. *See* **Chimneys**

Smokeless powder. *See* **Gunpowder**

Smoking 178; 613.8
> *See also* **Cigarettes; Cigars; Tobacco; Tobacco habit; Tobacco pipes**
> *xx* **Tobacco**

Smuggling 364.1
> *x* Contraband trade
> *xx* **Crime; Tariff**

Snakes 597.96
> *See also* names of specific snakes, e.g. **Rattlesnakes;** etc.
> *x* Serpents; Vipers
> *xx* **Reptiles**

Snorkeling. *See* **Skin diving**

Snow 551.57
> *xx* **Meteorology; Rain and rainfall; Storms; Water; Weather**

Snowmobiles 629.2
> *xx* **All terrain vehicles; Vehicles**

Soap 668
> *See also* **Detergents, Synthetic**
> *xx* **Cleaning; Cleaning compounds**

Soap box derbies 796.6
> *x* Racing

Soap carving. *See* **Soap sculpture**

Soap sculpture 736
> *x* Soap carving
> *xx* **Modeling; Sculpture**

Soaring flight. *See* **Gliding and soaring**

Sobriquets. *See* **Nicknames**

Soccer 796.334
> *xx* **Ball games; College sports; Football**

Social action 302
> *See also* **Social work;** also subjects with the subdivision *Citizen participation,* e.g. **City planning—United States—Citizen participation;** etc.
> *x* Action, Social; Activism, Social
> *xx* **Social policy; Social problems; Social work**

Social adjustment 158; 303.3
> *See also* **Socially handicapped**
> *x* Adjustment, Social
> *xx* **Human behavior; Human relations; Social psychology**

Social alienation. *See* **Alienation (Social psychology)**

Social anthropology. *See* **Ethnology**

Social aspects. *See* subjects with the subdivision *Social aspects,* e.g. **Genetic engineering—Social aspects;** etc.

Social behavior. *See* **Human behavior**

Social case work   361.3
> *See also* **Counseling; Parole; Probation**
> *x* Case work, Social; Family social work
> *xx* **Counseling; Social work**

Social change   303.4; 909
> *See also* **Community development; Moderniza-**
> **tion; Sociobiology; Urbanization**
> *x* Change, Social; Cultural change; Social evolu-
> tion
> *xx* **Anthropology; Evolution; Progress; Social sci-**
> **ences; Sociology**

Social classes   305.5; 323.3
> *See also* **Aristocracy; Class consciousness; Elite**
> **(Social sciences); Labor; Middle classes; No-**
> **bility; Upper classes**
> *x* Class distinction; Rank; Social distinctions
> *xx* **Caste; Equality; Manners and customs; Social**
> **conflict; Sociology**

Social conditions   909
> Use for general materials relating to several or
> all of the following topics: labor, poverty,
> education, health, housing, recreation, mo-
> ral conditions.
> *See also*

Cost of living	**Social movements**
Counter culture	**Social problems**
Economic conditions	**Social surveys**
Labor	**Standard of living**
Moral conditions	**Urbanization**
Quality of life	

> also names of groups of people and names of
> countries, cities, etc. with the subdivision
> *Social conditions,* e.g. **Indians of North**
> **America—Social conditions; Jews—Social**
> **conditions; Blacks—Social conditions;**
> **United States—Social conditions; Chicago**
> **(Ill.)—Social conditions;** etc.
> *x* Social history
> *xx* **Social ethics; Sociology**

Social conflict   303.6
> *See also* **Conflict of generations; Role conflict;**
> **Social classes**
> *x* Class conflict; Class struggle; Conflict, Social
> *xx* **Social psychology; Sociology**

Social conformity.   *See* **Conformity**

Social customs.   *See* **Manners and customs;** and
> names of ethnic groups, countries, cities,
> etc. with the subdivision *Social life and cus-*
> *toms,* e.g. **Indians of North America—**
> **Social life and customs; Jews—Social life**
> **and customs; United States—Social life and**
> **customs;** etc.

Social democracy.   *See* **Socialism**

Social distinctions.   *See* **Social classes**

Social drinking.   *See* **Drinking of alcoholic bever-**
> **ages**

Social ecology.   *See* **Human ecology**

Social equality.   *See* **Equality**

Social ethics 177
   See also
   Bioethics   **Political ethics**
   Citizenship   **Sexual ethics**
   Crime   **Social conditions**
   Friendship   **Social problems**
     x Ethics, Social
     xx **Ethics; Social problems**
Social evolution. *See* **Social change**
Social group work **361.3; 361.4; 362**
     x Group work, Social
     xx **Associations; Clubs; Social work**
Social groups **302.3**
   See also **Elite (Social sciences); Leadership;**
      Problem solving, Group; Social psychology;
      Social values
     x Group dynamics; Groups, Social
     xx **Sociology**
Social history. *See* **Social conditions**
Social hygiene. *See* **Prostitution; Public health;**
      Sexual hygiene; Venereal diseases
Social insurance. *See* **Social security**
Social learning. *See* **Socialization**
Social life and customs. *See* **Manners and customs;**
      and names of ethnic groups, countries, cit-
      ies, etc. with the subdivision *Social life and*
      customs, e.g. **Indians of North America—**
      Social life and customs; Jews—Social life
      and customs, United States—Social life and
      customs; etc.
Social medicine (May subdiv. geog.) **362.1**
      Use for materials on the study of social, genetic,
      and environmental influences on human
      disease and disability, as well as the promo-
      tion of health measures to protect both the
      individual and the community.
   See also **Hospices; Medical ethics**
     x Medical care—Social aspects; Medical sociol-
      ogy; Medicine, Social; Medicine—Social as-
      pects
     xx **Medical ethics; Public health; Public welfare;**
      Sociology
Social movements **303.4**
   See also **Anti-apartheid movement; Antinuclear**
      movement; Sanctuary movement (Refugee
      aid)
     xx **Social conditions; Social problems; Social psy-**
      chology
Social planning. *See* **Social policy**
Social policy **361.6**
   See also **Economic policy; Land reform; Social**
      action; also names of countries, cities, etc.
      with the subdivision *Social policy,* e.g.
      United States—Social policy; etc.
     x National planning; Planning, National; Social
      planning; State planning
     xx **Economic policy**

Social problems   361; 363
> *See also*

Charities	**Men—Social conditions**
Children—Employment	**Prostitution**
Community centers	**Public health**
Crime	**Race discrimination**
Discrimination	**Race relations**
Divorce	**Social action**
Ethnic relations	**Social ethics**
Eugenics	**Social movements**
Homeless people	**Social surveys**
Housing	**Standard of living**
Illegitimacy	**Substance abuse**
Immigration and emigra-	**Suicide**
tion	**Unemployed**

Juvenile delinquency
> *x* Reform, Social; Social reform; Social welfare
> *xx* **Social conditions; Social ethics; Sociology**

Social problems and the church.   *See* **Church and social problems**

Social problems in education.   *See* **Educational sociology**

Social psychology   302
> *See also*

Alienation (Social psychol-	**Interviewing**
ogy)	**National characteristics**
Attitude (Psychology)	**Political psychology**
Class consciousness	**Psychology, Applied**
Crowds	**Social adjustment**
Discrimination	**Social conflict**
Ethnopsychology	**Social movements**
Human relations	**Violence**

> *x* Mass psychology; Psychology, Social
> *xx* **Crowds; Ethnopsychology; Psychology; Social groups; Sociology**

Social reform.   *See* **Social problems**

Social role   302
> *See also* **Role conflict; Role playing; Sex role**
> *x* Role, Social

Social sciences   300
> Use for general and comprehensive materials dealing with the various branches of the social sciences, such as sociology, political science, economics, etc.
> *See also* **Cross cultural studies; Economics; Political science; Social change; Sociology**
> *x* Social studies

Social security   368.4
> *See also* **Insurance, Health; Insurance, Unemployment; Old age pensions; Workers' compensation**
> *x* Insurance, Social; Insurance, State and compulsory; Insurance, Workers'; Labor—Insurance; Security, Social; Social insurance; State and insurance
> *xx* **Pensions**

Social service.   *See* **Social work**

Social settlements   361.7
> *See also* **Boys' clubs; Community centers; Girls' clubs; Playgrounds;** also names of settle-

Social settlements—*Continued*

    ments, e.g. **Hull House;** etc.

   x Church settlements; Neighborhood centers; Settlements, Social

  xx **Charities; Social work; Welfare work in industry**

Social studies. *See* **Geography; History; Social sciences**

Social surveys (May subdiv. geog.) **301**

    Use for materials on the methods employed in conducting surveys of social and economic conditions of communities and also for surveys of individual regions or cities. In the latter case a second heading may be used for the name of a region or city followed by the subdivision *Social condtions.*

  See also **Educational surveys**

   x Community surveys; Surveys

  xx **City planning; Regional planning; Social conditions; Social problems; Sociology**

Social surveys—United States 301

   x United States—Social surveys

Social values 303.3

    Use for materials on the principles and standards of human interaction within a particular group.

  See also **Quality of life**

   x Group values

  xx **Conformity; Human relations; Quality of life; Social groups; Values**

Social welfare. *See* **Charities; Public welfare; Social problems; Social work**

Social work 361.3

    Use for materials on the methods employed in welfare work, public or private. Materials on privately supported welfare activities are entered under **Charities.** Materials on tax-supported welfare activities are entered under **Public welfare.**

  See also

Charities	**Public welfare**
Community organization	**Social action**
Crisis centers	**Social case work**
Group homes	**Social group work**
Hotlines (Telephone counseling)	**Social settlements**
	Welfare work in industry

   x Philanthropy; Social service; Social welfare; Welfare work

  xx **Social action**

Social work with the elderly 362.6

    Use same form for social work with other classes of people.

  xx **Elderly**

Socialism (May subdiv. geog.) **320.5; 335**

  See also

Capitalism	**Individualism**
Communism	**Industry—Government policy**
Dialectical materialism	
Equality	**Labor**
Government ownership	**Labor unions**

Socialism—*Continued*

> **National socialism**   **Syndicalism**
> **Proletariat**   **Utopias**
>
> *x* Collectivism; Marxism; Social democracy
> *xx* **Capitalism; Communism; Cooperation; Democracy; Economics; Equality; Individualism; Labor; National socialism; Political science; Sociology; Syndicalism**

Socialism—United States 320.5; 335

> *x* United States—Socialism

Socialization 303.3

> Use for materials on the process by which individuals acquire group values and learn to function effectively in society.
>
> *See also* **Peer pressure**
> *x* Children—Socialization; Social learning
> *xx* **Acculturation; Child rearing; Education; Sociology**

Socialization of industry. *See* **Government ownership; Industry—Government policy**

Socialized medicine. *See* **Charities, Medical; Insurance, Health; Insurance, Hospitalization; Medicine, State**

Socially handicapped 362

> *x* Culturally deprived; Culturally handicapped; Disadvantaged; Underprivileged
> *xx* **Handicapped; Social adjustment**

Socially handicapped children 362.7

> *x* Culturally deprived children; Culturally handicapped children; Disadvantaged children; Underprivileged children
> *xx* **Handicapped children**

Socials. *See* **Church entertainments**

Societies 060

> Use for general materials about societies, etc. The headings enumerated below represent various types of societies and associations. Add others as needed. Materials about, and publications of, societies devoted to specific subjects are entered under the subject with the subdivision *Societies,* e.g. **Agriculture—Societies;** etc.
>
> *See also*
>
> **Associations**   **Labor unions**
> **Boys' clubs**   **Men—Societies**
> **Choral societies**   **Parents' and teachers' associations**
> **Clubs**
> **Cooperative societies**   **Secret societies**
> **Educational associations**   **Women—Societies**
> **Girls' clubs**
>
> also general subjects with the subdivision *Societies,* e.g. **Agriculture—Societies;** etc.; and names of individual societies
> *x* Learned societies
> *xx* **Associations; Clubs**

Societies, Cooperative. *See* **Cooperative societies**

Society and art. *See* **Art and society**

Society and language. *See* **Sociolinguistics**

Society, Nonliterate folk 306

> *See also* **Man, Nonliterate; Nomads**

Society, Nonliterate folk—*Continued*

    x Folk society, Nonliterate; Illiterate societies;
        Nonliterate folk society; Preliterate society;
        Primitive society; Society, Primitive

    xx **Civilization; Ethnology; Sociology**

Society of Friends 289.6

    x Friends, Society of; Quakers

    xx **Congregationalism**

Society of Jesus. *See* **Jesuits**

Society, Primitive. *See* **Society, Nonliterate folk**

Society, Upper. *See* **Upper classes**

Sociobiology 304.2; 304.5

    Use for materials on the biological basis of so-
        cial behavior, especially as transmitted ge-
        netically.

    x Biology—Social aspects; Biosociology

    xx **Psychology, Comparative; Social change**

Sociolinguistics 302.2

    Use for materials on the study of the social as-
        pects of language, particularly linguistic be-
        havior as determined by sociocultural fac-
        tors.

    x Language and society; Society and language;
        Sociology and language

    xx **Language and languages; Sociology**

Sociology (May subdiv. by religion adjective form,
        e.g. **Sociology, Christian;** etc.) **301**

    Use for systematic studies on the structure of so-
        ciety. General materials dealing with sociol-
        ogy, political science, economics, etc. are en-
        tered under **Social sciences.**

    See also

Aristocracy	**Race relations**
Cities and towns	**Slavery**
Civilization	**Social change**
Communism	**Social classes**
Educational sociology	**Social conditions**
Equality	**Social conflict**
Ethnic relations	**Social groups**
Ethnopsychology	**Social medicine**
Family	**Social problems**
Heredity	**Social psychology**
Human ecology	**Social surveys**
Immigration and emigra-	**Socialism**
tion	**Socialization**
Individualism	**Society, Nonliterate folk**
Labor	**Sociolinguistics**
Population	**Unemployed**

    xx **Social sciences**

Sociology and language. *See* **Sociolinguistics**

Sociology, Christian 261

    See note under **Church and social problems.**

    See also **Christianity and economics; Liberation
        theology**

    x Christian sociology

    xx **Church and social problems**

Sociology, Educational. *See* **Educational sociology**

Sociology, Rural 307.7

    Use for materials on the discipline of rural soci-
        ology and the theory of social organization

Sociology, Rural—*Continued*
>   in rural areas. Materials on the rural condi-
>   tions of particular regions, countries, cities,
>   etc. are entered under the place with the
>   subdivision *Rural conditions.* Descriptive,
>   popular and literary materials on living in
>   the country are entered under **Country life.**
>   *See also* **Country life; Farm life; Peasantry; Ur-**
>   **banization;** also names of countries, states,
>   etc. with the subdivision *Rural conditions,*
>   e.g. **United States—Rural conditions;** etc.
>   *x* Rural sociology
>   *xx* **Country life; Farm life; Peasantry**

Sociology, Urban 307.7
>   *See also* **Cities and towns; City life; Urban re-**
>   **newal; Urbanization**
>   *x* Urban sociology
>   *xx* **Cities and towns**

Sodium content of food. *See* **Food—Sodium con-**
tent

Softball 796.357
>   *xx* **Baseball**

Software, Computer. *See* **Computer software**

Soil conservation 631.4
>   *See also* **Erosion; Soil erosion**
>   *x* Conservation of the soil
>   *xx* **Erosion; Natural resources; Soil erosion**

Soil erosion 631.4
>   *See also* **Soil conservation**
>   *x* Top soil loss
>   *xx* **Erosion; Soil conservation**

Soil fertility. *See* **Soils**

Soil mechanics. *See* **Soils (Engineering)**

Soilless agriculture. *See* **Aeroponics; Hydroponics**

Soils 631.4
>   *See also*

Agricultural chemistry	**Fertilizers and manures**
Clay	**Irrigation**
Compost	**Reclamation of land**
Drainage	**Soils (Engineering)**

>   also headings beginning with the word **Soil**
>   *x* Soil fertility
>   *xx* **Agricultural chemistry; Agriculture; Geology,**
>   **Economic**

Soils—Bacteriology 631.4
>   *See also* **Bacteriology, Agricultural**
>   *xx* **Bacteriology, Agricultural; Sanitary engineer-**
>   **ing**

Soils (Engineering) 620.1
>   *x* Earthwork; Soil mechanics
>   *xx* **Foundations; Roads; Soils; Structural engi-**
>   **neering**

Soils, Lunar. *See* **Lunar soil**

Solar batteries 621.31
>   *x* Batteries, Solar; Solar cells; Sun powered bat-
>   teries
>   *xx* **Electric batteries; Photovoltaic power genera-**
>   **tion; Solar radiation**

Solar cells. *See* **Photovoltaic power generation; So-**
lar batteries

Solar eclipses. *See* **Eclipses, Solar**
Solar energy 621.47
> *See also* **Photovoltaic power generation; Solar engines; Solar heating**
> *x* Solar power
> *xx* **Energy resources; Renewable energy resources; Solar radiation; Sun**
Solar engines 621.47
> *xx* **Engines; Solar energy**
Solar heat. *See* **Solar heating**
Solar heating 621.47; 697
> *See also* names of applications, e.g. **Solar homes;** etc.
> *x* Solar heat
> *xx* **Heating; Solar energy**
Solar homes 697; 728
> *xx* **Architecture, Domestic; Houses; Solar heating**
Solar physics. *See* **Sun**
Solar power. *See* **Solar energy**
Solar radiation 621.47
> *See also* **Solar batteries; Solar energy; Sunspots**
> *x* Radiation, Solar; Sun—Radiation
> *xx* **Meteorology; Space environment**
Solar system 523.2
> *See also* **Comets; Earth; Meteors; Moon; Planets; Sun;** also names of planets, e.g. **Saturn (Planet);** etc.
> *xx* **Astronomy; Planets; Stars; Sun**
Solder and soldering 671.5
> *See also* **Alloys; Welding**
> *x* Brazing
> *xx* **Metals; Metalwork; Plumbing; Welding**
Soldiers (May subdiv. geog.) **355-359**
> *See also* **Mercenary soldiers; Missing in action;** also names of countries with the subdivision *Army—Military life,* e.g. **United States. Army—Military life;** etc.
> *x* Army life; Soldiers' life
> *xx* **Armies; Military personnel**
Soldiers' bonus. *See* **Pensions, Military**
Soldiers, Disabled. *See* **Physically handicapped**
Soldiers' handbooks. *See* **United States. Army—Handbooks, manuals, etc.**
Soldiers—Hygiene. *See* **Military health**
Soldiers' life. *See* **Soldiers;** and names of countries with the subdivision *Army—Military life,* e.g. **United States. Army—Military life;** etc.
Soldiers' songs. *See* **War songs**
Soldiers—United States 355-359
> *x* G.I.'s; GIs; United States—Soldiers
Solid geometry. *See* **Geometry**
Solid waste disposal. *See* **Refuse and refuse disposal; Salvage (Waste, etc.)**
Solids 530.4; 531; 536; 541
> *xx* **Chemistry, Physical and theoretical; Physics**
Solitaire (Game) 795.4
> *x* Patience (Game)
Solution achievement. *See* **Problem solving**
Somatology. *See* **Physical anthropology**

Sonar   621.389

   x Echo ranging; Sound navigation

   xx **Signals and signaling**

Sonata   781

   xx **Musical form**

Sonatas   781

   xx **Orchestral music**

Song books.   *See* **Songbooks**

Song writing.   *See* **Composition (Music); Music, Popular (Songs, etc.)—Writing and publishing**

Songbooks   784

   See also **School songbooks**

   x Community songbooks; Song books

   xx **Songs**

Songbooks, School.   *See* **School songbooks**

Songs (May subdiv. geog. adjective form, e.g. **Songs, American;** etc.) **784**

   Use for collections of songs that include both words and music, and for materials about songs. Collections of songs that contain the words but not the music are entered under **Poetry.**

   Names of all types of songs are not included in this list but are to be added as needed.

   See also

Ballads	etc.)
Black songs	**National songs**
Carols	**School songbooks**
Children's songs	**Sea songs**
Folk songs	**Songbooks**
Hymns	**State songs**
Lullabies	**Students' songs**
Music, Popular (Songs,	**War songs**

   also general subjects, names of classes of persons, and of schools, colleges, etc. with the subdivision *Songs and music,* e.g. **Aeronautics—Songs and music; Cowhands—Songs and music; United States Military Academy—Songs and music;** etc.; and names of individual songs

   xx **Poetry—Collected works; Vocal music**

Songs, African   784.7

   x African songs; Folk songs, African; Folk songs, Black (African)

Songs, American   784.7

   See also **Black songs; Folk songs—United States; National songs, American**

   x American songs; United States—Songs

Songs, National.   *See* **National songs**

Songs, Popular.   *See* **Music, Popular (Songs, etc.)**

Songwriters.   *See* **Composers; Lyricists**

Sons and fathers.   *See* **Fathers and sons**

Sons and mothers.   *See* **Mothers and sons**

Soothsaying.   *See* **Divination**

Soporifics.   *See* **Narcotics**

Sorcery.   *See* **Occult sciences; Witchcraft**

Sororities.   *See* **Fraternities and sororities**

Sorrow.   *See* **Joy and sorrow**

Soubriquets.   *See* **Nicknames**

Soul 128; 233

   See also **Immortality; Personality; Psychology; Reincarnation; Spiritual life**

   x Spirit

   xx **Future life; Man (Theology); Personality; Philosophy; Reincarnation**

Sound 534; 620.2

   See also

Architectural acoustics	**Phonetics**
Hearing	**Soundproofing**
Music—Acoustics and	**Sounds**
physics	**Ultrasonics**
Noise	**Vibration**

   x Acoustics

   xx **Music; Music—Acoustics and physics; Physics; Pneumatics; Radiation**

Sound effects 534; 620.2

Sound insulation. *See* **Soundproofing**

Sound navigation. *See* **Sonar**

Sound recording. *See* **Sound—Recording and reproducing**

Sound—Recording and reproducing 621.389

   See also **Compact disc players; High-fidelity sound systems; Intercommunication systems; Stereophonic sound systems;** also methods of recording, e.g. **Magnetic recorders and recording;** etc.

   x Sound recording

   xx **Motion pictures; Phonograph; Radio**

Sound recordings 789

   See also **Talking books**

   x Audiodiscs; Audiorecords; Discography; Discs, Sound; Phonodiscs; Phonograph records; Phonorecords; Recordings, Sound; Records, Phonograph

   xx **Audiovisual education; Audiovisual materials**

Sound waves 534; 620.2

   See also **Ultrasonic waves**

   xx **Vibration; Waves**

Soundproofing 693.8

   x Insulation (Sound); Sound insulation

   xx **Architectural acoustics; Sound**

Sounds 534; 620.2

   xx **Sound**

Soups 641.8

   xx **Cookery**

South Africa 968

   x Africa, South; Republic of South Africa; Union of South Africa

South Africa—History 968

South Africa—Race relations 320.5; 968

   See also **Anti-apartheid movement**

   x Apartheid

   xx **Race relations**

South America 980

   xx **America; Latin America**

South America—Exploration. *See* **America—Exploration**

South American literature. *See* **Latin American literature**

South Atlantic States. *See* **Atlantic States**
South Korea. *See* **Korea (South)**
South Pole 998
  See also **Antarctic regions**
  x Polar expeditions
  xx **Antarctic regions; Polar regions**
South Sea Islands. *See* **Islands of the Pacific**
South (U.S.). *See* **Southern States**
Southeast Asia 915.9; 959
  Use for materials on Southeast Asia including
    Burma, Thailand, Malaysia, Singapore, In-
    donesia, Vietnam, Kampuchia, Laos, and
    the Philippines.
  x Asia, Southeast
Southern Africa. *See* **Africa, Southern**
Southern States 975
  x South (U.S.)
  xx **United States**
Southern States—History 975
  xx **Slavery—United States**
Southwest, New. *See* **Southwestern States**
Southwest, Old. *See* **Old Southwest**
Southwestern States 979
  Use for materials on that part of the United
    States which corresponds roughly with the
    old Spanish province of New Mexico, in-
    cluding the present Arizona, New Mexico,
    southern Colorado, Utah, Nevada, and Cali-
    fornia.
  x Southwest, New
  xx **United States**
Sovereigns. *See* **Kings, queens, rulers, etc.; Monar-
    chy; Roman emperors**
Soviet bloc. *See* **Communist countries**
Soviet invasion of Czechoslovakia. *See* **Czechoslo-
    vakia—History—1968- , Intervention**
Soviet literatures. *See* **Soviet Union—Literatures**
Soviet Union 947
  Materials on the Russian empire or the Union of
    Soviet Socialist Republics are entered under
    Soviet Union, regardless of time period. Ap-
    propriate period subdivisions may be
    added.
  The adjective **Russian** is used to refer to the So-
    viet Union and to the Russian language and
    literature, e.g. **Artificial satellites, Russian;
    Russian literature;** etc. Materials on the cit-
    izens of the Soviet Union are entered under
    Russians.
  See also **Russians**
  x Russia; U.S.S.R.; Union of Soviet Socialist
    Republics; USSR
Soviet Union—Communism. *See* **Communism—
    Soviet Union**
Soviet Union—History 947
Soviet Union—History—1905, Revolution 947.08
Soviet Union—History—1917- 947.084
**Soviet Union—History—1917-1921, Revolution
    947.084**
  x Revolution, Russian; Russian revolution

Soviet Union—History—1917-1921,
   Revolution—*Continued*
   xx **Revolutions**
Soviet Union—History—1925-1953 947.084
Soviet Union—History—1939-1940, War with
   Finland. *See* **Russo-Finnish War, 1939-**
   1940
Soviet Union—History—1953- 947.085
Soviet Union—Literatures 891.7; 894
   Use for materials discussing several of the litera-
      tures of the Soviet Union. Materials discuss-
      ing literature in the Russian language, which
      is the principal state and cultural language
      of the Soviet Union, are entered under
      Russian literature.
   x Literatures of the Soviet Union; Soviet litera-
      tures
Soybean 633.3
   xx **Forage plants**
Space age. *See* **Astronautics and civilization**
Space and time 115
   See also **Fourth dimension; Personal space**
   x Time and space
   xx **Relativity (Physics)**
Space-based weapons. *See* **Space weapons**
Space biology 574.1
   Use for materials on the biology of people, ani-
      mals, and plants while in outer space. Life
      indigenous to outer space is entered under
      Life on other planets.
   See also **Life on other planets**
   x Astrobiology; Bioastronautics; Cosmic biol-
      ogy; Cosmobiology; Exobiology; Extrater-
      restrial life
   xx **Biology; Space sciences**
Space chemistry 523.02
   x Cosmic chemistry; Cosmochemistry
   xx **Chemistry**
Space colonies 999
   Use for materials on communities established in
      space or on natural extraterrestrial bodies.
      Materials on bases established on natural
      extraterrestrial bodies for specific functions
      other that colonization are entered under
      Extraterrestrial bases. Materials on
      manned installations in space or on natural
      extraterrestrial bodies for specific functions,
      such as servicing space ships, are entered
      under **Space stations.**
   See also **Extraterrestrial bases**
   x Colonies, Space; Communities, Space; Outer
      space—Colonies
   xx **Astronautics and civilization; Extraterrestrial**
      bases
Space commercialization. *See* **Space industrializa-**
   tion
Space communication. *See* **Astronautics—**
   Communication systems; Interstellar com-
   munication
Space craft. *See* **Space ships**

Space environment 629.4

See also **Cosmic rays; Solar radiation**

  x Environment, Space; Extraterrestrial environ-
    ment; Space weather

  xx **Astronomy; Outer space**

Space exploration (Astronautics). *See* **Outer
    space—Exploration**

Space flight 629.4

See also

Astrodynamics	**Navigation (Astronautics)**
Astronauts	**Orbital rendezvous (Space**
Extravehicular activity	**flight)**
(Space flight)	**Outer space—Exploration**
Interplanetary voyages	**Space medicine**

  also names of projects, e.g. **Gemini project;** etc.

  x Humans in space; Man in space; Manned
    space flight; People in space; Rocket flight;
    Space flight, Manned; Space travel

  xx **Aeronautics—Flights; Astrodynamics; As-
    tronautics; Interplanetary voyages; Naviga-
    tion (Astronautics); Space medicine**

Space flight—Law and legislation. *See* **Space law**

Space flight, Manned. *See* **Space flight**

Space flight to the moon 629.45

  Use same form for space flight to other planets.

  See also **Apollo project; Moon—Exploration**

  x Flight to the moon; Lunar expeditions; Moon,
    Voyages to; Voyages to the moon

  xx **Astronautics**

Space gardening. *See* **Aeroponics**

Space heaters 644

  See also **Fireplaces; Stoves**

  xx **Heating**

Space industrial processing. *See* **Space industrial-
    ization**

Space industrialization 629.44

  x Commercial endeavors in space; Industrial
    uses of space; Manufacturing in space;
    Space commercialization; Space industrial
    processing; Space manufacturing; Space sta-
    tions—Industrial applications

  xx **Industrialization**

Space laboratories. *See* **Space stations**

Space law 341.4

  See also **Airspace law**

  x Aerospace law; Artificial satellites—Law and
    legislation; Astronautics—Law and legisla-
    tion; Law, Space; Space flight—Law and
    legislation; Space stations—Law and legisla-
    tion

  xx **Astronautics and civilization; International
    law; Law**

Space manufacturing. *See* **Space industrialization**

Space medicine 616.9

  See also **Aviation medicine; Life support systems
    (Space environment); Space flight; Weight-
    lessness**

  x Aerospace medicine; Bioastronautics

  xx **Aviation medicine; Space flight; Space sci-
    ences**

Space navigation. *See* **Navigation (Astronautics)**
Space nutrition. *See* **Astronauts—Nutrition**
Space optics 535
> *See also* **Astronautical instruments; Astronomical instruments; Remote sensing**
> *xx* **Optics; Remote sensing; Space sciences**
Space orbital rendezvous. *See* **Orbital rendezvous (Space flight)**
Space, Outer. *See* **Outer space**
Space, Personal. *See* **Personal space**
Space photography 778.3
> *See also* **Lunar photography;** also objects with the subdivision *Photographs from space,* e.g. **Earth—Photographs from space; Moon—Photographs from space;** etc.
> *x* Astronautics, Photography in; Photography in astronautics; Photography, Space
> *xx* **Photography**
Space platforms. *See* **Space stations**
Space power. *See* **Astronautics and civilization**
Space probes 629.43
> Use only for space exploration by remote control from earth.
> *See also* types of probes, e.g. **Lunar probes; Mars probes;** etc.; also names of space vehicles and space projects, e.g. **Mariner project;** etc.
> *x* Probes, Space
> *xx* **Outer space—Exploration; Space vehicles**
Space rescue operations 629.45
> *x* Manned space flight—Rescue work; Rescue operations, Space; Space ships—Rescue work
> *xx* **Rescue work**
Space research. *See* **Outer space—Exploration; Space sciences**
Space rockets. *See* **Space vehicles**
Space sciences 500.5
> Use for general materials and for scientific results of space exploration and scientific applications of space flight.
> *See also* **Astronautics; Astronomy; Geophysics; Outer space; Space biology; Space medicine; Space optics**
> *x* Science and space; Space research
> *xx* **Astronautics; Astronomy; Science**
Space sciences—International cooperation 500.5
Space ships 629.45
> Use for materials on space vehicles with people on board. Materials on spacecraft both with and without people are entered under **Space vehicles.**
> *See also* **Orbital rendezvous (Space flight); Rocket planes**
> *x* Space craft
> *xx* **Astronautics; Life support systems (Space environment); Rocketry; Space vehicles**
Space ships—Accidents. *See* **Astronautics—Accidents**
Space ships—Pilots. *See* **Astronauts**

Space ships—Rescue work. *See* **Space rescue operations**

Space shuttles 629.44

Use for materials on vehicles used to transport equipment and personnel to a space station.

See also names of individual space shuttles, e.g. **Challenger (Space shuttle);** etc.

x Reusable space vehicles; Shuttles, Space; Space vehicles, Reusable

xx **Space vehicles**

Space stations 629.44

See note under **Space colonies.**

See also **Orbital rendezvous (Space flight)**

x Laboratories, Space; Orbital laboratories; Orbiting vehicles; Sky laboratories; Space laboratories; Space platforms

xx **Artificial satellites; Astronautics; Space vehicles**

Space stations—Industrial applications. *See* **Space industrialization**

Space stations—Law and legislation. *See* **Space law**

Space suits. *See* **Astronauts—Clothing**

Space telecommunication. *See* **Interstellar communication**

Space television. *See* **Television in astronautics**

Space travel. *See* **Interplanetary voyages; Space flight**

Space vehicles 629.47

Use for materials on vehicles with and without people on board. Materials on space vehicles with people on board are entered under **Space ships.**

See also **Artificial satellites; Astronautics; Lunar excursion module; Space probes; Space ships; Space shuttles; Space stations**

x Space rockets

xx **Artificial satellites; Astronautics; Rocketry**

Space vehicles—Accidents. *See* **Astronautics—Accidents**

Space vehicles—Extravehicular activity. *See* **Extravehicular activity (Space flight)**

Space vehicles—Guidance systems 629.47

Space vehicles—Instruments. *See* **Astronautical instruments**

Space vehicles—Piloting 629.45

x Piloting (Astronautics)

xx **Astronauts; Navigation (Astronautics)**

Space vehicles—Propulsion systems 629.47

Space vehicles—Recovery 629.4

x Recovery of space vehicles

Space vehicles, Reusable. *See* **Space shuttles**

Space vehicles—Thermodynamics 629.47

xx **Thermodynamics**

Space vehicles—Tracking 629.46; 629.47

x Tracking of satellites

Space walk. *See* **Extravehicular activity (Space flight)**

Space warfare 358

Use for materials on interplanetary warfare, attacks on earth from outer space, and warfare

Space warfare—*Continued*
>
> among the nations of earth in outer space.
>
> *See also* **Space weapons**
>
> *x* Earth—Space attack and defense; Interplane-
> tary warfare; Interstellar warfare; Space
> wars; Star Wars; War, Space; Warfare,
> Space
>
> *xx* **Outer space**

Space wars. *See* **Space warfare**

Space weapons 358

> *x* Space-based weapons; Star Wars weapons;
> Weapons, Space
>
> *xx* **Munitions; Space warfare**

Space weather. *See* **Space environment**

Spain 946

> May be subdivided like United States except for
> *History.*

Spain—History 946

Spain—History—1898, War of 1898. *See* **United
States—History—1898, War of 1898**

Spain—History—1936-1939, Civil War 946.081

Spain—History—1939-1975 946.082

Spain—History—1975- 946.083

Spanish America. *See* **Latin America**

Spanish-American War, 1898. *See* **United States—
History—1898, War of 1898**

Spanish Armada. *See* **Armada, 1588**

Spanish language 460

> May be subdivided like **English language.**

Spanish literature 860

> May use same subdivisions and names of liter-
> ary forms as for **English literature.**
>
> *See also* **Latin American literature**

Sparring. *See* **Boxing**

Spas. *See* **Health resorts, spas, etc.**

Spastic paralysis. *See* **Cerebral palsy**

Speakers (Recitation books). *See* **Readings and recitations**

Speaking. *See* **Debates and debating; Lectures and
lecturing; Preaching; Public speaking; Rhetoric; Voice**

Speaking choirs. *See* **Choral speaking**

Spear fishing 799.1

> *xx* **Fishing**

Special collections in libraries. *See* **Libraries—
Special collections**

Special education 371.9

> *See also* **Mainstreaming in education;** also classes
> of exceptional children with the subdivision
> *Education,* e.g. **Mentally handicapped chil-
> dren—Education;** etc.
>
> *x* Education, Special
>
> *xx* **Education; Mainstreaming in education**

Special libraries 026; 027.6

> Use for materials on libraries covering special-
> ized subjects, containing special format ma-
> terials, or serving a specialized clientele.
>
> *See also* types of special libraries, e.g. **Business
> libraries; Corporate libraries; Government li-
> braries; Music libraries;** etc.

Special libraries—*Continued*
    x Libraries, Special
    xx **Libraries**
Special Olympics 796.4
    x Olympics, Special
    xx **Olympic games; Sports for the handicapped**
Specialists exchange programs. *See* **Exchange of persons programs**
Specie. *See* **Money**
Specimens, Preservation of. *See* **Taxidermy; Zoological specimens—Collection and preservation;** and names of natural specimens with the subdivision *Collection and preservation,* e.g. **Birds—Collection and preservation;** etc.

Spectacles. *See* **Eyeglasses**

Specters. *See* **Apparitions; Ghosts**

Spectra. *See* **Spectrum analysis**

Spectrochemical analysis. *See* **Spectrum analysis**

Spectrochemistry. *See* **Spectrum analysis**

Spectroscopy. *See* **Spectrum analysis**

Spectrum analysis 535

    See also **Light; Mass spectrometry**
    x Analysis, Spectrum; Spectra; Spectrochemical analysis; Spectrochemistry; Spectroscopy
    xx **Astronomy; Astrophysics; Chemistry; Light; Optics; Radiation; Sun**
Speculation 332.64

    See also **Investments; Real estate investment; Securities; Stock exchange**
    xx **Finance; Investments; Stock exchange**
Speech 372.6; 410; 612

    See also **Language and languages; Phonetics; Speech therapy; Voice**
    xx **Language and languages; Language arts; Phonetics; Voice**
Speech correction. *See* **Speech therapy**
Speech disorders 157; 616.85
    x Defective speech; Speech pathology; Stammering; Stuttering
Speech, Liberty of. *See* **Free speech**
Speech pathology. *See* **Speech disorders**
Speech recognition, Automatic. *See* **Automatic speech recognition**
Speech therapy 616.85
    x Speech correction
    xx **Speech**
Speeches, addresses, etc. 808.85; 815.08; etc.

    See also **After dinner speeches; Lectures and lecturing; Toasts;** also general subjects with the subdivision *Addresses and essays,* e.g. **Agriculture—Addresses and essays; United States—History—Addresses and essays; World War, 1939-1945—Addresses and essays;** etc.
    x Addresses; Orations
Speeches, addresses, etc., American 815.08
    x American orations; American speeches

Speeches, addresses, etc., English 825
>   *x* English orations; English speeches
>   *xx* **English literature**

Speed 531
>   *x* Velocity
>   *xx* **Motion**

Speed reading. *See* **Rapid reading**

Speed, Supersonic. *See* **Aerodynamics, Supersonic**

Speleology. *See* **Caves**

Spellers 421
>   *xx* **English language—Spelling**

Spelling. *See* names of languages with the subdivision *Spelling,* e.g. **English language—Spelling**; etc.

Spelling reform 421
>   *x* English language—Spelling reform; Orthography; Phonetic spelling
>   *xx* **English language—Spelling**

Spells. *See* **Charms**

Spherical trigonometry. *See* **Trigonometry**

Spices 641.3; 664
>   *See also* names of spices

Spiders 595.4
>   *x* Arachnida

Spies 327.1; 355.3
>   *See also* **Secret service; World War, 1939-1945—Underground movements**
>   *x* Intelligence agents
>   *xx* **Espionage; Military art and science; Secret service; Subversive activities**

Spinal paralysis, Anterior. *See* **Poliomyelitis**

Spinning 677; 746.1
>   *xx* **Textile industry**

Spiral gearing. *See* **Gearing**

Spires 726
>   *x* Steeples
>   *xx* **Architecture; Church architecture**

Spirit. *See* **Soul**

Spirit, Holy. *See* **Holy Spirit**

Spiritism. *See* **Spiritualism**

Spirits. *See* **Angels; Apparitions; Demonology; Ghosts; Spiritualism; Witchcraft**

Spirits, Alcoholic. *See* **Liquors and liqueurs**

Spiritual healing 615.8
>   Use for materials on the use of faith, prayer, or religious means to treat illness. Materials on psychic or psychological means to treat illness are entered under **Mental healing.**
>   *See also* **Christian Science; Mental healing; Miracles; Therapeutics, Suggestive**
>   *x* Divine healing; Evangelistic healing; Faith cure; Faith healing; Healing, Spiritual
>   *xx* **Christian Science; Medicine and religion; Mental healing; Mind and body; Subconsciousness; Therapeutics, Suggestive**

Spiritual life 248
>   *See also* **Faith; Meditation; Sanctification**
>   *x* Life, Spiritual
>   *xx* **Ethics; Human behavior; Mysticism; Religion; Soul; Theology**

Spiritualism 133.9
> *See also* **Apparitions; Clairvoyance; Ghosts; Psychical research; Psychokinesis**
> *x* Spiritism; Spirits
> *xx* **Apparitions; Future life; Ghosts; Occult sciences; Psychical research; Supernatural**

Spirituals (Songs) 784.7
> *See also* **Black songs; Blues (Songs, etc.)**
> *x* Black spirituals
> *xx* **Black music; Black songs; Music, American**

Splicing. *See* **Knots and splices**

Splicing of genes. *See* **Genetic engineering**

Spoils system. *See* **Corruption in politics**

Sponges 593.4
> *xx* **Invertebrates**

Spontaneous abortion. *See* **Miscarriage**

Spontaneous combustion. *See* **Combustion**

Sports (May subdiv. geog.) **796**
> *See also*

Aeronautical sports	**Outdoor life**
Amusements	**Physical education**
Athletics	**Professional sports**
Coaching (Athletics)	**Rodeos**
College sports	**School sports**
Games	**Water sports**
Gymnastics	**Winter sports**
Olympic games	

> also names of sports, e.g. **Baseball; Basketball; Football;** etc.; and names of competitions
> *xx* **Amusements; Athletics; Games; Outdoor life; Physical education; Play; Recreation**

Sports cars 629.2
> *See also* names of specific sports cars
> *xx* **Automobiles**

Sports coaching. *See* **Coaching (Athletics)**

Sports—Corrupt practices 796
> *x* Cheating in sports; Corrupt practices; Corruption in sports; Sports scandals

Sports—Equipment and supplies 796.028
> *x* Equipment and supplies

Sports for the handicapped 796
> *See also* **Special Olympics**

Sports—Medical aspects. *See* **Sports medicine**

Sports medicine 613.7; 615; 617
> *x* Athletic medicine; Physical education—Medical aspects; Sports—Medical aspects
> *xx* **Medical care; Medicine**

Sports scandals. *See* **Sports—Corrupt practices**

Spot welding. *See* **Electric welding**

Spraying and dusting 632
> *See also* **Aeronautics in agriculture; Fungicides; Herbicides; Insecticides**
> *x* Dusting and spraying
> *xx* **Agricultural pests; Fruit—Diseases and pests; Fungicides; Herbicides; Insecticides**

Spun glass. *See* **Glass fibers**

Sputniks. *See* **Artificial satellites, Russian**

Square dancing 793.3
> *xx* **Folk dancing**

Square root 513

   xx **Arithmetic**

Squirrels 599.32

   See also **Chipmunks**

SSTs. *See* **Supersonic transport planes**

St. Dominic, Order of. *See* **Dominicans**

St. Francis, Order of. *See* **Franciscans**

St. Valentine's Day. *See* **Valentine's Day**

Stabilization in industry. *See* **Business cycles; Economic conditions**

Stage. *See* **Acting; Actors and actresses; Drama; Theater**

Stage lighting 792

   x Television—Stage lighting; Theaters—Stage lighting

Stage scenery. *See* **Theaters—Stage setting and scenery**

Stage setting. *See* **Theaters—Stage setting and scenery**

Stagecoaches. *See* **Carriages and carts**

Stained glass. *See* **Glass painting and staining**

Stamina, Physical. *See* **Physical fitness**

Stammering. *See* **Speech disorders**

Stamps, Postage. *See* **Postage stamps**

Standard book numbers. *See* **Publishers' standard book numbers**

Standard of living 339.4

   See also **Cost of living**

   x Living, Standard of

   xx **Quality of life; Social conditions; Social problems; Wealth**

Standard of value. *See* **Money**

Standard time. *See* **Time**

Standards of output. *See* **Production standards**

Star Wars. *See* **Space warfare**

Star Wars weapons. *See* **Space weapons**

Stars 523.8

   See also

Astrology	**Galaxies**
Astronomy	**Meteors**
Astrophysics	**Planets**
Black holes (Astronomy)	**Solar system**

   also names of groups of stars and specific stars, e.g. **Pulsars; Sirius;** etc.

   x Constellations; Double stars; Sidereal system

   xx **Astronomy; Planets**

Stars—Atlases 523.8

   x Astronomy—Atlases; Atlases, Astronomical

   xx **Atlases**

Stars, Falling. *See* **Meteors**

Starvation 363.8

   See also **Famines; Fasting; Hunger; Malnutrition**

   xx **Fasting; Hunger; Malnutrition**

Starvation, Self-imposed. *See* **Anorexia nervosa**

State aid to education 379

   x Education—State aid

   xx **Education—Finance; Education—Government policy**

State aid to libraries 021.8

   x Libraries—State aid

State aid to libraries—*Continued*
  xx **Libraries—Government policy; Library finance**
State and agriculture. *See* **Agriculture—Government policy**
State and church. *See* **Church—Government policy**
State and education. *See* **Education—Government policy**
State and energy. *See* **Energy resources—Government policy**
State and environment. *See* **Environment—Government policy**
State and industry. *See* **Industry—Government policy**
State and insurance. *See* **Social security**
State and railroads. *See* **Railroads—Government policy**
State and science. *See* **Science—Government policy**
State and the arts. *See* **Arts—Government policy**
State birds 598
  xx **Birds**
State church. *See* **Church—Government policy**
State constitutions. *See* **Constitutions, State**
State debts. *See* **Debts, Public**
State encouragement of the arts. *See* **Arts—Government policy**
State-federal relations. *See* **Federal-state relations**
State flowers 582
  Use same form for other state symbols.
  x Flowers, State
  xx **Flowers**
State governments 353.9
  Use for general materials on state government. Materials on the government of a particular state are entered under the name of the state with the subdivision *Politics and government.*
  See also **Constitutions, State; Federal government; Federal-state relations; Governors; State-local relations;** also names of states with the subdivision *Politics and government,* e.g. **Ohio—Politics and government;** etc.
  x United States—State governments
  xx **Constitutions, State; Federal government; Political science**
State, Heads of. *See* **Heads of state**
State libraries 027.5
  Use for materials on government libraries, maintained by state funds, that preserve state records and publications for use by state officials and residents.
  x Libraries, State
  xx **Government libraries**
State-local relations 342; 351.09
  x City-state relations; Local-state relations
  xx **Local government; Municipal government; State governments**
State-local tax relations. *See* **Intergovernmental tax relations**

586

State medicine. *See* **Medicine, State**
State of the Union messages. *See* **Presidents—**
　　　　United States—Messages
State ownership. *See* **Government ownership**
State ownership of railroads. *See* **Railroads—**
　　　　Government policy
State planning. *See* **Regional planning; Social pol-**
　　　　icy; and names of states with the subdivi-
　　　　sion *Economic policy* or *Social policy,* e.g.
　　　　Ohio—Economic policy; Ohio—Social pol-
　　　　icy; etc.
State police. *See* **Police, State**
State regulation of industry. *See* **Industry—**
　　　　Government policy
State rights 320.1; 342
　　x Secession; States' rights
　　xx **Political science; Slavery—United States**
State songs 784.7
　　xx **Songs**
State, The 320.1
　　See also **Political science; Public interest**
　　x Administration; Commonwealth, The; Wel-
　　　　fare state
　　xx **Political science**
States, New 321
　　x New nations
　　xx **Developing countries**
States' rights. *See* **State rights**
Statesmen (May subdiv. geog.) **920; 923**
　　See also **Diplomats; Heads of state; Politicians**
　　xx **Diplomats; Politicians**
Statics 531
　　See also **Dynamics; Hydrostatics; Strains and**
　　　　stresses
　　xx **Dynamics; Mechanics; Physics**
Statistical inference. *See* **Probabilities**
Statistics 310
　　Use for materials on the theory and methods of
　　　　statistics.
　　See also **Average; Census; Probabilities; Sam-**
　　　　pling (Statistics); Vital statistics; also gen-
　　　　eral subjects and names of countries, cities,
　　　　etc. with the subdivision *Statistics,* e.g.
　　　　Agriculture—Statistics; United States—
　　　　Statistics; Chicago (Ill.)—Statistics; etc.
　　xx **Economics**
Statistics—Graphic methods 001.4
　　x Diagrams, Statistical
　　xx **Graphic methods**
Statues. *See* **Monuments; Sculpture**
Statutes. *See* **Law**
Steam 536
　　xx **Heat; Power (Mechanics); Water**
Steam engineering 621.1
　　See also **Mechanical engineering; Power (Me-**
　　　　chanics); Steam engines; Steam navigation;
　　　　Steam power plants
　　xx **Engineering; Mechanical engineering**
Steam engines 621.1
　　See also **Condensers (Steam); Farm engines;**

Steam engines—*Continued*
  Locomotives; Marine engines; Steam turbines
  xx **Engines; Heat engines; Machinery; Mechanics; Steam engineering**
Steam fitting. *See* **Pipe fitting**
Steam heating 697
  xx **Heating**
Steam navigation 386; 387; 623.8
  See also **Marine engineering; Navigation; Steam
  turbines; Steamboats**
  x Navigation, Steam
  xx **Navigation; Steam engineering; Steamboats;
  Transportation**
Steam power plants 621.1
  x Power plants, Steam
  xx **Power plants; Steam engineering**
Steam pumps. *See* **Pumping machinery**
Steam turbines 621.1
  xx **Steam engines; Steam navigation; Turbines**
Steamboats 387.2
  See also **Steam navigation**
  x Steamships
  xx **Boats and boating; Naval architecture; Ocean
  travel; Shipbuilding; Ships; Steam naviga-
  tion**
Steamships. *See* **Steamboats**
Steel 669; 672
  See also **Building, Iron and steel; Iron;** also head-
  ings beginning with the word **Steel**
  xx **Metalwork**
Steel construction. *See* **Building, Iron and steel;
  Steel, Structural**
Steel engraving. *See* **Engraving**
Steel industry and trade 338.4; 672
  See also **Iron industry and trade**
  x Industries
  xx **Industry; Iron industry and trade; Ironwork**
Steel industry and trade—Quality control 338.4; 672
  xx **Quality control**
Steel, Structural 691
  See also **Building, Iron and steel**
  x Steel construction; Structural steel
  xx **Building, Iron and steel; Building materials;
  Civil engineering**
Steeples. *See* **Spires**
Steers. *See* **Beef cattle**
Stencil work 686.2
  See also **Silk screen printing**
  xx **Decoration and ornament; Painting**
Stenography. *See* **Shorthand**
Stereophonic sound systems 621.389
  xx **High-fidelity sound systems; Sound—
  Recording and reproducing**
Stereophotography. *See* **Photography, Stereoscopic**
Sterility in animals. *See* **Infertility**
Sterility in humans. *See* **Infertility**
Sterilization (Birth control) 613.9
  See also **Infertility; Vasectomy**
  xx **Birth control; Infertility**

Stewardesses, Airline. *See* **Airlines—Flight atten-
    dants**
Stewards, Airline. *See* **Airlines—Flight attendants**
Stills. *See* **Distillation**
Stimulants 613.8
    See also **Alcohol; Liquors and liqueurs; Narcotics**
    x Intoxicants
    xx **Narcotics; Temperance; Therapeutics**
Stock and stock breeding. *See* **Livestock**
Stock control. *See* **Inventory control**
Stock exchange 332.6
    See also **Bonds; Foreign exchange; Investments;
        Securities; Speculation; Stocks; Wall Street
        (New York, N.Y.)**
    x Securities exchange; Stock market
    xx **Commerce; Exchange; Finance; Investments;
        Speculation; Stocks**
Stock judging. *See* **Livestock judging**
Stock market. *See* **Stock exchange**
Stock raising. *See* **Livestock**
Stockings. *See* **Hosiery**
Stocks 332.6
    See also **Bonds; Corporations; Investments; Stock
        exchange**
    x Dividends; Shares of stock
    xx **Bonds; Commerce; Investments; Securities;
        Stock exchange**
Stockyards. *See* **Meat industry and trade**
Stoics 188
    xx **Ethics; Philosophy, Ancient**
Stokers, Mechanical 621.1
    x Mechanical stokers
STOL aircraft. *See* **Short take off and landing air-
    craft**
Stomach 612
    See also **Digestion**
Stone 552; 553.5; 693
    See also **Masonry; Petrology; Quarries and quar-
        rying; Rocks; Stonecutting;** also names of
        stones, e.g. **Marble;** etc.
    xx **Building materials; Geology, Economic; Pe-
        trology; Quarries and quarrying; Rocks**
Stone Age 930
    See also **Archeology; Man, Prehistoric; Stone im-
        plements**
    x Eolithic period; Neolithic period; Paleolithic
        period; Prehistory
    xx **Archeology**
Stone-cutting. *See* **Stonecutting**
Stone implements 930
    x Flint implements; Implements, utensils, etc.
    xx **Archeology; Stone Age**
Stone quarries. *See* **Quarries and quarrying**
Stonecutting 693
    x Stone-cutting
    xx **Masonry; Stone**
Stones, Precious. *See* **Precious stones**
Stoneware. *See* **Pottery**
Storage batteries 621.31
    See also **Electric batteries**

Storage batteries—*Continued*
  x Batteries, Electric
  xx **Electric batteries**
Storage devices, Computer. *See* **Computer storage devices**
Storage in the home 643; 648; 684.1
  x Home storage
  xx **Home economics**
Stores. *See* **Chain stores; Cooperative societies; Department stores; Discount stores; Retail trade; Supermarkets**
Stories. *See* **Anecdotes; Fairy tales; Fiction; Legends; Romances; Stories in rhyme; Stories without words; Storytelling;** and literary and musical forms with the subdivision *Stories, plots, etc.,* e.g. **Ballets—Stories, plots, etc.; Operas—Stories, plots, etc.;** etc.; also subjects with the subdivision *Fiction,* e.g. **Slavery—United States—Fiction;** etc.; and such phrase headings that do not lend themselves to subdivision, e.g. **Bible stories; Humorous stories; Mystery and detective stories; School stories; Science fiction; Sea stories; Short stories;** etc.
Stories in rhyme E; Fic
  x Stories
  xx **Rhyme**
Stories without words E
  x Nonword stories; Picture books for children, Wordless; Stories; Wordless stories
  xx **Picture books for children**
Storms (May subdiv. geog.) **551.5**
  See also

Blizzards	**Snow**
Cyclones	**Thunderstorms**
Dust storms	**Tornadoes**
Hurricanes	**Typhoons**
Meteorology	**Winds**
Rain and rainfall	

  also other kinds of storms
  xx **Hurricanes; Meteorology; Ocean; Rain and rainfall; Tornadoes; Weather; Winds**
Storytelling 027.62; 372.6
  See also **Folklore; Short story**
  x Stories
  xx **Children's literature; Folklore; Short story**
Storytelling—Collections 808.85
  Use for collections of stories compiled primarily for oral presentation.
Stoves 697
  xx **Heating; Space heaters**
Strain (Psychology). *See* **Stress (Psychology)**
Strains and stresses 531; 620.1; 624.1
  See also **Strength of materials**
  x Architectural engineering; Stresses
  xx **Architecture; Mechanics; Statics; Strength of materials; Structures, Theory of**
Strangers and children. *See* **Children and strangers**
Strategic materials. *See* **Materials**

Strategy 355.4

See also **Armies; Military art and science; Naval art and science; Tactics;** also countries and areas of the world with the subdivision *Strategic aspects,* c.g. **Middle East— Strategic aspects;** etc.

x Military strategy; Naval strategy

xx **Military art and science; Naval art and science; War**

Stratigraphic geology. *See* **Geology, Stratigraphic**

Stratosphere 551.5

xx **Atmosphere, Upper**

Straw votes. *See* **Public opinion polls**

Strawberries 634

xx **Berries**

Stream animals 591.52

x River animals

xx **Animals; Rivers; Wildlife**

Streamlining. *See* **Aerodynamics**

Street cars. *See* **Street railroads**

Street cleaning 363.7; 628

See also **Refuse and refuse disposal**

xx **Cleaning; Municipal engineering; Public health; Refuse and refuse disposal; Roads; Sanitary engineering; Streets**

Street lighting. *See* **Streets—Lighting**

Street railroads 388.4

See also **Cable railroads; Electric railroads; Subways**

x Interurban railroads; Railroads, Street; Street cars; Trams; Trolley cars

xx **Cable railroads; Electric railroads; Local transit; Public utilities; Railroads; Transportation**

Street traffic. *See* **City traffic; Traffic engineering; Traffic regulations**

Streets (May subdiv. geog.) **388.4; 625.8**

See also **City traffic; Pavements; Roads; Street cleaning**

x Alleys; Avenues; Boulevards; Thoroughfares

xx **Cities and towns; Civil engineering; Pavements; Roads; Transportation**

Streets—Chicago (Ill.) 388.409

x Chicago (Ill.)—Streets

Streets—Lighting 628.9

x Cities and towns—Lighting; Street lighting

xx **Lighting**

Strength of materials 620.1

See also **Building materials; Strains and stresses;** also special materials and forms with the subdivision *Testing,* e.g. **Concrete—Testing;** etc.

x Architectural engineering; Materials, Strength of; Resistance of materials

xx **Architecture; Building; Building, Iron and steel; Building materials; Civil engineering; Materials; Mechanics; Strains and stresses; Structures, Theory of**

Strength training. *See* **Weight lifting**

Stress (Physiology) 612; 616.8

    See also **Job stress**

    x Physiological stress; Tension (Physiology)

Stress (Psychology) 157

    See also **Burn out (Psychology); Job stress; Separation anxiety in children**

    x Anxiety; Emotional stress; Psychological stress; Strain (Psychology); Tension (Psychology)

    xx **Psychology**

Stresses. *See* **Strains and stresses**

Strikes and lockouts (May subdiv. geog.) **331.89**

    May also subdivide by industry or occupation and then geographically.

    See also **Arbitration, Industrial; Collective bargaining; Injunctions; Labor unions; Sabotage; Syndicalism**

    x Lockouts; Picketing; Sit-down strikes; Work stoppages

    xx **Arbitration, Industrial; Collective bargaining; Industrial relations; Injunctions; Labor; Labor disputes; Labor unions**

Strikes and lockouts—Automobile industry—United States 331.89

Strikes and lockouts—United States 331.89

    x United States—Strikes and lockouts

Strikes, Hunger. *See* **Hunger strikes**

String orchestra music 785.06

    xx **Orchestral music**

Stringed instruments 787

    See also names of stringed instruments, e.g. **Guitar; Violin;** etc.

    x Bowed instruments

    xx **Musical instruments**

Strip films. *See* **Filmstrips**

Structural botany. *See* **Botany—Anatomy**

Structural drafting. *See* **Mechanical drawing**

Structural engineering 624.1

    See also **Building; Foundations; Hydraulic structures; Soils (Engineering); Structures, Theory of**

    x Engineering, Structural

    xx **Architecture; Building materials; Civil engineering; Engineering; Structures, Theory of**

Structural failures 624.1

    See also types of structural failures, e.g. **Building failures;** etc.

    x Collapse of structures; Failures, Structural

    xx **Reliability (Engineering)**

Structural materials. *See* **Building materials**

Structural psychology. *See* **Gestalt psychology**

Structural steel. *See* **Steel, Structural**

Structures, Offshore. *See* **Drilling platforms**

Structures, Theory of 624

    See also **Building; Strains and stresses; Strength of materials; Structural engineering**

    x Architectural engineering; Theory of structures

    xx **Building, Iron and steel; Structural engineering**

Stucco 693
   xx **Building materials; Decoration and ornament;**
       Plaster and plastering
Student activities 371.8
   See also **After school programs; College and**
       school drama; College and school journal-
       ism; School assembly programs; School
       sports
   x Extracurricular activities
Student aid. *See* **Scholarships, fellowships, etc.;**
       Student loan funds
Student busing. *See* **Busing (School integration)**
Student clubs. *See* **Students—Societies**
Student councils. *See* **Self-government (in educa-**
       tion)
Student customs. *See* **Student life**
Student evaluation of teachers 371.1
   x Student rating of teachers; Teachers, Student
       rating of
Student government. *See* **Self-government (in edu-**
       cation)
Student guidance. *See* **Educational counseling**
Student life 371.8
   x Student customs
   xx **Students**
Student loan funds 371.2; 378
   See also **Scholarships, fellowships, etc.**
   x Loan funds, Student; Student aid
   xx **Scholarships, fellowships, etc.**
Student movement. *See* **Youth movement**
Student protests, demonstrations, etc. *See* **Stu-**
       dents—Political activity; Youth movement
Student rating of teachers. *See* **Student evaluation**
       of teachers
Student revolt. *See* **Students—Political activity;**
       Youth movement
Student self-government. *See* **Self-government (in**
       education)
Student societies. *See* **Students—Societies**
Student-teacher interaction. *See* **Teacher-student**
       relationships
Student teaching 371.1
   x Practice teaching; Teachers—Practice teaching
   xx **Teachers—Training; Teaching**
Student violence. *See* **School violence**
Students (May subdiv. geog.) **371.8**
   See also **School children; Student life;** also types
       of students, e.g. **College students;** etc.; also
       headings beginning with the words **College**
       and **School**
   x School life
Students and libraries. *See* **Libraries and students**
Students—Counseling. *See* **Educational counseling**
Students, Foreign 370.19
   x College students, Foreign; Foreign students
Students—Grading and marking. *See* **Grading and**
       marking (Students)
Students' military training camps. *See* **Military**
       training camps

Students—Political activity 324; 371.8
    x Politics and students; Student protests, dem-
        onstrations, etc.; Student revolt
    xx **Youth movement**
Students—Societies 371.8
    See also **Fraternities and sororities**
    x School clubs; Student clubs; Student societies
Students' songs 784.6
    x College songs
    xx **Songs**
Students—United States 371.8
    x United States—Students
Study abroad. *See* **Foreign study**
Study, Courses of. *See* **Education—Curricula;** and
    types of education and schools with the sub-
    division *Curricula,* e.g. **Library education—**
    Curricula; Colleges and universities—
    Curricula; etc.
Study, Foreign. *See* **Foreign study**
Study, Method of 371.3
    See also **Independent study;** also subjects with
    the subdivision *Study and teaching,* e.g.
    Art—Study and teaching; etc.
    x Learning, Art of; Method of study; Study
        skills
    xx **Education; Teaching**
Study overseas. *See* **Foreign study**
Study skills. *See* **Study, Method of**
Stunt men and women 791; 791.43
    xx **Acrobats and acrobatics**
Stuttering. *See* **Speech disorders**
Style in dress. *See* **Costume; Fashion**
Style, Literary 808
    See also **Criticism; Letter writing; Literature—**
    History and criticism; Rhetoric
    x Literary style
    xx **Criticism; Literature; Rhetoric**
Style manikins. *See* **Models, Fashion**
Style manuals. *See* **Printing—Style manuals**
Sub-Saharan Africa. *See* **Africa, Sub-Saharan**
Subconsciousness 127; 154.2
    See also

Consciousness	**Mind and body**
Dreams	**Personality disorders**
Hallucinations and illu-	**Psychoanalysis**
sions	**Sleep**
Hypnotism	**Spiritual healing**
Mental healing	**Telepathy**
Mental suggestion	

    xx **Consciousness; Hypnotism; Mental healing;**
    Mind and body; Psychical research; Psy-
    choanalysis; Psychology; Psychology,
    Pathological; Therapeutics, Suggestive
Subculture. *See* **Counter culture**
Subgravity state. *See* **Weightlessness**
Subject dictionaries. *See* **Encyclopedias and dictio-**
    naries
Subject headings 025.4
    See also **Classification—Books**
    x Thesauri

Subject headings—*Continued*

   xx **Cataloging; Catalogs, Subject; Indexes**

Submarine boats. *See* **Submarines; Submersibles**

Submarine cables. *See* **Cables, Submarine**

Submarine diving. *See* **Diving, Submarine**

Submarine engineering. *See* **Ocean engineering**

Submarine exploration. *See* **Underwater exploration**

Submarine geology 551.46

   See also **Ocean bottom; Plate tectonics**

   x Geology, Submarine; Marine geology; Underwater geology

   xx **Geology; Oceanography; Plate tectonics**

Submarine medicine 616.9

   x Medicine, Submarine; Underwater medicine; Underwater physiology

   xx **Medicine**

Submarine oil well drilling. *See* **Oil well drilling, Submarine**

Submarine photography. *See* **Photography, Submarine**

Submarine research stations. *See* **Undersea research stations**

Submarine telegraph. *See* **Cables, Submarine**

Submarine vehicles. *See* **Submersibles**

Submarine warfare 359.4

   See also **Submarines; Torpedoes; World War, 1939-1945—Naval operations—Submarine**

   x Naval warfare; Warfare, Submarine

   xx **Naval art and science; War**

Submarines 359.3; 623.8

   Use for materials on submarines only. Materials on other underwater craft are entered under **Submersibles.**

   See also **Nuclear submarines**

   x Boats, Submarine; Submarine boats; U boats

   xx **Boats and boating; Naval art and science; Ships; Submarine warfare; Submersibles; Warships**

Submarines, Nuclear. *See* **Nuclear submarines**

Submersibles 623.8

   See note under **Submarines.**

   See also types of submersibles, e g. **Bathyscaphe; Submarines; Undersea research stations;** etc.

   x Boats, Submarine; Deep diving vehicles; Deep sea vehicles; Deep submergence vehicles; Oceanographic submersibles; Submarine boats; Submarine vehicles; Undersea vehicles; Underwater exploration devices

   xx **Oceanography—Research; Underwater exploration**

Subscription television 384.55

   See also **Home Box Office**

   x Pay television, Subscription; Television, Subscription

   xx **Television**

Subsidies 338.9

   See also headings beginning with **Federal aid to . . .**

Subsidies—*Continued*
  x Bounties; Grants; Subventions
  xx **Economic assistance, Domestic; Economic policy; Industry—Government policy**
Subsistence economy 331.2; 339.4
  See also **Barter; Poverty**
  xx **Cost of living; Poverty**
Substance abuse 362.2; 616.86
  See also **Alcoholism; Drug abuse; Tobacco habit**
  x Abuse of substances; Addiction; Addictive behavior
  xx **Social problems**
Substitute products
  See also **Synthetic products;** also types of substitute products, e.g. **Sugar substitutes;** etc.
  x Ersatz products
  xx **Commercial products; Synthetic products; Waste products**
Subterranean economy. *See* **Underground economy**
Subtraction 513
  xx **Arithmetic**
Suburban areas. *See* **Metropolitan areas**
Suburban homes. *See* **Architecture, Domestic**
Suburban life 307.7
  See also names of cities with the subdivision *Suburbs and environs,* e.g. **Chicago (Ill.)— Suburbs and environs;** etc.
Subventions. *See* **Subsidies**
Subversive activities 322.4
  See also **Espionage; Internal security; Political crimes and offenses; Sabotage; Spies; Terrorism**
  x Fifth column
  xx **Insurgency; Internal security**
Subways 388.4
  x Railroads, Underground; Underground railroads
  xx **Civil engineering; Local transit; Railroads; Street railroads; Transportation; Tunnels**
Success 158
  See also **Ability; Leadership; Life skills; Saving and thrift; Self-realization**
  x Fortune; Personal development
  xx **Business ethics; Self-realization; Wealth**
Succession, Intestate. *See* **Inheritance and succession**
Suffering 152.1; 214
  See also **Good and evil; Joy and sorrow; Pain**
  xx **Pain**
Suffrage 324.6
  See also **Naturalization; Representative government and representation; Voter registration;** also classes of people with the subdivision *Suffrage,* e.g. **Blacks—Suffrage; Women— Suffrage;** etc.
  x Franchise; Voting
  xx **Citizenship; Constitutional law; Democracy; Elections; Political science; Representative government and representation**
Suffragettes. *See* **Women—Suffrage**

Sugar 641.3; 664
  See also **Syrups;** also types of sugar, e.g. **Maple sugar;** etc.
Sugar substitutes 664
  x Artificial sweeteners; Nonnutritive sweeteners
  xx **Substitute products**
Suggestion, Mental. *See* **Mental suggestion**
Suggestive therapeutics. *See* **Therapeutics, Suggestive**
Suicide 179; 362.2
  See also **Right to die**
  xx **Medical jurisprudence; Right to die; Social problems**
Suing (Law). *See* **Actions and defenses**
Suites 785.8
  xx **Musical form; Orchestral music**
Suits (Law). *See* **Actions and defenses**
Sulfa drugs. *See* **Sulfonamides**
Sulfonamides 615
  x Sulfa drugs
Sulfur. *See* **Sulphur**
Sulphur 546; 553.6; 661
  x Sulfur
Summer camps. *See* **Camps**
Summer employment 331.1
  See also **Youth—Employment**
  xx **Youth—Employment**
Summer homes. *See* **Architecture, Domestic; Houses**
Summer resorts
  See also **Health resorts, spas, etc.**
  x Resorts
  xx **Health resorts, spas, etc.**
Summer schools 371.2
  x Vacation schools
  xx **Playgrounds; Public schools; Schools**
Summer schools, Religious 377
  x Bible classes; Vacation church schools; Vacation schools, Religious
  xx **Schools**
Sun 523.7
  See also **Solar energy; Solar system; Spectrum analysis; Sunspots**
  x Solar physics
  xx **Astronomy; Solar system**
Sun-dials. *See* **Sundials**
Sun—Eclipses. *See* **Eclipses, Solar**
Sun (in religion, folklore, etc.). *See* **Sun worship**
Sun powered batteries. *See* **Solar batteries**
Sun—Radiation. *See* **Solar radiation**
Sun-spots. *See* **Sunspots**
Sun worship 291.2
  x Sun (in religion, folklore, etc.)
  xx **Religion**
Sunday schools 268
  See also **Bible—Study**
  x Bible classes
  xx **Church work; Religious education**
Sundials 681.1
  x Horology; Sun-dials

Sundials—*Continued*
  xx **Clocks and watches; Garden ornaments and furniture; Time**
Sunken cities. *See* **Cities and towns, Ruined, extinct, etc.**
Sunken treasure. *See* **Buried treasure**
Sunspots 523.7
  x Sun-spots
  xx **Meteorology; Solar radiation; Sun**
Super markets. *See* **Supermarkets**
Superhighways. *See* **Express highways**
Superintendents of schools. *See* **School superintendents and principals**
Superior children. *See* **Gifted children**
Supermarkets 658.8
  x Stores; Super markets
  xx **Grocery trade; Retail trade**
Supernatural 133; 398.2
  See also

Divination	**Psychical research**
Miracles	**Revelation**
Occult sciences	**Spiritualism**
Prophecies (Occult sciences)	**Superstition**

  xx **Miracles; Religion**
Supersonic aerodynamics. *See* **Aerodynamics, Supersonic**
Supersonic airliners. *See* **Supersonic transport planes**
Supersonic transport planes 629.133
  x S.S.T.'s; SSTs; Supersonic airliners
Supersonic waves. *See* **Ultrasonic waves**
Supersonics. *See* **Ultrasonics**
Superstition 001.9; 398
  See also

Alchemy	**Exorcism**
Apparitions	**Fairies**
Astrology	**Folklore**
Charms	**Fortune telling**
Demonology	**Ghosts**
Divination	**Occult sciences**
Dreams	**Vampires**
Errors	**Witchcraft**

  x Delusions; Traditions
  xx **Demonology; Divination; Errors; Folklore; Ghosts; Occult sciences; Religion; Supernatural**
Supervision of employees. *See* **Personnel management**
Supervision of schools. *See* **School supervision**
Supervisors 331.7
  x Foremen and foreladies; Managers
  xx **Factory management; Personnel management**
Supplementary employment 331.1
  x Double employment; Dual employment; Employment, Supplementary; Moonlighting; Second job; Secondary employment
  xx **Labor; Part-time employment**
Support of children. *See* **Child support**

Supreme Court—United States. *See* **United States. Supreme Court**

Surf. *See* **Ocean waves**

Surf riding. *See* **Surfing**

Surface effect machines. *See* **Ground effect machines**

Surfing 797.1
> *x* Surf riding
> *xx* **Water sports**

Surgeons 610.69; 617.092; 920
> *See also* **Physicians**
> *x* Medical profession
> *xx* **Physicians**

Surgery 617
> *See also* **Anesthetics; Antiseptics; Cryosurgery; Orthopedics; Transplantation of organs, tissues, etc.; Vivisection;** also names of diseases and names of organs and regions of the body with the subdivision *Surgery,* e.g. **Cancer—Surgery; Heart—Surgery;** etc.
> *x* Operations, Surgical
> *xx* **Medicine**

Surgery, Cosmetic. *See* **Surgery, Plastic**

Surgery, Orthopedic. *See* **Orthopedics**

Surgery, Plastic 617
> *x* Cosmetic surgery; Plastic surgery; Surgery, Cosmetic
> *xx* **Transplantation of organs, tissues, etc.**

Surgical transplantation. *See* **Transplantation of organs, tissues, etc.**

Surnames. *See* **Names, Personal**

Surrealism 709.04; 759.06
> *xx* **Art; Postimpressionism (Art)**

Surrogate mothers 306.8
> *xx* **Mothers**

Surveillance, Electronic. *See* **Eavesdropping**

Surveying 526.9
> *See also* **Geodesy; Mine surveying; Topographical drawing**
> *x* Land surveying
> *xx* **Civil engineering; Geodesy; Geography; Measurement**

Surveys. *See* types of surveys, e.g **Educational surveys; Library surveys; Social surveys;** etc.

Survival (after airplane accidents, shipwrecks, etc.) 613.6
> *See also* **Wilderness survival**
> *x* Castaways
> *xx* **Aeronautics—Accidents; Shipwrecks**

Survival of the fittest. *See* **Natural selection**

Survival skills 613.6
> Use for materials on skills needed to survive in a hazardous environment, usually stressing self-reliance and economic self-sufficiency.
> *See also* types of survival, e.g. **Wilderness survival;** etc.
> *x* Emergency survival; Human survival skills
> *xx* **Civil defense; Human ecology; Life skills; Man—Influence of environment**

Suspended sentence. *See* **Probation**

Suspense fiction. *See* **Gothic fiction**

Suspension bridges. *See* **Bridges**

Swamp animals 591.52
  xx **Animals; Marshes; Wildlife**

Swamps. *See* **Marshes**

Swedish language 439.7
  May be subdivided like **English language.**
  xx **Scandinavian languages**

Swedish literature 839.7
  May use same subdivisions and names of liter-
    ary forms as for **English literature.**
  xx **Scandinavian literature**

Swimming 797.2
  See also **Diving; Marathon swimming; Synchro-
    nized swimming**
  xx **Water sports**

Swimming pools 725; 797.2028

Swindlers and swindling 364.1
  See also **Counterfeits and counterfeiting; Credit
    card crimes; Fraud; Impostors and impos-
    ture; Quacks and quackery**
  x Con artists; Con game; Confidence game
  xx **Crime; Criminals; Fraud; Impostors and im-
    posture**

Swine. *See* **Pigs**

Switchboard hotlines. *See* **Hotlines (Telephone
    counseling)**

Switches, Electric. *See* **Electric switchgear**

Symbiosis. *See* **Botany—Ecology**

Symbolic numbers. *See* **Symbolism of numbers**

Symbolism 809
  See also **Heraldry; Signs and symbols;** also types
    of symbolism in religions, e.g. **Christian art
    and symbolism; Religious art and symbol-
    ism;** etc.
  x Devices (Heraldry); Emblems
  xx **Art; Mythology; Signs and symbols**

Symbolism in literature 809
  Use same form for symbolism in other subjects.
  See also **Allegories**
  xx **Literature**

Symbolism of numbers 133.3
  See also **Cabala; Three (The number)**
  x Number symbolism; Numerology; Sacred
    numbers; Symbolic numbers
  xx **Cabala; Christian art and symbolism; Magic;
    Mysticism; Numerals**

Symbols. *See* **Abbreviations; Signs and symbols**

Sympathy 152.4
  See also **Bereavement**
  x Compassion; Consolation; Pity
  xx **Bereavement; Emotions; Human behavior**

Symphonic poems 785.3

Symphonies 785.1
  Use for musical scores.
  xx **Orchestral music**

Symphony 785.1
  Use for materials on the symphony as a musical
    form.
  xx **Musical form**

Symptoms. *See* **Diagnosis**
Synagogues (May subdiv. geog.) **726**
    xx **Architecture; Judaism**
Synchronized swimming 797.2
    x Ballet, Water; Water ballet
    xx **Swimming**
Syndicalism 335
    See also **Anarchism and anarchists; Communism;**
        Socialism
    xx **Labor; Labor unions; Socialism; Strikes and**
        lockouts
Synfuels. *See* **Synthetic fuels**
Synods. *See* **Councils and synods**
Synonyms. *See* names of languages with the subdi-
    vision *Synonyms and antonyms,* e.g.
        English language—Synonyms and ant-
        onyms; etc.
Synthesizer music. *See* **Electronic music**
Synthesizer (Musical instrument) 789.9
    xx **Musical instruments, Electronic**
Synthetic chemistry. *See* **Chemistry, Organic—**
    Synthesis
Synthetic detergents. *See* **Detergents, Synthetic**
Synthetic fabrics 677
    See also names of synthetic fabrics, e.g. **Nylon;**
        Rayon; etc.
    x Fabrics, Synthetic
    xx **Fabrics; Synthetic products**
Synthetic food. *See* **Food, Artificial**
Synthetic fuels 662
    x Artificial fuels; Nonfossil fuels; Synfuels
    xx **Fuel; Synthetic products**
Synthetic products 677; 678
    See also **Chemurgy; Substitute products;** also
        names of types of synthetic products and
        names of specific products, e.g. **Food, Artifi-**
        cial; Plastics; Rayon; Rubber, Artificial;
        Synthetic fabrics; Synthetic fuels; etc.
    xx **Chemistry, Organic—Synthesis; Chemistry,**
        Technical; Chemurgy; Plastics; Substitute
        products
Synthetic rubber. *See* **Rubber, Artificial**
Syphilis 616.95
    xx **Venereal diseases**
Syrups 641.3
    xx **Sugar**
System analysis 001.6; *004.2; *621.392
    See also **System design; Systems engineering**
    x Linear system theory; Network theory; Sys-
        tems analysis
    xx **Cybernetics; Mathematical models; System**
        theory
System design 001.64; *004.2
    x Design, System; Systems design
    xx **Electronic data processing; System analysis**
System engineering. *See* **Systems engineering**
System theory 003
    See also **Cybernetics; Operations research; Sys-**
        tem analysis; Systems engineering
    x Systems, Theory of; Theory of systems

Systems analysis.   *See* **System analysis**
Systems design.   *See* **System design**
Systems engineering 620.7
 See also **Bionics; Operations research; Reliability
  (Engineering)**
 x System engineering
 xx **Automation; Cybernetics; Design, Industrial;
  Engineering; Operations research; System
  analysis; System theory**
Systems reliability.   *See* **Reliability (Engineering)**
Systems, Theory of.   *See* **System theory**
T groups.   *See* **Group relations training**
T.I.R.O.S. (Meteorological satellite).   *See* **Tiros
  (Meteorological satellite)**
T.V.   *See* **Television**
Table decoration.   *See* **Table setting and decoration**
Table etiquette 395
 xx **Eating customs; Etiquette**
Table setting and decoration 642
 See also **Flower arrangement; Tableware**
 x Table decoration
 xx **Decoration and ornament**
Table talk.   *See* **Conversation**
Table tennis.   *See* **Ping-pong**
Tables (Systematic lists).   *See* scientific and eco-
  nomic subjects with the subdivision *Tables,
  etc.,* e.g. **Trigonometry—Tables, etc.;** etc.
Tableware 642; 738; 739; 748.2
 See also **Glassware; Pottery; Silverware**
 xx **Table setting and decoration**
Tactics 355.4
 See also **Biological warfare; Guerrilla warfare**
 x Military tactics
 xx **Military art and science; Strategy**
Tadpoles.   *See* **Frogs**
Tailoring 646.4; 687
 See also **Dressmaking; Uniforms, Military**
 x Garment making
 xx **Clothing and dress; Clothing trade; Dressmaking; Fashion**
Taiwan 915.1; 951
 Use for materials discussing the post-1948 Re-
  public of China or the island of Taiwan, re-
  gardless of time period. Materials discussing
  mainland China or the People's Republic of
  China, regardless of time period, are entered
  under **China.**
 Appropriate period subdivisions may be added
  as needed.
 x China (Republic of China, 1949-   ); Formosa;
  Nationalist China; Republic of China,
  1949-
Talent.   *See* **Genius; Gifted children; Musical ability**
Tales.   *See* **Fables; Fairy tales; Folklore; Legends**
Talismans.   *See* **Charms**
Talk shows 791.44; 791.45
 xx **Interviewing; Radio programs; Television pro-
  grams**
Talking.   *See* **Conversation**

Talking books 027.6
    x Books, Talking; Cassette books
    xx **Blind—Books and reading; Sound recordings**
Talking pictures. *See* **Motion pictures**
Tall tales 398.2; 808.83; 813; etc.; Fic
    xx **Folklore; Legends; Wit and humor**
Talmud 296.1
    xx **Hebrew literature; Jewish literature; Judaism**
Tanks (Military science) 355
    x Armored cars (Tanks); Cars, Armored (Tanks)
Tanning 675
    See also **Hides and skins; Leather**
    xx **Chemistry, Technical; Hides and skins;
        Leather**
Taoism 299
    xx **Religions**
Tap dancing 793.3
    See also **Clog dancing**
    xx **Dancing**
Tape recorder music. *See* **Electronic music**
Tape recorders. *See* **Magnetic recorders and re-
        cording**
Tapestry 746.3
    xx **Decoration and ornament; Decorative arts; In-
        terior design; Needlework**
Tariff (May subdiv. geog.) **336.2; 382.7**
    See also **Balance of trade; Free trade and protec-
        tion; Smuggling**
    x Custom duties; Customs (Tariff); Duties; Ex-
        ports; Government regulation of commerce;
        Imports; Revenue
    xx **Commerce; Commercial policy; Economic pol-
        icy; Finance; Free trade and protection;
        Taxation; Trusts, Industrial**
Tariff question—Free trade and protection. *See*
        Free trade and protection
Tariff—United States 336.2; 382.7
    x United States—Tariff
Tarot 133.3; 795.4
    Use for materials on the cards and the game.
    xx **Card games; Fortune telling**
Tartans 391
    x Highland costume; Scottish tartans
    xx **Clans**
Taste 152.1
    xx **Senses and sensation**
Taste (Esthetics). *See* **Esthetics**
Taverns. *See* **Restaurants, bars, etc.**
Tax credits 336.2
    xx **Income tax**
Tax relations, Intergovernmental. *See* **Intergovern-
        mental tax relations**
Tax sharing. *See* **Intergovernmental tax relations;
        Revenue sharing**
Taxation (May subdiv. geog.) **336.2**
    See also

Assessment	**lations**
Income tax	**Internal revenue**
Inheritance and transfer tax	**Sales tax**
	Tariff
Intergovernmental tax re-	**Tithes**

603

Taxation—*Continued*

 also subjects with the subdivision *Taxation,* e.g.
  Real estate investment—Taxation; etc.

 x Direct taxation; Duties; Revenue; Taxes

 xx **Assessment; Estate planning; Finance; Political science**

Taxation of income. *See* **Income tax**

Taxation of legacies. *See* **Inheritance and transfer tax**

Taxation of sales. *See* **Sales tax**

Taxation—United States 336.2

 x United States—Taxation

Taxes. *See* **Taxation**

Taxidermy 579

 See also **Zoological specimens—Collection and preservation;** also names of specimens with the subdivision *Collection and preservation,* e.g. **Birds—Collection and preservation;** etc.

 x Specimens, Preservation of

 xx **Zoological specimens—Collection and preservation**

Tea rooms. *See* **Restaurants, bars, etc.**

Teacher-parent conferences. *See* **Parent-teacher conferences**

Teacher-parent relationships. *See* **Parent-teacher relationships**

Teacher-student relationships 371.1; 378

 x Pupil-teacher relationships; Student-teacher interaction

 xx **Children and adults; Human relations; Teaching**

Teacher training. *See* **Teachers colleges; Teachers—Training**

Teachers 371.1; 920

 See also **Educational associations; Educators; School superintendents and principals; Teaching**

 x College teachers; Faculty (Education); Professors

 xx **Education; Educators**

Teachers and parents. *See* **Parent-teacher relationships**

Teachers colleges 378

 Use for general and historical materials about teachers colleges. Materials dealing with their educational functions are entered under **Teachers—Training.**

 See also **Teachers—Training;** also names of teachers colleges

 x Normal schools; Teacher training; Training colleges for teachers

 xx **Colleges and universities; Education—Study and teaching; Teachers—Training**

Teachers, Exchange of. *See* **Teachers, Interchange of**

Teachers' institutes. *See* **Teachers' workshops**

Teachers, Interchange of 370.19

 x Exchange of teachers; Interchange of teachers; Teachers, Exchange of

 xx **Exchange of persons programs; International**

Teachers, Interchange of—*Continued*
      education
Teachers—Practice teaching. *See* **Student teaching**
Teachers, Student rating of. *See* **Student evaluation**
      of teachers
Teachers—Training 371.1
    Use for materials dealing with the history and
        methods of training teachers, including the
        educational functions of teachers colleges.
        Materials on the study of education as a sci-
        ence are entered under **Education—Study**
        and teaching.
    See also **Student teaching; Teachers colleges;**
        Teachers' workshops
    x Teacher training
    xx **Education—Study and teaching; Teachers col-**
        leges; Teaching
Teachers' workshops 371.1
    x Teachers' institutes; Workshops, Teachers'
    xx **Teachers—Training**
Teaching 371.1
    Use for materials on the art and method of
        teaching.
    See also

Classroom management	**School superintendents**
Education	**and principals**
Educational psychology	**School supervision**
Examinations	**Student teaching**
Home instruction	**Study, Method of**
Kindergarten	**Teacher-student relation**
Lectures and lecturing	**ships**
Montessori method of edu-	**Teachers—Training**
cation	**Teaching teams**
Project method in teaching	**Tutors and tutoring**
School discipline	

    also subjects with the subdivision *Study and*
        teaching, e.g. **Science—Study and teaching;**
        etc.
    x Instruction; Pedagogy; School teaching
    xx **Education; Schools—Administration; Teach-**
        ers
Teaching—Aids and devices 371.3
    See also Audiovisual materials; Bulletin boards;
        Motion pictures in education; Programmed
        instruction; Radio in education; Teaching
        machines; Television in education
Teaching at home. *See* **Home instruction**
Teaching, Computer. *See* **Computer assisted in-**
      struction
Teaching—Data processing. *See* **Computer assisted**
      instruction
Teaching—Experimental methods. *See* **Educa-**
      tion—Experimental methods
Teaching, Freedom of. *See* **Academic freedom**
Teaching machines 371.3
    x Automatic teaching; Tutorial machines
    xx **Programmed instruction; Teaching—Aids and**
        devices
Teaching teams 371.1
    x Team teaching

Teaching teams—*Continued*
> *xx* **Teaching**

Teachings of Jesus. *See* **Jesus Christ—Teachings**

Team teaching. *See* **Teaching teams**

Tearooms. *See* **Restaurants, bars, etc.**

Technical assistance (May subdiv. geog. adjective form) **338.91; 361.6**
> See note under **Economic assistance.**
> *See also* **Community development; Developing countries; Industrialization**
> *x* Aid to developing areas; Assistance to developing areas; Foreign aid program
> *xx* **Community development; Developing countries; Economic assistance; Economic policy; Industrialization; International cooperation; International economic relations**

Technical assistance, American 338.973; 361.6
> *x* American technical assistance; United States—Technical assistance

Technical chemistry. *See* **Chemistry, Technical**

Technical education 370.11; 373.2; 374
> *See also*

Apprentices	**Industrial arts education**
Correspondence schools and courses	**Occupational retraining**
	Occupational training
Employees—Training	**Professional education**
Evening and continuation schools	**School shops**
	Vocational education

> also technical subjects with the subdivision *Study and teaching,* e.g. **Engineering—Study and teaching;** etc.
> *x* Education, Industrial; Education, Technical; Industrial education; Industrial schools; Technical schools; Trade schools
> *xx* **Education; Education, Higher; Employees—Training; Industrial arts education; Professional education; Technology; Vocational education**

Technical schools. *See* **Technical education**

Technical services (Libraries). *See* **Library technical processes**

Technical terms. *See* **Technology—Dictionaries**

Technical writing 808
> *x* Scientific writing
> *xx* **Authorship; Technology—Language**

Technique. *See* subjects with the subdivision *Technique,* e.g. **Fiction—Technique; Love stories—Technique; Painting—Technique;** etc.

Technology 600
> *See also*

Building	**Machinery**
Chemistry, Technical	**Manufactures**
Engineering	**Mills and millwork**
Industrial arts	**Technical education**
Inventions	

> *x* Applied science; Arts, Useful; Useful arts
> *xx* **Industrial arts**

Technology and civilization 303.4
> Use same form for technology and other subjects

Technology and civilization—*Continued*
>*See also* **Computers and civilization; Machinery in industry**
>*x* Civilization and technology
>*xx* **Civilization**

Technology—Dictionaries 603
>*x* Technical terms

Technology—Language 601; 603
>*See also* **Technical writing**

Teenage consumers. *See* **Young consumers**

Teenage drinking. *See* **Youth—Alcohol use**

Teenage mothers. *See* **Adolescent mothers**

Teenage pregnancy. *See* **Pregnancy, Adolescent**

Teenage prostitution. *See* **Prostitution, Juvenile**

Teenagers. *See* **Youth**

Teenagers and alcohol. *See* **Youth—Alcohol use**

Teenagers and drugs. *See* **Youth—Drug use**

Teenagers, Runaway. *See* **Runaway children**

Teeth 611; 612; 617.6
>*See also* **Dentistry**
>*x* Anatomy, Dental
>*xx* **Dentistry**

Teeth—Diseases 617.6
>*See also* **Water—Fluoridation**
>*x* Medicine, Dental

Telecommunication 384; 621.38
>*See also*

Artificial satellites in telecommunication	**Interstellar communication**
Broadcasting	**Microwave communication systems**
Cables, Submarine	**Radio**
Computer networks	**Telecommuting**
Data transmission systems	**Telegraph**
Electronic publishing	**Telephone**
Intercommunication systems	**Television**

>also subjects with the subdivision
>*Communication systems,* e.g.
>**Astronautics—Communication systems;** etc.
>*x* Electric communication; Mass communication
>*xx* **Communication**

Telecommuting 331.2
>Use for materials on employment at home with computers, word processors, etc. connected to a central work site, permitting employees to substitute telecommunications for transportation.
>*See also* **Home computers**
>*x* Alternate work site; At-home employment; Cottage industry, Electronic; Electronic cottage; Flexiplace; Home labor; Home work (Employment); Homework (Employment); Work at home; Working at home
>*xx* **Automation; Home business; Management; Telecommunication**

Teleconferencing 384.6; 651.7
>*x* Conference calls (Teleconferencing); Telephone—Conference calls
>*xx* **Telephone**

Telegraph 384.1; 621.382

 See also **Cables, Submarine; Cipher and tele-**
  graph codes

 xx **Electric engineering; Electric wiring; Electric-**
  ity; Public utilities; Telecommunication

Telegraph codes. *See* **Cipher and telegraph codes**

Telegraph, Submarine. *See* **Cables, Submarine**

Telekinesis. *See* **Psychokinesis**

Telemarketing 384.55; 621.388; 658.8

 Use for materials on the use of electronic media
  as a form of marketing that bypasses retail
  outlets in the advertising and selling of
  goods.

 x Electronic marketing

 xx **Cable television; Direct selling; Marketing;**
  Teletext systems

Telematiques. *See* **Teletext systems**

Telepathy 133.8

 See also **Clairvoyance; Mind reading**

 x Mental telepathy; Thought transference

 xx **Clairvoyance; Extrasensory perception; Mind**
  reading; Psychical research; Subconscious-
  ness

Telephone 384.6; 621.385

 See also **Teleconferencing; Video telephone**

 xx **Electric engineering; Electric wiring; Electric-**
  ity; Public utilities; Telecommunication

Telephone—Conference calls. *See* **Teleconferenc-**
  ing

Telephone counseling. *See* **Hotlines (Telephone**
  counseling)

Telephone directories. *See* names of cities with the
  subdivision *Directories—Telephone,* e.g.
  Chicago (Ill.)—Directories—Telephone;
  etc.

Telephotography 778.3

 xx **Photography**

Teleprocessing networks. *See* **Computer networks**

Telereference. *See* **Teletext systems**

Telescope 522

 xx **Astronomical instruments**

Teletext systems 384.55; 621.388; *384.3

 Use for works on the transmission of computer-
  based data from a central source to the
  home television.

 See also types of information transmitted, e.g.
  Electronic mail systems; Telemarketing; etc.

 x Broadcast videotex systems; Interactive videotex systems; Telematiques; Telereference;
  Television data system; Television reference system; Videotext systems; Viewdata
  systems

 xx **Data transmission systems; Electronic publish-**
  ing; Information storage and retrieval sys-
  tems; Television broadcasting

Television 384.55; 621.388

 See also

Closed-circuit television	**systems**
Color television	**Public television**
Microwave communication	**Subscription television**

Television—*Continued*
>   **Video art**   **Videodiscs**
>   **Video telephone**   **Videotapes**
>   *x* T.V.; TV
>   *xx* **Telecommunication**
Television actors and actresses. *See* **Actors and actresses**
Television advertising 659.14
>   *x* Advertising, Television; Commercials, Television; Television commercials
>   *xx* **Advertising**
Television and children 384.55; 791.45
>   Use for materials dealing with the effect of television on children.
>   Use same form for television and other subjects.
>   *See also* **Motion pictures and children**
>   *x* Children and television
>   *xx* **Children; Motion pictures and children**
Television and infrared observation satellite. *See* **Tiros (Meteorological satellite)**
Television and youth 384.55; 791.45
>   *x* Youth and television
>   *xx* **Youth**
Television authorship 791.45; 808
>   *See also* **Television plays—Technique**
>   *x* Television writing
>   *xx* **Authorship**
Television broadcasting 384.55
>   *See also*
>   **Cable television**   **Television in education**
>   **Equal time rule (Broad-**   **Television in politics**
>   **casting)**   **Television programs**
>   **Fairness doctrine (Broad-**   **Television scripts**
>   **casting)**   **Videotape recorders and**
>   **Teletext systems**   **recording**
>   *xx* **Broadcasting; Mass media; Radio broadcasting**
Television broadcasting—Vocational guidance 384.55
>   *xx* **Vocational guidance**
Television, Cable. *See* **Cable television**
Television—Censorship 384.55
>   *xx* **Censorship**
Television, Closed-circuit. *See* **Closed-circuit television**
Television, Color. *See* **Color television**
Television commercials. *See* **Television advertising**
Television data system. *See* **Teletext systems**
Television drama. *See* **Television plays**
Television—Equipment and supplies 621.388
>   *See also* **Videodisc players; Videotape recorders and recording**
Television games. *See* **Video games**
Television in astronautics 621.388; 629.47
>   *x* Space television; Television, Space
>   *xx* **Astronautics—Communication systems**
Television in education 371.33
>   Use same pattern for television in other subjects.
>   *See also* **Closed-circuit television**
>   *x* Education and television; Educational

Television in education—*Continued*
>television
>*xx* **Audiovisual education; Closed-circuit television; Teaching—Aids and devices; Television broadcasting**

Television in politics 324.7
>*See also* **Equal time rule (Broadcasting); Fairness doctrine (Broadcasting)**
>*xx* **Politics, Practical; Television broadcasting**

Television journalism. *See* **Broadcast journalism**

Television news. *See* **Broadcast journalism**

Television plays 808.82; 812; etc.
>Use for individual television plays, for collections of plays and for materials about them. Materials on how to write television plays are entered under **Television plays—Technique.**
>*x* Scenarios; Television drama
>*xx* **Drama; Television programs; Television scripts**

Television plays—Technique 808.2
>*See also* **Radio plays—Technique**
>*x* Play writing; Playwriting
>*xx* **Drama—Technique; Radio plays—Technique; Television authorship**

Television—Production and direction 384.55; 791.45

Television programs 791.45
>*See also* types of television programs and specific programs, e.g. **Music videos; Talk shows; Television plays;** etc.
>*x* Programs, Television
>*xx* **Television broadcasting**

Television, Public. *See* **Public television**

Television—Receivers and reception 621.388
>*See also* **Video games**
>*x* Television sets

Television reference system. *See* **Teletext systems**

Television—Repairing 621.388

Television scripts 791.45
>*See also* **Radio scripts; Television plays**
>*xx* **Radio scripts; Television broadcasting**

Television sets. *See* **Television—Receivers and reception**

Television, Space. *See* **Television in astronautics**

Television—Stage lighting. *See* **Stage lighting**

Television stations 384.55

Television, Subscription. *See* **Subscription television**

Television writing. *See* **Television authorship**

Telstar project 621.3841
>*x* Bell System Telstar satellite; Project Telstar
>*xx* **Artificial satellites in telecommunication**

Temperament 155.2
>*See also* **Character**
>*xx* **Character; Mind and body; Psychology; Psychology, Physiological**

Temperance 178; 241
>Use for general materials on the temperance question and the temperance movement.
>*See also* **Alcohol—Physiological effect; Alcohol-**

Temperance—*Continued*
>	ism; **Drinking of alcoholic beverages; Narcotic habit; Prohibition; Stimulants**
>	*x* Abstinence; Drunkenness; Intemperance; Intoxication; Total abstinence
>	*xx* **Alcoholism; Drinking of alcoholic beverages; Human behavior; Prohibition**

Temperature 536
>	*See also* **Heat; Low temperatures; Thermometers and thermometry**
>	*xx* **Heat; Thermometers and thermometry**

Temperature, Animal and human. *See* **Body temperature**

Temperature, Body. *See* **Body temperature**

Temperatures, Low. *See* **Low temperatures**

Temples (May subdiv. geog.) **726**
>	*See also* **Mosques**
>	*xx* **Archeology; Architecture; Architecture, Ancient; Architecture, Asian; Church architecture**

Temporal power of the Pope. *See* **Popes—Temporal power**

Temporary employment 331.2
>	*x* Employment, Temporary
>	*xx* **Employment**

Ten commandments 222
>	*x* Commandments, Ten; Decalogue

Tenant and landlord. *See* **Landlord and tenant**

Tenant farming. *See* **Farm tenancy**

Tenement houses 363.5
>	*See also* **City planning; Housing**
>	*xx* **Cities and towns; Houses; Housing**

Tennis 796.342
>	*x* Lawn tennis
>	*xx* **Games**

Tennis—Tournaments 796.342
>	*x* Tournaments
>	*xx* **Contests**

Tenpins. *See* **Bowling**

Tension (Physiology). *See* **Stress (Physiology)**

Tension (Psychology). *See* **Stress (Psychology)**

Tents 796.54
>	*xx* **Camping**

Tenure of land. *See* **Land tenure**

Tenure of office. *See* **Civil service**

Terminal care 362.1; 649.8
>	*See also* **Hospices; Life support systems (Medical environment); Terminally ill; Terminally ill children**
>	*xx* **Death**

Terminally ill 362.1; 649.8
>	*x* Dying patients; Fatally ill patients
>	*xx* **Death; Sick; Terminal care**

Terminally ill children 362.1; 649.8
>	*x* Dying children; Fatally ill children
>	*xx* **Terminal care**

Terminals, Computer. *See* **Computer terminals**

Termination of pregnancy. *See* **Abortion**

Terminology. *See* **Names;** and subjects with the subdivision *Terminology,* e.g.

Terminology—*Continued*
> Botany—Terminology; etc.

Terns 598
> *xx* **Water birds**

Terra cotta 620.1; 693
> *xx* **Building materials; Decoration and ornament; Pottery**

Terrain sensing, Remote. *See* **Remote sensing**

Terrapins. *See* **Turtles**

Terrariums 635.9
> *See also* **Gardens, Miniature**
> *x* Vivariums
> *xx* **Indoor gardening**

Terrestrial physics. *See* **Geophysics**

Territorial waters (May subdiv. geog.) **341.4**
> *See also* **Continental shelf; Maritime law**
> *x* 3 mile limit; 200 mile limit; Economic zones (Maritime law); Three mile limit; Two hundred mile limit
> *xx* **Continental shelf; Maritime law; Shipping**

Territorial waters—United States 341.4
> *x* United States—Territorial waters

Terror, Reign of. *See* **France—History—1789-1799, Revolution**

Terrorism (May subdiv. geog.) **322.4**
> *See also* **Hostages; Sabotage**
> *x* Political violence
> *xx* **Anarchism and anarchists; Assassination; Insurgency; Political crimes and offenses; Revolutions; Subversive activities**

Terrorism—United States 303.6; 322.4
> *x* United States—Terrorism

Test pilots. *See* **Air pilots; Airplanes—Testing**

Test tube babies. *See* **Fertilization in vitro, Human**

Test tube fertilization. *See* **Fertilization in vitro**

Tests. *See* **Educational tests and measurements; Examinations; Mental tests**

Teutonic peoples 572.9363
> *See also* **Anglo-Saxons**
> *x* Goths; Nordic peoples; Ostrogoths; Saxons; Visigoths
> *xx* **Ethnology**

Textbooks 371.3
> Use for materials about textbooks, not for textbooks of a subject. The latter are entered under the name of subject only, e.g. **Arithmetic; Geography;** etc.
> *x* School books

Textile chemistry 677
> *See also* **Dyes and dyeing**
> *x* Chemistry, Textile
> *xx* **Chemistry, Technical; Textile industry**

Textile design 746
> *See also* **Textile painting**
> *xx* **Commercial art; Decoration and ornament; Design**

Textile fibers. *See* **Fibers**

Textile industry 677
> *See also*
>
> **Bleaching**   **Textile chemistry**
> **Cotton manufacture**   **Textile printing**
> **Dyes and dyeing**   **Weaving**
> **Spinning**   **Yarn**
>
> also names of articles manufactured, e.g **Carpets; Hosiery;** etc
>
> *xx* **Weaving** ʿ

Textile painting 746.6
> *xx* **Painting; Textile design**

Textile printing 746.6
> *See also* **Silk screen printing**
>
> *x* Block printing; Printing, Textile
>
> *xx* **Textile industry**

Textiles. *See* **Fabrics**

Theater (May subdiv. geog.) **792**
> Use for materials dealing with drama as acted on the stage, and with the historical, moral, and religious aspects of the theater. Materials dealing with drama from a literary point of view are entered under **Drama; American drama; English drama;** etc.
>
> *See also*
>
> **Acting**
> **Actors and actresses**   **Mysteries and miracle**
> **Amateur theater**   **plays**
> **Arena theater**   **Opera**
> **Ballet**   **Pantomimes**
> **Children's plays**   **Passion plays**
> **Drama**   **Puppets and puppet plays**
> **Dramatic criticism**   **Shadow pantomimes and**
> **Experimental theater**   **plays**
> **Little theater movement**   **Shakespeare, William, 1564-**
> **Masks (Plays)**   **1616—Stage history**
> **Morality plays**   **Theaters**
> **Motion pictures**   **Vaudeville**
>
> also names of wars with the subdivision *Theater and the war,* e.g. **World War, 1939-1945—Theater and the war;** etc.
>
> *x* Histrionics; Stage
>
> *xx* **Acting; Actors and actresses; Amusements; Drama; Drama in education; Performing arts**

Theater, Amateur. *See* **Amateur theater**

Theater criticism. *See* **Dramatic criticism**

Theater-in-the-round. *See* **Arena theater**

Theater—Little theater movement. *See* **Little theater movement**

Theater—Production and direction 792
> *See also* **Motion pictures—Production and direction**
>
> *x* Direction (Theater); Play direction (Theater); Play production
>
> *xx* **Amateur theater**

Theater—United States 792
> *x* United States—Theater

Theaters (May subdiv. geog.) **725**
> Use for materials dealing only with theater buildings, their architecture, construction, decoration, sanitation, etc.

Theaters—*Continued*
    x Opera houses; Playhouses
    xx **Architecture; Centers for the performing arts;**
        Theater
Theaters—Stage lighting. *See* **Stage lighting**
Theaters—Stage setting and scenery 792
    See also **Scene painting**
    x Scenery (Stage); Stage scenery; Stage setting;
        Theatrical scenery
Theatrical costume. *See* **Costume**
Theatrical makeup. *See* **Makeup, Theatrical**
Theatrical scenery. *See* **Theaters—Stage setting**
    and scenery
Theatricals, College. *See* **College and school drama**
Thefts, Art. *See* **Art thefts**
Theism 211
    See also **Atheism; Christianity; Deism; God**
    xx **Atheism; Deism; God; Philosophy; Rational-**
        ism; Religion; Theology
Theme parks. *See* **Amusement parks**
Theological education. *See* **Theology—Study and**
    teaching
Theology 230; 291
    See also

Atheism	**Natural theology**
Baptism	**Predestination**
Christianity	**Providence and govern-**
Church	**ment of God**
Conversion	**Religion**
Creeds	**Religion and science**
Deism	**Revelation**
Eschatology	**Sacraments**
Faith	**Sacrifice**
God—Christianity	**Sanctification**
Good and evil	**Secularism**
Grace (Theology)	**Sin**
Holy Spirit	**Spiritual life**
Immortality	**Theism**
Liturgies	**Trinity**
Man (Theology)	**Worship**
Mysticism	

    xx **Christianity; Creation; God—Christianity; Re-**
        ligion
Theology, Devotional. *See* **Devotional exercises;**
    Prayers
Theology, Doctrinal 230; 240
    See also **Liberation theology; Love (Theology);**
        Regeneration (Theology)
    x Christian doctrine; Doctrinal theology; Dog-
        matic theology
Theology, Natural. *See* **Natural theology**
Theology of liberation. *See* **Liberation theology**
Theology, Pastoral. *See* **Pastoral work**
Theology—Philosophy. *See* **Christianity—**
    Philosophy
Theology—Study and teaching 230; 291
    See also **Catechisms; Christian education;**
        Church and education; Religious education
    x Education, Theological; Religion—Study and
        teaching; Theological education

Theology—Study and teaching—*Continued*
   xx **Christian education; Church and education;**
        Religious education
Theoretical chemistry. *See* **Chemistry, Physical**
       and theoretical
Theory of games. *See* **Game theory**
Theory of graphs. *See* **Graph theory**
Theory of numbers. *See* **Number theory**
Theory of structures. *See* **Structures, Theory of**
Theory of systems. *See* **System theory**
Theosophy 299
   See also **Reincarnation; Yoga**
   xx **Mysticism; Religions**
Therapeutics 615
   See also

Antiseptics	**Medicine**
Chemistry, Medical and	**Naturopathy**
pharmaceutical	**Nursing**
Diet in disease	**Nutrition**
Drugs	**Stimulants**
Electrotherapeutics	**X rays**
Materia medica	

      also names of diseases and groups of diseases,
         e.g. **Smallpox; Fever; Nervous system—**
         Diseases; etc.; names of food with the sub-
         division *Therapeutic use,* e.g.
         Corn—Therapeutic use; etc.; names of
         drugs, e.g. **Narcotics;** etc.; and names of
         types of therapy, e.g. **Diet therapy; Hydro-**
         therapy; Occupational therapy; Pet therapy;
         Phototherapy; Physical therapy; Radiother-
         apy; etc.
   x Therapy
   xx **Materia medica; Medicine—Practice; Pathol-**
      ogy
Therapeutics, Suggestive 615.8
   See also **Hypnotism; Mental healing; Mental**
      suggestion; Psychology, Pastoral; Psycho-
      therapy; Spiritual healing; Subconsciousness
   x Suggestive therapeutics
   xx **Hypnotism; Mental healing; Mental sugges-**
      tion; Psychotherapy; Spiritual healing
Therapy. *See* **Therapeutics**
Thermal insulation. *See* **Insulation (Heat)**
Thermal waters. *See* **Geothermal resources; Gey-**
      sers
Thermoaerodynamics. *See* **Aerothermodynamics**
Thermodynamics 536
   See also **Aerothermodynamics; Heat; Heat en-**
      gines; Heat pumps; Quantum theory; also
      subjects with the subdivision
      Thermodynamics, e.g. **Space vehicles—**
      Thermodynamics; etc.
   xx **Chemistry, Physical and theoretical; Dynam-**
      ics; Heat; Heat engines; Physics; Quantum
      theory
Thermometers and thermometry 536
   See also **Temperature**
   xx **Heat; Meteorological instruments; Tempera-**
      ture

Thermonuclear bomb. *See* **Hydrogen bomb**
Thesauri. *See* **Subject headings;** and names of languages with the subdivision *Synonyms and antonyms,* e.g. **English language—Synonyms and antonyms;** etc.
Theses. *See* **Dissertations, Academic**
Thieves. *See* **Robbers and outlaws**
Think tanks. *See* **Problem solving, Group**
Thinking. *See* **Thought and thinking**
Third parties (U.S. politics) 324.2
Third World. *See* **Developing countries**
Third World War. *See* **World War III**
Thirteenth century 909.07
> *x* 1200-1299 (13th century)
> *xx* **Europe—History—476-1492; Middle Ages**
Thirty Years' War, 1618-1648 909.08; 940.2
> *xx* **Europe—History—1492-1789; Germany—History—1517-1740**
Thoroughfares. *See* **Roads; Streets**
Thought and thinking 153.4
> *See also* **Attention; Critical thinking; Intellect; Logic; Memory; Perception; Reasoning**
> *x* Thinking
> *xx* **Educational psychology; Intellect; Logic; Psychology**
Thought control. *See* **Brainwashing**
Thought transference. *See* **Telepathy**
Threatened animals. *See* **Rare animals**
Threatened plants. *See* **Rare plants**
Threatened species. *See* **Endangered species**
Three mile limit. *See* **Territorial waters**
Three (The number) 513
> *xx* **Numerals; Symbolism of numbers**
Thrift. *See* **Saving and thrift**
Throat 611; 612
> *See also* **Voice**
Thunderstorms 551.5
> *See also* **Lightning**
> *xx* **Meteorology; Storms**
Tidal waves. *See* **Ocean waves**
Tides 525
> *xx* **Astronomy; Moon; Navigation; Oceanography; Physical geography**
Tie dyeing 667
> *xx* **Dyes and dyeing**
Tiles 620.1; 693; 738.6
> *xx* **Bricks; Building materials; Ceramics; Clay industries; Pottery**
Timber. *See* **Forests and forestry; Lumber and lumbering; Trees; Wood**
Time 529
> *See also* **Calendars; Chronology; Clocks and watches; Day; Night; Periodicity; Sundials**
> *x* Standard time
> *xx* **Longitude; Periodicity**
Time and space. *See* **Space and time**
Time management 646.7; 650.1; 658
> *x* Allocation of time; Personal time management; Time—Organization; Time, Use of; Use of time

Time management—*Continued*
   xx **Leisure; Management**
Time—Organization. *See* **Time management**
Time production standards. *See* **Production standards**
Time sharing (Real estate). *See* **Timesharing (Real estate)**
Time study 658.5
   See also **Motion study**
   xx **Efficiency, Industrial; Factory management; Job analysis; Motion study; Personnel management; Production standards**
Time, Use of. *See* **Time management**
Timesharing (Real estate) 333.3; 333.5; 643
   x Condominium timesharing; Real estate timesharing; Time sharing (Real estate); Vacation home timesharing
   xx **Condominiums; Housing**
Tin 669
   See also **Pewter**
Tinsmithing. *See* **Tinwork**
Tinwork 671
   x Tinsmithing
   xx **Metalwork**
Tires 678
   x Rubber tires
   xx **Wheels**
Tiros (Meteorological satellite) 551.6
   x T.I.R.O.S. (Meteorological satellite); Television and infrared observation satellite
   xx **Meteorological satellites**
Tissue donation. *See* **Donation of organs, tissues, etc.**
Tissues—Transplantation. *See* **Transplantation of organs, tissues, etc.**
Tithes 254.8
   xx **Church finance; Ecclesiastical law; Taxation**
Toadstools. *See* **Mushrooms**
Toasts 808.5; 808.85
   See also **After dinner speeches**
   x Healths, Drinking of
   xx **After dinner speeches; Epigrams; Speeches, addresses, etc.**
Tobacco 633.7
   See also **Smoking**
   xx **Smoking**
Tobacco habit 178; 613.8; 616.86
   xx **Habit; Smoking; Substance abuse**
Tobacco pipes 688
   x Pipes, Tobacco
   xx **Smoking**
Toes. *See* **Foot**
Toilet preparations. *See* **Cosmetics**
Toleration 303.6
   See also **Academic freedom; Discrimination; Freedom of conscience; Religious freedom**
   x Bigotry; Intolerance
   xx **Discrimination; Human relations**
Toll roads. *See* **Express highways**

Tombs (May subdiv. geog.) **726**
> *See also* **Brasses; Catacombs; Cemeteries; Epitaphs; Mounds and mound builders**
> *x* Burial; Graves; Mausoleums; Rock tombs; Sepulchers; Vaults (Sepulchral)
> *xx* **Archeology; Architecture; Cemeteries; Monuments; Shrines**

Tongue twisters 818
> *xx* **Children's poetry; Folklore; Nonsense verses**

Tools 621.9
> *See also* **Agricultural machinery; Carpentry—Tools; Machine tools; Machinery; Power tools;** also names of specific tools, e.g **Saws;** etc.
> *x* Implements, utensils, etc.

Top soil loss. *See* **Soil erosion**

Topographical drawing 526.8
> *See also* **Map drawing**
> *xx* **Drawing; Map drawing; Surveying**

Topology 514
> *See also* **Algebras, Linear; Fractals; Graph theory**
> *x* Analysis situs; Position analysis; Rubber sheet geometry
> *xx* **Algebras, Linear; Geometry; Set theory**

Tories, American. *See* **American Loyalists**

Tornadoes (May subdiv. geog.) **551.5**
> *See also* **Cyclones; Storms**
> *xx* **Meteorology; Storms; Winds**

Torpedoes 623.4
> *xx* **Explosives; Naval art and science; Submarine warfare**

Tort liability of professions. *See* **Malpractice**

Tortoises. *See* **Turtles**

Total abstinence. *See* **Temperance**

Totalitarianism 321.9
> *See also* **Communism; Dictators; Fascism; National socialism**
> *x* Authoritarianism

Totems and totemism 299
> *xx* **Ethnology; Indians of North America—Religion; Mythology**

Touch 152.1; 612
> *x* Feeling
> *xx* **Senses and sensation**

Tourism. *See* **Tourist trade**

Tourist accommodations. *See* **Hotels, motels, etc.; Youth hostels**

Tourist trade 910.2
> *See also* **Travel**
> *x* Tourism
> *xx* **Travel**

Tournaments. *See* subjects with the subdivision *Tournaments,* e.g. **Tennis—Tournaments;** etc.

Town life. *See* **City life**

Town meeting. *See* **Local government**

Town planning. *See* **City planning**

Towns. *See* **Cities and towns**

Township government. *See* **Local government**

Toxic dumps.   *See* **Hazardous waste sites**
Toxic substances.   *See* **Hazardous substances; Poi-
sons and poisoning**
Toxicology.   *See* **Poisons and poisoning**
Toy and movable books   E
    x Movable books; Pop-up books
    xx **Picture books for children**
Toys   688.7
    See also names of kinds of toys, e.g. **Dollhouses;
Dolls; Electric toys; Electronic toys;** etc.
    x Miniature objects
    xx **Amusements**
Track and field.   *See* **Track athletics**
Track athletics   796.4
    See also names of specific track sports, e.g.
Running; etc.
    x Field athletics; Track and field
    xx **Athletics; College sports**
Tracking and trailing   799.2-799.3
    See also **Animal tracks**
    x Trailing
    xx **Animals—Habits and behavior; Hunting**
Tracking of satellites.   *See* **Artificial satellites—
Tracking; Space vehicles—Tracking**
Tracks of animals.   *See* **Animal tracks**
Traction engines.   *See* **Tractors**
Tractors   629.2; 631.5
    x Traction engines
    xx **Agricultural machinery; Farm engines**
Trade.   *See* **Business; Commerce**
Trade agreements (Labor).   *See* **Arbitration, Indus-
trial; Labor contract**
Trade and professional associations   380.1; 650
    Use for materials on business or professional or-
ganizations whose aim is the protection or
advancement of their common interests
without regard to the relations of employer
and employee.
    x Professional associations
    xx **Associations**
Trade, Balance of.   *See* **Balance of trade**
Trade barriers.   *See* **Commercial policy**
Trade, Boards of.   *See* **Chambers of commerce**
Trade fairs.   *See* **Fairs**
Trade marks.   *See* **Trademarks**
Trade, Restraint of.   *See* **Restraint of trade**
Trade routes   387
    x Ocean routes; Routes of trade; Sea routes
    xx **Commerce; Geography, Commercial; Trans-
portation**
Trade schools.   *See* **Technical education**
Trade unions.   *See* **Labor unions**
Trade waste.   *See* **Industrial wastes; Waste products**
Trademarks   341.7
    See also **Brand name products; Patents**
    x Company symbols; Corporate symbols; Trade
marks
    xx **Brand name products; Commerce; Manufac-
tures; Patents**
Trades.   *See* **Industrial arts; Occupations**

Traditions.   *See* **Folklore; Legends; Manners and
customs; Rites and ceremonies; Superstition**
Traffic accidents   363.1
See also **Drunk driving**
x Automobile accidents; Automobiles—
Accidents; Highway accidents
xx **Accidents; Traffic regulations**
Traffic, City.   *See* **City traffic**
Traffic control.   *See* **Traffic engineering**
Traffic engineering   388.4
Use for materials on the planning of the flow of
traffic and related topics, largely as they
concern street transportation in cities and
metropolitan areas.
See also **Car pools; City traffic; Express high-
ways; Local transit**
x Street traffic; Traffic control; Traffic regulation
xx **Engineering; Highway engineering; Transpor-
tation**
Traffic regulation.   *See* **Traffic engineering**
Traffic regulations   388.4
See also **Automobiles—Law and legislation;
Traffic accidents**
x Street traffic
xx **Automobiles—Law and legislation; Transpor-
tation**
Tragedy   792.1
xx **Drama**
Trailer parks   796.54
See also **Mobile home parks**
xx **Campgrounds**
Trailers.   *See* **Automobiles—Trailers; Travel trailers
and campers**
Trailers, Home.   *See* **Mobile homes**
Trailing.   *See* **Tracking and trailing**
Train wrecks.   *See* **Railroads—Accidents**
Trained nurses.   *See* **Nurses**
Training camps, Military.   *See* **Military training
camps**
Training colleges for teachers.   *See* **Teachers col-
leges**
Training, Occupational.   *See* **Occupational training**
Training of animals.   *See* **Animals—Training**
Training of children.   *See* **Child rearing**
Training of employees.   *See* **Employees—Training**
Training, Vocational.   *See* **Occupational training**
Trains, Railroad.   *See* **Railroads**
Tramps   305.5
See also **Begging**
x Hoboes; Vagabonds; Vagrants
xx **Begging; Homeless people**
Trams.   *See* **Street railroads**
Transactional analysis   158
xx **Human relations**
Transatlantic flights.   *See* **Aeronautics—Flights**
Transcendental meditation   158
xx **Meditation**
Transcendentalism   141
See also **Idealism**

Transcendentalism—*Continued*
   xx **Idealism; Philosophy**
Transcontinental journeys (U.S.). *See* **Overland journeys to the Pacific (U.S.)**
Transcultural studies. *See* **Cross cultural studies**
Transexuality. *See* **Transsexuality**
Transfer tax. *See* **Inheritance and transfer tax**
Transformation (Genetics). *See* **Genetic transformation**
Transformers, Electric. *See* **Electric transformers**
Transistors 621.3815
   xx **Electronics; Semiconductors**
Transit systems. *See* **Local transit**
Translating and interpreting 418
   x Interpreting and translating; Machine translating; Mechanical translating
   xx **Language and languages**
Transmission of data. *See* **Data transmission systems**
Transmission of power. *See* **Electric lines; Electric power distribution; Power transmission**
Transmissions, Automobile. *See* **Automobiles—Transmission devices**
Transmutation (Chemistry) 546; 547
   Use for modern discussions on the transmutation of metals. Materials dealing with the medieval attempts to transmute baser metals into gold are entered under **Alchemy.**
   See also **Cyclotron**
   x Metals, Transmutation of; Transmutation of metals
   xx **Alchemy; Atoms; Nuclear physics; Radioactivity**
Transmutation of metals. *See* **Alchemy; Transmutation (Chemistry)**
Transplantation of organs, tissues, etc. 617
   See also **Donation of organs, tissues, etc.; Surgery, Plastic;** also names of organs of the body with the subdivision *Transplantation,* e.g. **Heart—Transplantation;** etc.
   x Medical transplantation; Organ transplantation; Prosthesis; Surgical transplantation; Tissues—Transplantation
   xx **Donation of organs, tissues, etc.; Preservation of organs, tissues, etc.; Surgery**
Transplantation of organs, tissues, etc.—Moral and religious aspects 174
   xx **Bioethics**
Transportation 380
   Use for general materials on the transportation of persons or goods.
   See also

Aeronautics, Commercial	**Harbors**
Bridges	**Inland navigation**
Canals	**Local transit**
Car pools	**Merchant marine**
Commerce	**Ocean travel**
Electric railroads	**Pipelines**
Express service	**Postal service**
Freight and freightage	**Railroads**

Transportation—*Continued*

Roads	**Trade routes**
Shipping	**Traffic engineering**
Steam navigation	**Traffic regulations**
Street railroads	**Trucking**
Streets	**Vehicles**
Subways	**Waterways**

  also subjects with the subdivision
    Transportation, e.g. **School children—**
    Transportation; World War, 1939-1945—
    Transportation; etc.
  x Locomotion
  xx **Commerce**
Transportation, Highway 388.3
  See also **Automobiles; Buses; Trucks**
  x Highway transportation
Transportation, Military 355.8
  See also **Vehicles, Military**
  x Military motorization; Military transporta-
    tion; Motorization, Military
  xx **Military art and science**
Transsexuality 612
  x Change of sex; Sex change; Transexuality
  xx **Reproductive system; Sex role**
Trapping 639
  See also **Fur trade; Game and game birds; Hunt-**
    ing
  xx **Game and game birds; Hunting**
Travel 910.2
  Use for materials on the art of travel, advice, en-
    joyment, etc. Descriptions of actual voyages
    are entered under **Voyages and travels** or
    under names of places with the subdivision
    Description and travel.
  See also **Automobiles—Touring; Health resorts,**
    spas, etc.; Ocean travel; Tourist trade; Voy-
    ages and travels; Voyages around the world;
    also names of countries, states, etc. with the
    subdivision *Description and travel,* e.g.
    United States—Description and travel; etc.
  x Group travel
  xx **Manners and customs; Tourist trade; Voyages**
    and travels
Travel trailers and campers 629.2
  See also **Mobile homes; Vans**
  x Campers and trailers; House trailers; Pickup
    campers; Trailers
  xx **Automobiles—Trailers; Camping; Recre-**
    ational vehicles
Travelers (May subdiv. geog. adjective form, e.g.
    Travelers, German; etc.) **910.92; 920**
  See also **Explorers**
  x Voyagers
  xx **Explorers; Voyages and travels**
Travelers, American 910.92; 920
  x American travelers; United States—Travelers
Traveling sales personnel. *See* **Sales personnel**
Travels. *See* **Overland journeys to the Pacific**
    (U.S.); Scientific expeditions; Voyages and
    travels; Voyages around the world; and

Travels—*Continued*
> names of countries, states, etc. with the sub-
> division *Description and travel,* e.g. **United
> States—Description and travel;** etc.

Travesties. *See* **Parodies**

Tray gardens. *See* **Gardens, Miniature**

Treason 364.1
> *x* Collaborationists; High treason
> *xx* **Crime; Political crimes and offenses**

Treasure trove. *See* **Buried treasure**

Treaties 341.3; 341.6
> *See also* **Arbitration, International;** also names of
> countries with the subdivision *Foreign rela-
> tions—Treaties,* e.g. **United States—
> Foreign relations—Treaties;** etc.; and
> names of wars with the subdivision
> *Treaties,* e.g. **World War, 1939-1945—
> Treaties;** etc.
> *xx* **Congresses and conventions; Diplomacy; In-
> ternational law; International relations**

Tree planting 635.9
> *See also* **Reforestation; Trees; Windbreaks**
> *x* Planting
> *xx* **Forests and forestry; Reforestation; Trees**

Trees (May subdiv. geog.) **582.16; 635.9**
> Use for materials on the structure, care, charac-
> teristics and use of trees.
> Names of all trees are not included in this list
> but are to be added as needed, in the singu-
> lar form, e.g. **Oak;** etc.
> *See also*

Dwarf trees	**Nurseries (Horticulture)**
Evergreens	**Nuts**
Forests and forestry	**Plants**
Fruit culture	**Pruning**
Grafting	**Shrubs**
Landscape gardening	**Tree planting**
Leaves	**Wood**
Lumber and lumbering	

> also names of trees, e.g. **Oak;** etc.
> *x* Arboriculture; Timber
> *xx* **Botany; Forests and forestry; Landscape gar-
> dening; Tree planting**

Trees in art. *See* **Plants in art**

Trees—United States 582.16
> *x* United States—Trees

Trent Affair, 1861 973.7
> *xx* **United States—History—1861-1865, Civil
> War**

Trial by jury. *See* **Jury**

Trial by publicity. *See* **Freedom of the press and
fair trial**

Trial marriage. *See* **Unmarried couples**

Trials 345; 347
> May be subdivided by topic, e.g. **Trials (Mur-
> der);** etc.
> *See also* **Courts martial and courts of inquiry;
> Crime**
> *xx* **Crime; Criminal law**

Trials (Murder) 345
    x Murder trials
    xx **Murder**
Tricks 793.5
    See also **Card tricks; Magic**
    xx **Magic**
Tricycles 629.2; 796.6
    x Cycling; Trikes
    xx **Bicycles and bicycling**
Trigonometry 516.2
    x Plane trigonometry; Spherical trigonometry
    xx **Geometry; Mathematics**
Trigonometry—Tables, etc. 516.2
    See also **Logarithms**
    x Tables (Systematic lists)
    xx **Mathematics—Tables, etc.**
Trikes. *See* **Tricycles**
Trinity 231
    See also **God—Christianity; Holy Spirit; Jesus
        Christ**
    xx **God—Christianity; Holy Spirit; Jesus Christ;
        Jesus Christ—Divinity; Theology; Unitari-
        anism**
Tripoline War. *See* **United States—History—1801-
        1805, Tripolitan War**
Trivia. *See* **Curiosities and wonders**
Trolley cars. *See* **Street railroads**
Tropical diseases. *See* **Tropical medicine**
Tropical fish 597; 639.3
    xx **Fishes**
Tropical jungles. *See* **Jungles**
Tropical medicine 614
    See also names of tropical diseases, e.g. **Yellow
        fever;** etc.
    x Diseases, Tropical; Hygiene, Tropical; Medi-
        cine, Tropical; Tropical diseases
    xx **Medicine; Tropics**
Tropical rain forests. *See* **Rain forests**
Tropics
    See also **Jungles; Tropical medicine;** also sub-
        jects with the subdivision *Tropics,* e.g.
        Agriculture—Tropics; etc.
Troubadours 791.092; 920
    xx **French poetry; Minstrels; Poets**
Trout fishing 799.1
    xx **Fishing**
Truancy (Schools). *See* **School attendance**
Truck farming. *See* **Vegetable gardening**
Truck freight. *See* **Trucking**
Trucking 388.3
    x Truck freight
    xx **Freight and freightage; Transportation**
Trucks 629.2
    See also **Materials handling;** also names of spe-
        cific makes and models
    x Automobile trucks; Motor trucks
    xx **Automobiles; Materials handling; Transporta-
        tion, Highway**
Trust companies 338.8; 658
    See also **Banks and banking; Investment trusts**

Trust companies—*Continued*

    x Companies, Trust

    xx **Banks and banking; Business; Corporations**

Trusts, Industrial 338.8; 658.1

    See also

Antitrust law	**Monopolies**
Capitalism	**Railroads—Consolidation**
Competition	**Restraint of trade**
Corporations	**Tariff**
Interstate commerce	

    x Business combinations; Cartels; Combinations, Industrial; Industrial combinations; Industrial mergers; Industrial trusts; Mergers, Industrial

    xx **Capital; Commerce; Competition; Corporation law; Corporations; Economics; Monopolies; Restraint of trade**

Trusts, Industrial—Law and legislation. *See* **Antitrust law**

Truth 111

    See also **Agnosticism; Knowledge, Theory of; Pragmatism; Reality; Skepticism; Truthfulness and falsehood**

    x Certainty

    xx **Belief and doubt; Faith; Knowledge, Theory of; Philosophy; Pragmatism; Skepticism**

Truth in advertising. *See* **Advertising, Fraudulent**

Truthfulness and falsehood 177

    See also **Honesty**

    x Credibility; Falsehood; Lying; Untruth

    xx **Honesty; Human behavior; Truth**

Tuberculosis 616.9

    xx **Lungs—Diseases**

Tugboats 623.8

Tuition. *See* **College costs; Colleges and universities—Finance; Education—Finance**

Tumbling 796.4

    xx **Acrobats and acrobatics**

Tumors 616.99

    See also **Cancer**

Tuning 781.91

    See also names of instruments with the subdivision *Tuning,* e.g. **Piano—Tuning;** etc.

    xx **Musical instruments**

Tunnels 624.1

    See also **Boring; Excavation; Subways**

    xx **Civil engineering**

Turbines 621.2; 621.406

    See also **Gas turbines; Steam turbines**

    xx **Engines; Hydraulic engineering; Hydraulic machinery; Wheels**

Turkeys 636.5

    xx **Poultry**

Turning 621.9

    See also **Lathes; Woodwork**

    x Lathe work; Wood turning

    xx **Carpentry; Lathes; Woodwork**

Turnpikes (Modern). *See* **Express highways**

Turtles 597.92

    x Terrapins; Tortoises

Turtles—*Continued*

   xx **Reptiles**

Tutorial machines. *See* **Teaching machines**

Tutors and tutoring 371.3

      Use for materials on instruction provided to an individual or small group by a professional teacher, peer, or individual with appropriate training or experience.

   See also **Independent study; Individualized instruction**

   xx **Home instruction; Teaching**

TV. *See* **Television**

Twentieth century 909.82

      See note under **Nineteenth century.**

   x 1900-1999 (20th century)

   xx **History, Modern—1900-1999 (20th century)**

Twenty-first century 909.83

   x 2000-2099 (21st century)

Twins 618.2

   See also **Brothers and sisters**

   xx **Birth, Multiple; Brothers and sisters**

Two hundred mile limit. *See* **Territorial waters**

Type and type founding 686.2

   See also **Advertising layout and typography; Initials; Linotype; Printing—Specimens; Typesetting**

   xx **Founding; Initials; Printing; Printing—Specimens; Typesetting**

Type specimens. *See* **Printing—Specimens**

Typesetting 686.2

   See also **Linotype; Printing; Type and type founding**

   x Composition (Printing)

   xx **Printing; Type and type founding**

Typewriters 652.3; 681

   xx **Office equipment and supplies**

Typewriting 652.3

   xx **Business education; Office practice; Writing**

Typhoid fever 616.9

   x Enteric fever

Typhoons 551.5

      See note under **Cyclones.**

   See also **Hurricanes**

   xx **Hurricanes; Storms; Winds**

Typography. *See* **Printing**

U boats. *See* **Submarines**

U.F.O.'s. *See* **Unidentified flying objects**

U.H.F. radio. *See* **Radio, Shortwave**

U.N. *See* **United Nations**

U.S. *See* **United States**

U.S.A. *See* **United States**

U.S.S.R. *See* **Soviet Union**

UFOs. *See* **Unidentified flying objects**

UHF radio. *See* **Radio, Shortwave**

Ultrahigh frequency radio. *See* **Radio, Shortwave**

Ultrasonic waves 534.5

   x Supersonic waves; Waves, Ultrasonic

   xx **Sound waves; Ultrasonics**

Ultrasonics 534.5

   See also **Ultrasonic waves**

Ultrasonics—*Continued*
   x Inaudible sound; Supersonics
   xx **Sound**
Ultraviolet rays   535.8; 621.36
   x Rays, Ultra-violet
   xx **Electromagnetic waves; Phototherapy; Radiation; Radiotherapy**
Umbrellas and parasols   391; 685
   x Parasols
UN.   *See* **United Nations**
Unbelief.   *See* **Skepticism**
Unborn child.   *See* **Fetus**
Unconventional warfare.   *See* **Guerrilla warfare**
Undenominational churches.   *See* **Community churches**
Under water exploration.   *See* **Underwater exploration**
Underdeveloped areas.   *See* **Developing countries**
Undergraduates.   *See* **College students**
Underground aliens.   *See* **Aliens, Illegal**
Underground, Anticommunist.   *See* **Anticommunist movements**
Underground architecture   624.1; 690; 720
   See also **Basements; Earth sheltered houses**
   x Underground design
   xx **Architecture**
Underground design.   *See* **Underground architecture**
Underground economy
   See also **Aliens, Illegal; Barter**
   x Economy, Underground; Income, Untaxed; Subterranean economy
   xx **Economics**
Underground films.   *See* **Experimental films**
Underground houses.   *See* **Earth sheltered houses**
Underground literature   809
   See also **Underground press**
Underground movements (World War, 1939-1945).   *See* **World War, 1939-1945—Underground movements**
Underground press   070.4
   x Alternative press; Press, Underground
   xx **Press; Underground literature**
Underground railroad   326
   See also **Slavery—United States**
   xx **Slavery—United States**
Underground railroads.   *See* **Subways**
Underprivileged.   *See* **Socially handicapped**
Underprivileged children.   *See* **Socially handicapped children**
Undersea engineering.   *See* **Ocean engineering**
Undersea exploration.   *See* **Underwater exploration**
Undersea research habitats.   *See* **Undersea research stations**
Undersea research stations   551.46
   See also **Aquanauts;** also names of special research projects and stations, e.g. **Sealab project;** etc.
   x Manned undersea research stations; Sea laboratories; Submarine research stations; Un-

Undersea research stations—*Continued*
     dersea research habitats; Underwater research stations

  xx **Oceanography—Research; Skin diving; Submersibles; Underwater exploration**
Undersea technology. *See* **Oceanography**
Undersea vehicles. *See* **Submersibles**
Understanding. *See* **Intellect; Knowledge, Theory of**
Undertakers and undertaking 393
  x Funeral directors; Morticians
Underwater drill (Petroleum). *See* **Oil well drilling, Submarine**
Underwater exploration 551.46; 627
  See also **Aquanauts; Diving, Submarine; Marine biology; Skin diving; Submersibles; Undersea research stations**
  x Exploration, Submarine; Exploration, Underwater; Submarine exploration; Under water exploration; Undersea exploration
  xx **Adventure and adventurers; Diving, Submarine; Oceanography—Research; Skin diving**
Underwater exploration devices. *See* **Submersibles**
Underwater geology. *See* **Submarine geology**
Underwater medicine. *See* **Submarine medicine**
Underwater photography. *See* **Photography, Submarine**
Underwater physiology. *See* **Submarine medicine**
Underwater research stations. *See* **Undersea research stations**
Underwater swimming. *See* **Skin diving**
Underwriting. *See* **Insurance**
Unemployed 331.13
  See also **Economic assistance, Domestic; Food relief; Insurance, Unemployment; Labor supply; Occupational retraining**
  xx **Charities; Economic assistance, Domestic; Labor; Labor supply; Poor; Public welfare; Social problems; Sociology; Unemployment**
Unemployment 331.13
  See also **Employment agencies; Insurance, Unemployment; Unemployed**
  xx **Employment; Human resources; Labor supply**
Unemployment insurance. *See* **Insurance, Unemployment**
Unfair competition. *See* **Competition, Unfair**
Unfair trade practices. *See* **Competition, Unfair**
Ungraded schools. *See* **Nongraded schools**
Unicameral legislatures. *See* **Legislative bodies**
Unidentified flying objects 001.9
  x Flying saucers; Saucers, Flying; U.F.O.'s; UFOs
  xx **Aeronautics; Astronautics**
Uniforms, Military 355.1; 355.8
  x Costume, Military; Military costume; Military uniforms; Naval uniforms; Uniforms, Naval
  xx **Costume; Tailoring**
Uniforms, Naval. *See* **Uniforms, Military**
Union churches. *See* **Community churches**

Union of South Africa. *See* **South Africa**
Union of Soviet Socialist Republics. *See* **Soviet Union**
Union shop. *See* **Open and closed shop**
Unions, Labor. *See* **Labor unions**
Unisexuality. *See* **Androgyny**
Unison speaking. *See* **Choral speaking**
Unitarianism 288
> *See also* **Jesus Christ—Divinity; Trinity**
> *xx* **Congregationalism; Jesus Christ—Divinity**
United Brethren. *See* **Moravians**
United Nations 341.23
> *x* U.N.; UN
> *xx* **Arbitration, International; International cooperation; International organization**
United Nations—Armed forces 341.23
> *x* Peace keeping forces
United Nations—Finance 341.23
United Nations—Information services 341.23
> *xx* **Information services**
United Nations—Officials and employees 341.23
> *x* Employees and officials; Officials
United Nations—Yearbooks 341.2305
> *x* Annuals
> *xx* **Yearbooks**
United States 973
> The subject subdivisions under this heading may be used under the name of any country or region, with the exception of the period divisions of history. For subdivisions that may be used under names of states, see **Ohio;** under names of cities, see **Chicago (Ill.).**
> Most of these subdivisions are examples of the directions given in the general references under various headings throughout the list. See references are supplied more liberally than any library may need but they were included here in order to show what subjects are given geographic treatment, not only as a subdivision under the name of a country, but also as a heading subdivided by the country or by national adjective.
> Corporate entries, that is those official bodies which may be used as author entries and as subjects, are included only when they have been used as examples or as references or when they are subdivided by subject. Corporate entries are distinguished by using a period between parts instead of the dash, e.g. **United States. Army.**
> *See also* **Americans;** also names of regions of the United States and groups of states, e.g. **Atlantic States; Gulf States (U.S.); Middle West; Mississippi River Valley; New England; Old Northwest; Old Southwest; Oregon Trail; Pacific Northwest; Southern States; Southwestern States; West (U.S.);** etc.; and headings beginning with the word **American.**

United States—*Continued*
    x U.S.; U.S.A.; US; USA
United States—Actors and actresses. *See* **Actors**
    and actresses, American
United States—Agriculture. *See* **Agriculture—**
    United States
United States—Air—Pollution. *See* **Air—**
    Pollution—United States
United States—Animals. *See* **Animals—United**
    States
United States—Antiques. *See* **Antiques—United**
    States
United States—Antiquities 973
    See also **Indians of North America—Antiquities**
    x Prehistory
    xx **Antiquities; Archeology; Man, Prehistoric**
United States—Appropriations and expenditures
    351.72
    x Federal spending policy; Government spend-
      ing policy
    xx **Budget—United States**
United States—Architecture. *See* **Architecture,**
    American
United States—Archives. *See* **Archives—United**
    States
United States—Armed forces 355
    See also official names and branches of the
      armed forces, e.g. **United States. Army;**
      United States. Navy; etc.
    x Military forces
United States—Armed forces—Military life 355.1
    x Military life
    xx **Military personnel**
United States. Army 355
    Subdivisions used under this subject may be
      used under armies of other countries.
    x Army
    xx **Armies; Military history; United States—**
      Armed forces
United States. Army—Appointments and retirements
    355.1
    x United States. Army—Retirements
United States. Army—Biography 920
    x Military biography
United States. Army—Chaplains 355.3; 920
    xx **Chaplains**
United States. Army—Crimes and
    misdemeanors. *See* **Military offenses—**
    United States
United States. Army—Demobilization 355.2
United States. Army—Desertions. *See* **Desertion,**
    Military—United States
United States. Army—Enlistment. *See* **United**
    States. Army—Recruiting, enlistment, etc.
United States. Army—Examinations 355.1
    x Army tests

United States. Army—Handbooks, manuals, etc.
355
x Soldiers' handbooks; United States. Army—
Officers' handbooks; United States.
Army—Soldiers' handbooks
United States. Army—Insignia 355.1
xx **Insignia**
United States. Army—Medals, badges, decorations,
etc. 355.1
xx **Insignia; Medals**
United States. Army—Military life 355.1
x Army life; Military life; Soldiers' life
xx **Military personnel; Soldiers**
United States. Army—Music. *See* **United States.**
Army—Songs and music
United States. Army—Officers 355.3
United States. Army—Officers' handbooks. *See*
United States. Army—Handbooks, manuals,
etc.
United States. Army—Ordnance and ordnance stores
355.8
xx **Ordnance**
United States. Army—Parachute troops 356
x United States—Parachute troops
xx **Parachute troops**
United States. Army—Recruiting, enlistment, etc.
355.2
x Enlistment; Recruiting and enlistment; United
States. Army—Enlistment
United States. Army—Retirements. *See* **United**
States. Army—Appointments and retire-
ments
United States. Army—Soldiers' handbooks. *See*
United States. Army—Handbooks, manuals,
etc.
United States. Army—Songs and music 784.7
x United States. Army—Music
United States—Art. *See* **Art, American**
United States—Artificial satellites. *See* **Artificial**
satellites, American
United States—Artists. *See* **Artists, American**
United States—Astronautics. *See* **Astronautics—**
United States
United States—Atlases. *See* **United States—Maps**
United States—Authors. *See* **Authors, American**
United States—Ballads. *See* **Ballads, American**
United States—Banks and banking. *See* **Banks and**
banking—United States
United States—Bibliography 015.73
xx **Bibliography**
United States—Bicentennial celebrations. *See*
American Revolution Bicentennial, 1776-
1976
United States—Biculturalism. *See* **Biculturalism—**
United States
United States—Bilingualism. *See* **Bilingualism—**
United States
United States—Bio-bibliography 016; 920
x Bio-bibliography

United States—Biography 920
   xx **Biography**
United States—Biography—Dictionaries 920
   xx **Biography—Dictionaries; Encyclopedias and**
       dictionaries
United States—Biography—Portraits 920
   x United States—History—Portraits
   xx **Portraits**
United States—Birds. *See* **Birds—United States**
United States—Botany. *See* **Botany—United States**
United States—Boundaries 973
   x Frontiers
   xx **Boundaries**
United States—Budget. *See* **Budget—United States**
United States—Campaign funds. *See* **Campaign**
       funds—United States
United States—Capital punishment. *See* **Capital**
       punishment—United States
United States—Cathedrals. *See* **Cathedrals—**
       United States
United States—Catholic Church. *See* **Catholic**
       Church—United States
United States—Catholics. *See* **Catholics—United**
       States
United States—Census 317.3; 351.81
   xx **Census**
United States—Centennial celebrations, etc. 351.85
   See also **American Revolution Bicentennial,**
       1776-1976
United States—Children. *See* **Children—United**
       States
United States—Children—Employment. *See* **Chil-**
       dren—Employment—United States
United States—Christmas. *See* **Christmas—United**
       States
United States—Church—Government policy. *See*
       Church—Government policy—United States
United States—Church history 277.3
   See also **United States—Religion**
   x United States—Religious history
   xx **Church history; United States—Religion**
United States—Church of England. *See* **Church of**
       England—United States
United States—Churches. *See* **Churches—United**
       States
United States—Cities and towns. *See* **Cities and**
       towns—United States
United States—City planning. *See* **City planning—**
       United States
United States—Civil defense 363.3
   xx **Civil defense**
United States—Civil service. *See* **Civil service—**
       United States
United States—Civilization 973
   See also **Americana**
   x American civilization
   xx **Civilization**
United States—Civilization—1960-1970 973.92
United States—Civilization—1970- 973.92
United States—Civilization—Foreign influences 973

United States—Climate 551.6973
   xx **Climate; Weather**
United States—Collective settlements. *See* **Collective settlements—United States**
United States—Colleges and universities. *See* **Colleges and universities—United States**
United States—Colonies 325.73; 973
   x United States—Insular possessions; United States—Territories and possessions
   xx **Colonies**
United States—Commerce 381; 382
   xx **Commerce**
United States—Commercial policy 338.973; 381
   xx **Commercial policy; Economic policy**
United States—Communism. *See* **Communism—United States**
United States—Composers. *See* **Composers, American**
United States. Congress 328.73
   x Congress—United States
   xx **Legislative bodies**
United States. Congress. House 328.73; 342
   x Representatives—United States
United States. Congress. Senate 328.73; 342
   x Senators—United States
United States—Constitution 342.73; 973.3
   xx **Constitutions**
United States—Constitutional history 342
   xx **Constitutional history, United States—History; United States—History—1783-1809**
United States—Constitutional law 342
   xx **Constitutional law**
United States—Consular service. *See* **United States—Diplomatic and consular service**
United States—Country life. *See* **Country life—United States**
United States—Courts. *See* **Courts—United States**
United States—Crime. *See* **Crime—United States**
United States—Dancing. *See* **Dancing—United States**
United States—Debts, Public. *See* **Debts, Public—United States**
United States—Declaration of independence 973.3
   x Declaration of independence (U.S.)
United States—Decoration and ornament. *See* **Decoration and ornament, American**
United States—Decorative arts. *See* **Decorative arts—United States**
United States—Defenses 355.4
   x Defenses, National; National defenses
   xx **Fortification**
United States—Description and travel 917.3
   x Description; Journeys; Travels
   xx **Discoveries (in geography); Explorers; Geography; Travel; Voyages and travels**
United States—Description and travel—Guidebooks 917.302
   x Guidebooks; United States—Guidebooks

United States—Description and travel—Maps. *See*
    United States—Maps
United States—Description and travel—Views
    917.3022
  x Scenery
  xx **Pictures; Views**
United States—Diplomatic and consular service
    327.73; 351.89
  x United States—Consular service
  xx **Diplomatic and consular service**
United States—Directories 973.025
  Use for lists of names and addresses. Lists of
    names without addresses are entered under
    United States/Registers.
  See also **United States—Registers**
  xx **Directories; United States—Registers**
United States—Dramatists. *See* **Dramatists, Amer-**
    ican
United States—Drawing. *See* **Drawing, American**
United States—Earthquakes. *See* **Earthquakes—**
    United States
United States—Economic assistance. *See* **Eco-**
    nomic assistance, American
United States—Economic conditions 330.973
  May be subdivided by period using the subdivi-
    sions under **United States—History,** e.g.
    United States—Economic conditions—1600-
    1775, Colonial period; etc.
  x National resources; United States—History,
    Economic; United States—Natural re-
    sources
  xx **Economic conditions; Natural resources—**
    United States; Poverty
United States—Economic policy 338.973
  x National planning; Planning, Economic; Plan-
    ning, National
  xx **Economic policy**
United States—Education. *See* **Education—United**
    States
United States—Elderly. *See* **Elderly—United**
    States
United States—Elections. *See* **Elections—United**
    States
United States—Emigration. *See* **United States—**
    Immigration and emigration
United States—Employees. *See* **United States—**
    Officials and employees
United States—Engraving. *See* **Engraving, Ameri-**
    can
United States—Environmental policy. *See* **Envi-**
    ronment—Government policy—United
    States
United States—Ethics. *See* **Ethics, American**
United States—Ethnology. *See* **Ethnology—United**
    States
United States—European War, 1914-1918. *See*
    World War, 1914-1918—United States
United States—Excavations (Archeology). *See* **Ex-**
    cavations (Archeology)—United States

United States—Executive departments 353.03
  See also **Presidents—United States—Staff**
  x Executive departments
United States—Executive departments—
  Reorganization 353.03
  x Administrative agencies—Reorganization; Executive departments—Reorganization; Government reorganization; Reorganization of administrative agencies
United States—Executive power. *See* **Executive power—United States**
United States—Exploration. *See* **America—Exploration; United States—Exploring expeditions; West (U.S.)—Exploration**
United States—Exploring expeditions 508.73; 973
  Use for materials on exploration within the United States and for explorations in other countries which are sponsored by the United States. Materials on early exploration in territory that became a part of the United States are entered under **America—Exploration.**
  See also names of expeditions, e.g. **Lewis and Clark Expedition (1804-1806);** etc.
  x Explorations; Exploring expeditions; United States—Exploration
  xx **America—Exploration; Explorers**
United States—Famines. *See* **Famines—United States**
United States—Farm life. *See* **Farm life—United States**
United States—Fascism. *See* **Fascism—United States**
United States—Festivals. *See* **Festivals—United States**
United States—Fiction Fic
  xx **Fiction**
United States—Finance. *See* **Finance—United States**
United States—Fiscal policy. *See* **Fiscal policy—United States**
United States—Fisheries. *See* **Fisheries—United States**
United States—Fishes. *See* **Fishes—United States**
United States—Fishing. *See* **Fishing—United States**
United States—Flags. *See* **Flags—United States**
United States—Flowers. *See* **Flowers—United States**
United States—Folk art. *See* **Folk art, American**
United States—Folk dancing. *See* **Folk dancing, American**
United States—Folk music. *See* **Folk music—United States**
United States—Folk songs. *See* **Folk songs—United States**
United States—Folklore. *See* **Folklore—United States**
United States—Foreign economic relations 330.973
  x Foreign economic relations—United States

United States—Foreign opinion (May subdiv. geog.
  adjective form) **303.3**
  x Anti-Americanism; Antiamericanism; Foreign
    opinion
  xx **Public opinion**
United States—Foreign opinion, French 303.3
  x Foreign opinion; French foreign opinion—
    United States
United States—Foreign policy. *See* **United
  States—Foreign relations**
United States—Foreign population 325.73
  See also **United States—Immigration and emi-
    gration;** also **Mexican Americans; Mexi-
    cans—United States;** and similar headings
  x Foreign population; Foreigners; Population,
    Foreign
  xx **Americanization; Immigration and emigration;
    Minorities; United States—Immigration
    and emigration**
United States—Foreign relations (May subdiv. geog.)
  327.73
  See also **Monroe Doctrine; United States—
    Neutrality**
  x Foreign policy; Foreign relations; United
    States—Foreign policy
  xx **Diplomacy; Imperialism; International rela-
    tions; United States—Neutrality; World
    politics**
United States—Foreign relations—Iran 327.73
  See also **Iran hostage crisis, 1979-1981**
United States—Foreign relations—Treaties 327.73
  x United States—Treaties
  xx **Treaties**
United States—Forests and forestry. *See* **Forests
  and forestry—United States**
United States—Furniture. *See* **Furniture, American**
United States—Gazetteers 910.3
  xx **Gazetteers**
United States—Geographical names. *See* **Names,
  Geographical—United States**
United States—Geography 917.3
  xx **Geography**
United States—Geology. *See* **Geology—United
  States**
United States—Government. *See* **United States—
  Politics and government**
United States—Government buildings. *See* **United
  States—Public buildings**
United States—Government employees. *See*
  United States—Officials and employees
United States—Government publications 025.17
  x Official publications; United States—Public
    documents
  xx **Government publications**
United States—Governmental investigations. *See*
  Governmental investigations—United States
United States—Graphic arts. *See* **Graphic arts,
  American**
United States—Guidebooks. *See* **United States—
  Description and travel—Guidebooks**

United States—Hippies. *See* **Hippies—United States**

United States—Historians. *See* **Historians, American**

United States—Historic buildings. *See* **Historic buildings—United States**

United States—**Historical geography** 557.73
 x Historical geography
 xx **Geography, Historical**

United States—**Historical geography—Maps 557.73; 912**
 xx **United States—Maps**

United States—**History** 973
 See also **Americana; United States—Constitutional history**
 x American history

United States—**History—1600-1775, Colonial period 973.2**
 Use for the period from the earliest permanent English settlements on the Atlantic coast to the American Revolution, i.e. 1600-1775. Materials dealing with the period of discovery are entered under **America—Exploration.**
 See also **Bacon's Rebellion, 1676; King Philip's War, 1675-1676; Pilgrims (New England colonists); Pontiac's Conspiracy, 1763-1765; Puritans; United States—History—1689-1697, King William's War; United States—History—1755-1763, French and Indian War**
 x American colonies; Colonial history (U.S.)

United States—History—1675-1676, King Philip's War. *See* **King Philip's War, 1675-1676**

United States—**History—1689-1697, King William's War 973.2**
 x King William's War, 1689-1697
 xx **Indians of North America—Wars; United States—History—1600-1775, Colonial period**

United States—**History—1755-1763, French and Indian War 973.2**
 See also **Pontiac's Conspiracy, 1763-1765**
 x French and Indian War
 xx **Indians of North America—Wars; United States—History—1600-1775, Colonial period**

United States—**History—1775-1783, Revolution 973.3**
 May be subdivided like **United States—History—1861-1865, Civil War.**
 See also **American Loyalists; Canadian Invasion, 1775-1776; Fourth of July**
 x American Revolution; Revolution, American; War of the American Revolution
 xx **Revolutions**

United States—History—1775-1783, Revolution—Centennial celebrations, etc. *See* **American Revolution Bicentennial, 1776-1976**

United States—History—1783-1809 973.4
> *See also* **Lewis and Clark Expedition (1804-**
> **1806); Louisiana Purchase; United States—**
> **Constitutional history**
> *x* Confederation of American colonies

United States—History—1783-1865 973.5

United States—History—1801-1805, Tripolitan War
> **973.4**
> *x* Tripoline War
> *xx* **Pirates**

United States—History—1812-1815, War of 1812
> **973.5**
> *x* War of 1812

United States—History—1815-1861 973.5; 973.6
> *See also* **Black Hawk War, 1832**

United States—History—1845-1848, War with Mex-
> **ico 973.6**
> *x* Mexican War, 1845-1848

United States—History—1861-1865, Civil War
> **973.7**
> *See also* **Confederate States of America; Slav-**
> **ery—United States; Trent Affair, 1861**
> *x* American Civil War; Civil War—United
> States; War of Secession (U.S.)
> *xx* **War**

United States—History—1861-1865, Civil War—
> **Biography 920**

United States—History—1861-1865, Civil War—
> **Campaigns 973.7**
> *See also* names of battles, e.g. **Gettysburg (Pa.),**
> **Battle of, 1863;** etc.
> *xx* **Battles**

United States—History—1861-1865, Civil War—
> **Causes 973.7**
> *x* Secession

United States—History—1861-1865, Civil War—
> **Centennial celebrations, etc. 973.7**

United States—History—1861-1865, Civil War—
> **Drama 808.82; 812; etc.**
> *xx* **Drama**

United States—History—1861-1865, Civil War—
> **Fiction Fic**
> *xx* **Historical fiction**

United States—History—1861-1865, Civil War—
> **Health aspects 973.7**

United States—History—1861-1865, Civil War—
> **Medical care 973.7**

United States—History—1861-1865, Civil War—
> **Naval operations 973.7**

United States—History—1861-1865, Civil War—
> **Personal narratives 973.7**
> Use for miscellaneous accounts and reports writ-
> ten by soldiers, officers, journalists and
> other observers. Accounts limited to a spe-
> cial topic are entered under the specific sub-
> ject.

United States—History—1861-1865, Civil War—
> **Pictorial works 973.7022**
> *x* Illustrations
> *xx* **Pictures**

United States—History—1861-1865, Civil War—
       Prisoners and prisons 973.7
United States—History—1861-1865, Civil
       War—Reconstruction. *See* **Reconstruction**
       (1865-1876)
United States—History—1861-1865, Civil War—
       Sources 973.7
   xx **History—Sources**
United States—History—1865-1898 973.8
   See also **Reconstruction (1865-1876)**
United States—History—1898, War of 1898 973.8
   x American-Spanish War, 1898; Hispano-
       American War, 1898; Spain—History—
       1898, War of 1898; Spanish-American War,
       1898
United States—History—1898-1919 973.9; 973.91
United States—History—1900-1999 (20th century)
       973.9
United States—History—1914-1918, European
       War. *See* **World War, 1914-1918—United**
       States
United States—History—1914-1918, World
       War. *See* **World War, 1914-1918—United**
       States
United States—History—1919-1933 973.91
United States—History—1933-1945 973.917
United States—History—1939-1945, World
       War. *See* **World War, 1939-1945—United**
       States
United States—History—1945-1953 973.918
United States—History—1953-1961 973.921
United States—History—1961-1974
       973.922-973.924
   See also **Watergate Affair, 1972-1974**
United States—History—1974- 973.925
United States—History—Addresses and essays 973
   x Addresses
   xx **Essays; Lectures and lecturing; Speeches, ad-**
       dresses, etc.
United States—History—Bibliography 016.973
United States—History—Chronology 973
   xx **Chronology, Historical**
United States—History—Dictionaries 973.03
United States—History—Drama 808.82; 812; etc.
United States—History, Economic. *See* **United**
       States—Economic conditions
United States—History—Examinations, questions,
       etc. 973.076
   See also **United States—History—Study and**
       teaching
   xx **United States—History—Study and teaching**
United States—History—Fiction Fic
United States—History—Historiography 973.07
   xx **Historiography**
United States—History, Local 973
   x History, Local; Local history
United States—History, Military 355
   x History, Military; United States—Military
       history
   xx **Military history**

United States—History, Naval 359
 x History, Naval; United States—Naval history
 xx **Naval battles; Naval history; Sea power**
United States—History—Outlines, syllabi, etc.
     973.02
 xx **United States—History—Study and teaching**
United States—History—Periodicals 973.05
United States—History—Poetry 808.81; 811; etc.
United States—History, Political. *See* **United**
     States—Politics and government
United States—History—Portraits. *See* **United**
     States—Biography—Portraits
United States—History—Societies 973.06
 xx **History—Societies**
United States—History—Sources 973
 xx **History—Sources**
United States—History—Study and teaching 973.07
 See also **United States—History—Examinations,**
     questions, etc.; United States—History—
     Outlines, syllabi, etc.
 xx **United States—History—Examinations, ques-**
     tions, etc.
United States—Hospitals. *See* **Hospitals—United**
     States
United States—Hostages. *See* **Hostages, American**
United States—Hotels, motels, etc. *See* **Hotels,**
     motels, etc.—United States
United States—Hunting. *See* **Hunting—United**
     States
United States—Illustrators. *See* **Illustrators, Amer-**
     ican
United States—Immigration and emigration 325.73
 See also **United States—Foreign population;** also
     names of nationality groups, e.g. **Mexican**
     Americans; Mexicans—United States; etc.
 x Foreign population; Population, Foreign;
     United States—Emigration
 xx **Americanization; Colonization; Immigration**
     and emigration; United States—Foreign
     population
United States—Industries 338.09; 658; 670
 x Industries; United States—Manufactures
 xx **Industrial arts**
United States—Industry—Government policy. *See*
     Industry—Government policy—United
     States
United States—Insular possessions. *See* **United**
     States—Colonies
United States—Intellectual life 973
 x Intellectual life
United States—Intelligence service. *See* **Intelli-**
     gence service—United States
United States—Internal security. *See* **Internal se-**
     curity—United States
United States—Irrigation. *See* **Irrigation—United**
     States
United States—Labor. *See* **Labor—United States**
United States—Labor unions. *See* **Labor unions—**
     United States
United States—Lakes. *See* **Lakes—United States**

640

United States—Land settlement. *See* **Land settlement—United States**

United States—Law. *See* **Law—United States**

United States—Legends. *See* **Legends—United
States**

United States—Libraries. *See* **Libraries—United
States**

United States. Library of Congress. *See* **Library of
Congress**

United States—Literary landmarks. *See* **Literary
landmarks—United States**

United States—Literature. *See* **American literature**

United States—Mail. *See* **Postal service—United
States**

United States—Manners and customs. *See* **United
States—Social life and customs**

United States—Manufactures. *See* **United States—
Industries**

United States—Maps 912
    See also **United States—Historical geography—
Maps**
    x United States—Atlases; United States—
Description and travel—Maps
    xx **Atlases; Maps; Road maps**

United States—Medicine. *See* **Medicine—United
States**

United States—Merchant marine. *See* **Merchant
marine—United States**

United States—Military history. *See* **United
States—History, Military**

United States—Military offenses. *See* **Military offenses—United States**

United States—Military personnel. *See* **Military
personnel—United States**

United States—Military policy 355
    xx **Military policy**

United States—Militia 355.3
    See also **United States. National Guard**
    x Militia

United States—Mines and mineral resources. *See*
**Mines and mineral resources—United
States**

United States—Monetary policy. *See* **Monetary
policy—United States**

United States—Moral conditions 973
    xx **Moral conditions**

United States—Municipal government. *See* **Municipal government—United States**

United States—Museums. *See* **Museums—United
States**

United States—Music. *See* **Music, American**

United States—Musicians. *See* **Musicians, American**

United States—Muslims. *See* **Muslims—United
States**

United States—Names, Geographical. *See* **Names,
Geographical—United States**

United States—Names, Personal. *See* **Names, Personal—United States**

United States—National characteristics. *See* **Na-
tional characteristics, American**
United States. National Guard 355.3
   x National Guard (U.S.)
   xx **United States—Militia**
United States—National parks and reserves. *See*
   National parks and reserves—United States
United States—National security 350; 355
   xx **National security**
United States—National songs. *See* **National
songs, American**
United States—Natural disasters. *See* **Natural di-
sasters—United States**
United States—Natural history. *See* **Natural histo-
ry—United States**
United States—Natural monuments. *See* **Natural
monuments—United States**
United States—Natural resources. *See* **Natural re-
sources—United States; United States—
Economic conditions**
United States—Nature study. *See* **Nature study—
United States**
United States—Naval history. *See* **United States—
History, Naval**
United States. Navy 359
   Subdivisions used under this subject may be
   used under navies of other countries.
   x Naval administration; Navy; Sea life
   xx **Naval history; Navies; Sailors; Sea power;
United States—Armed forces; Warships**
United States. Navy—Biography 920
   x Military biography; Naval biography
United States. Navy—Enlistment. *See* **United
States. Navy—Recruiting, enlistment, etc.**
United States. Navy—Handbooks, manuals, etc. 359
   x United States. Navy—Officers' handbooks
United States. Navy—Insignia 359.1
   xx **Insignia**
**United States. Navy—Medals, badges, decorations,
etc. 359.1**
   xx **Insignia; Medals**
United States. Navy—Officers 359.3
United States. Navy—Officers' handbooks. *See*
   **United States. Navy—Handbooks, manuals,
etc.**
**United States. Navy—Recruiting, enlistment, etc.
359.2**
   x Enlistment; Recruiting and enlistment; United
States. Navy—Enlistment
United States. Navy—Sealab project. *See* **Sealab
project**
United States—Neutrality 327.1; 327.73
   See also **United States—Foreign relations**
   xx **Neutrality; United States—Foreign relations**
United States—Novelists. *See* **Novelists, American**
United States—Occupations 331.7
   xx **Occupations**
United States of Europe (proposed). *See* **European
federation**

**United States—Officials and employees 351.1; 353.
001**
> *See also* **Civil service—United States**
> *x* Government employees; Officials; United
>   States—Employees; United States—
>   Government employees
> *xx* **Civil service—United States**

United States—Painters. *See* **Painters, American**

United States—Painting. *See* **Painting, American**

United States—Parachute troops. *See* **United
   States. Army—Parachute troops**

United States—Parks. *See* **Parks—United States**

United States—Peoples. *See* **Ethnology—United
   States**

United States—Personal names. *See* **Names, Personal—United States**

United States—Petroleum. *See* **Petroleum—United
   States**

United States—Philosophers. *See* **Philosophers,
   American**

United States—Philosophy. *See* **Philosophy, American**

United States—Physical geography. *See* **Physical
   geography—United States**

United States—Plants, Cultivated. *See* **Plants, Cultivated—United States**

United States—Poets. *See* **Poets, American**

United States—Police. *See* **Police—United States**

United States—Politicians. *See* **Politicians—
   United States**

United States—Politics and government 973
> May be subdivided by period using the subdivi-
>   sions under **United States—History**, e.g.
>   **United States—Politics and government—
>   1600-1775, Colonial period;** etc.
> *x* Administration; American government;
>   American politics; Civics; Civil govern-
>   ment; Government; Politics; United
>   States—Government; United States—
>   History, Political
> *xx* **Comparative government; Political science;
>   Politics, Practical; Public administration;
>   World politics**

United States—Popular culture 973
> *See also* **Americana**
> *xx* **Popular culture**

United States—Population 304.6; 317.3
> *xx* **Population**

United States—Postal service. *See* **Postal service—
   United States**

United States—Pottery. *See* **Pottery, American**

United States—Presidents. *See* **Presidents—United
   States**

United States—Prints. *See* **Prints, American**

United States—Prisons. *See* **Prisons—United
   States**

United States—Propaganda. *See* **Propaganda,
   American**

United States—Protests, demonstrations, etc. *See*
  **Protests, demonstrations, etc.—United
  States**
United States—Public buildings 725
  x United States—Government buildings
  xx **Public buildings**
United States—Public debts. *See* **Debts, Public—
  United States**
United States—Public documents. *See* **United
  States—Government publications**
United States—Public health. *See* **Public health—
  United States**
United States—Public lands 333.1
  x Public lands
United States—Public schools. *See* **Public
  schools—United States**
United States—Public works 351.86
  xx **Public works**
United States—Race relations 305.8; 323.1
  See also **Black Muslims**
  xx **Anthropology; Minorities; Race relations**
United States—Refugees. *See* **Refugees, American**
United States—Registers 973.025
  Use for lists of names without addresses. Lists of
  names that include addresses are entered
  under **United States—Directories.**
  See also **United States—Directories**
  x Registers of persons
  xx **United States—Directories**
United States—Religion 277.3
  See also **United States—Church history**
  xx **Religion; United States—Church history**
United States—Religious history. *See* **United
  States—Church history**
United States—Rural conditions 307.7
  x Rural conditions
  xx **Sociology, Rural**
United States—Schools. *See* **Schools—United
  States**
United States—Science. *See* **Science—United
  States**
United States—Sculptors. *See* **Sculptors, American**
United States—Sculpture. *See* **Sculpture, American**
United States—Secret service. *See* **Secret service—
  United States**
United States—Separation of powers. *See* **Separa-
  tion of powers—United States**
United States—Shipping. *See* **Shipping—United
  States**
United States—Social conditions 973
  xx **Poverty; Social conditions**
United States—Social life and customs 973
  x Customs, Social; Social customs; Social life
  and customs; United States—Manners and
  customs
  xx **Ethnology; Manners and customs**
United States—Social policy 973
  x National planning; Planning, National
  xx **Social policy**

United States—Social surveys. *See* **Social surveys—United States**

United States—Socialism. *See* **Socialism—United States**

United States—Soldiers. *See* **Soldiers—United States**

United States—Songs. *See* **Songs, American**

United States—State governments. *See* **State governments**

United States—Statistics 317.3
   x Burial statistics
   xx **Statistics**

United States—Strikes and lockouts. *See* **Strikes and lockouts—United States**

United States—Students. *See* **Students—United States**

United States. Supreme Court 347
   x Supreme Court—United States

United States. Supreme Court—Biography 920

United States—Tariff. *See* **Tariff—United States**

United States—Taxation. *See* **Taxation—United States**

United States—Technical assistance. *See* **Technical assistance, American**

United States—Territorial expansion 973

United States—Territorial waters. *See* **Territorial waters—United States**

United States—Territories and possessions. *See* **United States—Colonies**

United States—Terrorism. *See* **Terrorism—United States**

United States—Theater. *See* **Theater—United States**

United States—Travelers. *See* **Travelers, American**

United States—Treaties. *See* **United States—Foreign relations—Treaties**

United States—Trees. *See* **Trees—United States**

United States—Universities. *See* **Colleges and universities—United States**

United States—Urban renewal. *See* **Urban renewal—United States**

United States—Veterans. *See* **Veterans—United States**

United States—Vice-presidents. *See* **Vice-presidents—United States**

United States—Women. *See* **Women—United States**

United States—World War, 1914-1918. *See* **World War, 1914-1918—United States**

United States—World War, 1939-1945. *See* **World War, 1939-1945—United States**

United States—Youth. *See* **Youth—United States**

United States—Zoology. *See* **Zoology—United States**

United Steelworkers of America 331.88
   xx **Labor unions**

Universal bibliographic control. *See* **Bibliographic control**

Universal history. *See* **World history**

Universal language. *See* **Language, Universal**

Universe 113; 523.1

    See also **Astronomy; Creation; Earth; Life on other planets**

    x Big bang theory; Cosmogony; Cosmography; Cosmology; Expanding universe

    xx **Creation; Earth; Metaphysics; Philosophy**

Universities. *See* **Colleges and universities**

University degrees. *See* **Degrees, Academic**

University extension 378

    See also **Adult education; Correspondence schools and courses**

    xx **Colleges and universities; Education, Higher**

University graduates. *See* **College graduates**

University libraries. *See* **Academic libraries**

University students. *See* **College students**

Unmarried couples 306.7

    x Cohabitation; Common law marriage; Living together; Marriage, Open ended; Nonmarital relations; Open ended marriage; Trial marriage; Unmarried people

    xx **Lifestyles; Sexual ethics; Shared housing; Single people**

Unmarried men. *See* **Single men**

Unmarried mothers 306.7

    x Mothers, Unmarried; Unwed mothers

    xx **Single parent family; Single women**

Unmarried people. *See* **Single people; Unmarried couples**

Unmarried women. *See* **Single women**

Unskilled workers. *See* **Labor**

Untruth. *See* **Truthfulness and falsehood**

Unwed mothers. *See* **Unmarried mothers**

Upholstery 684.1

    See also **Drapery; Furniture**

    xx **Furniture; Interior design**

Upper atmosphere. *See* **Atmosphere, Upper**

Upper classes 305.5

    x Fashionable society; High society; Society, Upper

    xx **Aristocracy; Social classes**

Uranium 669

    xx **Radioactivity**

Urban areas. *See* **Cities and towns; Metropolitan areas**

Urban-federal relations. *See* **Federal-city relations**

Urban life. *See* **City life**

Urban planning. *See* **City planning**

Urban renewal (May subdiv. geog.) **307**

    Use for materials on urban redevelopment and the economic, sociological, and political factors involved. Architectural and engineering aspects are entered under **City planning.**

    See also **City planning; Community development; Community organization**

    x Slum clearance

    xx **City planning; Community organization; Metropolitan areas; Sociology, Urban**

Urban renewal—Chicago (Ill.) 307

    x Chicago (Ill.)—Urban renewal

Urban renewal—United States 307
   x United States—Urban renewal
Urban sociology. *See* **Sociology, Urban**
Urban traffic. *See* **City traffic**
Urban transportation. *See* **Local transit**
Urbanization (May subdiv. geog.) **301; 307.7**
   xx **Cities and towns; Social change; Social condi-
      tions; Sociology, Rural; Sociology, Urban**
US. *See* **United States**
USA. *See* **United States**
Use of time. *See* **Time management**
Used merchandise. *See* **Secondhand trade**
Useful arts. *See* **Industrial arts; Technology**
USSR. *See* **Soviet Union**
Utensils, Kitchen. *See* **Household equipment and
      supplies**
Utilitarianism 144
   See also **Pragmatism; Secularism**
   xx **Ethics; Pragmatism**
Utilities, Public. *See* **Public utilities**
Utilization of waste. *See* **Recycling (Waste, etc.);
      Salvage (Waste, etc.)**
Utopias 321
   x Ideal states
   xx **Political science; Socialism**
V.C.R.'s. *See* **Videotape recorders and recording**
V.D. *See* **Venereal diseases**
V.T.O.L.'s. *See* **Vertically rising airplanes**
Vacation church schools. *See* **Summer schools, Re-
      ligious**
Vacation home timesharing. *See* **Timesharing
      (Real estate)**
Vacation schools. *See* **Summer schools**
Vacation schools, Religious. *See* **Summer schools,
      Religious**
Vacations 331.25; 658.3
   See also **Holidays**
   xx **Holidays; Recreation**
Vaccination 614.4
   See also **Immunity; Smallpox**
   x Immunization; Inoculation
   xx **Communicable diseases; Immunity; Public
      health; Smallpox**
Vacuum tubes 537.5; 621.3815
   See also **Amplifiers, Vacuum tube; Cathode ray
      tubes; Electronics**
   x Electron tubes
   xx **X rays**
Vagabonds. *See* **Tramps**
Vagrants. *See* **Tramps**
Valentine's Day 394.2
   x Saint Valentine's Day; St. Valentine's Day
   xx **Holidays**
Valuation 338.5
   Use for general materials only. Materials on val-
      uation of special classes of property are en-
      tered under the class, e.g. **Real estate;** etc.
      Materials on valuation for taxing purposes
      are entered under **Assessment.**
   x Appraisal; Capitalization (Finance)

Valuation—*Continued*
　xx **Assessment**
Values 170; 171
　Use for materials on moral and esthetic values.
　See also **Social values**
　x Axiology; Human values; Worth
　xx **Esthetics; Ethics; Psychology**
Vampires 398
　xx **Animals, Mythical; Superstition**
Van life 728.7
　x Vanning; Vans—Social aspects
　xx **Mobile home living; Vans**
Van pools. *See* **Car pools**
Vanishing animals. *See* **Rare animals**
Vanishing species. *See* **Endangered species**
Vanning. *See* **Van life**
Vans 728.7
　See also **Van life**
　xx **Travel trailers and campers**
Vans—Social aspects. *See* **Van life**
Variation (Biology) 575.2
　See also **Adaptation (Biology); Evolution; Mendel's law; Natural selection**
　x Mutation (Biology)
　xx **Biology; Botany; Evolution; Genetics; Heredity; Zoology**
Varnish and varnishing 667; 698
　See also **Lacquer and lacquering**
　x Finishes and finishing
　xx **Lacquer and lacquering; Painting, Industrial; Wood finishing**
Varsity sports. *See* **College sports**
Vascular system. *See* **Cardiovascular system**
Vasectomy 613.9
　xx **Sterilization (Birth control)**
Vases 666; 731; 738.3
　See also **Glassware; Pottery**
　xx **Glassware; Pottery**
Vassals. *See* **Feudalism**
Vatican City 914.5
　Use for materials discussing the independent papal state of Vatican City, consisting of the Vatican Palace, Saint Peter's Basilica, Saint Peter's Square, the Vatican Gardens, etc. and certain palaces and churches not located within Vatican City but which are under its jurisdiction.
Vatican City—Foreign relations. *See* **Catholic Church—Relations (Diplomatic)**
Vatican Council (2nd : 1962-1965) 262
　xx **Councils and synods**
Vaudeville 792.7
　xx **Amusements; Theater**
Vaults (Sepulchral). *See* **Tombs**
VCRs. *See* **Videotape recorders and recording**
VD. *See* **Venereal diseases**
Vedas 294.5
　xx **Hinduism; Sacred books**
Vegetable anatomy. *See* **Botany—Anatomy**

Vegetable gardening 635

> *See also* **Vegetables**
>
> *x* Kitchen gardens; Market gardening; Truck
> farming
>
> *xx* **Gardening; Horticulture; Vegetables**

Vegetable kingdom. *See* **Botany; Plants**

Vegetable oils. *See* **Essences and essential oils; Oils
and fats**

Vegetable pathology. *See* **Plants—Diseases**

Vegetables 633; 635

> Names of all vegetables are not included in this
> list but are to be added as needed, e.g.
> **Celery; Potatoes;** etc.
>
> *See also* **Cookery—Vegetables; Root crops; Vege-
> table gardening; Vegetarianism;** also names
> of vegetables, e.g. **Celery; Potatoes;** etc.
>
> *xx* **Botany; Food; Vegetable gardening**

Vegetables—Canning. *See* **Vegetables—
Preservation**

Vegetables—Marketing. *See* **Farm produce—
Marketing**

Vegetables—Preservation 641.4

> *x* Vegetables—Canning
>
> *xx* **Canning and preserving**

Vegetarian cookery 641.5

> *See also* **Cookery—Vegetables**
>
> *x* Cookery, Vegetarian
>
> *xx* **Cookery**

Vegetarianism 613.2

> *xx* **Diet; Food; Vegetables**

Vehicles 629.2

> *See also* types of vehicles and individual vehi-
> cles, e.g. **All terrain vehicles; Automobiles;
> Recreational vehicles; Snowmobiles;** etc.
>
> *xx* **Transportation**

Vehicles, Military 355.8

> *x* Army vehicles; Military vehicles
>
> *xx* **Transportation, Military**

Vehicles, Recreational. *See* **Recreational vehicles**

Velocity. *See* **Speed**

Veneers and veneering 674; 698

> *xx* **Cabinet work; Furniture**

Venereal diseases 616.95

> *See also* names of venereal diseases, e.g.
> **Syphilis;** etc.
>
> *x* Hygiene, Social; Social hygiene; V.D.; VD
>
> *xx* **Prostitution; Sexual hygiene**

Ventilation 697

> *See also* **Air conditioning; Chimneys; Heating**
>
> *xx* **Air; Air conditioning; Heating; Home econom-
> ics; Hygiene; Sanitation; Sanitation, House-
> hold**

Ventriloquism 793.8

> *xx* **Amusements; Voice**

Verbal abuse. *See* **Invective**

Verbal learning 153.1; 370.15

> Use for materials on the process of learning and
> understanding written or spoken language,
> ranging from learning to associate two non-
> sense syllables to solving problems pres-

Verbal learning—*Continued*
  ented in verbal terms.
  x Learning, Verbal
  xx **Language and languages; Learning, Psychology of**
Vermin. *See* **Household pests; Pests**
Vers libre. *See* **Free verse**
Versification 808.1
  See also **Poetry; Rhyme**
  x English language—Versification; Meter; Prosody
  xx **Authorship; Poetics; Rhythm**
Vertebrates 596
  See also **Amphibians; Birds; Fishes; Mammals; Reptiles**
  xx **Animals; Zoology**
Vertical take off airplanes. *See* **Vertically rising airplanes**
Vertically rising airplanes 629.133
  x Airplanes, Vertically rising; V.T.O.L.'s; Vertical take off airplanes; VTOLs
  xx **Airplanes; Ground effect machines**
Vessels (Ships). *See* **Ships**
Veterans (May subdiv. geog.) **355.1**
  See also **Hospitals, Military; Military personnel; Pensions, Military**
  x Ex-service men; War veterans
  xx **Military personnel; Pensions, Military**
Veterans Day 394.2
  x Armistice Day
Veterans—Education 355.1
  x Education of veterans
  xx **Reconstruction (1914-1939); Reconstruction (1939-1951)**
Veterans—Employment 331.5; 355.1
  x Employment of veterans
  xx **Employment; Reconstruction (1914-1939); Reconstruction (1939-1951)**
Veterans—Hospitals. *See* **Hospitals, Military**
Veterans—Law and legislation 343
  xx **Military law**
Veterans—United States 355.1
  x G.I.'s; GIs; United States—Veterans
Veterinary medicine 636.089
  See also **Animals—Diseases;** also names of animals with the subdivision *Diseases,* e.g. **Cattle—Diseases;** etc.
  x Medicine, Veterinary
  xx **Livestock**
Viaducts. *See* **Bridges**
Vibration 531; 620.3
  See also **Light; Sound waves; Waves**
  xx **Mechanics; Sound**
Vicarious atonement. *See* **Atonement—Christianity**
Vice. *See* **Crime;** and names of specific vices, e.g. **Gambling; Prostitution;** etc.
Vice-presidents (May subdiv. geog.) **353.03; 920**
  xx **Presidents**
Vice-presidents—United States 920
  x United States—Vice-presidents

Victimless crimes. *See* **Crimes without victims**

Victims of atomic bombings. *See* **Atomic bomb victims**

Victims of crime 362.8
 x Crime victims
 xx **Crime**

Video art 709.04; 791.43; 791.45
 Use for materials on works of art created with the use of television and videorecording technology.
 x Art, Electronic; Art, Video; Electronic art
 xx **Art; Art, Modern—1900-1999 (20th century); Television; Videotape recorders and recording**

Video cassette recorders and recording. *See* **Videotape recorders and recording**

Video cassettes. *See* **Videotapes**

Video disc players. *See* **Videodisc players**

Video discs. *See* **Videodiscs**

Video games 688.7
 Use for materials on electronic games played by means of images on a video screen.
 x Electronic games; Games, Electronic; Games, Video; Television games
 xx **Electronic toys; Games; Television—Receivers and reception**

Video recordings. *See* **Videodiscs; Videotapes**

Video tapes. *See* **Videotapes**

Video telephone 384.6; 621.386
 x Picture telephone; Videophone
 xx **Data transmission systems; Telephone; Television**

Videocassettes. *See* **Videotapes**

Videodisc players 621.388
 Use for materials on electronic units resembling a record player that play back pictures and sound from prerecorded discs onto a television receiver.
 See also **Videodiscs**
 x Video disc players
 xx **Television—Equipment and supplies**

Videodiscs 621.388
 Use for materials on plastic discs that play back optically encoded, prerecorded sound and pictures through a television receiver.
 x Discs, Video; Video discs; Video recordings
 xx **Audiovisual materials; Optical storage devices; Television; Videodisc players**

Videophone. *See* **Video telephone**

Videorecorders. *See* **Videotape recorders and recording**

Videos, Music. *See* **Music videos**

Videotape recorders and recording 621.388; 778.59
 Use for materials on electromechanical devices that make possible the electronic recording and playback of video or video and audio materials on magnetic tape.
 See also **Video art; Videotapes**
 x V.C.R.'s; VCRs; Video cassette recorders and recording; Videorecorders

Videotape recorders and recording—*Continued*
    xx **Magnetic recorders and recording; Television broadcasting; Television—Equipment and supplies**

Videotapes 621.388; 778.59
    Use for materials dealing with magnetic tapes on which video or video and audio material are recorded and reproduced by the videotape recorder.
    x Cassette tape recordings, Video; Video cassettes; Video recordings; Video tapes; Videocassettes
    xx **Audiovisual materials; Motion pictures; Television; Videotape recorders and recording**

Videotext systems. *See* **Teletext systems**

Vietnam War, 1961-1975 959.704
    May use appropriate subdivisions under **World War, 1939-1945.**
    x Vietnamese War, 1961-1975

Vietnamese War, 1961-1975. *See* **Vietnam War, 1961-1975**

Viewdata systems. *See* **Teletext systems**

Views
    Use for collections of pictures of many places.
    See also names of countries, states, etc. with the subdivision *Description and travel—Views,* e.g. **United States—Description and travel—Views;** etc.; and names of cities with the subdivision *Description—Views,* e.g. **Chicago (Ill.)—Description—Views;** etc.
    x Geography—Pictorial works; Scenery

Vigilance committees 364.1; 364.4
    xx **Crime; Criminal law; Lynching**

Vikings 936
    Use for materials on early Scandinavian people. Materials on the people since the 10th century are entered under **Scandinavians.**
    See also **Normans**
    x Norsemen; Northmen
    xx **Normans; Scandinavians**

Villages 307.7
    See also **Community development; Local government**
    xx **Cities and towns; Local government**

Villas. *See* **Architecture, Domestic**

Vines. *See* **Climbing plants**

Vineyards. *See* **Grapes**

Violence 303.6
    See also types of violence, e.g. **Family violence; School violence;** etc.
    xx **Aggressiveness (Psychology); Social psychology**

Violin 787.1
    x Fiddle
    xx **Stringed instruments**

Violin music 787.1

Violinists, violoncellists, etc. 920; 927
    x Violoncellists
    xx **Musicians**

Violoncellists. *See* **Violinists, violoncellists, etc.**

Violoncello 787
   x Cello
Vipers. *See* **Snakes**
Virgin Mary. *See* **Mary, Blessed Virgin, Saint**
Viruses 576
   x Microbes
   xx **Microorganisms**
Visceral learning. *See* **Biofeedback training**
Viscosity 532; 620.1
   xx **Hydrodynamics; Mechanics**
Visigoths. *See* **Teutonic peoples**
Vision 612; 617.7
   See also **Color sense; Eye; Optical illusions**
   x Sight
   xx **Eye; Optics; Senses and sensation**
Vision disorders 362.4; 617.7
   See also **Blind; Color blindness**
   x Defective vision
Visions 133.8
   See also **Apparitions; Dreams; Hallucinations**
      and illusions
   xx **Apparitions**
Visitation rights (Domestic relations) 305.8
   Use for materials on the legal right of parents or
      grandparents to visit their children or grand-
      children in situations of separation, divorce,
      etc.
   xx **Domestic relations**
Visiting animals. *See* **Pet therapy**
Visitors' exchange programs. *See* **Exchange of per-**
      sons programs
Visual data processing. *See* **Optical data processing**
Visual instruction. *See* **Audiovisual education**
Visual literacy 153; 707
   Use for materials on the ability to interpret and
      evaluate visual objects and symbols, such as
      television, motion pictures, artworks, etc.
   x Literacy, Visual
   xx **Arts; Literacy; Semiotics**
Vital records. *See* **Registers of births, etc.**
Vital statistics 312
   See also **Census; Mortality; Population; Registers**
      of births, etc.
   x Burial statistics; Death rate; Marriage statis-
      tics; Mortuary statistics; Records of births,
      etc.
   xx **Registers of births, etc.; Statistics**
Vitamins 574.1; 615; 641.1
   xx **Food; Nutrition; Physiological chemistry**
Vivariums. *See* **Terrariums**
Vivisection 179
   See also **Animal abuse**
   x Antivivisection
   xx **Animal abuse; Surgery**
Vocabulary 413; 423; etc.
   See also **Words, New**
   x Words
Vocal culture. *See* **Singing; Voice**

Vocal music   784
> *See also*

Cantatas	Operas
Carols	Operetta
Choral music	Oratorios
Folk songs	Singing
Hymns	Songs

> *x* Music, Vocal
> *xx* **Music; Singing**

Vocation, Choice of. *See* **Vocational guidance**
Vocational education   370.11; 373.2; 374
> See note under **Occupational training.**
> *See also*

Blind—Education	Occupational training
Deaf—Education	Professional education
Employees—Training	Technical education
Industrial arts education	Vocational guidance
Occupational retraining	

> also names of industries, professions, etc. with
> the subdivision *Study and teaching,* e.g.
> **Agriculture—Study and teaching; Medi-
> cine—Study and teaching;** etc.
> *x* Career education; Education, Vocational
> *xx* **Education; Human resources policy; Profes-
> sional education; Technical education**

Vocational guidance   371.4
> Use for materials on the activities and programs
> designed to help people plan, choose, and
> succeed in their careers. Consider also
> **Educational counseling.**
> *See also*

Blind—Education	Job hunting
Career changes	Occupations
Deaf—Education	Paraprofessions and para-
Educational counseling	professionals
Employment	Professions

> also fields of knowledge and industries and
> trades with the subdivision *Vocational guid-
> ance,* e.g. **Law—Vocational guidance; Tele-
> vision broadcasting—Vocational guidance;**
> etc.
> *x* Career guidance; Choice of profession, occu-
> pation, vocation, etc.; Employment guid-
> ance; Guidance, Vocational; Job placement
> guidance; Occupational guidance; Vocation,
> Choice of
> *xx* **Counseling; Educational counseling; Employ-
> ment; Occupations; Professions; Vocational
> education**

Vocational training. *See* **Occupational training**
Vocations. *See* **Occupations; Professions**
Voice   784.9
> *See also* **Automatic speech recognition; Phonet-
> ics; Public speaking; Respiration; Singing;
> Speech; Ventriloquism**
> *x* Speaking; Vocal culture; Voice culture
> *xx* **Language and languages; Phonetics; Public
> speaking; Singing; Speech; Throat**

Voice culture. *See* **Singing; Voice**
Volatile oils. *See* **Essences and essential oils**

Volcanoes (May subdiv. geog.) **551.2**
> *See also* names of volcanoes
> *x* Eruptions
> *xx* **Geology; Mountains; Physical geography**

Volleyball 796.32

Volume (Cubic content) 389; 530.8
> *x* Cubic measurement
> *xx* **Geometry; Measurement; Weights and measures**

Volume feeding. *See* **Food service**

Voluntarism 361.7; 361.8
> *See also* **Associations; Charities; Foster grandparents;** also names of volunteer programs, e.g. **Foster grandparents program;** etc.
> *x* Volunteer work; Volunteering; Volunteerism; Volunteers
> *xx* **Associations; Charities**

Voluntary associations. *See* **Associations**

Volunteer military service. *See* **Military service, Voluntary**

Volunteer work. *See* **Voluntarism**

Volunteering. *See* **Voluntarism**

Volunteerism. *See* **Voluntarism**

Volunteers. *See* **Voluntarism**

Volunteers in church work. *See* **Lay ministry**

Voter registration 324.6
> *x* Registration of voters
> *xx* **Elections; Suffrage**

Voting. *See* **Elections; Suffrage**

Voting, Cumulative. *See* **Proportional representation**

Voyagers. *See* **Explorers; Travelers**

Voyages and travels 910.4
> *See also*

Adventure and adventurers	**Sailors**
Aeronautics—Flights	**Scientific expeditions**
Discoveries (in geography)	**Seafaring life**
Explorers	**Shipwrecks**
Northeast Passage	**Travel**
Northwest Passage	**Travelers**
Ocean travel	**Voyages around the world**
Overland journeys to the	**Whaling**
Pacific (U.S.)	**Yachts and yachting**
Pilgrims and pilgrimages	

> also names of countries, continents, etc. with the subdivision *Description and travel,* e.g. **United States—Description and travel;** etc.; also names of regions, e.g. **Antarctic regions;** etc. and names of individual ships; and classes of people and individuals with the subdivision *Voyages and travels,* e.g. **Popes—Voyages and travels;** etc.
> *x* Journeys; Travels
> *xx* **Adventure and adventurers; Discoveries (in geography); Explorers; Geography; Travel**

Voyages around the world 910.4
> *x* Circumnavigation; Journeys; Travels
> *xx* **Travel; Voyages and travels**

Voyages to the moon. *See* **Space flight to the moon**

VTOLs. *See* **Vertically rising airplanes**

Wage-price controls. *See* **Wage-price policy**
Wage-price policy 339.2
    x Price controls; Price-wage policy; Wage-price
        controls
    xx **Inflation (Finance); Prices; Wages**
Wages 331.2; 658.3
    See also **Cost of living; Equal pay for equal work;
        Job analysis; Nonwage payments; Prices;
        Profit sharing; Wage-price policy**
    x Compensation; Overtime
    xx **Cost of living; Economics; Labor; Labor con-
        tract; Prices**
Wages—Annual wage 331.2
    x Annual income; Annual wage plans; Guaran-
        teed annual income; Guaranteed income
    xx **Income**
Wages—Minimum wage 331.2
    x Minimum wage
Wagons. *See* **Carriages and carts**
Waiters and waitresses 642
    x Waitresses
Waitresses. *See* **Waiters and waitresses**
Wakefulness. *See* **Insomnia**
Walking 796.5
    See also **Hiking**
    x Locomotion
    xx **Hiking**
Walking in space. *See* **Extravehicular activity
    (Space flight)**
Wall decoration. *See* **Mural painting and decora-
    tion**
Wall painting. *See* **Mural painting and decoration**
Wall Street (New York, N.Y.) 332.6
    Use for materials on the activities of Wall Street
        as a financial district. Historical and de-
        scriptive materials on Wall Street as a street
        are entered under **Streets—New York
        (N.Y.)**.
    xx **Stock exchange**
Wallpaper 676
    See also **Paper hanging**
    xx **Interior design; Paper hanging**
Walls 694; 721
    See also **Foundations; Masonry; Mural painting
        and decoration**
    xx **Building; Carpentry; Civil engineering; Foun-
        dations; Masonry**
Walt Disney World (Fla.) 791.06
    x Disney World (Fla.)
    xx **Amusement parks**
War 172; 303.6; 355
    See also

Aeronautics, Military	law)
Armies	**Military art and science**
Arms control	**Military law**
Battles	**Military personnel**
Chemical warfare	**Munitions**
Guerrilla warfare	**Naval art and science**
International law	**Navies**
Intervention (International	**Peace**

656

War—*Continued*

    Psychological warfare   **Submarine warfare**

    Strategy   **World War III**

      also names of wars, battles, etc., e.g. **United States—History—1861-1865, Civil War; Gettysburg (Pa.), Battle of, 1863;** etc.

      x Fighting; Wars

      xx **Armies; International law; Military art and science; Peace**

War and civilization 172; 303.4

    Use same form for war with other subjects.

    x Civilization and war

    xx **Civilization; Progress**

War and industry. *See* **War—Economic aspects**

War and religion 201; 261.8

    See also **Conscientious objectors; Pacifism; World War, 1939-1945—Moral and religious aspects**

    x Christianity and war; Church and war; Religion and war

War, Articles of. *See* **Military law**

War crime trials 341.6

    xx **World War, 1939-1945—Atrocities**

War crimes. *See* names of wars with the subdivision *Atrocities,* e.g. **World War, 1939-1945—Atrocities;** etc.; and names of specific atrocities

War cripples. *See* **Physically handicapped**

War debts. *See* **Debts, Public;** and names of wars with the subdivision *Finance,* e.g. **World War, 1939-1945—Finance;** etc.

War Economic aspects 330.1

    Use for materials discussing the economic causes of war and the effect of war on industry and trade.

    See also **Industrial mobilization; Munitions; World War, 1939-1945—Human resources;** also names of wars with the subdivision *Economic aspects,* e.g. **World War, 1939-1945—Economic aspects;** etc.

    x Economics of war; Industry and war; War and industry

War of 1812. *See* **United States—History—1812-1815, War of 1812**

War of 1914. *See* **World War, 1914-1918**

War of 1939-1945. *See* **World War, 1939-1945**

War of nerves. *See* **Psychological warfare**

War of Secession (U.S.). *See* **United States—History—1861-1865, Civil War**

War of the American Revolution. *See* **United States—History—1775-1783, Revolution**

War pensions. *See* **Pensions, Military**

War poetry 808.81; 811; etc.

    See also **War songs;** also names of wars with the subdivision *Poetry,* e.g. **World War, 1939-1945—Poetry;** etc.

    xx **Poetry—Collected works; War songs**

War protest movements. *See* names of wars with the subdivision *Protests, demonstrations, etc.,* e.g. **World War, 1939-1945—Protests,**

War protest movements—*Continued*
      demonstrations, etc.; etc.
War ships. *See* **Warships**
War songs 784.7
    See also **War poetry; World War, 1939-1945—**
      Songs and music
    x Battle songs; Soldiers' songs
    xx **National songs; Songs; War poetry**
War, Space. *See* **Space warfare**
War use of animals. *See* **Animals—War use**
War use of dogs. *See* **Dogs—War use**
War veterans. *See* **Veterans**
War work. *See* names of wars with the subdivision
    War work, e.g. **World War, 1939-1945—**
    War work; etc.
Warfare, Space. *See* **Space warfare**
Warfare, Submarine. *See* **Submarine warfare**
Warm air heating. *See* **Hot air heating**
Wars. *See* **Military history; Naval history; War;**
    and names of wars, e.g. **World War, 1939-**
    1945; etc.
Wars of the Roses, 1455-1485. *See* **Great Britain—**
    History—1455-1485, War of the Roses
Warships 359.3; 623.8
    See also **Aircraft carriers; Navies; Submarines;**
    also names of countries with the subhead
    Navy, e.g. **United States. Navy;** etc.; and
    names of individual warships
    x Battle ships; Battleships; War ships
    xx **Naval architecture; Naval art and science; Na-**
      vies; Sea power; Ships
Washing. *See* **Laundry**
Wasps 595.79
    x Hymenoptera
    xx **Insects**
Waste as fuel. *See* **Waste products as fuel**
Waste disposal. *See* **Industrial wastes; Refuse and**
    refuse disposal; Sewage disposal; Waste
    products
Waste (Economics) 339.4
    xx **Economics**
Waste products 604.6; 628.4
    See also **Industrial wastes; Recycling (Waste,**
    etc.); Refuse and refuse disposal; Salvage
    (Waste, etc.); Substitute products
    x By-products; Junk; Products, Waste; Trade
      waste; Waste disposal
    xx **Chemistry, Technical; Industrial wastes; Man-**
      ufactures; Recycling (Waste, etc.); Refuse
      and refuse disposal; Salvage (Waste, etc.)
Waste products as fuel 333.79; 662; 665
    See also **Biomass energy**
    x Energy conversion from waste; Organic waste
      as fuel; Waste as fuel
    xx **Biomass energy; Salvage (Waste, etc.)**
Waste products—Recycling. *See* **Recycling (Waste,**
    etc.); Salvage (Waste, etc.)
Waste reclamation. *See* **Recycling (Waste, etc.);**
    Salvage (Waste, etc.)
Wastes, Hazardous. *See* **Hazardous wastes**

Watches. *See* **Clocks and watches**
Water 551.4; 553.7
  See also

Floods	**Lakes**
Fog	**Ocean**
Frost	**Ponds**
Geysers	**Rain and rainfall**
Glaciers	**Rivers**
Hydraulic engineering	**Sea water**
Hydrotherapy	**Snow**
Ice	**Steam**

  x Hydrology
  xx **Earth sciences; Hydraulic engineering; Hy-
      draulics**
Water—Analysis 546
  x Chemical analysis
  xx **Chemistry, Analytic; Water—Pollution**
Water animals. *See* **Freshwater animals; Marine
      animals**
Water ballet. *See* **Synchronized swimming**
Water birds 598
  See also names of water birds, e.g. **Terns;** etc.
  x Aquatic birds; Birds, Aquatic; Water fowl;
      Wild fowl
  xx **Birds**
Water color painting. *See* **Watercolor painting**
Water colors. *See* **Watercolor painting**
Water conduits. *See* **Aqueducts**
Water conservation 333.91
  See also **Water supply**
  x Conservation of water
  xx **Water supply**
Water cure. *See* **Hydrotherapy**
Water—Detergent pollution. *See* **Detergent pollu-
      tion of rivers, lakes, etc.**
Water farming. *See* **Hydroponics**
Water flow. *See* **Hydraulics**
Water—Fluoridation 628.1
  x Fluoridation of water
  xx **Teeth—Diseases**
Water fowl. *See* **Water birds**
Water—Heavy water. *See* **Deuterium oxide**
Water—Oil pollution. *See* **Oil pollution of water**
Water plants. *See* **Freshwater plants; Marine plants**
Water—Pollution 363.7; 628.1
  See also **Acid rain; Industrial wastes; Refuse and
      refuse disposal; Sewage disposal; Water—
      Analysis; Water supply;** also types of pollu-
      tion, e.g. **Detergent pollution of rivers, lakes,
      etc.; Oil pollution of water;** etc.
  x Pollution of water; Rivers—Pollution
  xx **Environmental health; Industrial wastes; Pol-
      lution; Public health; Refuse and refuse dis-
      posal; Rivers; Sewage disposal; Water sup-
      ply**
Water power 333.9; 621.2
  See also **Dams; Hydraulic engineering; Hydrau-
      lic machinery; Hydroelectric power plants**
  x Hydroelectric power
  xx **Energy resources; Hydraulics; Power (Me-**

Water power—*Continued*
>> chanics); Renewable energy resources; Rivers; Water resources development

Water—Purification 628.1
>> *See also* **Sea water conversion**
>> *x* Purification of water
>> *xx* **Sanitation; Water supply**

Water resources development 333.9
>> *See also* **Hydroelectric power plants; Inland navigation; Irrigation; Water power; Water supply**

Water rights 333.9
>> *xx* **Irrigation; Rivers**

Water skiing 797.1
>> *x* Skiing, Water
>> *xx* **Skis and skiing; Water sports**

Water sports 797
>> *See also*

Boats and boating	**Skin diving**
Canoes and canoeing	**Surfing**
Diving	**Swimming**
Fishing	**Water skiing**
Rowing	**Yachts and yachting**
Sailing	

>> also names of other water sports
>> *x* Aquatic sports
>> *xx* **Sports**

Water supply (May subdiv. geog.) **628.1**
>> *See also*

Aqueducts	**Water conservation**
Dams	**Water—Pollution**
Forest influences	**Water—Purification**
Irrigation	**Wells**
Reservoirs	

>> *x* Waterworks
>> *xx* **Civil engineering; Municipal engineering; Public health; Public utilities; Reservoirs; Sanitary engineering; Sanitation; Water conservation; Water—Pollution; Water resources development; Wells**

Water supply engineering 628.1
>> *See also* **Boring; Hydraulic engineering**
>> *xx* **Civil engineering; Engineering; Hydraulic engineering**

Water transportation. *See* **Shipping**

Watercolor painting 751.42
>> *x* Water color painting; Water colors; Watercolors
>> *xx* **Painting**

Watercolors. *See* **Watercolor painting**

Watergate Affair, 1972-1974 351.9; 973.924
>> *xx* **Corruption in politics; Misconduct in office; United States—History—1961-1974**

Watering places. *See* **Health resorts, spas, etc.**

Waterways 386
>> Use for general materials on rivers, lakes, and canals as highways for transportation or commerce.
>> *See also* **Canals; Inland navigation; Lakes; Rivers**

Waterways—*Continued*
  xx **Transportation**
Waterworks. *See* **Water supply**
Wave mechanics 530.1
  xx **Mechanics; Quantum theory; Waves**
Waves 551.47
  See also **Electric waves; Light; Ocean waves; Radiation; Sound waves; Wave mechanics**
  xx **Hydrodynamics; Vibration**
Waves, Electromagnetic. *See* **Electromagnetic waves**
Waves, Ultrasonic. *See* **Ultrasonic waves**
Wealth 330.1
  See also

Capital	**Money**
Capitalists and financiers	**Poverty**
Economic conditions	**Profit**
Income	**Property**
Income tax	**Standard of living**
Inheritance and succession	**Success**
Millionaires	

  x Distribution of wealth; Fortune; Fortunes; Riches
  xx **Capital; Economics; Finance; Millionaires; Money; Property**
Weapons and weaponry. *See* **Arms and armor; Firearms**
Weapons, Atomic. *See* **Nuclear weapons**
Weapons, Enhanced radiation. *See* **Neutron weapons**
Weapons, Neutron. *See* **Neutron weapons**
Weapons, Nuclear. *See* **Nuclear weapons**
Weapons, Space. *See* **Space weapons**
Weariness. *See* **Fatigue**
Weather 551.6
  See note under **Climate.**
  See also

Climate	**Snow**
Humidity	**Storms**
Meteorology	**Weather forecasting**
Rain and rainfall	**Winds**

  also names of countries, cities, etc. with the subdivision *Climate,* e.g. **United States—Climate;** etc.
  xx **Climate; Meteorology**
Weather—Control 551.68
  x Artificial weather control; Cloud seeding; Control; Rain making; Weather modification
Weather—Folklore 551.6
  x Weather lore
  xx **Folklore; Meteorology; Weather forecasting**
Weather forecasting 551.6
  See also **Meteorology in aeronautics; Weather—Folklore**
  xx **Forecasting; Meteorology; Weather**
Weather lore. *See* **Weather—Folklore**
Weather modification. *See* **Weather—Control**
Weather satellites. *See* **Meteorological satellites**
Weather stations. *See* **Meteorology—Observatories**

Weaving 746.1; 746.4

> *See also* **Basket making; Beadwork; Lace and lace making; Looms; Textile industry;** also names of woven articles, e.g. **Carpets;** etc.
>
> *x* Hand weaving
>
> *xx* **Carpets; Handicraft; Textile industry**

Weddings 392

> *See also* **Marriage customs and rites**
>
> *xx* **Marriage**

Weed killers. *See* **Herbicides**

Weedicides. *See* **Herbicides**

Weeds 632

> *xx* **Agricultural pests; Botany; Botany, Economic; Gardening**

Week 529

> *xx* **Calendars; Chronology**

Weight control. *See* **Reducing**

Weight lifting 796.4

> *See also* **Bodybuilding**
>
> *x* Bodybuilding (Weight lifting); Powerlifting; Pumping iron; Strength training; Weight training
>
> *xx* **Athletics; Bodybuilding; Exercise**

Weight training. *See* **Weight lifting**

Weightlessness 531

> *x* Free fall; Gravity free state; Subgravity state; Zero gravity
>
> *xx* **Man—Influence of environment; Space medicine**

Weights and measures 389

> *See also* **Decimal system; Electric measurements; Measurement; Measuring instruments; Metric system; Volume (Cubic content)**
>
> *x* Cambistry; Measures; Metrology
>
> *xx* **Measurement**

Welding 671

> *See also* **Electric welding; Solder and soldering**
>
> *x* Oxyacetylene welding
>
> *xx* **Blacksmithing; Forging; Ironwork; Metalwork; Solder and soldering**

Welding, Electric. *See* **Electric welding**

Welfare agencies. *See* **Charities**

Welfare state. *See* **Economic policy; Public welfare; State, The**

Welfare work. *See* **Charities; Public welfare; Social work**

Welfare work in industry 658.3

> *See also* **Counseling; Housing; Social settlements**
>
> *xx* **Industrial management; Labor; Social work**

Well boring. *See* **Boring**

Well drilling, Oil. *See* **Oil well drilling**

Wells 551.49; 627

> *See also* **Boring; Natural gas; Petroleum; Water supply**
>
> *x* Artesian wells
>
> *xx* **Boring; Hydraulic engineering; Water supply**

West Africa. *See* **Africa, West**

West Germany. *See* **Germany (West)**

West Indian literature (French) 840

> *x* French literature—West Indian authors

West (U.S.) 978

    Use for the region west of the Mississippi River.

    See also **Pacific Northwest; Pacific States;** also names of individual states in this region

    x Western States

    xx **United States**

West (U.S.)—Exploration 978

    x United States—Exploration

Western and country music. *See* **Country music**

Western civilization. *See* **Civilization, Occidental**

Western Europe. *See* **Europe**

Western States. *See* **West (U.S.)**

Westminster Abbey 726

    xx **Abbeys**

Whales 599.5

    xx **Mammals, Marine**

Whaling 639

    xx **Fisheries; Hunting; Voyages and travels**

Wheat 633.1

    See also **Flour**

    x Breadstuffs

    xx **Flour; Grain**

Wheels 531; 629.2

    See also **Gearing; Tires; Turbines**

    x Car wheels

Which-way stories. *See* **Plot-your-own stories**

Whistle blowing 174; 351.9; 352

    Use for materials on the practice of calling public attention to corruption, mismanagement, or waste in government, business, the military, etc.

    x Blowing the whistle

    xx **Corruption in politics; Public interest**

Whittling. *See* **Wood carving**

Wholistic medicine. *See* **Holistic medicine**

Widows 305.4; 306.8

    See also **Remarriage; Single parent family**

    xx **Family; Married women; Single parent family; Single women; Women**

Wife abuse 362.8

    x Abuse of wives; Battered wives; Battered women; Wife battering; Wife beating

    xx **Family violence; Married women**

Wife battering. *See* **Wife abuse**

Wife beating. *See* **Wife abuse**

Wigs 391

    xx **Costume; Hair and hairdressing**

Wild animals. *See* **Animals; Wildlife**

Wild children. *See* **Feral children**

Wild flowers 582.13

    x Flowers, Wild; Wildflowers

    xx **Flowers**

Wild flowers—Conservation. *See* **Plant conservation**

Wild fowl. *See* **Game and game birds; Water birds**

Wilderness areas 333.78

    x Preservation of natural scenery; Protection of natural scenery

    xx **Forest reserves; National parks and reserves; Natural monuments**

Wilderness survival 613.6; 796.5

    x Bush survival; Outdoor survival

    xx **Camping; Outdoor life; Survival (after airplane accidents, shipwrecks, etc.); Survival skills**

Wildflowers. *See* **Wild flowers**

Wildlife (May subdiv. geog.) **333.95; 639**

    Names of all categories of wildlife are not included in this list but are to be added as needed.

    See also

Alpine animals	**Game and game birds**
Dangerous animals	**Jungle animals**
Desert animals	**Marine animals**
Extinct animals	**Rare animals**
Forest animals	**Stream animals**
Freshwater animals	**Swamp animals**
Furbearing animals	

    x Feral animals; Wild animals

    xx **Animals**

Wildlife and pesticides. *See* **Pesticides and wildlife**

Wildlife conservation 639.9

    See also

Birds—Protection	serves
Forest reserves	**Natural resources**
Game preserves	**Pesticides and wildlife**
Game protection	**Rare animals**
National parks and re-	**Wildlife refuges**

    x Conservation of wildlife; Preservation of wildlife; Protection of wildlife

    xx **Conservation of natural resources; Endangered species; Nature conservation; Rare animals; Zoology, Economic**

Wildlife refuges 639.9

    See also names of specific refuges

    x Refuges, Wildlife; Sanctuaries, Wildlife; Wildlife sanctuaries

    xx **Wildlife conservation**

Wildlife sanctuaries. *See* **Wildlife refuges**

Will. *See* **Brainwashing; Free will and determinism**

Wills 346

    See also **Executors and administrators; Inheritance and succession**

    x Bequests; Legacies

    xx **Executors and administrators; Genealogy; Inheritance and succession; Registers of births, etc.**

Wills, Living. *See* **Right to die**

Wind. *See* **Winds**

Wind instruments 788

    See also **Bands (Music);** also names of wind instruments, e.g. **Flute;** etc.

    x Brass instruments; Woodwind instruments

    xx **Bands (Music); Musical instruments**

Wind power 621.4

    See also **Windmills**

    xx **Energy resources; Power (Mechanics); Renewable energy resources; Windmills**

Windbreaks 634.9

    x Shelterbelts

Windbreaks—*Continued*
    xx **Tree planting**
Windmills 621.4
    See also **Wind power**
    xx **Irrigation; Wind power**
Window dressing. *See* **Show windows**
Window gardening 635.9
    See also **House plants**
    x Greenhouses, Window; Window greenhouses; Windowbox gardening; Windowsill gardening
    xx **Flower gardening; Flowers; Gardening; Indoor gardening**
Window greenhouses. *See* **Window gardening**
Windowbox gardening. *See* **Window gardening**
Windows 721
    See also **Glass; Show windows**
    xx **Architecture—Details; Building**
Windows, Stained glass. *See* **Glass painting and staining**
Windowsill gardening. *See* **Window gardening**
Winds 551.3; 551.5
    See also **Cyclones; Hurricanes; Storms; Tornadoes; Typhoons**
    x Gales; Wind
    xx **Meteorology; Navigation; Physical geography; Storms; Weather**
Windsurfing 797.1
    x Board sailing; Sailboarding
    xx **Sailing**
Wine and wine making (May subdiv. geog.) **664**
    See also **Fermentation; Grapes**
    xx **Alcoholic beverages; Fermentation; Grapes**
Winter resorts 613; 796.9
    See also **Health resorts, spas, etc.**
    x Resorts
    xx **Health resorts, spas, etc.**
Winter sports 796.9
    See also names of winter sports, e.g. **Ice hockey; Ice skating; Skis and skiing; Sleds and sledding;** etc.
    x Ice sports
    xx **Sports**
Wire agencies. *See* **News agencies**
Wireless. *See* **Radio**
Wiretapping 363.2
    See also **Eavesdropping**
    xx **Criminal investigation; Eavesdropping; Privacy, Right of**
Wiring, Electric. *See* **Electric wiring**
Wishes 153.8
    xx **Motivation (Psychology)**
Wit and humor 808.7; 817; etc.
    See also

Anecdotes	**Jokes**
Chapbooks	**Nonsense verses**
Comedy	**Parody**
Epigrams	**Practical jokes**
Humorists	**Puns and punning**
Humorous poetry	**Satire**
Humorous stories	**Tall tales**

Wit and humor—_Continued_
    also **American wit and humor; English wit and humor;** etc.; and subjects with the subdivision _Anecdotes, facetiae, satire, etc.,_ e.g.
      Music—Anecdotes, facetiae, satire, etc.; etc.
    _x_ Facetiae; Humor
    _xx_ **Laughter; Literature**
Witchcraft 133.4
    See also **Charms; Demonology; Occult sciences; Witches**
    _x_ Black art (Magic); Black magic (Witchcraft); Delusions; Necromancy; Sorcery; Spirits; Wizardry
    _xx_ **Demonology; Exorcism; Folklore; Occult sciences; Superstition**
Witches 133.4
    _x_ Covens
    _xx_ **Witchcraft**
Witnesses 345; 347
    _x_ Cross-examination
Wives. _See_ **Married women**
Wives of presidents—United States. _See_ **Presidents—United States—Spouses**
Wives, Runaway. _See_ **Runaway adults**
Wizardry. _See_ **Witchcraft**
Wolf children. _See_ **Feral children**
Woman. _See_ **Women**
Woman power. _See_ **Human resources**
Women (May subdiv. geog.) **305.4; 323.3**
    See also

Black women	**Widows**
Girls	**World War, 1939-1945—**
Married women	**Women**
Mothers	**Young women**
Single women	

    also headings beginning with the words **Women** and **Women's**
    _x_ Woman
Women air pilots 629.132
    _xx_ **Air pilots**
Women artists 704
    Use same form for the attainments of women in other occupations and professions, e.g.
      Women physicians; etc.
    _xx_ **Artists; Women—Employment**
Women authors 809
    See also **American literature—Women authors**
    _xx_ **Authors**
Women—Biography 920
    _x_ Heroines
    _xx_ **Biography**
Women, Black. _See_ **Black women**
Women—Civil rights 323.4
    See also **Feminism; Women—Suffrage; Women's movement**
    _x_ Emancipation of women; Rights of women; Women—Emancipation; Women—Equal rights; Women's rights
    _xx_ **Civil rights; Feminism; Sex discrimination; Women—Suffrage**

Women—Clothing. *See* **Women's clothing**
Women—Clubs. *See* **Women—Societies**
Women—Diseases 618.1
    x Diseases of women
Women—Dress. *See* **Women's clothing**
Women—Education 376
    See also **Coeducation**
    x Education of women
    xx **Coeducation**
Women—Emancipation. *See* **Women—Civil rights**
Women—Employment 331.4
    See also **Equal pay for equal work; Self-
        employed women;** also **Women artists;
        Women physicians;** and similar headings
    x Employment of women; Girls—Employment;
        Women—Occupations; Working girls;
        Working women
    xx **Discrimination in employment; Labor; Labor
        supply**
Women—Enfranchisement. *See* **Women—Suffrage**
Women—Equal rights. *See* **Women—Civil rights**
Women—Health and hygiene 613
    x Health and hygiene
    xx **Health**
Women in art 704.9
    Use for materials on women depicted in works
        of art. Materials on the attainments of
        women in the area of art are entered under
        Women artists.
    xx **Art**
Women in business. *See* **Businesswomen**
Women in literature 809
    Use for materials on the theme of women in
        works of literature. Materials on the attain-
        ments of women in the area of literature are
        entered under **Women authors.**
    xx **Characters and characteristics in literature;
        Literature**
Women in motion pictures 791.43
    Use for materials discussing the portrayal of
        women in motion pictures. Materials dis-
        cussing all aspects of women's involvement
        in motion pictures are entered under
        Women in the motion picture industry.
    xx **Motion pictures**
Women in the Bible 220.8
    x Bible—Women; Heroines
    xx **Bible—Biography**
Women in the motion picture industry 338.4; 791.43
    See note under **Women in motion pictures.**
    xx **Motion picture industry**
Women judges 347.092; 920
    xx **Judges**
Women—Occupations. *See* **Women—Employment**
Women physicians 610.69
    xx **Physicians; Women—Employment**
Women police. *See* **Police**
Women—Political activity 324
    See also **Women politicians**
    xx **Politics, Practical**

Women politicians 920
  xx **Politicians; Women—Political activity**
Women—Psychology 155.3
  x Feminine psychology
Women—Rights. *See* **Feminism**
Women, Self-employed. *See* **Self-employed women**
Women, Single. *See* **Single women**
Women—Social conditions 305.4
  See also **Divorce; Prostitution; Women—
    Societies; Women's movement**
Women—Societies 367
  See also **Girls' clubs**
  x Women—Clubs; Women's clubs; Women's
    organizations
  xx **Clubs; Societies; Women—Social conditions**
Women—Suffrage 324.6
  See also **Women—Civil rights**
  x Suffragettes; Women—Enfranchisement
  xx **Suffrage; Women—Civil rights**
Women—United States 305.4
  See also **Presidents—United States—Spouses**
  x United States—Women
Women's clothing 646
  x Women—Clothing; Women—Dress
  xx **Clothing and dress**
Women's clubs. *See* **Women—Societies**
Women's liberation movement. *See* **Women's
    movement**
Women's movement 323.3; 323.4
  See also **Feminism**
  x Women's liberation movement
  xx **Feminism; Women—Civil rights; Women—
    Social conditions**
Women's organizations. *See* **Women—Societies**
Women's rights. *See* **Feminism; Women—Civil
    rights**
Wonders. *See* **Curiosities and wonders**
Wood 674
  Use for materials on the chemical and physical
    properties of different kinds of wood and
    how they are used.
  See also **Forests and forestry; Lumber and lum-
    bering; Plywood; Woodwork;** also kinds of
    wood, e.g. **Oak;** etc.
  x Timber
  xx **Building materials; Forest products; Forests
    and forestry; Fuel; Trees**
Wood block printing. *See* **Wood engraving; Wood-
    cuts**
Wood carving 736
  x Carving (Arts); Carving, Wood; Whittling
  xx **Decoration and ornament; Furniture; Sculp-
    ture; Woodwork**
Wood engraving 761
  x Block printing; Wood block printing
  xx **Engraving**
Wood finishing 684; 698
  See also **Lacquer and lacquering; Varnish and
    varnishing**
  x Finishes and finishing

Wood finishing—*Continued*
  xx **Painting, Industrial**
Wood—Preservation 674
  x Preservation of wood
Wood turning. *See* **Turning**
Woodcuts 761
  x Block printing; Wood block printing
Woods. *See* **Forests and forestry**
Woodwind instruments. *See* **Wind instruments**
Woodwork 684
  See also **Cabinet work; Carpentry; Furniture;
     Turning; Wood carving**
  xx **Architecture—Details; Cabinet work; Carpen-
     try; Decorative arts; Turning; Wood**
Woodworking machinery 621.9; 684
  See also special kinds of machines, e.g. **Lathes;**
     etc.
  xx **Machinery**
Wool 677
  See also **Dyes and dyeing; Yarn**
  x Animal products
  xx **Fibers; Yarn**
Word books. *See* **Picture dictionaries**
Word games 793.7
  See also names of specific word games, e.g.
     Crossword puzzles; etc.
  xx **Games; Literary recreations**
Word processing 651.7; *652
  xx **Office management; Office practice**
Word processor keyboards. *See* **Keyboards (Elec-
     tronics)**
Wordless stories. *See* **Stories without words**
Words. *See* **Vocabulary**
Words, New 422
  x Coinage of words; New words
  xx **Semantics; Vocabulary**
Work 331.1
  See also **Employee morale; Job satisfaction; La-
     bor; Work ethics**
Work at home. *See* **Home business; Telecommuting**
Work ethics 174
  x Ethics, Work
  xx **Ethics; Labor; Work**
Work performance standards. *See* **Performance
     standards**
Work satisfaction. *See* **Job satisfaction**
Work standards. *See* **Production standards**
Work stoppages. *See* **Strikes and lockouts**
Work stress. *See* **Job stress**
Workers' compensation 368.4
  x Compensation; Employers' liability; Insur-
     ance, Workers' compensation; Workmen's
     compensation
  xx **Insurance, Accident; Insurance, Health; Occu-
     pational diseases; Social security**
Workers' participation in management. *See* **Man-
     agement—Employee participation**
Working animals 636.08
  See also headings for animals in specific work-
     ing situations, e.g. **Animals—War use; Ani-**

Working animals—*Continued*
        mals in police work; **Dogs—War use;** etc.
   x Animals, Working
   xx **Animals; Domestic animals; Zoology, Economic**
Working at home. *See* **Home business; Telecommuting**
Working boys. *See* **Children—Employment**
Working classes. *See* **Labor**
Working day. *See* **Hours of labor**
Working girls. *See* **Children—Employment; Women—Employment**
Working hours. *See* **Hours of labor**
Working parents, Children of. *See* **Children of working parents**
Working robots. *See* **Robots, Industrial**
Working women. *See* **Women—Employment**
Workmen's compensation. *See* **Workers' compensation**
Workshop councils. *See* **Management—Employee participation**
Workshops, Teachers'. *See* **Teachers' workshops**
World. *See* **Earth**
World economics. *See* **Commercial policy; Economic conditions; Economic policy; Geography, Commercial**
World, End of the. *See* **End of the world**
World government. *See* **International organization**
World history 909
   See also **Geography; History, Ancient; History, Modern; Middle Ages—History**
   x History, Universal; Universal history
   xx **History**
World language. *See* **Language, Universal**
World organization. *See* **International organization**
World politics 909
   See note under **International relations.**
   See also **Geopolitics; International organization; International relations; World War III; World War, 1914-1918; World War, 1939-1945;** also names of countries with the subdivisions *Foreign relations* and *Politics and government,* e.g. **United States—Foreign relations; United States—Politics and government;** etc.
   x International politics
   xx **Geopolitics; International organization; International relations; Political science**
World politics—1945-1965 909.82
   x Cold war; Power politics
World politics—1965- 909.82
   x Power politics
World War III 355
   x Third World War
   xx **War; World politics**
World War, 1914-1918 (May subdiv. geog.)
      940.3-940.4
   May be subdivided like **World War, 1939-1945.** Here are listed references applicable only to this war.

World War, 1914-1918—*Continued*

    x European War, 1914-1918; War of 1914

    xx **Europe—History—1914-1945; History, Modern—1900-1999 (20th century); World politics**

World War, 1914-1918—Economic aspects 940.3

    xx **Reconstruction (1914-1939)**

World War, 1914-1918—Gas warfare 940.4

    xx **Poisonous gases—War use**

World War, 1914-1918—Peace 940.3

    See also **League of Nations**

World War, 1914-1918—Reconstruction. *See* **Reconstruction (1914-1939)**

World War, 1914-1918—Territorial questions 940.3

    See also **Mandates**

World War, 1914-1918—United States 940.3

    x United States—European War, 1914-1918; United States—History—1914-1918, European War; United States—History—1914-1918, World War; United States—World War, 1914-1918

World War, 1939-1945 (May subdiv. geog.)
    940.53-940.54

    Subdivisions used under this heading may be used under other wars.

    See also names of battles, sieges, etc., e.g.
    Ardennes, Battle of the, 1944-1945; Pearl Harbor (Oahu, Hawaii), Attack on, 1941; etc.

    x European War, 1939-1945; War of 1939-1945; Wars

    xx **Europe—History—1914-1945; History, Modern—1900-1999 (20th century); World politics**

World War, 1939-1945—Addresses and essays 940.53

    x Addresses

    xx **Essays; Lectures and lecturing; Speeches, addresses, etc.**

World War, 1939-1945—Aerial operations 940.54

    x Air warfare

    xx **Aeronautics, Military**

World War, 1939-1945—Amphibious operations 940.54

    xx **World War, 1939-1945—Naval operations**

World War, 1939-1945—Antiwar movements. *See* **World War, 1939-1945—Protests, demonstrations, etc.**

World War, 1939-1945—Armistices 940.54

    x Armistices

World War, 1939-1945—Arms. *See* **World War, 1939-1945—Equipment and supplies**

World War, 1939-1945—Art and the war 940.54

    xx **Art**

World War, 1939-1945—Atrocities 940.54

    See also **War crime trials;** also names of specific atrocities and crimes

    x Atrocities, Military; Military atrocities; War crimes

World War, 1939-1945—Battles, sieges, etc. *See*
      World War, 1939-1945—Campaigns; World
      War, 1939-1945—Naval operations

World War, 1939-1945—Biography 920

World War, 1939-1945—Blacks 940.54

World War, 1939-1945—Blockades 940.54

World War, 1939-1945—Campaigns (May subdiv.
    geog.) **940.54**
   See also **Pearl Harbor (Oahu, Hawaii), Attack**
     on, 1941; also names of battles, campaigns,
     sieges, etc., **Ardennes, Battle of the, 1944-**
     1945; Pearl Harbor, (Oahu, Hawaii), Attack
     on, 1941; etc.
   x World War, 1939-1945—Battles, sieges, etc.
   xx **Battles**

World War, 1939-1945—Cartoons. *See* **World**
      War, 1939-1945—Humor, caricatures, etc.

World War, 1939-1945—Causes 940.53
   See also **National socialism**

World War, 1939-1945—Censorship 940.54

World War, 1939-1945—Charities. *See* **World**
      War, 1939-1945—Civilian relief; World
      War, 1939-1945—War work

World War, 1939-1945—Chemical warfare 940.54
   xx **Chemical warfare**

World War, 1939-1945—Children 940.53
   xx **Children**

World War, 1939-1945—Civilian defense. *See*
     Civil defense

World War, 1939-1945—Civilian evacuation. *See*
     World War, 1939-1945—Evacuation of ci-
     vilians

World War, 1939-1945—Civilian relief 940.54
   See also **World War, 1939-1945—Refugees**
   x World War, 1939-1945—Charities
   xx **Charities; Economic assistance; Food relief;**
     Reconstruction (1939-1951); World War,
     1939-1945—Food supply; World War,
     1939-1945—Medical care; World War,
     1939-1945—Refugees; World War, 1939-
     1945—War work

World War, 1939-1945—Collaborationists 940.53
   x Fifth column; Quislings
   xx **World War, 1939-1945—Occupied territories**

World War, 1939-1945—Congresses 940.53
   xx **Congresses and conventions**

World War, 1939-1945—Conscientious objectors
     940.53
   See also **World War, 1939-1945—Draft resisters**
   xx **Conscientious objectors; World War, 1939-**
     1945—Protests, demonstrations, etc.

World War, 1939-1945—Correspondents. *See*
      World War, 1939-1945—Journalists

World War, 1939-1945—Desertions 940.54
   xx **Desertion, Military**

World War, 1939-1945—Destruction and pillage
     940.54

World War, 1939-1945—Diplomatic history   940.53
 See also World War, 1939-1945—Governments
   in exile
World War, 1939-1945—Displaced persons.   *See*
   World War, 1939-1945—Refugees
World War, 1939-1945—Draft resisters   940.54
 xx Military service, Compulsory—Draft resisters;
   World War, 1939-1945—Conscientious objectors
World War, 1939-1945—Economic aspects   940.53
   Use for materials dealing with the economic
   causes of the war and the effect of the war
   on commerce and industry.
 See also Reconstruction (1939-1951); World
   War, 1939-1945—Finance; World War,
   1939-1945—Human resources; World War,
   1939-1945—Reparations
 xx Reconstruction (1939-1951); War—Economic
   aspects
World War, 1939-1945—Education and the war
   940.53
 xx Education
World War, 1939-1945—Engineering and construction   940.54
 xx Military engineering
World War, 1939-1945—Equipment and supplies
   940.54
 x World War, 1939-1945—Arms; World War,
   1939-1945—Military supplies; World War,
   1939-1945—Munitions; World War, 1939-
   1945—Ordnance; World War, 1939-1945—
   Supplies; World War, 1939-1945—
   Weapons
 xx Munitions
World War, 1939-1945—Evacuation of civilians
   940.54
 x Civilian evacuation; Evacuation of civilians;
   World War, 1939-1945—Civilian evacuation
 xx Civil defense; World War, 1939-1945—
   Refugees
World War, 1939-1945—Fiction   Fic
World War, 1939-1945—Finance   940.53
   Use for materials on the cost and financing of
   the war, including war debts, and the effect
   of the war on financial systems, including
   inflation.
 x War debts
 xx Debts, Public; World War, 1939-1945—
   Economic aspects
World War, 1939-1945—Food question.   *See*
   World War, 1939-1945—Food supply
World War, 1939-1945—Food supply   940.53
 See also World War, 1939-1945—Civilian relief
 x World War, 1939-1945—Food question
 xx Food relief
World War, 1939-1945—Forced repatriation   940.53
 See also World War, 1939-1945—Refugees
 xx World War, 1939-1945—Prisoners and prisons; World War, 1939-1945—Refugees

World War, 1939-1945—Governments in exile
940.53
 x Governments in exile
 xx **World War, 1939-1945—Diplomatic history**
World War, 1939-1945—Guerrillas. *See* **World
  War, 1939-1945—Underground movements**
World War, 1939-1945—Health aspects 940.54
 xx **Military health; Sanitation**
World War, 1939-1945—Hospitals. *See* **World
  War, 1939-1945—Medical care**
World War, 1939-1945—Human resources 940.54
 xx **Armies; Human resources; Labor; Labor sup-
  ply; War—Economic aspects; World War,
  1939-1945—Economic aspects**
**World War, 1939-1945—Humor, caricatures, etc.
 940.53**
 x Humor; World War, 1939-1945—Cartoons
 xx **Cartoons and caricatures**
World War, 1939-1945, in literature. *See* **World
  War, 1939-1945—Literature and the war**
World War, 1939-1945, in motion pictures. *See*
  **World War, 1939-1945—Motion pictures
  and the war**
World War, 1939-1945—Influence 940.53
World War, 1939-1945—Jews 940.54
 See also **Holocaust, Jewish (1933-1945)**
 xx **Holocaust, Jewish (1933-1945)**
World War, 1939-1945—Jews—Rescue 940.54
 x Rescue of Jews, 1939-1945
 xx **Jews—Persecutions**
World War, 1939-1945—Journalists 940.54
 x World War, 1939-1945—Correspondents;
  World War, 1939-1945—War correspon-
  dents
World War, 1939-1945—Literature and the war
 x World War, 1939-1945, in literature
 xx **Literature**
World War, 1939-1945—Maps 940.54
World War, 1939-1945—Medical care 940.54
 See also **World War, 1939-1945—Civilian relief**
 x World War, 1939-1945—Hospitals
 xx **Armies—Medical care; Hospitals, Military;
  Medicine, Military; Military health**
World War, 1939-1945—Military supplies. *See*
  **World War, 1939-1945—Equipment and
  supplies**
World War, 1939-1945—Missing in action 940.54
 xx **Missing in action; World War, 1939-1945—
  Prisoners and prisons**
**World War, 1939-1945—Moral and religious aspects
 940.53; 940.54**
 x World War, 1939-1945—Religious aspects
 xx **War and religion**
**World War, 1939-1945—Motion pictures and the
 war**
 x World War, 1939-1945, in motion pictures
 xx **Motion pictures**
World War, 1939-1945—Munitions. *See* **World
  War, 1939-1945—Equipment and supplies**

World War, 1939-1945—Museums 940.54
xx **Museums**
World War, 1939-1945—Naval operations 940.54
   See also **World War, 1939-1945—Amphibious operations**
   x Naval warfare; World War, 1939-1945—Battles, sieges, etc.
   xx **Naval battles**
World War, 1939-1945—Naval operations—Submarine 940.54
   x World War, 1939-1945—Submarine operations
   xx **Submarine warfare**
World War, 1939-1945—Occupied territories 940.54
   Use for general treatment of the subject. For occupation of specific countries, use the name of the country with the subdivision *History—1940-1945, German occupation* or *History— 1945- , Allied occupation,* e.g. **Netherlands—History—1940-1945, German occupation; Japan—History—1945-1952, Allied occupation;** etc.
   See also **Japan—History—1945-1952, Allied occupation; World War, 1939-1945—Collaborationists; World War, 1939-1945—Underground movements;** also names of countries with the subdivision *History—1940-1945, German occupation,* e.g. **Netherlands—History—1940-1945, German occupation;** etc.
   xx **Military occupation; World War, 1939-1945—Territorial questions**
World War, 1939-1945—Ordnance. *See* **World War, 1939-1945—Equipment and supplies**
World War, 1939-1945—Peace 940.53
   xx **Peace**
World War, 1939-1945—Personal narratives 940.53; 940.54
   Use for autobiographical materials that relate experiences of persons in connection with the war.
   x Personal narratives
   xx **Autobiographies; Biography**
World War, 1939-1945—Pictorial works 940.53
World War, 1939-1945—Poetry
   xx **War poetry**
World War, 1939-1945—Prisoners and prisons 940.54
   See also **World War, 1939-1945—Forced repatriation; World War, 1939-1945—Missing in action**
   xx **Concentration camps; Prisoners of war**
World War, 1939-1945—Propaganda 940.54
   xx **Propaganda**
World War, 1939-1945—Protests, demonstrations, etc. 940.54
   See also **World War, 1939-1945—Conscientious objectors**
   x Antiwar movements; Protest movements

World War, 1939-1945—Protests, demonstrations,
    etc.—*Continued*
    (War); War protest movements; World
    War, 1939-1945—Antiwar movements
World War, 1939-1945—Psychological aspects
    940.53
  xx Psychological warfare
World War, 1939-1945—Public opinion 940.54
  xx Public opinion
World War, 1939-1945—Railroads. *See* World
    War, 1939-1945—Transportation
World War, 1939-1945—Reconstruction. *See* Re-
    construction (1939-1951)
World War, 1939-1945—Refugees 940.53
  See also World War, 1939-1945—Civilian relief;
    World War, 1939-1945—Evacuation of ci-
    vilians; World War, 1939-1945—Forced re-
    patriation
  x Displaced persons; World War, 1939-1945—
    Displaced persons
  xx Refugees, Political; World War, 1939-1945—
    Civilian relief; World War, 1939-1945—
    Forced repatriation
World War, 1939-1945—Regimental histories
    940.54
World War, 1939-1945—Religious aspects. *See*
    World War, 1939-1945—Moral and reli-
    gious aspects
World War, 1939-1945—Reparations 940.53
  x Reparations (World War, 1939-1945)
  xx Reconstruction (1939-1951); World War,
    1939-1945—Economic aspects
World War, 1939-1945—Resistance
    movements. *See* World War, 1939-
    1945—Underground movements
World War, 1939-1945—Secret service 940.54
  xx Secret service
World War, 1939-1945—Social aspects 940.53
World War, 1939-1945—Social work. *See* World
    War, 1939-1945—War work
World War, 1939-1945—Songs and music 784.6
  xx Military music; War songs
World War, 1939-1945—Sources 940.53
  xx History—Sources
World War, 1939-1945—Submarine
    operations. *See* World War, 1939-1945—
    Naval operations—Submarine
World War, 1939-1945—Supplies. *See* World War,
    1939-1945—Equipment and supplies
World War, 1939-1945—Territorial questions
    940.53
  See also World War, 1939-1945—Occupied ter-
    ritories
  xx Boundaries
World War, 1939-1945—Theater and the war
  xx Theater
World War, 1939-1945—Transportation 940.54
  x World War, 1939-1945—Railroads
  xx Transportation

World War, 1939-1945—Treaties 940.53
   xx Treaties
World War, 1939-1945—Underground movements
     940.54
    x Underground movements (World War, 1939-
      1945); World War, 1939-1945—Guerrillas;
      World War, 1939-1945—Resistance move-
      ments
    xx **Guerrilla warfare; Spies; World War, 1939-**
      1945—Occupied territories
World War, 1939-1945—United States 940.53
    x United States—History—1939-1945, World
      War; United States—World War, 1939-
      1945
World War, 1939-1945—War correspondents. *See*
      World War, 1939-1945—Journalists
World War, 1939-1945—War work 940.53
    See also **World War, 1939-1945—Civilian relief**
    x War work; World War, 1939-1945—Charities;
      World War, 1939-1945—Social work
World War, 1939-1945—Weapons. *See* **World**
      War, 1939-1945—Equipment and supplies
World War, 1939-1945—Women 940.54
   xx **Women**
World's Fair (1989: Paris, France). *See* **Expo '89**
    (Paris, France)
World's fairs. *See* **Exhibitions; Fairs**
Worms 595.1
   xx **Invertebrates**
Worry 157
   x Anxiety
   xx **Mental health; Nervous system—Diseases**
Worship 248.3; 264; 291.3
   See also **Devotional exercises; Prayer; Public**
    worship; Sacrifice
   x Devotion
   xx **Religion; Theology**
Worth. *See* **Values**
Wounded, First aid to. *See* **First aid**
Wounds and injuries 617
   See also **Fractures**
   x Injuries
   xx **Accidents**
Wrapping of gifts. *See* **Gift wrapping**
Wrecks. *See* **Shipwrecks;** and subjects with the
    subdivision *Accidents,* e.g.
    Railroads—Accidents; etc.
Wrestling 796.8
   See also **Judo**
Writers. *See* **Authors;** and classes of writers, e.g.
    Dramatists; Historians; Journalists; etc.
Writing 411
    Use for general materials on the history and art
     of writing and on elegant handwriting. Prac-
     tical guides are entered under **Handwriting.**
     Materials on handwriting as an expression
     of the writer's character are entered under
     Graphology.

Writing—*Continued*
> *See also*

Abbreviations	**Graphology**
Alphabet	**Handwriting**
Autographs	**Hieroglyphics**
Calligraphy	**Picture writing**
Ciphers	**Shorthand**
Cryptography	**Typewriting**

> *xx* **Alphabet; Ciphers; Communication; Handwriting; Language and languages; Language arts**

Writing (Authorship). *See* **Authorship; Creative writing; Journalism**

Wrought iron work. *See* **Ironwork**

X-15 (Rocket aircraft) 629.133
> *xx* **Rocket planes**

X rays 537.5
> *See also* **Gamma rays; Radiologists; Radiotherapy; Vacuum tubes**
> *x* Radiography; Rays, Roentgen; Roentgen rays
> *xx* **Electricity; Electromagnetic waves; Light; Radiation; Radioactivity; Radiotherapy; Therapeutics**

Xerography 686.4
> *xx* **Copying processes and machines**

Yacht basins. *See* **Marinas**

Yacht racing. *See* **Boat racing**

Yachts and yachting 797.1
> *See also* **Marinas; Sailing**
> *x* Regattas
> *xx* **Boatbuilding; Boats and boating; Ocean travel; Sailing; Ships; Voyages and travels; Water sports**

Yard sales. *See* **Garage sales**

Yarn 677
> *See also* **Cotton; Flax; Wool**
> *xx* **Textile industry; Wool**

Yearbooks 050
> *See also* **Almanacs; Calendars;** also general subjects and names of organizations with the subdivision *Yearbooks,* e.g.
> **Literature—Yearbooks; United Nations—Yearbooks;** etc.
> *x* Annuals
> *xx* **Almanacs; Serial publications**

Yeast 641.3
> *xx* **Fermentation**

Yellow fever 616.9
> *xx* **Tropical medicine**

Yiddish language 437
> May be subdivided like **English language.**
> *x* German Hebrew; Jewish language; Jews—Language; Judaeo-German
> *xx* **Hebrew language**

Yiddish literature 837
> May use same subdivisions and names of literary forms as for **English literature.**
> *xx* **Jewish literature**

Yippies. *See* **Hippies**

Yoga 181; 613.7

   xx **Hinduism; Philosophy, Hindu; Theosophy**

Yom Kippur 296.4

   x Atonement, Day of; Day of Atonement

   xx **Fasts and feasts—Judaism**

Yom Kippur War, 1973. *See* **Israel-Arab War, 1973**

Yosemite National Park (Calif.) 719; 979.4

   xx **National parks and reserves**

Young adults. *See* **Youth**

Young adults' library services 027.62

   See also **Children's libraries; School libraries (High school); Young adults' literature**

   x Libraries and young adults; Libraries, Young adults'; Library services to young adults; Young people's libraries

   xx **Children's libraries; School libraries (High school); Youth**

Young adults' literature 028.5

   x Youth—Literature

   xx **Young adults' library services**

Young consumers 640.73; 658.8

   x Children as consumers; Teenage consumers; Youth market

   xx **Consumers**

Young men 305.2; 305.3

   See also **Boys; Youth**

   xx **Boys; Men; Youth**

Young people's libraries. *See* **Young adults' library services**

Young women 305.2; 305.4

   See also **Girls; Youth**

   xx **Girls; Women; Youth**

Youth (May subdiv geog.) 305.2

   See also

Adolescence	Runaway children
Boys	Television and youth
Children	Young adults' library ser-
Church work with youth	vices
Dropouts	Young men
Girls	Young women

   x Adolescents; Teenagers; Young adults

   xx **Boys; Children; Girls; Young men; Young women**

Youth—Alcohol use 613.8; 616.86

   See also **Drinking age**

   x Alcohol and teenagers; Alcohol and youth; Alcohol use; Drinking and youth; Teenage drinking; Teenagers and alcohol

   xx **Alcoholism; Drinking of alcoholic beverages**

Youth and drugs. *See* **Youth—Drug use**

Youth and narcotics. *See* **Youth—Drug use**

Youth and television. *See* **Television and youth**

Youth—Attitudes 155.5; 305.2

   xx **Attitude (Psychology)**

Youth—Drug use 613.8; 616.86

   x Drug use; Drugs and teenagers; Drugs and youth; Teenagers and drugs; Youth and drugs; Youth and narcotics

   xx **Drug abuse; Drug addicts; Drugs; Juvenile**

Youth—Drug use—*Continued*
        delinquency; Narcotic habit
Youth—Employment 331.3
    See also Summer employment
    x Child labor; Employment of youth
    xx Age and employment; Labor; Labor supply;
        Summer employment
Youth hostels 647
    x Hostels, Youth; Tourist accommodations
Youth—Literature. *See* Young adults' literature
Youth market. *See* Young consumers
Youth movement 322.4
    See also Students—Political activity
    x Student movement; Student protests, demon-
        strations, etc.; Student revolt
    xx Protests, demonstrations, etc.
Youth—Religious life 268
    See also Jesus people
Youth, Runaway. *See* Runaway children
Youth—United States 305.2
    x American youth; United States—Youth
Zen Buddhism 294.3
    xx Buddhism
Zeppelins. *See* Airships
Zero gravity. *See* Weightlessness
Zinc 669
    See also Brass
Zionism 956.94
    See also Jews—Restoration
    xx Jews—Restoration
Zip code (May subdiv. geog.) 383; 912
    x Postal delivery code
    xx Postal service
Zodiac 133.5; 523
    xx Astronomy
Zoning 346.04; 352.9
    x City planning—Zone system; Districting (in
        city planning)
    xx City planning
Zoogeography. *See* Biogeography
Zoological gardens. *See* Zoos
Zoological specimens—Collection and preservation
        579
    See also Taxidermy; also names of specimens
        with the subdivision *Collection and preser-*
        vation, e.g. Birds—Collection and preserva-
        tion; etc.
    x Collections of natural specimens; Preservation
        of zoological specimens; Specimens, Preser-
        vation of
    xx Collectors and collecting; Taxidermy
Zoology (May subdiv. geog.) 590; 591
    See also

Anatomy, Comparative	Natural history
Animals	Physiology, Comparative
Embryology	Poisonous animals
Evolution	Psychology, Comparative
Fossils	Variation (Biology)

Zoology—*Continued*

also names of divisions, classes, etc. of the animal kingdom, e.g. **Invertebrates; Vertebrates; Birds; Mammals;** etc.; and names of animals

x Animal kingdom; Animal physiology; Fauna

xx **Animals; Biology; Natural history; Nature study; Science**

Zoology, Economic 591.6

Use for general materials on animals injurious and beneficial to man and to agriculture, and for materials on the extermination of wild animals, venomous snakes, etc.

See also

Agricultural pests	**Pests**
Domestic animals	**Pests—Control**
Furbearing animals	**Wildlife conservation**
Insects, Injurious and beneficial	**Working animals**

x Animals, Useful and harmful; Biology, Economic; Economic zoology

Zoology of the Bible. *See* **Bible—Natural history**

Zoology—United States 591.973

x United States—Zoology

Zoos 590.74

See also names of zoos

x Zoological gardens

xx **Animals; Parks**